TEACH WITH INSIGHT!
STANDARD LESSON RESOURCES™

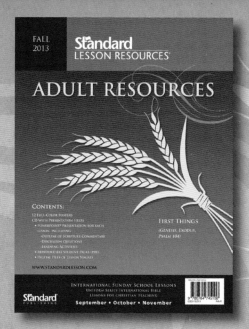

Adult Resources

Engage students with maps, charts, posters, and a CD with PowerPoint® presentations and reproducible student activity pages.

978-0-7847-4510-6

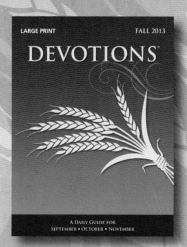

Devotions®

Enhance your weekly study through daily Scripture reading tied to each week's lesson.

Pocket Size
978-0-7847-4467-3

Large Print
978-0-7847-4514-4

The Essential Book of Teacher Tips

The perfect complement to *Standard Lesson Commentary®* or any ISSL Curriculum, this book provides:

- 52 informative articles with over 150 ideas for effective lesson presentations
- Undated articles to use throughout the year every year

978-0-7847-3529-9

Seek®

Continue your lesson with this weekly take home paper that includes articles, stories, questions, and daily Bible readings.

978-0-7847-4513-7

Available at your local Christian retailer or www.standardlesson.com

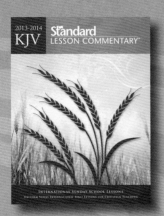 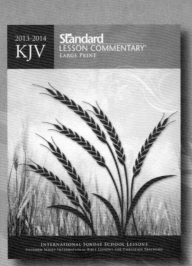 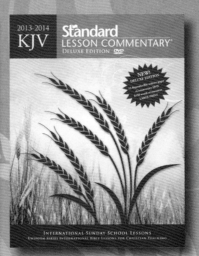 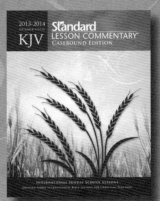
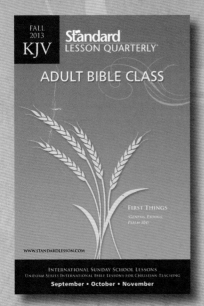

2013-2014

KJV

Standard
LESSON COMMENTARY®

Edited by
Ronald L. Nickelson

King James
Version

Volume 61

Jonathan
Underwood,
Senior Editor

Standard®
PUBLISHING

Cincinnati, Ohio

IN THIS VOLUME

Scripture taken from the *King James Version*.

Lessons based on International Sunday School Lessons © 2010 by the Lesson Committee.

INDEX OF PRINTED TEXTS

The printed texts for 2013–2014 are arranged here in the order in which they appear in the Bible.

DVD-ROM AVAILABLE

The *Standard Lesson Commentary*® is available in an electronic format in special editions of this volume. The DVD contains the full text of the King James *Standard Lesson Commentary*® and *The NIV*® *Standard Lesson Commentary*® powered by QuickVerse® from WORDsearch® Bible Study Software, additional study helps, and a collection of presentation helps that can be projected or reproduced as handouts. Order 020510213 (KJV) or 020520213 (NIV). Some 200 additional books and resources are available by FREE download from www.wordsearchbible.com/products/free.

For questions regarding the installation, registration, or activation of the DVD, contact WORDsearch Customer Service at (800) 888-9898 or (512) 615-9444, Mon–Fri, 8 a.m. to 8 p.m.; or Sat, 10 a.m. to 5 p.m. (Central Time). For problems with the DVD, contact WORDsearch Technical Support at (888) 854-8400, Mon–Fri, 9 a.m. to 5 p.m. (Central Time) or by e-mail at Support@WORDsearchBible.com.

Logos users! You can purchase the *Standard Lesson eCommentary* as a direct download from www.logos.com/standard. This is a separate purchase from the print edition.

CUMULATIVE INDEX

A cumulative index for Scripture passages used in the STANDARD LESSON COMMENTARY *for September 2010–August 2014 is provided below.*

FIRST THINGS

Special Features

Lessons

Unit 1: First Days

Unit 2: First Nation

Unit 3: First Freedom

QUARTERLY QUIZ

Use these questions as a pretest or as a review. The answers are on page iv of This Quarter in the Word.

Lesson 1

1. Psalm 104 echoes the promise to Noah that ___ will never again cover the earth. *Psalm 104:6, 9*

2. The psalmist notes that when God sends out His Spirit, the earth is destroyed. T/F. *Psalm 104:30*

Lesson 2

1. God said that is was not good for Adam to be what? (alone, nagged, sleepy?) *Genesis 2:18*

2. God gave names to all of the animals of the earth after He created them. T/F. *Genesis 2:20*

Lesson 3

1. When confronted, whom did Adam blame for his sin? (Eve, the serpent, himself?) *Genesis 3:12*

2. God told Eve that her sorrow would be increased in _____. *Genesis 3:16*

Lesson 4

1. The token or sign of God's covenant with Noah was the _____. *Genesis 9:13*

2. What did God promise Noah? (great wealth, never again to destroy the world by flood, many children?) *Genesis 9:15*

Lesson 5

1. What building material did the people of Babel use? (stone, concrete, brick?) *Genesis 11:3*

2. Before the Tower of Babel, the people of the earth spoke a single language. T/F. *Genesis 11:6*

Lesson 6

1. Abram's home city was _____ of the Chaldees. *Genesis 15:7*

2. Abram's deep sleep by God also involved what? (darkness, moonlight, owls?) *Genesis 15:12*

Lesson 7

1. Sarah reacted with _____ when hearing that she would become pregnant. *Genesis 18:12*

2. Sarah's son was named Isaac by Abraham. T/F. *Genesis 21:3*

Lesson 8

1. Ishmael and Hagar escaped death when Abraham rescued them. T/F. *Genesis 21:17-19*

2. Ishmael became skilled as a what? (farmer, archer, builder?) *Genesis 21:20*

Lesson 9

1. Jacob dreamed of a ladder with _____ ascending and descending on it. *Genesis 28:12*

2. Jacob promised to give half of all his possessions to God. T/F. *Genesis 28:22*

Lesson 10

1. God called Moses to rescue His people from the land of _____. *Exodus 3:10*

2. Moses wanted to know what about the Lord? (His name, His location, His oath?) *Exodus 3:13*

Lesson 11

1. The feast to remember being saved from the plague of death was called _____. *Exodus 12:11*

2. The Hebrews protected their houses from the plague of death by burning incense in the doorways. T/F. *Exodus 12:13*

Lesson 12

1. What did the Lord use to part the Red Sea? (firestorm, earthquake, wind?) *Exodus 14:21*

2. The escape through the Red Sea occurred at night. T/F. *Exodus 14:21, 22, 24*

Lesson 13

1. What was the main structure of the tabernacle? (an earthen mound, a stone tower, a tent?) *Exodus 40:19*

2. When the tabernacle was finished, a cloud covered it, and it was filled with the _____ of the Lord. *Exodus 40:34*

QUARTER AT A GLANCE

IN RECENT YEARS, the theme of "man vs. ____" has been used to form the title of certain television shows. There's *Man vs. Wild,* where the main character pits himself against severe conditions to demonstrate how he can survive. Another is *Man vs. Food,* where the show's star exhibits a "talent" for consuming all kinds of food.

As we read the Bible, it may seem that the title *Man vs. God* would be fitting! Such conflict plays an important part in the lessons for this quarter, which examine God's creative work as described primarily in Genesis and Exodus, the first two books of the Old Testament.

Genesis: God Uses Individuals

When God created the man and the woman in His image (lesson 2), He created them with great potential and with great responsibility. Sadly, however, we do not have to read far into Genesis until we see the "man vs. God" scenario arise (lesson 3). Yet even after Adam and Eve's disobedience, God announced His plan to reverse the curse of sin by means of the seed of the woman (Genesis 3:15). This is the first reference in Scripture to the coming of Jesus.

The Lord's response to "man vs. God" was to establish a relationship with those created in His image. In spite of man's continual failure to be faithful to God, God remained faithful in His intention to rebuild that relationship. We see this in God's covenant with Noah and his sons (lesson 4). Following the judgment rendered at Babel (lesson 5) came the call of Abram and the establishment of a covenant with him (lesson 6).

The remaining chapters of Genesis record how God worked to fulfill that covenant. This was not a smooth road by any means; the account sometimes reads like that of a highly dysfunctional family! The issue became not only "man vs. God" but "man/woman vs. man/woman." Conflicts arose —between Abram (Abraham) and Sarai (Sarah), between Isaac and Ishmael, between Jacob and Esau, etc. But the Lord was not deterred; He kept His covenant promise intact.

Exodus: God Creates a Nation

In time, Abraham's descendants became the great nation that God had promised. That nation's enslavement set the stage for God's call of Moses and the people's deliverance (lesson 10). God established the Passover (lesson 11) as a means for His people to remember the event that marked their freedom. This deliverance was given a dramatic exclamation point at the Red Sea (lesson 12).

However, such freedom was not a license for God's people to live as they pleased. If they tried to do so, then the "man vs. God" conflict would present itself anew. To remind the Israelites where their allegiance lay, God provided the tabernacle. This was a visible symbol of His presence for the Israelites throughout their travel to the land of promise (lesson 13).

God Himself Takes Action

Sadly, the rest of the Old Testament becomes an account of the never-ending "man vs. God" struggle. We know from the New Testament that insti-

> *The Lord's response to "man vs. God" was to establish a relationship with those created in His image.*

tutions such as the Passover and the tabernacle were not able to address completely the "man vs. God" problem. They are part of the shadow that the Old Testament law represents (Hebrews 10:1).

Ultimately, God took definitive action to reverse sin's destruction by sending the seed of the woman (Jesus). His death as an atoning sacrifice provided the genuine remedy. Only when *Immanuel* ("God with us") came was the conflict of "man vs. God" completely addressed.

GET THE SETTING

by Lloyd M. Pelfrey

AS A NEW NATION under God, Israel needed to know several things: the reasons for the journey to Canaan, the patriarchal roots of Israelite faith, and the power of God in creation. Moses wrote the book of Genesis to provide answers, beginning with this majestic statement: "In the beginning God created the heaven and the earth." How was that different from creation concepts held by other nations?

Creation Accounts

About 100 years ago, it was popular to suggest that Genesis 1 and 2 were borrowed from a "Babylonian Genesis." This document was found in Nineveh, where it was part of the famous clay-tablet library of Ashurbanipal, who was king of Assyria from 668 to 627 BC.

The document is titled *Enuma Elish,* meaning "when on high." It does indeed feature parallels with the Genesis account of creation, but the contrasts are even more striking. The plot begins with the murder of Apsu, a male god representing fresh water. This caused his spouse Tiamat, a female deity representing salt water, to want to avenge his death. The great god Ea then selected Marduk, the god of Babylon, to fight Tiamat, and Marduk (depicted to the right) killed her. He then used the water to create Heaven and earth, and he used her blood to make humankind. This contrasts sharply with the dignified, majestic simplicity of Genesis!

The Egyptians, for their part, had a dozen or so creation stories, and we recall that Moses had been trained with "all the wisdom of the Egyptians" (Acts 7:22). In fact, each continent, nation, or people group had its own theory of how things came to be (cosmogony). They are consistent in that there were gods involved. The usual goal of such accounts is to honor the chief god of a geographic area. The methods of creation tend to exaggerate the ways that new life is observed in nature: through mating (often among the gods), the use of eggs, and vivid imaginations about each of these methods.

Covenants

Moses also showed how God used covenants in promising Canaan to the descendants of the patriarchs. Genesis 6:18, where God said He would establish a covenant with Noah, features the Bible's first use of the word *covenant.* The word is then used several times in Genesis 9 when that covenant is established (lesson 4). Numerous accounts of a worldwide flood have been found among the tribes and territories of the earth. Most such accounts have one family that escaped the deluge in some kind of boat.

The word *covenant* has other backgrounds as well. Genesis 15:18 (lesson 6) uses the expression "made a covenant," and in Hebrew it is literally "cut a covenant." This figure of speech is based on the fact that it was customary to cut (sacrifice) animals when making a covenant. This is demonstrated in the clay tablets discovered at Mari (northeastern Syria), which describe a covenant ceremony of the early second millennium BC that used the foal of a donkey as the sacrificial animal.

When the people of a region heard the word *covenant,* they usually thought about treaties or agreements between individuals or nations. A conquered nation (the vassal) might be offered an agreement by the conqueror (the suzerain). The regular formula included a preamble, historical review, stipulations, and consequences for disobedience. The gods were often cited as witnesses. Copies were made, and memorial stones were sometimes erected.

Creation and *covenant* were important concepts in antiquity! Do you see how and why these concepts are still vital in the New Testament era?

THIS QUARTER IN THE WORD

Mon, Aug. 26	God Knows Our Every Need	Matthew 6:25-34
Tue, Aug. 27	The Greatness of the Creator	Psalm 104:1-4
Wed, Aug. 28	Nourishment for All Creatures	Psalm 104:10-18
Thu, Aug. 29	The Cycle of Days and Seasons	Psalm 104:19-23
Fri, Aug. 30	The Exalted God of Creation	Psalm 97:1-9
Sat, Aug. 31	Praise God, the Creator	Psalm 104:31-35
Sun, Sep. 1	God, Our Creator and Sustainer	Psalm 104:5-9, 24-30
Mon, Sep. 2	Living Creatures of Every Kind	Genesis 1:20-25
Tue, Sep. 3	Made in the Image of God	Genesis 1:26-31
Wed, Sep. 4	Formed from the Dust	Genesis 2:1-9
Thu, Sep. 5	In the Likeness of God	Genesis 5:1-5
Fri, Sep. 6	Made a Little Lower than God	Psalm 8
Sat, Sep. 7	Created in the Likeness of God	Ephesians 4:17-24
Sun, Sep. 8	Created Male and Female	Genesis 2:18-25
Mon, Sep. 9	Obeying God's Voice	Exodus 19:3-8
Tue, Sep. 10	The Blessing in Obedience	Deuteronomy 11:26-32
Wed, Sep. 11	Choosing the Life of Obedience	Deuteronomy 30:11-20
Thu, Sep. 12	Obeying God Above All	Acts 5:27-42
Fri, Sep. 13	The Enticement to Disobey	Genesis 3:1-7
Sat, Sep. 14	The Punishment for Disobedience	Genesis 3:18-24
Sun, Sep. 15	The Consequences of Disobedience	Genesis 3:8-17

Mon, Nov. 11	Called to Live in Freedom	Galatians 5:13-21
Tue, Nov. 12	Setting Apart the Firstborn	Exodus 13:11-16
Wed, Nov. 13	Guided by Pillars of Cloud and Fire	Exodus 13:17-22
Thu, Nov. 14	Pharaoh's Change of Heart	Exodus 14:5-9
Fri, Nov. 15	The Lord Will Fight for You	Exodus 14:10-14
Sat, Nov. 16	Guarded from the Approaching Enemy	Exodus 14:15-20
Sun, Nov. 17	The Lord Saved Israel That Day	Exodus 14:21-30
Mon, Nov. 18	Offering Our Possessions	Exodus 35:4-9
Tue, Nov. 19	Offering Our Skills	Exodus 35:10-19
Wed, Nov. 20	Stirred Hearts and Willing Spirits	Exodus 35:20-29
Thu, Nov. 21	Skills for Every Kind of Work	Exodus 35:30-35
Fri, Nov. 22	An Overabundance of Offerings	Exodus 36:2-7
Sat, Nov. 23	Blessing the Faithful Workers	Exodus 39:32-43
Sun, Nov. 24	God Affirms the Completed Work	Exodus 40:16-30, 34, 38

Answers to the Quarterly Quiz on page 2

Lesson 1—1. water. 2. false. **Lesson 2**—1. alone. 2. false. **Lesson 3**—1. Eve. 2. childbirth. **Lesson 4**—1. (rain)bow. 2. never again to destroy the world by flood. **Lesson 5**—1. brick. 2. true. **Lesson 6**—1. Ur. 2. darkness. **Lesson 7**—1. laughter. 2. true. **Lesson 8**—1. false. 2. archer. **Lesson 9**—1. angels. 2. false. **Lesson 10**—1. Egypt. 2. His name. **Lesson 11**—1. Passover. 2. false. **Lesson 12**—1. wind. 2. true. **Lesson 13**—1. a tent. 2. glory.

LESSON CYCLE CHART

International Sunday School Lesson Cycle, September 2010–August 2016

Year	Fall Quarter (Sep, Oct, Nov)	Winter Quarter (Dec, Jan, Feb)	Spring Quarter (Mar, Apr, May)	Summer Quarter (Jun, Jul, Aug)
2010–2011	The Inescapable God (Exodus, Psalms)	Assuring Hope (Isaiah, Matthew, Mark)	We Worship God (Matthew, Mark, Philippians, 1 & 2 Timothy, Jude, Revelation)	God Instructs His People (Joshua, Judges, Ruth)
2011–2012	Tradition and Wisdom (Proverbs, Ecclesiastes, Song of Solomon, Matthew)	God Establishes a Faithful People (Genesis, Exodus, Luke, Galatians)	God's Creative Word (John)	God Calls for Justice (Pentateuch, History, Psalms, Prophets)
2012–2013	A Living Faith (Psalms, Acts, 1 Corinthians, Hebrews)	Jesus Is Lord (John, Ephesians, Philippians, Colossians)	Undying Hope (Daniel, Luke, Acts, 1 & 2 Thessalonians, 1 & 2 Peter)	God's People Worship (Isaiah, Ezra, Nehemiah)
2013–2014	First Things (Genesis, Exodus, Psalm 104)	Jesus and the Just Reign of God (Luke, James)	Jesus' Fulfillment of Scripture (Pentateuch, 2 Samuel, Psalms, Prophets, Gospels, Acts, Revelation)	The People of God Set Priorities (Haggai, Zechariah, 1 & 2 Corinthians)
2014–2015	Sustaining Hope (Job, Isaiah, Jeremiah, Ezekiel, Habakkuk)	Acts of Worship (Psalms, Daniel, Matthew, Luke, John, Ephesians, Hebrews, James)	The Spirit Comes (Mark, John, Acts, 1 Corinthians, 1–3 John)	God's Prophets Demand Justice (Isaiah, Jeremiah, Ezekiel, Amos, Micah, Zechariah, Malachi)
2015–2016	The Christian Community Comes Alive (Acts)	Sacred Gifts and Holy Gatherings (Pentateuch, Song of Solomon, Hosea, Micah, Gospels)	The Gift of Faith (Mark, Luke)	Toward a New Creation (Zephaniah, Romans)

"God"	"Hope"	"Worship"	"Community"	"Tradition"	"Faith"	"Creation"	"Justice"

A Passion for Teaching

Teacher Tips by Brent Amato

IN ANY TEACHER TRAINING, should we not consider inspiration before implementation, motivation before methodology, passion before presentation? Think about teachers who have captivated you. I suspect one characteristic of those teachers was their sincere enthusiasm that flowed from hearts passionate about their role.

There are three major sources of passion for Christian teaching. These three are available to all who aspire to be excellent teachers.

Who Is Teaching: You in Christ!

Realize in the truest and best sense that it is not *just you* who is teaching, but rather *you in Christ.* This "you" is filled with the Holy Spirit (1 Corinthians 6:19; Galatians 2:20). Always keep in mind your spiritual resources for teaching. This means moving beyond secular, human-based credentials to spiritual, God-based power (1 Corinthians 2:1, 3-5; Colossians 3:16). This enables you to identify your insecurities and anxieties about teaching so you can give them over to the Lord (1 Peter 5:7). When you do, you can move beyond Moses' self-doubting responses to God's call (Exodus 3:11; 4:10, 13) to confident acceptance of that call.

Realize that your role is more than a teacher—you are nothing less than a steward of the gospel (compare 1 Corinthians 4:1, 2; 1 Timothy 1:11, 12)! Be faithful and teach, looking forward to the day you will hear the commendation of our Lord: "Well done, thou good and faithful servant" (Matthew 25:21, 23).

Realize also that we cannot fully comprehend the impact of a Spirit-filled, spiritually gifted teacher (John 14:12). *Passionately teach!*

What You Are Teaching: God's Word!

Realize that you are teaching nothing less than the Word of God (1 Thessalonians 2:13)! When you hold your Bible in your hand, think of yourself as Moses holding the tablets at Mount Sinai.

The Bible is the inspired Word of God (2 Timothy 3:16a). The Word of God identifies and meets your students' deepest needs (Hebrews 4:12).

Realize that the Bible is profitable for all whom you teach (2 Timothy 3:16b, 17); it will not fail to accomplish God's purpose for them (Isaiah 55:11). *Passionately teach!*

Whom You Are Teaching: Your Students!

Realize that you are influencing your students individually and corporately in your church. Realize also that your students may change from week to week in the ways they respond and react to the sown Word. Like Peter, one student may walk into class as a coward in the courtyard one week (Matthew 26:69-75), but as a bold preacher in a public forum the next (Acts 2:14-36). Like Thomas, another student may come as a person of great courage one week (John 11:16), as a doubter the next (20:24, 25), and as a devout worshipper the third (20:26-28).

Realize the truth in the observation, "Everyone is a potential winner. Some people are disguised as losers; don't let their appearance fool you." God knows which students will yield that hundredfold crop (Matthew 13:8, 23), so let Him worry about that. Your goal as a teacher should be that every lesson will promote spiritual maturity for the building of the body of Christ as you sow the Word (Ephesians 4:11-16). *Passionately teach!*

Teaching as a Passion

Realize how awesome it is for a Christian to be privileged to teach the Bible to others! Make it your goal to be like Apollos, who not only was "fervent in the spirit and taught diligently the things of the Lord" (Acts 18:25), but also was open to being taught "the way of God more perfectly" (18:26). The old cliché "leaders are readers" includes the idea that teachers never stop learning. This too is part of your passion to teach.

GOD CREATES

DEVOTIONAL READING: Matthew 6:25-34
BACKGROUND SCRIPTURE: Psalm 104

PSALM 104:5-9, 24-30

5 Who laid the foundations of the earth, that it should not be removed for ever.

6 Thou coveredst it with the deep as with a garment: the waters stood above the mountains.

7 At thy rebuke they fled; at the voice of thy thunder they hasted away.

8 They go up by the mountains; they go down by the valleys unto the place which thou hast founded for them.

9 Thou hast set a bound that they may not pass over; that they turn not again to cover the earth.

. . . .

24 O LORD, how manifold are thy works! in wisdom hast thou made them all: the earth is full of thy riches.

25 So is this great and wide sea, wherein are things creeping innumerable, both small and great beasts.

26 There go the ships: there is that leviathan, whom thou hast made to play therein.

27 These wait all upon thee; that thou mayest give them their meat in due season.

28 That thou givest them they gather: thou openest thine hand, they are filled with good.

29 Thou hidest thy face, they are troubled: thou takest away their breath, they die, and return to their dust.

30 Thou sendest forth thy spirit, they are created: and thou renewest the face of the earth.

KEY VERSE

O LORD, how manifold are thy works! in wisdom hast thou made them all: the earth is full of thy riches.
—**Psalm 104:24**

First Things

Unit 1: First Days

Lessons 1–5

Lesson Aims

After participating in this lesson, each student will be able to:

1. List evidence of God's ability to create and sustain.

2. Match elements of the lesson text with their parallels in Genesis 1 and 2.

3. Write a poem or song of praise to God for His provision and sustaining power.

Lesson Outline

Introduction
    A. First Things First
    B. Lesson Background: The Psalms
I. Sovereign Power (Psalm 104:5-9)
    A. Creating the Earth (v. 5)
    B. Commanding the Waters (vv. 6-9)
      Breathtaking!
II. Sustaining Care (Psalm 104:24-30)
    A. Providing Variety (vv. 24-26)
      His Creativity, Our Blessing
    B. Providing Food (vv. 27, 28)
    C. Providing Life (vv. 29, 30)
Conclusion
    A. The Importance of Beginning Well
    B. Prayer
    C. Thought to Remember

Introduction

A. First Things First

Being first at something is generally considered a mark of distinction. To be the first in one's family to graduate from college or to be the first runner to cross the finish line are noteworthy.

Sometimes being first implies being a pacesetter or establishing a pattern that others will follow. When Neil Armstrong became the first human to set foot on the moon, it marked a dramatic step forward in the American space program. Jackie Robinson's becoming the first African-American to play major league baseball in 1947 opened the door for other African-Americans to do the same.

The first book of the Bible, Genesis, begins with the familiar "In the beginning God created the heaven and the earth" (Genesis 1:1). It is with good reason that the first "main character" in the Bible is God. As the Creator, He is the ultimate "first." In this case, it is impossible for anyone to imitate His "firstness" even remotely. Hear His words given through the prophet Isaiah: "Thus saith the Lord the King of Israel, and his redeemer the Lord of hosts; I am the first, and I am the last; and beside me there is no God" (Isaiah 44:6). The only one who has ever made a similar claim truthfully is Jesus, who was God "made flesh" (John 1:1, 14; Revelation 1:17; 22:13).

B. Lesson Background: The Psalms

Today's lesson deals with God's creative activity as described in Psalm 104. The Psalms have been described as "Israel's hymnal"; as such they cover a wide range of topics, just as any church hymnal does.

One of these topics is creation—and specifically God's glory and splendor as seen throughout His creation. Psalm 19:1-6 is a prime example of this; the first verse affirms, "The heavens declare the glory of God; and the firmament sheweth his handywork." Psalm 104 (today's text) is an especially sweeping tribute to God as Creator. Nearly all of its 35 verses highlight the ways in which He demonstrates His loving care for all He has made.

When discussing authorship of the Psalms, many automatically think of King David. That is certainly appropriate since 73 of the 150 psalms are attributed to David in their titles. Two other psalms that have no title are credited to David in the New Testament: Psalm 2 (in Acts 4:25, 26) and Psalm 95 (in Hebrews 4:7). A psalm without a title is often referred to as an "orphan psalm." That is the case with Psalm 104, today's text. But that fact does not detract from its ability to instruct us about God (see 2 Timothy 3:16).

I. Sovereign Power
(PSALM 104:5-9)

Psalm 104 begins and ends with the writer exhorting himself to bless the Lord; this is parallel to Psalm 103, which begins and ends the same way. In the first four verses of Psalm 104, we can see in poetic language the theme of this preaching-to-self: God is pictured as "clothed with honour and majesty" (v. 1); light is His "garment" (v. 2). He is portrayed as a master designer and builder "who stretchest out the heavens like a curtain" (v. 2) and lays the "beams of his chambers in the waters" (v. 3; these are the waters "above the firmament" in Genesis 1:7) as though the heavens were a building with various levels or "floors."

He also makes the clouds His "chariot," and He walks "upon the wings of the wind" (Psalm 104:3). Paganism uses chariot imagery in descriptions of certain fictional deities; such imagery is used here (and elsewhere in Scripture) to present the Lord as the supreme one. He in truth holds the power that they hold only in myth. Only He can make "his angels spirits; his ministers a flaming fire" (v. 4; compare Hebrews 1:7).

HOW TO SAY IT

Baal	*Bay*-ul.
Canaan	*Kay*-nun.
Canaanite	*Kay*-nun-ite.
Elijah	Ee-*lye*-juh.
Elisha	Ee-*lye*-shuh.
Galilee	*Gal*-uh-lee.
Haggai	*Hag*-eye or *Hag*-ay-eye.
leviathan	luh-*vye*-uh-thun.
Noah	*No*-uh.

A. Creating the Earth (v. 5)

5. Who laid the foundations of the earth, that it should not be removed for ever.

The picture of God as the divine architect continues. The Scriptures teach that at the end of time, when Jesus returns, the old earth will indeed be removed (2 Peter 3:10). What the psalmist is saying is that no human being—no power other than that of the Creator himself—can remove or move the earth from its established position.

The earthquakes that occur throughout the world should caution us against placing too much trust in "things on the earth" (Colossians 3:2). The writer of Hebrews contrasts the shakiness of this world with the kingdom of God, which "cannot be moved" (Hebrews 12:26-28; compare Haggai 2:21). It just stands to reason that the one who *laid the foundations of the earth* has the ability to move or remove it whenever He wishes.

What Do You Think?
Does the way you pray match the way you *should* pray when the world seems out of control? Why, or why not?
Talking Points for Your Discussion
- During crises that touch you personally
- During crises that don't touch you personally

B. Commanding the Waters (vv. 6-9)

6. Thou coveredst it with the deep as with a garment: the waters stood above the mountains.

Previously in this psalm, God is portrayed as clothing himself with honor and majesty, covering himself with light (vv. 1, 2). Here He covers the earth *with the deep*—that is, with deep waters—that at one time *stood above the mountains*. This appears to describe the setting of Genesis 1:2: "And the earth was without form, and void; and darkness was upon the face of the deep." At that point nothing was visible except the waters.

7, 8. At thy rebuke they fled; at the voice of thy thunder they hasted away. They go up by the mountains; they go down by the valleys unto the place which thou hast founded for them.

The waters are characterized almost as a rebellious child; they receive a rebuke from the Lord, and in response they flee to their assigned places. Thunder is often associated with pagan deities in antiquity, but the Scriptures tell us that thunder is the voice of God. Psalm 29:3 in particular notes, "The voice of the Lord is upon the waters: the God of glory thundereth: the Lord is upon many waters" (compare 2 Samuel 22:14; Job 37:4, 5; Psalms 18:13; 77:18). It is interesting to see the idea of God's thunderous voice alongside that of His self-adornment with majesty, etc., in Job 40:9, 10.

We should also consider what the Old Testament says about God's sovereignty over creation in contrast with how the pagan peoples of Old Testament times view the world. For pagans, the world is often a fearsome, terrifying place. Natural disasters are seen as an indication that "the gods" need to be appeased in some way. The peoples who worship these fictitious gods are not sure what they have done to cause the gods' wrath. Consequently, these people live in a state of perpetual uncertainty regarding the gods they worship.

The Old Testament, however, is quite clear in its acknowledgment of the world as the creation of the one true God, who is personal, powerful, and sovereign. He is to be trusted and faithfully served by those made in His image. The ancient Israelites are not a seafaring people, yet they know that the sea is not a place of uncontrolled chaos. Like everything else in the world, the waters are the handiwork of God.

Visual for Lesson 1. *Point to this visual as you ask, "How has your study of creation helped you better appreciate the Creator?"*

What Do You Think?
How will you use this passage to remind yourself that God is in control?
Talking Points for Your Discussion
- In times of physical uncertainty (natural disasters, health problems, etc.)
- In times of relational uncertainty (divorce, etc.)
- In times of spiritual uncertainty (satanic attack, etc.)
- Other

❧ BREATHTAKING! ❧

On the Enhanced Fujita Scale, an EF5 tornado is the most destructive. The year 2011 saw several of these devastate various areas of Mississippi, Alabama, Tennessee, Missouri, and Oklahoma. At the heart of the affected areas, it didn't matter how well the homes were built. The EF5 funnels leveled everything.

How small we feel when we view the forces of nature! How much more difficult it is to imagine the power that creates and maintains all that is! How can we quantify the power of the Almighty? How can we grasp its magnitude? It's possible to read the poetry of Psalm 104 and miss the reality of it. The Lord truly can control the forces of nature with a word. In His perfect expression of the Almighty Father, Jesus spoke to a storm and calmed it (Matthew 8:23-27).

Knowing that the master of all elements and forces is watching us should draw us to godly fear and reverence. Knowing that His powerful love and grace work continually to draw us back to Him should take our breath away.   —V. E.

9. Thou hast set a bound that they may not pass over; that they turn not again to cover the earth.

Again we see an affirmation of God's control over His creation. "This is my Father's world" is what an old hymn declares, and thus it has always been. The waters go to their appointed places; they do not act independently of their Creator. This verse describes what happens in Genesis 1:9: "And God said, Let the waters under the heaven be gathered together unto one place, and let the dry land appear: and it was so."

The language of this verse could also apply to the flood of Noah's day (see lesson 4). The statement that the waters will *turn not again to cover the earth* is reminiscent of God's promise to Noah and his sons following the flood (Genesis 9:11, 15).

In addition, the prominence of water in these verses and the emphasis on God's control of them calls to mind the various miracles in the Bible involving water. Included in this list is the parting of the Red Sea to allow the Israelites to escape the Egyptians (Exodus 14:21, 22; see lesson 12), the parting of the Jordan River to allow the Israelites to enter Canaan (Joshua 3:14-17), the parting of the Jordan by both Elijah and Elisha (2 Kings 2:8, 13, 14), and Jesus' stilling of a storm on the Sea of Galilee (Mark 4:35-39). The "rebuke" in Psalm 104:7 may be compared with Jesus' command of "Peace, be still," which brought immediate calm to that storm.

II. Sustaining Care
(PSALM 104:24-30)

While the first part of our printed text highlights God's work in creation, the next portion describes God's faithfulness in sustaining His creation. The psalmist calls attention to this in verses 10-23 (not in today's text), where he gives examples of God's providential care on earth and in the heavens. All of this bears witness that what people often call "the natural world" is in reality "the supernatural world," for it all exhibits the gracious hand of God.

A. Providing Variety (vv. 24-26)

24. O LORD, how manifold are thy works! in wisdom hast thou made them all: the earth is full of thy riches.

The psalmist pauses in the midst of his examples of God's care for His creation to reflect on and extol God's many wonderful works. The Creator is indeed creative! This is abundantly clear from the variety of creatures in the world. The distinctions in size, color, speed, and other characteristics are amazing! Humans in their limited

wisdom have studied and categorized these creatures; but at the same time, sadly, people often have failed to give credit to the wisdom that made these creatures in the first place.

That wisdom is God's alone. May we never lose our sense of wonder at our Creator's magnificent craftsmanship. Such variety provides a vast source of riches for us to enjoy—the kind of wealth that has nothing to do with the size of one's bank account!

What Do You Think?
  What situations other than Sunday worship prompt you to praise God? Why?
Talking Points for Your Discussion
  - With family
  - Among friends
  - At work
  - Alone
  - Other

❧ *HIS CREATIVITY, OUR BLESSING* ❧

My husband is an entomologist. Because of this, I have learned more about insects than I ever thought I would. Did you know there are more varieties of beetles—more than 350,000 types—than all of the other types of creatures combined? There are certainly even more that humans have yet to discover.

Bugs aren't the only place to notice variety. Our family has relocated many times, and whenever we meet new neighbors and coworkers, we find that each person is unique. We have never found a duplicate.

Psalm 104 points to the Father's creativity. He delights in variety. He never runs out of fresh ideas and ways to bless us. It is criminal for us to put God in a box of our limited understanding, to think He cannot show us the way out of our current challenges. It will take all of eternity to fathom and enjoy the infinite facets of His wisdom. But it is our privilege to praise Him and His ways *now*. Indeed, we fail in our role as children of God when we neglect to praise Him for the many wonders He has placed in the ample "playground" He has made for us.

—V. E.

25. So is this great and wide sea, wherein are things creeping innumerable, both small and great beasts.

The psalmist now focuses on one area of creation where variety is especially evident: the *great and wide sea*. Documentaries that have filmed ocean life have captured some of this for all to see. These programs provide us with a sense of just how impressive are the number and size *(both small and great)* of the creatures that dwell in the waters. The psalmist acknowledges this, even without the benefit of the technology we possess today.

> **What Do You Think?**
> How do modern discoveries affect your view of God and His creation?
> *Talking Points for Your Discussion*
> - Regarding living organisms
> - Regarding forces of nature
> - Regarding psychology
> - Regarding secular views of evolution
> - Other

26. There go the ships: there is that leviathan, whom thou hast made to play therein.

Certain occupations allow people to appreciate in a special way the magnitude and wonder of God's creative activity. Here the psalmist describes those who travel in ships as having a special window through which to see the splendor of creation. In particular *that leviathan* is cited as a creature that God has *made to play* in the waters.

What exactly is a leviathan? Obviously it is some kind of creature of the water, though specifically which one is subject to much speculation. Some think it is a crocodile. Job 41, where leviathan is described in much more detail, may support this. In particular, Job 41:14 notes that "his teeth are terrible round about" (with *terrible* meaning "capable of inciting terror"). However, Job 41 also uses much figurative language in describing leviathan (see vv. 18-21), so we are cautious about making a firm identification. The notation regarding "the heads of leviathan" in Psalm 74:14 adds to our caution.

In any case, leviathan is clearly a creature to be feared according to the way Job 41 pictures it. Isaiah 27:1, a passage where the judgment of God is described, mentions "the piercing serpent, even leviathan that crooked serpent." This seems to connect leviathan with the serpent as the latter is used in Scripture to portray Satan.

Accounts from ancient Canaanite literature mention a many-headed sea serpent that is defeated by the god Baal. Here in Psalms, though, the focus is more on leviathan as simply a creature of the water—just one of many that God has created. And leviathan is clearly under the control of the Creator, who considers it as one of the many creatures He allows *to play* in His "swimming pool."

Perhaps a connection to pagan myths is a part of the psalmist's reason for mentioning leviathan; the psalmist may want to convey that the true God, the Creator, is far superior to any power associated with paganism. Since the true God has created the sea creatures, any discussion of a god needing to defeat a sea serpent is laughable.

B. Providing Food (vv. 27, 28)

27. These wait all upon thee; that thou mayest give them their meat in due season.

All creatures depend on the Lord. How sad that humans, though made in the image of God, often refuse to acknowledge Him as the giver of "every good gift and every perfect gift" (James 1:17). Worse still is our tendency to complain about God's provisions from time to time (compare Numbers 11:6).

> **What Do You Think?**
> What effort will you make in the week ahead to turn your complaints into praise?
> *Talking Points for Your Discussion*
> - While stuck in traffic
> - In seeing high prices while grocery shopping
> - While working in an unfulfilling job
> - Other (be specific)

28. That thou givest them they gather: thou openest thine hand, they are filled with good.

Sometimes we feed certain animals by allowing them to eat from our hands. God's power to give in this regard is infinitely greater than ours. Moses warned the Israelites not to forget that the

Lord is the source of their blessings and cautioned them not to think that "the might of mine hand hath gotten me this wealth" (Deuteronomy 8:17).

C. Providing Life (vv. 29, 30)

29, 30. Thou hidest thy face, they are troubled: thou takest away their breath, they die, and return to their dust. Thou sendest forth thy spirit, they are created: and thou renewest the face of the earth.

The imagery here should stir self-reflection: do we acknowledge our constant, day-by-day need for God? Do we realize just how terrifying our existence would be without His sustaining presence?

The Lord holds the power of life and death over all His creatures. When these creatures die, they *return to their dust* just as humans do (Genesis 3:19; Ecclesiastes 12:7). God's Spirit then provides life to new creatures so that the earth is repopulated with them. It is noteworthy that the Hebrew word translated as *breath* and *spirit* in these two verses is the same. This is part of the parallelism that characterizes so much of Hebrew poetry, a parallelism that may be less evident in a translation. The fact that the psalmist recognizes that God is the one who *renewest the face of the earth* affirms God to be not only the Creator but also as "Re-creator."

The psalmist concludes Psalm 104 with his own expression of praise to the Lord. He will not allow the creatures of this world to outpraise him! "I will sing unto the Lord as long as I live: I will sing praise to my God while I have my being" (v. 33). The concluding declaration in verse 35 is this: "Let the sinners be consumed out of the earth, and let the wicked be no more." Those who deny God's creative activity or seek to squelch the witness of creation to His greatness will themselves be squelched. The undeniable truth is that God is the Creator. Humanity ignores or defies that fact to its own destruction (compare Daniel 4:28-32).

Conclusion

A. The Importance of Beginning Well

In the classic movie *Mary Poppins,* a very proper nanny offers her services to the Banks household, where two rather impudent children live. One of the chores the children need to attend to is cleaning their rooms. To encourage the children to get this task done, Mary presents it as a game—a game she calls, "Well Begun Is Half-Done." Her point is that starting any job properly is the key to completing it well and on time.

The importance of the "well begun" principle can also be applied to the understanding of one's purpose for living. If we have no sense of beginnings or origins or cannot with confidence answer the question, "How did we get here?" then the reason for our existence is shrouded in mystery. So, for that matter, is the issue of our future. If we do not know where we came from, how can we know for sure where we're going? But if we know our beginnings, then we are more than "half done"; we are well on our way to grasping our purpose for living and to knowing what the future holds.

This lesson begins a series of studies entitled "First Things." We should think of *first* not just in terms of things that happened first (in a chronological sense), but also in terms of what is of first importance. If God is in control of "first things" (creation), then "middle things" (the present) have purpose, and "last things" (the future) are in His hands as well.

B. Prayer

Lord of all creation, we join with the psalmist in voicing our praise to You for Your marvelous handiwork. We know that what You have made continues to declare Your glory in spite of humanity's determined efforts to silence that declaration. Thank You for Your constant and faithful care. In Jesus' name, amen.

C. Thought to Remember

God is the one who creates and sustains.

VISUALS FOR THESE LESSONS

The visual pictured in each lesson (example: page 12) is a small reproduction of a large, full-color poster included in the *Adult Resources* packet for the Fall Quarter. That packet also contains the very useful *Presentation Helps* on a CD for teacher use. Order No. 020019213 from your supplier.

INVOLVEMENT LEARNING

Some of the activities below are also found in the helpful student book, Adult Bible Class.
Don't forget to download the free reproducible page from www.standardlesson.com to enhance your lesson!

Into the Lesson

Option: Place in chairs copies of the "God's Creation" word-search puzzle from the reproducible page, which you can download. Learners can begin working on this as they arrive.

Create eight large cards with the following entries, one each: *light / sky / land and sea / plants / sun and moon / sea creatures and birds / land animals / man.* Have the following headings displayed on the board as learners arrive: Day 1 / Day 2 / Day 3 / Day 4 / Day 5 / Day 6 / Day 7. Affix the cards to the board randomly. Say, "Let's do a little review. As you can see, I have the elements of creation on the cards. Keep your Bibles closed as we match each to its day of creation. Then we'll check our conclusions with Scripture."

After completing the exercise and checking answers against Genesis 1, say, "Do you know that Genesis 1 is not the only place in the Bible that speaks of creation? This morning we'll look at a parallel passage."

Into the Word

Divide the class into four small groups or study pairs and make these assignments: Group 1—Psalm 104:5-9; Group 2—Psalm 104:24-30; Group 3—Genesis 1:1-13; Group 4—Genesis 1:14-31. Ask each group to read its assigned text, summarize it, and identify the theme of the passage. When the groups are ready, ask them to share findings. *(Possible responses for summaries and themes: Group 1: an introduction to the creation process / God's power in creation. Group 2: creation of the sea and the creatures that inhabit it / awe at what God has created. Group 3: creation days 1 to 3 / God is the Creator of all that exists. Group 4: creation days 4 to 6 / God's pleasure with all that He created.)* Add information from the commentary to the groups' presentations where appropriate.

When you have completed the Scripture analysis, say, "Sometimes critics of the Bible will claim that passages like these are proof that the Bible is flawed because passages that refer to the same event do not record those events in the same way. Let's see how such passages complement, rather than contradict, one another."

Distribute identical handouts with today's text and Genesis 1:1-31. Ask learners to work in their groups or pairs to put the verses from these two passages into a single sequence so that the two accounts flow as one. *Option:* Distribute scissors and tape so learners can physically arrange the texts. *(Possible compilation: Genesis 1:1→Psalm 104:5→Genesis 1:2→Psalm 104:6→Genesis 1:3-7 →Psalm 104:7, 8→Genesis 1:8, 9→Psalm 104:9→ Genesis 1:10-21→Psalm 104:25, 26→Genesis 1:22-25→Psalm 104:27-30→Genesis 1:26-31.)*

Compare and contrast the results. Differing sequences will provide an opportunity for a close examination of the two passages.

Into Life

Say, "Our lesson reminds us of the greatness of God and the majesty of His creation. Sadly, God's creation becomes tainted by sin. One kind of sin occurs when people dehumanize others, who are made in God's image." Ask for examples of how this has occurred throughout history; jot answers on the board. *(Possible responses: slavery, genocide, abortion, euthanasia, sex trafficking.)* Discuss ways that "the average person" may be guilty of dehumanizing others; jot answers on the board. *(Possible responses: bigotry, prejudice, stereotyping).* Brainstorm ways to counteract the tendency to dehumanize.

In addition to or instead of the above: Distribute copies of the "Mighty Works" activity from the reproducible page; allow three minutes for completion. Discuss results and—in the spirit of a lesson on creation—give a token prize for the most creative set of responses.

Conclude by singing the hymn, "This Is My Father's World."

God's Image: Male and Female

DEVOTIONAL READING: Psalm 8

BACKGROUND SCRIPTURE: Genesis 1, 2; 5:1, 2

GENESIS 2:18-25

18 And the LORD God said, It is not good that the man should be alone; I will make him an help meet for him.

19 And out of the ground the LORD God formed every beast of the field, and every fowl of the air; and brought them unto Adam to see what he would call them: and whatsoever Adam called every living creature, that was the name thereof.

20 And Adam gave names to all cattle, and to the fowl of the air, and to every beast of the field; but for Adam there was not found an help meet for him.

21 And the LORD God caused a deep sleep to fall upon Adam, and he slept: and he took one of his ribs, and closed up the flesh instead thereof;

22 And the rib, which the LORD God had taken from man, made he a woman, and brought her unto the man.

23 And Adam said, This is now bone of my bones, and flesh of my flesh: she shall be called Woman, because she was taken out of Man.

24 Therefore shall a man leave his father and his mother, and shall cleave unto his wife: and they shall be one flesh.

25 And they were both naked, the man and his wife, and were not ashamed.

KEY VERSE

The LORD God said, It is not good that the man should be alone; I will make him an help meet for him.

—**Genesis 2:18**

First Things

Unit 1: First Days

LESSONS 1–5

LESSON AIMS

After participating in this lesson, each student will be able to:

1. Summarize the process by which God created woman.

2. Explain what was "not good" about the man's being alone and what that says about the importance of marriage.

3. Write a note of encouragement to a couple newly married or preparing to enter into marriage.

LESSON OUTLINE

Introduction

A. An Unforgettable Wedding

Many weddings took place on April 29, 2011. But one in particular was quite out of the ordinary: the marriage of Prince William to Catherine Middleton. Millions witnessed the ceremony on TV and the Internet; an estimated one million people lined the procession route from Buckingham Palace to Westminster Abbey. Depending on where a person lived, a significant adjustment in one's scheduling was required in order to witness the event as it happened. For example, a pub in Cincinnati, Ohio, opened its doors at 5:45 a.m. so patrons could witness the exchange of vows on its TV.

The lesson text for today records another unforgettable "wedding," if we may use that term. It was unforgettable because it was the very first. This memorable occasion was not witnessed by millions of people. No cheering crowds were there; in fact, only three parties (not counting animals) were present: God, the first man, and the first woman. The account, however, has been read by hundreds of millions of people, for it is recorded in God's sacred Word, in Genesis 2:22, 23.

This record still has much to teach us about the meaning and the significance of marriage. It highlights a truth that today's world desperately needs to recognize: the origin of marriage is divine, not human. It is indeed "holy matrimony."

B. Lesson Background

Today's lesson and the next three are drawn from the book of Genesis. Today's text deals with part of God's actions on the sixth day of creation. According to Genesis 1:24-31, this is the day God created land animals and the first humans. The picture becomes fuller when we see the first man (Adam) being placed "into the garden of Eden to dress it and to keep it" (Genesis 2:15).

Some students maintain that the creation account in Genesis 2 is an entirely different, and even contradictory, account from that found in Genesis 1. But Genesis 2 should be considered supplementary, not contradictory, to Genesis 1. Some suggest that Genesis 2 is like the effect of a zoom lens, focusing especially on the events of the sixth day, primarily those involving the man and the woman created in God's image.

The focus within Genesis 2 on the creation of the man and the woman is most appropriate given the special place that human beings have in God's creative activity. Only humans are said to be created in the image of God (Genesis 1:26, 27), as what might be called the grand finale of God's work. He saves the best for last, as confirmed by the additional details provided in Genesis 2.

I. Problem
(Genesis 2:18-20)
A. God States the Need (v. 18)

18. And the Lord God said, It is not good that the man should be alone; I will make him an help meet for him.

The phrase "and God saw that it was good" appears at various stages of His creative work (Genesis 1:10, 12, 18, 21, 25). The assessment of the creation as "very good" concludes the entire account (Genesis 1:31). However, we now learn of a situation that *is not good*: the fact that the man should be alone. So God determines that He *will make him an help meet for him.* The word *meet* in this context carries with it the idea of "appropriate." Therefore the help to be provided for the man is someone who will serve as an appropriate companion.

Thus something of the purpose for the creation of woman is already hinted at even before her creation takes place. She will complete the man, helping him become what he would not be capable of becoming were he to remain alone.

What Do You Think?
How can the church do a better job of ministering to those who are now "alone" as widows and widowers?
Talking Points for Your Discussion
- In church programming
- In church budgeting
- Cooperating with community-based seniors programs
- Other

B. Adam Sees the Need (vv. 19, 20)

19. And out of the ground the Lord God formed every beast of the field, and every fowl of the air; and brought them unto Adam to see what he would call them: and whatsoever Adam called every living creature, that was the name thereof.

The line *out of the ground the Lord God formed every beast of the field* reflects what has already occurred on the sixth day of creation (see Genesis 1:24, 25). While the waters are said to have brought forth the various sea creatures and birds on the fifth day (1:20), all creatures are made from the ground or dust as noted in Psalm 104:29 (see last week's lesson). The man himself also has been formed "of the dust of the ground" by the Lord God (Genesis 2:7).

But now we come to new information: all of the creatures that God has made are brought before Adam for naming by the man. We wonder if this naming procedure includes each and every subcategory of creature "after his kind" (Genesis 1:25). Some think that that would take too long for a single day, so they propose that Adam names only the broader categories of animals and birds rather than the much more numerous subcategories.

It is noteworthy that this verse includes the first time in the Genesis account that the name *Adam* appears. In the Hebrew text, the word *Adam* is actually the same as that which is translated "the man" in Genesis 2:18 (the Hebrew language has no capital letters to designate proper names). Of perhaps greater significance at this time is the fact that the name *Adam* comes from the Hebrew word meaning "ground" in Genesis 2:7. This calls attention to the material from which he is created.

20. And Adam gave names to all cattle, and to the fowl of the air, and to every beast of the field; but for Adam there was not found an help meet for him.

Adam proceeds to name the various creatures. But in the process a sobering truth dawns: although they come from the ground as he does, none is quite like him. *For Adam there was not found an help meet for him.* Thus the state of being alone, which God has already said is "not good" for the man, is recognized by the man himself.

Perhaps we have been wondering to this point why God doesn't just name all the creatures himself. This may be the reason: having Adam do the naming allows him to come to his own conclusion regarding his need.

II. Provision
(GENESIS 2:21-23)
A. Man Sleeps (v. 21)

21. And the LORD God caused a deep sleep to fall upon Adam, and he slept; and he took one of his ribs, and closed up the flesh instead thereof.

God now acts to address the man's incompleteness. This is a multistep process, the first of which is for God to cause *a deep sleep to fall upon Adam.*

The Hebrew word rendered *deep sleep* is used in two other places where the Lord acts in a literal, physical way on individuals: regarding Abram in Genesis 15:12 (lesson 6), and regarding Saul and his companions in 1 Samuel 26:12. (Other uses of this word are found in Job 4:13; 33:15; Proverbs 19:15; and Isaiah 29:10.) It is during this divinely induced anesthesia that the Lord proceeds to the next two steps: removing one of Adam's ribs, then closing the flesh.

B. God Shapes (v. 22)

22. And the rib, which the LORD God had taken from man, made he a woman, and brought her unto the man.

This very brief account of God's creation of a woman raises a question: why create the woman from the man's rib? Many have suggested a special symbolism: woman is made from the "side" of the man so that she will be neither "above" him nor "beneath" him, but always by his side to encourage him. The Bible is silent regarding such symbolism. Scripture simply pulls back the curtain on this very sacred moment, gives us a quick glimpse of what happens, and then closes the curtain. We

would not know of this account at all had not God chosen to reveal it to us.

The primary point behind the description of the woman's creation seems to be the special care that God takes to solve the man's incompleteness. The woman is not created from the dust of the ground as was the man; rather, she is created from the man. The psychological importance of this fact is revealed in the next verse.

C. Man Speaks (v. 23)

23. And Adam said, This is now bone of my bones, and flesh of my flesh: she shall be called Woman, because she was taken out of Man.

When Adam awakens from his surgery, the recovery time is apparently very brief. He beholds in amazement the new individual before him and immediately understands that she is not like any of the creatures he has previously seen and named. The phrase *This is now* is somewhat difficult to translate from Hebrew into smooth English that will fit with the rest of the sentence. Literally it reads, "This is the time." Perhaps an exclamation such as "At last!" fits the setting.

Adam acknowledges what makes God's newest creation unique: she is *bone of my bones, and flesh of my flesh.* Adam is aware of the procedure he has just undergone. But rather than feel like he is "missing something" (a rib), he experiences a sense of completeness. His feeling of being alone has been remedied. He clearly sees a special individual before him—one with whom he senses a genuine kinship.

Adam then proceeds to "name" this new creation, just as he has previously named the creatures brought before him: *She shall be called Woman.* Earlier we noted that the Hebrew words for *ground* and *Adam* (or *the man*) are drawn from the same noun. Here, however, a different word for *man* is used by Adam when he says of the woman that *she was taken out of Man.* The word for man that is related to the word *ground* will not do here, for this new individual has not come from the ground as Adam has. Since she has been *taken out of Man,* her designation, *Woman,* is taken out of the different word for man that Adam uses (in fact, it is the feminine form of that word).

HOW TO SAY IT

Corinthians	Ko-*rin*-thee-unz (*th* as in *thin*).
Ephesians	Ee-*fee*-zhunz.
Moses	*Mo*-zes or *Mo*-zez.

We should note at this point that the name Adam gives his new companion is really more of a description that recognizes what distinguishes her from the other residents in the Garden of Eden. Adam will not actually name her *Eve* until later, after the fall (Genesis 3:20). Out of all the designations that Adam has assigned on this sixth day, we can be sure that *woman* will be the one he will cherish most!

What Do You Think?
  What are some ways that husbands and wives can use their similarities and differences to become a more complete reflection of the image of God?
Talking Points for Your Discussion
  - In thoughts (Hebrews 10:24)
  - In words (Proverbs 16:24)
  - In actions (Galatians 5:13)

❧ *DOING THINGS GOD'S WAY* ❧

Private citizens and governments around the world are intensely debating the definition of marriage. Can two people of the same gender be married? Isn't it discrimination to view same-sex couples as less than married so long as they are committed to each other? God is love—isn't it unloving to be biased in our view of people?

This question is answered directly in God's Word: God calls homosexual behavior an "abomination" (Leviticus 18:22; compare Romans 1:26, 27; 1 Corinthians 6:9). Today's text reveals the perfect and deliberate design of God: marriage of one man to one woman.

Make no mistake: the cultural trend of redefining marriage involves the twisting of God's design and purpose for marriage and family. God loves every person He has ever made. He always desires what is best for each of us. As His children, we must not behave disrespectfully, but always graciously honor others as His image bearers. But behaviors that God abhors are never to be called "good" (Isaiah 5:20). God does not sanction homosexual relationships; we shouldn't either. The loving thing to do is to point people to God and His ways.   —V. E.

III. Principles
(GENESIS 2:24, 25)
A. One Flesh (v. 24)

24. Therefore shall a man leave his father and his mother, and shall cleave unto his wife: and they shall be one flesh.

Moses wrote the first five books of the Bible, and that fact raises a question about this verse: is Moses quoting Adam here, or is this Moses' own inspired commentary? Being the first human, Adam never has the experience of leaving *his father and mother,* thus suggesting that this is Moses' commentary. Of course, the Holy Spirit could inspire Adam to make this statement, but it is probably better to see the words as those of Moses.

Three significant stages in a marriage relationship are set forth in this verse. The first is that *a man [shall] leave his father and his mother.* Marriage involves the creation of a new bond; this is a bond with one's spouse, a bond that supersedes any close ties with parents. This does not mean that no further involvement occurs with the parents; the idea, rather, is that the parental bond is no longer the most significant relationship in the lives of the husband and wife.

Second, the man is to *cleave unto his wife.* The Hebrew word translated as *cleave* means "cling to" or "stick to." It implies an especially tight bonding or loyalty. That is why the first step of fully leaving father and mother must be made. Marriage counselors can attest to the fact that many problems in marriages occur because loyalty to one or both parents continues to trump loyalty to one's spouse.

The third step is a result of the cleaving: the husband and wife become *one flesh.* This speaks primarily to the unity that is to characterize marriage in the sight of God. That oneness is rooted in the process by which woman was created. God actually did make two out of one by creating woman from man's rib; two then become one in marriage. The intimacy that this creates certainly includes the sexual relationship, but it cannot be limited to that. True intimacy means a sharing of every aspect of life lest the oneness be compromised.

The vital importance of Genesis 2:24 is seen in the fact that it is quoted four times in the New Testament (see Matthew 19:1-6 and its parallel in Mark 10:1-8; 1 Corinthians 6:12-20; and Ephesians 5:22-33). These timeless words continue to proclaim God's design concerning marriage: one man and one woman becoming one flesh for life.

❧ ONE WEAK MOMENT ❧

Shortly after moving our family for a new job, my husband moved us again in order to get a job he would enjoy more. I agreed, but the transition proved to be more difficult than I had expected. While he was enjoying his dream job, I was miserable, struggling to rebuild my life. Then the thought hit me: *I could move back to California—to the place where I enjoyed work, friends, and climate!*

My mother, sister, grandmother, and even great-grandmother had been divorced, so why couldn't I? I was independent, and knew I could survive. There were only two problems with my solution. First, my friends in California were Christians and would not support my leaving my husband for this reason. The second reason was even more troubling: although I knew I could live without a husband, I was sure I couldn't live without God. The Bible is clear that God desires spouses to stay together (Malachi 2:16; Mark 10:9). I just couldn't

figure out how to be right with God while choosing not be right with my husband.

When I finally told God "okay," I felt Him lift me out of despair. Looking back, I can't imagine the damage that one decision would have brought me, my children, and my spouse (who happens to be my best friend). My discontentment phase is barely memorable from this point in life. This Scripture shows that marriage is a priority union. This isn't to diminish the value of the extended family, but to show God's point of view for this special, for-life relationship.   —V. E.

B. No Shame (v. 25)

25. And they were both naked, the man and his wife, and were not ashamed.

This is an interesting way to conclude this account. The issue of nakedness has not been mentioned thus far, but it will become a critical issue in the next chapter of Genesis, where Adam and Eve's disobedience is recorded. One of the consequences of their sin will be recognizing their nakedness and covering themselves (Genesis 3:7).

At this point, however, innocence characterizes the relationship between the first man and the first woman. The fact that their nakedness produces no sense of shame reflects not only that innocence but also the degree of intimacy between them. When sin intrudes, their innocence will depart. Their intimacy will be damaged badly, as shown by Adam's attempt to blame his wife, in whom he had originally expressed delight (Genesis 3:12, next week's lesson).

Conclusion
A. The State of the Union (of Marriage)
For as long as most of us can remember, God's ideal for marriage has been under assault in West-

ern society. "Living together" (which used to be called "shacking up") has gained acceptance, even from some who have been brought up in the church. No doubt this cavalier attitude toward marriage is just one of many consequences that the Western world has experienced as a result of its rejection of a Judeo-Christian framework that defines marriage on biblical terms.

But this is not the time (nor is it ever) for the church to wave the white flag in surrender. We cannot allow the culture to set the terms of the marriage issue. Churches can offer sermons, retreats, and Bible studies on God's plan for marriage. Premarital counseling can be offered (or made mandatory) to those considering marriage in the church. Youth should be instructed during (or before) the high-school years about the biblical teaching concerning marriage and how the Christian marriage can serve as a model of the relationship between Christ and the church.

That last point is crucial. Ultimately, the assault on marriage undermines a key witnessing tool of the church. Strong marriages are an essential part of how the church witnesses on behalf of Jesus to a lost world (compare 1 Timothy 5:14, 15). When Paul uses marriage to illustrate the relationship between Christ and the church in Ephesians 5, he cites Genesis 2:24. That illustration remains a vital part of the church's message to whatever culture it is confronting. Marriage is meant to honor the Creator, and it is meant to honor the head of the church, Jesus Christ.

B. Singled Out?

Unmarried Christians who are content to remain single may feel a bit uncomfortable by the declaration, "It is not good that the man should be alone" (Genesis 2:18). They may discover that their lifestyle allows them to serve the Lord with a freedom and flexibility that would not be theirs if they were married.

The single lifestyle is not inconsistent with the overall teaching of Scripture. Paul, whose high regard for marriage we have already noted, told the Corinthians that a married person has additional cares to address (1 Corinthians 7:32-34). Jesus acknowledged that some remain unmarried

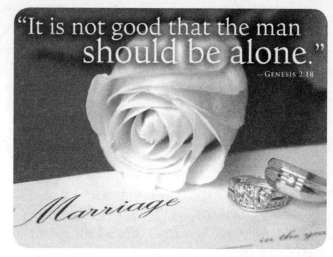

"It is not good that the man should be alone." — GENESIS 2:18

Visual for Lesson 2. *Point to this visual as you ask, "What are some things the church can do to uphold and promote the biblical view of marriage?"*

"for the kingdom of heaven's sake" (Matthew 19:12). Genesis 2:18 must be seen in its immediate setting. It was certainly not good for Adam to remain alone for several reasons, among them God's desire for humans to "be fruitful, and multiply, and replenish the earth" (Genesis 1:28). Adam could not do that alone!

Living in a world affected by sin, we know that there are situations where singleness may be the preferred state in which one should live. Jeremiah was told to remain single and childless because of the hard times that God's people were to face (Jeremiah 16:1-4). Marriage would have made that man's prophetic task more difficult. One could even say that God demonstrated mercy toward Jeremiah through His command not to marry or have children: Jeremiah would be spared the heartache of seeing his wife and children suffer, and his family would be spared the heartache of seeing a husband and father suffer.

C. Prayer

Father, may we give marriage the respect it deserves. In these troubled times, we pray for the strength and courage to speak on behalf of marriage as You created and ordained it. In the name of Jesus, whose bride is the church, amen.

D. Thought to Remember

Marriage is "holy matrimony" because it was created by God.

INVOLVEMENT LEARNING

Some of the activities below are also found in the helpful student book, Adult Bible Class.
Don't forget to download the free reproducible page from www.standardlesson.com to enhance your lesson!

Into the Lesson

Contact learners in advance to ask that they bring one of their wedding pictures to class. Have participants place their pictures in a basket next to the door as they arrive.

After everyone is seated, mix up the pictures; then show them one at a time, asking learners to identify who is in the picture. Allow those pictured to tell how long they have been married. (If your class is of such a size that many won't be able to see details of the pictures, you can collect pictures in advance and scan them for projection.)

Alternative: Place in chairs copies of the "Match the Phrases" exercise from the reproducible page, which you can download. Learners can begin working on this as they arrive. Wrap up either this segment or the one above by saying, "Even though today's Scripture will be very familiar to many of us, we want to make sure we study it in the context of marriage."

Into the Word

Divide the class into four small groups or study pairs; distribute the following instructions: *Task Group*—Identify a task that God gave the first man to perform in today's text and a negative result of that task. *Not-Good Group*—Identify what God declared to be "not good" at the stage of the creation account in today's text; also identify God's solution. *Marriage Group*—Identify what is to happen when people get married. *Process Group*—Describe the steps of the process by which woman was created and Adam's reaction.

Ask groups to present their findings. (*Expected responses: Task Group—task was to name the creatures; negative result was that no "help meet" for the man was found [Genesis 2:19, 20]. Not-Good Group—the man was alone; God would provide a "help meet for him" [2:18]; Marriage Group—attachment to spouse is to supersede attachment to parents, sometimes called "leave and cleave" [2:24,*

25]; Process Group—the steps were deep sleep, rib removal, closure of wound, creation of woman, and Adam's recognition of "flesh of my flesh" [2:21-23].)

Use the following discussion questions to explore the text more fully. You can use these either for a whole-class discussion or as assignments to small groups.

1. What significance is there in the fact that God allowed Adam to be aware of his need before God filled it? (*Genesis 2:20b*)

2. What significance is there in the fact that the creation procedures for the first man and the first woman were different? (*Genesis 2:7, 21, 22*)

3. Why is the need to sever ties with parents an important foundation for a God-honoring marriage? (*Genesis 2:24a*)

4. What does "one flesh" signify in addition to the sexual aspect of marriage? (*Genesis 2:24b*)

After the discussion, say, "I hope that today's lesson has made us more aware of the importance to God of marriage. Now let's put this knowledge into action."

Into Life

Work together as a class to make a list of best practices for keeping a marriage strong; expect responses from personal experience, from books on marriage, and from Scripture. Jot responses on the board. *Option:* If your class does not include engaged couples, you can start this segment by saying, "Let's compile some 'Helpful Hints' from our collective wisdom that we can pass along to engaged couples as they contemplate their forthcoming marriages. I will mail our list to the engaged couples in our church."

Alternative: Have learners complete the "Encouragement for Marriage" activity on the reproducible page. Furnish copies of the church directory to assist learners in identifying those to receive the notes. Ask learners to mail their completed notes, or you can collect the notes to mail yourself.

KNOWLEDGE OF GOOD AND EVIL

DEVOTIONAL READING: Deuteronomy 30:11-20
BACKGROUND SCRIPTURE: Genesis 3

GENESIS 3:8-17, 21, 23

8 And they heard the voice of the LORD God walking in the garden in the cool of the day: and Adam and his wife hid themselves from the presence of the LORD God amongst the trees of the garden.

9 And the LORD God called unto Adam, and said unto him, Where art thou?

10 And he said, I heard thy voice in the garden, and I was afraid, because I was naked; and I hid myself.

11 And he said, Who told thee that thou wast naked? Hast thou eaten of the tree, whereof I commanded thee that thou shouldest not eat?

12 And the man said, The woman whom thou gavest to be with me, she gave me of the tree, and I did eat.

13 And the LORD God said unto the woman, What is this that thou hast done? And the woman said, The serpent beguiled me, and I did eat.

14 And the LORD God said unto the serpent, Because thou hast done this, thou art cursed above all cattle, and above every beast of the field; upon thy belly shalt thou go, and dust shalt thou eat all the days of thy life:

15 And I will put enmity between thee and the woman, and between thy seed and her seed; it shall bruise thy head, and thou shalt bruise his heel.

16 Unto the woman he said, I will greatly multiply thy sorrow and thy conception; in sorrow thou shalt bring forth children; and thy desire shall be to thy husband, and he shall rule over thee.

17 And unto Adam he said, Because thou hast hearkened unto the voice of thy wife, and hast eaten of the tree, of which I commanded thee, saying, Thou shalt not eat of it: cursed is the ground for thy sake; in sorrow shalt thou eat of it all the days of thy life.

. . . .

21 Unto Adam also and to his wife did the LORD God make coats of skins, and clothed them.

. . . .

23 Therefore the LORD God sent him forth from the garden of Eden, to till the ground from whence he was taken.

KEY VERSES

And the LORD God said, Behold, the man is become as one of us, to know good and evil: and now, lest he put forth his hand, and take also of the tree of life, and eat, and live for ever: therefore the LORD God sent him forth from the garden of Eden, to till the ground from whence he was taken. —**Genesis 3:22, 23**

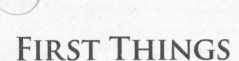

First Things

Lesson Aims

After participating in this lesson, each student will be able to:

1. Describe the consequences of the sin of Adam and Eve as well as God's promise of hope.

2. Match the descriptions of both the consequences of sin and God's promise of hope with specific examples from modern life.

3. Confess and repent of one "hidden sin" in his or her life.

Lesson Outline

Introduction

A. Surviving the Fall

May 30, 2011, was an unusually hot Memorial Day in the Bronx section of New York City. From the fifth floor of an apartment, 14-month-old Xania Angel Samuels tumbled out of an open window to the ground below. She survived the plunge and was rushed to the hospital with head trauma. Xania had been wearing her favorite pink winter coat when she fell, and the heavy coat—which she insisted on wearing on what was the hottest day of the year to that point—probably cushioned the impact and saved her life.

Today's lesson text from Genesis 3 includes the consequences of what is often termed "the fall" of Adam and Eve, caused by their disobedience to God. Clothing did not protect them from those consequences, but clothing was provided as a part of God's care for them after their fall. Today's text will also show how God looked ahead and foretold a special plan to "cover" all of humanity and shield it from the effects of the fall by administering His own "head trauma" to the serpent.

B. Lesson Background

Last week we studied God's creation of woman as an appropriate helper for man. A situation that God had previously called "not good" was then made good and complete. But the happy ending of chapter 2 is quickly countered by the opening of chapter 3. The first three words are ominous: "Now the serpent . . ."

Nowhere does the record in Genesis associate the serpent with Satan (the devil). But we know from other Scriptures that the serpent is the instrument of Satan to carry out his hideous designs against the man and the woman, to ruin the perfection that God the Creator established in Eden (2 Corinthians 11:3; Revelation 12:9).

The serpent's first words were intended to cast doubt on the authority of God's word: "Yea, hath God said, Ye shall not eat of every tree of the garden?" (Genesis 3:1). In a blatant denial of the Creator's established consequences for disobedience, the serpent brazenly assured the woman, "Ye shall not surely die" (v. 4). Such a lie is in keeping with the devil's tactics (John 8:44). Tragically, the woman fell into the devil's trap as did the man (Genesis 3:6).

Thus far our consideration of "First Days" in this unit of studies has been positive. It now takes a tragic turn in the opposite direction as we see unfolding before us the chaos that the first sin brings upon the human race and, indeed, all creation. Genesis 3:7 tells us that after the man and the woman had eaten from the forbidden tree, "The eyes of them both were opened, and they knew that they were naked." Thus the consequences of sin are apparent even before the Lord confronts the guilty parties. The innocence and lack of shame that had characterized the man and woman's relationship (2:25) were gone, and they covered themselves with garments made of fig leaves (3:7). Then they had to face the one whose command they had disobeyed.

I. Confronting the Problem
(GENESIS 3:8-13)

A. Hearing (v. 8a)

8a. And they heard the voice of the LORD God walking in the garden in the cool of the day.

It may seem odd that God is described as *walking in the garden,* since "God is a spirit" (John 4:24). The language is most likely a way of portraying the closeness that has characterized the relationship between God and the two humans to this point. One may assume that Adam and Eve's "walk" up to now has pleased God, and they have welcomed the opportunity to walk with Him whenever He comes into the garden. That situation is about to change.

B. Hiding (v. 8b)

8b. And Adam and his wife hid themselves from the presence of the LORD God amongst the trees of the garden.

Adam and his wife no longer welcome the sound of God's approach. *The trees of the garden* that have been given to them for their pleasure and enjoyment (Genesis 2:16) are now used as a shield to hide behind. The two are trying to avoid having to face the Lord.

C. God Addresses the Man (vv. 9-12)

9. And the LORD God called unto Adam, and said unto him, Where art thou?

God already knows where Adam is, of course. God asks *Where art thou?* because Adam needs to know that God desires a word with him.

10. And he said, I heard thy voice in the garden, and I was afraid, because I was naked; and I hid myself.

Adam's admission of being afraid signals the end of the closeness that has characterized the relationship that he and Eve have enjoyed between themselves and God to this point. The nakedness that had produced no shame previously (Genesis 2:25) is now a source of shame. Adam is not fully naked at this point since both he and Eve have clothed themselves (3:7). But even though Adam has covered his physical nakedness, he senses that he has not covered it enough to be comfortable in the presence of God.

It is tragically, painfully clear at this point that the serpent has lied. Yes, the eyes of the two humans are open as the serpent had promised (Genesis 3:5, 7); but "knowing good and evil" (v. 5) is not the pleasurable experience that the serpent had led them to believe it would be. Adam "knows" he is guilty of the evil of breaking God's commandment; he "knows" he can no longer be close with God. It would have been far better

HOW TO SAY IT

Corinthians	Ko-*rin*-thee-unz (*th* as in *thin*).
Ephesians	Ee-*fee*-zhunz.
Xania	*Zan*-yuh.

for him simply to have trusted and obeyed God than to possess the bitter knowledge that he has acquired through disobedience.

11. And he said, Who told thee that thou wast naked? Hast thou eaten of the tree, whereof I commanded thee that thou shouldest not eat?

Again, it is not information that God seeks as He questions Adam. Rather, the questions are designed to get Adam to realize something. The second of the Lord's questions goes straight to the heart of the matter: has Adam disobeyed the clear command given him by his Creator?

12. And the man said, The woman whom thou gavest to be with me, she gave me of the tree, and I did eat.

Adam avoids giving direct answers to the Lord's questions. Instead, Adam points an accusing finger at the woman—the very person whom he had earlier described ecstatically as "bone of my bones, and flesh of my flesh" (Genesis 2:23)! Now it appears that he wants nothing to do with her. Adam even suggests that some blame be placed upon the Lord since Eve is *the woman whom thou gavest to be with me.* Perhaps Adam is implying that being "alone" would not have been such a bad thing after all, in contrast with what the Lord had stated (2:18).

Adam is correct when he says *she gave me of the tree, and I did eat.* That is indeed what happened according to Genesis 3:6. But for Adam to create a scenario that absolves him of all guilt and responsibility is a consequence of the fall that humans continue to practice and perfect. We call it "blame-shifting."

D. God Addresses the Woman (v. 13)

13. And the LORD God said unto the woman, What is this that thou hast done? And the woman said, The serpent beguiled me, and I did eat.

Now God speaks to the woman. The tone appears a bit softer than that used with the man. Perhaps this is because the man had received from the Lord himself the command not to eat from the forbidden tree (Genesis 2:17), while the woman apparently knows of the command from the man. Even so, the woman knew about this command before breaking it (3:2, 3).

Eve admits more of the truth than Adam does. Her statement *the serpent beguiled me* may reveal some blame-shifting on her part, but the key word *beguiled* indicates that she knows that a deception has occurred. The serpent is the source of the deception. The bliss and delight that he implied would belong to the man and the woman are nowhere to be found.

❧ RATIONALIZING VS. REPENTING ❧

One day I heard myself praying (actually, mentally jabbering) about reasons for my behavior. I was doing quite the spin job, if I do say so myself!

Suddenly, it was as if I were listening from another point of view—outside of myself. I could clearly see I had made a mistake and was trying to make myself sound free from guilt. Then a realization struck: God already knew. He knew not only what I had done, but also every subtle nuance of motive behind my behavior. He knew the whole story better than I did myself.

Reclining in my comfortable hearth chair, I paused. It was obvious that my many unspoken thoughts were ridiculous attempts to buoy myself above the rising sense of guilt and shame. Like the prodigal son of Luke 15:11-20, I came to my senses. I asked God to show me His point of view, and the truth of God's Word flooded my mind. I knew where I was wrong and why. Gone was the unease I had felt only minutes before. God's grace was tangible from the first moment I relinquished my excuses and repented (compare Psalm 51).

It's easy to be angry with Adam and Eve. They sinned, and their choice has wreaked havoc on themselves and us. But God is waiting with grace and forgiveness. —V. E.

II. Pronouncing Consequences
(GENESIS 3:14-17)
A. For the Serpent (vv. 14, 15)

14. And the LORD God said unto the serpent, Because thou hast done this, thou art cursed above all cattle, and above every beast of the field; upon thy belly shalt thou go, and dust shalt thou eat all the days of thy life.

Since the serpent has been the instrument of deception, God addresses him first in judgment. God's pronouncement of a curse on the serpent *above all cattle, and above every beast of the field* seems to say that all other creatures will suffer negative effects as a result of sin's entrance into the world (see Romans 8:22, 23), but the serpent will be punished more severely than they.

Some suggest that the words *upon thy belly shalt thou go* imply that the serpent stands upright prior to this curse. But this phrase may mean that the serpent's crawling will now carry with it a meaning of contempt that was not present previously. The idea of eating dust likely signifies humiliation or shame, which it does elsewhere in Scripture (see Psalm 72:9; Isaiah 49:23; Micah 7:17).

15. And I will put enmity between thee and the woman, and between thy seed and her seed; it shall bruise thy head, and thou shalt bruise his heel.

The enmity, or hostility, mentioned here is reflected to some extent in the aversion most people have to snakes. But the language of this verse, especially toward the end, points to a deeper spir-

itual hostility that understands the seed of the serpent to be linked with Satan and all who carry out his evil intentions (compare John 8:44). Satan's continuing desire is to ruin lives by deceit (just as he ruined Eve's), thereby thwarting God's righteous purposes toward those created in His image (compare Revelation 12:9).

In time, however, one seed (descendant) of the woman fulfills God's purpose by dealing Satan a death blow. This is pictured here as striking the enemy's head. Jesus does this by means of His death on the cross (Hebrews 2:14, 15; compare 1 John 3:8). That Satan is to *bruise his heel* indicates that Satan inflicts a measure of suffering on the Son of God, but this in no way causes the kind of damage that Jesus inflicts on Satan.

> *What Do You Think?*
> How should the fact that Christ crushes Satan affect how we approach our spiritual battles?
> *Talking Points for Your Discussion*
> - Regarding God's task (Zechariah 4:6; 1 Corinthians 10:13)
> - Regarding our task (Ephesians 4:26, 27; 1 Peter 5:8, 9; James 4:7)

B. For the Woman (v. 16)

16. Unto the woman he said, I will greatly multiply thy sorrow and thy conception; in sorrow thou shalt bring forth children; and thy desire shall be to thy husband, and he shall rule over thee.

God turns His attention to the woman. Childbearing was to occur as a part of God's plan prior to the fall (Genesis 1:28), but now the process of multiplying through childbearing will be accompanied by a multiplying of sorrow, referring primarily to the pain involved in giving birth.

Some suggest that a part of this sorrow includes the understanding that any child will enter a world greatly tainted by sin. Who can foresee what aspects of the curse of sin lie ahead for a newborn baby as he or she matures? Despite a parent's best intentions, a child will experience the sorrows of life in a fallen world—and for some that sorrow will be especially tragic.

Another consequence for the woman is stated, one that affects the relationship between husband and wife: *and thy desire shall be to thy husband, and he shall rule over thee*. This has been interpreted in various ways. One idea is that it means she will still desire her husband in spite of the pain of childbirth, and that he will use that to dominate her in the relationship.

It seems better, however, to view this statement as a description of the tension, in the sense of a power struggle, that will characterize the relationship between a husband and a wife as a result of the fall. The harmony and unity that was so eloquently expressed by Adam when the Lord brought the woman to him (Genesis 2:23) will now be a struggle to maintain.

No man should interpret the language of this verse as a license to mistreat his wife. He must honor God in the way he treats his spouse, a principle discussed by Paul, who uses Christ's love for the church as a model (Ephesians 5:25).

C. For the Man (v. 17)

17. And unto Adam he said, Because thou hast hearkened unto the voice of thy wife, and hast eaten of the tree, of which I commanded thee, saying, Thou shalt not eat of it: cursed is the ground for thy sake; in sorrow shalt thou eat of it all the days of thy life.

Now addressing the man, God makes Adam's blame clear: he *hast hearkened unto the voice of [his] wife* rather than to God's voice. Then the man's punishment is pronounced: *cursed is the ground for thy sake*. Like the woman, the man will experience his own version of sorrow; it will come in his efforts to bring forth food from the ground. God had placed the man in the Garden of Eden "to dress it and to keep it" (Genesis 2:15). This task was intended to be a source of satisfaction as the man worked in harmony with his Creator. Now, however, such work will be much more of a drudgery or toil.

Thus the important tasks given for the man and the woman will still be done: children will to be born and crops will be harvested. But the struggle to carry out these duties will always be a reminder of the high price of disobeying God.

III. Enacting the Pronouncement
(Genesis 3:21, 23)
A. Caring for the Couple (v. 21)

21. Unto Adam also and to his wife did the Lord God make coats of skins, and clothed them.

Following the devastating announcements of discipline, God proceeds to demonstrate an act of grace: He makes *coats of skins* for the couple. The two have already made coverings of fig leaves for themselves (Genesis 3:7), and we wonder if the additional covering of skins foreshadows the system of animal sacrifices that God will institute later. Nothing is said in the Bible about this. The immediate message to Adam and Eve is what should not be overlooked: the God who has just disciplined them still cares deeply for them.

What Do You Think?

When was a time that God provided for you in the midst of a problem of your own making? How did Hebrews 12:5-11 apply to that situation?

Talking Points for Your Discussion

- Alienating a family member
- Incurring too much debt
- Behaving dishonestly
- Other

❧ CLOTHING FROM GOD ❧

Corporal punishment, time-outs, loss of privileges. Discipline of children can be a controversial topic. Experts seem to agree that the one thing children need when receiving discipline is reassurance of the parent's love. I've seen it dozens of times with children barely old enough to walk: when reprimanded, they rush to the parent's arms. They do so to be reassured that they have not lost the loving relationship with their parent.

The first sin shattered the blissful harmony between God and humans. The consequences pronounced on the first man and woman were surely difficult. What kept the consequences from being unbearable for those two was what God did next. God reassured them of His continuing love by providing them appropriate covering.

God is still busy loving His rebellious children. He sees us attempting to clothe our sin through our own efforts, attempts that end up being only "filthy rags" (Isaiah 64:6). In response, He sends Jesus, who covers our sin with "the robe of righteousness" (61:10). There is probably no better statement of God's love than John 3:16.   —V. E.

B. Casting Out the Couple (v. 23)

23. Therefore the LORD God sent him forth from the garden of Eden, to till the ground from whence he was taken.

Perhaps this verse offers one reason why the Lord has clothed the couple: to prepare them for life away *from the garden of Eden*, from which they are now expelled. In verse 22 (not in today's text), God gives the reason for their eviction—so that they, in their fallen condition, will not eat of the tree of life and live forever. This is an act of discipline, but it is also one of grace. Sin-cursed humanity must be protected from itself. Unchecked sin would be catastrophic.

The Hebrew word translated *till* is the same as that translated "dress" in Genesis 2:15. The man will continue to do the work he was doing in the garden, only now he will do so with the grim awareness that the ground from which he has been made is cursed (3:17). He has no one to blame for this sad outcome but himself.

Conclusion

A. The Right Kind of Knowledge

Even before Adam and Eve ate of "the tree of the knowledge of good and evil" (Genesis 2:17), there was a sense in which they knew the distinction between good and evil. They knew that eating from the forbidden tree was evil, or wrong. But the serpent implied that something was lacking in their knowledge, and that the Lord was holding out on them. The serpent promised that eating of the tree would open their eyes so they would be "knowing good and evil" (3:5).

After the two had eaten from the tree, the serpent's words partly came true: "And the eyes of them both were opened" (Genesis 3:7). But what did they then "know"? That they were naked.

Visual for Lesson 3

Use this visual to start a discussion that compares immediate vs. delayed consequences of sin.

What was their response? "And they sewed fig leaves together, and made themselves aprons."

Consider the irony: the man and the woman, who were then "wise" (moderns might call them "sophisticated") in the realization of their nakedness, proceeded to exercise utter foolishness by trying to cover it up on their own! So whatever "knowledge" they gained was obtained at the price of their ability to think in a spiritually pleasing, God-honoring fashion. Theirs was not the heavenly outcome that the serpent promised; it was hellish, with the loss far, far outweighing whatever gain was achieved.

So it is with any attempt to obtain knowledge apart from our Creator's desires. The irony of Adam and Eve's disobedience and "cover-up" is exemplified by modern humanity's sad plight: we have access to more knowledge than any previous generation, yet spiritually and morally many are woefully ignorant.

B. Prayer

Father, we live in a time when many freely and proudly boast that they have rejected You. May we who claim to be Your people live lives that will not give them further reason to boast. May our faith in and devotion to You be unmistakably clear. In Jesus' name, amen.

C. Thought to Remember

Knowledge without God is ultimately ignorance.

INVOLVEMENT LEARNING

Some of the activities below are also found in the helpful student book, Adult Bible Class.
Don't forget to download the free reproducible page from www.standardlesson.com to enhance your lesson!

Into the Lesson

Option: Place in chairs copies of the "Mixed-up Consequences" activity from the reproducible page, which you can download. Learners can begin working on this as they arrive.

Before class, read a plot overview of the epic poem *Paradise Lost,* by John Milton (easy to find on the Internet). Then print out these three sections of the poem: verses 412–433, verses 734–759, and verses 996–1003 of Book 9. Say, "Today we are going to study the section of Genesis where sin enters the world and humanity is sentenced to suffer its consequences. To set the context, let me read some verses from John Milton's *Paradise Lost.*" (If your learners are not familiar with this classic work, summarize the plot overview for them.) After you have read the three sections from *Paradise Lost,* allow a few minutes for reactions.

Alternative: Ask learners to call out the names of public figures whose secret sin was discovered; jot responses on the board. (Save this list for the end of class; put learner responses off to one side because you will need much of the board for the Into the Word segment.) After several names are listed, discuss the consequences each person faced, as well as the ripple effects or collateral damage of his or her sin.

After either opening, say, "Now let's spend some time today studying what the Bible has to say about the immediate and far-reaching consequences of Adam and Eve's choices."

Into the Word

Mark off the top half of the board in two sections. At the top of the left section, write *Consequences of Sin*; at the top of the right section, write *God's Promise of Hope.* Say, "As we read today's text, be alert to the consequences of Adam and Eve's sin," then ask one or more volunteers to read the text aloud. After the reading, ask learners what consequences of sin they see; jot responses on the board under the left heading. (See the lesson commentary for expected responses.)

After all responses have been entered under the left heading, probe deeper by asking your learners to distinguish between immediate consequences and far-reaching consequences. As learners offer their suggestions, put an *I* next to the entries on the board that are immediate and an *F* next to the ones that are far-reaching. (Immediate consequences are found in verses 8-12; far-reaching consequences are found in verses 14-19, 23.)

Say, "Now let's consider the hope we have, the way out that God provides us from the quagmire of sin." Ask for reactions to verse 15; jot those reactions on the board. Use the lesson commentary on this verse to add information that learners miss.

Into Life

Option 1: If you began the lesson reading from *Paradise Lost,* conclude by reading verses 1–16 and 47b–62 from Book 10 and verses 270–284 and 402–410 from Book 12. Discuss how the poem deals with Christ as the one whom God provides to judge and save Adam and Eve.

Option 2: If you began the lesson by asking for a listing of names of public figures whose secret sin was discovered, return to that list now. As a class, discuss what would have been appropriate actions for those individuals to take if they had wanted to repent of their secret sin and guard against its recurrence. (Some of these individuals may have already done so; if that knowledge is available, discuss what they did.) Discuss why repentance and accountability are necessary steps for Christians to take when battling sin.

Option 3: Distribute copies of the "No More Secret Sins" activity from the reproducible page. Since this calls for personal confession, you may wish to distribute it as a take-home exercise.

Conclude class with a prayer of thanksgiving for God's provision of salvation through Jesus.

AN EVERLASTING COVENANT

DEVOTIONAL READING: Isaiah 54:9-14

BACKGROUND SCRIPTURE: Genesis 6:9–9:28

GENESIS 9:1, 3-6, 8-17

1 And God blessed Noah and his sons, and said unto them, Be fruitful, and multiply, and replenish the earth.

· ·

3 Every moving thing that liveth shall be meat for you; even as the green herb have I given you all things.

4 But flesh with the life thereof, which is the blood thereof, shall ye not eat.

5 And surely your blood of your lives will I require; at the hand of every beast will I require it, and at the hand of man; at the hand of every man's brother will I require the life of man.

6 Whoso sheddeth man's blood, by man shall his blood be shed: for in the image of God made he man.

· ·

8 And God spake unto Noah, and to his sons with him, saying,

9 And I, behold, I establish my covenant with you, and with your seed after you;

10 And with every living creature that is with you, of the fowl, of the cattle, and of every beast of the earth with you; from all that go out of the ark, to every beast of the earth.

11 And I will establish my covenant with you; neither shall all flesh be cut off any more by the waters of a flood; neither shall there any more be a flood to destroy the earth.

12 And God said, This is the token of the covenant which I make between me and you and every living creature that is with you, for perpetual generations:

13 I do set my bow in the cloud, and it shall be for a token of a covenant between me and the earth.

14 And it shall come to pass, when I bring a cloud over the earth, that the bow shall be seen in the cloud:

15 And I will remember my covenant, which is between me and you and every living creature of all flesh; and the waters shall no more become a flood to destroy all flesh.

16 And the bow shall be in the cloud; and I will look upon it, that I may remember the everlasting covenant between God and every living creature of all flesh that is upon the earth.

17 And God said unto Noah, This is the token of the covenant, which I have established between me and all flesh that is upon the earth.

KEY VERSE

I will establish my covenant with you; neither shall all flesh be cut off any more by the waters of a flood; neither shall there any more be a flood to destroy the earth. —**Genesis 9:11**

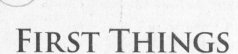

FIRST THINGS

Unit 1: First Days

LESSONS 1–5

LESSON AIMS

After participating in this lesson, each student will be able to:

1. Summarize what God said about the sacredness of human life in His covenant with Noah and his descendants.

2. Evaluate modern arguments about the death penalty in light of Genesis 9:6.

3. Explain the significance of the rainbow to an unbeliever.

LESSON OUTLINE

Introduction
  A. Judgment Day
  B. Lesson Background
 I. Commands (GENESIS 9:1, 3-6)
  A. Duty (v. 1)
  B. Diet (vv. 3, 4)
  C. Demand (vv. 5, 6)
 II. Covenant (GENESIS 9:8-11)
  A. Participants (vv. 8-10)
    God's Care
  B. Promise (v. 11)
 III. Confirmation (GENESIS 9:12-17)
  A. Sign (vv. 12, 13)
    What Comes to Mind
  B. Significance (vv. 14-17)
Conclusion
  A. Today's Floods
  B. Prayer
  C. Thought to Remember

Introduction

A. Judgment Day

Judgment Day was supposed to occur on May 21, 2011, according to radio preacher Harold Camping. Many of Camping's followers purchased space on billboards throughout the U.S., encouraging people to "save the date" and prepare for the end.

Of course, the date came and went with no judgment except the predictable one that Camping was foolish for having made such a prediction. He was scorned by non-Christians and Christians alike, the latter citing Jesus' clear teaching that no one except God the Father knows the day or the hour of Jesus' return (Mark 13:32). Camping's adjusted prediction for Judgment Day to occur on October 21, 2011, only added to the scorn. Camping turned out to be just another in a long line of "date setters" whose failures proved they were not speaking for God.

Noah, by contrast, received a direct communication from the Lord about a day of judgment—a judgment that was to be carried out by means of a flood. Noah was also told how to prepare for that day, eventually being given an exact timetable as to when God's judgment would be carried out (Genesis 7:4). What made Noah worthy of this honor was the fact that he "was a just man and perfect in his generations, and . . . walked with God" (6:9). Noah obeyed God's commands fully (6:22; 7:5).

While we do not know the time of the coming, final Judgment Day (and we should be extremely suspicious of anyone who claims to know), we *do* know what God's expectations of us are. They are essentially what He has required from His people since day one and what He required from Noah: *obedience.*

B. Lesson Background

Last week's lesson text focused on the aftermath of the first sin, committed by Adam and Eve in the Garden of Eden. Today's Scripture brings us to the aftermath of God's judgment by means of the great flood. God brought the flood on the world because of the level of corruption and depravity that those made in His image had

• 34 •

reached (Genesis 6:5). The exception to this spiritual quagmire was Noah, who "found grace in the eyes of the Lord" (v. 8). God commanded Noah to build an ark, which provided deliverance from the flood for him, his sons, their wives (1 Peter 3:20), and those creatures that Noah was told to take aboard.

The subsequent rains lasted 40 days and nights (Genesis 7:12). Over a year passed from the time the rains began until the earth dried out after the waters receded (comparing 7:11 with 8:13, 14). The Lord then brought forth from the ark Noah, his family, and the living creatures that had been given refuge there. Noah built an altar to the Lord and offered sacrifices (8:20). The Lord responded with a promise that He would never again destroy all living creatures as He had done by means of the flood (vv. 21, 22). The Lord's next words, part of today's printed text, were directed specifically to Noah and his sons.

I. Commands
(GENESIS 9:1, 3-6)
A. Duty (v. 1)

1. And God blessed Noah and his sons, and said unto them, Be fruitful, and multiply, and replenish the earth.

God had made the man and the woman on the sixth day of creation, instructing them to "be fruitful, and multiply, and replenish the earth" (Genesis 1:28). Now, after the judgment carried out through the great flood, God begins what we might call a "re-creation" with *Noah and his sons.* Eight people are to fulfill the mandate given to Adam and Eve (Genesis 7:13; 1 Peter 3:20).

> *What Do You Think?*
> Do we still have an obligation to "be fruitful, and multiply"? Why, or why not?
> *Talking Points for Your Discussion*
> - Current world population of seven billion people
> - The moral issues of birth control
> - Jeremiah 16:1, 2; 29:6
> - Luke 23:29
> - 1 Timothy 5:14

B. Diet (vv. 3, 4)

3. Every moving thing that liveth shall be meat for you; even as the green herb have I given you all things.

Humanity's diet now is expanded beyond the vegetation permitted in Genesis 1:30, and meat becomes a new source of protein. We may wonder why God gives such permission at this particular time since creatures are not especially numerous. Unclean animals had been taken aboard the ark in twos, while clean animals had been taken by sevens (Genesis 7:2, 3)—and some of the latter have already been sacrificed (8:20). But capture of creatures for food will not be easy since they now fear humans (9:2). It seems that just as man has to "sweat" to produce food from the ground (3:19), he now will be required to exercise a similar effort to obtain meat from earth's creatures.

4. But flesh with the life thereof, which is the blood thereof, shall ye not eat.

God next imposes a limitation on the new allowance concerning humanity's diet: people are forbidden to eat *flesh* (or meat) with its blood. The restriction and the reason for it will be restated in the Mosaic law at Leviticus 17:10-14 and Deuteronomy 12:16, 23-25. Taken together, the passages from Genesis, Leviticus, and Deuteronomy imply that blood either is or somehow represents a creature's "life force."

One may suggest that the center of life is in the heart or the brain, but these organs function only if the supply of blood to them is maintained. To cut off the blood supply means certain death. John H. Walton and Victor H. Matthews observe that "the draining of the blood before eating the meat was a way of returning the life force of the animal to the God who gave it life. This offers recognition that [individuals] have taken the life with permission and are partaking of God's bounty as his guests."

Some suggest that this principle remains intact today (compare Acts 15:20, 29). Others point to Jesus' "purging" of all meats (Mark 7:18, 19) as a basis for saying that dietary regulations from the Old Testament are no longer binding. This may be one of those areas where differences of opinion can exist without passing judgment on those who hold them (Romans 14:1-4).

GOD'S PROMISE
IS EVERLASTING

Visual for Lesson 4. *Use this visual to introduce the discussion question that is associated with Genesis 9:16.*

C. Demand (vv. 5, 6)

5. And surely your blood of your lives will I require; at the hand of every beast will I require it, and at the hand of man; at the hand of every man's brother will I require the life of man.

God expands on the previous stipulation. So important is the principle that "life is in the blood" that He states *and surely your blood of your lives will I require.* God will, first of all, require a reckoning for human life that is taken by *every beast* that is responsible for so doing. God declares that He will keep a record of every person killed by a member of the animal kingdom, and He will hold the deadly animal accountable.

Of course, animals do not understand the concept of guilt; even so, they are accountable to their Creator for their actions. How much more, then, is this the case with those created in God's image —beings who *are* capable of understanding guilt! Both this verse and the next address our accountability to God in this regard.

6. Whoso sheddeth man's blood, by man shall his blood be shed: for in the image of God made he man.

God requires of humans that the life of a murderer *(whoso sheddeth man's blood)* must be taken as punishment for the heinous act. This principle is later embedded within the Law of Moses, where a distinction is made between premeditated murder and what we would call involuntary man-

slaughter (Exodus 21:12-14). The reason for the kind of punishment we see in our text is based on our uniqueness as creatures made *in the image of God.* So passionate is God about preserving and protecting this uniqueness that destroying a life must be disciplined to the ultimate degree: life for life (see also Leviticus 24:17; Numbers 35:31).

The Old Testament basis for capital punishment is thus quite clear. To take the life of a murderer is to be considered an act of the utmost respect for life—life as a creative gift of God. Capital punishment is not a barbaric, inhuman act; instead, it is a just response to a deed that has demonstrated the ultimate contempt for the one who creates life.

Capital punishment is controversial today, even within Christianity. Some may question whether the principle of "life for life" is still valid, given the fact that we are no longer under the old law, but are under grace (Romans 6:14). To this concern we can point out that although Jesus has indeed "abolished in his flesh . . . the law of commandments contained in ordinances" (Ephesians 2:15) by "nailing it to his cross" (Colossians 2:14), the requirement of Genesis 9:6 predates the Law of Moses. Further, the New Testament itself seems to indicate that capital punishment is still valid (Romans 13:4; Acts 25:11).

> **What Do You Think?**
> How does the fact of being made in God's image influence your stand on moral issues today?
> *Talking Points for Your Discussion*
> ▪ Regarding capital punishment
> ▪ Regarding abortion
> ▪ Regarding your view of people of other races
> ▪ Regarding your response to the needs of those with mental or physical disabilities

II. Covenant
(GENESIS 9:8-11)
A. Participants (vv. 8-10)

8, 9. And God spake unto Noah, and to his sons with him, saying, And I, behold, I establish my covenant with you, and with your seed after you.

God has already told Noah "with thee will I establish my covenant" (Genesis 6:18), the first time the word *covenant* appears in the Bible. Following the great flood, God addresses not only Noah but also his three sons (see 5:32; 6:10; 7:13; and 9:18). God's covenant includes not only them but their *seed,* or descendants (compare 1 Chronicles 1:4-27). Therefore the covenant about to be explained embraces all human beings.

10. And with every living creature that is with you, of the fowl, of the cattle, and of every beast of the earth with you; from all that go out of the ark, to every beast of the earth.

God's covenant also applies to *every living creature.* Therefore the prohibitions and warnings that were given earlier regarding these creatures and humans are balanced with the establishment of a special covenant with both parties. The nature of that covenant is explained next.

❧ GOD'S CARE ❧

James Herriot was the pen name of James Alfred Wight (1916–1995), an English veterinarian who wrote delightful books about animals and their owners in rural Yorkshire. The books became bestsellers because of their charm and Herriot's winsome manner of describing people and animals.

Herriot's first significant book was *All Creatures Great and Small,* and this title also has been used as the name for a series of four books. He took this title from the nineteenth-century hymn "All Things Bright and Beautiful," of which the refrain's first four lines read as follows:

> All things bright and beautiful,
> All creatures great and small,
> All things wise and wonderful,
> The Lord God made them all.

All four lines became titles of Herriot's books. In these titles, he acknowledges God's creation and His care for all of His creatures.

Genesis records this care. God's promise and covenant to never again flood the entire earth applies also to animals. God's concern for them has a message for us: if God cares for creatures not created in His image, what does this say about His care for those who *are* created in His image? See Matthew 10:29-31. —J. B. N.

B. Promise (v. 11)

11. And I will establish my covenant with you, neither shall all flesh be cut off any more by the waters of a flood; neither shall there any more be a flood to destroy the earth.

The specifics of the Lord's covenant are provided: never again will He use *the waters of a flood* to *cut off* life and *destroy the earth* as He has just done. The next destruction of the earth will be by fire, not water (2 Peter 3:6-12).

What Do You Think?
  How would you respond to the various ways that people deny *judgment* or *justice* to be an essential aspect of God's nature?
Talking Points for Your Discussion
  ▪ "God's love means that everyone will be saved in the end."
  ▪ "The injustice in the world shows that God doesn't care about justice."
  ▪ "Love and judgment are incompatible for God."

III. Confirmation
(GENESIS 9:12-17)
A. Sign (vv. 12, 13)

12, 13. And God said, This is the token of the covenant which I make between me and you and every living creature that is with you, for perpetual generations: I do set my bow in the cloud, and it shall be for a token of a covenant between me and the earth.

Once more the all-inclusive nature of the covenant is emphasized: it is for Noah and his sons (both instances of the pronoun *you* are plural in Hebrew) along with *every living creature.* Moreover, the covenant is *for perpetual generations,* which is another way of describing "your seed after you" in Genesis 9:9 (above).

The visual reminder of the *bow* (or rainbow) is the token of that covenant. The noun *bow* generally describes an instrument of death, used for hunting or warfare (Genesis 27:3; 48:22; etc.). Genesis 9:13, 14, 16 and Ezekiel 1:28 are the only places in the Old Testament where this word signifies a rainbow. Perhaps the symbolism in God's declaration lies in the fact that He is laying aside an instrument of destruction in keeping with His promise not to destroy the earth again by means of a flood.

Some believe that this is the first appearance of a rainbow, marking its significance as part of the covenant that God is establishing. Others maintain that the rainbow has already been seen on previous occasions after rainfalls, but the rainbow becomes the token of God's covenant only after He speaks the words in the verse before us.

> **What Do You Think?**
> How are modern covenants and contracts different from the covenant in today's text? Why is it important to grasp these distinctions?
> *Talking Points for Your Discussion*
> - Regarding wedding vows
> - Regarding business deals
> - Regarding product warranties
> - Other

❧ WHAT COMES TO MIND ❧

Various cultural myths and symbolisms have been attached to rainbows down through the years. As children we were told that Irish leprechauns place pots of gold at the ends of rainbows; some of us even tried to find such pots. Rainbows are sometimes used in works of art to represent peace and tranquility, with mountain views, buildings, etc., positioned under the rainbow's arc. The unchristian New Age Movement of the latter half of the twentieth century used images of rainbows as part of its identity.

Something is missing in all these representations. It is no mere coincidence that rainbows are formed out of droplets of water suspended in the air—it is, after all, a *rain*bow. God uses rain droplets to remind us that water will never flood the whole earth again.

There is no physical reality to a rainbow since its appearance is due to light passing through water droplets. Yet the lack of physical reality does not detract in the least from God's powerful promise never again to destroy the earth by water. Is that the first thing that comes into your mind when you see a rainbow?   —J. B. N.

B. Significance (vv. 14-17)

14, 15. And it shall come to pass, when I bring a cloud over the earth, that the bow shall be seen in the cloud: and I will remember my covenant, which is between me and you and every living creature of all flesh; and the waters shall no more become a flood to destroy all flesh.

God's memory never fails, of course. So the phrase *I will remember* does not imply that God might somehow forget certain details and needs a rainbow to be reminded of them. In a passage such as this, the phrase *I will remember* carries with it the idea that God is about to act to fulfill a promise He has made. A similar usage is found in Exodus 2:24, where God hears the cries of the Israelites in bondage in Egypt and "remembered his covenant." God's response in Exodus 3 is to call Moses to be Israel's deliverer. In the case at hand, God takes personal charge of being the deliverer as He continuously ensures that *the waters shall no more become a flood to destroy all flesh.*

16. And the bow shall be in the cloud; and I will look upon it, that I may remember the everlasting covenant between God and every living creature of all flesh that is upon the earth.

This verse reemphasizes what has already been stated. As we ponder what God himself promises to remember, we realize that the rainbow ultimately is meant to help *us* remember something, in the more traditional sense of the word *remember*. God knows how prone we are to forget His works in spite of how great and mighty they are. So He provides memory devices such as the visual aid of a rainbow to help us remember.

> **What Do You Think?**
> How does each of the following serve to remind you of the promises God has made and how He has kept them?
> *Talking Points for Your Discussion*
> - The lives of godly people
> - The nature of certain places
> - The anniversary of a "deliverance event"
> - The significance of certain objects
> - Other

17. And God said unto Noah, This is the token of the covenant, which I have established between me and all flesh that is upon the earth.

A final reaffirmation of the rainbow's importance is given to Noah himself. This is only fitting since this account of the flood began with God's message to Noah about how corrupt the earth had become (Genesis 6:13) and of God's intention to establish His covenant with Noah (6:18).

When Noah is first introduced in Scripture, he is called "a just man and perfect in his generations" (Genesis 6:9). Because Noah faithfully did "according to all that God commanded him" (6:22), he is now given the privilege to witness God's "re-creative" activity and to hear God announce the terms of a covenant with *all flesh that is upon the earth*. It is still true that those who faithfully obey and serve God receive numerous blessings, privileges, and insights that remain only mysteries to those who, like the vast majority in Noah's day, remain entrenched in their wickedness (Matthew 13:10-16; Colossians 1:26).

Conclusion

A. Today's Floods

This writer is preparing this lesson during 2011, the rainiest year on record in Cincinnati, where he lives. The months of April and November in 2011 were themselves the wettest Aprils and Novembers on record. This weather pattern caused some parts of the U.S. to suffer greatly from floods and tornadoes. Skeptics may look at a promise of God such as that found in today's text and mockingly ask, "What covenant? Look, I don't care if the flood was worldwide or not; if God is in charge of the world, can't He keep a flood or a tornado from devastating whole towns and communities and disrupting the lives of millions of people? What good can possibly come by His letting such disasters occur?"

Living in a fallen world—a world still under the curse of sin—can present followers of the Lord Jesus Christ with some very challenging questions. We know that ultimately God will bring about "new heavens and a new earth" (2 Peter 3:13). But at times we may wonder why He doesn't step in and fix some of what's wrong with the earth we live in now.

An important part of our witness occurs in the midst of the tragedies that are an inescapable part of life in a fallen world. We are able in such circumstances to show the difference our faith in Christ makes. This is not because we are exempt from tragedies or because life automatically gets better by turning to Jesus. Rather, it is because Christian faith gives us a unique perspective on the tragedies of this present world. The cross of Christ becomes our "token" or sign by which we view life (especially the difficult side) in a fallen world. Just as God used the tragedy of the cross to accomplish His purpose of providing salvation from sin, so He can use the disasters of this life for a higher, eternal purpose (Romans 8:28).

We must remember that we have not had a clear message from God regarding any flood that has occurred since the days of Noah. Noah's flood is the only one specifically tied with the judgment of God. Current floods (and other disasters) can be situations in which Christians demonstrate in tangible ways the love of Christ to cynics. When we do, we allow these circumstances to testify to God's grace rather than His judgment.

B. Prayer

Father, the covenant You made with Noah is just one example of Your faithfulness. Thank You for the many precious promises found in Your Word. May we find strength and endurance in them whenever life in this sinful world makes us especially weary. In Jesus' name, amen.

C. Thought to Remember

God is a covenant maker
and a covenant keeper.

HOW TO SAY IT

Colossians	Kuh-*losh*-unz.
Deuteronomy	Due-ter-*ahn*-uh-me.
Ephesians	Ee-*fee*-zhunz.
Leviticus	Leh-*vit*-ih-kus.
Mosaic	Mo-*zay*-ik.
Noah	*No*-uh.

INVOLVEMENT LEARNING

Some of the activities below are also found in the helpful student book, Adult Bible Class.
Don't forget to download the free reproducible page from www.standardlesson.com to enhance your lesson!

Into the Lesson

Begin class by saying, "Today I thought we'd take a little test to see how well we know the story of Noah's flood. As I read each sentence, raise your hand if the statement is true." (If you think your learners will hesitate to answer publicly in this manner, have them jot their true/false responses on a piece of paper; assure them that you won't collect their answers.)

1. God told Noah to make an ark of oak. *False, Genesis 6:14;* 2. Noah took only two of every animal into the ark. *False, Genesis 7:2, 3;* 3. Noah did exactly as God told him. *True, Genesis 6:22;* 4. It rained for 40 days and nights. *True, Genesis 7:12;* 5. Noah, his family, and the animals left the ark as soon as the rain stopped. *False, Genesis 8:6-10;* 6. Noah sent out a raven to see whether the waters had subsided. *True, Genesis 8:7;* 7. Noah built an altar and offered sacrifices to God after leaving the ark. *True, Genesis 8:20.*

Alternative: As a pretest, distribute copies of the "Re-Creation" activity from the reproducible page, which you can download. Allow a few minutes for completing, but don't discuss the results. The correct answers will be apparent as you work through the text in the next segment.

Say, "Even when we've read or heard a text numerous times, there is still much to learn from it. As we study today's text, let's see what new understanding we can gain."

Into the Word

Before class, reproduce the 15 verses of today's Scripture text on 15 handouts, one verse each. Form learners into pairs or groups of three. Distribute the handouts, as evenly as possible, to the pairs or groups. Ask learners to identify whether there is anything in the verses they have been given that suggests how God views humanity.

Call for conclusions by having a member of each pair or group read a verse aloud and iden-

tify the discovery. Jot responses on the board. Responses should resemble the following: *God thinks highly enough of humans to (1) want them to repopulate the earth (v. 1), (2) provide them food (v. 3), (3) want them to view human life as sacred (vv. 4-6), and (4) establish a covenant (vv. 12-17).*

Say, "We can see from Genesis 9:6 that God values human life—so much so that He requires 'life for life' justice. Many today disagree about the appropriateness or validity of the death penalty. Let's consider both secular and Christian arguments for and against capital punishment. What are they?" Write on the board *Secular Arguments* and *Christian Arguments* as two column headings; mark off two areas under each of these as *For* and *Against.* Jot responses in the appropriate areas. Be prepared to challenge learners' positions with observations from the lesson commentary. Remind learners that they must reconcile this issue in light of Scripture, not secular viewpoints.

Wrap up by saying, "Regardless of our personal convictions concerning capital punishment, I think we can all agree that today's text shows us how precious we are to God. How is our value to God connected with the symbol of the rainbow He has granted us to have?" Use the lesson commentary to fill in gaps in learners' understanding.

Into Life

Ask learners to brainstorm how the concept of the sacredness of human life is being attacked today; jot responses on the board *(possibilities: abortion, euthanasia, embryonic stem cell research, genocide).* Then ask learners to discuss ways that they can "make a holy noise" on these issues *(possibilities: participate in a March for Life; volunteer at a local senior center; etc.).*

Option: Distribute copies of the "A Sacred Promise" activity from the reproducible page. Provide colored pencils to enable learners to create their symbols as directed.

GOD SCATTERS THE NATIONS

DEVOTIONAL READING: 2 Chronicles 34:22-28
BACKGROUND SCRIPTURE: Genesis 11:1-9

GENESIS 11:1-9

1 And the whole earth was of one language, and of one speech.

2 And it came to pass, as they journeyed from the east, that they found a plain in the land of Shinar; and they dwelt there.

3 And they said one to another, Go to, let us make brick, and burn them throughly. And they had brick for stone, and slime had they for morter.

4 And they said, Go to, let us build us a city and a tower, whose top may reach unto heaven; and let us make us a name, lest we be scattered abroad upon the face of the whole earth.

5 And the LORD came down to see the city and the tower, which the children of men builded.

6 And the LORD said, Behold, the people is one, and they have all one language; and this they begin to do: and now nothing will be restrained from them, which they have imagined to do.

7 Go to, let us go down, and there confound their language, that they may not understand one another's speech.

8 So the LORD scattered them abroad from thence upon the face of all the earth: and they left off to build the city.

9 Therefore is the name of it called Babel; because the LORD did there confound the language of all the earth: and from thence did the LORD scatter them abroad upon the face of all the earth.

KEY VERSE

The LORD scattered them abroad from thence upon the face of all the earth: and they left off to build the city.
—**Genesis 11:8**

Photo: Hemera Technologies / Photos.com / Thinkstock

FIRST THINGS

Unit 1: First Days

LESSONS 1–5

LESSON AIMS

After participating in this lesson, each student will be able to:

1. Recount the events surrounding the attempt to construct the Tower of Babel and the Lord's thwarting of that attempt.

2. Tell why the people were wrong in what they were trying to do at Babel and compare that error with similar sins of today.

3. Identify signs that the tower builders' sinful attitude exists in his or her church and suggest a plan for dealing with it.

LESSON OUTLINE

Introduction

A. A Tale of Two Towers

John Tower served as a United States senator from Texas for nearly 24 years. After leaving the Senate, Tower continued to be involved in American politics until his death in a plane crash in 1991. In contrast with his last name, John Tower stood only 5'5" tall. "My name is Tower," he would tell people, "but I don't."

Today's text tells about the attempt to build the Tower of Babel—a project undertaken by people who wanted to "tower" over everyone, including God. Because of their misplaced motivation, God brought judgment on them and abruptly halted their efforts. As a result, their tower—didn't.

B. Lesson Background

Some refer to the first 11 chapters of Genesis as *primeval history.* This means that Genesis 1–11 records events that happened in the earliest ages of history. It should be emphasized that these events are indeed *history*—they are not to be placed in the realm of myth or fiction. Certainly, the testimonies of Jesus and the New Testament writers are crucial here; all of them treat the Old Testament record with the utmost respect and assume the historicity of any event to which they refer. These include events in Genesis 1–11 (see Matthew 24:37-39; Romans 5:12-14; 1 Corinthians 15:45; 2 Corinthians 11:3; and 1 Peter 3:18-20).

Genesis 10, which immediately precedes today's text, includes what is called *the table of nations.* This describes where the families of the sons of Noah settled after the flood. The chapter concludes with this statement: "These are the families of the sons of Noah, after their generations, in their nations: and by these were the nations divided in the earth after the flood" (Genesis 10:32). Verses 5, 20, and 31 reveal more than one language being spoken by these descendants. The account of the Tower of Babel (today's text) tells how this dividing of humanity in terms of languages occurred.

We cannot know with certainty how many years passed between Noah's flood and the point where Genesis 11 begins. Time is not Scripture's primary concern here (which is often true within these early chapters of Genesis). The focus is more on people, especially their relationship with God. That focus lets us see the blessings that accompany obedience and the discipline that accompanies disobedience.

After reading the account of the flood in the previous chapters of Genesis, one is led to ask, "Will people change after such a severe act of judgment? Will anything be different?" Sadly, Noah, who is described in such impressive terms earlier (Genesis 6:9), becomes guilty of drunkenness (9:20, 21). One of his sons reacts to Noah's subsequent nakedness in a disrespectful manner (9:22-27). Thus, even at this point it is clear that while sin has been judged, it has not been eliminated.

I. The Setting
(GENESIS 11:1, 2)

A. One Language (v. 1)

1. And the whole earth was of one language, and of one speech.

This account begins with what appears to be a positive statement. The term *one speech* is literally "the same words" in the Hebrew text. This may indicate that the vocabulary within this common language is understood by all people. Or perhaps it indicates that any dialects or diverse speech patterns at this point are not important enough to affect the ability of people to understand one another.

HOW TO SAY IT

Babel	*Bay*-bul.
Babylon	*Bab*-uh-lun.
cherubims	*chair*-uh-bims.
Eiffel	*Eye*-fuhl.
Euphrates	You-*fray*-teez.
Hiddekel	*Hid*-eh-kell.
Japheth	*Jay*-feth.
Pisa	*Pea*-zuh.
primeval	pry-*me*-vuhl.
Shinar	*Shy*-nar.
Tigris	*Tie*-griss.
ziggurat	*zig*-oo-rat.

B. One Location (v. 2)

2. And it came to pass, as they journeyed from the east, that they found a plain in the land of Shinar; and they dwelt there.

As people journey *from the east*, they eventually find an appropriate place to settle down. Shinar is the region around Babylon, located in the broad Tigris-Euphrates valley. The Garden of Eden may have been in this vicinity, since the Tigris and Euphrates Rivers are mentioned in connection with the garden's location. (See Genesis 2:14, where *Hiddekel* is another name for the Tigris River). Thus the people are still in "eastern" territory.

East has been very significant in Genesis thus far. The Garden of Eden is described as being "eastward" (Genesis 2:8). After Adam and Eve's sin and expulsion from the garden, the Lord stationed cherubims on the east side of Eden to prevent reentry (3:24). Cain made his home "on the east of Eden" following his murder of Abel (4:16). Thus the direction of east has been associated with ominous developments to this point. The account before us will provide yet another one.

What Do You Think?
> If offered a chance to relocate (better job, etc.), how do you know if it's God's will to do so?

Talking Points for Your Discussion
- Providing for your family
- Opportunities for Christian witness
- Opportunity to be involved with a strong church or to help a struggling one
- Other

II. The Scheme
(GENESIS 11:3, 4)

A. Resources (v. 3)

3. And they said one to another, Go to, let us make brick, and burn them throughly. And they had brick for stone, and slime had they for morter.

After having decided to settle in Shinar, the people determine to build permanent structures in which to live. The phrase *Go to* means something like "Come on."

The bricks to be used for construction have to be burned (or baked)—perhaps in a kiln or oven of some kind. Stone would be cheaper to use since stones do not have to be fabricated as bricks must be. But if no stone quarry is nearby and clay is available, the people will have to adopt a more expensive brick-making process. The fact that they are willing to do so shows their determination.

The word *slime* may be confusing to us at first since we naturally do not connect that term with building materials! It probably refers to bitumen, a tarry substance used as an adhesive or sealant (see also Genesis 14:10; Exodus 2:3). Although this material will serve as a binder between the bricks, it is nothing like our modern cement.

B. Resolution (v. 4)

4a. And they said, Go to, let us build us a city and a tower, whose top may reach unto heaven;

Now the people's goals become more specific and loftier. The tower that is part of the planning should not be thought of in terms of, say, the Leaning Tower of Pisa or the Eiffel Tower. Most likely a tower at this time resembles what is called *a ziggurat*. This is a pyramid-like structure with steps that lead upward to a platform on which may be found an altar or shrine for worship of a particular god.

The height of the structure is thought to bring the worshipper closer to the heavens and thus closer to his or her god or gods. The same thinking is behind the construction of the "high places" often mentioned in the Old Testament (example: Leviticus 26:30). We should note, however, that the text before us does not specifically link this structure to any pagan gods or practices.

❧ THE RIGHT KIND OF ELEVATION ❧

In the fifth century AD, there was a classification of monks known as "pillar saints." They built pillars for themselves, resided on these pillars, and achieved wide acclaim. Perhaps the most famous of these individuals was Simeon Stylites (the word *stylites* itself means "pillar"—think "stylus"), who lived AD 390–459. He started out on a pillar that was about 6 feet high, but gradually increased it until the platform was about 60 feet off the ground.

Many people were attracted to him because of his austerity and holiness. No doubt he was a holy man, but he was also eccentric and a bit bizarre. When insects came and laid their eggs on him, he often would cut himself so worms could feed on his bodily fluids. One time when a worm fell off his arm, Simeon replaced it and exclaimed, "Eat what God has given you!"

Many came to Simeon for spiritual counsel, including rulers and emperors. Because he was suspended between Heaven and earth, people thought him to be closer to Heaven, so obviously his words of counsel would have more spiritual value. Those who began the Tower of Babel also thought they could get closer to Heaven by building a tower. They were unsuccessful, and my guess is that the altitude of Simeon did not help much either. Not too many people today think they can get closer to God by increasing their elevation above the ground. Our problem is more along the lines of elevating our minds. See Daniel 4:29, 30; Romans 12:3; Colossians 2:18; etc.   —J. B. N.

4b. And let us make us a name, lest we be scattered abroad upon the face of the whole earth.

Now we see the problem with the proposed tower: *let us make us a name* clearly indicates that the people's desire is for self-promotion. God is completely absent from their goals and plans.

> *What Do You Think?*
> How do people attempt to "make a name" for themselves today? Under what circumstances, if any, can this be a good thing to do?
> *Talking Points for Your Discussion*
> ▪ Proverbs 3:4; 29:23
> ▪ John 3:30
> ▪ Romans 12:16
> ▪ Galatians 6:4

Second, the people claim that they do not want to be *scattered abroad upon the face of the whole earth.* By making a name for themselves—by constructing a tower and a city that will give them a sense of achievement and a permanent place to live, respectively—the people think they will have no need to move anywhere else. The problem with this thinking is that it seems to reveal defiance of God's mandate to "be fruitful, and multiply, and replenish the earth" (Genesis 1:28; 9:1). Again, it is painfully evident that although sin was judged by the great flood, it has not been eliminated.

III. The Sovereign God
(GENESIS 11:5-9)
A. He Sees (v. 5)

5. And the LORD came down to see the city and the tower, which the children of men builded.

Much as God came "walking in the garden" to confront Adam and Eve (Genesis 3:8), here God is described as coming *down to see* what these builders are up to. The language used is probably an ironic (and darkly humorous) way of pointing out the futility of the people's efforts: here they are desiring to build "a tower, whose top may reach unto heaven" (v. 4), yet the fact that the Lord comes down to observe their vain undertaking reveals that the tower isn't high enough!

The phrase *children of men* may be viewed from a couple of angles. It may describe who these self-important individuals really are: despite their high and haughty aims, they are still "children of men," nothing more. If taken in a literal sense as "sons of Adam," then perhaps the message is that these individuals, who desire to be so independent, are in reality acting no differently from their first ancestor. Adam did not escape the consequences of disobeying God, and neither will these people.

B. He Speaks (vv. 6, 7)

6. And the LORD said, Behold, the people is one, and they have all one language; and this they begin to do: and now nothing will be restrained from them, which they have imagined to do.

The idea of being of "one language, and of one speech" (Genesis 11:1) may appear to be a plus at first since this can promote unity of purpose and cooperation. But the Lord sees the situation quite differently. If the unified people are allowed to engage in such a defiant act of self-important disobedience, then *nothing will be restrained from them, which they have imagined to do.*

This language is similar to the way the Lord described His concern over humanity's having access to the tree of life after the first sin was committed: "Behold, the man is become as one of us, to know good and evil: and now, lest he put forth his hand, and take also of the tree of life, and eat, and live for ever" (Genesis 3:22)—then came eviction from the garden. God was concerned about the consequences of humans in a sinful condition having the potential of living forever in that condition.

The issue is much the same here at Babel: that unrestrained human freedom would have devastating consequences. Unity of purpose may seem an ideal goal, but if that unity is devoid of reverence for God and His authority, then the results will be disastrous. "All things are possible for man," some may arrogantly claim, but history has repeatedly illustrated that these "things" often are the most repulsive, barbaric acts imaginable. We can only wonder how many times God has looked at humanity's so-called "proud achievements" and simply shaken His head in sorrow at what amounts to nothing more than Babel revisited.

What Do You Think?
 What are some ways we can use our freedom to
  glorify God?
Talking Points for Your Discussion
 ▪ Regarding freedom of speech
 ▪ Regarding freedom of thought
 ▪ Regarding freedom of behavior
 ▪ Regarding freedom of movement
 ▪ Regarding freedom of association

---

7. Go to, let us go down, and there confound their language, that they may not understand one another's speech.

God couches His counterplan in language similar to what the builders themselves have used. *Go to* was used by the builders in verses 3, 4; here the Lord introduces His intentions in the same way. The people had said *let us* (v. 3); the Lord says the same here. The *us* in the Lord's case is most likely a reference to the Trinity.

God's words *let us* in Genesis 1:26 included granting dominion to humans; now, however, the same words serve to restrict humans' dominion, particularly their self-centered schemes in rebellion against God. God therefore declares that He will confound the people's language so that they can no longer *understand one another's speech*. With conversation stymied, the people's efforts to complete their city and tower will come to nothing.

What Do You Think?

What more can you or your church do to bridge language barriers for Christ?

Talking Points for Your Discussion

- Concerning those in your community who do not speak English
- Concerning the training of missionaries
- Concerning support for Bible translation efforts
- Other

❧ *WHAT GOD HEARS* ❧

In the 1994 movie *Nell*, Jodie Foster plays the part of a reclusive girl raised by her mother in the backcountry of the North Carolina hills. The mother had experienced a stroke, leaving her with severely impaired speech. After the mother died, Nell was discovered by the local doctor.

No one could understand Nell's slurred speech at first. Eventually, a researcher discovered that Nell's language was indeed English, but she had learned it from her mother, whose impediment had made Nell's speech virtually unrecognizable. Nell was taken to court to decide whether she should be institutionalized. Both sides argued their cases, then Nell spoke up, to everyone's surprise. The doctor had to interpret for her, but Nell was able to explain her situation, and she was granted her freedom to return to the hills.

Speech is a wonderful gift, a marvelous tool of communication. But when speech is misunderstood, the results can be both frustrating and devastating. We all feel inadequate to speak to God at one time or another. Our speech seems slurred, the right words won't come. It is at such times that we rely on the fact that "the Spirit itself maketh intercession for us with groanings which cannot be uttered" (Romans 8:26). Thank God for that heavenly language!   —J. B. N.

C. He Scatters (vv. 8, 9)

8. So the LORD scattered them abroad from thence upon the face of all the earth: and they left off to build the city.

Thus the people who don't want to be scattered (v. 4) are now scattered out of sheer frustration at their inability to live in harmony. The fact that they proceed to move *upon the face of all the earth* puts back in motion God's original intention for humanity. *The city* that had begun with such enthusiasm and fervor remains unfinished.

What Do You Think?

What lessons did you learn from a time when God closed a door on an unfinished plan or project?

Talking Points for Your Discussion

- A church building project
- A business venture
- A service opportunity
- A family or group event
- A personal goal
- Other

---

9. Therefore is the name of it called Babel; because the LORD did there confound the language of all the earth: and from thence did the LORD scatter them abroad upon the face of all the earth.

There appears to be a twofold play on words here involving the name *Babel*. First, *Babel* means "gate of God" in the language of the ancient Babylonians. But this city hardly lives up to such a presumptuous label! Instead of reaching "unto heaven" (v. 4), the builders have become scattered *upon the face of all the earth*. Instead of making a name for themselves as they originally intended (v. 4), they have become humiliated.

As noted previously, Genesis 10 elaborates on the "scattering" in describing the movements of Noah's three sons (Japheth, Ham, and Shem) and their descendants. At the conclusion of each son's account is the note of division according to "tongues" or languages (vv. 5, 20, 31). Thus the "one language" mentioned at the outset of this lesson becomes many.

The other play on words involves the Hebrew word translated as *confound*. This sounds very much like the name *Babel* and is an apt description of what has occurred as a result of God's intervention. (Of course, English gives us a similarly sounding word, *babble,* which implies confusion or nonsense.) Perhaps the intended lesson of this double meaning is that no matter how one looks at this endeavor, *Babel* means "confusion, failure, and frustration."

Conclusion

A. Humanity's "Bridges to Nowhere"

The phrase *bridge to nowhere* was used in the U.S. presidential campaign of 2008 to mock a "pork barrel" project: a bridge to be constructed primarily for the purpose of bringing dollars into a certain congressional district regardless of need for the bridge. An Internet search reveals that at least 11 bridges, primarily in the U.S., have been given this negative label. Sometimes bridges were built with all good intentions, but lack of forethought resulted in an unused or unusable bridge for one reason or another.

Genesis 1–11 records earliest humanity's *bridges to nowhere* in relation to God, and today's lesson sketches one of those. The people intended their tower to bridge the gap between earth and Heaven, but God intervened to ensure that the effort went nowhere. But God didn't just put a stop to faulty plans; He replaced those plans with a better one.

B. God's "Bridge to Somewhere"

Genesis 1–11 is rich with descriptions of God's actions to put humanity back on the right path. God's path is the path to somewhere important: an eternal, sin-free fellowship with Him. Perhaps you have seen artistic depictions of a canyon with the words "sinful people" on one side and "Holy God" on the other side. The two sides in such depictions are separated by the chasm of sin and death, but the chasm is bridged by the cross of Christ (John 3:16; 5:24; Hebrews 2:14, 15; 1 Peter 2:24; etc.).

Many Bible students have noted how the events that transpired on the Day of Pentecost served to reverse what occurred at Babel. Babel involved a confusion of language. But at Pentecost the gift of tongues (or languages) on those speak-

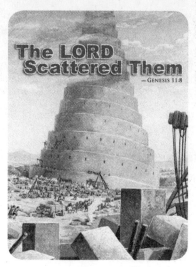

Visual for Lesson 5

Point to this visual as you contrast what happened at Babel with what happened on Pentecost.

ing brought about an amazing unity. Each person present could hear proclaimed in his or her native language "the wonderful works of God" (Acts 2:11). Many languages were present at Pentecost, yet God brought about a unity that those at Babel could not achieve because their plans were divorced from God's plans.

Paul Kissling sees what happened in Jerusalem at Pentecost as a "down payment on the reversal of the curse of Babel." The complete reversal will occur in the new Jerusalem, a place where a unity will be demonstrated that those at Babel could not have imagined. John pictures it for us in Revelation 7:9, 10: "After this I beheld, and, lo, a great multitude, which no man could number, of all nations, and kindreds, and people, and tongues, stood before the throne, . . . and cried with a loud voice, saying, Salvation to our God which sitteth upon the throne, and unto the Lamb."

Babel—and all undertakings similar to it—will be long forgotten.

C. Prayer

Our Father, we pray for the nations of our world to humble themselves before You. May we set the example as we remember that You resist the proud but give grace unto the humble (James 4:6). In Jesus' name, amen.

D. Thought to Remember

We can reach Heaven only on God's terms.

INVOLVEMENT LEARNING

Some of the activities below are also found in the helpful student book, Adult Bible Class.
Don't forget to download the free reproducible page from www.standardlesson.com to enhance your lesson!

Into the Lesson

Before class, do an Internet search for the tallest buildings in the world. Have some pictures of these on display without identification as learners arrive. Ask learners to identify the buildings.

Alternative: Ask learners to name some of the tallest skyscrapers in the world. *(Possible responses: Shanghai World Financial Center, Trump International Hotel and Tower, Empire State Building.)* Say, "Today we will read about the first record of an attempt to build a tall structure and why God was displeased with those who tried to build it."

Into the Word

Option: As a pretest, distribute copies of the "Bringing Order to Confusion" activity from the reproducible page, which you can download. Check answers against the Scripture text. You can use this activity to lead into the next exercise.

Divide the board into four columns. Writing left to right, put *Event / Cause / Effect* as headers for the first three columns. Leave the rightmost column unlabeled for the time being. Then divide learners into four groups and give the following Scripture assignments: Group 1, Genesis 11:1, 2; Group 2, Genesis 11:3, 4; Group 3, Genesis 11:5-7; Group 4, Genesis 11:8, 9. Ask groups to read their verses then identify the event, the possible cause of the event, and the effect of that event. Advise that most of the causes will be inferences rather than concrete evidence from the text.

When groups are ready, call for findings and jot them on the board. Expected and possible responses: *Group 1*—event: found a good place to live together; cause: common language; effect: common purpose, common goals, unity. *Group 2*—event: made bricks, built a city and tower; cause: wanted to achieve own purpose rather than God's; effect: made a name for themselves, maintained solidarity. *Group 3*—event: God came down to see; cause: God read man's heart; effect:

God confused their language. *Group 4*—event: people scattered; cause: God wanted to thwart man's plan; effect: God's will prevailed over man's.

Lead the class in discussing each event and its stated or possible causes and effects. Allow learners to defend their inferences concerning causes.

Title the fourth column on the board as *Motives.* Ask, "What was behind the people's desire to build a city with a tower?" Record answers in the fourth column. If someone responds by quoting "let us make us a name" from Genesis 11:4, immediately push deeper by asking, "What does that imply?" *(Possible responses: wanted to exclude God from their plans, were being disobedient to God's command to "replenish the earth.")* Brainstorm modern examples of similar sins.

Into Life

Say, "It's usually fairly easy to spot the 'mote' in someone else's eye, but if we are going to be the church God has called us to be, then we must make sure we have no 'beams' in our own eyes (see Matthew 7:3-5)." Ask learners to evaluate their church as a body of believers to see if it is guilty of the sins of the people of Babel. (Caution: be sure to make this discussion about the church *as a body,* not mentioning any particular individual; do not allow this to become a gripe session.)

Use the following questions to lead the discussion: 1. Which attitudes of the people of Babel can become a problem when the church engages in a building project, and what can be done to prevent that from happening? 2. Is it possible for a church to become "too big"? Why, or why not?

Conclude with a prayer for God's protection on your church so that wrong attitudes don't develop. Ask for God to give wisdom to your church's leadership. As learners depart, distribute copies of the "My Own Babel" exercise from the reproducible page. This should be a take-home activity since it calls for responses that are very personal.

THE PROMISE OF A FUTURE

DEVOTIONAL READING: Hebrews 11:8-16
BACKGROUND SCRIPTURE: Genesis 12:1-7; 13; 15; 17:8

GENESIS 15:5-21

5 And he brought him forth abroad, and said, Look now toward heaven, and tell the stars, if thou be able to number them: and he said unto him, So shall thy seed be.

6 And he believed in the LORD; and he counted it to him for righteousness.

7 And he said unto him, I am the LORD that brought thee out of Ur of the Chaldees, to give thee this land to inherit it.

8 And he said, Lord GOD, whereby shall I know that I shall inherit it?

9 And he said unto him, Take me an heifer of three years old, and a she goat of three years old, and a ram of three years old, and a turtledove, and a young pigeon.

10 And he took unto him all these, and divided them in the midst, and laid each piece one against another: but the birds divided he not.

11 And when the fowls came down upon the carcases, Abram drove them away.

12 And when the sun was going down, a deep sleep fell upon Abram; and, lo, an horror of great darkness fell upon him.

13 And he said unto Abram, Know of a surety that thy seed shall be a stranger in a land that is not theirs, and shall serve them; and they shall afflict them four hundred years;

14 And also that nation, whom they shall serve, will I judge: and afterward shall they come out with great substance.

15 And thou shalt go to thy fathers in peace; thou shalt be buried in a good old age.

16 But in the fourth generation they shall come hither again: for the iniquity of the Amorites is not yet full.

17 And it came to pass, that, when the sun went down, and it was dark, behold a smoking furnace, and a burning lamp that passed between those pieces.

18 In the same day the LORD made a covenant with Abram, saying, Unto thy seed have I given this land, from the river of Egypt unto the great river, the river Euphrates:

19 The Kenites, and the Kenizzites, and the Kadmonites,

20 And the Hittites, and the Perizzites, and the Rephaims,

21 And the Amorites, and the Canaanites, and the Girgashites, and the Jebusites.

KEY VERSE

In the same day the LORD made a covenant with Abram, saying, Unto thy seed have I given this land, from the river of Egypt unto the great river, the river Euphrates. —**Genesis 15:18**

FIRST THINGS

Unit 2: First Nation

LESSONS 6–9

LESSON AIMS

After participating in this lesson, each student will be able to:

1. Describe the ways that God confirmed His promises to Abram.

2. Explain the importance of the words *believe* and *covenant* in this lesson.

3. Write a prayer that confesses a weakness in believing God's promises.

LESSON OUTLINE

Introduction

A. Unbelievable!

The word *unbelievable* is a choice word to use in response to an account that has an unexpected outcome. Entering the phrase *unbelievable stories* in an Internet search engine provides examples from war, sports, and other backgrounds.

Consider, for example, "the amazin' Mets" of 1969. The previous year, baseball's New York Mets finished ninth in the 10-team National League. The Mets had come into existence in 1962, and the team had never finished higher than that in its 7-year history. To tell anyone in 1968 that the Mets would win the World Series the following year would have drawn laughter. Yet on October 6, 1969—exactly 44 years ago today—the New York Mets won the National League pennant. The Mets then went on to defeat the Baltimore Orioles in the 1969 World Series. *Unbelievable!*

The lesson for today is about a promise with unbelievable dimensions—that Abram would have descendants and that they would be more than the stars he could see and count.

B. Lesson Background

After the Tower of Babel event (last week's lesson), the people clustered by language groups and migrated to different areas of the earth (see Genesis 10:5, 20, 31). Cities and civilizations developed. Groups such as the Sumerians and Akkadians became powerful. Their artifacts and clay tablets reveal much about them.

God's redemptive plan, for its part, was moving forward according to His schedule. That plan involved relocating a man named Abram from Ur of the Chaldees (or Kasdim) to the land of Canaan. Several sites are mentioned as possibilities for the location of Ur, but the one that is about 170 miles south of Babylon seems to have the best evidence. Ur was a progressive city that some consider as one of the largest cities of antiquity. Estimates of its population are as high as 65,000. Abram and his family left this thriving commercial area and moved to Haran in northern Mesopotamia. Genesis 11:31 states that Terah (Abram's father) is the one who led in the relocation.

Abram was called to leave Haran after his father died (Genesis 12:1; Acts 7:4), and God gave the seven special promises found in Genesis 12:2, 3. The seventh promise has messianic implications: all the families of the earth would be blessed because of Abram.

So Abram journeyed to Canaan. He built his first altar to the Lord in Canaan when he was at Shechem (Genesis 12:6, 7). It was here that Abram received a promise that this was the land that would be given to his descendants. Famine drove the family to Egypt, and then they returned to Canaan (12:10–13:1). Abram and his nephew, Lot, both prospered, but they had to go their separate ways (13:2-12). Again, God promised the land to Abram (13:14, 15).

The "adventures" that follow in Genesis 14 lead up to God's covenant with Abram in Genesis 15. In the opening verses of Genesis 15, we see Abram assured of the Lord's favor. That assurance includes the promise of a son to become Abram's heir. Abram's name is not changed to *Abraham* until Genesis 17, and that distinction will be maintained in this lesson.

I. A People in the Future
(GENESIS 15:5, 6)
A. Declaration (v. 5)

5. And he brought him forth abroad, and said, Look now toward heaven, and tell the stars, if thou be able to number them: and he said unto him, So shall thy seed be.

This verse continues "the word of the Lord" that Abram is receiving beginning in Genesis 15:4. The fact that Abram is instructed to look toward *the stars* indicates that this communication is taking place at night. To do so, Abram is called out of his tent or place of sleep, perhaps as part of the vision or perhaps in a wakeful state. God has already noted the future of Abram's offspring in Genesis 13:16. That proliferation is restated here in terms of the number of stars.

The estimate of the number of stars visible to the naked eye varies, depending on the time of the night and whether a person is in the northern or southern hemisphere. One study says that

the grand total of stars visible to the naked eye is 9,110. A report in 2010 suggested that there are 300 sextillion stars in the universe. For Abram, who does not have a telescope, there is certainly "more here than meets the eye"! The primary point is not a specific number of descendants, however, but that there will be many of them.

What Do You Think?
How have God's promises been confirmed for you at different stages of your faith journey?
Talking Points for Your Discussion
- In "good" times
- In times of conflict
- In times of hardship
- Other

❧ YOU, THE STAR ❧

Recently I spent some time at a cabin in the mountains of New Mexico, at an elevation of 7,300 feet. The nighttime sky was incredible. There were far more stars visible than I am used to seeing. Urban areas, with their "light pollution," cause many stars to be obscured altogether. The difference in a rural setting is amazing!

On a cloudless night in a rural area, one can see the Milky Way stretching from horizon to horizon. The Milky Way, the galaxy within which our solar system is located, is called that because it appears as a milky substance in the heavens. It contains at least 200 billion stars. Those stars were in existence when God said "so shall thy seed be."

We don't know the exact number of stars in the universe, but God does. And if He can know each star by its name (Psalm 147:4), He can certainly count the number of Abraham's descendants and know each of us by name as well. Today, it's spiritual, not physical, descent from Abraham that counts (Luke 3:8; John 8:39-47; Galatians 3:7). Let your light shine!   —J. B. N.

B. Decisions (v. 6)

6. And he believed in the LORD; and he counted it to him for righteousness.

We now see Abram's reaction and the Lord's approval of that reaction. This is the first time that a form of the word *believed* occurs in the Bible. This case involves Abram's trust that God will fulfill what He has said. The importance of this is seen in the fact that this verse is quoted three times in the New Testament: in Romans 4:3; Galatians 3:6; and James 2:23 (compare Romans 4:9, 22; Hebrews 11:8-12).

This is not the first time that faith is demonstrated in the Bible, however. Hebrews 11 notes that Abel, Enoch, and Noah, who preceded Abram, obeyed God in faith. To have faith does not mean discarding reason or believing what you know is not true. As Abram considers the creation and the fact that God can give life and speak into being what did not previously exist (Romans 4:17), then it is reasonable that God can use Abram's "dead" body and the "deadness" of his wife's womb (4:19) to provide a son.

The Lord's response to Abram's faith is to count or credit that faith to him *for righteousness*. The Hebrew word translated *counted it . . . for* occurs over 100 times in the Old Testament, and it is often translated as some form of *think*. If God thinks a person to be righteous, that is what really matters. Abram's faith is the key to his being counted as righteous in the mind of God.

Both Old and New Testaments affirm that no one is righteous in terms of never sinning (Ecclesiastes 7:20; Romans 3:10). Righteousness is not something that a person can earn "by the deeds of the law" (Romans 3:20). But God's gracious provisions mean that He can count a person as righteous. Abram's belief is the basis for that here. Our faith is also a basis (Romans 4:5).

II. A Possession in the Future
(GENESIS 15:7-11)

A. Purpose and Question (vv. 7, 8)

7. And he said unto him, I am the LORD that brought thee out of Ur of the Chaldees, to give thee this land to inherit it.

The Lord leaves no doubt that He is the one who brought Abram *out of Ur of the Chaldees*. The purpose was not just to move Abram away from a certain place, but to bring him to Canaan in order to give him that land as an inheritance. This reaf-

firms similar statements in Genesis 12. There also are similarities between the verse before us and the opening statement by the Lord as He gives the Ten Commandments to Israel (Exodus 20:2). When God speaks through Moses hundreds of years later, God will affirm that not only is He bringing the people out of slavery in Egypt, but also into the land of promise (see Exodus 13:3-5).

We may wonder what is so special about Canaan that the Lord chooses it for a people, a temple, and the place where the Messiah is to be born. Canaan is the crossroads of the ancient world, lying between Africa and Asia. Commerce to the west, among the nations around the Mediterranean, always thrives. These factors will help spread the concept of "one God" in all directions.

What Do You Think?
  What helps you trust God when He overrides your
    plan with one of His own?
Talking Points for Your Discussion
  ▪ Concerning your church
  ▪ Concerning your vocation
  ▪ Concerning your family
  ▪ Other

8. And he said, Lord GOD, whereby shall I know that I shall inherit it?

At first glance, we may think that Abram's question reveals doubt on his part. The total context, however, indicates that God does not perceive Abram to be expressing skepticism (contrast Luke 1:18-20). Abram does believe, but his question suggests that it would be helpful to have a symbol or sign to confirm the events of the vision. That is about to happen!

B. Command and Response (vv. 9-11)

9. And he said unto him, Take me an heifer of three years old, and a she goat of three years old, and a ram of three years old, and a turtledove, and a young pigeon.

The vision of the night seems to have ended, although some students consider the entire event to be a vision. The statement to Abram seems to involve activities of the day and into the next night. As the new day dawns, Abram receives instructions on gathering five kinds of animals. The fact that the heifer, goat, and ram are to be 3 years old seems to have no special significance. Such animals have reached maturity, and they have a youthful vigor.

10. And he took unto him all these, and divided them in the midst, and laid each piece one against another: but the birds divided he not.

Abram complies with God's commands, and his actions show that he understands that these animals are not to be burnt offerings. The ritual about to be described is found also in Jeremiah 34:18, 19, and in the records provided by other nations of that part of the world.

The four-legged animals are cut in half, and the pieces are laid so that the two parts of each animal are placed side by side (juxtaposed). There is a space between the halves, and that space is essential to what is about to take place as verse 17 will make clear. The two birds are not cut apart; it is usually assumed they are laid opposite one other.

11. And when the fowls came down upon the carcases, Abram drove them away.

Various kinds of birds are attracted to such a scene, and normally this is God's method of "cleaning up" an ecological problem. This time the situation is different. A sacred, significant ritual is pending, and Abram wants to preserve the animals for the ceremony that is to come. He therefore drives away the intruders so that they will not mutilate the carcasses.

C. Situations and Outcomes (vv. 12-16)

12. And when the sun was going down, a deep sleep fell upon Abram; and, lo, an horror of great darkness fell upon him.

Either in reality or as part of the vision, God moves to bring two things upon Abram: *a deep sleep* that is beyond what is normal (see the commentary on Genesis 2:21 in lesson 2) and a sense of oppressive, *great darkness*. The interpretation is not provided, but it is usually believed that the darkness causes Abram to be aware of the suffering that his descendants will experience (next verse).

13. And he said unto Abram, Know of a surety that thy seed shall be a stranger in a land that is not theirs, and shall serve them; and they shall afflict them four hundred years.

The pronouncement by God provides understanding to the oppression that Abram feels. Exodus 12:40, 41 states that the total time spent in Egypt is exactly 430 years. This is not a contradiction to the 400 years noted here, for the Israelites will be protected by Joseph during their early years, and those years may not be counted as part of the centuries of slavery. In addition, large numbers are often rounded (compare Acts 7:6).

14. And also that nation, whom they shall serve, will I judge: and afterward shall they come out with great substance.

The name of the oppressing nation is not given, but Egypt is obviously the one that fulfills the prophecy. The judgment that the Lord will declare will be severe indeed (see Exodus 7:14–11:10; 12:29, 30; 14:23-31). God will indeed execute justice on that nation, and then Abram's descendants will leave.

When the Israelites are thrust out of Egypt after the deaths of all firstborn Egyptians, the Israelites will be given things of value (Exodus 12:33-36). In one sense, this too will be justice, for the Israelites finally will be compensated for their hard labor as slaves.

HOW TO SAY IT

Akkadians	Uh-*kay*-dee-unz.
Al-'Arish	Awl-A-*reesh*.
Amorites	*Am*-uh-rites.
Canaanites	*Kay*-nun-ites.
Chaldees	*Kal*-deez.
Girgashites	*Gur*-guh-shites.
Hittites	*Hit*-ites or *Hit*-tites.
Hivites	*Hi*-vites.
Jebusites	*Jeb*-yuh-sites.
Kenites	*Ken*-ites.
Mediterranean	*Med*-uh-tuh-**ray**-nee-un.
Mesopotamia	*Mes*-uh-puh-**tay**-me-uh.
Perizzites	*Pair*-ih-zites.
Rephaims	*Ref*-a-ims.
Shechem	*Shee*-kem or *Shek*-em.
Sumerians	Sue-*mer*-ee-unz.
Terah	*Tair*-uh.

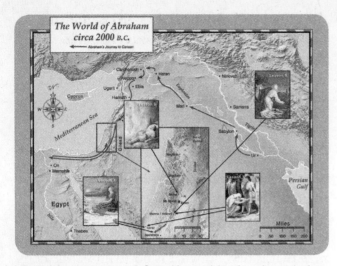

The World of Abraham circa 2000 B.C.
← Abraham's Journey to Canaan

Visual for Lessons 6 & 9. *Keep this visual posted throughout this unit of lessons to give your learners a geographical perspective.*

❧ SURPRISING TURNAROUNDS ❧

Some time ago, I read a story about a janitor who worked at a small liberal arts college. He never earned a big salary, but he often asked the economics professors about investing. When the janitor died at a ripe old age, he bequeathed the college $3 million from his estate! Here was a man in a "low" position who surprised everyone.

We all like stories like that, don't we? But such stories go back a long way. Abram moved from a center of civilization to endure the hardships (even famine) of a less prosperous area, only to end up very rich (Genesis 13:2). Starting with little more than the shirt on his back, Jacob reversed that trip and ended up wealthy (30:43).

The children of Israel suffered while in Egypt, but ultimately they gained their freedom and left "with great substance." That was a surprising turnaround, but earthly reversals of fortune ultimately are not as important as heavenly ones. The story of the rich man and Lazarus is crucial in this regard (Luke 16:19-31). Make sure you don't allow your earthly circumstances to distract you from the ultimate turnaround that awaits. —J. B. N.

15. And thou shalt go to thy fathers in peace; thou shalt be buried in a good old age.

Assurance is given to Abram that he will not experience this enslavement himself. Abram is between 75 and 86 years old at this point (Gene-

sis 12:4; 16:16), and he will be 175 at the time of his death (25:7). He will indeed die "in a good old age, an old man, and full of years" (25:8, 9).

16. But in the fourth generation they shall come hither again: for the iniquity of the Amorites is not yet full.

Abram now receives a different time factor: the liberation of his descendants will be *in the fourth generation.* It is thus obvious that a generation is considered to be about 100 years at this time. The longevity of Abram, Isaac, and Jacob—who die at ages 175, 180, and 147, respectively—demonstrates this (Genesis 25:7; 35:28; 47:28).

Another factor is that the present occupants of Canaan, here called *the Amorites,* will also experience divine judgment. The name of one of the largest groups is used to represent all of them (compare Genesis 15:19, 20, below).

> *What Do You Think?*
> How do you see the faith and actions of past generations bearing fruit in your life today?
> *Talking Points for Your Discussion*
> - Regarding physical ancestors
> - Regarding spiritual ancestors

III. A Promise to Abram
(GENESIS 15:17-21)
A. Covenant Confirmed (v. 17)

17. And it came to pass, that, when the sun went down, and it was dark, behold a smoking furnace, and a burning lamp that passed between those pieces.

The Jeremiah passage cited above with verse 10 shows that this type of covenant requires that the participants walk in the open path between the halves of each animal. According to ancient texts, the implication is that the ones entering into the covenant are making a solemn commitment, and that they will experience death (as represented by the slain animals) if they violate their parts of the covenant. The covenant in view here is known as *a grant covenant*; it does not place any demands on the recipient. God is binding himself to do as He has promised, and Abram is not required to walk between the halves of the animals.

Neither does God personally do any walking. Instead, He uses *a smoking furnace* (a clay oven) and *a burning lamp* to go *between those pieces*. A clay oven is an inverted bowl, probably about two feet high, with a hole near the top that allows a draft to keep the fire burning. The seriousness of this ceremony leaves no doubt: God intends to fulfill His grant.

B. Covenant Stated (vv. 18-21)

18. In the same day the Lord made a covenant with Abram, saying, Unto thy seed have I given this land, from the river of Egypt unto the great river, the river Euphrates.

This verse is significant in that it is the first time that the word *covenant* is used to describe God's promises to Abram. It also provides an answer to the question that Abram asked earlier (v. 8) about an assurance that he will inherit the land.

The promised land is described in two ways. The first description is in terms of geographical points. *The river of Egypt unto the great river, the river Euphrates* describes the range from the southwest to the far north and east. The Egyptian boundary refers to a small stream (the Wadi Al-'Arish) that is recognized as the point where a person enters Egypt when coming from Canaan.

What Do You Think?
What will you do to ensure that you are leaving a legacy of faith for future generations?
Talking Points for Your Discussion
- Through behavior modeled
- Through evident spiritual disciplines
- Through personal teaching
- Other

19. The Kenites, and the Kenizzites, and the Kadmonites,

A second way to describe the promised land is by listing its inhabitants. According to this verse and the next two, there are 10 tribal groups. A comparison with Deuteronomy 7:1 reveals that the Hivites are not mentioned here, but the verse before us adds three not discussed there (compare Exodus 3:8 in lesson 10, which has the same groups as Deuteronomy 7:1, differently ordered).

20, 21. And the Hittites, and the Perizzites, and the Rephaims, and the Amorites, and the Canaanites, and the Girgashites, and the Jebusites.

Commentary on Exodus 3:8, 17 in lesson 10 provides a bit more depth on the people groups that inhabit the promised land. The reaction of Abram to these stunning promises is not given. It is assumed that his faith in God is made even stronger by what transpires in the ceremony.

What Do You Think?
What obstacles, spiritual and otherwise, will have to be cleared out of the way to enable you to serve God as you should?
Talking Points for Your Discussion
- Urgent issues displacing important issues
- Perfectionism
- Procrastination
- Other

Conclusion
A. Standing on the Promises

God is a maker of promises! He made promises of land, children, and forgiveness of sin. He also promised consequences for disobedience. The promises began in the Garden of Eden, and they were made through the centuries until the completion of His revelations as recorded in the Bible.

Someone observed that the gospel consists of four things: facts to be believed, commands to be obeyed, promises to be received, and warnings to be heeded. Each factor is important to the believer who is standing on the promises of God. May we exhibit the faith of Abram in believing God's promises—and acting on them.

B. Prayer

Thank You, Almighty God, for these examples of covenant love and for the promises that You have revealed about the glorious future for all who follow Christ. In Jesus' name, amen.

C. Thought to Remember

Expect God to keep His promises— because He will!

INVOLVEMENT LEARNING

Some of the activities below are also found in the helpful student book, Adult Bible Class.
Don't forget to download the free reproducible page from www.standardlesson.com to enhance your lesson!

Into the Lesson

Option: Place in chairs copies of the "Abram and Me" activity from the reproducible page, which you can download. Learners can begin working on this as they arrive. Wait until the Into Life segment to discuss results.

As learners arrive, have on display a large clear-glass jar filled with sand. Display next to it a sign reading, "Guess the number, get a prize!" After your class assembles, hold up the jar and say, "We've all seen 'guess the number' contests, often involving jelly beans, marbles, etc. Such contests are easy to determine a winner since it's a simple matter to dump out the jelly beans and count them after the contest deadline. But who would actually want to do that with grains of sand?"

Point out Genesis 15:5. Say, "God tells Abram that his descendants will be as the stars. In 22:17, God adds the illustration of sand. God can count these things, but we need not do so. Our task, as Abram's, is to take God at His word."

Into the Word

Recruit a volunteer to appear as Abram in Bible-times dress to deliver the following monologue:

After the great flood and the foolishness of a tower to Heaven—two stories I had heard repeated many times growing up—my ancestor Shem and his descendants settled in a fertile area near two rivers. I was living in the same area, at Haran, when God spoke to me. I do not understand why He spoke to *me,* of all people, regarding His plans! My wife was not able to have children, but God said He would make a great nation of me. After we had journeyed to Canaan, then to Egypt, and then back to Canaan, God spoke once more. He had more startling news: He would give me a son, my own flesh and blood, as an heir! How could I believe such a thing at my age? But I must. For God is true.

After thanking "Abram," let the class comment on both the scriptural and the "poetic license" aspects of the monologue, but do not let this discussion drag out.

Use the commentary to explain the ceremony of Genesis 15:9-17. Then pose the following questions to your class, allowing time for response between each. Some responses will be conjectural since the Scripture references noted do not provide the complete answer in every instance.

1. What question from Abram elicited this ceremony by God? *(v. 8)*

2. Why did Abram drive away the birds of prey? *(v. 11)*

3. What was Abram's state of consciousness during the ceremony? *(v. 12)*

4. What part did God's revelation of the foreign captivity have in assuring Abram of His promise? *(v. 13)*

5. Why was Abram assured that he would live a long life and die in peace? *(v. 15)*

6. How did a listing of the tribal groups occupying Canaan offer assurance to Abram? *(vv. 19-21)*

Into Life

Option: If you used the "Abram and Me" activity above, ask learners what the hidden message is. Use that to make a transition to this segment.

Give each learner a slip of paper that reads "Believing God is not always easy" on one side and "God counts belief as righteousness" on the other. Say, "Keep this slip of paper with you in the week ahead. Before you pray at various times, first read both sides of the paper. Then relate the two truths on the paper for the issue of prayer that is presenting itself at the time."

Alternative: Distribute copies of the "The Desperate Father and Me" activity from the reproducible page. Have someone read aloud Mark 9:17-26. Discuss the mixture of belief and unbelief that is honestly confessed in verse 24; have learners fill in the blanks per instructions and exchange results with someone. Close with a prayer for belief.

A PROMISE TO SARAH

DEVOTIONAL READING: Isaiah 51:1-6

BACKGROUND SCRIPTURE: Genesis 17:15-17; 18:9-15; 21:1-7

GENESIS 17:15-17

15 And God said unto Abraham, As for Sarai thy wife, thou shalt not call her name Sarai, but Sarah shall her name be.

16 And I will bless her, and give thee a son also of her: yea, I will bless her, and she shall be a mother of nations; kings of people shall be of her.

17 Then Abraham fell upon his face, and laughed, and said in his heart, Shall a child be born unto him that is an hundred years old? and shall Sarah, that is ninety years old, bear?

GENESIS 18:9-15

9 And they said unto him, Where is Sarah thy wife? And he said, Behold, in the tent.

10 And he said, I will certainly return unto thee according to the time of life; and, lo, Sarah thy wife shall have a son. And Sarah heard it in the tent door, which was behind him.

11 Now Abraham and Sarah were old and well stricken in age; and it ceased to be with Sarah after the manner of women.

12 Therefore Sarah laughed within herself, saying, After I am waxed old shall I have pleasure, my lord being old also?

13 And the LORD said unto Abraham, Where-fore did Sarah laugh, saying, Shall I of a surety bear a child, which am old?

14 Is any thing too hard for the LORD? At the time appointed I will return unto thee, according to the time of life, and Sarah shall have a son.

15 Then Sarah denied, saying, I laughed not; for she was afraid. And he said, Nay; but thou didst laugh.

GENESIS 21:1-7

1 And the LORD visited Sarah as he had said, and the LORD did unto Sarah as he had spoken.

2 For Sarah conceived, and bare Abraham a son in his old age, at the set time of which God had spoken to him.

3 And Abraham called the name of his son that was born unto him, whom Sarah bare to him, Isaac.

4 And Abraham circumcised his son Isaac being eight days old, as God had commanded him.

5 And Abraham was an hundred years old, when his son Isaac was born unto him.

6 And Sarah said, God hath made me to laugh, so that all that hear will laugh with me.

7 And she said, Who would have said unto Abraham, that Sarah should have given children suck? for I have born him a son in his old age.

KEY VERSE

Sarah conceived, and bare Abraham a son in his old age, at the set time of which God had spoken to him.

—**Genesis 21:2**

FIRST THINGS

Unit 2: First Nation

LESSONS 6–9

LESSON AIMS

After participating in this lesson, each student will be able to:

1. Describe the reactions of Abraham and Sarah to the promise of a son.

2. Explain the significance of laughing in each section of today's text.

3. Suggest a way to show God that he or she trusts God's plans.

LESSON OUTLINE

Introduction

A. Making Promises

The investors had to promise that they would not tell anyone about the project, which was top secret. Anyone who violated this nondisclosure agreement would forfeit his or her investment. The supposed project involved a method of producing energy so that a unit the size of a small box could provide electricity for a city.

If this sounds too good to be true, it was. Those who received the funds for the imaginary project were master manipulators. They spent the money on themselves, declared bankruptcy, and depended on the investors to keep their promises not to spill the beans. Someone, however, finally talked. Did he lose what he invested? Yes—and so did the ones who kept the promise.

Some people make promises to God that are intended to manipulate God into doing what they want. The phrase *foxhole religion* describes another category of suspect promises. The one making this type of promise commits his or her future, with all sincerity, to God if God will only spare the person from imminent danger. But the promise may fade from memory once the danger has passed.

Today's lesson is about promises that God made to Sarah about her having a son. God's promises are not like ours—He never manipulates; His memory doesn't fade. When God promises, He keeps His word, and we receive the benefits.

B. Lesson Background

God made several promises to Abram. When Abram's family left Haran, the Lord said that He would make Abram to be a great nation (Genesis 12:2). Abram entered Canaan at age 75, and he was told that this was the land that God planned to give to his descendants (12:7). After Abram and nephew Lot went their separate ways, Abram was again told that all the land he could see would be given to his descendants (13:15).

But Abram and his wife were childless. With the passing of the years, Abram may have been thinking again how he could "help" God resolve this problem of Abram's having a proper heir. In Genesis 16, Abram's wife, Sarai (renamed Sarah in today's lesson), offered a culturally acceptable way that could fulfill what had been promised: she would give Hagar, her maidservant, to Abram. The resulting offspring would be from Abram's body, and Sarai could have a son through Hagar. This attempt to run ahead of God turned out to be a bad idea, as Genesis 16:4b-6 shows.

The Lord appeared to Abram 13 years later to reveal new dimensions of the covenant (Genesis 17:1). First, Abram's name (meaning "exalted father") was changed to Abraham (meaning "father of a multitude"; 17:5). It was strange for a man who had only one son (Ishmael) to have such a name! Even so, Abraham's acceptance of the name shows that he understood that to change a person's name shows that you have authority over that person. Today's text takes us into a second name change initiated by the authority of God.

I. Prediction
(GENESIS 17:15-17)

Between God's changing of Abram's name (Genesis 17:3-5) and the changing of Sarai's name (today's text) comes the Lord's introduction of the practice of circumcision for all males who are in Abraham's household. This is a sign of the covenant (v. 11).

The seriousness of God's intent is seen in His declaration that failure to undergo circumcision is the same as breaking the covenant (v. 14). Abraham's two parts of the covenant are to understand it (vv. 1-14) and implement it (vv. 23-27). Sandwiched between these two is God's declaration of Sarai's role.

HOW TO SAY IT

Abraham	*Ay*-bruh-ham.
Abram	*Ay*-brum.
Hagar	*Hay*-gar.
Ishmael	*Ish*-may-el.
Keturah	Keh-*too*-ruh.
Mamre	*Mam*-reh.
Sarai	*Seh*-rye.
Yahweh *(Hebrew)*	*Yah*-weh.
Zacharias	Zack-uh-*rye*-us.

A. Name Given (v. 15)

15. And God said unto Abraham, As for Sarai thy wife, thou shalt not call her name Sarai, but Sarah shall her name be.

Abraham's wife, Sarai, has not been mentioned in any previous communications from God regarding Abraham's having a son, so this section of Scripture is a first in that regard (see v. 16, next). Just before that happens, she is mentioned as another person whose name is being changed. This time, however, there is no difference in meaning: both *Sarah* and *Sarai* mean "princess." An example of this meaning is found in 1 Kings 11:3, where it is given in the plural form as "princesses."

Some suggest that the minor change in the name may be a difference in dialect. The unchanged meaning fits Sarah's forthcoming status, as verse 16 reveals.

❧ *YOUR NEW NAME* ❧

Fans of professional wrestling know that Terrance Gene Bollea gained fame on TV under a different name. In another case, Angelo Siciliano, the bodybuilder of the 1940s, marketed his system for muscle development by giving himself a name that created a mental image of success in that regard. If you're a baseball fan of any era, you probably know the nickname by which George Herman Ruth, Jr. was called.

Did the three well-known substitute names come to mind? They are Hulk Hogan, Charles Atlas, and Babe Ruth, respectively. Hogan's professional moniker added to his cachet as a TV personality, while Siciliano's new name conjured up visions of a Titan from Greek mythology. Both changes were successful in terms of marketing. Ruth's nickname is a bit different because he didn't choose the new name for himself; rather, it was imposed upon him by teammates and fans.

We see several name changes in the Bible, and Sarah's is one of those. She didn't choose her new name, God did. The new name had the same meaning as the old one, but the change symbolized the authority and power God had over her life. This is a marvelous thing because "him that overcometh . . . I will write upon him my new name" (Revelation 3:12). —C. R. B.

B. Son Promised (v. 16)

16. And I will bless her, and give thee a son also of her: yea, I will bless her, and she shall be a mother of nations; kings of people shall be of her.

Sarah is to be the mother of the special son promised to Abraham. For this to happen at her advanced age (see v. 17, next), she will need a blessing from the Lord, and that is what He provides.

The blessing for Abraham and Sarah reaches into the future and includes kings and royalty among their descendants. Thus it is quite appropriate for Sarah's changed name still to mean "princess." The fulfillment for this aspect of the promise begins when Saul becomes Israel's first genuine king more than 1,000 years later. The final king in the long line is Jesus Christ, the "King of kings" (Revelation 17:14).

C. Father Laughs (v. 17)

17. Then Abraham fell upon his face, and laughed, and said in his heart, Shall a child be born unto him that is an hundred years old? and shall Sarah, that is ninety years old, bear?

Abraham's reaction is to fall to the ground in laughter. Some have said that this reflects skepticism, similar to Sarah's in Genesis 18. This negative view doesn't fit the man who looked at the stars of the heavens and believed God (Genesis 15:6). We conclude that Abraham combines an attitude of worship with laughter that results from an inner joy (compare Romans 4:19-21).

When Abraham looks ahead, he realizes that at the time of the birth he will be 100 years old and Sarah will be 90 (compare Genesis 17:1, 24). These facts cause him to ask himself the two questions we see here. The implications are staggering,

and Abraham knows that the promised outcome is beyond what is considered normal.

Genesis 17:19 (not in today's text) should also be mentioned, for there God informs Abraham that the name of the son is to be *Isaac.* The name means "he laughs," and it points to the laughter here and to what occurs in the next section of our study.

II. Promise
(GENESIS 18:9-15)

The opening verses of Genesis 18 provide the background for the dialogue that is a part of the printed text for today. Abraham is near Mamre, and three men are suddenly standing in front of him (see Hebrews 13:2). This probably takes place a short time after the first segment of our lesson.

To have guests show up is special, for they can bring news from far away. Therefore Abraham instructs Sarah and a servant to prepare a meal of hospitality (Genesis 18:6, 7). The men ask the questions we see next.

A. Listening and Laughing (vv. 9-12)

9. And they said unto him, Where is Sarah thy wife? And he said, Behold, in the tent.

In the culture of the day, it is not customary for a man to inquire about the wife of another man. Therefore Abraham is probably curious about the inquiry we see here. Perhaps there is something about these men that causes Abraham to accept the question, so he replies that she is *in the tent.*

10. And he said, I will certainly return unto thee according to the time of life; and, lo, Sarah thy wife shall have a son. And Sarah heard it in the tent door, which was behind him.

One of the guests speaks, and in so doing he states that he will return later. Opinions vary on the figure of speech *according to the time of life* used to describe when the return will occur. One view is that it will be at the beginning of another year from the present moment. Another opinion is that it will be when the dormancy of winter is changing to the new life of spring. Romans 9:9 offers the translation "at this time will I come," but this doesn't help much in pointing to one interpretation over the other. Genesis 18:1 implies that this conversation takes place in the heat of summer, so the interpretations of the timing of the promised return vary by only a few months in any case.

As the special guest continues, Sarah has positioned herself on the other side of the tent flap, directly behind the one who is speaking. What she overhears is a shocking statement to one of her age, for the man announces that at the time of his return she will *have a son*.

11. Now Abraham and Sarah were old and well stricken in age; and it ceased to be with Sarah after the manner of women.

At this point, Abraham is 99 and Sarah is 89 years of age (compare Genesis 17:17, above). Sarah's age means that she is no longer experiencing the monthly cycle that is associated with the ability to conceive children. We may compare the life situation of these two with that of Zacharias and Elisabeth in Luke 1:5-7.

What Do You Think?
  How have you seen God work through someone in a way not usually associated with his or her stage of life? How has this increased your faith?
Talking Points for Your Discussion
  - Through a child
  - Through a teenager
  - Through an elderly person

12. Therefore Sarah laughed within herself, saying, After I am waxed old shall I have pleasure, my lord being old also?

Sarah quickly evaluates the announcement by the stranger to be preposterous, and this prompts a silent laughter *within herself*. To burst forth in laughter would reveal that she is eavesdropping on the conversation of the men.

Sarah is fully aware that both she and her husband are *waxed old*. To her, it is quite unreasonable to think that she can conceive and bear a child (compare Romans 4:17, 19). Therefore both Abraham's laughter of delight and the laughter of Sarah's doubt are reflected in the name of their son to be born (see the commentary on 17:17).

At some point, Sarah's doubt gives way to faith since Hebrews 11:11 says, "Through faith also Sara herself received strength to conceive seed, and was

delivered of a child when she was past age, because she judged him faithful who had promised."

What Do You Think?
  What helps you overcome doubt that threatens your trust in God's promises?
Talking Points for Your Discussion
  - When events seem to contradict God's promises
  - When God seems to be doing nothing
  - When people around you are giving in to doubt
  - Other

B. Response and Reaction (vv. 13-15)

13. And the Lord said unto Abraham, Wherefore did Sarah laugh, saying, Shall I of a surety bear a child, which am old?

The most important fact of this verse is that the speaker is now designated as *the Lord*. When the four letters of this word are all capital letters, it indicates that this is the divine name *Yahweh*. The three guests were earlier called "men" (Genesis 18:2), and Hebrews 13:2 uses the term "angels." The word *angel* can mean "messenger," and that is the situation here. The speaker is the Lord himself, and He is the special messenger from Heaven.

Some scholars believe that this is a manifestation of God the Son before He is born as a babe in Bethlehem. The special nature of this messenger is seen in the bold pronouncement and in being able to know the unexpressed thoughts and silent laughter of Sarah.

14. Is any thing too hard for the Lord? At the time appointed I will return unto thee, according to the time of life, and Sarah shall have a son.

The Lord's responses continue with a rhetorical question and an affirmation. The thrust of the question *Is any thing too hard for the Lord?* is repeated in different circumstances in both the Old and New Testaments. As a question, we see it in Jeremiah 32:27. As a statement, we see it in Jeremiah 32:17; Matthew 19:26; Luke 1:37; and Romans 4:21. The difficult statement *I will return unto thee, according to the time of life* is identical in Hebrew to the one found in Genesis 18:10 (above), except for the added word *certainly* there.

15. Then Sarah denied, saying, I laughed not; for she was afraid. And he said, Nay; but thou didst laugh.

Sarah reacts with a feeble attempt to defend herself. Perhaps she rationalizes that there has been no audible laughter, but God knows a person's heart and thoughts (compare Matthew 9:4; 12:25).

III. Fulfillment
(GENESIS 21:1-7)

We may assume that Sarah's unusual pregnancy runs the usual nine months in duration. During this time Lot and his daughters are rescued from catastrophe (Genesis 19), and Abraham repeats a cowardly act (compare Genesis 20 with 12:10-20).

A. Birth of the Son (vv. 1, 2)
1. And the LORD visited Sarah as he had said, and the LORD did unto Sarah as he had spoken.

The first verse of Genesis 21 is a general statement that is intended to show that the Lord keeps His promises to Sarah. Although not recorded, Sarah's laughter of disbelief probably turns into a laughter of joy during her pregnancy. We would like to know more about such things (compare Genesis 25:22; Luke 1:41).

What Do You Think?

How has reaching a dream or goal later in life than you planned influenced your faith walk?

Talking Points for Your Discussion
- Regarding marriage
- Regarding children
- Regarding a financial goal
- Regarding an education goal
- Other

---

2. For Sarah conceived, and bare Abraham a son in his old age, at the set time of which God had spoken to him.

The general statement of verse 1 is followed by a summary of the basic facts surrounding the conception and birth of the child of Abraham and Sarah. It has been 25 years since God first made a promise to Abraham that involved his becoming a great nation (Genesis 12:2), but God's plans are fulfilled at the scheduled time (compare Galatians 4:4).

B. Naming the Son (vv. 3, 4)
3. And Abraham called the name of his son that was born unto him, whom Sarah bare to him, Isaac.

Abraham follows the stipulations and revelations of the God-given covenant. The name given to the son is therefore Isaac (meaning "he laughs"), just as God had said (Genesis 17:19). This name serves as a constant reminder to the parents of the different types of laughter that Abraham and Sarah expressed in their reactions to the promises of God. The lineage of Jesus continues to move forward (Matthew 1:2; Luke 3:34).

4. And Abraham circumcised his son Isaac being eight days old, as God had commanded him.

The ritual of circumcision as a sign of the covenant was introduced a year earlier, when Abraham was 99 years old (Genesis 17:10-14, 24). The practice is now applied to the covenantal son of Abraham (Genesis 17:19; Acts 7:8) when the infant is *eight days old,* just *as God had commanded.* Devout Jews of the New Testament era are careful to continue obedience to this command (see Luke 1:59; 2:21; Philippians 3:5).

C. Parents of the Son (vv. 5-7)
5. And Abraham was an hundred years old, when his son Isaac was born unto him.

The factor of Abraham's age is important. It is one way of showing that what has transpired has been through divine intervention. To establish a time line of Abraham's life from the point of his call (as Abram) to his death, see Genesis 12:4; 16:3, 16; 17:1, 17, 24; 21:5; 25:7.

6, 7. And Sarah said, God hath made me to laugh, so that all that hear will laugh with me. And she said, Who would have said unto Abraham, that Sarah should have given children suck? for I have born him a son in his old age.

Sarah, age 90, now speaks of the joy that has come into her life with the birth of a son. We can presume that this joy stays with her for the remaining 37 years of her life (Genesis 23:1).

The word *laugh* carries a special meaning for Sarah. A form of it is the name of her son, and she is confident that others will laugh when they learn that God has granted her a son. The promises of God about Sarah's having a son are fulfilled, and that is a source of shared joy. A key part of this joy is the relief at having the stigma of barrenness removed (compare 1 Samuel 1:1–2:11; Psalm 113:9; Luke 1:25).

What Do You Think?
What things have you seen that confirm for you that nothing is impossible with God?
Talking Points for Your Discussion
▪ Spiritual issues in your own life
▪ Spiritual issues in the lives of others
▪ Relational issues in your own life
▪ Relational issues in the lives of others
▪ Other

❧ RHETORICAL QUESTIONS ❧

In Shakespeare's *The Merchant of Venice,* the Jewish character Shylock asks, "Hath not a Jew eyes? Hath not a Jew hands, organs, dimensions, senses, affections, passions? . . . If you prick us, do we not bleed?" Shylock asks rhetorical questions —questions spoken not to seek information, but to make a point that should be self-evident.

Occasionally, rhetorical questions are used to sell products. A TV ad for Dial® soap in the 1960s asked, "Aren't you glad you use Dial? Don't you wish everybody did?" Other rhetorical questions are intended to amuse. For example, you may have seen this one: "If lawyers are disbarred and clergymen defrocked, doesn't it follow that electricians can be delighted, musicians denoted, cowboys deranged, models deposed, tree surgeons debarked, and dry cleaners depressed?"

We have seen a series of rhetorical questions in today's study, concluding with the one in Genesis 21:7. The obvious answer to "Who would have said unto Abraham, that Sarah should have given children suck?" is *no one!* Joyous Sarah then exults, "I have borne him a son in his old age!" This calls for another question: Is there anything too difficult for God? Well, is there?   —C. R. B.

Conclusion
A. Abraham's Children

Ishmael, Isaac, . . . and the list of Abraham's descendants continues beyond that. It includes the sons born to Keturah, whom Abraham married after Sarah died (Genesis 25:1, 2; 1 Chronicles 1:32). The list features Jacob, his 12 sons, and many others who became part of the nation of Israel. Romans 4:16 says that Abraham is the father of all who believe. The popular children's chorus of a few years ago was correct when it stated that Father Abraham has many sons; that is great doctrine.

Our belief includes intellectual assent, but it is more than that. These lessons from Genesis are not just to be discussed academically. They should help us develop a stronger, deeper faith in God and give us a blessed assurance that the promises He has made about the future will come to pass. Just look at what God did for Abraham and Sarah!

B. Prayer

Father in Heaven, thank You for making it possible for me to be one of Your children. May my life be an instrument to lead others to become Your children as well. In Jesus' name, amen.

C. Thought to Remember
Nothing is too difficult for the Lord.
Nothing.

Visual for Lesson 7. *Point to this visual as you have Jeremiah 32:17, 27; Matthew 19:26; Luke 1:37; and Romans 4:21 read aloud. Discuss.*

INVOLVEMENT LEARNING

Some of the activities below are also found in the helpful student book, Adult Bible Class.
Don't forget to download the free reproducible page from www.standardlesson.com to enhance your lesson!

Into the Lesson

Have on display a banner reading *A Time to Laugh.* (An artistic class member might enjoy preparing this.) If available, play as class begins a sound track of people laughing. (You can download such a sound track from the Internet, or you can record your own family and friends laughing.)

Alternative: Distribute copies of the "What Makes It Funny?" activity from the reproducible page, which you can download. Use this to start a whole-class discussion on the idea of laughter, according to the instructions.

Say, "Laughter may or may not always be appropriate. As we take a closer look at today's text, we'll see what prompted the laughter of Abraham and Sarah and whether or not their laughter was appropriate."

Into the Word

Ask three volunteers to read aloud today's texts of Genesis 17:15-17; 18:9-15; and 21:1-7, one section each.

In light of the fact that several questions appear in today's text, use the format of the TV show *Jeopardy* to give answers to which learners must ask the questions that go with them. Possible answers and expected questions are as follows. You may wish to show answers on small posters rather than simply reading them.

1. One hundred years old. *What was Abraham's age when Isaac was born? (17:17; 21:5)*

2. Ninety years old. *What was Sarah's age when Isaac was born? (17:17)*

3. This person denied having laughed. *Who was Sarah? (18:15)*

4. This person fell to the ground in laughter. *Who was Abraham? (17:17)*

5. She was formerly known as Sarai. *Who was Sarah? (17:15)*

6. He mentioned Sarah's laughter to Abraham. *Who was the Lord? (18:13)*

7. He was eight days old when circumcised. *Who was Isaac? (21:4)*

8. This person predicted laughter by others. *Who was Sarah? (21:6)*

9. This is mentioned either 7 or 10 times. *What is a form of the word* laugh*? (mentioned 7 times, in 17:17; 18:12, 13, 15; and 21:6, but since the name Isaac means "laughter," one might add 3 more per 21:3, 4, 5)*

Divide your class into two segments called *The Abraham Side* and *The Sarah Side.* Say, "Play the part of a prosecutor as you make a case for the laughter of your 'defendant' (Abraham or Sarah) to have reflected lack of faith." Let sides offer their arguments. Use the commentary to support and challenge the arguments. (*Option:* Let each segment challenge the arguments of the other.)

Ask three learners to take turns reading the verses of Romans 4:16-25 aloud. Note that a key idea is God's ability to give life to the dead. This ability extends not only to the "dead" reproductive organs of Abraham and Sarah, but also to God's Son (who was dead in the tomb) and to people dead in sin!

Into Life

Say, "The Romans 4 passage affirms that Abraham was fully persuaded that God was able to do what He promised (see v. 21)." Give each learner a slip of paper with this commitment statement: "I fully believe that God is able to do what He promises, and I will demonstrate that confidence by _____ this week." Challenge learners to use the slip as a Bible bookmark for a time and to complete the statement only when they have considered an appropriate response.

Option: Distribute copies of the "Believing God" activity from the reproducible page. Have learners complete this in small groups and discuss. This will provide an additional opportunity to carry the truth of the study into daily living.

BLESSINGS FOR ISHMAEL AND ISAAC

DEVOTIONAL READING: Hebrews 11:17-22
BACKGROUND SCRIPTURE: Genesis 15–17; 21:9-21; 26:1-25

GENESIS 21:12-14, 17-21

12 And God said unto Abraham, Let it not be grievous in thy sight because of the lad, and because of thy bondwoman; in all that Sarah hath said unto thee, hearken unto her voice; for in Isaac shall thy seed be called.

13 And also of the son of the bondwoman will I make a nation, because he is thy seed.

14 And Abraham rose up early in the morning, and took bread, and a bottle of water, and gave it unto Hagar, putting it on her shoulder, and the child, and sent her away: and she departed, and wandered in the wilderness of Beersheba.

. . . .

17 And God heard the voice of the lad; and the angel of God called Hagar out of heaven, and said unto her, What aileth thee, Hagar? fear not; for God hath heard the voice of the lad where he is.

18 Arise, lift up the lad, and hold him in thine hand; for I will make him a great nation.

19 And God opened her eyes, and she saw a well of water; and she went, and filled the bottle with water, and gave the lad drink.

20 And God was with the lad; and he grew, and dwelt in the wilderness, and became an archer.

21 And he dwelt in the wilderness of Paran: and his mother took him a wife out of the land of Egypt.

GENESIS 26:2-5, 12, 13

2 And the LORD appeared unto him, and said, Go not down into Egypt; dwell in the land which I shall tell thee of:

3 Sojourn in this land, and I will be with thee, and will bless thee; for unto thee, and unto thy seed, I will give all these countries, and I will perform the oath which I sware unto Abraham thy father;

4 And I will make thy seed to multiply as the stars of heaven, and will give unto thy seed all these countries; and in thy seed shall all the nations of the earth be blessed;

5 Because that Abraham obeyed my voice, and kept my charge, my commandments, my statutes, and my laws.

. . . .

12 Then Isaac sowed in that land, and received in the same year an hundredfold: and the LORD blessed him.

13 And the man waxed great, and went forward, and grew until he became very great.

KEY VERSE

God said unto Abraham, . . . In Isaac shall thy seed be called. And also of the son of the bondwoman will I make a nation, because he is thy seed. —**Genesis 21:12, 13**

FIRST THINGS

Unit 2: First Nation

LESSONS 6–9

LESSON AIMS

After participating in this lesson, each student will be able to:

1. Describe God's separate blessings on Isaac and Ishmael.

2. Explain the superior blessing of Isaac over that of Ishmael even though Ishmael was born first.

3. Suggest a means of sharing one's faith in Christ with a Muslim.

LESSON OUTLINE

Introduction

A. Moses Easterly Lard

Mary Lard was the mother of six. Her husband had moved the family to western Missouri, but his death from smallpox in about 1829 left her to rear the children alone. In 1830, she made one of the most heart-wrenching decisions that a mother can make. Deciding that there was no way she could feed six children, she told the two oldest sons that they would have to leave. She gave each a small New Testament and bid her farewells with quivering lips. As the boys walked away, they heard their mother scream, a sound they never forgot.

The boy named Moses never told what happened during the next few years. Did the two live off the land, steal, or work for others, perhaps living in barns or caves? Moses Lard had another problem: he could not read. He became an apprentice to a tailor and taught himself to read during that time. He would take letters from signs, put them together in different ways, and ask people about the sounds or the words that resulted.

Moses Lard eventually began to preach, and he caught the attention of Alexander Doniphan, later to be a hero of the Mexican-American War (1846–1848). That man made arrangements for Lard to attend college. Lard graduated in 1849, age 30, as the valedictorian of the class, in spite of having to work to support his family. Lard's ministries included preaching, writing a commentary on the book of Romans, and being a debater and an editor. That's "not bad" for one who had to teach himself to read!

Today's lesson offers certain parallels in that it involves a decision to break up a family because circumstances seemed to require it. Even so, troubling family circumstances can yield good outcomes (Genesis 17:20; 25:12-18).

B. Lesson Background

Only four verses separate last week's lesson from this one. Since the backgrounds are therefore the same, the Lesson Background of last week need not be repeated here. Instead, we will pay some attention to the literary method that Moses used in writing the book of Genesis.

The first part of the book of Genesis is *general history* (what we also called *primeval history* in lesson 5). As Moses introduces new people or nations throughout this section, the emphasis very quickly moves to the person or entity that he intends to feature at that point. For example, Genesis 1:1 refers to the heavens and earth, but the next verse focuses immediately on the earth. Genesis 2 sharpens the focus to the first humans. The accounts of the first sin and the first murder are set forth in Genesis 3 and 4, but the goal is to get to another son of Adam and Eve—namely, Seth. Notice the focus on him in Genesis 5:1-3. In Genesis 5:6-26, we see repeatedly that a certain descendant "begat sons and daughters," but the only one mentioned by name in each case is the one leading to Noah and the flood.

After the flood, the biblical record gives information about the descendants of Noah's three sons—Shem, Ham, and Japheth (Genesis 9:18, 19). There are 70 founders of nations or people groups mentioned in the table of nations in Genesis 10. The incident of the Tower of Babel (lesson 5) provides an explanation for the presence of different languages among the peoples of the world. After that, the emphasis quickly returns to Shem and his descendants (Genesis 11:10-26). The plan seems to be to move as quickly as possible to Abram, a son of Terah.

The second part of the book of Genesis could be called *personal history*. It is about people who have purpose in the plan of God to bring the Messiah into the world at just the right time (Galatians 4:4). This section of Genesis begins with Genesis 11:27. The focus is on the descendants of Abram that continue through Isaac, Jacob, and the latter's 12 sons. Others are mentioned as they take their places on the stage of history. In this light, the goal for Moses, the author, is to provide an explanation on how the nation of Israel came into existence.

I. Promises for Ishmael
(GENESIS 21:12-14, 17-21)

Children are weaned between the ages of 2 and 3. The weaning of Isaac when he reaches this age becomes the basis of "a great feast" for the family of Abraham (Genesis 21:8). Big brother Ishmael is age 16 or 17 (see 17:24, 25; 21:5), and for some reason he begins to mock little Isaac (21:9). Sarah, a protective mother of Isaac, her only son, demands that her husband expel Hagar and her son from the household (21:10). Abraham is reluctant to do so because Ishmael is his son (21:11). It is at this point that God intervenes.

A. Intervention (vv. 12, 13)

12. And God said unto Abraham, Let it not be grievous in thy sight because of the lad, and because of thy bondwoman; in all that Sarah hath said unto thee, hearken unto her voice; for in Isaac shall thy seed be called.

Abraham has genuine concerns for Hagar, who is the *bondwoman* or slave, and Ishmael (*the lad*, son of Abraham and Hagar). It is also possible that Abraham is influenced by the customs of the time that make it illegal to dismiss the son of a bondwoman. We should remember that Ishmael was Abraham's only son for 14 years. Abraham's grief of Genesis 21:11 is quite understandable!

So God speaks words of reassurance and direction to Abraham. God's first pronouncement is that Sarah is right, *for in Isaac shall thy seed be called.* Isaac is indeed the son of the covenant. This fact contradicts the Islamic belief today that the covenant of promise goes through Ishmael.

Genesis 16:1 tells us that Hagar is an Egyptian. If she was given to Abraham (as Abram) by

HOW TO SAY IT

Beersheba	Beer-*she*-buh.
Gerar	*Gear*-rar (G as in get).
Hagar	*Hay*-gar.
Haran	*Hair*-un.
Isaac	*Eye*-zuk.
Ishmael	*Ish*-may-el.
Japheth	*Jay*-feth.
Nahor	*Nay*-hor.
Paran	*Pair*-un.
patriarchs	*pay*-tree-arks.
primeval	pry-*me*-vuhl.
Sinai	*Sigh*-nye or *Sigh*-nay-eye.
Terah	*Tair*-uh.

Pharaoh in Genesis 12:14, it means she has been uprooted once already from familiar surroundings since Abraham is no longer in Egypt. Hagar tried to leave previously, of her own volition, because Sarah made her life miserable (Genesis 16). This time, however, Hagar is being expelled.

> ### What Do You Think?
> What can your church do to address the issue of dysfunctional families? What will be your part in this?
>
> *Talking Points for Your Discussion*
> - Prevention (premarital counseling, etc.)
> - Intervention (family systems counseling, etc.)
> - Other

13. And also of the son of the bondwoman will I make a nation, because he is thy seed.

Abraham's fears about what will happen to Ishmael are relieved: because Ishmael is a son of Abraham, the descendants of Ishmael will become a nation. Ishmael is a primary ancestor of many Arab peoples today (compare Genesis 25:12-18; 1 Chronicles 1:29).

B. Dismissal (v. 14)

14. And Abraham rose up early in the morning, and took bread, and a bottle of water, and gave it unto Hagar, putting it on her shoulder, and the child, and sent her away: and she departed, and wandered in the wilderness of Beersheba.

Abraham obeys God's instructions without delay. Hagar and Ishmael are supplied with the basic necessities to begin their journey. The skin-bottle for the water is the normal container for liquids. We can only wonder if Hagar also receives gold or silver as part of her means to sustain herself.

The youthfulness of Ishmael is shown by the word *child*. Even so, he is at least 16 years old, as previously noted. Hagar's departure toward *the wilderness of Beersheba* indicates a move in a southeasterly direction.

⅍ THE DANGER OF IMPATIENCE ⅍

Troubled, dysfunctional families are far too common these days. The evidence of such trouble is often seen when a spouse—usually the wife—is found to be suffering from abuse. The abuser may use physical violence or the threat of it to exert control. The threats are themselves psychologically abusive.

The relationships within Abraham's family were troubled. We see abuse on the part of Sarah in Genesis 16:6 against Hagar. After Sarah bore Isaac, the child of God's promise, the stress between the two women reached a boiling point —again. Sarah demanded that Abraham "cast out" Hagar and Ishmael (21:10).

No doubt, Abraham thought he was doing the right thing (or, at least, the best thing in the circumstances) in sending the two away in order to restore peace in the home. Today this might be considered domestic abuse or, at least, "failure to support." But God was there to provide and protect when Abraham was not. We keep in mind that all this anguish could have been avoided had not Abraham and Sarah decided in their impatience to "help" God's plan by deciding to conceive a child by Hagar. Do you ever try to move faster than God wants you to?   —C. R. B.

> ### What Do You Think?
> What are the limits of "tolerance," if any? Why?
>
> *Talking Points for Your Discussion*
> - Within families (Judges 11:1, 2; Acts 16:1)
> - Within the church (John 1:14, 17; Romans 14; 1 Corinthians 5:11; 6:7, 8)
> - In relationships with unbelievers (1 Corinthians 5:9, 10; 15:33)
> - Other

C. Assurance (vv. 17, 18)

17. And God heard the voice of the lad; and the angel of God called to Hagar out of heaven, and said unto her, What aileth thee, Hagar? fear not; for God hath heard the voice of the lad where he is.

Verses 15, 16 (not in today's text) indicate that the skin-bottle is soon empty. We do not know how much water has been supplied by Abraham or if Hagar has been able to refill the bottle to this point. In any case, the heat of the desert creates a great need for water, and it runs out.

Hagar (v. 16) and Ishmael are vocal in their distress. God responds because of *the voice of the lad,* but He directs his message to Hagar.

18. Arise, lift up the lad, and hold him in thine hand; for I will make him a great nation.

Hagar is not in the immediate presence of her son at this point; he is "a good way off, as it were a bowshot" (v. 16) when the angel of God speaks. The instruction to *hold him in thine hand* carries more than the idea of "physical holding"; Hagar is to be a guiding, steadying influence on her son. The angel of the Lord previously had told Hagar some things about the future of Ishmael when she ran away (see Genesis 16:11, 12). Now the promise is expanded: *I will make him a great nation.*

D. Development (vv. 19-21)

19. And God opened her eyes, and she saw a well of water; and she went, and filled the bottle with water, and gave the lad drink.

God providentially supplies water. The presence of a well in this episode bears a similarity to the earlier occasion when Hagar fled from Sarah (Genesis 16:7). At that time, the angel of the Lord came to Hagar at a well (or "fountain," as it is called in 16:7), and it was given a name as a reminder of the event (16:14).

20. And God was with the lad; and he grew, and dwelt in the wilderness, and became an archer.

Two things combine to enable the hardy mother and son to survive in this rugged area. First is the fact that God is *with the lad.* Can any affirmation be better than that? Second, Ishmael develops his skill as an archer; this helps son and mother have an adequate food supply.

21. And he dwelt in the wilderness of Paran: and his mother took him a wife out of the land of Egypt.

The new home of Hagar and Ishmael *in the wilderness of Paran* means that the two have moved farther south. The region of Paran is in the Sinai Peninsula, which is just east of Egypt (compare Numbers 10:12). Ishmael needs a wife in order for him to become a great nation, so in a culture of arranged marriages, his mother turns to her native Egypt to meet that need (compare Genesis 24:1-4).

The rest of the story for Ishmael has several factors of interest. Genesis 25:7-9 states that Ishmael and Isaac are together again to bury Abraham when he dies at the age of 175. At that time Ishmael is age 89 and Isaac is 75. We can only wonder about the conversations and the farewells that took place!

Genesis 25:12-18 specifies that Ishmael has 12 sons and names them. The general regions where they live are listed. Ishmael will die at the age of 137, and the promises made to Abraham and Hagar indeed come to pass.

What Do You Think?
  When did you see a plan fail, only to end up with a good (or better) outcome because it did? What did this experience teach you about God?
  Talking Points for Your Discussion
  - At work
  - At church
  - During a move
  - Other

II. Blessings for Isaac
(Genesis 26:2-5, 12, 13)

Isaac experiences many important events prior to the blessings listed in the next segment of today's printed text. His famous near-sacrifice is recorded in Genesis 22. The chapter that follows tells of the death of his mother at age 127, when Isaac is 37 years old and still single (compare 17:17 with 23:1). Abraham sends a trusted servant back to his relatives to secure a wife for Isaac (24:15), and that servant returns with Rebekah, who marries Isaac when he is 40 (25:20). She is a granddaughter of Nahor, Abraham's brother (and also a great-granddaughter of his other brother, Haran; see 11:29). Isaac at age 60 becomes the father of twins, Esau and Jacob (25:26).

A famine in Canaan then prompts Isaac to move his household elsewhere. The latter part of Genesis 26:1 seems to indicate that Isaac is already in Gerar. Isaac may intend this place to be no more than a stopover on the way to Egypt, but it ends up becoming a more permanent place of residence, as we shall see.

A. Promises (vv. 2, 3)

2. And the LORD appeared unto him, and said, Go not down into Egypt; dwell in the land which I shall tell thee of.

Abraham had gone to Egypt in order to escape a famine over 100 years earlier. Egypt nearly always has good crops because of the annual surge of the Nile River. Isaac's descendants will go to Egypt in the days of Jacob also to escape a famine, but that is more than 100 years in the future at this point. From the time that Abram enters Canaan at age 75 (Genesis 12:4), there is a total of 215 years until grandson Jacob and the others go to Egypt (46:1-27). The Lord will command Jacob to do so at that time (46:3), but for now the Lord commands the opposite for Isaac, Jacob's father.

3. Sojourn in this land, and I will be with thee, and will bless thee; for unto thee, and unto thy seed, I will give all these countries, and I will perform the oath which I sware unto Abraham thy father.

Isaac needs to stay put. As Isaac does so, the Lord intends to bless him and *perform the oath* given to Abraham on more than one occasion.

This is the first of only two times that God provides a special message for Isaac (the other one is in Genesis 26:24). In addition, the Lord reveals to Rebekah, Isaac's wife, that she will have twins (25:23). This limited communication does not diminish Isaac's role as one of the great patriarchs. He is a man of faith, and this is affirmed in Hebrews 11:20. Isaac lives as God desires.

What Do You Think?

Under what circumstances would it be wise to advise someone to relocate rather than staying put? When would that be bad advice? Why?

Talking Points for Your Discussion

- Issues of God's call to mission work
- Issues of responsibility to family
- Issues of economic conditions
- Other

❧ TOWARD GREENER GRASS? ❧

"The grass is always greener on the other side of the fence" is a well-worn proverb. It's truth is said to be demonstrated by the fact that cattle and horses can be see standing at a fence row as they nibble at the grass growing just on the other side. If we look closely, however, we may see good reason for the livestock's behavior: the grass on their side of the fence may have already been eaten! So too we humans may have good reasons for seeking "greener grass."

Good things may come from such a desire. Think of the great explorers of centuries past. Whatever motivated them, we are the beneficiaries of their efforts. But bad things can also come from a desire to reach "greener grass" if we are merely trying to sidestep or escape our problems.

For Isaac and his family, Egypt seemed like a better place to live than Gerar. The annual flooding of the Nile River meant famines were less frequent there. Egypt's civilization seems to have been more advanced than other's. But God told Isaac not to go. There is a time to move on and a time to stay put; this is a matter for prayer. Our greatest personal growth may come in working through today's obstacles rather than bailing out.

—C. R. B.

B. Posterity (vv. 4, 5)

4. And I will make thy seed to multiply as the stars of heaven, and will give unto thy seed all these countries; and in thy seed shall all the nations of the earth be blessed.

The comparison with *the stars of heaven* is similar to what was stated to Abram (before being renamed Abraham) in Genesis 15:5 (see lesson 6). The statement to Abram was given as much as 20 years before Isaac was born. Isaac surely has heard about it second hand, but it is good for him to hear it personally.

A second part of this blessing is also similar to what was promised to Abram—that those who descend from Isaac will receive territories of the various people-groups that inhabit the land of Canaan. See comments on Genesis 15:19-21 in lesson 6.

The most important part of this revelation is that through Isaac's *seed shall all the nations of the earth be blessed.* This phrase is reminiscent of the promise given to Abram in Genesis 12:3, just before he left Haran to begin his sojourn to the land that God would show him.

5. Because that Abraham obeyed my voice, and kept my charge, my commandments, my statutes, and my laws.

The faith that pleases God is the obedient faith that Paul speaks of in Romans 1:5; 16:26. Such faith has been demonstrated by Abraham, and now Isaac hears the same challenge directly from God.

This verse is fascinating because it hints that there are different types of obligations for the patriarchs. We would like to know more about God's *commandments, statutes,* and *laws* at this point in history, but God has chosen not to make further explanations part of the divine record. (This is over 500 years before Moses gives the law to Israel at Sinai.) We can only wonder about things such as the sacrificing of animals by Abel (Genesis 4:4), Noah (8:20), and Abraham (22:7).

What Do You Think?
   What personal stories can you tell of someone's faithfulness producing benefits for a future generation?
Talking Points for Your Discussion
   ▪ Regarding a minister
   ▪ Regarding a teacher
   ▪ Regarding an ancestor
   ▪ Other

C. Prosperity (vv. 12, 13)

12. Then Isaac sowed in that land, and received in the same year an hundredfold: and the LORD blessed him.

That land refers to the area around Gerar (Genesis 26:6). Verses 7-11 (not in today's text) give the account of Isaac's imitating his father with a falsehood in the same area (compare 20:1-13). After being rebuked by the local king, Isaac remains in the area and becomes very successful. The primary reason is the blessing of the Lord.

13. And the man waxed great, and went forward, and grew until he became very great.

The blessings from God continue! Isaac has grain for his own use, and he can sell any surplus. The verses that follow show that his wealth includes herds, flocks, and servants. Truly Isaac is blessed both spiritually and materially. This will cause problems with neighbors, but those pagans eventually come to see that Isaac is "blessed of the Lord" (Genesis 26:29).

Conclusion
A. It's Not a License!

It is good to be reminded of the promises and blessings for Ishmael and Isaac, for we know that neither was perfect in the sight of the Lord. Little is known about Ishmael, except that as a teenager he mocked his little brother. God still made promises to him. Isaac, for his part, seems to have been a very godly person. His falsehood to the people of Gerar is a blemish on his record, but God still blessed him.

It is also good to know that God loves sinners and blesses them (us). But the fact that God blessed others after they sinned is not to be used as a license to justify sin. God forgives, but genuine repentance comes first.

B. Prayer

Thank You, Almighty God, for blessing those who helped bring the Messiah into the world. May I do my part in sharing the good news about Jesus so that others may be blessed. In His name, amen.

C. Thought to Remember
When blessed, remember the source.

Visual for Lesson 8. *Start a discussion by pointing to this visual as you ask, "Under what circumstances is it most important to do this? Why?"*

INVOLVEMENT LEARNING

Some of the activities below are also found in the helpful student book, Adult Bible Class.
Don't forget to download the free reproducible page from www.standardlesson.com to enhance your lesson!

Into the Lesson

Option 1: Distribute copies of the "God Bless You!" activity from the reproducible page, which you can download. Have learners work individually on this brief exercise to introduce the concept of *blessing*.

Option 2: Prepare flash cards for the following words related to mental states and emotions: *confusion, discontentment, contempt, despair, hope, jealousy, joy, kindness, resolution, satisfaction, sorrow.* Before class, ask one of your more "expressive" students to be prepared to stand before the class and demonstrate the emotions as you reveal cards (one by one) that only he or she can see. Ask the class to guess each emotion being dramatized, then show the card. Comment: "A range of human emotions fill the first part of our text today. Let's see if we can sort things out."

Into the Word

Distribute large flash cards as described in Option 2 above (whether or not you chose to do that option) to various learners. Say, "As we listen to Genesis 21:8-21, hold up your card if you think the verse being read reflects the emotion on your card."

Have a good oral reader stand before the group to read Genesis 21:8-21 (which includes verses not in the printed text). Ask your reader to pause after reading each verse to allow time for learners to raise their cards. Class members may offer a variety of responses; encourage free discussion. You may wish to make your own list before class for comparison.

Next, distribute handouts that list the enumerated principles below. Say, "As we work our way through Genesis 26:2-5, 12, 13, think of how these statements *are* or *are not* apparent in God's dealings with Isaac. Jot notes on your handout." Read the text slowly, stopping after each verse to allow time for learners to make the connections.

1. When God says, "Stop!" then one must stop. 2. With God, a promise to the father is a promise to the son. 3. One of the greatest promises is that many will be blessed by the faithful obedience of the one. 4. Physical blessings may be considered spiritual blessings if recognized as coming from God. 5. Wealth is a blessing if one is aware that it comes from God's grace. 6. Heading away from the place of God's promise is heading in the wrong direction. 7. Faith passed from one generation to the next is an indication the older generation is doing something right.

Option: If you chose Option 1 under Into the Lesson, use discoveries to compare and contrast with the blessings of Ishmael and Isaac as you work through the two sections of today's text.

Into Life

Option 1: Explore your learners' understanding of Islam's view of Isaac and Ishmael by asking, "What do Muslims believe about the two sons of Abraham discussed in today's lesson?" Do your own research in advance so you can correct misperceptions. At a minimum, you should note that Muslims believe they have inherited Ishmael's legacy, thus their claim that they too are "children of Abraham." Ask, "What are some strategies for presenting Jesus as the Son of God to Muslims?"

To challenge your learners to grow in this area, distribute copies of the "Witnessing to the Descendants of Ishmael" activity from the reproducible page as take-home work.

Option 2: Have learners pair off and discuss this question: "What is the most difficult decision regarding a personal relationship you have ever had to make?" After a few minutes, ask for volunteers to reveal in general terms (no names mentioned) what was discussed. (Caution: this intensely personal question may bring back painful memories that are best left undisturbed.) Ask, "How do we grow in Christ through such times of pain?

THE BLESSING PASSES TO JACOB

DEVOTIONAL READING: John 4:1-15
BACKGROUND SCRIPTURE: Genesis 27, 28; 32:22-30; 35:9-15

GENESIS 28:1A, 10-22

1a And Isaac called Jacob, and blessed him.

. . . .

10 And Jacob went out from Beersheba, and went toward Haran.

11 And he lighted upon a certain place, and tarried there all night, because the sun was set; and he took of the stones of that place, and put them for his pillows, and lay down in that place to sleep.

12 And he dreamed, and behold a ladder set up on the earth, and the top of it reached to heaven: and behold the angels of God ascending and descending on it.

13 And, behold, the LORD stood above it, and said, I am the LORD God of Abraham thy father, and the God of Isaac: the land whereon thou liest, to thee will I give it, and to thy seed;

14 And thy seed shall be as the dust of the earth, and thou shalt spread abroad to the west, and to the east, and to the north, and to the south: and in thee and in thy seed shall all the families of the earth be blessed.

15 And, behold, I am with thee, and will keep thee in all places whither thou goest, and will bring thee again into this land; for I will not leave thee, until I have done that which I have spoken to thee of.

16 And Jacob awaked out of his sleep, and he said, Surely the LORD is in this place; and I knew it not.

17 And he was afraid, and said, How dreadful is this place! this is none other but the house of God, and this is the gate of heaven.

18 And Jacob rose up early in the morning, and took the stone that he had put for his pillows, and set it up for a pillar, and poured oil upon the top of it.

19 And he called the name of that place Bethel: but the name of that city was called Luz at the first.

20 And Jacob vowed a vow, saying, If God will be with me, and will keep me in this way that I go, and will give me bread to eat, and raiment to put on,

21 So that I come again to my father's house in peace; then shall the LORD be my God:

22 And this stone, which I have set for a pillar, shall be God's house: and of all that thou shalt give me I will surely give the tenth unto thee.

KEY VERSE

Behold, I am with thee, and will keep thee in all places whither thou goest, and will bring thee again into this land; for I will not leave thee, until I have done that which I have spoken to thee of. —**Genesis 28:15**

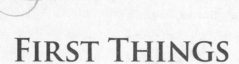

FIRST THINGS

Unit 2: First Nation

LESSONS 6–9

LESSON AIMS

After participating in this lesson, each student will be able to:

1. Summarize the context and content of Jacob's dream at Bethel and his reaction to it.

2. Compare and contrast the "awakening" of someone to God's presence today with Jacob's sudden awareness of God's presence.

3. Suggest one or two ways to demonstrate actively his or her awareness of God's presence.

LESSON OUTLINE

Introduction
    A. If? Because? Regardless?
    B. Lesson Background
I. Isaac Blesses (GENESIS 28:1a)
II. Jacob Dreams (GENESIS 28:10-15)
    A. Sleep Achieved (vv. 10, 11)
    B. Imagery Perceived (vv. 12, 13a)
    C. Promise Received (vv. 13b-15)
      Jacob's Dream as Ours
III. Jacob Reacts (GENESIS 28:16-22)
    A. Great Fear (vv. 16, 17)
      "I Didn't Know . . ."
    B. Stone Memorial (v. 18)
    C. New Name (v. 19)
    D. Special Vow (vv. 20-22)
Conclusion
    A. What Next?
    B. Prayer
    C. Thought to Remember

Introduction

A. If? Because? Regardless?

It is interesting to classify levels of faith by the three words above. Examples of the three levels abound.

The "if" level. This level is characterized by an attitude of "If (and only if) God will do *this*, then I will do *that*." Some people bargain with God to coax Him to do what they want. In other words, their obedience to God is conditional. A statement by Jacob that is part of today's lesson may seem, at first glance, to demonstrate this level. We will evaluate this in our discussion of Genesis 28:20, 21.

The "because" level. We may perceive this level of faith in passages such as Exodus 18:11; Judges 17:13; 1 Kings 17:24; and 2 Kings 5:15. Particularly interesting is Job 1:9-11. There Satan claims that Job fears God *because* God has blessed him so much; but if God were to remove the blessings, then Job would curse God. Job proved that his faith was not what Satan thought. Instead, Job's faith was at the next level.

The "regardless" level. Job 13:15 speaks to this level of faith. This level also is demonstrated by Daniel's three friends who refused to bow to an idol near Babylon. The three men stated that God was able to deliver them; but even if God chose not to deliver them, they still would not bow to the image (Daniel 3:16-18).

These three levels of faith and today's lesson text invite each of us to consider this question: Which level of faith describes my own?

B. Lesson Background

The final segment of last week's lesson saw Isaac becoming ever more prosperous (Genesis 26:13). That prosperity, however, brought negative consequences in the forms of jealousy, sabotage, and expulsion (vv. 14-16). As a result, Isaac ended up moving to the southeast, toward Beersheba (v. 23), a place where his father, Abraham, had lived.

It was at Beersheba that the elderly Isaac decided that it was time for him to give the formal patriarchal blessing to his older son, Esau (Genesis 27:4). This was in spite of the fact that God had told Rebekah that the older would serve the younger

(25:23). Isaac may have reasoned that Esau should have the blessing because Esau already had wives (26:34) whereas Jacob was still a bachelor.

Things did not go as Isaac had planned because Rebekah schemed for Jacob to receive the blessing instead (Genesis 27:5-29). This was accomplished, but then Esau threatened to kill his brother (27:41). Rebekah heard about the threat, and she developed a plan to put her favored son 550 miles away: she appealed to Isaac that Jacob should return to her relatives in order to secure a proper wife (26:34, 35; 27:46). Our text for today picks up with Isaac's reaction to this plan.

I. Isaac Blesses
(Genesis 28:1a)
1a. And Isaac called Jacob, and blessed him.

Isaac has already blessed Jacob once (Genesis 27:27-29); that blessing was for prosperity and dominance. The blessing we see here is for Jacob to find a proper wife. Rebekah has expressed to Isaac, her husband, her displeasure with Esau's wives. They are "daughters of Heth" (27:46); Heth is the ancestor of the Hittites (10:15; 23:10; 26:34).

Genesis 28:1b-5 (not in today's text) describes Isaac's instructions for Jacob to secure a wife in far away Padanaram. Verses 6-9 reveal Esau's sensitivity about his parents' feelings toward his wives; in an attempt to compensate, he marries a first cousin, a daughter of Ishmael.

What Do You Think?
When was a time you were blessed by respecting someone else's wishes?
Talking Points for Your Discussion
- Concerning a parent
- Concerning a friend
- Concerning your church's leadership
- Other

II. Jacob Dreams
(Genesis 28:10-15)
A. Sleep Achieved (vv. 10, 11)
10. And Jacob went out from Beersheba, and went toward Haran.

As Jacob departs, he may wonder if he will ever see his parents again. This concern seems to enter into the vow that he makes later (v. 21, below). Jacob does see his father again (Genesis 35:27-29). But as far as can be determined, Jacob does not see his mother again; the last time Rebekah is understood to be living is here in chapter 28.

Genesis 26:34 states that Esau is 40 years old when he marries two Hittite women. Jacob's age when he leaves his parents to find a wife is not stated. Circumstantial data based on subsequent events are used by some scholars to suggest that he is 77 years old when he leaves his parents, with an alternative view that he is 57. Jacob's destination is Haran, the place where grandfather Abraham was living before he left for Canaan (Genesis 11:31).

11. And he lighted upon a certain place, and tarried there all night, because the sun was set; and he took of the stones of that place, and put them for his pillows, and lay down in that place to sleep.

Travel at night is difficult and unwise in an era before streetlights. Therefore, it is time to stop when the sun sets. The *certain place* where Jacob stops is named Luz, which Jacob will rename Bethel per verse 19, below. This is almost 60 miles from Jacob's starting point in Beersheba, so this is probably his second or third night on the road, depending on his speed of travel.

Two meals per day are customary, and perhaps Jacob has the second of these before bedding down for the night. His meal may be something his mother prepared for him, which is possible at this stage of the journey. But Jacob will have to live off the land as the journey progresses (v. 20).

We may wonder how Jacob intends to get much sleep if he is using stones for pillows! But this will be no ordinary night of sleep in any case.

B. Imagery Perceived (vv. 12, 13a)
12. And he dreamed, and behold a ladder set up on the earth, and the top of it reached to heaven: and behold the angels of God ascending and descending on it.

Jacob's sleep this night involves dreaming, and this becomes a spiritual highlight. This is the first of several times that the Lord communicates directly with Jacob, and it is the second time that dreams are used by God to give a message to someone. (The first time is in Genesis 20:3.) Dreams become very important in the remainder of Genesis; they involve Jacob and Laban plus four other people in the days of Joseph.

As Jacob looks he sees *the angels of God ascending and descending* on some kind of ladder. An Internet search will reveal numerous artistic efforts to depict this. Some students propose that this ladder is something like the ancient ziggurats, which have sets of stairs to connect different levels. Archaeologists have discovered that the steps of the ziggurats were for gods to come down from Heaven; the purpose of the tower at Babel was to reach to the heavens (see lesson 5).

Jacob's dream is different: it has angels moving in both directions between Heaven and earth. Jesus used phrases from this verse in his discussion with Nathanael (see John 1:51).

13a. And, behold, the LORD stood above it.

Jacob is probably aware of the pagan concepts mentioned above. If he is, then he realizes that what he sees in his dream is different from paganism in an important way: the Lord is standing above the ladder, and there is no movement on His part to come to earth.

What Do You Think?
What's the difference between dreams from God and "regular" dreams? How do those differences serve as a caution about claiming "God told me . . ." because of a dream?

Talking Points for Your Discussion
- The content of the dream
- The uniqueness of the dream
- The circumstances of the dream
- Jeremiah 23:25-32
- Revelation 22:18, 19
- Other

C. Promise Received (vv. 13b-15)

13b. And said, I am the LORD God of Abraham thy father, and the God of Isaac: the land whereon thou liest, to thee will I give it, and to thy seed.

Jacob secured his brother's birthright by bargaining for it, and he received his father's patriarchal blessing by deception. But Jacob is now given a promise that is immensely more important than either of those two: the announcement that the blessings promised through Abraham and Isaac are to continue through him. This is the most important part of the dream. Jacob also learns that his mission will be successful; the fact that the land will be given to Jacob's seed means that he will have a wife and at least one child.

The promise about possessing the land was first given to Abraham (Genesis 12:6, 7), then repeated after he returned from Egypt (15:18-21; lesson 6). The land-promise to Abraham was to that man's "seed," while the restatement here is to both Jacob's seed and to Jacob himself.

We may wonder why God applies the word *father* to Abraham instead of Isaac since Abraham was actually Jacob's grandfather. The word *father* is used in the Bible also to describe "ancestors"; likewise, the word *son* is used to describe "successors." Abraham was Jacob's "father" in a special way.

14. And thy seed shall be as the dust of the earth, and thou shalt spread abroad to the west, and to the east, and to the north, and to the south: and in thee and in thy seed shall all the families of the earth be blessed.

The Lord's message continues, and a phrase is used that Jacob probably has heard before—that the posterity of this family *shall be as the dust of the earth.* This phrase was used when Abraham separated from Lot and as Abraham was promised all the land he could see (Genesis 13:14-18). Jacob may have heard about this from his grandfather personally, for Jacob was 15 when Abraham died (computed from 21:5; 25:7, 20, 26).

The part of the message about the blessing to come on *all the families of the earth* was first stated in Genesis 12:3, when Abraham was leaving Haran (the place Jacob is now headed). This has been God's larger plan all along. It is not a new element.

15. And, behold, I am with thee, and will keep thee in all places whither thou goest, and will bring thee again into this land; for I will not leave thee, until I have done that which I have spoken to thee of.

The story of the assurance that Jacob received of the Lord's presence for the journey will be passed along to the Israelites by Moses just before that man's death hundreds of years later (Deuteronomy 31:6). However, the message of assurance in the verse before us is not merely for Jacob himself. God has bigger plans in mind, as seen in the last phrase of Genesis 28:14, above. The Lord will bring to pass all the things that He has declared. Jacob knows that his mission will be successful, and he learns that he will be able to return to Canaan.

❧ JACOB'S DREAM AS OURS ❧

We use the word *dream* in various ways. Very often this word has a sense of "unreality" attached to it. All of us have told stories of the weird things we dream of while asleep. Those as well as most of our daydreams are nothing more than fantasies (compare Psalm 73:20; Isaiah 29:8).

Dream-fantasies make for good songwriting. "I Dream of Jeannie with the Light Brown Hair" is the first line of a song of similar name published in 1854. Moving into the twentieth century, we have songs such as "Dream a Little Dream of Me." There is even a list of "25 Hit Songs Named After Dreams" on the Internet!

The message God gave to Jacob was not a fantasy composed to entertain people at a social gathering. God's dream-message to Jacob renewed the promise that God would be with His people to be a blessing to the nations. This dream-message is important to us as well; we help bring it ever closer to fulfillment as we carry out the Great Commission (Matthew 28:19, 20).
—C. R. B.

III. Jacob Reacts
(GENESIS 28:16-22)
A. Great Fear (vv. 16, 17)

16, 17. And Jacob awaked out of his sleep, and he said, Surely the LORD is in this place; and I knew it not. And he was afraid, and said, How dreadful is this place! this is none other but the house of God, and this is the gate of heaven.

As Jacob awakes, he quickly reacts to what he has experienced. The statement *the Lord is in this place* may seem curious at first. Doesn't Jacob know that God is everywhere? About 1,000 years later, David will affirm in Psalm 139:7-12 that he cannot escape from God, for God is indeed everywhere. Jacob may not realize that fact at this point in his life, or he simply may be reacting from terror since the word *dreadful* conveys the idea of "fear."

The positions of the standing Lord and the moving angels draw Jacob's conclusion that *this is the gate of heaven*. We think of a gate as something that allows or blocks access to something else. Therefore Jacob's present location seems to be a special piece of geography. The phrase *the house of God* will be considered when we get to verse 19.

> **What Do You Think?**
> In what places or situations have you sensed God's presence where you otherwise felt isolated? Why was that?
> *Talking Points for Your Discussion*
> ▪ During a military deployment
> ▪ During a personal crisis
> ▪ While convalescing
> ▪ During a family conflict
> ▪ Other

HOW TO SAY IT

Babel	*Bay*-bul.
Babylon	*Bab*-uh-lun.
Beersheba	Beer-*she*-buh.
Bethel	*Beth*-ul.
Canaan	*Kay*-nun.
Esau	*Ee*-saw.
Haran	*Hair*-un.
Hittite	*Hit*-ites or *Hit*-tite.
Ishmael	*Ish*-may-el.
Nathanael	Nuh-*than*-yull (*th* as in *thin*).
patriarchal	pay-tree-*are*-kul.
Rebekah	Reh-*bek*-uh.
ziggurats	*zig*-oo-rats.

❧ "I DIDN'T KNOW . . ." ❧

Douglas "Wrong Way" Corrigan (1907–1995) became famous for his transatlantic flight of 1938. Taking off from Brooklyn, New York, he flew nonstop to Ireland although his flight plan

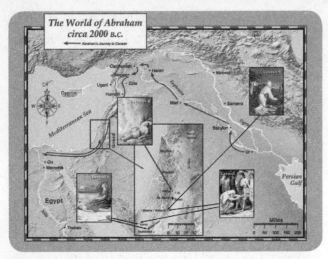

Visual for Lessons 6 & 9. *Wrap up this unit of lessons by summarizing the faith that was evident as you point to the four smallest insets in sequence.*

called for him to fly to Long Beach, California. He claimed to have discovered he was going the wrong way about 26 hours into the 28-hour flight, citing navigational error due to heavy cloud cover. Although the evidence pointed to an intentional "error," Corrigan stuck to his story of not knowing he was going the wrong direction. Some claims of "I didn't know" are hard to swallow!

Jacob's claim, "Surely the Lord is in this place; and I knew it not" is more believable. He did not claim to have ended up in Bethel by navigational error, and he was not out to set up a profitable tourist attraction. With the revelation of the New Testament, we must acknowledge that "surely the Lord is in this place" wherever we go; the "and I knew it not" part of Jacob's statement is not available to us. May we not live in self-imposed ignorance to the evidence of God's presence in our lives!   —C. R. B.

B. Stone Memorial (v. 18)

18. And Jacob rose up early in the morning, and took the stone that he had put for his pillows, and set it up for a pillar, and poured oil upon the top of it.

A custom then as now is to erect memorials to commemorate events, battles, etc. Large stone pillars or slabs of stone are used to help both present and future generations remember what happened in a place. What Jacob is doing here fits this pattern (see also Genesis 31:45-53; 35:1-15, 20).

Some suggest that this procedure is in conflict with what Moses stresses in Deuteronomy 16:22—that the people of Israel are not to set up sacred images or stones, for the Lord hates them. The resolution of this supposed conflict is simple. If an erected stone is to involve the worship of other gods, then the Lord's statement applies. A stone memorial is entirely different, however (compare Exodus 24:4; Joshua 4:1-9).

The next act involving Jacob's memorial stone is to dedicate or consecrate it. This is done by pouring oil on the top of the stone. Oil is connected with consecration or anointing in many places in the Old Testament; the one we see here is the first.

C. New Name (v. 19)

19. And he called the name of that place Bethel: but the name of that city was called Luz at the first.

Jacob does two more things before resuming his journey. In verse 17 he declared that the place where he has just slept is "the house of God"; now Jacob determines to use this expression as the name for this location, which is about 11 miles north of Jerusalem. The syllable *beth* means "house of" in Hebrew, and *el* is a shortened word for "God." Therefore *Bethel* means "house of God." Since *Bethel . . . was called Luz at the first,* we may wonder why Moses, who wrote this account, states that Abram "removed from [Haran] unto a mountain on the east of Bethel, and pitched his tent, having Bethel on the west" (Genesis 12:8). Undoubtedly, Moses did this for the sake of clarity.

Bethel will play an important part in the history of Israel. The town becomes a center of idol worship after the nation splits apart in about 930 BC (1 Kings 12:25-33), but Bethel's idolatrous altar will be destroyed by a godly king hundreds of years after that (2 Kings 23:15). Archaeologists have not been able to determine with certainty the location of Bethel.

D. Special Vow (vv. 20-22)

20. And Jacob vowed a vow, saying, If God will be with me, and will keep me in this way that I go, and will give me bread to eat, and raiment to put on.

Jacob's final decision involves something that is not recorded in the Bible until now: the making of a vow to God. Vows made to deities often include conditions: "only if the deity will do *this* will I then do *that.*" While many people attempt to negotiate terms with God, that does not seem to be the case for Jacob. For Jacob, the context of his situation is one of appreciation, not the "if" level of faith that was cited in the lesson Introduction. Reverence is a factor motivating him to want to do something for the God of Abraham and Isaac, who has now affirmed that the special promises will continue through Jacob.

What Do You Think?
Are vows to God appropriate in the New Testament era? Why, or why not?
Talking Points for Your Discussion
- Matthew 5:33-37; 23:16-22
- Acts 18:18; 21:18-26
- Hebrews 6:16
- James 5:12

21, 22. So that I come again to my father's house in peace; then shall the LORD be my God: and this stone, which I have set for a pillar, shall be God's house: and of all that thou shalt give me I will surely give the tenth unto thee.

Jacob's financial holdings are negligible as he makes this vow. He has only what is with him. If Jacob is ever able to return to his *father's house,* then Jacob will do his best to fulfill his sincere desires to make this place *God's house* and to *give the tenth* of all he has. This verse is usually viewed from the perspective of what Jacob accumulates while he is away (see Genesis 30:43), but he does not know of any future wealth at this point.

The tithe or tenth in the ancient world is usually a tax given to a ruler. The context shows that Jacob's desire to give a tenth to God is in appreciation for God's working through him to accomplish God's purposes. Jacob reasons that he first has to return *(come again to my father's house in peace)* in order to receive his inheritance. The birthright portion is ordinarily twice what anyone else receives (compare Deuteronomy 21:17), and Jacob is in possession of that birthright.

Admittedly, Jacob has his faults; one such fault will present itself years later when Jacob rebukes his favorite son for having a dream (Genesis 37:10)! But one emphasis here is that Jacob sincerely wants to pass something back to God because of what God promises him. God will remind Jacob of his vow years later (31:13, 38).

What Do You Think?
When did a sense of God's presence make a difference in how you reacted to a difficult time in your life? How did things turn out?
Talking Points for Your Discussion
- During an "alone time" of intense soul-searching
- During a church conflict
- During a family conflict
- Other

Conclusion
A. What Next?

We would like to know more about Jacob's mind-set as he left Beersheba. His brother intended to kill him, and he had to leave for his own safety. His scheming had not produced what he had wanted, so he ended up on the road, alone.

In some cases, it is a good thing to have everything go wrong and to end up at the bottom. From this position it is easier to look up to God and to trust in Him. Even then, some people seem to experience more than their "share" of poverty and/or persecution. To be a Christian in some cultures is to be oppressed continually.

Regardless of the situations of life, the real question is *What responses to my situation will be pleasing to God?* Jacob made good choices at Bethel. Each person has choices to make in "the house of God." What will yours be?

B. Prayer

Father, I want to honor You in all circumstances. Please grant me the wisdom to make right choices throughout this day. In Jesus' name, amen.

C. Thought to Remember
Christians are always in Bethel,
the house of God.

INVOLVEMENT LEARNING

Some of the activities below are also found in the helpful student book, Adult Bible Class.
Don't forget to download the free reproducible page from www.standardlesson.com to enhance your lesson!

Into the Lesson

Hold up a bed pillow as class begins. Ask, "Does anyone need some sleep?" After some reactions, say, "Well, Jacob certainly needed some sleep." Then pull out a large, rounded rock and say, "Here's what Jacob found to rest his head on. Anyone want to try it? You might need to wrap your coat around it a few times!"

Next, display the words *If / Because / Regardless* vertically on the board, with *If* at the top. Put the word *Faith* on a strip of poster board, and hold this strip alongside each of the other three words in sequence as you lead the class in saying in unison the two-word phrases that result: *"if" faith / "because" faith / "regardless" faith.* Ask, "What are the differences among these types or levels of faith?" Use the lesson Introduction to clarify learners' responses. Say, "Let's see how today's text can help move us to the *regardless* level.

Into the Word

Display the stub of an airplane boarding pass (actual or created), a compass, a flashlight, a stone, a toy ladder, an angel figurine, some seeds, a globe, a bottle of olive oil, a contract, and a church offering envelope. Draw attention to each item briefly in the order given; then return each to a table in front of the group. Say, "See if you can tell me how each of these relate to the story in today's text." Have the text read aloud.

Learners should note the following connections as the story unfolds: the ticket represents Jacob's journey; the compass represents Jacob's travel in a certain direction and the four directions of verse 14; the flashlight is for the nighttime scene; the stone represents Jacob's "pillow"; the ladder is for the conduit between earth and Heaven; the angel represents those Jacob sees ascending and descending; the seeds stand for Jacob's future family; the globe suggests that "all the families of the earth [will] be blessed"; the oil represents the ded-

ication of the pillar; the contract illustrates God's promise and Jacob's vow; the envelope represents the tithe Jacob promises.

Bring the text into modern experience by asking this question: "In what ways can Jacob's experience be similar to the ways people today might sense God's special presence?" Learners may note that a sense of God's closeness may be sudden and unexpected and/or may occur when in a quiet, thoughtful state of mind.

Follow up by asking, "What aspects of Jacob's experience should we *not* expect to be repeated today? Why?" This may lead into a discussion of individuals who claim that "God told me" such and such. Be prepared to address the dangers of "them that prophesy out of their own hearts" because of "a vain vision" and "a lying divination" (Ezekiel 13:1, 2, 7). Discuss the infrequent nature of God-given dreams in the Bible.

Into Life

Option 1: Give each learner a card with this incomplete statement: "God is here, and I know it because . . ." Say, "We all need to raise our awareness of the personal presence of God. This week, carry this card and jot notes when you sense God's nearness. As the week concludes, ask yourself this question: 'What similarities do I see in the occasions I have noted?'"

Option 2: Distribute copies of the "When and Where" activity from the reproducible page, which you can download. Ask learners to take a few minutes to complete it. Ask for volunteers to share thoughts with the class, but don't put anyone on the spot.

Option 3: The "Why and How" activity on the reproducible page can help reinforce the idea of giving more attention to the way God is at work in one's life. This can be a take-home exercise if you think learners will hesitate to share the personal responses.

GOD PREPARES FOR DELIVERANCE

DEVOTIONAL READING: Exodus 4:10-16
BACKGROUND SCRIPTURE: Exodus 1–4

EXODUS 3:7-17

7 And the LORD said, I have surely seen the affliction of my people which are in Egypt, and have heard their cry by reason of their taskmasters; for I know their sorrows;

8 And I am come down to deliver them out of the hand of the Egyptians, and to bring them up out of that land unto a good land and a large, unto a land flowing with milk and honey; unto the place of the Canaanites, and the Hittites, and the Amorites, and the Perizzites, and the Hivites, and the Jebusites.

9 Now therefore, behold, the cry of the children of Israel is come unto me: and I have also seen the oppression wherewith the Egyptians oppress them.

10 Come now therefore, and I will send thee unto Pharaoh, that thou mayest bring forth my people the children of Israel out of Egypt.

11 And Moses said unto God, Who am I, that I should go unto Pharaoh, and that I should bring forth the children of Israel out of Egypt?

12 And he said, Certainly I will be with thee; and this shall be a token unto thee, that I have sent thee: When thou hast brought forth the people out of Egypt, ye shall serve God upon this mountain.

13 And Moses said unto God, Behold, when I come unto the children of Israel, and shall say unto them, The God of your fathers hath sent me unto you; and they shall say to me, What is his name? what shall I say unto them?

14 And God said unto Moses, I AM THAT I AM: and he said, Thus shalt thou say unto the children of Israel, I AM hath sent me unto you.

15 And God said moreover unto Moses, Thus shalt thou say unto the children of Israel, The LORD God of your fathers, the God of Abraham, the God of Isaac, and the God of Jacob, hath sent me unto you: this is my name for ever, and this is my memorial unto all generations.

16 Go, and gather the elders of Israel together, and say unto them, The LORD God of your fathers, the God of Abraham, of Isaac, and of Jacob, appeared unto me, saying, I have surely visited you, and seen that which is done to you in Egypt:

17 And I have said, I will bring you up out of the affliction of Egypt unto the land of the Canaanites, and the Hittites, and the Amorites, and the Perizzites, and the Hivites, and the Jebusites, unto a land flowing with milk and honey.

KEY VERSES

The LORD God of your fathers, the God of Abraham, of Isaac, and of Jacob, appeared unto me, saying, I have surely visited you, and seen that which is done to you in Egypt: and I have said, I will bring you up out of the affliction of Egypt. —**Exodus 3:16b, 17a**

FIRST THINGS

Unit 3: First Freedom

LESSON AIMS

After participating in this lesson, each student will be able to:

1. Summarize God's call to Moses and Moses' reaction to it.

2. Explain the meaning and significance of God's name.

3. Plan a specific way to be a voice for someone facing oppression today.

LESSON OUTLINE

Introduction

A. Prince of Egypt

In 1998, DreamWorks Animation released the animated film *Prince of Egypt*. This popular movie retells the story of the deliverance of the Israelites from Egypt.

As is often the case with cinematic retellings, the producers take considerable liberty with the story. Although the Bible says nothing about Moses' life growing up as the adopted son of Pharaoh's daughter, the movie furnishes abundant details. In the movie, Moses is adopted not by Pharaoh's daughter, but by the queen. That makes Moses the stepson of Pharaoh and kid brother to Ramses, who is next in line to succeed his father as Pharaoh. Moses therefore ends up wielding considerable power as Royal Chief Architect under his brother, who is crown prince in charge of all of Pharaoh's temple building projects.

Moses is oblivious to his humble origins as the son of a Hebrew slave at first. But Miriam, his sister by birth, reveals the truth to him. Although he is reluctant to accept it, this truth is confirmed by a disturbing dream and a frank conversation with his stepparents.

DreamWorks Animation is not alone in filling the gaps in Moses' backstory. It is quite common for preachers, Sunday school teachers, and even Bible scholars to infer a great deal from the simple statement, "And the child grew, and she brought him unto Pharaoh's daughter, and he became her son" (Exodus 2:10). Who can blame them? Moses is a pivotal figure in both biblical and world history. Three of the major world religions (Christianity, Judaism, and Islam) claim Moses as a core prophet. Today we will look at what Scripture does have to say about the event that changed the course of Moses' life and world history.

B. Lesson Background

In Genesis 15, God appeared to Abraham in a vision to reaffirm the promise to make a great nation of that man. God sealed His Word with a covenant ceremony (lesson 6). Though this was certainly good news to Abraham, a dark cloud hovered over this promise: God also revealed to

Abraham that his descendants would be enslaved in Egypt for 400 years (v. 13).

That is precisely what happened. Abraham's grandson Jacob was forced to relocate all of Abraham's descendants to Egypt in about 1877 BC to survive a famine (Genesis 45–50). Things went well at first. Through divine providence, Jacob's son Joseph had received Pharaoh's favor and was able to settle all of his extended family in the rich land of Goshen.

The Israelites multiplied as time passed, but the memory of Joseph's favor evaporated from the Egyptian establishment (Exodus 1:8). The Israelites came to be seen as a threat within their host country. So the Pharaohs followed the well-trod path of paranoid power-bearers: they intensified their grip and oppressed this minority (vv. 9-11).

Things seemed bleak for Abraham's descendants, but the birth of Moses changed everything. Because Pharaoh had issued a decree that all Israelite boys were to be killed at birth, Moses' mother placed him in the river in "an ark of bulrushes" (Exodus 2:3). Pharaoh's daughter soon discovered him and proceeded to ask Moses' mother to nurse the infant. The daughter then adopted Moses as her own (vv. 5-10).

The next we hear of Moses is when he killed an Egyptian for mistreating a Hebrew slave (Exodus 2:12). Unlike the animated film, however, Pharaoh exhibited no special affection for Moses and ordered him to be executed (v. 15). Moses fled and found a new home among the Midianites, who lived east of Egypt (vv. 11-22).

Then Moses found God—or God found Moses! While tending sheep, Moses saw a bush that burned without being consumed (Exodus 3:2, 3). Moses listened as God revealed His will to Moses, who was 80 years old at the time (7:7).

I. God Sees
(Exodus 3:7-10)
A. Awareness of Suffering (v. 7)

7. And the LORD said, I have surely seen the affliction of my people which are in Egypt, and have heard their cry by reason of their taskmasters; for I know their sorrows.

Our passage begins with God. In so doing, the verse before us establishes something that Christians have long claimed by faith: God sees and hears. The God of Israel, who later reveals himself as the God of Jesus, sees the plight and hears the cries of His people. He is neither blind nor deaf (contrast Psalms 115:4-7; 135:15-17).

After 400 years of exile, Abraham's descendants may have grown callous to claims about God's promise to make them a great nation. The fact that the reception Moses later receives from his own people runs both hot (Exodus 4:29-31) and cold (5:19-21; 6:9) testifies that time has taken its toll on their faith. The Lord is appearing to Moses at a time when the people fear for their lives. The new Pharaoh has not only increased their labor (1:8-14), but also is murdering their baby boys (1:15-22). The taskmasters have become ruthless in using the Hebrews as slaves to carry out backbreaking labor in the heat of the sun (1:11-14). In an environment like this, the last thing the Hebrews want is for someone to stir up trouble and provoke Pharaoh to make their lives even more miserable.

> *What Do You Think?*
> Do biblical examples of complaint and despair ever serve as models of how we should pray? Why, or why not?
> *Talking Points for Your Discussion*
> - Job 6:1-4
> - Psalm 44:23-26
> - Lamentations 3:44

❧ THE ALL-SEEING GOD ❧

George Orwell's dark novel *1984* presents the specter of government as an all-seeing Big Brother, capable of intruding into every aspect of people's lives. The fear of the ever-increasing ability of government to "watch us" has intensified over the six decades since the book's appearance. As one website claims, "If you think the government is watching your every move, that's crazy—but if you think the government is too good or too honest to try it, that's naïve."

Surveillance is not limited to the government, however. We all know that we are being watched by cameras on private property such as banks and shopping malls—any place where criminal activity is likely. And the proliferation of cellphone cameras in the hands of the masses means that *whatever* we do in public (and sometimes in private) has the potential of appearing online for everyone to see. Our cherished privacy is no more.

But there has never been such a thing as privacy from God's eyes! As God saw the suffering of the ancient Hebrews, so also He sees everything about our lives. Whether you find that fact to be comforting or frightening speaks volumes about your spiritual condition. —C. R. B.

B. Declaration of Solution (vv. 8, 9)

8. And I am come down to deliver them out of the hand of the Egyptians, and to bring them up out of that land unto a good land and a large, unto a land flowing with milk and honey; unto the place of the Canaanites, and the Hittites, and the Amorites, and the Perizzites, and the Hivites, and the Jebusites.

God's response is not merely that of declaring His awareness. He is not the kind of god whom people imagine as knowing what is going on but choosing not to get involved. The true God acts! He steers world history toward its appointed end. Central to God's plans for world history is His desire to form Abraham's descendants into a people to bless all nations (Genesis 12:1-3).

That blessing requires the Hebrews to occupy a particular plot of land between the Mediterranean

Sea and the Jordan River: the land of Canaan (or Palestine). This is the first of 20 passages in the Old Testament to refer to this land as *flowing with milk and honey.* This phrase conveys an image of a fertile land that is ideally suited for farming and animal husbandry. When compared with many other parts of the world today, Palestine may not seem all that fertile. But when compared with the lands around it in Moses' day, it stands out as prime real estate in what is called the Fertile Crescent.

The commentary on verse 17 below discusses the particular people groups listed in this verse (see also lesson 6).

9. Now therefore, behold, the cry of the children of Israel is come unto me: and I have also seen the oppression wherewith the Egyptians oppress them.

The all-knowing God is about to teach both His people and the Egyptians that He is no mere tribal or territorial deity. *The children of Israel* will eventually learn that their God is the God of all nations; the oppressive wickedness of Egypt draws God's attention just as much as the well-being of Israel does.

All this will be evident when God unleashes the 10 plagues on Egypt (Exodus 7–12). After that, God will continue His judgment because the Egyptians will have much to learn as the oppressors become the oppressed. What the Egyptians will not learn until much later is that God's people must be released so that God can use them to incorporate Egypt and all other nations into His saving purposes in Christ (Matthew 28:19; Galatians 3:8).

C. Commissioning of Moses (v. 10)

10. Come now therefore, and I will send thee unto Pharaoh, that thou mayest bring forth my people the children of Israel out of Egypt.

Up to this point, Moses may be thrilled at what he is hearing. The focus so far has been on God's saving actions on Israel's behalf. Now, however, God is recruiting Moses to implement the plan!

Moses' assignment is far more dangerous than merely speaking to the Hebrews and organizing their departure. He must return to the capital city, where a warrant out for his arrest was once issued

HOW TO SAY IT

Amorites	*Am*-uh-rites.
Canaanites	*Kay*-nun-ites.
Girgashites	*Gur*-guh-shites.
Jebusites	*Jeb*-yuh-sites.
Mediterranean	*Med*-uh-tuh-**ray**-nee-un.
Midianites	*Mid*-ee-un-ites.
Miriam	*Meer*-ee-um.
patriarchs	*pay*-tree-arks.
Perizzites	*Pair*-ih-zites.
Pharaoh	*Fair*-o or *Fay*-roe.
Rephaims	*Ref*-a-ims.
Yahweh *(Hebrew)*	*Yah*-weh.

(Exodus 2:11-15). Even though a new king sits on the throne (2:23), it is always the wrong time (by human thinking) to ask a powerful king to release his most productive labor force!

> **What Do You Think?**
> When was a time you moved from saying, "Somebody needs to do this" to "I need to do this"? What motivates us to make this shift?
>
> *Talking Points for Your Discussion*
> - Urgency of the need
> - Plea from a significant source
> - Intersection of need and personal abilities

II. God Explains
(EXODUS 3:11-15)

A. Doubt and Assurance (vv. 11, 12)

11. And Moses said unto God, Who am I, that I should go unto Pharaoh, and that I should bring forth the children of Israel out of Egypt?

Like prophets after him, Moses is reluctant to be God's spokesman. Hundreds of years later, Isaiah will voice his awareness of his own moral impurity (Isaiah 6:5), and Jeremiah will claim to be too young for the job (Jeremiah 1:6). From our perspective, Moses may seem like the perfect candidate. As one who grew up around palace circles (Exodus 2:10), he speaks the language and is acquainted with royal customs. At the very least, his education surpasses that of most of the Israelites of his day (Acts 7:22).

But Moses doesn't seem to see it that way. From his perspective, he is a misfit. We can imagine him thinking that the "purebred" Egyptians look down on him for his Israelite origins. The Israelites, on the other hand, may be suspicious of him for his past connections with their oppressors. When Moses killed a slave driver who was abusing an Israelite, his Egyptian connections were not strong enough to protect him from Pharaoh's wrath, and Moses' Hebrew affiliation was too weak to gain him a sympathetic reception from the very people he was trying to defend (Exodus 2:11-15; Acts 7:24-26).

In addition to all that, Moses is now age 80 (Exodus 7:7), and it has been 40 years since he has been in Egypt (Acts 7:23, 30). Having found a stable home where he is both welcome and trusted, God now is calling him to leave it all behind and march defiantly into the heart of the Egyptian empire! It is little wonder, then, that the elderly Moses deems himself unfit for this mission.

> **What Do You Think?**
> When was a time you hesitated in your response to a perceived call from God? What contributed to your ultimate decision, right or wrong?
>
> *Talking Points for Your Discussion*
> - Becoming aware of God's bigger plan (Acts 10:9-20, 34, 35)
> - Focusing on the personal danger (Esther 4:11)
> - Seeing the need (Nehemiah 1:1–2:5)
> - Other

❧ RELUCTANT TO SERVE ❧

Civil war ravaged the West African nation of Liberia from 1989 to 1996. Factions fought one another for seven years, killing 200,000 people and sending 1,000,000 refugees packing. The end of the war did see the end of oppression, however. Finally, in 2005, the "most free, fair and peaceful elections in Liberia's history" brought Ellen Johnson Sirleaf into office as the first democratically elected female president in Africa. She was a reluctant public servant, but nevertheless she provided a stability to the nation that her power-hungry predecessors had not.

Some people look for every opportunity to grab power (see 2 Samuel 15; 1 Kings 1). Others, like Moses, avoid—even outright resist—such opportunities. The key issue in both cases is *motive*. Do we seek power only to enrich ourselves and stroke our egos? Do we avoid such opportunities because of a preference for our current comfort zone? Throughout history, people have responded properly to God's call to serve as leaders. When God calls, be prepared to answer!   —C. R. B.

12. And he said, Certainly I will be with thee; and this shall be a token unto thee, that I have sent thee: When thou hast brought forth the people out of Egypt, ye shall serve God upon this mountain.

Visual for
Lesson 10

When God CALLS, He EMPOWERS.

Point to this visual as you ask, "When did you first discover the truth of this statement personally?"

God is unconcerned with self-doubts. The reason: the Israelites' release is not going to be won on the basis of Moses' diplomatic skills. It is going to be won with a show of God's power. All God needs is a willing messenger. Once Moses adjusts to God's reality, Moses will fit that bill perfectly.

The nature of God's token or sign is worth noting. When humans ask for signs, we often want something like a down payment as to the outcome that is being promised. We want a demonstration of power that is sufficient to convince us that the other party can be trusted to deliver on the promise. Yet God is not like us. Here the sign that He will deliver what He promises will be His fulfillment of the promise. It is as if God is saying to Moses, "Do you doubt that I can pull off the release of your people? You will see it for yourself when they are worshipping me on the very ground on which you are now standing!"

B. Question and Answer (vv. 13-15)

13. And Moses said unto God, Behold, when I come unto the children of Israel, and shall say unto them, The God of your fathers hath sent me unto you; and they shall say to me, What is his name? what shall I say unto them?

The questions that Moses asks are valid from a human standpoint. When a potentially life-changing (and life-threatening) opportunity is placed before us, we want to know who stands behind the opportunity. If we are being asked to

step out and take a significant risk, the promise of a nameless benefactor is usually not enough for us.

Yet the request we see here is more difficult than Moses realizes. The God of Israel is not like the fictitious gods that the world concocts—gods with names, addresses, shapes, and fickle personalities that Moses knew of during his time in Egypt. So God needs to change Moses' perspective. As God does so, He will lay a right foundation for His people to understand His sovereign transcendence.

> *What Do You Think?*
> How do we know when it's time to move from questioning and planning to action in the service of God?
> *Talking Points for Your Discussion*
> - Valid questions vs. questions of doubt
> - Gathering data vs. overanalyzing
> - Getting counsel vs. stalling
> - Taking responsibility vs. taking the easy way
> - Other

14. And God said unto Moses, I AM THAT I AM: and he said, Thus shalt thou say unto the children of Israel, I AM hath sent me unto you.

God's self-identification *I AM THAT I AM* includes the ideas of God "who is what He is" and "who will be who He will be" (compare Revelation 1:4, 8; 4:8). This self-identification does not allow the hearer to draw on a prior frame of reference that will fall short of who God is. God is not the best of human experience taken to the nth degree. He is unlike any other being that we might name or experience that we might have.

For this reason, it is crucial that the Christian understanding of God begins with God's self-revelation in Scripture, especially as seen in Jesus (John 8:58). To build doctrine on any other foundation leads to idolatry, regardless of best intentions.

15. And God said moreover unto Moses, Thus shalt thou say unto the children of Israel, the LORD God of your fathers, the God of Abraham, the God of Isaac, and the God of Jacob, hath sent me unto you: this is my name for ever, and this is my memorial unto all generations.

God takes two steps further. First, he gives Moses a shorthand way of saying the "I AM

THAT I AM" of verse 14 by providing the name *the Lord* or "Yahweh" (which is our best approximation). This word is built on the same root Hebrew word that comes across in English as "I AM THAT I AM." God reveals His personal divine name to Moses in this verse.

Second, God makes it clear that He will not be known only by what He does in the future (Exodus 3:12), but also by what He began to reveal of himself by His actions to the Israelites' forefathers Abraham, Isaac, and Jacob. God's self-revelation to enslaved Israel will be consistent with His prior self-disclosure to those three patriarchs.

III. God Sends
(EXODUS 3:16, 17)
A. Elders Assembled (v. 16)

16. Go, and gather the elders of Israel together, and say unto them, The LORD God of your fathers, the God of Abraham, of Isaac, and of Jacob, appeared unto me, saying, I have surely visited you, and seen that which is done to you in Egypt.

Before God sends Moses to Pharaoh, He sends Moses to his own people. They stand in a privileged relationship of knowledge of God's plans (compare Amos 3:7). Moses will visit Pharaoh soon enough, but God's people must first get on board with the plan. Their first reception of His message is quite positive according to Exodus 4:29-31.

What Do You Think?
Without direct communication from God such as Moses received, how do you discern what God is calling you to do?
Talking Points for Your Discussion
- Holy Spirit guidance
- Spiritual giftedness
- Closed and opened doors of opportunity
- Counsel by fellow Christians
- Other

B. Plan Announced (v. 17)

17. And I have said, I will bring you up out of the affliction of Egypt unto the land of the Canaanites, and the Hittites, and the Amorites, and the Perizzites, and the Hivites, and the Jebusites, unto a land flowing with milk and honey.

The six groups listed here (as well as v. 8, above) are small tribes that occupy various plots of land in Canaan. They are never as powerful as Israel is in the days of David and Solomon, so they are easily controlled by stronger nations around them. These groups are named in various passages throughout the Old Testament, but especially Exodus through Joshua. In some passages, the Girgashites, Kenites, Kadmonites, and Rephaims are also listed (example: Genesis 15:20, 21; see commentary on this passage in lesson 6); in other places, the Hivites are left out (example: Nehemiah 9:8); and in still other places, just one or a few are named to represent the grouping (example: Genesis 15:16).

Because of Israel's failure to obey God fully, these six people groups remain in the land after the Israelites settle into it (Judges 3:5). They are still there during Solomon's day (2 Chronicles 8:7). Regarding *a land flowing with milk and honey,* see commentary on Exodus 3:8, above.

Conclusion
A. Servant of God

Though we cannot be sure what Moses' life was like as an adopted son of Pharaoh's daughter, we know what it was like after God laid claim to him. Moses learned that the holy God sees and hears, that God's power is all that is needed to accomplish God's mission, that God's name is unlike any other name, and that God's people have an important role to play in His plans. We who would continue to serve this God by seeking first His kingdom must take to heart these lessons!

B. Prayer

Lord God, we, like Moses, come before You with doubt that we are fit to be used of You to accomplish anything of lasting value for the world. Please prove us wrong! In Jesus' name, amen.

C. Thought to Remember

Join God in delivering people from sin-slavery.

INVOLVEMENT LEARNING

Some of the activities below are also found in the helpful student book, Adult Bible Class.
Don't forget to download the free reproducible page from www.standardlesson.com to enhance your lesson!

Into the Lesson

Have on display this question: *What's in a name?* Have five learners ready to read these quotes regarding names, one each: (1) "The name of a man is a numbing blow from which he never recovers" (Marshall McLuhan); (2) "That which we call a rose, by any other name would smell as sweet" (William Shakespeare, in *Romeo and Juliet*); (3) "Tigers die and leave their skins; people die and leave their names" (Japanese proverb); (4) "Proper names are poetry in the raw. Like all poetry they are untranslatable" (W. H. Auden); (5) "A good name is rather to be chosen than great riches" (Proverbs 22:1). Learners may wish to comment on these ideas as each is presented. Note that today's study revolves around a "name question."

Into the Word

Prepare in advance 16 blank dialogue balloons (typical of comic strips) cut from 8½" x 11" sheets of white paper. Say, "In today's text we are privileged to overhear a very personal conversation. I have a collection of dialogue balloons to help us get a handle on this." Distribute the dialogue balloons and markers; if your class is small, give two or more to some learners. Then assign from Exodus 3 these verses: 3, 4a, 4b, 5, 6, 7, 8, 9, 10, 11, 12, 13, 14, 15, 16, 17. Do not assign back-to-back verses to the learners having more than one dialogue balloon. (Verses 3-6 are not part of today's printed text, but are an important part of the conversation.)

Say, "In as few words as possible, summarize what the speaker says in your assigned verse(s). When you finish, give your balloon(s) to me." After all are submitted, shuffle them. Comment: "Now we have a jumbled conversation, so I need your help in reassembling the ideas. As I read a quote, tell me if it is early, middle, or late in the conversation, and I will post it accordingly. Close your Bibles!"

Read a dialogue balloon, receive responses, and affix the dialogue balloon to the wall or board with masking tape. Repeat for all. When you finish, ask learners if the arrangement looks proper for representing the sequence of the text. If they do not think so, ask, "How should this be fixed?" Rearrange as necessary.

Option. You can note that this is one of the longest recorded conversations between God and a person in the Scriptures. Ask if learners can recall other long conversations. For each identified, ask, "What would you say is the key issue involved?" One example is God and Isaiah in Isaiah 6; the issue (similar to this one in Exodus 3) is Isaiah's becoming God's spokesperson to His people.

Into Life

Option: For a transition to this segment, distribute copies of the "Talking with God" activity from the reproducible page, which you can download. Ask learners to summarize God's conversation with Moses using only the two dialogue balloons, then complete the bottom half of the exercise as indicated. Ask for volunteers to reveal responses.

Say, "Broadly speaking, there are two types of oppressions today: physical and spiritual. Who are some of the cruel taskmasters of each?" Let learners respond freely. In the *physical oppression* area, learners may mention dictators, those involved in human trafficking, etc.; if someone mentions "government policy," be careful not to allow the discussion to drift into one of partisan politics. The obvious answer in the *spiritual oppression* area is Satan, but learners may also mention some of his human ambassadors.

As the list grows, ask simply, "How do you see yourself as a deliverer for those oppressed by such powers?" Ask also, "What, if anything, can our class do corporately?"

Alternative: Distribute copies of the "Oppression and Deliverance" activity from the reproducible page. This exercise poses similar questions, but with more focus on Scripture background.

BEGINNING OF
PASSOVER

DEVOTIONAL READING: John 1:29-37
BACKGROUND SCRIPTURE: Exodus 6:2-30; 12

EXODUS 12:1-14

1 And the LORD spake unto Moses and Aaron in the land of Egypt, saying,

2 This month shall be unto you the beginning of months: it shall be the first month of the year to you.

3 Speak ye unto all the congregation of Israel, saying, In the tenth day of this month they shall take to them every man a lamb, according to the house of their fathers, a lamb for an house:

4 And if the household be too little for the lamb, let him and his neighbour next unto his house take it according to the number of the souls; every man according to his eating shall make your count for the lamb.

5 Your lamb shall be without blemish, a male of the first year: ye shall take it out from the sheep, or from the goats:

6 And ye shall keep it up until the fourteenth day of the same month: and the whole assembly of the congregation of Israel shall kill it in the evening.

7 And they shall take of the blood, and strike it on the two side posts and on the upper door post of the houses, wherein they shall eat it.

8 And they shall eat the flesh in that night, roast with fire, and unleavened bread; and with bitter herbs they shall eat it.

9 Eat not of it raw, nor sodden at all with water, but roast with fire; his head with his legs, and with the purtenance thereof.

10 And ye shall let nothing of it remain until the morning; and that which remaineth of it until the morning ye shall burn with fire.

11 And thus shall ye eat it; with your loins girded, your shoes on your feet, and your staff in your hand; and ye shall eat it in haste: it is the LORD's passover.

12 For I will pass through the land of Egypt this night, and will smite all the firstborn in the land of Egypt, both man and beast; and against all the gods of Egypt I will execute judgment: I am the LORD.

13 And the blood shall be to you for a token upon the houses where ye are: and when I see the blood, I will pass over you, and the plague shall not be upon you to destroy you, when I smite the land of Egypt.

14 And this day shall be unto you for a memorial; and ye shall keep it a feast to the LORD throughout your generations; ye shall keep it a feast by an ordinance for ever.

KEY VERSE

This day shall be unto you for a memorial; and ye shall keep it a feast to the LORD throughout your generations; ye shall keep it a feast by an ordinance for ever. —**Exodus 12:14**

FIRST THINGS

Unit 3: First Freedom

LESSONS 10–13

LESSON AIMS

After participating in this lesson, each student will be able to:

1. Recall the details of the first Passover, just before the Israelites left Egypt.

2. Explain the importance of keeping alive the memory of events that have spiritual significance.

3. Brainstorm ways to make the "visual aids" of baptism and the Lord's Supper more meaningful in his or her church.

LESSON OUTLINE

Introduction
   A. A Beginning to Remember
   B. Lesson Background
 I. When to Eat the Lamb (EXODUS 12:1-7)
   A. The First Month (vv. 1, 2)
   B. The Tenth Day (vv. 3-5)
   C. The Fourteenth Day (vv. 6, 7)
 II. How to Eat the Lamb (EXODUS 12:8-11)
   A. Proper Action (vv. 8-10)
      Learning to Cook
   B. Proper Attire (v. 11)
      No Hurry?
 III. Why to Eat the Lamb (EXODUS 12:12-14)
   A. Passing Through (v. 12)
   B. Passing Over (v. 13)
   C. Passing On (v. 14)
Conclusion
   A. An Unforgettable Ending
   B. Prayer
   C. Thought to Remember

Introduction

A. A Beginning to Remember

People like to remember how things began. Nations celebrate their origins with holidays, solemn ceremonies, and raucous parades. Families celebrate marriages and the anniversaries that follow with parties, gifts, and cakes. Organizations celebrate their founding with employee picnics, commemorative products, and contests.

We need to celebrate important events because it is all too easy to forget what has brought us to the point where we are now. "The daily grind" may consume our time and energy to the point that unless we plan to slow down and contemplate what is important, we will not say the "deeper" things that need to be said, think what needs to be thought, and do what needs to be done. Important people and historic moments will fade from memory as we forget what made them special.

Forgetfulness can lead to disaster as mistakes are repeated and purposes (reasons for being) are lost. The meaning of life can get swallowed up by life's demands; the direction God has given world history can be replaced with a pointless, repetitive cycle.

God knows the importance of remembering beginnings. He gave the ancient Israelites three practices by which to remember their founding event, the exodus from Egypt: (1) the rite of the firstborn son, (2) the meal of unleavened bread, and (3) the celebration of the Passover feast. Today's lesson focuses on the third of these.

B. Lesson Background

The Passover feast, like other commemorations, must be considered within the historical context in which it occurred. Further, we must look not just to the immediate context, but also to the larger context of history for fullest comprehension.

For Passover, that context goes all the way back to Genesis 1. In the first 11 chapters of Genesis, we see God's good creation collapsing under the weight of human sinfulness. Not even the catastrophic event of the great flood could cure what ailed the world. Rather than forsake humanity, however, God formed a people through whom

He would bless all nations. They would be His vehicle for ushering in the Messiah to reconcile a wounded world to Him.

This people began with Abraham and Sarah. Generations later, the growing nation of their descendants found itself enslaved within the confines of Egyptian civilization. Pharaoh, feeling threatened by their growth, suppressed them with harsh toil and deadly population control. After centuries of progressively worse treatment, the cries of the Hebrews moved God to action. He raised up a figure who would lead the Israelites out of Egypt as God willed to develop them as a light to the nations.

Moses was that leader. Through Moses, God unleashed a barrage of plagues against the Egyptians. These plagues eventually broke Pharaoh's stubborn will, but he has not yet conceded defeat as today's text begins. In anticipation of the tenth and final plague, God established the Passover instructions as specified in today's text. By these, generations of Israelites were to remember their exemption from the associated catastrophe (Exodus 12:24-27).

I. When to Eat the Lamb
(Exodus 12:1-7)

A. The First Month (vv. 1, 2)

1, 2. And the Lord spake unto Moses and Aaron in the land of Egypt, saying, This month shall be unto you the beginning of months: it shall be the first month of the year to you.

Having shocked Egypt with nine devastating plagues to this point, God is on the verge of delivering His people from their oppressors. From God's perspective, the "what for" of this deliver-

HOW TO SAY IT

Abib	*A*-bib.
Abraham	*Ay*-bruh-ham.
Levites	*Lee*-vites.
Messiah	Meh-*sigh*-uh.
Nisan	*Nye*-san.
Pharaoh	*Fair*-o or *Fay*-roe.
purtenance	*purt*-nunts.

ance matters more than the "what from." God is not liberating all oppressed peoples throughout the world; He is liberating a specific group of slaves for His mission of forming a new people that He will use to bless all nations.

If the Hebrew people are to bless the nations, they will need to live differently from their oppressors. To become a light, they will have to exhibit a life rhythm different from that of the Egyptians. One feature of this new rhythm is a distinctive calendar. Since (1) deliverance from Egypt marks the founding moment in Israel's national history and (2) the Passover is the most important event to mark this deliverance, then (3) God decrees that this observance should occur in the month that is to mark the beginning of Israel's new year. This observance therefore takes place in the month of Abib (Exodus 13:4), later called Nisan (Esther 3:7).

> *What Do You Think?*
> What are some ways that Christians are to "live differently" from unbelievers? How will you improve in this regard?
> *Talking Points for Your Discussion*
> - Regarding church involvement
> - Regarding family life
> - Regarding ethical standards
> - Regarding compassion
> - Ephesians 4:17–5:20

B. The Tenth Day (vv. 3-5)

3. Speak ye unto all the congregation of Israel, saying, In the tenth day of this month they shall take to them every man a lamb, according to the house of their fathers, a lamb for an house.

God's calendar for Israel is populated with special months and days. A key pattern in this calendar is the use of significant numbers, especially 10 and multiples of 7. The number 10 corresponds both to the number of plagues God sends on Egypt and the number of commandments He gives Israel (Exodus 20). It is fitting, then, that God instructs His people to begin preparation for Passover on *the tenth day* of the first month of their year. On this day, one man in each house is required to select a lamb. The emphasis here is that God's requirement applies to every household.

4. And if the household be too little for the lamb, let him and his neighbour next unto his house take it according to the number of the souls; every man according to his eating shall make your count for the lamb.

God recognizes that not all households are equally blessed in numbers of people and financial resources. It is crucial, however, that the smaller and/or poorer households not be excluded from Israel's shared life. God therefore allows—and requires—households to combine resources so that all may participate. Everyone must join in if this practice is to have the desired effect of uniting God's people according to their common history and mission.

What Do You Think?

With Thanksgiving approaching, what can you do to include a "little" household in your own celebration of thanks to God?

Talking Points for Your Discussion

- Regarding widows, widowers, and other singles
- Regarding a homeless person
- Regarding stranded travelers (bad weather, hospital emergency room, etc.)
- Other

---

5. Your lamb shall be without blemish, a male of the first year: ye shall take it out from the sheep, or from the goats.

Not just any animal may be selected for the Passover meal. The animal must *be without blemish,* as with all sacrifices in Israel's worship life that God will establish later (compare Exodus 29:1; Leviticus 22:21; Numbers 19:2; etc.). To offer an animal with a defect would communicate that this practice is not very important (see Malachi 1:8, 12-14). The Israelites must offer their best because their God is the best thing that has ever happened to them!

The animal must also be *a male of the first year.* Its gender may represent Israel's firstborn sons, who are to be spared the tenth plague—the plague that will take the lives of Egypt's firstborn males

(Exodus 11:5; 12:29, 30). The lamb's young age may represent Israel's youthful vigor as a nation.

It is not essential that the animal to be sacrificed be a sheep, which is what we normally associate with the word *lamb.* A young goat will do just as well. God recognizes that not all households have access to both, so He leaves the option open.

C. The Fourteenth Day (vv. 6, 7)

6. And ye shall keep it up until the fourteenth day of the same month: and the whole assembly of the congregation of Israel shall kill it in the evening.

Four days after selecting the lambs, the households within Israel must slaughter them. The time appointed for this, *in the evening,* is after the sun begins to set but before darkness falls completely. Responsibility for slaughtering the animals transfers eventually from heads of households to Levites and/or priests as time passes (2 Chronicles 35:1-11; Ezra 6:20).

7. And they shall take of the blood, and strike it on the two side posts and on the upper door post of the houses, wherein they shall eat it.

The purpose for smearing blood on the doorposts is discussed in verse 13, below. This practice and that of eating inside one's house are not permanent features of this feast. After the Israelites settle into the promised land, the celebration will be centralized in "the place which the Lord thy God shall choose to place his name in" (Deuteronomy 16:6).

II. How to Eat the Lamb
(EXODUS 12:8-11)

A. Proper Action (vv. 8-10)

8a. And they shall eat the flesh in that night, roast with fire,

The fact that the people are to *eat the flesh in that night* implies haste in the preparation of the Passover lamb. There is no time for marinating the meat extensively. The symbolic value of this practice requires that it be eaten hastily (see v. 11).

8b. And unleavened bread;

The "haste factor" also applies to the bread of the meal. Leavened bread (that is, bread made with yeast) requires time to rise. But there will not be enough time for such a process because the Israelites will have only a narrow window of time to depart after God strikes Egypt with the final plague. The people must be ready to go.

8c. And with bitter herbs they shall eat it.

The use of *bitter herbs* points to the bitterness of Israel's oppression in Egypt (Exodus 1:14; Numbers 9:11). Lettuce and endive are the most common bitter herbs that are native to the region.

> *What Do You Think?*
> Is it appropriate for Christians to remind themselves periodically of the bitterness of their lives while slaves to sin? Why, or why not?
>
> *Talking Points for Your Discussion*
> - Rejoicing in deliverance (Romans 5:11)
> - Feeling overwhelmed with regret (1 Corinthians 15:9)

9. Eat not of it raw, nor sodden at all with water, but roast with fire; his head with his legs, and with the purtenance thereof.

The meat must be prepared properly. God makes clear in Genesis 9:4 that all lifeblood is sacred to Him (see lesson 4). For this reason, the people must not eat meat that has blood still in it. The people must drain all blood, effectively returning it to the author of life. God will stress this repeatedly after the exodus (Deuteronomy 12:16, 23-25; 15:23). In the instructions in Leviticus 17:10-13 (which the Israelites have not received at this point), God even will require that blood poured onto the ground be covered with dust (contrast Ezekiel 24:7).

Roasting animals is one way to make sure that no blood remains. Meat that is consumed raw or after having been boiled *(sodden . . . with water)* is much more likely to have blood still in it. *Purtenance* refers to the inner organs (compare Exodus 29:13, 17, 22).

❧ LEARNING TO COOK ❧

Would you like to be a great chef? The Internet offers many descriptions of self-proclaimed "world-class" cooking schools. One such institution in New York proclaims itself to be "the best culinary school in the world." It boasts that its stu-

CHRIST OUR PASSOVER
IS SACRIFICED FOR US
— 1 CORINTHIANS 5:7B

Visual for Lesson 11. *Use this visual to start a discussion regarding the connection between Passover and Christ's sacrifice.*

dents spend in excess of 1,300 hours in the kitchen or bakeshop. Offered are degrees for professionals and certificates for those who are merely "food enthusiasts." Do you suppose that includes those of us who just like to eat?

A cooking school in California asserts that its name "is synonymous with expertise, refinement, and culinary excellence—qualities meticulously nurtured" in its programs. A school in Chicago that specializes in French pastry boasts that it provides "an intense focus on contemporary aesthetics." Wouldn't most of us rather eat a pastry than merely stare at it?

Kidding aside, what the Hebrew cooks prepared on the evening of the Passover had to be done quickly; there was no time for culinary-school aesthetics and refinement. It was God's recipe that had to be followed for that simple meal. And so it is with God's other "recipes" as seen in, for example, Matthew 28:19, 20; John 3:36; Acts 2:38; and James 1:6. Don't try to "improve" God's recipes—just follow them in faith!   —C. R. B.

10. And ye shall let nothing of it remain until the morning; and that which remaineth of it until the morning ye shall burn with fire.

The practice of completely burning the sacrificial lamb anticipates two features of Israel's future practices of eating and sacrificing. First, it anticipates the eating of manna (Exodus 16:11-36). As the Israelites journey toward the promised land, God will provide food by raining down manna from Heaven. Yet God will insist that the Israelites collect only enough manna to eat each day. With one exception (see Exodus 16:21-23), nothing shall remain for future consumption. This practice will remind the Israelites of their dependence on God for their daily bread. In destroying the leftovers of the Passover feast, the people will learn that God is the source of their sustenance. We echo this lesson when we ask our heavenly Father to give us our daily bread (Matthew 6:11).

Second, the Israelites acknowledge the sacredness of the meal by ensuring that the animal is entirely consumed by the combination of eating and burning. The meat may not be used partially for a sacred feast on one day with leftovers being used the next day to feed livestock or to serve as an afternoon snack. It is sacred food. This will be the imagery of the burnt offerings of Israel's forthcoming sacrificial system (Leviticus 1:1-9).

B. Proper Attire (v. 11)

11. And thus shall ye eat it; with your loins girded, your shoes on your feet, and your staff in your hand; and ye shall eat it in haste: it is the LORD's passover.

The command to have *your loins girded, your shoes on your feet, and your staff in your hand* speaks not only to behavior, but also to the attitude the people are to have as they prepare to head onward in faith. Once the Passover meal is eaten, there is to be no hesitation as with Lot's wife (Genesis 19:26). The attire God specifies is dress for the road (compare Luke 12:35).

What Do You Think?

In what ways can and should Sunday morning worship prepare us to be "ready to go" for service to God?

Talking Points for Your Discussion

- The role of the sermon
- The role of the Lord's Supper
- The role of Christian fellowship
- The role of corporate prayer
- Other

Even after slavery was outlawed in America in the 1860s, the de facto law of the land in parts of the U.S. continued to limit the freedoms of former slaves and their descendants. The U.S. Supreme Court decision Plessy v. Ferguson of 1896 made things worse by upholding a "separate but equal" law, which permitted continued segregation.

This situation took a dramatic turn in 1954. That was the year of the landmark Brown v. Board of Education of Topeka decision in which the U.S. Supreme Court overturned Plessy v. Ferguson. The civil rights movement of the 1960s followed.

Thomas Jefferson, himself a slave owner, had penned the words "all men are created equal" for the U.S. Declaration of Independence in 1776. Looking back from our vantage point in the year 2013, we wonder why it took so long to put into practice the truth of that statement! Patience is often a virtue (Psalms 37:7; 40:1). But "taking our time" is sinful when we delay making changes that we know we should.

God is patient and longsuffering (Romans 9:22; 1 Peter 3:20). But the Bible also shows God acting quickly and demanding that we do so as well. It was so on the night of the Passover, and it is so today as God calls us to a new life in Jesus, a life free from the slavery of sin. There should be no delay. "How shall we, that are dead to sin, live any longer therein?" (Romans 6:2).   —C. R. B.

III. Why to Eat the Lamb
(EXODUS 12:12-14)

A. Passing Through (v. 12)

12. For I will pass through the land of Egypt this night, and will smite all the firstborn in the land of Egypt, both man and beast; and against all the gods of Egypt I will execute judgment: I am the LORD.

Time after time, the hardness of Pharaoh's heart kept him from releasing God's people. So God is about to inflict a strict judgment on Pharaoh and his people. As God's chosen people, Israel is God's firstborn (Exodus 4:22), the people to whom He is entrusting the responsibility of carrying His legacy. If Pharaoh refuses to honor God's exclusive claim on His firstborn, then Pharaoh and his people will have to forfeit *their* firstborn.

There also may be a tie-in with Pharaoh's decision to kill all newborn Israelite boys (Exodus 1:16). By taking the life of only the firstborn of Egypt, God is not giving Pharaoh the equal measure he deserves. Nevertheless, God is about to send a powerful message to Pharaoh that he has no rightful claim on the lives of God's people. For Pharaoh to kill every Hebrew newborn boy is an act of genocide since all the Hebrew females eventually would be absorbed into the Egyptian nation. Were that to happen, Abraham's descendants would no longer be distinguishable as a people-group.

B. Passing Over (v. 13)

13. And the blood shall be to you for a token upon the houses where ye are: and when I see the blood, I will pass over you, and the plague shall not be upon you to destroy you, when I smite the land of Egypt.

God does not want to punish the Israelites along with the Egyptians. So He uses the lambs' blood that is smeared on the doorposts (v. 7, above) as the distinguishing mark regarding who shall live. In anticipation of Jesus, the lambs' blood is to "cover" God's people, and they will be spared from death. Of course, God does not need the blood to tell who is who. But the Israelites need to learn to follow God's instructions since they are in the process of becoming His set-apart people.

C. Passing On (v. 14)

14. And this day shall be unto you for a memorial; and ye shall keep it a feast to the LORD throughout your generations; ye shall keep it a feast by an ordinance for ever.

The lessons God is teaching the Israelites through the Passover event are relevant to future generations. If the lessons are not to be forgotten, then God's people will have to instill them into each subsequent generation (compare Deuteronomy 6:20-25). This is the purpose of the meal. It is to serve as a permanent fixture in the calendar of Old Testament Israel. As the Israelites continue to observe Passover, their children will not forget who they are, where they came from, and where they are going as God's chosen people.

> *What Do You Think?*
> What traditions can we establish in our family celebrations to pass along spiritual truths to children and grandchildren?
> *Talking Points for Your Discussion*
> - Regarding Thanksgiving
> - Regarding Christmas
> - Regarding Easter
> - Regarding birthdays

Conclusion

A. An Unforgettable Ending

People may try to avoid remembering how certain things come to an end (jobs, marriages, the lives of loved ones, etc.). Endings tend to be sad because we do not like to let go. We do not like the instability that the end of something familiar brings into our lives. An ending of something often signals entrance into the unknown as comfortable routines must be abandoned and new ones developed.

Yet endings sometimes are gateways to new beginnings that far outshine the past. The Passover was just such a gateway. In this vein, Christ has given us the Lord's Supper for us to remember the end of Jesus' earthly life that leads to resurrection life in Him. The facts surrounding the ending of Jesus' earthly ministry belong in our memory because they are the foundation of our new life in Him. It is thus fitting that Jesus instituted the Lord's Supper in the context of the Passover meal. Remembering what Jesus has done is a vital foundation to being able to "teach all nations" as Jesus would have us do (Matthew 28:19).

B. Prayer

Thank You, God, for new beginnings! As we think of Passover, let us not forget the new beginning You brought by sending Your spotless lamb, Jesus, to die on our behalf. In His name, amen.

C. Thought to Remember

God's deliverance is always there for us.

INVOLVEMENT LEARNING

Some of the activities below are also found in the helpful student book, Adult Bible Class.
Don't forget to download the free reproducible page from www.standardlesson.com to enhance your lesson!

Into the Lesson

Option: Place in chairs copies of the "Egyptians Fall, Part 1" exercise from the reproducible page, which you can download. Learners can begin working on this as they arrive. (*Alternative:* Distribute this at the end of class as a take-home activity.)

Prepare a 2014 calendar that fits on a single 8½" by 11" sheet of paper. (Search for "calendar template" on the Internet.) Give each learner a copy. Also bring a full-color decorative calendar to hang before the group. Say, "Circle what you consider to be 'special days' in the coming year." Allow two or three minutes, then ask, "Who has a special day marked in January?" Continue naming the remaining 11 months as your class members raise hands in response. (Keep this moving rapidly; you want only shows of hands, not discussions of which days are special and why.)

Comment: "Wow—that's a lot of special days! Some of those are important personally; others involve family members; still others involve larger groups, such as our church as a whole. Each special day has its own significance. Today's study is about one of the most significant days on the calendar of Old Testament Israel—it's Passover."

Into the Word

Distribute handouts with *Time to* printed across the top; have the word *REMEMBER* vertically down the middle of the page. (*Alternative:* Distribute blank sheets of paper and have learners write these words themselves, in the desired arrangement.) Read the lesson text read aloud, then say, "Close your Bibles for a memory test! I'm going to ask some questions and give some completion statements. We are going to work down through the eight letters of the word *remember* in sequence. Jot each one-word answer so that it intersects with the letter under consideration. Here goes."

R: How was the lamb to be cooked? (*roasted, v. 9*); *E:* What part of the meal was to be bitter?

(*herbs, v. 8*); *M:* Leftover meat was to be burned before what time of day? (*morning, v. 10*); *E:* On which day of the month was the lamb to be taken and set aside? (*tenth, v. 3*); *M:* What was declared to be "the first"? (*month, v. 2*); *B:* What was to be put on doorposts? (*blood, v. 7*); *E:* In what manner was the meal to be eaten? (*haste, v. 11*); *R:* Other than Moses, to whom was the Lord speaking? (*Aaron, v. 1*).

Discuss results and review the Scripture text to correct any misconceptions or deficiencies.

Note that Passover was about a new way to worship God for Old Testament Israel in celebration of a salvation event. Ask simply, "What do you see that is 'new' in today's text?" Expect learners to point out the new calendar and a new observance (Passover) on that calendar; learners may then point out more "newnesses" in relation to those two: a new use of blood; a new spirit of community inclusion, etc. Continue: "Which Passover elements are given new significance for us as we observe the Lord's Supper? Why?" (See 1 Corinthians 11:23-25.)

Into Life

Launch a brainstorming session as you say, "The procedures of the Passover celebration result in 'visual aids' to make the feast meaningful and memorable to succeeding generations. What can we do to make the Lord's Supper and baptism more meaningful in terms of the 'visual aids' that they provide for us?" (*Option:* Divide the class in half, one to discuss the Lord's Supper in this regard and one to discuss baptism.)

Option: Distribute copies of the "A New Day, A New Way" activity from the reproducible page. Ask a learner to read 1 Corinthians 5:7 aloud. Use this text to launch a discussion of attitudes, speech, and behaviors that are sinful "leaven." Learners can use the cutout of the exercise as a memory tool in the week ahead, as noted.

BEGINNING OF FREEDOM

DEVOTIONAL READING: Galatians 5:13-21
BACKGROUND SCRIPTURE: Exodus 13:17-22; 14

EXODUS 14:13, 14, 21-30

13 And Moses said unto the people, Fear ye not, stand still, and see the salvation of the LORD, which he will shew to you to day: for the Egyptians whom ye have seen to day, ye shall see them again no more for ever.

14 The LORD shall fight for you, and ye shall hold your peace.

. . . .

21 And Moses stretched out his hand over the sea; and the LORD caused the sea to go back by a strong east wind all that night, and made the sea dry land, and the waters were divided.

22 And the children of Israel went into the midst of the sea upon the dry ground: and the waters were a wall unto them on their right hand, and on their left.

23 And the Egyptians pursued, and went in after them to the midst of the sea, even all Pharaoh's horses, his chariots, and his horsemen.

24 And it came to pass, that in the morning watch the LORD looked unto the host of the Egyptians through the pillar of fire and of the cloud, and troubled the host of the Egyptians,

25 And took off their chariot wheels, that they drave them heavily: so that the Egyptians said, Let us flee from the face of Israel; for the LORD fighteth for them against the Egyptians.

26 And the LORD said unto Moses, Stretch out thine hand over the sea, that the waters may come again upon the Egyptians, upon their chariots, and upon their horsemen.

27 And Moses stretched forth his hand over the sea, and the sea returned to his strength when the morning appeared; and the Egyptians fled against it; and the LORD overthrew the Egyptians in the midst of the sea.

28 And the waters returned, and covered the chariots, and the horsemen, and all the host of Pharaoh that came into the sea after them; there remained not so much as one of them.

29 But the children of Israel walked upon dry land in the midst of the sea; and the waters were a wall unto them on their right hand, and on their left.

30 Thus the LORD saved Israel that day out of the hand of the Egyptians; and Israel saw the Egyptians dead upon the sea shore.

KEY VERSE

Thus the LORD saved Israel that day out of the hand of the Egyptians. —**Exodus 14:30**

FIRST THINGS

Unit 3: First Freedom

LESSONS 10–13

LESSON AIMS

After participating in this lesson, each student will be able to:

1. Tell how Israel escaped from Egypt by crossing the Red Sea.

2. Compare and contrast the Israelites' deliverance from bondage through crossing the Red Sea with the role of baptismal water in delivering believers from the bondage of sin (1 Corinthians 10:1, 2).

3. Sing a song of praise to God, giving thanks for salvation.

LESSON OUTLINE

Introduction

A. From Despair to Deliverance

We were supposed to fly directly across Lake Michigan and down the Wisconsin coast to Chicago's Midway Airport. However, the storm was so strong we had to hug the shoreline of Michigan, flying south, bumping hard every second. I knew we were in trouble when the businessmen who took this flight daily were visibly frightened. It seemed that the plane would break apart any second. Our seat belts hardly held us in place as we bounced around. There was no way to fly out of it.

After more than an hour with teeth chattering and hearts pounding, we emerged into smooth air just south of the airport. The evening sun was setting, and rays were filtering through the storm clouds. We landed safely, and everyone clapped for joy for the "great salvation" we had just experienced. We had moved quickly from despair to deliverance.

Perhaps our emotions were a bit like what the Israelites experienced at the Red Sea. Their exodus has become a figure of the Christian experience of salvation and freedom from sin.

B. Lesson Background

To understand the miraculous nature of the exodus events, one must look back to the very beginnings of the book of Exodus itself. In the first place, young Moses was saved from a death sentence by divine circumstances to be reared in Pharaoh's household (Exodus 2:1-10; Acts 7:20-22). But at age 40, Moses killed an Egyptian overseer and had to flee for his own life. He then spent 40 years as a shepherd before being confronted by God in the burning bush (Exodus 2:11–3:22; Acts 7:23-32). Moses thus became the man to lead God's people out of Egypt (Exodus 3–6).

The miracles of the plagues reached a climax with the death of the firstborn in Egypt (Exodus 7–11). When Pharaoh finally let the people go, God did not lead them by a northern route, the most direct way to Canaan (13:17); rather, He led them toward the south "through the way of the wilderness of the Red sea" (13:18). By the time the Israelites "encamped in Etham, in the edge of the wilderness" (13:20), the people had seen many miracles performed by God through Moses. Thus they should have been confident in the outcome of what was coming next.

When we read Exodus 14:2, we see that God had deliberately led the people into an impossible position (from a human point of view), with their backs to the sea. God placed Israel in this position —with no apparent way to escape the Egyptian army—in order that He might show His glory to the Israelites.

An Israelite countermarch tricked Pharaoh into thinking that the Israelites were confused in their attempt to escape into the wilderness (v. 3). God used this opportunity to "harden Pharaoh's heart" so Pharaoh would chase after the Israelites with his army (vv. 4-6). This he did, with his 600 "chosen" chariots plus many other chariots and horsemen (vv. 7-9). The Israelites reacted with great fear and consternation (v. 10). With sarcasm, "they said unto Moses, Because there were no graves in Egypt, hast thou taken us away to die in the wilderness?" (v. 11). Time for another miracle!

I. Terrifying Situation
(EXODUS 14:13, 14)
A. Watch Closely (v. 13)

13. And Moses said unto the people, Fear ye not, stand still, and see the salvation of the LORD, which he will shew to you to day: for the Egyptians whom ye have seen to day, ye shall see them again no more for ever.

Ancient Egypt is a culture obsessed with a religion of death. The pyramids, which are monumental tombs for the Pharaohs, testify to this fact. The pyramids were built long before the time of Moses, and it is against this "religion of death" backdrop that Moses speaks words of encouragement.

The Hebrew word for *stand still* is a special form that means "to take one's stand within oneself." Thus the phrase *stand still* is addressed more to the hearer's attitude than to physical posture. In other words, the Israelites are to be calm and confident, not wavering in their trust in God. All they have to do is wait and *see the salvation of the Lord.*

The word *see,* used three times, is emphasized in this verse. At the end of the chapter, at the conclusion of the great salvation accomplished by God, the Israelites will *see* "Egyptians dead upon the sea shore," they will *see* God's "great work" (Exodus 14:30, 31). Moses addresses the people's fears most appropriately as he predicts that *the Egyptians whom ye have seen to day, ye shall see them again no more for ever.* Death is about to become a sudden reality for many Egyptians, whose culture is fixated on a religion of death.

B. Do Nothing (v. 14)

14. The LORD shall fight for you, and ye shall hold your peace.

The Lord is the "man of war" (Exodus 15:3) who announces His strategy and goals from the beginning (see 6:2-8). The exodus events, wilderness experiences, and conquest of Canaan are and will be God's battle. The Lord has His part in what is about to happen, and the Israelites have theirs: it is to shut up and watch. Unfortunately, the people are beginning to develop the bad habit of running off at the mouth when silence would indicate faith.

What Do You Think?
What was the most terrifying experience of your life? How did you grow spiritually as a result?
Talking Points for Your Discussion
- Lessons learned about God's power
- Lessons learned about your own tendencies
- Lessons learned about spiritual "blind spots"
- Other

❧ THE FIGHT-OR-FLIGHT RESPONSE ❧

Stress-filled situations can trigger the fight-or-flight mechanism that seems to be built in to most of God's creatures. The leader (alpha male) of a wolf pack will fight if challenged for leadership. A deer will flee for her life when sensing a predator nearby.

Humans demonstrate the same two responses in stressful situations. God seems to have hardwired us for either "fight or flight" when danger looms. Many people will flee from a burning building while others remain inside to help others escape. Those fleeing want to save their own lives; those remaining inside are fighting for the lives of loved ones. But no one simply hangs around inside a burning building to see what will happen next!

In anticipation of the Egyptian attack, Moses' commands of "fear ye not," "stand still," and "hold your peace" challenged his people to override their fight-or-flight instinct. They could do so by replacing that instinct with trust in God. The Bible requires that we use godly wisdom as we evaluate situations in this regard. There are indeed times to fight (2 Corinthians 10:3-5; 1 Timothy 6:12; etc.) and circumstances to flee (Acts 9:23-25; 1 Corinthians 6:18; 10:14; etc.). How are you training yourself to make godly choices?   —C. R. B.

II. Miraculous Intervention
(EXODUS 14:21-28)

A. Israelites Escape (vv. 21, 22)

21. And Moses stretched out his hand over the sea; and the LORD caused the sea to go back by a strong east wind all that night, and made the sea dry land, and the waters were divided.

There are two things in Exodus 14:15-20 (not in today's text) that we should note as we move to verse 21. First, verse 16 tells us that Moses is stretching out not just *his hand*, but the "rod" that has been the visible means of God's power throughout the plagues. This rod has been important from the beginning of this deliverance (see Exodus 4:17). Many times the text recounts that Moses stretches out this rod to do signs and miracles (see Exodus 7:19, 20; 8:5, 16, 17; 9:23; 10:13; 17:9-12). However, Moses eventually uses the rod in a way that displeases God (see Numbers 20:11).

We may wonder why God even bothers to use Moses and his rod to get things done. It seems to be a principle that God prefers to work through the human instrument. God usually finds someone to push His plan forward (example: Isaiah 6:8), but sometimes He doesn't (example: Ezekiel 22:30). Yet even when the human instrument is involved, we know that the signs and miracles ultimately come from God.

This is no less true when God uses natural forces to accomplish a task, with the miracle being in the intensity and timing of those forces. For example, consider how God uses the wind in the verse before us. We experience wind almost daily as a natural, nonmiraculous force of nature that God has put in place for the normal functioning of the world. The miraculous element here is in the intensity and duration of the wind as God causes *the sea to go back by a strong east wind all that night* (compare also Exodus 10:13).

The way the text actually reads should cause healthy skepticism as we consider how Hollywood recreates accounts from the Bible. For example, Cecil B. DeMille's 1956 movie *The Ten Commandments* is inaccurate in showing the waters parting almost instantly as Charlton Heston, playing the part of Moses, raises his staff. That's not how it happened. God certainly could have done it that way, but He chose a different procedure.

The second thing to note from Exodus 14:15-20 is that the angel of God causes "the pillar of the cloud" to separate the Egyptian army from the Israelites; the result is "a cloud and darkness" to the Egyptians, but a source of light "by night" to the Israelites. This means that the Israelites can witness what is happening *all that night* while the Egyptians cannot.

22. And the children of Israel went into the midst of the sea upon the dry ground: and the waters were a wall unto them on their right hand, and on their left.

The fact that it is still night as *the children of Israel* cross *the sea upon the dry ground* is confirmed by the fact that God does not destroy the Egyptians until "the morning watch" (v. 24, below). Even though it is night, the Israelites have light to see by, as noted previously. Surely they recognize that God is indeed fighting for them (v. 14)! We take for granted that Moses leads the way into

HOW TO SAY IT

Canaan	*Kay*-nun.
Corinth	*Kor*-inth.
Egyptians	Ee-*jip*-shuns.
Etham	*E*-thum.
Pharaoh	*Fair*-o or *Fay*-roe.

the parted waters on *dry ground*; then the Israelites followed as sheep follow their shepherd (Isaiah 63:11).

As a conjecture, we might consider the possibility that God could have formed the walls of water *on their right hand, and on their left* by means of a strong jet stream of air that freezes the water as it piles up. As this happens, the seabed may become frozen mud. This theory does not contradict the fact that the text says *dry ground*. I live in Illinois, and on a cold winter's night I can walk across a field of frozen mud as dry ground since there will be no water on the bottom of my shoes after I cross. My conjecture fits well with the statement that "the depths were congealed in the heart of the sea" (Exodus 15:8).

I realize that this is my imagination at work, but it is plausible. It is also possible that the east wind is not cold and that the wind itself holds up the walls of water on both sides. The problem this theory presents is the great difficulty (if not impossibility) of the Israelites being able to walk through such a strong force of continual wind as they pass between the walls of water.

In any case, it is still a miracle! The mixed emotions of this journey between two walls of water surely include fear, excitement, joy, even helplessness. So the Israelites escape.

Point to this visual as you compare the Red Sea deliverance with our deliverance in Christ.

Visual for
Lesson 12

What Do You Think?

What characteristics of a leader will result in people following that leader? What does this tell us about Christian leadership development?

Talking Points for Your Discussion

- Regarding leaders in the church
- Regarding Christians who are leaders in business or government
- "Leaders are born" vs. "leaders are made"

B. Egyptians Pursue (v. 23)

23. And the Egyptians pursued, and went in after them to the midst of the sea, even all Pharaoh's horses, his chariots, and his horsemen.

What makes Pharaoh order his chariots and horsemen into the parted waters, clearly a frightening situation if there ever was one? It is God

fighting for Israel by hardening the hearts of the Egyptians (Exodus 14:4, 8, 17). They are remorseful for having let Israel go (v. 5). God had halted their pursuit temporarily (vv. 19, 20), but now they resume the chase. Hard hearts tend to throw caution to the wind.

C. God Fights (vv. 24, 25)

24. And it came to pass, that in the morning watch the LORD looked unto the host of the Egyptians through the pillar of fire and of the cloud, and troubled the host of the Egyptians,

There are several watches throughout the night, and *the morning watch* is the one that occurs from 2 to 6 a.m. God's divine presence is manifested by *the pillar of fire and of the cloud* as it has been before (Exodus 13:21, 22; 14:19). Ancient cultures often depict deity by a brilliant fire in the midst of clouds. It is in such a manifestation that God is presented as observing the Egyptian army and troubling them.

25. And took off their chariot wheels, that they drave them heavily: so that the Egyptians said, Let us flee from the face of Israel; for the LORD fighteth for them against the Egyptians.

Part of the troubling or confusion is accomplished by God's destroying the wheels of the chariots. If the previous conjecture regarding "frozen mud" is correct, it would be nothing for God to thaw the mud so that chariot wheels become mired, with the result that the wheels come off.

The result is panic among the charioteers. Such a result undoubtedly spreads among the rank and file of the Egyptian army, causing great confusion. Even the Egyptians are able to recognize that God is fighting for the Israelites (compare Exodus 14:14; Deuteronomy 1:30; 3:22)! The Egyptians' attempt to turn around and flee from the Israelites, now on the other side of the sea, further adds to the confusion and paralysis.

> **What Do You Think?**
>
> What battles has God fought for you? What made you realize that you needed to relinquish control and allow Him to fight that battle?
>
> *Talking Points for Your Discussion*
> - Psalms 37:7-9; 44:6, 7; 124:1-5
> - Romans 8:35-37
> - 2 Corinthians 1:8-11
> - 1 John 5:4, 5
> - Other

D. Egyptians Perish (vv. 26-28)

26. And the LORD said unto Moses, Stretch out thine hand over the sea, that the waters may come again upon the Egyptians, upon their chariots, and upon their horsemen.

God can, of course, simply speak the word and cause the waters to *come again upon the Egyptians* without any participation by Moses. But the people need to see that Moses is the leader that God has chosen, so God works through him to finish off the pursuers.

27. And Moses stretched forth his hand over the sea, and the sea returned to his strength when the morning appeared; and the Egyptians fled against it; and the LORD overthrew the Egyptians in the midst of the sea.

The phrase *when the morning appeared* again confirms that the crossing takes place at night. The Israelites can see their great deliverance unfolding. The doctrinal points of these events are clearly stated several times throughout the story: the Egyptians know (before they die!) the identity of the one true God (Exodus 14:4, 17, 18), and the Israelites acknowledge God with reverent fear and trust in Him and His servant Moses (14:13, 14, 30, 31).

> **What Do You Think?**
>
> How does your deliverance by God from past circumstances help you face the next battle?
>
> *Talking Points for Your Discussion*
> - In how you view trying circumstances (2 Kings 6:13-17)
> - In how you pray (Luke 22:42)
> - In how you help others going through difficult times (1 Peter 4:12-19)
> - Other

28. And the waters returned, and covered the chariots, and the horsemen, and all the host of Pharaoh that came into the sea after them; there remained not so much as one of them.

The fact that the returning waters are deep enough to cover *the chariots, and the horsemen, and all the host of Pharaoh* indicates that the Israelites are not crossing a shallow, marshy lake as some have proposed. Such a theory is disallowed by the fact that the army of Pharaoh at the Red Sea perishes in the manner described here.

Although there may be parts of the army left back in Egypt that did not pursue Israel, the power of Egypt is so weakened that it is no factor in Canaan until the days of the Israelite monarchy, hundreds of years later. The statement *there remained not so much as one of them* acts as a bookend with verse 13: "For the Egyptians whom ye have seen to day, ye shall see them again no more for ever."

⚜ POWER FROM ABOVE ⚜

The "Arab Spring" of 2011 led to profound changes in North Africa. Uprisings in Egypt and Libya toppled autocratic regimes in those two countries. The rebels and their Western allies used modern "from above" communication technology to coordinate efforts, as messages sent over social media via satellites, etc., brought a new level of sophistication to civil-disobedience movements.

The uprising in Libya saw another "from above" technology used in overthrowing the government: that of air power, as a combination of manned and drone aircraft assisted rebel forces. Such "from above" power proved to be decisive.

The ancient Israelites were the rebels against Pharaoh's entrenched power. That ancient tyrant discovered that he was no match for the power that came against him from above—the power of the one and only God Almighty. Modern technology is nice to have, but its presence also lends itself to a certain danger: the danger of relying on it to the exclusion of the ultimate power from above. Think back to the day before you read this lesson. How much time did you spend in prayer in comparison with the amount of time you spent fiddling with the various high-tech gadgets on which we all rely so much?   —C. R. B.

III. Victorious Resolution
(EXODUS 14:29, 30)

A. Summary of Deliverance (v. 29)

29. But the children of Israel walked upon dry land in the midst of the sea; and the waters were a wall unto them on their right hand, and on their left.

This is a repeat of verse 22 with slight variation in verbs and word order. It functions as a conclusion for this section of the story that stretches from verse 21 to verse 29.

What Do You Think?
What "Red Sea experience" are you facing right now? What will be God's part and what will be your part in the victory to come?
Talking Points for Your Discussion
- Regarding a pending confrontation
- Regarding a financial difficulty
- Regarding a difficult area of ministry
- Other

B. Evidence of Freedom (v. 30)

30. Thus the LORD saved Israel that day out of the hand of the Egyptians; and Israel saw the Egyptians dead upon the sea shore.

This is an epilogue to the story. Israel sees "the salvation of the Lord" (v. 13) as evidenced by *the Egyptians dead upon the sea shore.* The Egyptian charioteers and horsemen are no match for the divine warrior. The "Song of Moses" that follows celebrates this victory over Pharaoh's army

(see Exodus 15:1-21). The fact of this deliverance is restated often (see Deuteronomy 11:4; Joshua 2:10; 4:23; 24:6, 7; Judges 11:16; Isaiah 51:10; 63:11-13) and remembered frequently in Israel's hymns (see Psalms 66:6; 77:19, 20; 78:13, 53; 106:7, 9, 22; 114:3, 5; 136:13, 15). The result is that the Israelites fear God and trust not only Him but also Moses (Exodus 14:31, immediately following today's text). Sadly, subsequent events will show how fleeting that fear and trust to be.

Conclusion

A. Our Great Salvation

Hebrews 3 compares and contrasts the faithfulness of Moses as a servant of God with the faithfulness of Jesus as the Son of God. While Israel's deliverance from slavery was great, the Christian's salvation from sin is far greater. The apostle Paul uses the exodus event to warn his readers in Corinth by comparing their status in Christ with Israel's baptism unto Moses (1 Corinthians 10:1, 2). Because of the Israelites' subsequent unfaithfulness, they were condemned to die in the wilderness (v. 5). In spite of our baptism into Christ, we may suffer the same condemnation if we prove to be unfaithful (vv. 6-12).

We must show gratitude for our great salvation in Jesus Christ. We do this by obedience to Christ's law of love. We must not be as the generation that left Egypt after witnessing the miracles of the plagues only to express doubt, fear, and sarcasm as the pursuing army approached (Exodus 14:10-12). "Now all these things happened unto them for ensamples: and they are written for our admonition, upon whom the ends of the world are come" (1 Corinthians 10:11).

B. Prayer

Our Father, we praise You for the great salvation we have in Christ. May we never take Your grace for granted or cheapen it by shallow discipleship. Help us to keep our eyes on the promised eternal life. Till Jesus comes, amen.

C. Thought to Remember
Expect God's deliverance.

INVOLVEMENT LEARNING

Some of the activities below are also found in the helpful student book, Adult Bible Class.
Don't forget to download the free reproducible page from www.standardlesson.com to enhance your lesson!

Into the Lesson

Option: Place in chairs copies of the "Egyptians Fall, Part 2" exercise from the reproducible page, which you can download. Learners can begin working on this as they arrive. (*Alternative:* Distribute this at the end of class as a take-home activity.)

Prepare two small posters, each featuring the word *water*. Affix these to the door frame of your learning area, one poster on each side. As class begins, ask, "Will someone please explain the symbolism of our entrance today?" The symbolism, of course, relates to Israel's passing between the walls of water in today's text.

Say, "Last week's lesson was about a *passing over*, while this week's study is about a *passing through*. This was a real 'sight to see' for the ancient Israelites, and it will be for us as well."

Into the Word

To continue with the "sight to see" theme, say, "I have something for you to see: signs . . . not miraculous ones, but ones you might see along the way of life. See if you can associate them with an idea or verse from the text." Reveal the signs below in sequence. The signs can be simple words on sheets of paper, but making these appear as road signs will enhance their visual appeal. After revealing a sign, pause for associations with the text; expected responses are noted.

Dead End—The Israelites' feeling of being trapped.

Danger—The threat from Pharaoh's finest warriors.

Warning: High Wind—The strong, all-night wind to move the waters where God wanted them.

Warning: Severe Tire Damage—The destruction of Pharaoh's chariots.

Enter at Your Own Risk—Pharaoh's sending his army after the Israelites.

Water Unsafe for Swimming—The drownings that occurred.

Exit—God's deliverance.

Littering Permitted—The littering of the shoreline with the dead.

Scenic Overlook—Seeing the results of God's intervention.

One Way—The path of obedience and trust.

No U-Turn Allowed—The futility of the Egyptians' attempted retreat.

As learners respond, offer additional commentary as appropriate.

Alternative: If you wish to use small groups, distribute handouts titled *What a Sight to See . . . and Not See!* Have several blank lines below the title. Say, "In Exodus 14:13, God promises a sight to see and a sight never to be seen again. What are those two sights?" (*Answers: deliverance would be seen; pursuing Egyptians would not be seen again.*) Then say, "Read through today's text plus verses 15-20. As you do, make a list of what you would have seen if you had been one of the escaping Israelites."

Into Life

Say, "The deliverance of the Israelites prompted praise in song (Exodus 15, not in today's text). What are some of your favorite songs or hymns that express your praise in Jesus' deliverance from sin?" Encourage a time of unstructured sharing.

Alternative: Invite one of your musically talented learners to lead the class in a song, hymn, or chorus that speaks of the joy of our salvation in Christ (examples: "There Is Power in the Blood," "Redeemed," and "Shout to the North.")

Say, "Immediately following the events in today's text, Moses led the Israelites in a song of joyous praise (Exodus 15:1-18). Our salvation in Jesus should always elicit this kind of praise." Distribute copies of the "A Time to Sing" activity from the reproducible page for learners to use in their devotional times in the week ahead.

BEGINNING OF THE TABERNACLE

DEVOTIONAL READING: Hebrews 9:11-15
BACKGROUND SCRIPTURE: Exodus 35–40

EXODUS 40:16-30, 34, 38

16 Thus did Moses: according to all that the LORD commanded him, so did he.

17 And it came to pass in the first month in the second year, on the first day of the month, that the tabernacle was reared up.

18 And Moses reared up the tabernacle, and fastened his sockets, and set up the boards thereof, and put in the bars thereof, and reared up his pillars.

19 And he spread abroad the tent over the tabernacle, and put the covering of the tent above upon it; as the LORD commanded Moses.

20 And he took and put the testimony into the ark, and set the staves on the ark, and put the mercy seat above upon the ark:

21 And he brought the ark into the tabernacle, and set up the vail of the covering, and covered the ark of the testimony; as the LORD commanded Moses.

22 And he put the table in the tent of the congregation, upon the side of the tabernacle northward, without the vail.

23 And he set the bread in order upon it before the LORD; as the LORD had commanded Moses.

24 And he put the candlestick in the tent of the congregation, over against the table, on the side of the tabernacle southward.

25 And he lighted the lamps before the LORD; as the LORD commanded Moses.

26 And he put the golden altar in the tent of the congregation before the vail:

27 And he burnt sweet incense thereon; as the LORD commanded Moses.

28 And he set up the hanging at the door of the tabernacle.

29 And he put the altar of burnt offering by the door of the tabernacle of the tent of the congregation, and offered upon it the burnt offering and the meat offering; as the LORD commanded Moses.

30 And he set the laver between the tent of the congregation and the altar, and put water there, to wash withal.

· ·

34 Then a cloud covered the tent of the congregation, and the glory of the LORD filled the tabernacle.

· ·

38 For the cloud of the LORD was upon the tabernacle by day, and fire was on it by night, in the sight of all the house of Israel, throughout all their journeys.

KEY VERSE

The cloud of the LORD was upon the tabernacle by day, and fire was on it by night, in the sight of all the house of Israel, throughout all their journeys. —**Exodus 40:38**

FIRST THINGS

Unit 3: First Freedom

LESSONS 10–13

LESSON AIMS

After participating in this lesson, each student will be able to:

1. Match the tabernacle's furnishings with their functions.

2. Compare and contrast God's presence in the tabernacle with His presence in the temple in Jerusalem, in Jesus, in the church, and in the individual Christian.

3. Demonstrate God's presence in his or her life in a concrete way in the week ahead.

LESSON OUTLINE

Introduction
  A. Building My Tabernacle
  B. Lesson Background
  I. Constructing the Tabernacle (Exodus 40: 16-19)
    A. Obedience of Moses (v. 16)
      Doing It God's Way
    B. Date of Completion (v. 17)
    C. Structure of the Sanctuary (vv. 18, 19)
  II. Furnishing the Tabernacle (Exodus 40: 20-30)
    A. The Holy of Holies (vv. 20, 21)
    B. The Tent of Meeting (vv. 22-28)
    C. The Courtyard (vv. 29, 30)
      Building the Building and the Body
  III. Presence at the Tabernacle (Exodus 40: 34, 38)
    A. Cloud and Glory (v. 34)
    B. Cloud and Fire (v. 38)
Conclusion
  A. Living in God's Presence
  B. Prayer
  C. Thought to Remember

Introduction

A. Building My Tabernacle

One of the great experiences in my childhood was the opportunity to construct a model tabernacle in Vacation Bible School, using a kit from Standard Publishing. It was the mid-1950s, and I was in the fifth grade. My VBS group was taught by the preacher, and he led us in a weeklong Bible study (mostly from Exodus 25–40) of the tabernacle and its furnishings. I remember using gold, silver, and copper paint during craft time to cover the posts and bases of our model.

I felt like I was building something special, so I was aggravated when my friend Doug was sloppy with the paint. It seemed that he couldn't have cared less about how the model tabernacle looked. I was disappointed at the end result because "it just wasn't right." But when we had our closing program in the evening, I was surprised when I saw our project displayed. It was perfect! Only later did I learn that our teacher had busied himself that afternoon repainting and touching up. Of course, we boys took the credit in front of our parents and the congregation, but secretly we knew who had made the model tabernacle look so good.

I don't remember much about our lessons that week, but I still remember the experience of building the tabernacle. It made me think more deeply about God's presence. Our lesson today has something to teach us in that regard.

B. Lesson Background

Ancient Israel's tabernacle can be thought of as a portable temple. Exodus 40 is a conclusion to all the instructions regarding the tabernacle proper (Exodus 25–31) and how it was built (Exodus 35–39). We may call these multichapter sections "the two narratives of the tabernacle." Exodus 40:1-11 parallels the *in*struction narrative of Exodus 25–31, while Exodus 40:16-33 parallels the *constr*uction narrative of Exodus 35–39. Exodus 40:12-15 is not exactly a parallel; it deals with Aaron (Moses' brother) and his sons, about whom details are given in Exodus 28, 29 and Leviticus 8:1-13.

The golden calf story of Exodus 32–34 has been placed between the two narratives of the tabernacle. Knowing the reason for this deliberate placement helps us appreciate more fully the tabernacle's purpose.

Moses' delay on the mountain (Exodus 32:1) resulted in the Israelites becoming anxious, so they expressed to Aaron a desire to have a visible representation of deity ("gods"). Previously, the people had been very afraid even to listen to God lest they die, and they had implored Moses to intercede (see Exodus 20:18-20; Deuteronomy 5:23-27). What the people demanded of Aaron was a material, visible entity to substitute for Moses' intercession between them and the presence of the invisible God. Exodus 32–34 therefore represents false worship as God was, in effect, put back into nature in the form of a calf. By contrast, the tabernacle and its furnishings represented true worship where God's presence was rightly displayed.

I. Constructing the Tabernacle
(Exodus 40:16-19)

A. Obedience of Moses (v. 16)

16. Thus did Moses: according to all that the Lord commanded him, so did he.

At the beginning of the instructions, God had said to Moses, "let them make me a sanctuary; that I may dwell among them. According to all that I shew thee, after the pattern of the tabernacle, and the pattern of all the instruments thereof, even so shall ye make it" (Exodus 25:8, 9). Moses is to ensure that the tabernacle furnishings are made according to the instructions given to him on Mount Sinai (25:40). Moses also is to erect the tabernacle according to God's specifica-

HOW TO SAY IT

acacia	uh-*kay*-shuh.
Gabriel	*Gay*-bree-ul.
Herod	*Hair*-ud.
omnipresence	ahm-nih-**prez**-ence.
Pentecost	*Pent*-ih-kost.
shittim	shih-*teem*.
tabernacle	**tah**-burr-*nah*-kul.
Titus Flavius	*Ty*-tus *Flay*-vee-us.
Zacharias	Zack-uh-*rye*-us.

tions (26:30). The work itself is done primarily by many skilled workers (see 31:1-11; 35:4–38:23), but Moses is in charge of making sure that everything is done right.

By the time we reach the verse before us, the phrase *all that the Lord commanded him, so did he* (or a variation of it) has been repeated numerous times with regard to the tabernacle's construction. It will be repeated several more times between here and the end of the book. Moses is meticulous in his obedience.

What Do You Think?
What are some benefits of complete obedience to God? What may be the cost of such obedience?
Talking Points for Your Discussion
- Matthew 19:27-29
- John 13:14-17
- Acts 5:27-29, 40, 41
- James 1:25
- Other

❧ DOING IT GOD'S WAY ❧

Most of us have a stubborn streak. We like to do things a certain way, and we also prefer that others do things the way we want them done. Frank Sinatra's famous song "My Way" echoes this kind of stubborn individualism.

Sometimes the *my way* approach involves whole communities. For example, residents of the small village of Town Line, New York, voted in 1861 to secede from the Union, reportedly on a vote of 85 to 40. The village didn't officially end its break with the Union until a new vote was taken on January 24, 1946!

"Doing it my way" may mean having blinders on regarding the wisdom of a different course of action. It may mean ignoring the likely consequences of stubbornly pushing ahead when circumstances suggest that we would be wise to reconsider our position. If we're not careful, our stubbornness may lead us into the trap of convincing ourselves that our way "must be" God's way. That seems to have been the problem of Jesus' opponents during His ministry on earth. Do we ever repeat this error?
—C. R. B.

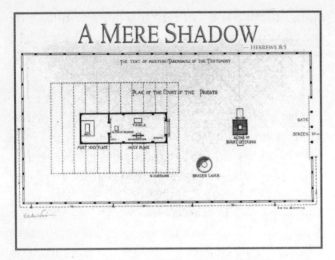

A MERE SHADOW
— HEBREWS 8:5

THE TENT OF MEETING TABERNACLE OF THE TESTIMONY

PLAN OF THE COURT OF THE PRIESTS

Visual for Lesson 13. *Point to this visual as you discuss why the tabernacle was "the example and shadow of heavenly things" (Hebrews 8:5).*

B. Date of Completion (v. 17)

17. And it came to pass in the first month in the second year, on the first day of the month, that the tabernacle was reared up.

The second year is a reference to the beginning of the exodus from Egypt. The Israelites had arrived in the wilderness of Sinai "in the third month . . . the same day" after their departure (Exodus 19:1). Therefore, the people have been in this area for 10 months by the time the tabernacle is finished. The raising of the tabernacle on the one-year anniversary of the exodus reinforces the idea that the Israelites are a distinct people. What a New Year's Day!

C. Structure of the Sanctuary (vv. 18, 19)

18. And Moses reared up the tabernacle, and fastened his sockets, and set up the boards thereof, and put in the bars thereof, and reared up his pillars.

The statement *Moses reared up the tabernacle* refers to the tabernacle proper—that is, the walls (see Exodus 26:15-30; 36:20-34). For each item listed in the verse before us, we will note references both to the instructions about it (in Exodus 25–31) and to its construction (in Exodus 35–39).

The foundation of the tabernacle consists of 100 *sockets*. There are 40 for the north and south walls each (Exodus 26:18-21). There are 14 for the west (back) side with 2 additional corner sockets to make a total of 16 there (26:22-25). The

remaining 4 are used for the pillars that are discussed below.

Placed in the sockets are 48 gold-covered *boards* made of shittim (acacia) wood. Each measures 10 cubits high by 1½ cubits wide (Exodus 26:16; 36:21). There are 20 boards on the north (26:20; 36:25), 20 on the south (26:18; 36:23), 6 on the west (26:22; 36:27), and 2 corner ones (26:23; 36:28).

There are four gold-covered *bars* to hold the boards in place. The middle bar apparently goes through the boards themselves for extra stability. Separating the most holy place (the holy of holies) from the holy place is a veil that hangs on four gold-covered *pillars* (26:31-35; 36:35, 36). We note five more pillars used for the entrance to the tabernacle (26:36, 37; 36:37, 38).

19. And he spread abroad the tent over the tabernacle, and put the covering of the tent above upon it; as the LORD commanded Moses.

The tent over the tabernacle and *the covering of the tent* consist of numerous curtains (Exodus 26:7-14; 36:14-19). These are made from layers of cloth and skin. There are many artists' sketches of what these coverings may have looked like.

II. Furnishing the Tabernacle
(EXODUS 40:20-30)

A. The Holy of Holies (vv. 20, 21)

20. And he took and put the testimony into the ark, and set the staves on the ark, and put the mercy seat above upon the ark.

The ark of the testimony (Exodus 25:10-22; 37:1-9) is the focal point of the tabernacle because it is the exact location for God's presence and revelation for Moses and the high priest. The special feature of the ark's covering is two cherubims molded of pure gold (25:17-22; 37:1-8).

The cherubims have wings that meet each other, and their faces look down on *the mercy seat,* the place where God will meet with Moses (Exodus 25:22; compare Numbers 7:89). The Israelites will come to envision the mercy seat to be God's "footstool," the place of His feet, while His throne is in Heaven itself (see 1 Chronicles 28:2; Psalm 99:5; 132:7; Lamentations 2:1). God establishes the sprinkling of blood on the mercy seat for forgiveness of sins (Leviticus 16:14-16). This foreshadows what Christ does for us (Hebrews 9; 1 Peter 1:2).

The testimony that is put into the ark refers to the stone tablets of the Ten Commandments. Other things will be put in later (Exodus 16:33, 34; Numbers 17:10, 11; compare Hebrews 9:4). *The staves* are used for carrying the ark since to touch the ark itself is to invite death (Exodus 37:4, 5; 25:14-16; 1 Chronicles 13:9, 10).

21. And he brought the ark into the tabernacle, and set up the vail of the covering, and covered the ark of the testimony; as the LORD commanded Moses.

The beautifully crafted *vail of the covering* is hung on four wooden pillars that are overlaid with gold and placed in silver sockets (Exodus 26:31-35; 36:35, 36); this vail (or veil) is designed to conceal *the ark of the testimony* (later known more commonly as "the ark of the covenant" per Numbers 10:33; etc.) from the priests. Only once a year will the high priest be allowed to enter into the holy of holies (Leviticus 16). Jesus' death and atonement for our sins has enabled every believer to enter into God's presence today; the veil has been torn asunder (see Matthew 27:51; Mark 15:38; Hebrews 9:11-14; 10:19-25; and 1 Peter 3:18).

What Do You Think?
  Thinking of the veil or curtain that Christ tore down in Mark 15:38, how can we ensure that we do not put up veils that may hinder relationships (ours or others') with God?
Talking Points for Your Discussion
  ▪ Veils of wrong priorities
  ▪ Veils of traditions
  ▪ Veils of legalism
  ▪ Other

B. The Tent of Meeting (vv. 22-28)

22, 23. And he put the table in the tent of the congregation, upon the side of the tabernacle northward, without the vail. And he set the bread in order upon it before the LORD; as the LORD had commanded Moses.

The table in the tent of the congregation, located on the north side of the holy place (Exodus 25:23-30; 37:10-16), is primarily for the "shewbread."

This consists of 12 cakes made of "fine flour," each cake representing a tribe (Leviticus 24:5-7). That is the reference of *set the bread in order.*

The bread represents God's provision in the wilderness. It is to be replaced every Sabbath with fresh bread (Leviticus 24:8). Only priests are allowed eat this bread and only in the holy place (Leviticus 24:9; see an exception in 1 Samuel 21:4; compare Matthew 12:3, 4). The table also includes utensils for wine and drink offerings (Exodus 37:16).

24, 25. And he put the candlestick in the tent of the congregation, over against the table, on the side of the tabernacle southward. And he lighted the lamps before the LORD; as the LORD commanded Moses.

The candlestick is made from a solid piece of gold; it is hammered out so that the candlestick rises from a base to form a middle stem with three branches on each side, modeled as a flowering almond tree (Exodus 25:31-36; 37:17-24). Thus, there are seven oil-filled bowls that provide light in the tabernacle (25:37; 27:20, 21).

The candlestick is probably about three and a half feet tall. (There is a depiction of it carved into the Arch of Triumph in Rome; the carving depicts the successful conclusion of the siege of Jerusalem by Titus Flavius in AD 70.) The candlestick is located on the south side, opposite the table of the shewbread.

What Do You Think?
  What do you need to do to make sure that Christ continues to be the candlestick or lamp that lights your way?
Talking Points for Your Discussion
  ▪ Psalm 119:105
  ▪ 1 John 1:7
  ▪ Revelation 1:12, 13

26, 27. And he put the golden altar in the tent of the congregation before the vail: and he burnt sweet incense thereon; as the LORD commanded Moses.

The golden altar is for burning incense; it is not to be used for burnt offerings (Exodus 30:1-10; compare 37:25-28). It is placed *before the vail,* behind which stands the ark of the covenant. The aroma of *sweet incense* wafts into the holy of holies to represent the prayers of the people rising into God's presence (see Exodus 30:34; compare Psalm 141:2; Revelation 5:8). Once per year, the high priest anoints the horns of this altar with blood for the atonement of the people (Exodus 30:10; Leviticus 16:18). This altar is part of the setting of Gabriel's appearance to Zacharias in Luke 1.

28. And he set up the hanging at the door of the tabernacle.

The curtain *at the door of the tabernacle* is similar in construction to the inner veil (Exodus 26:36; 36:37). This curtain hangs on five golden pillars. But unlike the four pillars for the veil set in silver sockets, the sockets for this entrance curtain are covered with brass (26:37; 36:38). This is probably because they can be seen from outside and so are considered part of the brass items in the courtyard (38:2-6; etc.).

What Do You Think?
What does the quality and particularity of the tabernacle furnishings have to say about how we should furnish church buildings, if anything?
Talking Points for Your Discussion
- Cost vs. value
- "'The best' is the enemy of 'good enough'"
- Matthew 26:8-13

C. The Courtyard (vv. 29, 30)

29. And he put the altar of burnt offering by the door of the tabernacle of the tent of the congregation, and offered upon it the burnt offering and the meat offering; as the LORD commanded Moses.

The altar of burnt offering is sometimes called "the brasen altar" (Exodus 38:30; 39:39; etc.). The sacrifices to be placed on it are described in Leviticus 1:1–7:38.

The horns of this altar (Exodus 27:2; 38:2) are sacred, and sinners can flee to them to avoid punishment. Others will flee to these horns in hopes of forgiveness or compassion from earthly enemies (see 1 Kings 1:50-53; 2:28-34). This altar foreshadows Christ, who is our perfect sacrifice and the altar for our redemption (see Hebrews 9:11-15).

30. And he set the laver between the tent of the congregation and the altar, and put water there, to wash withal.

The laver is a large bowl with a stand, both of brass (Exodus 30:17-21). These are made from "the lookingglasses of the women assembling . . . at the door of the tabernacle of the congregation" (38:8). These brass mirrors, highly polished and beautiful, were probably procured from the Egyptians during the exodus (12:35, 36).

The priests have to be "clean" each time they enter the tabernacle or offer sacrifices, so this laver is for washing in that regard. The penalty for priests not washing their feet and hands is death (Exodus 30:20, 21)! So the altar and laver go together (compare Ephesians 5:26; Titus 3:5).

❧ BUILDING THE BUILDING AND THE BODY ❧

Church building programs can be exciting experiences. Ideally, the process will unite the congregation in joyfully completing the task. But some congregations find the process to be a source of strife. In one church, the men on the board —good businessmen with good hearts—made fiscally responsible decisions on some aesthetic matters that aroused the ire of the artistically minded women of the church. In another church, the battle over the color of the carpet in the women's lounge caused several families to leave!

The source of such conflicts may be as simple as was stated by one combatant: "If this church is being built with my money, then I'm going to have a say in how it is built!" Danger looms when such a cantankerous spirit presents itself, and the damage can be significant.

Moses had lots of challenges in dealing with a fickle people, but dealing with a building committee was not one of them. God himself decided the sizes, shapes, colors, and materials of the tabernacle's architecture and furnishings. As for the building fund, the Egyptians had made a major contribution! Whether we are building a church building or the body of Christ, the continuous challenge is to keep our focus on what the divine architect, the master builder, would have us do. That's really the only way to keep our personal preferences in check.

—C. R. B.

III. Presence at the Tabernacle
(Exodus 40:34, 38)
A. Cloud and Glory (v. 34)

34. Then a cloud covered the tent of the congregation, and the glory of the Lord filled the tabernacle.

Although God is everywhere, He chooses to dwell among His people in a tent in a special way. No tent or temple can contain the Creator God, of course (Acts 17:24). But the purpose of the tabernacle is to have a symbol of God's presence. So after Moses sets up the tabernacle and consecrates it with oil, God manifests himself in a cloud that envelopes the tent, and thus His glory fills the tabernacle. God's divine presence is in the midst of His people, and His people can see it!

The parallel between this scene and the cloud and glory on Mount Sinai (Exodus 24:15-18) should encourage the people. God now moves the manifestation of His presence from Sinai to be with them on their journey (compare 13:21, 22; 14:19, 24; 16:10; 33:9, 10, 22; 34:5). This idea will develop more fully as time passes.

B. Cloud and Fire (v. 38)

38. For the cloud of the Lord was upon the tabernacle by day, and fire was on it by night, in the sight of all the house of Israel, throughout all their journeys.

In the fire and cloud hovering over the tabernacle, the Israelites have a visible, awe-inspiring symbol of God's presence in their midst. No one can deny it. All they can do is follow it. God is on a journey with His people and His people with Him (see Numbers 9:15-23; 10:11-28).

What Do You Think?

What "visual aids" have you found to be helpful reminders that Jesus is leading you on your journey?

Talking Points for Your Discussion
- Artwork displayed year round in your home
- Seasonal displays in your home
- The elements of the Lord's Supper
- Other

Conclusion
A. Living in God's Presence

Sin in the Garden of Eden resulted in humanity's losing the privilege of living in God's presence. But God has acted to reverse that situation. Freed from Egyptian bondage, Israel had God's presence in her midst by means of the tabernacle. Instead of cherubims turning away God's children by means of a sharp sword to guard the way to the tree of life (Genesis 3:24), the Israelites had images of cherubims marking the place of God's presence. Perhaps the candlestick stood for the tree of life as it illuminated the holy place.

The manifestation of God's presence was experienced anew when Solomon dedicated the temple (see 1 Kings 8:1–9:9; 2 Chronicles 7). That temple was destroyed in 586 BC because of sin. Rebuilt by the returned exiles, the temple was later enhanced by Herod the Great. Standing in its courts, Jesus declared himself to be the true temple (John 2:19-21; compare Mark 14:58). The apostle John declared "the Word was made flesh, and dwelt [literally, "tabernacled"] among us, (and we beheld his glory, the glory as of the only begotten of the Father,) full of grace and truth" (John 1:14). That was Jesus.

God made His presence known again on the Day of Pentecost. The result was the new temple described in 2 Corinthians 6:16 (see also 1 Corinthians 3:16, 17; Ephesians 2:19-22). Christ is the eternal high priest and the perfect sacrifice in an everlasting tabernacle (Hebrews 8:1–10:18). Today all Christians have access to the most holy place (Hebrews 10:19-22). In the new Jerusalem there will be no temple, for "the Lord God Almighty and the Lamb are the temple of it" (Revelation 21:22). Our future is to live in God's immediate presence forever!

B. Prayer

Our Father, help us realize Your presence as we worship. May we ever see our body of believers as Your dwelling place. In Jesus' name, amen.

C. Thought To Remember

Recognize and value God's presence in your life.

INVOLVEMENT LEARNING

Some of the activities below are also found in the helpful student book, Adult Bible Class.
Don't forget to download the free reproducible page from www.standardlesson.com to enhance your lesson!

Into the Lesson

Put the word *GOD* in bold lettering on eight or so index cards. Affix these cards randomly and conspicuously around your classroom; if your learning space has a window, be sure to put one on it (to represent His presence "out there" as well as "in here"). Save one to affix to yourself, ideally inside a coat or even lapel, to represent God's presence within the Christian.

As class begins, ask, "What are we talking about when we speak of God's omnipresence?" *(Expected response: "God is present everywhere.")* Indicate that your signs are a feeble way to represent God's presence at all times in all places. Point to the label you have put on yourself and say, "God lives especially within those who are committed to His will."

Note that today's study from Exodus 40 is a story of God's manifested presence in a special place and for a special time: the tabernacle of the not-yet-settled nation of Israel.

Into the Word

Distribute copies of the matching quiz below as a pretest. Say, "With Bibles closed, see if you can match each numbered item with its function for the tabernacle. When you finish, we'll go over the results as a class."

Items: 1. altar of burnt offerings; 2. ark; 3. boards; 4. candlestick; 5. golden altar; 6. laver; 7. staves; 8. table; 9. vail (or veil). ***Functions:*** A. for carrying the ark of the testimony; B. for ceremonial washing of hands and feet; C. for sacrifices; D. for the framework of the tabernacle; E. for separating the holy place from the most holy place; F. to burn incense; G. to hold lamps; H. to hold the bread; I. to hold the testimony and serve as a base for the mercy seat. *Answers: 1-C (v. 29); 2-I (v. 20); 3-D (v. 18); 4-G (vv. 24, 25); 5-F (vv. 26, 27); 6-B (v. 30); 7-A (v. 20); 8-H (vv. 22, 23); 9-E (vv. 21, 22, 26).*

Before going over the results, have three learners alternate reading the verses of Exodus 40:16-30 of today's text aloud (do not read verses 34 and 38 yet), then check responses. Lead your learners on an in-depth study of the temple furnishings and their functions by examining fuller explanations in the earlier chapters of Exodus (see the commentary for the cross-references). This will lay the foundation for discussing the climactic events of verses 34 and 38.

Read Exodus 40:34, 38 aloud. Compare and contrast the description of God's presence in these two verses with those of Exodus 19:16-20; 24:15-18; 1 Kings 8:1–9:9; 2 Chronicles 7; Acts 2:1-4; and/or Hebrews 12:18-24.

Into Life

Option 1: Distribute copies of the "'On the Go' Worship" activity from the reproducible page, which you can download. Have learners work on this in pairs or small groups. Stress that the questions need not all be dealt with nor need they be addressed in the sequence listed; learners are free to focus on only one or two questions that they find to be particularly convicting.

Option 2: Distribute copies of the "As the Lord Commanded" activity from the reproducible page; have learners work on this in pairs. Stress that this is not an exercise in "patting ourselves on the back" (see Luke 17:10). Rather, the idea is to remind us that Moses is a good model to emulate.

Option 3: Distribute peel-and-stick labels, and ask each learner to write *Feet on the Concrete* on his or hers. Say, "Take this home and post it where you will see it frequently in the week ahead. Each time you see it, let it remind you of this basic truth: 'God's presence is a concrete truth; that's where I stand; that's where I walk.' Let this truth encourage you to decide, 'I want to demonstrate my awareness of His presence in all that I do—and don't do—this week.'"

JESUS AND THE JUST REIGN OF GOD

Special Features

Lessons

Unit 1: God Sends Jesus

Unit 2: Jesus Ushers in the Reign of God

Unit 3: Live Justly in the Reign of God

QUARTERLY QUIZ

Use these questions as a pretest or as a review. The answers are on page iv of This Quarter in the Word.

Lesson 1
1. The angel Gabriel appeared to Mary in a city called _____. *Luke 1:26*
2. Mary's first reaction to the angel's greeting was one of joy. T/F. *Luke 1:29*

Lesson 2
1. Mary said that future generations would call her _____. *Luke 1:48*
2. Mary noted that God scatters the proud in the imagination of their what? (plans, minds, hearts?) *Luke 1:51*

Lesson 3
1. The name of the father of John the Baptist was _____. *Luke 1:67*
2. The birth of John the Baptist was seen as a sign that the Lord was raising a horn of what? (salvation, plenty, attack?) *Luke 1:69*

Lesson 4
1. Who was the Roman emperor when Jesus was born? (Augustus, Claudius, Nero?) *Luke 2:1*
2. The newborn Jesus was laid in a feeding trough that the Bible calls a _____. *Luke 2:7*

Lesson 5
1. It was revealed to Simeon that he would not die before he saw the Lord's _____. *Luke 2:26*
2. Anna the prophetess was from the tribe of Judah. T/F. *Luke 2:36*

Lesson 6
1. Jesus taught that He was the _____ of the Sabbath. *Luke 6:5*
2. Jesus healed the man with the deformed hand with a simple touch. T/F. *Luke 6:10*

Lesson 7
1. Jesus prayed "all night" before choosing His 12 apostles. T/F. *Luke 6:12*

2. Jesus surprised His audience when He taught that they should love their _____. *Luke 6:27*

Lesson 8
1. Jesus advised that one should try for the best seat when at a banquet. T/F. *Luke 14:8*
2. According to Jesus, if we humble ourselves, we will be _____. *Luke 14:11*

Lesson 9
1. What did the dogs do to Lazarus? (licked his sores, bit him, stole his bread crumbs?) *Luke 16:21*
2. After his death and while in torment, the rich man talks to _____. *Luke 16:24*

Lesson 10
1. According to James, receiving the engrafted Word will save our souls. T/F. *James 1:21*
2. James teaches that if we do not control our _____, our religion is worthless. *James 1:26*

Lesson 11
1. James states that is it OK to prefer rich folks over poor folks in the church. T/F. *James 2:2-4*
2. What does James call the command "Thou shalt love thy neighbour as thyself"? (golden rule, royal law, key to the Scriptures?) *James 2:8*

Lesson 12
1. Which woman is named by James to demonstrate being justified by works? (Bathsheba, Rachel, Rahab?) *James 2:25*
2. Faith without _____ is dead. *James 2:26*

Lesson 13
1. What does James call those who control their speech? (perfect, disciplined, patient?) *James 3:2*
2. James indicates that many people are successful in taming their tongues. T/F. *James 3:8*
3. The uncontrolled tongue is full of deadly _____. *James 3:8*

by Mark S. Krause

WE ALL HAVE suffered injustice, whether big or small. Perhaps we were overcharged for a car repair. Maybe we were punished for something we didn't do. Possibly we received a raw deal in the legal system. We move on, but we still want justice. We want fairness. We want evildoers, crooks, and cheats to be thwarted and punished. We don't want to wait, and we quickly quote the maxim "justice delayed is justice denied."

The Old Testament throbs with calls for justice. God desires justice more than sacrifice (Proverbs 21:3). King David famously counseled, "He that ruleth over men must be just" (2 Samuel 23:3). Amos thundered, "Let judgment run down as waters" (Amos 5:24). Yet the Old Testament also confronts us with an ongoing sense of justice denied, of justice perverted and delayed (example: Habakkuk 1:4). The prophets look forward to God's acting in a mighty way to bring true justice to the earth (see Isaiah 9:7).

God's justice is the underlying theme of this quarter's lessons from a New Testament perspective. **Unit 1: "God Sends Jesus"** features the text of the four great songs from the beginning of Luke's Gospel. The first of these is Mary's song of praise after learning of her miraculous pregnancy, sometimes called the "Magnificat" (Luke 1:46-55). The second is that of Zacharias (the father of John the Baptist), traditionally called the "Benedictus" (1:68-79). The third is the song of the angels to the shepherds of Bethlehem, the "Gloria in Excelsis" (2:14). The fourth is the song of praise and gratitude given by Simeon in the temple upon encountering the baby Jesus. It has been called the "Nunc Dimittis" (2:29-32).

In all four of these, there is an awareness of a righteous God acting to restore justice in Israel and the world. Mary celebrates her future son as the one who would bring down the proud and lift up the lowly (Luke 1:52), thus restoring a just society. Zacharias speaks of the Lord's providing a Savior to deliver the people from their enemies (1:69-71), thus giving them justice. The angels speak of a lasting peace on earth (2:14), a world peace where justice prevails. Simeon sees the baby as God's salvation, both to Israel and the other nations (2:30, 32), inaugurating God's reign of peace and justice throughout the earth.

But then (as now), the establishment of justice and peace is met with resistance. There are always those who profit from injustice, who thrive in a corrupt system, whether political, moral, or religious. **Unit 2: "Jesus Ushers in the Reign of God"** offers examples of Jesus' battling for justice as He overturns oppressive Sabbath traditions, calls for inclusion of the disenfranchised, and teaches a parable about a reversal of fortunes in eternity.

Finally, **Unit 3: "Live Justly in the Reign of God"** gives us a peek at the first-century church's struggle to implement the lessons of a just community as envisaged by Jesus. His church is to be blind to rank and privilege, a place where we all love our neighbors as we love ourselves. James calls this principle the "royal law" (James 2:8), the king of all rules for righteous living. Our call to jus-

> *We must remember that our salvation in Jesus is . . . justice diverted.*

tice is on the personal level, actualized in how we treat others.

For the Christian, justice is not merely a matter of the legal system and civic rights. Justice must begin with us, each of us individually. We must remember that our salvation in Jesus is neither justice denied nor justice delayed. It is, rather, *justice diverted* as Jesus willingly took the penalty of our sins upon himself. Since we have been declared righteous in this way, should we not show mercy to others?

Get the Setting

by Lloyd M. Pelfrey

The Bible says that Jesus came at exactly the right time (Galatians 4:4). An examination of history shows several key factors coming together to make this so. These factors are impressive individually, but their cumulative impact shows that Jesus' birth really did come at the right time.

On Earth, Peace

The heavenly multitude announced peace on earth to the shepherds. In a sense, that was not anything new, for similar proclamations had been made on previous occasions by Caesar Augustus, the Roman emperor at the time. (That's a depiction of him below; see Luke 2:1.)

Augustus first proclaimed peace in 29 BC, after he defeated Marc Antony and Cleopatra in 31 BC to end a civil war. A special ceremony was held at the temple of Janus, the two-headed god from which we get the word *January*. This temple had two doors or gates, with the statue of Janus situated between them. When the doors were open, it meant that Rome was at war. When the doors were shut, Rome was at peace. The fact that Augustus closed the gates three times indicated the restoration of peace after war had erupted.

The larger period of this Roman Peace (*Pax Romana* in Latin) lasted about 200 years, with minor uprisings quickly subdued. This period of peace meant that Joseph and Mary could travel in relative safety to Bethlehem, to Egypt, and back to Nazareth. Several decades later, this peace meant the same thing for the apostles and others as they took the gospel throughout the Roman Empire.

We keep in mind, however, that the peace announced to the shepherds was of a better kind! J. W. McGarvey observes that this was "Peace between God and man, and ultimately peace between man and man . . . his peace comes upon those who have accepted his Son."

Roman Roads

The roads of the Roman Empire were marvels of engineering, with portions still in use today. These highways were built primarily for commercial and military purposes so that trade and armies could move quickly throughout the empire. These roads also were important in helping fulfill the divine mandate to go into all the world and preach the gospel (Mark 16:15; Acts 1:8). Christ came on the scene when the transportation network of the ancient world was at its best!

Common Language

Over 500 years before Christ, Daniel prophesied that a goat from the west would conquer; that goat represented Greece (Daniel 8:5, 21). It is clear that Alexander the Great (356–323 BC) fulfilled that prophecy. He and his successors spread the Greek language far and wide.

By the time of Christ's birth, the Old Testament had been translated into Greek for the benefit of Greek-speaking Jews. The Day of Pentecost saw many languages being spoken, but the fact that the people could converse with one another about this miracle indicated the presence of a common language (Acts 2:6-12; compare John 19:20; Acts 21:37). Greek was that language, the universal language in which the New Testament was written.

Looking for the Next "Right Time"

God worked through pagan kings, ordinary people, and the rise and fall of empires to prepare for the first coming of the Lord at just the right time. We may therefore be assured that Christ's return will also be at just the right time.

THIS QUARTER IN THE WORD

Answers to the Quarterly Quiz on page 114

Lesson 1—1. Nazareth. 2. false. **Lesson 2**—1. blessed. 2. hearts. **Lesson 3**—1. Zacharias. 2. salvation. **Lesson 4**—1. Augustus. 2. manger. **Lesson 5**—1. Christ. 2. false. **Lesson 6**—1. Lord. 2. false. **Lesson 7**—1. true. 2. enemies. **Lesson 8**—1. false. 2. exalted. **Lesson 9**—1. licked his sores. 2. Abraham. **Lesson 10**—1. true. 2. tongues. **Lesson 11**—1. false. 2. royal law. **Lesson 12**—1. Rahab. 2. works. **Lesson 13**—1. perfect. 2. false. 3. poison.

MAP FEATURE

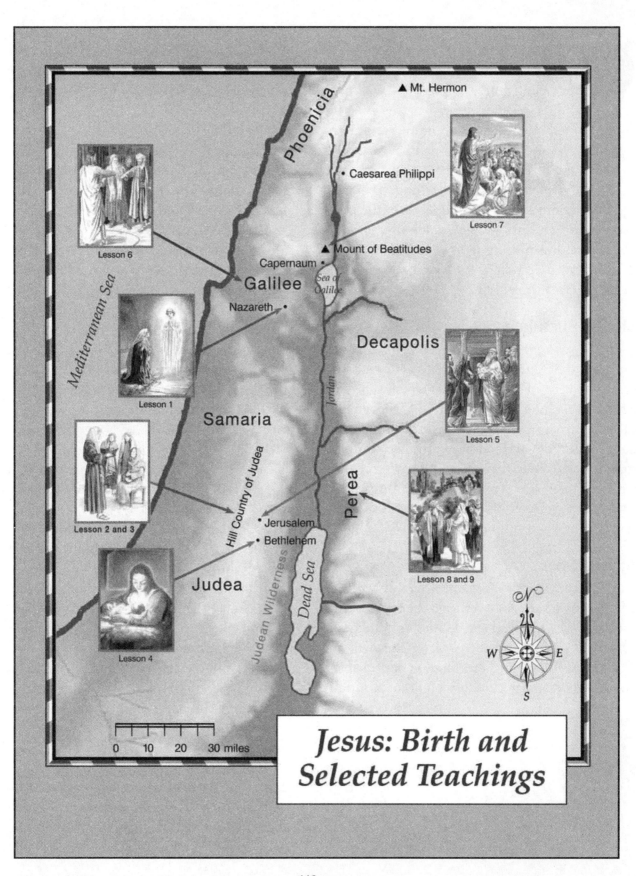

▲ Mt. Hermon

• Caesarea Philippi

Lesson 7

Phoenicia

Lesson 6

▲ Mount of Beatitudes

Capernaum •

Galilee

Sea of Galilee

Nazareth •

Mediterranean Sea

Decapolis

Lesson 1

Jordan

Lesson 5

Samaria

Hill Country of Judea

Perea

Lesson 2 and 3

• Jerusalem

• Bethlehem

Lesson 8 and 9

Judea

Judean Wilderness

Dead Sea

Lesson 4

N

W — E

S

0   10   20   30 miles

Jesus: Birth and Selected Teachings

• 119 •

YOU, THE STORYTELLER

Teacher Tips by Brent Amato

"ONCE UPON A TIME . . . ." From children to senior citizens, who hasn't been delighted and taught by a well-told story? Yet many teachers never use this effective teaching method. You can communicate or reinforce a truth by a dramatic telling of a story.

Creativity and variety are not only the spice of life but also the spice of teaching. The average teacher never gets beyond lecture (the most used and often least effective teaching method). The law of diminishing returns applies to repetitive teaching methodology. Why not surprise your learners with a story? Jesus did!

Stories Stimulate

A story can ignite the imagination and captivate both the mind and the heart. While facts and principles need to be taught and mentally grasped, effective teaching grabs much more. Storytellers call the learners to get out of their chairs in a Sunday school room and journey with them through time and space into the lives of interesting characters with interesting issues. The adventures, characters, and truths from your stories will speak in powerful ways to your learners.

Stories Stick

After teaching a variety of learners at a variety of levels in a variety of settings, I am no longer surprised at what students do and don't remember. Years, months, even weeks later, they will not recall my well-prepared presentation of principles, but they *will* remember a story I told that communicated something of value. Retention spans are precarious and almost always shorter than we teachers like to think. Here's where stories really

shine. If you've ever read, say, *The Chronicles of Narnia* by C. S. Lewis, you know firsthand the power of stories to stick.

"What stories could I tell?"

You can look to the perfect storyteller, Jesus Christ, and pick one of His stories. In fact, you will be doing just that when you get to the parables in lessons 8 and 9 of this quarter. The factual stories about Jesus are also ready-made for telling; an example is the birth narrative of Jesus in lesson 1. This story is so powerful that your learners probably already know it by heart!

You also can tell a story from your life. Pick one (serious or humorous) that relates to one of the aims for the lesson at hand, then watch your learners hang on every word. Not to be overlooked are the story illustrations that are part of the lessons in this commentary.

"But I'm not a storyteller!"

Sure you are! You've told stories to others all your life. But if storytelling doesn't come easily to you, here are some tips:

1. Write out your story and read it to the learners, being careful not be a "prisoner of the page."

2. Rehearse your story with another person, preferably someone with some drama background.

3. Gauge the length of the story to your audience so you don't "lose" them. I suggest no longer than a few minutes so that your story doesn't turn into a less interesting, less instructive monologue.

4. Ask open-ended questions about the story to involve learners in the educational process. Let them "jump on stage" in the drama of the story and try out a role.

The power of a well-told story to teach a truth cannot be overestimated. Surprise your learners with a story they weren't expecting. As you watch their minds and hearts light up, you'll know you're on your way to a great lesson!

THE ANGEL FORETELLS JESUS' BIRTH

DEVOTIONAL READING: Psalm 89:1-7
BACKGROUND SCRIPTURE: Luke 1:26-45

LUKE 1:26-40

26 And in the sixth month the angel Gabriel was sent from God unto a city of Galilee, named Nazareth,

27 To a virgin espoused to a man whose name was Joseph, of the house of David; and the virgin's name was Mary.

28 And the angel came in unto her, and said, Hail, thou that art highly favoured, the Lord is with thee: blessed art thou among women.

29 And when she saw him, she was troubled at his saying, and cast in her mind what manner of salutation this should be.

30 And the angel said unto her, Fear not, Mary: for thou hast found favour with God.

31 And, behold, thou shalt conceive in thy womb, and bring forth a son, and shalt call his name JESUS.

32 He shall be great, and shall be called the Son of the Highest: and the Lord God shall give unto him the throne of his father David:

33 And he shall reign over the house of Jacob for ever; and of his kingdom there shall be no end.

34 Then said Mary unto the angel, How shall this be, seeing I know not a man?

35 And the angel answered and said unto her, The Holy Ghost shall come upon thee, and the power of the Highest shall overshadow thee: therefore also that holy thing which shall be born of thee shall be called the Son of God.

36 And, behold, thy cousin Elisabeth, she hath also conceived a son in her old age: and this is the sixth month with her, who was called barren.

37 For with God nothing shall be impossible.

38 And Mary said, Behold the handmaid of the Lord; be it unto me according to thy word. And the angel departed from her.

39 And Mary arose in those days, and went into the hill country with haste, into a city of Juda;

40 And entered into the house of Zacharias, and saluted Elisabeth.

KEY VERSE

Behold, thou shalt conceive in thy womb, and bring forth a son, and shalt call his name JESUS.

—**Luke 1:31**

Jesus and the Just Reign of God

Unit 1: God Sends Jesus

Lessons 1–5

Lesson Aims

After participating in this lesson, each student will be able to:

1. Retell the story of the angel's announcement to Mary that she would give birth to the Son of God.

2. Explain the significance of Gabriel's statements and Mary's responses in the story's setting.

3. Write a statement of faith expressing belief in and the significance of the virgin birth.

Lesson Outline

Introduction

A. Destination Unknown

A generation ago, the "Destination Unknown" event was a staple on the church youth-group calendar. Only one or two leaders knew what the day held. The message that went out to everyone else was "Meet in the church parking lot at 9 a.m. Saturday. Wear old clothes and sturdy shoes; bring an old towel." The excitement came from the "unknown" aspect. This is what turned the ordinary into something mysterious, appealing to the teens' sense of adventure.

As we grow older, we realize that most of life is a series of "destination unknown" events. We make plans and pursue dreams, but often we end up in situations that we could not have anticipated. We sometimes wish that we could know what the future holds, hoping that such knowledge would give us an advantage.

Or perhaps we feel differently—that knowing in advance what is to happen would be overwhelming. Perhaps it is better for us not to know in advance the challenges and pressures that we will one day face. Life's "destination unknown" events compel us to trust in God. Our text today is a prime example of this truth.

B. Lesson Background: Foreign Domination

The appearance of Gabriel to Mary in today's text takes us to the cusp of the watershed moment of biblical history. We can understand it better if we keep in mind some key elements of the Bible's story line. The angelic appearance occurred when Israel was under the rule of the Roman Empire. The Romans conquered Judea in 63 BC; about 20 years later, they consolidated their power further through King Herod the Great. He was a ruthless local ruler who cooperated with Rome.

The Romans were skilled administrators, but their rule over Israel was still oppressive. Most offensive of all, the Romans were pagans—worshippers of false gods. Roman rule meant that the injustice and moral evils of that empire were sustained by allegiance to false gods who represented that evil.

The Roman Empire was not the first pagan kingdom to rule over Israel, of course. Before

Rome, the Greeks held sway during a part of the period of time between the Old and New Testaments. Before the rise of Greece, Persia was the great power. Before the Persians there were the Babylonians, and before them the Assyrians. Israel's history of being dominated by pagan empires went back many centuries.

Even so, the faithful of Israel clung to the ancient promise that God would not abandon His people. The God of all the nations of the earth had promised that He would restore His blessing to all the nations (Genesis 12:3; 18:18; 22:18). He had promised to Israel a king greater than David, a king whose throne would endure forever (2 Samuel 7:12, 13; Isaiah 9:6, 7; Jeremiah 23:5-8). Through generations, God's people held fast to their hope in God.

C. Lesson Background: Marriage Customs

An awareness of Jewish marriage customs in the biblical period will help us understand today's text. Marriages typically were arranged by families, with the input and approval of the prospective couple. Because the economy of the time was simpler, people were given responsibilities at what seems a young age to us. Thus, young women could be married as young as 13 years of age.

When a marriage was agreed to, the couple was considered legally bound, but they did not live together as husband and wife until the day of the marriage. On that day, the groom went to the bride's family's home, received his bride, and escorted her back to his family's home, where a feast of celebration was prepared. Prior to this wedding day, the groom and bride were forbidden to have sexual relations.

HOW TO SAY IT

Assyrians	Uh-*sear*-e-unz.
Babylonians	Bab-ih-*low*-nee-unz.
Gabriel	*Gay*-bree-ul.
Galilee	*Gal*-uh-lee.
Herod	*Hair*-ud.
Judea	Joo-*dee*-uh.
Nazareth	*Naz*-uh-reth.
Persians	*Per*-zhuns.
Zacharias	Zack-uh-*rye*-us.

I. Humble Setting
(LUKE 1:26-29)

A. Unremarkable Town (v. 26)

26. And in the sixth month the angel Gabriel was sent from God unto a city of Galilee, named Nazareth.

The story of Jesus' pending arrival is preceded by the announcement of John the Baptist's in Luke 1:24, 25. Both are part of the same movement of God to bring His promises to fulfillment.

Both pregnancies are announced in advance by the same angel: *Gabriel* (compare Daniel 8:16; 9:21). Jesus' birth comes after John's, since *the sixth month* here refers to the sixth month of Elisabeth's pregnancy with John. As the announcement will show, Jesus is to be far superior to John or any other person. John himself will say as much (see Luke 3:16).

Jesus' importance contrasts with the humble home of his parents. Nazareth is a small, insignificant town of low reputation (see John 1:46). It is located in Galilee, a region seen as less prestigious than Judea, where Jerusalem and the temple are found. As He has done throughout biblical history, God is at work among lowly, humble people to accomplish His purpose.

B. Unmarried Virgin (v. 27)

27. To a virgin espoused to a man whose name was Joseph, of the house of David; and the virgin's name was Mary.

We now understand the situation in which Gabriel's announcement is about to be made. The young woman, named Mary, is unmarried and has had no sexual experience. The name *Mary* is equivalent to the Old Testament name *Miriam*; that was the name of Moses' sister, who helped lead the exodus from Egypt (Exodus 15:20, 21). Mary is already *espoused* (or betrothed, engaged) to a certain man, and the two are awaiting the day of their marriage.

The man, named Joseph, is a descendant of Israel's great King David. We are reminded immediately of God's promise of a great Son of David, whose throne God has promised to establish forever (1 Chronicles 22:10).

C. Unexpected Blessing (vv. 28, 29)

28. And the angel came in unto her, and said, Hail, thou that art highly favoured, the Lord is with thee: blessed art thou among women.

The angel's words indicate that something extraordinary is about to happen. Following *hail,* a standard greeting, Mary's status as *highly favoured* indicates that she is about to receive a gift of God's grace—His favor on those who do not deserve it. Though Mary will faithfully respond to this announcement, there is no record that she is chosen by God because she is more outstanding than other young women of her time. Like all of God's human instruments, she receives God's undeserved blessing and calling. Ephesians 1:6 uses the same original-language word translated here as *highly favoured* to describe all Christians as "made us accepted."

The angel's affirmation *the Lord is with thee* reminds us of God's promise of the child whose name will be Immanuel, meaning "God with us" (Isaiah 7:14; 8:8; Matthew 1:23). It is by God's power that Mary will be used in the extraordinary way that the angel is about to announce. Through that event God will come to be with all of His people. The phrase *blessed art thou among women* is also found in Luke 1:42.

What Do You Think?

When have you seen God turn seemingly unfavorable circumstances into an advantage for His work? What does this say about how God may use you for that work?

Talking Points for Your Discussion
- Limited finances
- Limited education
- Limited physical abilities
- Other

---

29. And when she saw him, she was troubled at his saying, and cast in her mind what manner of salutation this should be.

We should not be surprised that Mary is *troubled* by what she hears. In the Bible, those to whom angels appear are commonly frightened, and with good reason (see Judges 6:22; Daniel 10:7-11; Luke 1:12).

II. Surprising Announcement
(LUKE 1:30-33)
A. Special Favor (v. 30)

30. And the angel said unto her, Fear not, Mary: for thou hast found favour with God.

The angel responds to Mary's fear with the reassurance that angels commonly give when they appear (compare Judges 6:23; Daniel 10:12; Luke 1:13). He reaffirms that he comes not with judgment, but with blessing. The word translated *favour* is the very one commonly translated "grace" in our New Testament.

B. Specific Name (v. 31)

31. And, behold, thou shalt conceive in thy womb, and bring forth a son, and shalt call his name JESUS.

Mary's blessing is to participate in the fulfillment of God's plan for the ages. But she will do so in a manner that seems entirely ordinary: by having a child. The angel instructs Mary to give her son a particular name, as is sometimes the case when God announces the pending birth of a child who will be significant in His plans (see Genesis 17:19; Isaiah 8:3; Hosea 1:2-9; Luke 1:13).

That name *Jesus* is derived from the Old Testament name *Joshua,* which itself is derived from the expression "The Lord saves." As Joshua was the leader of Israel in taking the land that God had promised, so Jesus will lead the greater fulfillment of God's promise to save.

What Do You Think?

What criteria should parents use in choosing names for their children? What improvements can Christians make in this regard?

Talking Points for Your Discussion
- Identification with a Bible character
- Inspiration from the name's meaning
- Association with a family member
- Other

C. Superior Kingdom (vv. 32, 33)

32. He shall be great, and shall be called the Son of the Highest: and the Lord God shall give unto him the throne of his father David.

The angel now gives a brief, tantalizing description of the promised son's significance. The fact that *He shall be great* indicates power, prominence, and authority belonging to a mighty ruler. *Son of the Highest* indicates a unique relationship with the one having all power: God himself. In the Old Testament, God's "son" is a term applied to the king whom God appoints (see 2 Samuel 7:12-16; 1 Chronicles 22:9, 10). Mary's child will surpass them all, as He will be a king who rules with unparalleled might because He is himself divine.

His role as king is stated again with the phrase *the throne of his father David*. The image of a throne that God establishes forever was part of the first promise made to David about his future son whom God would send (2 Samuel 7:13). This is the promise that God is now fulfilling.

33. And he shall reign over the house of Jacob for ever; and of his kingdom there shall be no end.

The description continues with terms that remind us further of the ancient promise of a great Son of David (2 Samuel 7:16; Isaiah 9:7). Israel's history is filled with kings who appeared on the scene, displayed great potential, but did not fulfill the expectations placed on them. In each case, the promised king whose throne God said He would establish forever had not yet come. But now, says the angel, that mighty king is on His way!

Surely the king whom the angel describes will challenge the power of Rome and all others who purport to rule without acknowledging God's power! But how this king will do so is to be seen, in part, in the setting of the angel's announcement: Jesus comes not to the throne room of political power, but to the humble peasant home of a young maiden.

❧ *A Humble Beginning* ❧

Abraham Lincoln was born in a log cabin, in 1809, to an uneducated farmer and his wife. The boy had only a few months of formal education in his early years. But the high principles of his father shaped his adult life significantly as he rose from lowly circumstances to become a man whom many consider the greatest of U.S. presidents. Lincoln's life demonstrates that it is foolish to judge the potential of a person by the circumstances of his or her family of origin.

Joseph and Mary were hardly the type of people of whom it would have been said, "There's a couple whose children will really amount to something." The two were poor, living in a small village far from the seats of power. But God chose them to bring His Son into the world and nurture Him to adulthood. Perhaps God saw something important in their character and spiritual qualities.

We remember that God looks at the heart as He chooses people for important tasks (1 Samuel 16:7). What does He see in you?   —C. R. B.

III. Unparalleled Explanation
(Luke 1:34-37)
A. Mary's Question (v. 34)

34. Then said Mary unto the angel, How shall this be, seeing I know not a man?

Mary understands that the conception the angel is describing will happen immediately. So of all the questions that may be swirling in her mind, one is prominent. She is unmarried, a virgin. She cannot have a child without a biological father, as everyone knows. Her statement *I know not a man* is a common, polite expression of her culture meaning, "I have not had sexual relations."

B. Angel's Response (vv. 35-37)

35. And the angel answered and said unto her, The Holy Ghost shall come upon thee, and the power of the Highest shall overshadow thee: therefore also that holy thing which shall be born of thee shall be called the Son of God.

The answer to Mary's question introduces something unprecedented: the promised child is to be conceived not by a union between a woman and man, but by the creative action of God's Holy Spirit. In keeping with the child's unique identity, He will have a unique beginning. For emphasis, the angel states twice that the child will be conceived by God's exceptional, miraculous, creative power. This one-of-a-kind action will affirm the child's one-of-a-kind status: He will be *holy*, distinctly set apart for God. The manner of His conception is fitting for one who is *the Son of God*.

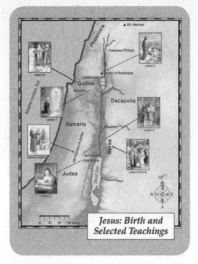

Visual for
Lessons 1 & 9

Jesus: Birth and
Selected Teachings

Post this map for the first two units of the quarter to give your learners a geographical perspective.

To understand what the angel is saying, we must understand what he does not say. The pagan world has many stories of gods who had sexual affairs with human women, fathering children through them. Those stories are very much unlike this account, for the women in those stories conceive their children by the usual sexual means, only with a supernatural person as father. Those are not stories of a virgin conceiving.

Mary, however, will conceive as a virgin because the Holy Spirit will accomplish a creative act, just as God's Spirit performed the first act of creation (Genesis 1, 2) and as God created the first man (Genesis 1:26, 27; 2:7). This marks Jesus as a person like no other, the *Son of God* in a way even greater than Adam was so designated (Luke 3:38).

36. And, behold, thy cousin Elisabeth, she hath also conceived a son in her old age: and this is the sixth month with her, who was called barren.

Throughout the account, we see parallels between the announcements of the pending arrivals of John the Baptist and Jesus. But here we see a difference: the miraculous conception of John has precedents regarding the presence of a biological father (example: Genesis 21:1-7), while the miraculous conception of Jesus does not. The God who by His creative power can give a child to an elderly, childless couple can also give a child to a virgin.

37. For with God nothing shall be impossible.

With this brief saying, the angel summarizes the whole matter. The God who called the universe into existence can do anything He chooses to do. He can cause childless couples to have children (Genesis 18:14). He can create a child within a virgin. He can welcome repentant rebels, no matter how stubbornly rebellious they have been. He can establish the reign of His Son by allowing Him to be tortured and killed. And He can raise the dead to new, everlasting life.

What Do You Think?
  What example can you give from your life of the truth of verse 37? How can you use this experience as part of your witness?
Talking Points for Your Discussion
  ▪ Physical healing
  ▪ Financial assistance
  ▪ Job opportunity
  ▪ Spiritual transformation
  ▪ Other

IV. Faithful Reaction
(LUKE 1:38-40)

A. Mary's Consent (v. 38)

38. And Mary said, Behold the handmaid of the Lord; be it unto me according to thy word. And the angel departed from her.

When promised the miracle of John's birth, the learned priest Zacharias responded with skepticism (Luke 1:18). The unlearned peasant Mary, by contrast, submits to the amazing announcement. A *handmaid* is a female slave, and with this expression Mary indicates her complete surrender to the message and mission just announced.

Mary is accepting more than we might realize at first glance. While she can be confident that her child is to be conceived miraculously, others will certainly not believe that. Even Joseph assumes that Mary must have been unfaithful (Matthew 1:18, 19). Mary willingly assumes the stigma of a seemingly illegitimate conception as she submits to the angel's announcement. The social cost of her obedience will be high. But she is willing to bear that cost, trusting that God's plan is best and right.

❧ MAKING ADJUSTMENTS ❧

A third-grade teacher had reached the limit of her patience. It seemed as though every one of her students was in a bad mood that day. So before sending them home, the teacher said, "Tomorrow, everyone come prepared to share a happy thought."

The next day came, and when it was Susie's time to share, she said, "I'm pregnant." Caught off guard, the teacher asked her to explain. Susie responded, "Last night my Mommy told my Daddy, 'I'm pregnant,' and Daddy said, 'Well, that's a happy thought!'" Little Susie obviously missed the sarcasm in her father's voice, and many a couple has faced an unplanned pregnancy with less than happy thoughts.

A pregnancy requires parents to adjust priorities. Certainly, Mary and Joseph ended up making profound adjustments in their plans for their life together (see Matthew 2:13-15). But the couple was open and available to God's plans. That's the key, isn't it, for all phases of life's journey? —C. R. B.

B. Mary's Trip (vv. 39, 40)

39, 40. And Mary arose in those days, and went into the hill country with haste, into a city of Juda; And entered into the house of Zacharias, and saluted Elisabeth.

Mary's first recorded action after the angel's departure is to travel south, uphill to a certain *city of Juda*. This trip away from home will result in a "change of scenery" where she may be able better to reflect on the momentous announcement. In going to Juda (Judea), Mary comes into the company of the one person who can best understand

her situation—her relative Elisabeth, also miraculously with child.

Conclusion

A. God's Unique Plan

Jesus' conception began the climax of God's saving plan. What God called Mary to do was unique. But the larger truth is that God consistently does His work through the seemingly weak. The child whom Mary bore was part of that pattern. Though all-powerful, He ministered among the weak and sick. Though without sin, He willingly associated with sinners (Luke 5:30-32).

We serve our mighty king not by lording it over people, but by serving them (Luke 22:25-27). We see God's kingdom advance not in the rich, powerful institutions of the world, but as the Spirit of God empowers His people from the inside. Like Mary, will we trust the God who issues the call?

B. Prayer

Lord, today we submit ourselves to You and Your power at work in us. In Jesus' name, amen.

C. Thought to Remember

Accept God's call.

VISUALS FOR THESE LESSONS

The visual pictured in each lesson (example: page 126) is a small reproduction of a large, full-color poster included in the *Adult Resources* packet for the Winter Quarter. That packet also contains the very useful *Presentation Helps* on a CD for teacher use. Order No. 020029213 from your supplier.

INVOLVEMENT LEARNING

Some of the activities below are also found in the helpful student book, Adult Bible Class.
Don't forget to download the free reproducible page from www.standardlesson.com to enhance your lesson!

Into the Lesson

Have the question *What's in a name?* displayed as learners arrive. Ask, "Do any of you know the meaning of your name?" After responses, ask, "Can some of you explain why you have the name you were given?" Expect responses that relate to family members, circumstances of birth, etc.

Alternative: Consult in advance a website such as www.babynames.com and find several names and associated meanings of members of your class. Read a meaning aloud and ask, "To whom in our class does this refer?" Do no more than six to keep this segment from dragging out.

After either alternative, relate the idea of the meaning of names to the commentary on verse 31 as a transition to the Into the Word segment.

Into the Word

Prepare handouts of the statements below. Leave space between each sentence to give learners room to correct any wrong words.

Distribute a handout and say, "If the statement is true, leave it as is. But if it is false, change or delete a word or phrase to make it correct." 1. In today's text, the angel Gabriel gave Mary and Joseph a message. 2. Mary's hometown apparently was Bethlehem. 3. Mary was pledged to be married to Joseph. 4. Mary was a virgin when Gabriel visited. 5. The first words Mary heard from the angel were, "Fear not, Mary." 6. Mary was told that she was blessed among all mankind. 7. Mary was troubled by the angel's words. 8. Mary was told that she would have a son. 9. Mary was not given the name for her unborn son. 10. Mary's son would be called "the Son of the Highest." 11. Mary's child would be given the throne of his father Abraham. 12. Mary asked how it was possible for her to have a baby since she was a virgin ("know not a man"). 13. Mary was told that the power of the Highest would overshadow her. 14. Mary's elderly relative Elisabeth had also con-

ceived and was in her seventh month. (*Answers:* 1. Delete "and Joseph." 2. Change "Bethlehem" to "Nazareth." 5. Change the words spoken to "Hail, thou that art highly favoured." 6. Change "all mankind" to "women." 9. Delete "not." 11. Change "Abraham" to "David." 14. Change "seventh" to "sixth." All other statements are true.)

To discuss the exchange between the angel Gabriel and Mary, pose the following questions, pausing for responses: 1. Why was Mary troubled by the angel's first words? 2. How did Gabriel reassure her? 3. Why might the angel's description of her future son have been overwhelming to Mary? 4. What question did Mary ask? 5. How do we know the angel was not upset with her question? 6. What information do we learn about how the baby was to be conceived? 7. Why was the information about Elisabeth good news to Mary?

Into Life

Stress to your learners that the doctrine of the virgin birth (or, more accurately, the virginal conception) is significant in Christian belief. Then write these two completion statements on the board: "I believe in the virgin birth because . . ." and "To me the virgin birth is significant because . . ." Allow several learners to respond to each statement; jot responses on the board. Suggest that learners prepare, in their times of personal devotion this week, a complete statement affirming the acceptance of God's plan for the incarnation of Jesus by means of a virgin birth. Instruct: "Make your statement a prayer of praise and submission, in the model of Mary in verse 38."

Option 1: Use the "I Believe" activity from the reproducible page, which you can download, to conclude the exercise above.

Option 2: Have learners complete the "Mary and I" activity. If you think the activity calls for responses that are too personal for class discussion, distribute copies as a take-home exercise.

MARY SINGS HER PRAISE

DEVOTIONAL READING: Psalm 111
BACKGROUND SCRIPTURE: Luke 1:46-56

LUKE 1:46-56

46 And Mary said, My soul doth magnify the Lord,

47 And my spirit hath rejoiced in God my Saviour.

48 For he hath regarded the low estate of his handmaiden: for, behold, from henceforth all generations shall call me blessed.

49 For he that is mighty hath done to me great things; and holy is his name.

50 And his mercy is on them that fear him from generation to generation.

51 He hath shewed strength with his arm; he hath scattered the proud in the imagination of their hearts.

52 He hath put down the mighty from their seats, and exalted them of low degree.

53 He hath filled the hungry with good things; and the rich he hath sent empty away.

54 He hath holpen his servant Israel, in remembrance of his mercy;

55 As he spake to our fathers, to Abraham, and to his seed for ever.

56 And Mary abode with her about three months, and returned to her own house.

KEY VERSE

Mary said, My soul doth magnify the Lord, and my spirit hath rejoiced in God my Saviour.

—Luke 1:46, 47

JESUS AND THE JUST REIGN OF GOD

Unit 1: God Sends Jesus

LESSONS 1–5

LESSON AIMS

After participating in this lesson, each student will be able to:

1. List some themes of Mary's song.

2. Explain why God's faithfulness—the source of Mary's praise—is important and foundational for people today.

3. Write a personal song of praise, like Mary's, for God's faithfulness.

LESSON OUTLINE

Introduction

A. A Christmas Musical

Many people say that their favorite movies and plays are musicals. While it may not be realistic for actors to break into song and dance in the middle of a conversation, audiences are taken up with the feelings that a song evokes.

Yet sometimes those hidden emotions actually do break out in song in real life. God's people have always expressed their love for Him, their fears about the present, their confidence in God's promises, etc., in song. From the ancient "Song of Moses" (Exodus 15) to contemporary worship compositions, the music of praise has always been part of the faith-filled life.

As befits the story of the Messiah's coming, Luke's Gospel includes four songs (or what are traditionally identified as songs) that celebrate what God did in sending His Son (1:46-55; 1:68-79; 2:14; and 2:29-32). We might say that Luke wrote the first Christmas musical! In so doing, he captured for all time the deepest feelings evoked by the momentous event of Christ's arrival. Today's lesson focuses on the first of the four songs.

B. Lesson Background

Today's text is part of the account of Mary's visit to Elisabeth, who became the mother of John the Baptist (Luke 1:39-45; see last week's lesson). Both women became mothers of children conceived by God's miraculous intervention, and both children became instrumental in fulfilling God's promises. But Mary's child was inherently superior, and so Elisabeth hailed her as "the mother of my Lord" (v. 43). The focus of attention was not on the mothers, but on their children—especially Mary's child—and what God was to accomplish through them.

Mary responded to Elisabeth's greeting with the song that is today's text. Like the Psalms and other poetry of the Old Testament, it derived its poetic qualities not from meter or rhyme, but from the expression of ideas in parallels. Two, three, or more statements follow one another to express similar concepts, creating a lyrical effect that conveys both thought and feeling.

The themes of Mary's song are familiar to readers of the Old Testament. Mary adapted traditional expressions of hope in God's promises as she reacted to God's announcement that He was about to fulfill those promises. Mary's song most closely resembles Hannah's prayer of praise after the birth of Samuel (see 1 Samuel 2:1-10).

For the Old Testament poets and prophets, the days when God would fulfill His promises lay in the uncertain future. Those poets and prophets could not say when or how God would fulfill His pledge to bless His people, restore them to himself, and make all nations His. They could only affirm God's faithfulness: if He has made a promise, then He will fulfill it—period. In times of distress, hope is to be found in God's rock-solid faithfulness.

In contrast with the Old Testament poets and prophets, Mary stood at the very threshold of fulfillment. She was pregnant with the child through whom God would act to do what He had promised. But the fulfillment of God's promise came at a cost: she was burdened with a pregnancy that appeared to all to be the result of sexual immorality. And beyond the birth of her child, she too could not say how God would go about fulfilling His pledge. Even so, she could, like the saints before her, celebrate God's faithfulness.

I. God's Great Deed
(LUKE 1:46-50)

A. Statement of Praise (vv. 46, 47)

46. And Mary said, My soul doth magnify the Lord.

Mary begins with a statement of God's greatness and her determination to acknowledge that greatness. To *magnify the Lord* is to proclaim His supreme importance and power, power that has

HOW TO SAY IT

Abraham	*Ay*-bruh-ham.
Magnificat	Mag-*nif*-ih-cot.
Messiah	Meh-*sigh*-uh.
Moses	*Mo*-zes or *Mo*-zez.
Philippians	Fih-*lip*-ee-unz.

been demonstrated in the miraculous conception of her child.

By saying that her *soul* exalts God, Mary speaks of the essence of her being—her very life or her inmost self. But by speaking of the part, she acknowledges the whole: as her soul praises, so she will act with all her being.

> *What Do You Think?*
>
> What occasion caused you to praise God more than any other? What did that experience say about what you consider most important?
>
> *Talking Points for Your Discussion*
> - Birth of a child
> - Deliverance from spiritual danger
> - Deliverance from physical danger
> - Special worship service
> - While enjoying nature
> - Other

47. And my spirit hath rejoiced in God my Saviour.

This statement stands parallel with the first one and emphasizes it by a certain repetition. God's greatness is the source of Mary's joy because God is acting as Savior—saving her and His people from the wretched condition of the world. God's greatness is manifested not just in His power, but in the way that He uses His power to save and to bless.

Mary's statement is quite powerful when we remember the circumstances in which she makes it: she is a young, pregnant, unmarried woman, and thus subject to all the scorn that comes to such a person. Yet she sees beyond that to focus on what God is doing.

B. Reasons for Praise (vv. 48-50)

48. For he hath regarded the low estate of his handmaiden: for, behold, from henceforth all generations shall call me blessed.

In identifying herself as being of *low estate*, Mary knows she has not been chosen by God because she is somehow outstanding in the way the world evaluates people. Like God's human instruments of the past, she has been chosen in her apparent insignificance. A *handmaiden* is literally a female slave, one for whom lowliness is assumed. In that regard she is like the nation of Israel when enslaved in Egypt, powerless to do anything except call on God for help.

So it is God's help to her, the blessing that God gives her in her weakness, that sets Mary apart. That blessing is not just for her but for all lowly people of all time, for she will give birth to the promised Christ. For that reason she can rightly affirm that generation after future generation will call her *blessed*—one who has received God's favor.

✵ FROM "NOBODY" TO "SOMEBODY" ✵

Steven Spielberg wanted to make movies, but he was denied admission to filmmaking school. So he started making 8mm films on his own at age 18. One day in 1965, Spielberg visited Universal Studios and had a chance meeting with Chuck Silvers, an editorial executive. Silvers liked Spielberg and invited him to come back "sometime."

Spielberg was there the next day, dressed in suit and tie and carrying his father's briefcase. He bluffed his way past the guard at the gate, found a vacant office, and put his name in plastic letters on the building's directory. For the next several months, he spent time with directors and writers, acting as if he belonged there.

The charade paid off. Ten years later, he was the director of *Jaws*, which grossed $470 million—the highest figure ever for a movie at that time. The list of Spielberg's subsequent successes is well known.

Mary was also a teenage "nobody" when her rise to fame began. But her ascendance was based on humility and integrity, not boldness and deception. This reminds us yet again that God looks at the heart in choosing people for important tasks.

—C. R. B.

49. For he that is mighty hath done to me great things; and holy is his name.

Again in parallel expression, Mary asserts that God's actions are the cause of her being blessed. She is like a slave (v. 48), but God *is mighty*. She is lowly, but the God whom she magnifies has done *great things*. To say that God's name is holy is to say that God is set apart, unlike any other. He is untouched by any form of evil, so much so that

His reputation in the world reflects this (compare Psalm 111:9).

50. And his mercy is on them that fear him from generation to generation.

Greatness is typically understood in terms of power. But Mary's song connects God's greatness to *his mercy* as well. He is the one who has the might and right to overpower and destroy all that is sinful. But out of His gracious love He offers mercy, withholding judgment as He forgives and restores those who have rebelled against Him. This has been His constant approach, but now that He has sent His Son, the basis and fulfillment of His mercy is coming to light. In all generations forward, God's mercy will prevail because of Jesus.

Mercy offered may not be mercy received, however. Mary sings that God's mercy goes to those who fear God (compare Psalm 103:13, 17). That fear means a profoundly solemn respect, a right estimate of God's greatness and one's own unworthiness. Recognizing that God is so holy and mighty and that we are so guilty and weak is what leads us to conclude that we have nothing but God's mercy on which to depend.

II. God's Great Plan
(LUKE 1:51-55)

A. To Demonstrate His Strength (v. 51)

51. He hath shewed strength with his arm; he hath scattered the proud in the imagination of their hearts.

The great drama of salvation, planned by God before creation itself, is now coming to its fulfillment. By sending His Son as a lowly child, God is paradoxically demonstrating to the world that His power is supreme. The mention of God's *arm* is a vivid word-picture of strength, not a literal description of a bodily existence for God. The arm is the means by which the warrior wields his weapons, and so God may be said figuratively to have the strongest of arms (compare Psalm 89:10).

The enemies whom the mighty, warrior God overcomes and scatters are called *the proud in the imagination of their hearts.* These are the people who live as if God were neither strong nor holy, as if God were irrelevant. Now God is demonstrating His power, showing them their true status, showing that He alone has true greatness. Ironically, He does so by sending His Son as a lowly child who becomes a lowly man who dies a lowly death. God's power is not like that of the world!

B. To Reverse the Situation (vv. 52, 53)

52. He hath put down the mighty from their seats, and exalted them of low degree.

Again in parallel fashion, Mary emphasizes that God is reversing the usual human order of things. *The mighty* are those who are powerful and impressive in the eyes of others. They have *seats* of power (what we often call "thrones"), a vivid figure of speech for the place of importance that they assume. These folks may see themselves in positions where they have no need of God. But God is now removing them from their positions, thus revealing their true status (compare Job 12:19).

By contrast, those *of low degree*—the humble and seemingly insignificant—are those whom God exalts (compare Job 5:11). Such people recognize their weakness as compared with God. The Christ who is coming into the world of Mary's day will be one of the lowly people, willingly taking lowliness on himself (compare Philippians 2:7). In so doing, He exalts all those who rightly know who they are in relation to God.

❧ *BRINGING DOWN THE MIGHTY* ❧

The "Arab Spring" of 2011 brought about the downfall of the autocratic leaders of Tunisia, Egypt, and Libya. If those leaders thought themselves to be immune from the will of the people, they found out otherwise!

History shows us that the vanity of despots can make them very reluctant to relinquish their tight control over the populace. In such cases, wealth, power, and pride form an oppressive, sometimes deadly, combination that can create the illusion of immunity. As a result, leaders feel free to do as they please, remaining accountable to no one. One need think only of Richard Nixon to realize that this kind of self-deception can occur even in democracies. Christian leaders also succumb to the power and prestige of leadership positions—remember Jim Bakker?

How different this is from our Lord! He left His place at the Father's side so that He might serve and save us (Philippians 2:5-8). In so doing, He provided us a model (see Mark 9:33-35).

—C. R. B.

What Do You Think?
  When was a time that a self-sufficient attitude interfered with your relationship with God? How did you overcome this problem?
Talking Points for Your Discussion
  - In handling finances
  - In dealing with a family problem
  - In dealing with a health issue
  - Other

53. He hath filled the hungry with good things; and the rich he hath sent empty away.

Mary has sung of the reversal of situations of the powerful and the lowly; in another parallel, she now sings of the reversal of *the rich* with *the hungry*. God has taught His people through generations that they need to depend on Him for their sustenance. He began by placing the first humans in a garden that He had prepared. Later,

Visual for Lesson 2. *Point to this visual as you ask, "How can we make Mary's song our own this Christmas season?"*

He took His people to a fruitful land that was not theirs, having freed them from slavery and provided them food and water in the desert. He still promises to feed His hungry people, to give them what they cannot supply for themselves (compare Psalm 107:9). By contrast, those who believe that they have plenty will be left unfilled. Their illusion that they already have everything they need is part of what Christ comes to destroy.

The themes of which Mary sings are important throughout Luke's Gospel. Jesus will later pronounce blessing on the poor and hungry but woe on the rich and well fed (Luke 6:20, 21, 24, 25). He will repeat that the least are the greatest in God's kingdom (9:46-48; 22:24-27). Jesus will also warn that riches put people in great peril (12:13-21; 18:18-30).

But what those texts teach is not a simple condemnation of the well-off and an exaltation of the deprived. Rather, they warn us about how we think of ourselves. Few of us probably use the words *rich* or *powerful* as self-descriptions. But on what do we rely, and where do we put our confidence? Having a measure of comfort and success can too easily give us a sense that we have everything we need, and that is the moment when we forget how much we need what God gives in Christ. If we want to be blessed by His coming, we have to understand ourselves as poor, lowly, and hungry—utterly dependent on what God gives us through Jesus.

C. To Fulfill His Promises (vv. 54, 55)

54. He hath holpen his servant Israel, in remembrance of his mercy.

What God is doing in Christ is carrying out what He has promised to His people from ancient times. Generation after generation, God gave promises to His people—to restore them from exile (Deuteronomy 30:1-3; Jeremiah 32:36-38), to send them a great king (2 Samuel 7:12-16; Isaiah 9:6, 7), and ultimately to bring blessing to all nations as God reclaims those nations as His (Genesis 12:1-3; Isaiah 49:6). These were God's promises of mercy, pledges that He would forgive and restore His people, that He would share His grace with all people despite their rebellion.

Now God is remembering those promises. It is not that He has forgotten them, but rather that "now is the time" He is acting on them (Galatians 4:4). In so doing, God is rescuing (the meaning of *holpen*) *his servant Israel*. That nation was designated by Isaiah as God's servant because God had promised to bring light to all nations through Israel (Isaiah 49:3-7; compare Psalm 98:3). God is now about to use Israel to bless all nations as He sends His Son as a part of Israel, to present himself to Israel, to die and rise as a member of Israel, and so to bring good news to all nations (Luke 24:46, 47). By this amazing, prophesied-but-unexpected means, God is fulfilling all His promises. This even includes fulfilling His purpose for all of creation: to make people His by His self-giving grace.

Mary and others of her day may expect that the fulfillment of God's promises will mean the defeat of the Roman Empire and the restoration of Israel's political and religious independence. After all, are not the Jewish people lowly, poor, and hungry as compared with mighty Rome? Are the Romans not pagans who hold Israel and Israel's God in contempt? But the way that God is fulfilling His promises is much different and much more potent than a shift in political power. It is, rather, a redefinition of power itself—as self-giving, merciful, gracious, and forgiving.

55. As he spake to our fathers, to Abraham, and to his seed for ever.

Mary's song makes clear that this fulfillment of God's promise is comprehensive. This promise was expressed generation after generation to Mary's Israelite forebears, all the way back to Abraham himself (Genesis 17:7). By Mary's time, that promise is centuries old—probably almost as distant in the past to her as Mary's time is to ours. It is our patience, not God's faithfulness, that the passing of time tests.

The word *seed* reminds us that God has promised to bless all nations through Abraham's progeny, or descendants (Genesis 22:16-18). It remains for the rest of Luke's Gospel to show us that Jesus is indeed the seed of Abraham who brings that promised blessing.

Thus the focus on God's promises looks both backward and forward. With the backward look, we are reminded that God's promises are ancient and take many generations to come to fruition. With the forward look, we are reminded that His promises and their fulfillment are matters of eternity. With Christ's coming, God's people receive a blessing that will endure forever, through all the changes that life brings and beyond this life to the life to come.

IV. Epilogue
(LUKE 1:56)

56. And Mary abode with her about three months, and returned to her own house.

Mary's visit with Elisabeth is a prolonged one. While at Elisabeth's house, Mary is away from the people of Nazareth, who naturally will assume that her pregnancy is the result of sexual immorality. We do not know at what point Joseph learns the real nature of Mary's pregnancy (Matthew 1:18-21), but it probably happens sometime after the *three months* of Mary's visit.

In any case, Mary is with the one person who is best able to understand her situation, as Elisabeth too is miraculously pregnant with a child of promise. They are two lowly people—the elderly, long-childless wife of an obscure priest, and a young peasant woman pregnant out of wedlock. God has called each to do something extraordinary, placing them in positions of difficulty but also of great joy. Both women understand more of what God is doing than do their contemporaries. But both will learn more about God's faithfulness as they see the fulfillment of His promises unfold.

What Do You Think?
What are some benefits and dangers of retreating from the world for a while?
Talking Points for Your Discussion
- Benefits
- Dangers

Conclusion
A. Our Faithful God

Many Christians would list Christmas carols among their favorite songs of worship. It's not hard to imagine Mary's song as being the first Christmas carol. In the history of the church, Mary's song has become a staple of Christian expression in worship. Often known by its first word in the Latin translation, "Magnificat," it has been set to many beautiful melodies. Clearly, Christians through the centuries have recognized that Mary's expression of praise for God's faithfulness is something that all His people should express continually.

In this light, Mary's song reflects many of the themes of other favorite carols: a sense of expectancy, the fact that our longing is about to be fulfilled, that something to be celebrated is taking place. Above all, Mary's song affirms what the Christmas story compels us to affirm today: that God is faithful to those promises, and that He fulfills them by sending Christ.

God's faithfulness prompts us to see our situation differently. If we are comfortable, God's faithfulness prompts us to see ourselves as weak and needy. If we are downtrodden, God's faithfulness prompts us to have hope. God will do no less than fulfill His word for each of His faithful—us.

B. Prayer

Father, we join Mary in singing Your praise for the gift of Your Son. We trust Your faithfulness in our lives. We submit ourselves to Your care in the name of Your Son, amen.

C. Thought to Remember

Sing of God's faithfulness!

INVOLVEMENT LEARNING

Some of the activities below are also found in the helpful student book, Adult Bible Class.
Don't forget to download the free reproducible page from www.standardlesson.com to enhance your lesson!

Into the Lesson

Ask the class, "What is your favorite movie musical?" After responses, ask, "What is it about actors breaking into song in the middle of a dramatic moment that appeals (or doesn't appeal) to you?" Someone may suggest that a song is one of the best ways to express intense emotion.

Alternative: Play a classical musical composition that is based on Mary's song of praise, her "Magnificat." An Internet search will reveal several downloadable versions. Ask for reactions.

After either alternative, say, "Today's text is an example of high emotion resulting in a song of joy and praise. Let's take a look."

Into the Word

Distribute handouts with the following lines and tunes of Christmas carols. Recruit a competent vocalist to sing each line to the suggested tune and then encourage the class to sing it with him or her. Note that each line is based on today's text. 1. "For me Mighty God has done great things; He's done great things to me" to the tune of "It Came Upon a Midnight Clear." 2. "Just as He promised to Abraham, a promise is now fulfilled" to the tune of "What Child Is This?" 3. "Look! His mercy comes to those who will fear His holy name" to the tune of "Hark, the Herald Angels Sing." 4. "O God, my soul doth magnify and glorify You, Lord" to the tune of "O Little Town of Bethlehem." 5. "Mighty from their thrones brought down, yet the lowly lifted high" to the tune of "We Three Kings." 6. "Lowly servant loved by God, He hath spoken to me" to the tune of "Good King Wenceslas." 7. "With His strong arm, the Lord has worked to scatter all the proud" to the tune of "The First Noel."

After each is sung, ask, "Where in the text do you see this sentiment expressed?" *(Suggested answers: 1–v. 49; 2–v. 55; 3–v. 50, 4–v. 46, 5–v. 52, 6–v. 48, 7–v. 51.)* Discuss.

Ask the class to look at verses 48, 51-54 and find a two-word phrase that appears in all five. (The phrase is *he hath*.) Now ask learners to note the adverb clause in verse 55, which is *as he spake*. Comment: "Mary's whole song is an emphatic statement that, with the birth of her child, God was about to do what He said He would. It is an exclamation of God's faithfulness. How does the Christmas story help you stand on the faithful promises of God?" Allow free response.

Option: Distribute copies of the "God Is Faithful" activity from the reproducible page, which you can download, to reinforce the idea of God's faithful fulfillment. You can have learners work individually or, to save time, divide the entries evenly among learners and have them report discoveries on their assigned passages.

Into Life

Give each learner a handout titled "Sing a Song of Christmas" that features the following stimulus questions: 1. What word best captures your emotional response to Jesus' coming? 2. In what way are you overwhelmed that He came to be your Savior? 3. What one great thing that God has done impresses you most? 4. In what ways does God's faithfulness challenge your own?

Next, ask learners (working individually) to pick one statement from Mary's song and write a line of personal praise to God that the statement implies that He has done. Ask for volunteers to share responses. *Option*: Challenge each learner to make his or her responses fit the tune of a favorite Christmas carol.

Option: Distribute copies of the "Magnify and Glorify" activity from the reproducible page as a take-home exercise to use in times of personal study and devotion this week.

Close by singing together one of the Christmas carols of the Into the Word segment using the traditional tune of the carol.

ZACHARIAS PROPHESIES ABOUT HIS SON, JOHN

DEVOTIONAL READING: Luke 1:59-66
BACKGROUND SCRIPTURE: Luke 1:57-80

LUKE 1:57, 58, 67-79

57 Now Elisabeth's full time came that she should be delivered; and she brought forth a son.

58 And her neighbours and her cousins heard how the Lord had shewed great mercy upon her; and they rejoiced with her.

. . . .

67 And his father Zacharias was filled with the Holy Ghost, and prophesied, saying,

68 Blessed be the Lord God of Israel; for he hath visited and redeemed his people,

69 And hath raised up an horn of salvation for us in the house of his servant David;

70 As he spake by the mouth of his holy prophets, which have been since the world began:

71 That we should be saved from our enemies, and from the hand of all that hate us;

72 To perform the mercy promised to our fathers, and to remember his holy covenant;

73 The oath which he sware to our father Abraham,

74 That he would grant unto us, that we being delivered out of the hand of our enemies might serve him without fear,

75 In holiness and righteousness before him, all the days of our life.

76 And thou, child, shalt be called the prophet of the Highest: for thou shalt go before the face of the Lord to prepare his ways;

77 To give knowledge of salvation unto his people by the remission of their sins,

78 Through the tender mercy of our God; whereby the dayspring from on high hath visited us,

79 To give light to them that sit in darkness and in the shadow of death, to guide our feet into the way of peace.

KEY VERSE

Thou, child, shalt be called the prophet of the Highest: for thou shalt go before the face of the Lord to prepare his ways; to give knowledge of salvation unto his people by the remission of their sins. —**Luke 1:76, 77**

JESUS AND THE JUST REIGN OF GOD

Unit 1: God Sends Jesus

LESSONS 1–5

LESSON AIMS

After participating in this lesson, each student will be able to:

1. Identify key themes of biblical promise in Zacharias's song.

2. Relate the key themes to their fulfillment in Christ.

3. Write a prayer of thanks to God for the promises in Zacharias's prayer and for how their fulfillment has been a blessing to him or her.

LESSON OUTLINE

Introduction
   A. The Prediction Business
   B. Lesson Background
 I. Promise Fulfilled (LUKE 1:57, 58)
   A. John's Birth (v. 57)
   B. People's Joy (v. 58)
     A Rejoicing That Never Dies
 II. Promises Reaffirmed (LUKE 1:67-79)
   A. Holy Spirit Empowers (v. 67)
   B. God's Promises Recalled (vv. 68-75)
   C. John's Role Stated (vv. 76-79)
     The Kind of Light We Need
Conclusion
   A. A Joyful Song
   B. Prayer
   C. Thought to Remember

Introduction

A. The Prediction Business

How many predictions have you heard this past week? Probably quite a few. "Experts" offer their confident forecasts of where the stock market is headed, what tomorrow's weather will be like, and which team will prevail in the big game. Of course, many predictions prove to be completely inaccurate. However, that does not stop people from making them or us from listening to them. The human desire to know the future seems insatiable.

Of course, only God knows the future. And only He can give us the kind of future that is truly worthwhile. God announced His plans for the future through prophets. God's prophets were more than mere human experts who could use personal expertise to project a likely future. God spoke through them to announce authoritatively what He would do to bring His will to reality.

God promised to bring about a future that would bless His people in ways that exceeded their hopes. In so doing God invited His people to trust Him, to look forward patiently in faith. Alongside the promised blessing came a warning: those who did not submit themselves to the God who controls the future would be judged as His enemies.

Though we commonly think of prophets in terms of the Old Testament, God continued to speak through prophets in the New Testament. At the birth of John the Baptist, Zacharias (his father) spoke in a way that recalled the great prophets of the Old Testament. In so doing, Zacharias prophesied that God was beginning the long-awaited time of fulfillment. John's birth signaled the start an important transition by God.

B. Lesson Background

Today's text forms the climax to the prophecy of John the Baptist's birth. Zacharias, an elderly, childless priest, had received from God's angel a pledge that he would become the father of a son who would announce the fulfillment of God's promises. Zacharias responded with disbelief; as a cautionary sign of judgment, God rendered him unable to speak for a time (Luke 1:5-22).

Zacharias's ultimate reaction, like Mary's song (Luke 1:46-55, lesson 2), is a poetic expression of praise to God. Employing parallel expressions typical of biblical poetry, Zacharias's song echoes key themes of prophetic promise from Israel's Scriptures. As God had fulfilled His surprising promise that Zacharias would become a father, so God would fulfill His greatest promises for all.

I. Promise Fulfilled
(LUKE 1:57, 58)

Mary visited Elisabeth (wife of Zacharias) in the sixth month of Elisabeth's pregnancy (Luke 1:26, 39), then departed for home after "about three months" (v. 56, last week's lesson). Since six plus three equals nine, we wonder if Mary stayed long enough to share the joy of the birth of the one who came to be known as John the Baptist. It seems likely that Mary did so, but the text doesn't say.

A. John's Birth (v. 57)

57. Now Elisabeth's full time came that she should be delivered; and she brought forth a son.

Luke has already pointed out that elderly, childless Elisabeth did indeed become pregnant as promised (Luke 1:24). Now the birth is narrated, and again God's promise proves faithful: the child born is a boy, as the angel had announced (v. 13).

B. People's Joy (v. 58)

58. And her neighbours and her cousins heard how the Lord had shewed great mercy upon her; and they rejoiced with her.

The birth of a child is always a cause for rejoicing, and John's birth, coming so late in his parents' lives, is especially so. The phrase *her cousins* refers to all kinds of relatives who join the celebration.

The celebration is not only for the birth, but also for the merciful gift of God that the child is. The situation of Zacharias and Elisabeth perhaps reminds those present of the situations of Abraham and Sarah, of Isaac and Rebekah, and of the parents of Samson. All had been childless, but to all God miraculously gave sons who advanced God's plan. Those present can anticipate that God again is about to do something great.

What Do You Think?
What was an occasion when family and friends rejoiced with you over an answer to a prayer that was a long time in coming? How can you use such occasions to witness for Christ?
Talking Points for Your Discussion
- For direction in life
- For a job
- For healing
- Other

❧ A REJOICING THAT NEVER DIES ❧

His Royal Highness, Prince William of Wales, was born to Princess Diana and Prince Charles on June 21, 1982. The fact that the royal birth brought an heir into the family was cause for great rejoicing, of course. Eventually, many British citizens rejoiced for another reason: Diana's popularity and public sympathy for her as a result of Charles's unfaithfulness to his marriage vows made many hope that occupancy of the throne would bypass Charles and go directly to William. Such is the fascination people still hold for those whose royal, titular power is largely symbolic in nature.

With the birth of John, a far more significant person than any earthly prince came into this world. The name *John* (Luke 1:63) means simply "God is gracious"—no fancy royal titles here! The task for which he was born was more important than being king of any nation: John was the one to "prepare . . . the way of the Lord" (Luke 3:4).

HOW TO SAY IT

Abraham	*Ay*-bruh-ham.
Assyria	Uh-*sear*-ee-uh.
Babylon	*Bab*-uh-lun.
Benedictus	Ben-eh-**dik**-tus.
Deuteronomy	Due-ter-*ahn*-uh-me.
Ezekiel	Ee-*zeek*-ee-ul or Ee-*zeek*-yul.
Isaac	*Eye*-zuk.
Isaiah	Eye-*zay*-uh.
Persians	*Per*-zhuns.
Rebekah	Reh-*bek*-uh.
Zacharias	Zack-uh-*rye*-us.

The rejoicing of June 21, 1982, died down long ago. The rejoicing for the birth of John the Baptist never should! Our rejoicing multiplies when we realize that we are privileged to carry on John's task of announcing Jesus to the world.—C. R. B.

II. Promises Reaffirmed
(LUKE 1:67-79)

In Luke 1:60-66 (not in today's text), John is circumcised and named. While others expect the boy to be named after his father, Elisabeth insists that he be named *John* (vv. 59, 60), the name that the angel commanded be given (v. 13). Zacharias—still without the power of speech—affirms in writing that the boy be called John (v. 63). With that, Zacharias's speech, lost for nine months, is restored (v. 64). So all realize that God is indeed at work (vv. 65, 66). Zacharias's song of praise follows.

A. Holy Spirit Empowers (v. 67)

67. And his father Zacharias was filled with the Holy Ghost, and prophesied, saying.

Zacharias's ability to speak has been miraculously withheld as a sign that God's promise to him can be trusted. Now the man's speech is not just restored, but is empowered by *the Holy Ghost*. This makes what Zacharias is about to say a prophecy, God's message as inspired by God's Spirit.

Throughout the Gospel of Luke and its companion volume, the book of Acts, the Holy Spirit is portrayed as empowering God's people to speak His word (see Luke 1:41; 2:25-35; 4:14; 12:12; Acts 2:4; 4:8, 31; 6:5; 11:28; 13:9). Zacharias's song is typical of such empowerment; the song is also exceptional as Zacharias witnesses a crucial event in God's plan unfold.

B. God's Promises Recalled (vv. 68-75)

68a. Blessed be the Lord God of Israel.

Like Mary's song in Luke 1:46-55, Zacharias's song has a long history of use in Christian worship. It is widely known by its first word in the Latin translation, "Benedictus," which reflects the first two words of this verse, *blessed be*. Echoes of this phrase in Israelite worship stretch to centuries before Christ (see Psalms 41:13; 72:18; 106:48).

In affirming that God is to be blessed, Zacharias calls on all people to praise and glorify God. The God who is worthy of such universal praise is none other than the God of Israel, the one who promised the Israelites that He would use them to bless all people (Genesis 12:1-3; Isaiah 42:6).

> *What Do You Think?*
> What are some ways you have found for praising or "blessing" God for His goodness to you? Which seems most meaningful, and why?
> *Talking Points for Your Discussion*
> - With words
> - With music
> - With actions
> - Other

68b. For he hath visited and redeemed his people.

A crucial aspect of God's promise is the pledge to once again "visit" His people to lead them out of bondage. Centuries before, God had warned Israel that disobedience would mean a return to the kind of bondage experienced in Egypt (Deuteronomy 29:16-28). If the people refused to listen after He had liberated them from slavery, then He would return them to domination by pagans. That was indeed what God did, as He allowed Assyria and Babylon to take His people into captivity in 722 and 586 BC, respectively.

In keeping with His promise, God restored the people to their land when the Persians overtook the Babylonian Empire. But that restoration did not fulfill all that God had promised; God's people remained under the control of the pagan nations of first Greece and then Rome after the decline of Persia. So the faithful continue to expect a future "visitation" of God, one to bring the fullness of God's promise to reality. With great joy, Zacharias is now announcing that the time of that visitation has arrived!

What Zacharias and others have yet to learn is that God is visiting them in a way greater than they anticipate: God is in the process of freeing His people from a bondage greater than that of political oppression. The bondage from which He will grant freedom is that of the great enemy,

Satan, and the evil that he inspires (Luke 4:1-13; 11:20-22; Hebrews 2:14; 1 John 3:8).

69. And hath raised up an horn of salvation for us in the house of his servant David.

The horn is a symbol of power and strength (Psalm 18:2). When a horned animal lifts its head, it asserts its power to those that threaten it. When Zacharias speaks of *an horn*, he echoes Old Testament texts such as 2 Samuel 22:3 and Psalm 132:17. For God's people, protection comes not from their own horn, but from the one that God raises for them. This signifies *salvation*. While that term can mean a rescue from mortal enemies, the story of Jesus shows us that God's salvation is greater than that of a political or military rescue.

The fact that this deliverance is associated with *the house of his servant David* recalls the promise that God would enable David's descendant to build God's house and establish a throne that would never end (1 Chronicles 17:11-14). To this point, all David's kingly descendants have been disappointments in that regard. But God continued to affirm this promise through His prophets (see Isaiah 9:6, 7; Jeremiah 23:5; Ezekiel 34:23). Now, says Zacharias, that promise is coming to fulfillment. When we remember that Mary's child belongs to David's house (Luke 1:27, 32), we realize through whom God will fulfill the promise.

70. As he spake by the mouth of his holy prophets, which have been since the world began.

What is happening as Zacharias speaks is nothing less than the fulfillment of the ancient prophets' message. Those prophets were *holy* because they were called by God. God's words became their words as God directed them to speak. The phrase *since the world began* translates a Greek phrase that is literally "from the ages." God's plan is just that ancient, having been established before the world's foundation (Ephesians 1:4). The birth of John signals something of utmost importance!

71. That we should be saved from our enemies, and from the hand of all that hate us.

This verse is strikingly similar to Psalm 106:10, which glorifies God for the people's deliverance at the Red Sea. But for Zacharias and other faithful Israelites, a great deal of their history is the story of domination by pagan nations (see comments on v. 68b, above). Zacharias and his fellow Israelites have no difficulty identifying those enemies!

> **What Do You Think?**
> What is the difference in your reactions to your physical enemies and to your spiritual enemies as led by Satan? In which area do you need the most improvement?
> *Talking Points for Your Discussion*
> - Reacting to physical enemies (Matthew 5:38-48; Luke 6:27-36)
> - Reacting to spiritual enemies (Luke 4:3-12; Ephesians 4:26, 27; 6:10-17; James 4:7)

72. To perform the mercy promised to our fathers, and to remember his holy covenant.

God had promised that He would one day do for Israel what He did in the exodus: bring the people back from exile to the land that He had promised them. God's promise equates to *his holy covenant*, the gracious agreement that He initiated as ruler of His people. The promise is ancient, made to the *fathers* of the nation. It is as old as Moses, of some 14 centuries previous. That man had warned that exile would be the consequence of disobedience, but he also promised that God would not abandon the nation to exile (Deuteronomy 30:1-5; compare Psalm 106:45, 46).

73. The oath which he sware to our father Abraham.

The supreme promise of God's covenant is the promise to bless all nations, the promise that He made multiple times to Abraham (Genesis 12:1-3; 18:18: 22:15-18). Israel's restoration will mean that people of all nations can come to know God and experience His blessing. God is determined to fulfill His promise to take back His world, whether Israel is obedient or not. Through the Holy Spirit's inspiration, Zacharias declares that the time has come.

74. That he would grant unto us, that we being delivered out of the hand of our enemies might serve him without fear.

God sent Moses to deliver the ancient Israelites from bondage in Egypt. Now that deliverance is about to be repeated. But the way it will happen —through Jesus' death and resurrection and the preaching of His name to all nations—will astonish even the faithful. As Zacharias speaks, the Israelites live in fear of their Roman overlords; the greater fear that God will eliminate, however, is the fear of death (Hebrews 2:15).

> **What Do You Think?**
> What was an occasion when God delivered you out of the hand of an enemy in a way you were not expecting? How has that experience enhanced your witness and praise?
>
> *Talking Points for Your Discussion*
> - Regarding a spiritual enemy
> - Regarding a physical enemy
> - Regarding a combination of the two

75. In holiness and righteousness before him, all the days of our life.

The people whom God redeems from bondage belong to Him. He purchases their freedom, so they are rightfully His "peculiar treasure" (Exodus 19:5), a claim that God made on Israel after He brought the people out of Egypt. So the Ten Commandments begin by reminding Israel, "I am the Lord thy God, which have brought thee out of the land of Egypt, out of the house of bondage" (20:2). Those whom God frees owe their lives in obedience to Him.

When God restores His people, He enables them to obey as they have not done before (Jeremiah 31:31-34). When God fulfills His promises, then His people are to demonstrate *holiness,* being set apart as His people, as well as *righteousness,* being obedient to His right way. We are able to present ourselves *in holiness and righteousness before him* because Jesus enables us to do so (Titus 2:11-14).

C. John's Role Stated (vv. 76-79)

76. And thou, child, shalt be called the prophet of the Highest: for thou shalt go before the face of the Lord to prepare his ways.

Zacharias now exults in what God will do through John: he is to be God's spokesman, guided by God's Spirit to speak God's message. Zacharias calls God *the Highest* to emphasize that God's authority is supreme. John, when his time arrives, can and will speak for no one greater.

The Gospels emphasize that John's calling is to *go before the face of the Lord to prepare his ways* (see Matthew 3:1-3; Mark 1:1-3; Luke 3:4-6; 7:27; John 1:23). That idea comes from Isaiah 40:3 and Malachi 3:1, passages that speak of preparing the way or road for God to visit His people and take them out of bondage. As the story line of the gospel develops, we learn that John the Baptist serves as the forerunner to Jesus in that regard. We understand the astonishing way that God fulfills His promise to visit His people as Jesus is revealed to be God in human flesh.

77. To give knowledge of salvation unto his people by the remission of their sins.

As a product of his time, Zacharias probably understands *salvation* to mean that God is about to rescue Israel from Roman oppression. Again, the rest of Luke's Gospel demonstrates that the salvation people most need is that of deliverance from the greater evil that oppresses. For this to happen, people need to turn to God and receive the cleansing forgiveness that He alone can give. This very thing is depicted in the baptism that John will administer "for the remission of sins" (Luke 3:3) in his role as the forerunner of Jesus (3:15).

78. Through the tender mercy of our God; whereby the dayspring from on high hath visited us.

God's gift of salvation comes to undeserving people. We are rebels against God. But God in His *tender mercy* gives us better than we deserve. God's mercy brings something like the dawning of a new day; *dayspring* simply means "dawn."

The "normal" dawn occurs daily in the eastern sky, whereas the unique dawn in this verse comes *from on high.* That is, God himself brings this special kind of dawn. The image of God's future blessing as a dawn comes from Malachi 4:2, 3, where the God-given dawn means healing, joy, and victory. Early copies of Luke differ as to whether the exact meaning is that the dawn "hath visited" or "will visit," but the point is clear either way: John's birth heralds the arrival of the time for God to fulfill His promise. It is a miraculous new morning.

79. To give light to them that sit in darkness and in the shadow of death, to guide our feet into the way of peace.

Darkness is a common image for the state of those who are far from God (Jeremiah 23:12; etc.). But God promises *to give light to them that sit in darkness,* whether they be the pagan nations (Isaiah 49:6) or Israel itself (9:2). Zacharias extends that promise to the final boundary of death (compare Psalm 23:4). Because we know the end of the story, we think of Jesus' resurrection from the dead and anticipate our own resurrection that it promises.

Zacharias closes his praise song with the image of God's guiding His people safely on a lighted path. That path leads to *peace,* which means not just the absence of hostility but the presence of blessing and wholeness. This is the destination that God promises by His mercy. This is the promise about to be fulfilled.

> *What Do You Think?*
>   What will you do personally this week to shine
>   Christ's light into the life of someone who lives
>   in spiritual darkness?
> *Talking Points for Your Discussion*
> - Personal testimony
> - Deed of kindness
> - Christlike lifestyle
> - Other

❧ THE KIND OF LIGHT WE NEED ❧

Paul Hellyer, a former Canadian Minister of Defence, takes a dim view of humanity's future in his book *Light at the End of the Tunnel: A Survival Plan for the Human Species,* published in 2010. He asserts that the year 2020 is the deadline for ending dependence on petroleum for energy. Exotic forms of energy already exist, he claims, but a "shadow government" controls their secret (which was learned from interplanetary visitors) for the benefit of a small number of people. One of Hellyer's imperatives is that all people must find ways to work together for the common good. Well, Mr. Hellyer, good luck on that one! Unless . . .

Two millennia ago, Zacharias announced the fact that light was coming. His son, John the Baptist, came on the scene as a witness to that light, Jesus Christ (John 1:6-9). From that heavenly visitor, we discover, among other things, the availabil-

Visual for Lesson 3. *Point to this visual as you ask, "How did someone prepare your heart to receive Jesus? What did you learn from this experience?"*

ity of the power of the Holy Spirit and the need for all of God's children to work together for the common good. Hellyer's book focuses on *survival*; in contrast, our New Testament focuses on *salvation*. Do we ever let a focus on the former distract us from the latter? —C. R. B.

Conclusion
A. A Joyful Song

Speechless for nine months, Zacharias offered an impressive, memorable song in celebration of John's birth. Layering phrase after phrase from the ancient prophets, he made clear to all that the time of fulfillment had arrived.

We are the beneficiaries of those promises and their fulfillment. We can know the promises and the gospel story that brings them to reality. We experience the salvation, mercy, knowledge, and light that God gives in Jesus Christ. Our expression of joy and thanks ought to be at least as vivid as Zacharias's, if not more so.

B. Prayer

Great God, we thank You that by Your mercy we have received the fulfillment of Your eternal promises in Jesus. May we live in full confidence of Your abiding faithfulness. In Jesus' name, amen.

C. Thought to Remember
Live in the light.

INVOLVEMENT LEARNING

Some of the activities below are also found in the helpful student book, Adult Bible Class.
Don't forget to download the free reproducible page from www.standardlesson.com to enhance your lesson!

Into the Lesson

Give three learners (preferably male) slips of paper with the following descriptions, one each. Ask these three to stand before the group and read the characterizations. As each finishes, ask, "Who am I?" and wait for responses.

1. I was the son of a 100-year-old man and his 90-year-old wife, who was barren. My parents both laughed when hearing the idea that I was on the way, but God and I got the "last laugh" when I was born. 2. I was born to a mother who had been barren for many years. But my father prayed, and God answered. My mother became pregnant . . . with twins! I was the younger one. 3. I was born to an elderly couple who had no children. My father doubted the angel's prediction and was struck speechless as a consequence. (*Answers:* 1. Isaac, whose name means "laughter"; 2. Jacob; 3. John the Baptist.) Use the final "who am I" as a transition to the next segment.

Into the Word

Recruit a learner to play the role of Zacharias for an interview. Use the following script.

Q: Zacharias, when the angel announced God's plan, you were skeptical. Why? **A:** My goodness, man, look at me! I am old; my wife is old. Have a child? It sounded preposterous.

Q: But God gave you a reason to believe?
A: God's kindness in teaching me through my enforced silence was a blessing. For nine months I pondered the marvel of His plan.

Q: Normally the father does not know if the child is a girl or a boy, but . . . **A:** *(interrupting)* I did not have to wonder. God said a son, and a son he was!

Q: How did your family and friends react? **A:** All of us were preparing for the day of his birth. And my, what a celebration of praise!

Q: On the day he was circumcised, how did you surprise everyone? **A:** The family had assumed our son would be named after me, but I hastily scribbled on a tablet, "His name is John!" Everyone was startled. That's when the Lord gave me the power to speak again, and I began to praise God. Talk about surprise!

Q: Your song of praise is a beautiful one. Had you been planning it for months? **A:** Mercy, no! It was not simply my song. It was the song of God's Spirit. I was overwhelmed in a way I had never been before, and the words simply flowed out.

Q: The way you began the song—do you see that as particularly important? **A:** Important? For hundreds of years we had no visit from God. He was silent. Redemption seemed to be nothing more than a hope. Now that hope was a reality!

After the interview, give each learner a copy of the script. Place learners into study teams for comparing it with today's lesson text to identify areas of accuracy and "poetic license."

Into Life

Ask the class to join you in a time of directed prayer. You can repeat some of the following ideas from Zacharias's song to stimulate prayer thoughts: visited by God / a redeemed people / salvation in our king / confirmation of God's promises / protected from our enemies / recipients of His mercy / serving God in holiness and righteousness / with a purpose to proclaim. Close the prayer with thanks for Zacharias's faith and submission.

Alternative: Distribute copies of the activity "John the Baptist and I" from the reproducible page, which you can download. This exercise will challenge learners to think about their roles as forerunners of Christ today.

Option: Distribute copies of the "Divine Illumination" activity from the reproducible page; have learners complete it as indicated. Ask volunteers to share results, but don't put anyone on the spot.

JESUS IS BORN

DEVOTIONAL READING: Galatians 4:1-7
BACKGROUND SCRIPTURE: Luke 2:1-20

LUKE 2:1-17

1 And it came to pass in those days, that there went out a decree from Caesar Augustus, that all the world should be taxed.

2 (And this taxing was first made when Cyrenius was governor of Syria.)

3 And all went to be taxed, every one into his own city.

4 And Joseph also went up from Galilee, out of the city of Nazareth, into Judaea, unto the city of David, which is called Bethlehem; (because he was of the house and lineage of David:)

5 To be taxed with Mary his espoused wife, being great with child.

6 And so it was, that, while they were there, the days were accomplished that she should be delivered.

7 And she brought forth her firstborn son, and wrapped him in swaddling clothes, and laid him in a manger; because there was no room for them in the inn.

8 And there were in the same country shepherds abiding in the field, keeping watch over their flock by night.

9 And, lo, the angel of the Lord came upon them, and the glory of the Lord shone round about them: and they were sore afraid.

10 And the angel said unto them, Fear not: for, behold, I bring you good tidings of great joy, which shall be to all people.

11 For unto you is born this day in the city of David a Saviour, which is Christ the Lord.

12 And this shall be a sign unto you; Ye shall find the babe wrapped in swaddling clothes, lying in a manger.

13 And suddenly there was with the angel a multitude of the heavenly host praising God, and saying,

14 Glory to God in the highest, and on earth peace, good will toward men.

15 And it came to pass, as the angels were gone away from them into heaven, the shepherds said one to another, Let us now go even unto Bethlehem, and see this thing which is come to pass, which the Lord hath made known unto us.

16 And they came with haste, and found Mary, and Joseph, and the babe lying in a manger.

17 And when they had seen it, they made known abroad the saying which was told them concerning this child.

KEY VERSE

She brought forth her firstborn son, and wrapped him in swaddling clothes, and laid him in a manger; because there was no room for them in the inn. —**Luke 2:7**

JESUS AND THE JUST REIGN OF GOD

Unit 1: God Sends Jesus

LESSONS 1–5

LESSON AIMS

After participating in this lesson, each student will be able to:

1. Summarize the story of the birth of Jesus according to Luke.

2. Explain the significance of Luke's listing of political rulers, the importance of the lineage of David, and the irony of the announcement of such an important birth being given first to shepherds.

3. Commit Luke 2:1-7 to memory.

LESSON OUTLINE

Introduction

A. The Power of Christmas

It has halted wars. It has altered economies. It unites families. It depletes bank accounts. It affects everyone's calendar. It is Christmas.

Though the Christmas holiday is influential, the true power of Christmas is in the Christmas story. As Luke tells it, Jesus' birth marks a sharp contrast between two kinds of power. One is the military and economic might of the Roman Empire; the other is the power of Jesus, the king whom God sent. He was God incarnate, the Creator himself entering the world as a human. He deliberately assumed a position of humility, lowliness, even poverty. Beginning in that unlikely position, He conquers the world.

B. Lesson Background

The Roman Empire conquered territories around the Mediterranean Sea in the centuries before Jesus' birth. By 63 BC, Rome had conquered the historic territory of Israel, although it took some years for the Romans to solidify their control. Caesar Augustus became emperor in 27 BC, and the great age of Roman power began to take shape. Subject peoples were taxed heavily. Those who did not submit to Roman authority could be fined, flogged, exiled, or executed.

Roman domination was more than a political and economic burden for the Jewish people. It was also a religious problem: as long as Rome ruled, God did not (or so it seemed). The reality of Roman occupation was a constant reminder that God had consigned Israel to a state of exile—even "exile" within its own borders—for generations.

The faithful looked to the promises of Scripture for hope. God had promised a great Son of David to rule over His people (2 Samuel 7:12-16). He had promised that beyond exile lay restoration (Isaiah 51:11), like the exodus of Moses' time. One day the pagan powers would be destroyed, and God would rule supreme over all nations (Daniel 7:1-14). Though centuries had passed since God gave His promises, the faithful looked beyond the failures of their forefathers and kept their trust in God's promise to take back His world.

These ideas intersect with Luke's story of Jesus' birth. The power of Rome is portrayed through its power to tax. We glimpse the oppression of Israel in the poverty of Jesus' family. The promise of God is clear as we hear again of David, whose promised Son is to rule over all.

I. Worldly Power
(LUKE 2:1-3)
A. Decree (vv. 1, 2)

1. And it came to pass in those days, that there went out a decree from Caesar Augustus that all the world should be taxed.

The Roman taxation system is familiar to Luke's readers. Recalling the familiar saying "All roads lead to Rome," the transportation network of the empire allows tax revenue to be moved efficiently to the imperial city. By this time, Caesar Augustus has been emperor for more than 20 years (see the Lesson Background), thus his power to tax, etc., is firmly established.

The expression *all the world* is quite interesting. Although Rome controls much territory, there are areas to the north, east, and south that the Romans know of but cannot conquer. Even so, the Romans commonly boast of their accomplishments, so they make exaggerated claims such as control of the whole world. Luke uses this claim to set the stage for a confrontation. Who will rule the entire world, Rome or God?

2. (And this taxing was first made when Cyrenius was governor of Syria.)

Luke ties the story of Jesus' birth to contemporary events to establish its precise setting. Even so, this verse presents a difficulty. Historical sources outside the Bible indicate that Cyrenius is *governor of Syria* in AD 6. But according to Matthew 2:1, Jesus is born in the time of Herod the Great. Other sources make clear that Herod dies in 4 BC. So we have strong reason to think that Jesus' birth is in 4 or 5 BC. (The curiosity of Jesus' birth coming in "BC," meaning "before Christ," is the result of a calculation error made in the early attempt to create a calendar based on Jesus' birth.)

There are two ways to understand Luke's statement without concluding that a mistake is involved. It is possible that the word translated *governor* refers to a different office; Cyrenius may have held a lesser position, perhaps as a taxation specialist, before becoming governor of the region per se. Or it is possible that the sentence structure in the original language means that this was the taxing *before* Cyrenius was governor of Syria. We have clear evidence that a census for taxation was taken in AD 6 when Cyrenius was governor; this led to riots (Acts 5:37) and a reorganization of Roman government in the region. Luke may therefore be saying, "This is not the notorious taxation under Cyrenius, but a lesser-known taxation before that."

Either way, the image of Roman power remains firm. Rome can demand taxes of its subjects whenever it chooses to do so. The pagan empire is supreme—or so it seems.

> *What Do You Think?*
> How do we distinguish between legitimate and illegitimate demands that a ruling authority makes on us? What reactions do those two kinds of demands call from you personally?
> *Talking Points for Your Discussion*
> - Mark 12:17
> - Acts 4:19; 5:29; 18:2; 23:5
> - Romans 13:1-7
> - 1 Peter 2:13-17
> - Other

B. Obedience (v. 3)

3. And all went to be taxed, every one into his own city.

Roman taxes that involve a census or enrollment constitute a kind of property tax. Every person with a claim to land must enroll in the tax ledger and pay the required amount. For most people, that means enrolling very close to home. But if a person owns property in another place, the tax census means a journey to that place for enrollment lest the property be forfeited.

❧ *ROMANS 8:28 IN ACTION* ❧

America's Great Recession that began in 2007 generated furious debate. Was the solution to the malaise to be found in more government spending funded by higher taxes? Or was the solution to be found in lowering taxes so that increased spending in the private sector would stimulate new hiring?

Regardless of one's view of tax policy to fix faltering economies, the vast majority of people accept the "necessary evil" of the government's power and need to levy taxes. But with the rare exception of someone like a Warren Buffett—the billionaire who in 2011 famously begged the government to raise his taxes—it's safe to assume that people want their taxes to be as low as possible.

Ironically, it was taxation that put Joseph and Mary on the road to Bethlehem, resulting in fulfillment of the prophecy in Micah 5:2. We might think of this as Romans 8:28 in action: "And we know that all things work together for good to them that love God." God still uses the various negative experiences of this world to accomplish His will. Watch for it!　　　　—C. R. B.

II. Lowly Infant
(LUKE 2:4-7)
A. David's City (v. 4)
4. And Joseph also went up from Galilee, out of the city of Nazareth, into Judaea, unto the city of David, which is called Bethlehem; (because he was of the house and lineage of David:).

Verses 4, 5 focus our attention on a single family that lives under Roman rule. Joseph and his location in Nazareth were introduced earlier (Luke 1:26, 27). Nazareth seems to be held in low esteem by the Jewish people of the time (John 1:45, 46). Bethlehem is also a lowly place—merely a small village of farmers and herdsmen. Joseph is traveling from one humble town to another.

HOW TO SAY IT

Bethlehem	*Beth*-lih-hem.
Caesar Augustus	*See*-zer Aw-*gus*-tus.
Cyrenius	Sigh-*ree*-nee-us.
Judaea	Joo-*dee*-uh.
Mediterranean	*Med*-uh-tuh-*ray*-nee-un.
Nazareth	*Naz*-uh-reth.
Pax Romana *(Latin)*	*Pahks* Ro-*mahy*-nah.
Zacharias	Zack-uh-*rye*-us.

Since Joseph's ancestors were from Bethlehem and he is going back there for the taxation enrollment, then Joseph likely has inherited a small piece of land in that area. If so, this implies that he lets others farm the land for a fee, since Joseph lives in Nazareth. This hardly makes Joseph prosperous, however. Farms in Judea are often small, yielding barely enough food for one's own family. The burden of Roman taxation makes survival even more difficult.

But Luke portrays Bethlehem as more than a tiny country village. He calls it *the city of David* and mentions David a second time in describing Joseph's connection with Bethlehem (compare Luke 1:26, 27). Luke wants us to think of the promise to David of a great descendant who will build God's house and rule an everlasting kingdom (see the Lesson Background).

B. David's Descendant (vv. 5-7)
5. To be taxed with Mary his espoused wife, being great with child.

Espoused means that Joseph and Mary are legally promised to each other for marriage (betrothed), but are not yet actually married. Readers understand by this point that Mary's pregnancy is a miracle, not the result of sexual immorality. But few, if any, in the family circles of Joseph and Mary are likely to believe a story of a miraculous, virginal conception. Thus Mary and Joseph's situation is difficult not only because of the taxation burden of Roman rule, but also because of social ostracism they face. Their situation is lowly indeed!

6. And so it was, that, while they were there, the days were accomplished that she should be delivered.

The phrase *and so it was* draws attention to the central event of the story: the birth of Jesus. Luke does not tell us how much time elapses between Joseph and Mary's arrival in Bethlehem and the birth of Jesus. But we do see that the one who will prove to be David's great son is born in David's own town (1 Samuel 16).

7. And she brought forth her firstborn son, and wrapped him in swaddling clothes, and laid him in a manger; because there was no room for them in the inn.

The fact that Jesus is Mary's firstborn is obvious by this point, since she is a virgin. But the mention of *firstborn son* suggests something a bit deeper, since the role of the firstborn son is that of primacy and authority (compare Deuteronomy 21:15-17; etc.).

Swaddling clothes are strips of cloth. The custom is to wrap babies securely with such strips for warmth and security. The infant Jesus receives the usual care of the culture in this regard (contrast Ezekiel 16:1-5). The use of *a manger* sends a different message, however. A manger is a feeding trough for animals, hardly the place one would place a baby. But this action yields a clue that the family has had to take shelter in a stable of some kind, perhaps one of the caves in the area that is used to shelter livestock. Their situation is lowly indeed!

Mention of an *inn* brings to modern minds the image of a place where overnight accommodations can be rented. But the word translated *inn* can refer more broadly to "a place of human habitation." Most Jewish travelers in Judea do not rent sleeping quarters such as we might in a modern motel. Rather, the custom is to extend to travelers the hospitality of one's home (compare Judges 19:12-21). It may be, then, that Mary and Joseph stay in a stable because this is the only accommodation available from those who normally would extend hospitality, but cannot due to so many people arriving for the census.

However we paint this picture in our minds, the larger circumstances are clear. Jesus is born into a poor family under Roman oppression, yet in a town that reminds us of God's promise of a great king. What shall we make of this situation?

> **What Do You Think?**
> How can we use the circumstances of Jesus' birth to demonstrate that lowliness and humility rather than "health and wealth" may be the reality for the obedient believer?
> *Talking Points for Your Discussion*
> - In the way we pray
> - In how we socialize
> - In how we handle our finances
> - Other

Visual for Lesson 4

Point to this visual as you ask, "What most causes people to say 'No Vacancy' to Jesus?"

III. Angelic Army
(LUKE 2:8-14)
A. The Scene (vv. 8, 9)

8. And there were in the same country shepherds abiding in the field, keeping watch over their flock by night.

The hill country around Bethlehem is suitable pastureland for sheep and goats (compare 1 Samuel 16:4, 11). The nighttime scene suggests tranquility, but that is about to change.

9. And, lo, the angel of the Lord came upon them, and the glory of the Lord shone round about them: and they were sore afraid.

As with Zacharias (Luke 1:11-20) and Mary (1:26-38), an angel appears to the shepherds. The accompanying *glory of the Lord* is a miraculous display of light (compare 9:29). The dark background of the night sky serves to highlight the scene. Those who encounter angels in the Bible commonly are afraid (Luke 1:12, 29; etc.), and we can understand why the shepherds are terrified!

B. The Announcement (vv. 10-12)

10. And the angel said unto them, Fear not: for, behold, I bring you good tidings of great joy, which shall be to all people.

As with earlier angelic appearances, the angel begins with *fear not* (compare Luke 1:13, 30). The word *behold* draws attention to what is about to be said. The angel's announcement contains *good tidings,* a term often used by the prophet to announce the promise of God's future restoration of blessing to His people (Isaiah 40:9; 52:7; 61:1).

To add a layer of emphasis, the angel also says that the good tidings will produce *great joy,* the consequence of God's promised blessing (Isaiah 55:12). The phrase *to all people* in the original language literally reads "to all the people," emphasizing the people of Israel. Though the blessing is first for Israel, ultimately it is a blessing for people of all nations who respond to God's offer.

> **What Do You Think?**
> What can your church do this Christmas season to ensure that the "good tidings of great joy" are available "to all people" in your community?
>
> *Talking Points for Your Discussion*
> - Transportation issues
> - Food issues
> - Clothing issues
> - Worship and program access
> - Other

11. For unto you is born this day in the city of David a Saviour, which is Christ the Lord.

There are now two kings in the story: Caesar Augustus and David's great Son. There are also two kingdoms: Rome's empire and God's promised reign. Israel may be a lowly nation and shepherds may be lowly people, but the angel still says that the child is born *unto you.* He is born for the benefit of all the lowly who seek refuge in God, as He will assume His position as king by first taking the position of lowliness (Luke 22:25-27).

That the child will be the supreme, divine king is seen in the description that the angel uses. The child is born *in the city of David* (Bethlehem; compare Micah 5:2), a reminder of the promise to David of a descendant who would become the great king. In the Roman Empire, the word *savior* usually refers to a prominent political or military ruler. Yet the Savior in Luke's narrative is neither of those, but He will outshine them all.

Christ means "anointed," referring to the action that designates someone as occupying an important office. *Lord* is a term of absolute authority. The great statement of Roman authority is "Caesar is lord" (compare John 19:15). But Israel's Lord is none other than the Lord God. The angel speaks of the newborn, for indeed He will be revealed to be God himself, entering the world as a human.

12. And this shall be a sign unto you; Ye shall find the babe wrapped in swaddling clothes, lying in a manger.

Though hailed as king, the child lies in a feeding trough for livestock. What an interesting sign for the shepherds! Certainly, it is an identifier: the child they are to seek will be found in an unusual place. But it is also a description: the divine king is born in a place of poverty, even rejection.

C. The Song of Celebration (vv. 13, 14)

13. And suddenly there was with the angel a multitude of the heavenly host praising God, and saying,

The one angel now has a lot of company! The word *host* refers to a great army (compare 1 Kings 22:19). In contrast with Rome's military might, this is the army of Heaven. The shepherds are thus granted a glimpse of God's supreme power.

The text has the army *saying* the praise, but most of us think in terms of the heavenly host *singing* (that is, "saying to music"). If we think of Luke's account of Jesus' birth as a musical (see the Introduction to lesson 2), then this song is the climax. The mighty army of Heaven sings praise for God, and humans get to hear it!

14. Glory to God in the highest, and on earth peace, good will toward men.

Whatever humans claim for themselves, God's claims are superior. Nothing will demonstrate His primacy more than what Jesus will accomplish. So Jesus' birth is the fitting moment for praise *to God in the highest.*

Rome's empire has brought a certain peace to the world. *Pax Romana,* Latin for "Roman peace," is a common slogan of the day. Rome imposes peace through force, but only God can bring real peace. His peace is not just the cessation of hostility. It means positive goodwill, harmony, and love among people. As the good news of Jesus is made known to the nations, people will be drawn together in loving fellowship, where former enemies can become sisters and brothers in Christ.

IV. Shepherds' Journey
(LUKE 2:15-17)

A. Deciding to Go (vv. 15, 16)

15. And it came to pass, as the angels were gone away from them into heaven, the shepherds said one to another, Let us now go even unto Bethlehem, and see this thing which is come to pass, which the Lord hath made known unto us.

God makes himself known not to the proud, but to the lowly (Luke 10:21). These lowly shepherds are the ones ready to receive with joy what God has to offer.

16. And they came with haste, and found Mary, and Joseph, and the babe lying in a manger.

With the energy of those who realize the magnitude of God's gift, the shepherds arrive to find a poor couple whose baby lies in a feeding trough. The great king is a child in a family as humble as those of the shepherds! That is God's plan.

> *What Do You Think?*
> Other than a nativity scene, what aspects of your Christmas celebration especially remind you of "the reason for the season"? Why is that?
> *Talking Points for Your Discussion*
> - Family traditions
> - Special church programs
> - Music
> - Certain decorations
> - Other

❧ OFFICIAL INVITATION ❧

On November 24, 2009, two gate-crashers somehow managed to join hundreds of guests at a White House state dinner. Having not been invited, the two had not undergone the background checks, etc., that invitees to such functions must undergo. The fact that these two managed to bypass the entire security process, even to the point of getting their picture taken with the president, caused quite an uproar!

God did a thorough background check before issuing invitations to see the newborn king. As a result, the shepherds were invited, as were the Magi (Matthew 2:1, 2). Herod wanted to come, but was denied (2:8, 12). Today, God extends an invitation for all to approach and accept Jesus. We all have criminal backgrounds because we all have broken God's laws. And that's precisely why He bids us come! How will you respond? —C. R. B.

B. Spreading the News (v. 17)

17. And when they had seen it, they made known abroad the saying which was told them concerning this child.

News like this cannot be kept secret, even though the shepherds do not yet have the entire gospel story. But what they know, they are ready to share. The God of Israel is fulfilling His promises for His lowly people, and He is doing so by means of a king born in lowliness.

> *What Do You Think?*
> What can we do this Christmas season to instill in ourselves the shepherds' level of excitement for sharing the good news about Jesus?
> *Talking Points for Your Discussion*
> - Things to do within large groups
> - Things to do within small groups
> - Things to do individually

Conclusion
A. Life Turned Upside Down

All the publicity seems to go to powerful governments, rich corporations, dynamic businesspeople, and famous entertainers. Perhaps we think that God's message would be better received if the church had a more powerful, prominent identity.

But the power of God does not operate like the power of the world. God's work confounds how we look at life. It turns life upside down, beginning in a stable, leading to a cross, climaxing at an empty tomb. It is the power to save for eternity.

B. Prayer

O God, may we rejoice anew in the greatest gift ever given! In the name of Jesus, that gift, amen.

C. Thought to Remember

Come to the manger yet again.

INVOLVEMENT LEARNING

Some of the activities below are also found in the helpful student book, Adult Bible Class.
Don't forget to download the free reproducible page from www.standardlesson.com to enhance your lesson!

Into the Lesson

Write *Taxes, Taxes, Taxes!* on the board. Ask learners to name all the taxes they can think of; jot responses on the board. Use the commentary to compare and contrast today's taxes with the burden of Roman taxation. Discuss especially the consequences for poor people, such as Joseph and Mary, as a transition to Bible study.

Alternative: Place in chairs copies of the "O Little Town of Bethlehem" activity from the reproducible page, which you can download. Learners can begin working on this as they arrive. Discuss results as a class. This will remind the class of the historical role of Bethlehem before Christ in setting the stage for today's Bible study.

Into the Word

Divide the class into two groups and have them do a responsive reading of today's text. Assign the odd-numbered verses to one group and the even-numbered verses to the other.

Before class, prepare handouts of a chart titled *A Royal Birth.* Below the title have three columns with these headings, one each: Circumstances / "Typical" Births of Royal Descent / King Jesus' Birth. Put the following five rows in the Circumstances column: 1. Obligation to pay taxes (Matthew 17:25, 26). 2. Assistance available for the birth. 3. Surroundings for the birth. 4. Messengers and method for spreading news of the birth. 5. First people to receive the news of the birth.

As you distribute the handouts, say, "The circumstances of Jesus' birth were quite different from what we might expect of a 'typical' birth of royal descent! Complete the chart by comparing and contrasting the two. The birth narratives of Matthew and Luke are available for answers in the third column; you may have to use your imagination to provide most answers for the middle column." Learners can work in small groups of three or four.

As groups work, draw this same chart on the board. Allow groups time to share answers with the class as a whole as you enter their responses on the chart you have on the board. Ask if there were any circumstances in which Jesus' birth was superior to that of a "typical" king.

Into Life

State, "Today's text, especially verses 1-7, are part of the Christian's basic doctrinal belief: that Jesus, Son of God, was born of the virgin Mary at a specific time in history to be God's Savior for all people. Let's work on memorizing those seven verses."

Distribute randomly to class members 15 slips of paper with the following phrases or clauses, one per slip: 1—And it came to pass in those days / 2—that there went out a decree from Caesar Augustus / 3—that all the world should be taxed / 4—(And this taxing was first made when Cyrenius was governor of Syria) / 5—And all went to be taxed, every one to his own city / 6—And Joseph also went up from Galilee / 7—out of the city of Nazareth, into Judaea / 8—unto the city of David, which is called Bethlehem / 9—(because he was of the house and lineage of David) / 10—to be taxed with Mary his espoused wife, being great with child / 11—And so it was, that, while they were there / 12—the days were accomplished that she should be delivered / 13—And she brought forth her firstborn son / 14—and wrapped him in swaddling clothes, and laid him in a manger / 15—because there was no room for them in the inn.

First, have learners read the slips aloud, in the correct sequence. Second, ask learners to do the same thing again, but without looking at their slips. Repeat these two steps as appropriate.

Option: Distribute copies of the "Angels and Shepherds and Me" activity from the reproducible page for learners to work on in pairs or as a take-home activity.

JESUS IS PRESENTED IN THE TEMPLE

DEVOTIONAL READING: Isaiah 49:8-13
BACKGROUND SCRIPTURE: Luke 2:21-40

LUKE 2:21, 22, 25-38

21 And when eight days were accomplished for the circumcising of the child, his name was called JESUS, which was so named of the angel before he was conceived in the womb.

22 And when the days of her purification according to the law of Moses were accomplished, they brought him to Jerusalem, to present him to the Lord.

. . . .

25 And, behold, there was a man in Jerusalem, whose name was Simeon; and the same man was just and devout, waiting for the consolation of Israel: and the Holy Ghost was upon him.

26 And it was revealed unto him by the Holy Ghost, that he should not see death, before he had seen the Lord's Christ.

27 And he came by the Spirit into the temple: and when the parents brought in the child Jesus, to do for him after the custom of the law,

28 Then took he him up in his arms, and blessed God, and said,

29 Lord, now lettest thou thy servant depart in peace, according to thy word:

30 For mine eyes have seen thy salvation,

31 Which thou hast prepared before the face of all people;

32 A light to lighten the Gentiles, and the glory of thy people Israel.

33 And Joseph and his mother marvelled at those things which were spoken of him.

34 And Simeon blessed them, and said unto Mary his mother, Behold, this child is set for the fall and rising again of many in Israel; and for a sign which shall be spoken against;

35 (Yea, a sword shall pierce through thy own soul also,) that the thoughts of many hearts may be revealed.

36 And there was one Anna, a prophetess, the daughter of Phanuel, of the tribe of Aser: she was of a great age, and had lived with an husband seven years from her virginity;

37 And she was a widow of about fourscore and four years, which departed not from the temple, but served God with fastings and prayers night and day.

38 And she coming in that instant gave thanks likewise unto the Lord, and spake of him to all them that looked for redemption in Jerusalem.

KEY VERSE

Mine eyes have seen thy salvation, which thou hast prepared before the face of all people.

—Luke 2:30, 31

JESUS AND THE JUST REIGN OF GOD

Unit 1: God Sends Jesus
LESSONS 1–5

LESSON AIMS

After participating in this lesson, each student will be able to:

1. Tell what happened when the infant Jesus was presented at the temple.

2. Explain the significance of the blessings of Simeon and Anna.

3. Identify a practical way to follow the example of Simeon and Anna in proclaiming the hope found in Jesus.

LESSON OUTLINE

Introduction
  A. "What Do You Want to Be?"
  B. Lesson Background
I. Obedient Parents (LUKE 2:21, 22)
  A. Circumcision and Naming (v. 21)
  B. Journey and Presentation (v. 22)
II. Devout Simeon (LUKE 2:25-35)
  A. Holy Status (vv. 25, 26)
  B. Faithful Action (v. 27)
  C. Effusive Praise (vv. 28-32)
  D. Amazed Parents (v. 33)
  E. Predicted Future (vv. 34, 35)
    Jesus: Still Spoken Against
III. Elderly Anna (LUKE 2:36-38)
  A. Holy Status (vv. 36, 37)
  B. Thankful Words (v. 38)
    Not an Either/Or Proposition
Conclusion
  A. Our Hopeful Expectation
  B. Prayer
  C. Thought to Remember

Introduction

A. "What Do You Want to Be?"

"What do you want to be when you grow up?" is a question children become accustomed to from adults. Some of us were annoyed by that question when we were younger. Most of us will admit that we have inflicted it on children ourselves.

When we see a child, we naturally think of the child's potential. What might she or he be in the future? The possibilities are intriguing and hopeful: an entrepreneur who starts a successful business, a scientist who makes a breakthrough discovery, an influential leader who shapes public policy—the list is endless. But with a few notable exceptions in the Bible, a child's future is uncertain, not yet written. It may be filled with greatness, tragedy, or both.

When Jesus was born, His parents already had an authoritative statement about His future (see Luke 1:32, 33). But how would that future as the ruler on David's throne take shape? A first glimpse at the answer comes in today's text.

B. Lesson Background

Our lesson is set in the Jerusalem temple against the background of the requirements of the Law of Moses. The temple was the center of ancient Israel's worship. In the wilderness just after the exodus from Egypt, God instructed Israel on building a tabernacle (in effect, a portable temple) for worship. The tabernacle and its successor, the temple, represented God's presence with His people. But as the Israelites descended further and further into sin, no king proved to be the one whose throne God would establish forever.

Finally, the temple was destroyed by the Babylonians when they sacked Jerusalem in 586 BC and took the people captive. The Jews were allowed to rebuild Jerusalem and its temple after that exile ended several decades later. That second temple was far less grand than the first. Yet God promised that the one who would build the true temple was still to come, and the glory of the ultimate temple of fulfillment would far outshine that of the one built by the returning exiles (Haggai 2:6-9).

Herod the Great, the client king who ruled Judea on Rome's behalf, began a massive project to rebuild the temple about two decades before Jesus' birth. The project was breathtaking, involving precut 55-ton stones, large columns to support vast colonnades, and huge stairs ascending to the temple mount. No doubt Herod wanted to legitimize himself as the promised temple-building king, but few took that idea seriously. The faithful still waited for God to send the true king. It is in that context that the infant Jesus is presented at the temple in today's text.

I. Obedient Parents
(LUKE 2:21, 22)
A. Circumcision and Naming (v. 21)

21. And when eight days were accomplished for the circumcising of the child, his name was called JESUS, which was so named of the angel before he was conceived in the womb.

One purpose of the Law of Moses, as given by God, was to establish Israel's identity as distinct from its pagan neighbors. A key command in this regard is circumcision. This was a sign of God's covenant, His pledge of blessing and terms of obedience, with Old Testament Israel. Centuries before God gave that law, He had commanded Abraham that his male descendants should be circumcised *eight days* after their birth (Genesis 17:12). Luke specifies that Jesus' parents fully obey this requirement.

Furthermore, the parents also obey the angel's instruction in naming Jesus (Luke 1:31). We are reminded of Zacharias and Elisabeth's similar obedience regarding the circumcision and naming of John (vv. 13, 59, 63).

B. Journey and Presentation (v. 22)

22. And when the days of her purification according to the law of Moses were accomplished, they brought him to Jerusalem, to present him to the Lord.

The Mosaic law features commands regarding things that are "clean" and "unclean." Some of these commands have a relationship to hygiene, but most have symbolic significance. Certain

common events can make a person unclean; for women, these include childbirth. At the end of a specified period of time, a woman who has given birth is to offer a sacrifice to mark the end of her uncleanness (Leviticus 12).

Mary's purification after the birth of her male child takes nearly six weeks (Leviticus 12:2, 4). At the time that she comes to the temple for her purification (12:6-8), she also presents Jesus *to the Lord*. The law specifies that a special gift is to be made at the birth of a firstborn (Exodus 13:2, 12, 13, 15; Numbers 18:15, 16), and Mary and Joseph are careful to obey this requirement as well (see Luke 2:23, 24, not in today's text).

Thus we see several of the law's commands coming together around the birth of this mother's first son. It is obedience to the Mosaic Law that brings to the temple for the first time the one who will fulfill God's promise to build the true temple. The stage is now set for the appearance of two other people who are lowly and righteous.

What Do You Think?

What more can your congregation do to stress to new parents the importance of honoring God as they welcome their new arrival?

Talking Points for Your Discussion
- Special presentations (parent dedication, etc.)
- Support groups
- Sermons and lessons
- Other

II. Devout Simeon
(LUKE 2:25-35)
A. Holy Status (vv. 25, 26)

25. And, behold, there was a man in Jerusalem, whose name was Simeon; and the same man was just and devout, waiting for the consolation of Israel: and the Holy Ghost was upon him.

A certain man named Simeon now comes on the scene. The description of his being *just* means that he carefully observes the Law of Moses; *devout* means that he is carefully respectful of God.

God's law includes promises in addition to commands. Simeon's *waiting for the consolation of*

Israel reveals a strong expectation and longing that God will fulfill those promises by bringing the answer to Israel's suffering (compare Isaiah 40:1). God's promises are centuries old, yet Simeon lives in hope that God will nevertheless fulfill them, and soon.

What Do You Think?

Which promises of God (and Scripture to support them) are especially important to you at the present time? Why?

Talking Points for Your Discussion

- For avoidance of temptation
- For guidance in making an important decision
- For a crisis involving a family member
- Other

The Holy Spirit's work in the Old Testament was primarily to empower the prophets to speak for God. The same is true of Simeon, as it is for others in Luke's Gospel. When Simeon speaks, we will listen to hear God's message.

26. And it was revealed unto him by the Holy Ghost, that he should not see death, before he had seen the Lord's Christ.

God has responded to Simeon's faithful expectancy with a personal promise. The time of fulfillment is indeed near, and God has pledged that Simeon will live to see the one who will bring that fulfillment. The word *Christ* means "anointed," therefore *the Lord's Christ* is the Lord's anointed one. This is none other than the king whom God has promised to His people, the great Son of David who is to build God's house, the true temple, and whose throne God intends to establish forever.

B. Faithful Action (v. 27)

27. And he came by the Spirit into the temple: and when the parents brought in the child Jesus, to do for him after the custom of the law.

God's Spirit, having promised Simeon that he is to see God's king, instructs that man to go to the temple on this particular day. It must be with a sense of expectation that Simeon receives this instruction! While there, Simeon sees Jesus' parents, with Jesus, arrive to perform their duties under the Law of Moses as previously discussed.

What Do You Think?

Have you ever had an experience of being led by the Holy Spirit to be in the right place at the right time? What happened? How do you know that the experience was not due to random chance?

Talking Points for Your Discussion

- To be a blessing to someone
- To be blessed by someone
- To witness to someone
- Other

C. Effusive Praise (vv. 28-32)

28. Then took he him up in his arms, and blessed God, and said.

Simeon not only sees the king, he also holds Him *in his arms*. If Simeon expects that God's king will appear in might and glory, he is surprised: what he witnesses is an infant-in-arms, the child of impoverished parents. Yet the aged prophet is more than happy to hold the baby. What can Simeon do but offer God praise, or bless God?

29. Lord, now lettest thou thy servant depart in peace, according to thy word.

In the original language, the emphasis of Simeon's words falls on two ideas: *now* and *peace*. Now the long-awaited time of fulfillment has come. That means peace for Simeon, as he can now die (*depart*) with renewed confidence that God's work will come to its climax.

30. For mine eyes have seen thy salvation.

Although the word *salvation* is among the most common in the New Testament, the word that appears here in the original language is unusual, occurring just a few times. Here and in Luke 3:6, the author draws on the Greek version of the Old Testament, known as the Septuagint. Isaiah 40:5 in that translation says that "all flesh shall see the salvation of God." However, Isaiah 40:5 from the Hebrew is somewhat different: "all flesh shall see *it*." The italicized *it* means that this word does not appear in the original, Hebrew language, and the translators have inserted this pronoun for smooth reading. Luke confirms the Septuagint's clarification that *it* refers to *thy salvation*, which uses the same unusual Greek word. Our next verse describes the extent of this salvation.

31. Which thou hast prepared before the face of all people.

Thinking back to the rare word for *salvation* in verse 30, we see Luke reminding the reader that God's promise is for *all people*. Again, see Luke 3:6, which affirms the same thing with the phrasing "all flesh." God's plan for the salvation of the nations is not a last-minute idea. It has been His central purpose for the world from the very beginning. He has prepared for this salvation throughout biblical history—through the times and events of the patriarchs, the exodus, the conquest of the promised land, the judges, Israel's united and divided monarchies, the Babylonian exile, and Israel's partial return to its land. What Simeon sees being fulfilled is what his people for generations have anticipated in preparation.

32. A light to lighten the Gentiles, and the glory of thy people Israel.

Using phrases from the prophet Isaiah, Simeon underlines the fulfillment of God's ancient promises. *Light to lighten the Gentiles* is the fulfillment of God's pledge to bless the nations (Genesis 12:1-3; Isaiah 42:6; 49:6). That is the ultimate purpose of His call to Israel, and so salvation that brings light to all nations is Israel's true glory (Isaiah 46:13).

D. Amazed Parents (v. 33)

33. And Joseph and his mother marvelled at those things which were spoken of him.

The common reaction to God's inspired words is marvel or amazement (Luke 1:63; 2:18; etc.). Even Jesus' parents, already recipients of God's revelation about Jesus, are in a state of awe as they hear Simeon's words. They still have much to learn about how God will fulfill His promises through Jesus.

E. Predicted Future (vv. 34, 35)

34a. And Simeon blessed them, and said unto Mary his mother, Behold, this child is set for the fall and rising again of many in Israel;

Simeon asks for God's blessing on the family, but his words to Mary take a dark turn. Because the child is "the glory of thy people Israel" (v. 32, above), we are not surprised that He is for the *ris-*

Visual for Lesson 5

Use this visual to introduce the discussion question associated with verse 25.

ing again of many in Israel. But Simeon's first prediction is that Jesus will be for *the fall . . . of many in Israel*!

Yet that is not a new prediction, as Isaiah 8:14 establishes. As the gospel story develops, Jesus repeatedly provokes division among His countrymen. Many believe in Him, but many refuse. Though He brings salvation, He also brings judgment. Every period of biblical history is a witness to division between the believing and the unbelieving. This will be no less true during Jesus' earthly ministry.

34b. And for a sign which shall be spoken against.

Although Jesus brings God's salvation, He also will be the object of violent opposition (compare Luke 6:11; 19:47). That opposition comes as no surprise in the divine plan. In fact, Jesus in the end will submit willingly to the violent plans of His opponents.

❧ JESUS: STILL SPOKEN AGAINST ❧

Christopher Hitchens (1949–2011) reached the peak of his notoriety as an atheist with the publication of his 2007 best seller, *God Is Not Great: How Religion Poisons Everything*. Hitchens believed organized religion to be "violent, irrational, intolerant, allied to racism, tribalism, and bigotry."

Less well-known is his brother, Peter, who became a Christian as an adult. His 2010 book, *The Rage Against God: How Atheism Led Me to*

Faith, refutes his brother's position. Peter's book describes how the "new atheists," such as his brother, willfully overlook the sins of atheism.

Simeon's prophecy that Jesus would be "a sign which shall be spoken against" is being continually fulfilled, as Christopher Hitchens's atheism makes clear. People of all times and places have spoken against Jesus. But others, such as Christopher's own brother, rise up to contest their arguments. If you have experienced family stress over your acceptance of Christ, you're not alone! Jesus himself predicted it (Luke 12:51-53). We should expect nothing to change in this regard until Jesus returns. Until then, there is something else that will not change: God's power to enable us to persevere (Hebrews 12:1).　　　　—C. R. B.

35. (Yea, a sword shall pierce through thy own soul also,) that the thoughts of many hearts may be revealed.

Jesus' mission is to die for the sins of humanity, and Luke's first hint regarding the cross is in the verse now before us. The great mystery of God's plan is that He brings victory, peace, and salvation to humanity by entering the world as a man and submitting to the worst treatment that the world can give. In so doing, Jesus receives the punishment that belongs to us. The pain that Jesus will endure will be pain to Mary as well, like a sword that cuts through her inmost being.

The revealing of what is inside every heart will be a result of Jesus' mission. God knows what is in a person's heart (Psalm 139:2), and we see that Jesus knows the thoughts of others in the gospel story line. As God through the gospel reveals the hidden, rebellious thoughts of humanity, we face a choice: to continue a masquerade of self-sufficiency or to cast ourselves on the mercy of the God who lays bare what is inside us.

III. Elderly Anna
(Luke 2:36-38)
A. Holy Status (vv. 36, 37)

36. And there was one Anna, a prophetess, the daughter of Phanuel, of the tribe of Aser: she was of a great age, and had lived with an husband seven years from her virginity.

Like Simeon, Anna is distinguished by her devotion to God and a prophetic empowerment by God's Spirit. She is an aged widow, having been married to a man who lived only seven years after the wedding. A woman without a husband in biblical times is often destitute. Bereft of family support, she may be able to do nothing but trust in God (Psalm 146:9; 1 Timothy 5:5).

Mention of *the tribe of Aser* (or Asher) identifies her ancestors as those who originally occupied the far northwestern part of Israel's territory (Joshua 19:24-31). Her continual presence in the temple (see the next verse), which is 75 miles or so from her ancestral territory, speaks to her devotion. The name *Phanuel* means "face of God."

37. And she was a widow of about four-score and four years, which departed not from the temple, but served God with fastings and prayers night and day.

The first phrase can be interpreted two ways: either (1) Anna is now about 84 years old or (2) she has been a widow for about 84 years. Either possibility fits the description of her being "of great age" in verse 36. Either possibility also means that she is old enough to remember when the Romans conquered the Jewish homeland in 63 BC.

Anna spends as much time as possible in the temple precincts, where her fastings represent mourning (compare Matthew 9:15). This expresses sadness for Israel's plight. So the prayers connected with her fastings are supplications to God to send the promised time of restoration. Devoted Anna awaits the arrival of God's king in His temple to restore His blessing to His people.

HOW TO SAY IT

Aser	*A*-ser.
Asher	*Ash*-er.
Babylonian	Bab-ih-*low*-nee-un.
Herod	*Hair*-ud.
Judea	Joo-*dee*-uh.
patriarchs	*pay*-tree-arks.
Phanuel	Fuh-*nyoo*-el.
Septuagint	Sep-*too*-ih-jent.
Simeon	*Sim*-ee-un.

B. Thankful Words (v. 38)

38. And she coming in that instant gave thanks likewise unto the Lord, and spake of him to all them that looked for redemption in Jerusalem.

Anna, like Simeon, immediately recognizes that Jesus is the very one whom God has promised. As we remember that Anna is a prophetess (v. 36), we understand that it is by the Holy Spirit's power that she, like Simeon, recognizes the role Jesus is to have. She cannot help but share this message with those who are waiting expectantly *for redemption in Jerusalem*. That redemption involves the arrival of the great king who is now at the center of attention. We are led to understand that among the temple worshippers are others like Simeon and Anna who are fervent in their expectation that God will do what He has promised for His people.

Luke uses a certain verb tense that emphasizes that Anna continually praises God and tells others about Jesus. We easily imagine that Anna shares the truth that has been revealed to her not only while Joseph, Mary, and Jesus are in the temple, but also after they have left.

"Preach the gospel at all times; when necessary, use words." This saying is commonly attributed to Francis of Assisi, although the earliest record of the statement comes two centuries after his death in 1226. Even so, the saying reflects a long-running tension regarding the best way to win the world to Christ: should it be through the spoken word or through deeds of Christian mercy?

The liberal "social gospel" of the early twentieth century stressed the work of medical and educational missions. By contrast, those more conservative in doctrine usually stressed verbal proclamation of the gospel (Romans 10:17). Missionaries in the latter group eventually came to acknowledge the value of deeds of mercy in opening minds to hear the gospel message. The false choice of "either words or deeds" is clear. Evangelism takes place by both words *and* deeds.

Anna became one who continually spoke of Jesus to all who would listen. Her deeds—the pattern of her devoted life—lent credibility to her message. And so it should be with us (see John 13:34, 35).   —C. R. B.

Conclusion

A. Our Hopeful Expectation

What would it have been like for us to have heard Simeon and Anna personally? Would we have received their messages with enthusiasm? Would we have reacted with skepticism, wondering "why now?" after so many centuries of waiting? Seeing God's plan with the benefit of hindsight, we now have more information than did either Simeon or Anna. This allows us to recognize what it means to follow Jesus in a life of surrender. And so we do, in hopeful expectation of the eternity with Him that awaits.

B. Prayer

Father, in Your Son You show us the only way to eternal life. Teach us to take up our crosses daily and follow Him. We pray in Jesus' name, amen.

C. Thought to Remember

Be like Simeon. Be like Anna.

INVOLVEMENT LEARNING

Some of the activities below are also found in the helpful student book, Adult Bible Class.
Don't forget to download the free reproducible page from www.standardlesson.com to enhance your lesson!

Into the Lesson

Wrap a large, empty box as if it were a present; cover the wrapping with question marks. As class begins, hold the box over your head and ask, "What's in it?" Someone will surely say, "We don't have any way of knowing!" Then ask, "Who *would* know?" The answer, of course, is, "The one who selected the gift and wrapped it."

Then compare this situation with the occasion of Simeon holding the baby Jesus in today's text. Say, "God knew what was in that 'gift'! It was His Son, and He revealed some of the baby's nature and future to Mary, to Joseph, and—in today's study—to Simeon and Anna. By revelation, each knew something significant about this indescribable gift wrapped in flesh and blood. Let's open God's Word and find out more." Direct learners to today's text.

Into the Word

Ask for three volunteers to read the following three segments aloud, one each: Luke 2:21, 22 / Luke 2:25-35 / Luke 2:36-38. Before the reading, instruct the class to be alert especially to what Simeon and Anna said and did.

Distribute 8½" x 11" handouts that feature a chart with three columns: the leftmost column will be very wide; the middle and rightmost columns will be very narrow. Label the three columns, left to right, as Description / Simeon / Anna.

Have the following entries as rows in the leftmost column: 1. Spent a lot of time at the temple. 2. Believed God's prophecies concerning a coming king. 3. Was old. 4. Received a personal promise from God to see the Messiah. 5. Noted for a strong prayer life. 6. Held the baby Jesus. 7. Realized the Messiah was for the Gentiles as well. 8. Is noted to have had the gift of prophecy. 9. Was from the tribe of Aser (or Asher). 10. Was widowed. 11. Spoke of Jesus as "the consolation of Israel." 12. Had a special message for Mary. 13. Spoke of the baby as being "redemption." 14. Got a noticeable reaction from Joseph and Mary. 15. Spoke of the baby as being "salvation." 16. Expressed a readiness to die, having seen the Messiah. 17. Was at the temple night and day. 18. Expressed personal thanks to God for the arrival of the Messiah. 19. Told many that the Messiah had arrived. 20. Was blessed by God.

Say, "Read through each of the short statements. As you look at today's text, put check marks under the appropriate name. If you consider the statement to be true for both, then put a check mark under both names." Answers are, of course, in today's text; allow time for sharing of reactions and impressions.

Alternative: The "Simeon, Anna, and Me" activity from the reproducible page, noted in the Into Life segment below, offers an abbreviated version of the above while including personal application. You may wish to use it as a transition.

Option: Distribute copies of the "Jesus' Middle Name?" activity from the reproducible page, which you can download. Have learners complete it in pairs. This exercise will allow a look at the text in a way that emphasizes the roles Jesus came to fulfill.

Into Life

Give each learner a name sticker with the letters *LSLA* on it. Explain that the letters stand for "Like Simeon, Like Anna." Suggest that learners wear the label in the week ahead. When questioned about the meaning of the letters, they can be prepared to say, "Like Simeon, Like Anna—I want to affirm publicly my belief that Jesus is the hope of the world for light and glory and redemption." This may offer an opportunity to speak further with the inquiring one about the lordship of Jesus.

Option: If you did not use the "Simeon, Anna, and Me" activity earlier, distribute copies now. Have learners complete this to check their spiritual maturity in relation to that of Simeon and Anna.

Honoring the Sabbath

Devotional Reading: John 5:2-17
Background Scripture: Luke 6:1-11

Luke 6:1-11

1 And it came to pass on the second sabbath after the first, that he went through the corn fields; and his disciples plucked the ears of corn, and did eat, rubbing them in their hands.

2 And certain of the Pharisees said unto them, Why do ye that which is not lawful to do on the sabbath days?

3 And Jesus answering them said, Have ye not read so much as this, what David did, when himself was an hungred, and they which were with him;

4 How he went into the house of God, and did take and eat the shewbread, and gave also to them that were with him; which it is not lawful to eat but for the priests alone?

5 And he said unto them, That the Son of man is Lord also of the sabbath.

6 And it came to pass also on another sabbath, that he entered into the synagogue and

taught: and there was a man whose right hand was withered.

7 And the scribes and Pharisees watched him, whether he would heal on the sabbath day; that they might find an accusation against him.

8 But he knew their thoughts, and said to the man which had the withered hand, Rise up, and stand forth in the midst. And he arose and stood forth.

9 Then said Jesus unto them, I will ask you one thing; Is it lawful on the sabbath days to do good, or to do evil? to save life, or to destroy it?

10 And looking round about upon them all, he said unto the man, Stretch forth thy hand. And he did so: and his hand was restored whole as the other.

11 And they were filled with madness; and communed one with another what they might do to Jesus.

Key Verse

Then said Jesus unto them, I will ask you one thing; Is it lawful on the sabbath days to do good, or to do evil? to save life, or to destroy it? —**Luke 6:9**

Photo: iStockphoto / Thinkstock

JESUS AND THE JUST REIGN OF GOD

Unit 2: Jesus Ushers in the Reign of God

LESSONS 6–9

LESSON AIMS

After participating in this lesson, each student will be able to:

1. Retell the story of Jesus and His disciples' being criticized for breaking the Sabbath.

2. Explain why breaking the Sabbath was so serious in Jesus' day and, in light of that, the significance of Jesus' being "Lord of the Sabbath."

3. Express his or her commitment to Jesus, who is Lord of the Sabbath and Lord of life.

LESSON OUTLINE

Introduction

A. Question Loading

"Have you stopped beating your wife?" In the give-and-take of daily conversation, one must be alert to questions that presuppose something to be true that is not true or has not been proven to be true. Such questions have been referred to as *loaded questions*. "Have you stopped beating your wife?" is the classic example. Note that this question has been "loaded" with the assumption that the person being questioned is a wife-beater. Whether he answers *no* or *yes*, he will be admitting to the wife-beating presupposition.

Today's lesson shows Jesus doing verbal battle with those who want to discredit Him. Question-loading is one of the techniques of His opponents. But the two encounters we will examine yielded results they did not anticipate.

B. Lesson Background

The two encounters in today's lesson involve issues of the Sabbath day. *Sabbath* is a Hebrew word meaning "rest" or "cease." This fact is fundamental for understanding God's requirements for Sabbath-keeping. Instructions regarding the Sabbath (the seventh day of the week) form a central component to the system of law of ancient Israel.

Even before receiving the law at Mount Sinai (Exodus 19 and following), the Israelites were instructed to gather and prepare a double portion of manna on the sixth day so there would be no working for food on the seventh (see Exodus 16:1-26). The principle of Sabbath-rest finds its most important expression as the fourth of the Ten Commandments, and it is the longest one in both Exodus 20:8-11 and Deuteronomy 5:12-15. To "remember" the Sabbath was to keep it holy. It was to be a day of rest, a cessation from all normal work activities. To work on this day was to break the Sabbath. Violators were subject to the death penalty (Exodus 31:12-17).

The Sabbath was instituted by God to be an enjoyable and necessary day for rest, reflection, and prayer. By the first century, however, it seems that some religious leaders of the Jews had elevated Sabbath-keeping to an oppressive art. Thus, keeping the Sabbath was more important than the benefits derived from keeping the Sabbath. Breaking the Sabbath as the Pharisees had defined it was an offense that marked one as religiously careless and sinful. The Gospels portray the Pharisees as masters of minutiae in this regard. Today's lesson finds Jesus at odds with some Pharisees over the issue of Sabbath-breaking. Matthew 12:1-8 and Mark 2:23-28 are parallels to our first segment; Matthew 12:9-14 and Mark 3:1-6 are parallels to our second segment.

I. Harvesting on the Sabbath
(Luke 6:1-5)

A. Loaded Question (vv. 1, 2)

1. And it came to pass on the second sabbath after the first, that he went through the corn fields; and his disciples plucked the ears of corn, and did eat, rubbing them in their hands.

Luke introduces us to another Sabbath day incident, which is called *the second sabbath after the first*. The prior Sabbath that Luke probably has in mind involves the incident of casting a demon out of a man (exorcism) in the Capernaum synagogue (Luke 4:31-37).

This particular confrontation occurs outdoors, as we see Jesus and His disciples walking through a field that has ripe heads of grain. When we see the word *corn* in the *King James Version*, we should not think of the yellow maize of western agriculture, which is unknown to Jesus' time and place. The text reflects an older use of the word *corn* to indicate any type of food grain. The grain is probably wheat or barley, and its harvestable condition places this episode in the April to June time frame.

While plucking heads of the ripe grain, the disciples are *rubbing them in their hands* in order to

HOW TO SAY IT

Ahimelech	A-*him*-uh-leck.
Assange	Eh-*sonzh*.
Capernaum	Kuh-*per*-nay-um.
Pharisees	*Fair*-ih-seez.
Sinai	*Sigh*-nye or *Sigh*-nay-eye.
synagogue	*sin*-uh-gog.

remove the chaff. The result is edible kernels of wheat or barley. This is a meager snack, but better than nothing when hungry. It is common for public pathways to go through private fields, so the disciples are not trespassing. It is also permissible to pluck and snack on this ripe grain while passing through a field as long as no sickle is used (see Deuteronomy 23:25).

2. And certain of the Pharisees said unto them, Why do ye that which is not lawful to do on the sabbath days?

Here is the loaded question. The assumption behind the question is that lawbreaking is happening. Therefore, for Jesus to answer the *why* as it is posed would be to admit to Sabbath-breaking. There is no issue about trespassing or stealing here. The issue, rather, is that both the plucking and rubbing of the grain heads are considered "work" (that is, reaping and threshing) by the Pharisees, and therefore a violation of the Sabbath (compare Luke 13:14; John 5:10).

It seems that Pharisees are accompanying Jesus and His disciples in order to see wrongdoing and accuse Him of it. They hope thereby to be able to discredit Him (see Luke 6:7, below).

What Do You Think?

What "loaded questions" do unbelievers ask Christians today? How do we respond in redemptive and Christ-honoring ways?

Talking Points for Your Discussion
- Concerning the existence of evil
- Concerning perceived contradictions in the Bible
- Concerning creation
- Other

B. Powerful Precedent (vv. 3, 4)

3, 4. And Jesus answering them said, Have ye not read so much as this, what David did, when himself was an hungred, and they which were with him; how he went into the house of God, and did take and eat the shewbread, and gave also to them that were with him; which it is not lawful to eat but for the priests alone?

Rather than answer the loaded question directly, Jesus responds by recalling a story from Israel's history that is recorded in 1 Samuel 21:1-6. In a desperate moment, David stopped at Nob to ask for some loaves of bread to satisfy the hunger of his party of men. The loaves he received were not ordinary loaves, but the specially prepared *shewbread* used in tabernacle ceremonies described in Leviticus 24:5-9.

One interpretation holds that David made his request on a Sabbath day; this interpretation is supported by 1 Samuel 21:6, which indicates that old bread had just been replaced by new bread, which Leviticus 24:8 says happens on the Sabbath. This makes the parallel to the situation of Jesus and His disciples tighter still. No one accused David of desecration or Sabbath-breaking because his need justified his request. We even read that the priest Ahimelech cooperated with him.

C. Authoritative Assertion (v. 5)

5. And he said unto them, That the Son of man is Lord also of the sabbath.

The Pharisees undoubtedly do not expect this answer! To this point in the Gospel of Luke, Jesus has used the title *Son of man* only once, on the occasion when He claimed the authority to forgive sins in Luke 5:24. Jesus now reasserts His authority as if to say, "You Pharisees don't control the Sabbath; I do."

This is a bold, audacious claim, since the Jews rightly see the Sabbath as established by God. As with forgiving sins, Jesus therefore is claiming authority that is reserved for God alone. The phrase *Lord also of the Sabbath* brings to mind the God of creation, who created the Sabbath by resting on the seventh day (Genesis 2:1-3; compare Exodus 20:11).

What Do You Think?

How can we practice the concept of Jesus' being "the Lord of our Sabbaths"? Or does Colossians 2:16 invalidate such a question? Explain.

Talking Points for Your Discussion
- Issue of adequate rest
- Issue of witness to unbelievers
- Issue of tolerance (Romans 14:5, 6)
- Other

Louis XIV (1638–1715) became the titular king of France at age 5 upon the death of his father. His subsequent reign of 72 years marks him as the longest reigning monarch in European history.

Louis believed in the divine right of kings, as did other regents of that era. The idea was that earthly monarchs had been placed in power by God himself. Thus, kings had absolute authority and were not accountable to any other individual or group, such as a parliament. One quote often attributed to Louis (although disputed by some historians) is, "I am the state." This is an elegant way of saying, "I make the rules around here, so don't you dare challenge me."

This kind of thinking is quite startling to those of us who live in democracies of the twenty-first century! Of course, Louis XIV was no more vain than many other leaders, ancient or modern. The Pharisees believed they were in charge when it came to matters of Jewish religion—they were the gatekeepers of the Law of Moses.

Jesus overturned their presumptions when He said He was Lord of the Sabbath. The fact is, Christ *is* in charge; He makes the rules. God does indeed establish both religious authorities (Matthew 23:2, 3a; Hebrews 13:17) and the "higher powers" of earthly governments (Romans 13:1-7). But those who occupy such positions must always be ready to say, with John the Baptist, "He must increase, but I must decrease" (John 3:30). —C. R. B.

II. Healing on the Sabbath
(LUKE 6:6-11)

A. Watchful Waiting (vv. 6, 7)

6. And it came to pass also on another sabbath, that he entered into the synagogue and taught: and there was a man whose right hand was withered.

In describing what happens *on another sabbath*, Luke does not specifically identify this as the very next Saturday. But we are to understand that this particular incident follows closely after the grain-plucking confrontation. We also are not told which synagogue this is, but the one in Capernaum is as good a candidate as any (see Luke

4:31). The critics of Jesus seem to have a ready-made opportunity to embarrass Him—they even may have set it up themselves.

Matthew and Mark also include this story (see the Lesson Background), but only Luke gives the detail that it is specifically the man's *right hand* that is withered. We are not told the cause of this particular disability. The word translated *withered* can describe land that is parched during a drought. The disability may be due to an injury that has not healed correctly, to a disease that causes the hand to contract and shrivel, or to a birth defect. At any rate, this is a hand that is less than fully useful for normal tasks of the hand.

It is possible that this condition causes social problems for the man, for the right hand is used for eating while the left hand is "the bathroom hand"; this is consistent with the Bible's depiction of the right hand as being the one of greater honor (Genesis 48:13, 14; Luke 20:42; 22:69; Galatians 2:9; etc.). The man's disability may serve to exclude him from social gatherings that involve communal eating; such functions involve taking food from a common dish with the right hand, something this man may be unable to do.

7. And the scribes and Pharisees watched him, whether he would heal on the sabbath day; that they might find an accusation against him.

This verse lends support to the proposal that this is all a setup by Jesus' critics—*the scribes and Pharisees*—and not a chance encounter. We discussed the Pharisees earlier; the scribes are another group who see Jesus as a threat to their interpretation of the law. Indeed, interpreting the law is their very livelihood.

What we see here is the "actions version" of the loaded question: attempting to put Jesus in an impossible, lose-lose situation. If He heals the man, He breaks the Sabbath and can be discredited as a lawbreaker. If He does not heal the man, He will be shown as lacking compassion, for He has not withheld His healing power before, and this is a pillar of His popularity (Luke 4:40; 5:15). What seems not to be questioned by Jesus' opponents is His power to heal the unfortunate man (compare Luke 13:14).

B. Compassionate Choice (vv. 8-10)

8a. But he knew their thoughts.

Jesus has divine insight into hidden motives (compare Luke 5:22; John 2:24, 25; Mark 2:8). The need of the man with the disability is not the concern of the scribes and Pharisees. He is simply a tool in their escalating battle against the new teacher, Jesus, who has won a great following and has cast the members of the religious hierarchy in an unfavorable light.

8b. And said to the man which had the withered hand, Rise up, and stand forth in the midst. And he arose and stood forth.

Jesus moves the confrontation forward by giving the man with the disability two simple commands so that what is about to happen will be plainly visible to all gathered. Jesus does not whisper to the man, "Meet me out back later when no one is looking, and I will heal you." So the tension in the story builds. What will Jesus do next?

9. Then said Jesus unto them, I will ask you one thing; Is it lawful on the sabbath days to do good, or to do evil? to save life, or to destroy it?

Rather than minister immediately to the man, Jesus first turns to His opponents and asks questions of His own. These are not unfair "loaded questions," but rhetorical questions—questions where the answer is obvious. Should we do good things on the Sabbath or evil things? Obvious answer: good things. Should we be savers of life on the Sabbath or killers? Obvious answer: savers.

Rhetorical questions are not asked to obtain information, but to make a point. Jesus' point here is similar to His point in the grain-plucking story: Sabbath rules should not prohibit good, lifesaving actions. If they do, then something is wrong. Mark 3:4 adds that Jesus' opponents do not answer.

10. And looking round about upon them all, he said unto the man, Stretch forth thy hand. And he did so: and his hand was restored whole as the other.

Jesus now gives the man another command. To *stretch forth* describes the spreading out of a folded-up tent. The mental picture we get is of a hand that may be tightly knotted, with the fingertips crunched against the palm. Jesus' command enables the man to spread his fingers, something he has been unable to do.

❧ CHALLENGING AUTHORITY ❧

WikiLeaks became a household word a few years ago, as did the name of its founder, Julian Assange. A journalist, computer hacker, and activist advocating "open governance," Assange's goal was to promote transparency in government by publicizing the findings of whistle-blowers.

In 2010, WikiLeaks started releasing a quarter of a million stolen American diplomatic cables, almost half of which were classified as either *confidential* or *secret*. Assange has been likened to Daniel Ellsberg, a RAND employee who leaked the Pentagon Papers in 1971. That leak led to claims that the government had lied to its citizens about various aspects of the Vietnam War.

Because Jesus boldly challenged the religious and political leaders of His day, some may see Him as a "revolutionary" in the same sense as Ellsberg and Assange. The comparison raises several questions: Is it accurate? Why, or why not? How do we know when to obey authority (Matthew 23:2, 3a;

Romans 13:1) and when to defy authority (Acts 4:19; 5:29)? The answers are not always easy to determine, but prayer will be a key.   —C. R. B.

C. Resulting Rage (v. 11)

11. And they were filled with madness; and communed one with another what they might do to Jesus.

The reaction of Jesus' opponents should disappoint and disgust us. A man has just had his life changed! He is now socially acceptable, employable, etc. There is no possibility of trickery by Jesus. He is not like the stage magician who reads the mind of a "volunteer" planted in the audience. Rather than express joy in the life-changing miracle, Jesus' opponents are blinded by rage, for He has outmaneuvered them.

Luke's conclusion to this section is ominous in what it foreshadows as the opponents begin to plot *what they might do to Jesus.* This is the beginning of a death conspiracy, as the parallels of Matthew 12:14 and Mark 3:6 indicate. Jesus' opponents are in danger of losing their control over the people. They have been thwarted, embarrassed, even humiliated, and they will not let this pass.

What Do You Think?
When have you seen Christians react negatively to something good that happened in the life of another person or church? How do we counteract such negativity?
Talking Points for Your Discussion
- Proverbs 14:30
- Acts 13:45
- 1 Corinthians 3:3; 13:4
- 2 Corinthians 12:20, 21
- Galatians 5:26
- Other

Conclusion
A. Modern Jews and the Sabbath
Rules for Sabbath-keeping can be very strict among observant Jews today. When I moved into a largely Jewish neighborhood in Los Angeles, I would see Orthodox Jews walking each Saturday morning to the community center where they held

services. It was important that their destination be no farther than a permitted "Sabbath-day walk" (compare Acts 1:12). They did not use automobiles to make the trip because car engines create fire for combustion, and making fire is considered "work" (see Exodus 35:3).

Some very observant Jews also believe that any use of electricity is "fire making," and therefore they will not turn on lights in their homes on the Sabbath. A Christian friend told me of a Jewish neighbor who asked him to come over to help with an issue in this regard one particular Sabbath: his Jewish friend wanted him to open the refrigerator and unscrew the lightbulb so that it would not turn on when the door was opened. This was something the Jewish family normally did before the Sabbath began, but that week they had forgotten. Without my friend's help, the family would not have opened the refrigerator, where their premade meals for the day were, lest they break the Sabbath by turning on a lightbulb.

B. Christians and the Sabbath

The above situation probably causes most of us to grimace a bit. It seems so hair-splitting, doesn't it? But on any level of particularity, the issue of being a Sabbath-keeper or a Sabbath-breaker is rarely asked among Christians these days. There are a couple of good reasons for this.

First, we realize that keeping the Sabbath is not the same as going to church on Sunday morning, and neither is missing a Sunday service a case of Sabbath-breaking. Please don't misunderstand: coming together with fellow Christians is a good thing and was faithfully practiced by the early church (see Acts 20:7; Hebrews 10:25). But taking an hour or two on Sunday morning to participate in teaching and worship activities at a church building does not define Sabbath-observance for the New Testament era. Second, Romans 14:5 and Colossians 2:16-23 establish that it would be a mistake to create "a Christian Sabbath" with scrupulous regulations that define all activities for a specific day. Keeping all this in mind will help keep us from becoming modern-day Pharisees.

Even so, the principle of having a period of rest, as the Sabbath was established to be, is bibli-

Visual for Lesson 6

Point to this visual as you ask, "Which areas of life are people most reluctant to yield to Jesus? Why?"

cal, God-ordained. This concept is not the same, however, as the old saying, "All work and no play makes Jack a dull boy." If we take time off from regular work only to cram the break with non-stop recreational activities, then we are not following the Sabbath principle. Have you ever returned from a vacation more tired than when you left? If so, that vacation was not any kind of Sabbath rest.

Mark's version of the grain-plucking incident offers an additional statement from Jesus: "The sabbath was made for man, and not man for the sabbath" (Mark 2:27). The Sabbath principle is to benefit us, not to oppress us. The psalmist wrote, "Be still, and know that I am God; I will be exalted among the heathen, I will be exalted in the earth" (Psalm 46:10). Nonstop activity works against our knowing God better. Slow down, be still, and take time to contemplate and reflect on your relationship with God! Don't just see a morning time of prayer and Bible reading as another thing to be crammed into a busy schedule. Refresh your relationship with God, weekly if not daily.

C. Prayer

God, You created; then You rested. May we too find rest from our busyness and find You in the stillness. May our knowledge of You advance as we slow down and listen. In Jesus' name, amen.

D. Thought to Remember

Honor the one who created the Sabbath.

INVOLVEMENT LEARNING

Some of the activities below are also found in the helpful student book, Adult Bible Class.
Don't forget to download the free reproducible page from www.standardlesson.com to enhance your lesson!

Into the Lesson

Give each learner a strip of paper with seven boxes that are 1½" square each. Have the letters *S-A-B-B-A-T-H* in the squares, one letter per square. (You can create five such strips from a single 8½" x 11" sheet turned sideways.) As class begins, say, "Read through Luke 6:1-11 silently and check off a letter on your strip each time you find the word *sabbath*. Take no more than two minutes."

When time is up, ask, "Do you have any left over?" (Everyone should have one remaining.) Then say, "Now turn to the parallel narrative in Mark 2:23–3:6 and focus on verse 27. There you will find at least one more occurrence of the word *sabbath* that is not in Luke's parallel. That will complete your strip! Today's study is obviously about the Sabbath: as God ordained it, as Jesus interpreted it, and as men distorted it."

Into the Word

Ask six learners to read aloud the following six segments, one segment each: Genesis 2:1-3; Exodus 16:23-29; Leviticus 25:1-7 plus 26:2; Deuteronomy 5:12-15; Nehemiah 10:31; Ezekiel 20:13-16. (Shrink or expand the list of segments at your discretion.) Note both the obedience and the disobedience related to Israel's keeping of the Sabbath. Use the Lesson Background to address the distortion of God's Sabbath requirements by the Jewish leaders of Jesus' day, emphasizing that the day had become one of oppression and burden rather than one of joy and rest.

Have the first episode of today's text (Luke 6:1-5) read aloud, then write the following words on the board: *critical, presumptuous, generous, authoritative, disabled, suspicious, obedient or submissive, challenging, delighted, angry, vindictive.* Pause as you write each word to allow learners to identify who experienced the description. Then have the second episode (Luke 6:6-11) read aloud and work through the list of descriptions in the same way.

Finally, go through the list of words a third time and ask as you pause at each, "Is this one a good thing or an evil thing?" Most answers are obvious, but sorting through differing viewpoints will enhance the lesson. Wrap up by noting that Jesus characterizes Sabbath choices as being choices between doing good or doing evil (see v. 9).

Alternative: Use the "Lord of the Sabbath" activity on the reproducible page, which you can download, as a different way to work through the text.

Into Life

Quote again Luke 6:5: "The Son of man is Lord also of the sabbath." Then ask, "What else is Jesus the Lord of?" After someone gives the obvious answer "everything," lead (or have someone else lead) the class in singing "He Is Lord," copyrighted 1986 by Word Music with an arrangement of a traditional tune by Tom Fettke. The words are based on Philippians 2:9-11 and will offer an appropriate "lordship focus" to conclude the study. (Most hymnals and Christian songbooks include a collection of titles that emphasize the lordship of Christ; you may find a choice that is better known by your class.)

Option: Instead of (or before) concluding with the above, distribute copies of the "Time to Rest" activity from the reproducible page. Begin by reading aloud Colossians 2:16, 17: "Let no man therefore judge you in meat, or in drink, or in respect of an holyday, or of the new moon, or of the sabbath days: which are a shadow of things to come; but the body is of Christ."

Next say, "Sabbath-keeping in and of itself is not an issue in the New Testament era. But the Sabbath principle of rest is still valuable, even critically important, in various ways. See how you think the Sabbath principle applies in the areas on this handout." Have learners complete it in small groups. When discussing results as a class, expect a wide variety of ideas. Ask for justification.

LIVING AS GOD'S PEOPLE

DEVOTIONAL READING: Matthew 18:21-35
BACKGROUND SCRIPTURE: Luke 6:12-49

LUKE 6:12, 13, 17-31

12 And it came to pass in those days, that he went out into a mountain to pray, and continued all night in prayer to God.

13 And when it was day, he called unto him his disciples: and of them he chose twelve, whom also he named apostles.

. . . .

17 And he came down with them, and stood in the plain, and the company of his disciples, and a great multitude of people out of all Judaea and Jerusalem, and from the sea coast of Tyre and Sidon, which came to hear him, and to be healed of their diseases;

18 And they that were vexed with unclean spirits: and they were healed.

19 And the whole multitude sought to touch him: for there went virtue out of him, and healed them all.

20 And he lifted up his eyes on his disciples, and said, Blessed be ye poor: for yours is the kingdom of God.

21 Blessed are ye that hunger now: for ye shall be filled. Blessed are ye that weep now: for ye shall laugh.

22 Blessed are ye, when men shall hate you, and when they shall separate you from their company, and shall reproach you, and cast out your name as evil, for the Son of man's sake.

23 Rejoice ye in that day, and leap for joy: for, behold, your reward is great in heaven: for in the like manner did their fathers unto the prophets.

24 But woe unto you that are rich! for ye have received your consolation.

25 Woe unto you that are full! for ye shall hunger. Woe unto you that laugh now! for ye shall mourn and weep.

26 Woe unto you, when all men shall speak well of you! for so did their fathers to the false prophets.

27 But I say unto you which hear, Love your enemies, do good to them which hate you,

28 Bless them that curse you, and pray for them which despitefully use you.

29 And unto him that smiteth thee on the one cheek offer also the other; and him that taketh away thy cloke forbid not to take thy coat also.

30 Give to every man that asketh of thee; and of him that taketh away thy goods ask them not again.

31 And as ye would that men should do to you, do ye also to them likewise.

KEY VERSE

Love your enemies, do good to them which hate you. —Luke 6:27

JESUS AND THE JUST REIGN OF GOD

Unit 2: Jesus Ushers in the Reign of God

LESSONS 6–9

LESSON AIMS

After participating in this lesson, each student will be able to:

1. List several qualities or characteristics of the disciples of Jesus from Luke 6.

2. Compare and contrast the behaviors cited under the blessings and woes of Luke 6:20-26 with what contemporary culture considers to be "the good life."

3. Role-play a Christian response to an insult or injury by an unbeliever.

LESSON OUTLINE

Introduction

A. Cheek-Turning

The 1982 movie *Gandhi* features a powerful recreation of a protest march that took place on May 21, 1930. In this scene, hundreds of men move forward to take control of the Dharasana Salt Works nonviolently. But the protesters are met with violence at the gate to the facility, where uniformed officers beat them with clubs. As each line of men falls, it is replaced by another line in a seemingly endless stream. The protesters offer no resistance whatsoever, passively accepting savage blows.

The protesters were following the teachings of Gandhi, who believed that the best way for India to win independence from the British was through nonviolent means. Mohandas Gandhi, the leader of this independence movement, had read the teachings of Jesus and seized on some of them to develop his philosophy of nonviolence. Chief among these was the instruction of Jesus to turn the other cheek after being struck (compare Luke 6:29, today's lesson).

If Jesus was talking about the Christian's proper response to an insult rather than how to react to the kind of bodily assault that can result in serious injury, then Gandhi's application of Jesus' teaching is open to question. Even so, we appreciate Gandhi and others who have advocated nonviolence. As we do, we take care to understand Jesus' teachings in this regard within the larger context of His message, a focus of this week's lesson.

B. Lesson Background

One of the most famous blocks of teaching in history is Jesus' Sermon on the Mount, found in Matthew 5–7. Much of the material in that sermon is found in the other Gospels, and an example of that is in Luke 6, today's text.

The setting of Luke 6:17 has Jesus coming down from a mountain to teach "in a plain." Therefore what follows is often referred to as Jesus' Sermon on the Plain. The apparent difference in geography from Matthew 5:1, combined with differences in the contents of Matthew 5–7 and Luke 6:17-49, lead some to believe that the Sermon on the

Mount and the Sermon on the Plain are different-yet-similar sermons, given in different locations.

On the other hand, the descriptions of "a mountain" (Matthew 5:1) and "the plain" (Luke 6:17) can refer to the same place when we realize that mountainous areas have level places here and there. Also, the different-yet-similar content of Matthew 5–7 and Luke 6:17-49 does not necessarily indicate different sermons by Jesus, since the Holy Spirit–inspired writers of the Gospels are known to abbreviate, summarize, and otherwise condense their accounts of Jesus' ministry (see John 21:25).

In any case, we should approach Luke's Sermon on the Plain in its own right. Delivered during Jesus' first general tour of Galilee (Luke 4:44), Jesus' popularity was rising as large crowds flocked to Him (as in today's lesson). But opposition was also rising, as we saw last week.

I. Praying and Choosing
(LUKE 6:12, 13)
A. Night (v. 12)

12. And it came to pass in those days, that he went out into a mountain to pray, and continued all night in prayer to God.

Last week's lesson saw Jesus heal a man on a Sabbath day, thereby enraging Jesus' opponents. Timewise, today's account is connected loosely as being *in those days*; we might say "some time later" as the setting shifts away from the confrontational atmosphere at a synagogue in Luke 6:6-11. Now Jesus seeks solitude so that He may have uninterrupted time for prayer. The fact that He goes *into a mountain* does not refer to a cave, but to an area

HOW TO SAY IT

beatitude	bee-*a*-tuh-tood (*a* as in *mat*).
Galilee	*Gal*-uh-lee.
Gennesaret	Geh-*ness*-uh-ret (*G* as in *get*).
Judaea	Joo-*dee*-uh.
Mohandas Gandhi	Mow-*hun*-daws *Gawn*-dee.
Sidon	*Sigh*-dun.
synagogue	*sin*-uh-gog.
Tyre	Tire.

dominated by a mountain. Jesus often withdraws for the purpose of prayer (Mark 1:35; 6:46; Luke 5:16; etc.), but this is the only occasion in the Gospels where we read of Jesus spending *all night* for this purpose. Luke is intent to present Jesus as a man of prayer (see Luke 9:18; 11:1; 22:41).

> *What Do You Think?*
> When was the last time you prayed with "all night" intensity, if ever? What does that experience (or lack of experience) say about your priorities in prayer?
> *Talking Points for Your Discussion*
> - Regarding a physical, spiritual, family, or financial issue
> - Regarding how you prioritize physical, spiritual, financial, and family issues

B. Day (v. 13)

13. And when it was day, he called unto him his disciples: and of them he chose twelve, whom also he named apostles.

Now we see why it is so important for Jesus to have prayed all night: He needs to select 12 men to begin a special relationship with Him. Jesus has many followers, but as *apostles*, these 12 disciples will receive the most intense ministry training from their mentor, Jesus. Apostles in the ancient world are those sent by a superior both to represent that person's authority and to accomplish a task. There can be little doubt that none but Jesus foresees the world-shaking results that will come from the work of these men, selected one day on a remote mountain in Galilee.

❧*THE CHURCH THAT DIDN'T BELIEVE IN PRAYER*❧

There's an old story about a small town that had always opted to be "dry" under state law that allowed local option regarding the sale of alcoholic beverages. But times changed as new people moved in, newcomers who eventually changed the local ordinance.

Soon thereafter, an entrepreneur began to build a bar for the sale of alcohol. A local church held an all-night prayer meeting to ask God to prevent the opening of the bar as its construction neared

WHAT IS JESUS SAYING ABOUT YOU?

Blessed are	Woe to	Imperatives
The poor	The rich	Love your enemies
The hungry	The full	Do good to those hating you
Those who weep	Those who laugh	Bless those cursing you
Those who are hated	Those spoken well of	Pray for those mistreating you
LUKE 6:20-22	LUKE 6:24-26	LUKE 6:27, 28

Visual for Lesson 7. *Have this visual displayed prominently as you work through the "three sets of four" of verses 20-28.*

completion. As the church prayed that night, a thunderstorm moved through the area, lightning struck the bar, and the building was destroyed by fire. The entrepreneur sued the church, alleging that the church's prayers had caused the fire. The church's attorney, wanting to absolve his client from liability, argued in court that the church's prayers had nothing to do with the event. After the judge had heard the preliminary statements, he said, "Regardless of how I decide this case, I can see one thing clearly: the bar owner believes in prayer, and the Christians do not."

The story is probably fictional, but the humorous twist at the end challenges us regarding our belief in prayer. Before Jesus' called His apostles, He spent the night in prayer. Should we treat the great decisions of our lives any less seriously?

—C. R. B.

II. Healing and Teaching
(LUKE 6:17-31)

A. Setting (v. 17a)

17a. And he came down with them, and stood in the plain, and the company of his disciples, and a great multitude of people out of all Judaea and Jerusalem, and from the sea coast of Tyre and Sidon.

The names of the 12 apostles are given in Luke 6:14-16 (not in today's text). As Jesus and His newly appointed 12 descend from the mountain,

they encounter a gathering crowd. We assume that this takes place somewhere near the Sea of Galilee, also known as "the lake of Gennesaret" (see Luke 5:1). Jesus' popularity is seen in the distances people travel to see Him: *Judaea and Jerusalem* are 70 or more miles to the south, while *the sea coast of Tyre and Sidon* is an area 40 to 60 miles to the north.

B. Expectations (vv. 17b-19)

17b, 18. Which came to hear him, and to be healed of their diseases; and they that were vexed with unclean spirits: and they were healed.

Luke describes two general types of healing: physical and spiritual. Whatever the problem, people are healed.

19. And the whole multitude sought to touch him: for there went virtue out of him, and healed them all.

Luke offers many summary statements in his Gospel and in Acts, but this is one of the most remarkable. In sweeping language, we are told that *the whole multitude* tries to touch Jesus. We can imagine hundreds if not thousands who seek healing (compare Luke 8:44; Acts 5:15; 19:11, 12). But this potentially chaotic scene is even more amazing for its results: everyone is healed! No one is excluded or overlooked. No one leaves disappointed.

This mass healing sets the scene for Jesus' next activity: teaching. The crowd understands that Jesus heals through the power of God; as a result, they are ready to listen. The fact that everyone needing healing has been served implies that there will be no more clamor in that regard to interrupt Jesus as He teaches. The newly selected apostles undoubtedly watch all this very closely. This is an important part of their preparation to be sent out later to do the same (Luke 9:1-6).

C. Blessings (vv. 20-23)

20. And he lifted up his eyes on his disciples, and said, Blessed be ye poor: for yours is the kingdom of God.

The pronouncements of Jesus that begin at this point are commonly known as *beatitudes*. A beatitude is a blessing given to a specific person or persons. It includes identification of those to be blessed and the nature of the future blessed state.

Some people associate blessings with "good luck" or "good fortune," but this way of thinking is foreign to the Bible. God's people are blessed because God blesses them in intentional ways, not because of the whims of fortune (compare Job 42:12).

In Jesus' first beatitude, the recipients of blessing are the poor. Every village in Jesus' day has poor people—those without adequate food, housing, and/or clothing. Unlike the similar beatitude "blessed are the poor in spirit" in Matthew 5:3, there is no spiritual qualification placed on the poverty of these recipients. Jesus addresses those on the bottom rung of the economic ladder, and His promise to them is priceless: *the kingdom of God.* They are given a share of the realm of the one who created and owns the universe—God himself.

21a. Blessed are ye that hunger now: for ye shall be filled.

The second beatitude is also directed to the poor, since to be hungry chronically is an aspect of poverty. Most of us who live in industrialized countries have never suffered from chronic hunger. We may miss a meal here or there, but what would it be like rarely to have enough food to satisfy one's hunger completely? It is to people in this state that Jesus promises *ye shall be filled.*

21b. Blessed are ye that weep now: for ye shall laugh.

This, the third beatitude, is similar to the one in Matthew 5:4. Both feature a blessing for those who are weeping or mourning, but the promised outcome is expanded here. In Matthew's beatitude, those who mourn "shall be comforted"; in Luke's version, the weeping not only will come to an end, it also will be transformed into laughter. In these first three beatitudes, then, the transformations indicate a 180° reversal in each case.

22, 23. Blessed are ye, when men shall hate you, and when they shall separate you from their company, and shall reproach you, and cast out your name as evil, for the Son of man's sake. Rejoice ye in that day, and leap for joy: for, behold, your reward is great in heaven: for in the like manner did their fathers unto the prophets.

The fourth beatitude focuses on the cost of following Jesus (compare Luke 9:23; 14:33). Despite standing for justice, being humble, and acting with compassion, the followers of Jesus will be met with hatred, rejection, reproach, and slander (compare John 15:19; 16:2; 1 Peter 4:14). The evil that permeates our world is seen no more clearly than when the followers of the Prince of Peace are hated and attacked because of their status as Christians (see Luke 21:16, 17). But this is nothing new, since the prophets of the Old Testament also suffered for telling the truth and living for God (compare Matthew 23:30, 31).

Jesus is not saying that such persecutions are blessings in and of themselves, however. The blessing lies in the promise that awaits: great reward in Heaven. We look forward to a time of no more tears (Revelation 21:4), when we will be with our Lord forever (1 Thessalonians 4:17). That is the ultimate time of fulfillment for all of these beatitudes.

What Do You Think?

In what ways can Christians be blessed by God *now* when suffering because of their faith? When have you seen (or experienced) this happen?

Talking Points for Your Discussion
- Immediate earthly blessings
- Longer-term earthly blessings

D. Woes (vv. 24-26)

24. But woe unto you that are rich! for ye have received your consolation.

The four beatitudes are followed by four corresponding woes. The designation *woe* comes from the Greek word that begins each one, literally "ou-ai." This is an expression of wailing, used in times of extreme distress, or as a warning of pending disaster (Isaiah 5:8; Revelation 8:13). The effect is the opposite of a blessing; it warns of coming ruin.

Each of the four woes corresponds (in order) to a beatitude. The first woe addresses the rich, promising that they have no future *consolation.* The verb translated *received* is used in the ancient world's commercial sector to indicate "paid in full." The wealth of the unrepentant rich will provide no comfort in the future, particularly after death, for their present riches are their full reward (compare Luke 16:19-26, lesson 9). It is inconsistent with Jesus' overall teaching, however, to see this as a blanket condemnation of wealth or rich people (see Matthew 27:57). Jesus ministers to rich and poor alike, for all need the saving message of His good news (see Luke 19:1-9).

25. Woe unto you that are full! for ye shall hunger. Woe unto you that laugh now! for ye shall mourn and weep.

Woes are now pronounced on the not-hungry and the not-sad, for they will end up with hunger and sadness. As with the rich, Jesus is not condemning those who are full and those who laugh merely because of such states of being. He is, rather, warning those who care little about the needs of others, never expecting themselves to be in need of food or comfort. If we trust only in ourselves, we eventually will find ourselves needy in ways we cannot overcome. If we trust in God, our needs will be met (Psalm 56:4).

❧ HAVING "ENOUGH" ❧

Poverty and hunger characterize the status of much of the world's population. One research institute reported at the end of 2011 that nearly a billion people go to bed hungry every night. The grim statistics of death from malnutrition seem to assault us at every turn.

Some advocacy groups call for the restructuring of the world's economic systems, but how this might be done is uncertain. Jesus offers His own perspective: God blesses the poor and hungry if their view of life includes the spiritual values that the Bible teaches. This might seem like "pretty thin soup" to those who must scramble to keep body and soul together. Perhaps we should hear Jesus speaking to those of us who have "enough," but keep wanting more; He is telling us that the happiness that results from full coffers and full bellies is fleeting.

True satisfaction comes only from living by divine principles, and that includes helping to met the needs of those who do not have enough. See 1 John 3:17.   —C. R. B.

26. Woe unto you, when all men shall speak well of you! for so did their fathers to the false prophets.

The fourth woe, a reverse of the fourth beatitude, is given with a historical perspective. Jesus'

disciples should not feel blessed when they are praised in public; they are to remember that such acclaim also was heaped on the false prophets in Israel's history (compare Jeremiah 14:13; Micah 2:11). Just as the fourth beatitude observes that the true prophets were reviled, so also the false prophets were welcomed, because they said what the people wanted to hear (see Jeremiah 5:31).

Again, we should not think that Jesus is condemning anyone who is popular with the public merely because of that fact. Jesus himself has received a favorable report by many (see Luke 4:14, 15). What Jesus denounces, rather, is the person who compromises truth for the sake of popularity (as did the false prophets). Those who proclaim God's truths without compromise are more likely to be shunned than accepted in the public arena.

> **What Do You Think?**
> What are some things we can do to gain a hearing by unbelievers while not compromising biblical truth in the process?
> *Talking Points for Your Discussion*
> - In tolerating various lifestyles (but see 1 Corinthians 5)
> - Regarding visible ministries to the needy (but see 2 Thessalonians 3:10)
> - In valuing freedom of expression (but see Titus 1:10, 11)
> - Other

E. Imperatives (vv. 27-30)

27, 28. But I say unto you which hear, Love your enemies, do good to them which hate you, bless them that curse you, and pray for them which despitefully use you.

Jesus now moves from four blessings and four woes to four commands to those desiring to be His disciples: *love, do good, bless,* and *pray for.* What makes Jesus' teaching startling is that the objects of these actions are those who should least receive them according to the way people normally think. We easily love those who love us, but our enemies? We do good things for our loved ones, but for those who hate us? We bless our friends in many ways, but those who curse us? We willingly pray for those we care about, but for our abusers? Even so, Proverbs 25:21 indicates that Jesus' teaching in this regard is nothing new.

29, 30. And unto him that smiteth thee on the one cheek offer also the other; and him that taketh away thy cloke forbid not to take thy coat also. Give to every man that asketh of thee; and of him that taketh away thy goods ask them not again.

Jesus follows the four commands with real-life illustrations. Slapping can be an act of violence, but in Jesus' world it is an insult. When we are insulted for our allegiance to Jesus, we should not retaliate in kind. When someone steals our *cloke* (outer garment), the robber should also be allowed to have our *coat* (inner garment). We are to exhibit generous behavior, always ready to give to others without expecting repayment.

As mentioned in this lesson's Introduction, Gandhi transformed these sayings into a theory of social action by nonviolence. Jesus is not teaching political philosophy, however, but a way of life.

What Do You Think?
What circumstances, if any, would be exceptions to what Jesus says here?
Talking Points for Your Discussion
- Matthew 25:7-9?
- Luke 12:39?
- Acts 23:2, 3?
- 2 Corinthians 11:20?
- Other?

F. Golden Rule (v. 31)

31. And as ye would that men should do to you, do ye also to them likewise.

The command to love enemies (v. 27) finds expression in a very practical way, in what we call the Golden Rule: we should treat others as we want to be treated. This maxim is probably what Paul has in mind when he refers to the "law of Christ" as being practiced when we give relief to those carrying heavy burdens (Galatians 6:2).

This is arguably the most influential item of Jesus' ethical teachings, perhaps the most important moral principle in history. It is the basis for any theory of respect for human rights and for

equal justice under law. There is equality of persons in the church, all members of which have the same Lord and Savior (Ephesians 4:4-6).

What Do You Think?
What are some practical ways you can put biblical principles into practice with regard to the Golden Rule?
Talking Points for Your Discussion
- Romans 14:3; 15:1, 2
- 1 Corinthians 8:13
- Philippians 2:3, 4
- Hebrews 13:2
- 1 Peter 4:9
- Other

Conclusion
A. Golden-Rule Living

I have a bad habit that my family often calls me on: when I am treated poorly by a salesperson, I am sometimes rude or abrupt in return. Poor service should not be rewarded, I rationalize in my self-centeredness. I am most successful in overcoming this bad behavior when I realize that I am breaking Jesus' Golden Rule. I am disobeying a central command of my Lord, a crucial guide to living.

Life presents an unending variety of situations that challenge us to react as Jesus would have us to. What do we do when we are slandered by a fellow employee? What do we do when someone posts a disrespectful comment on our Facebook wall? What do we do when we interact with one of life's army of rude people?

There is no catalog that lists detailed responses for every possible unpleasant encounter. However, we can always apply the Golden Rule. In so doing, we fulfill the law of our Lord. And, I suspect, our lives will be happier and more peaceful as a result.

B. Prayer

Lord, we are thankful that You do not treat us as we deserve as sinners. Help us act toward others in the gracious way You treat us. In Jesus' name, amen.

C. Thought to Remember

Make love your first response.

INVOLVEMENT LEARNING

Some of the activities below are also found in the helpful student book, Adult Bible Class.
Don't forget to download the free reproducible page from www.standardlesson.com to enhance your lesson!

Into the Lesson

Have displayed on the board as the class arrives the heading *My Favorite Sermon.* Ask, "Can you recall a sermon that struck you in a particularly effective way? Tell us about it." If a thought stimulus is needed, suggest such occasions as the day you decided to submit to the lordship of Jesus, an old-time revival meeting, or a funeral sermon.

After each response, probe deeper by asking the responder to tell exactly what made that particular sermon memorable. After a few minutes of discussion, direct your learners' attention to today's text by saying, "Well, the people in the audience of today's text certainly would never forget Jesus' sermon. Let's look at the reasons why."

Into the Word

Give each learner a handout that is blank except for the heading *Why I Found It Memorable.* Give this direction: "Assume you were in the crowd listening to Jesus on the day of our text. Look at verses 17-30 and make a list of elements of the occasion and words spoken that made the teaching event absolutely startling and memorable. Limit your list to four entries."

Allow learners no more than eight minutes to work. As they do, you may wish to stimulate discussion with these questions: What is there about the crowd itself you find to be fascinating? How do Jesus' principles differ from what your religious leaders back home teach? Which of Jesus' challenges will you find most difficult to follow? (*Option:* Include these questions, or others of your own choosing, on the handout.)

Ask for volunteers to share one memorable thing from their lists. Give one from your own list if you think it will encourage responses.

Option: Follow immediately by distributing copies of the "Hard Imperatives" activity from the reproducible page, which you can download. Discuss results and—most importantly—check to see if any learners had one or more of the hard imperatives as entries on their *Why I Found It Memorable* lists. Explore reasons why, or why not.

Into Life

Before class, invite two learners (L1 and L2) to stand before the group with you to role-play dramatic dialogues. In both situations, you the teacher (T) will play the role of antagonist.

Dialogue 1. **T:** "[name], you and I have known one another for a long time. I've never heard you say much about your religion, but to me Christianity is the most foolish thing I know of—believing in a man whose simpleminded followers claimed that He rose from the dead! Are you really that foolish?" **L1:** "Well, I suppose I am a fool, for Paul wrote about me in his letter to the Christians at Corinth when he said [quote all or part of 1 Corinthians 1:18-25]. So—I guess I am that foolish; I'm sorry you had not noticed before. It's my fault."

Dialogue 2. **T:** "[name], did you hear about what happened to those Christians in that Muslim country? Served them right. They had no business violating that country's law by distributing Bibles." **L2:** "Well, the legalism of such a restrictive belief certainly lends itself to such abuses. I have to admire the faith of anyone who stands by his or her convictions in spite of the cost. If you are convinced that you have learned vitally important truth, should you not share it with others?"

The above are just starters for the dialogues; participants should ad-lib the rest. (For greatest realism, even the dialogue-starters should be memorized, not read from scripts.) Let the dialogues continue as long as you choose. After each, discuss impressions with the class; be sure to relate the role-plays to Luke 6:22, 23, 26-28, and 31.

Alternative: Have learners complete in small groups the "The Good Life" activity from the reproducible page. (*Option:* This can be a take-home exercise.)

Enlarging Your Circle

DEVOTIONAL READING: Psalm 147:1-11
BACKGROUND SCRIPTURE: Luke 14:7-24

LUKE 14:7-18A, 21-24

7 And he put forth a parable to those which were bidden, when he marked how they chose out the chief rooms; saying unto them,

8 When thou art bidden of any man to a wedding, sit not down in the highest room; lest a more honourable man than thou be bidden of him;

9 And he that bade thee and him come and say to thee, Give this man place; and thou begin with shame to take the lowest room.

10 But when thou art bidden, go and sit down in the lowest room; that when he that bade thee cometh, he may say unto thee, Friend, go up higher: then shalt thou have worship in the presence of them that sit at meat with thee.

11 For whosoever exalteth himself shall be abased; and he that humbleth himself shall be exalted.

12 Then said he also to him that bade him, When thou makest a dinner or a supper, call not thy friends, nor thy brethren, neither thy kinsmen, nor thy rich neighbours; lest they also bid thee again, and a recompence be made thee.

13 But when thou makest a feast, call the poor, the maimed, the lame, the blind:

14 And thou shalt be blessed; for they cannot recompense thee: for thou shalt be recompensed at the resurrection of the just.

15 And when one of them that sat at meat with him heard these things, he said unto him, Blessed is he that shall eat bread in the kingdom of God.

16 Then said he unto him, A certain man made a great supper, and bade many:

17 And sent his servant at supper time to say to them that were bidden, Come; for all things are now ready.

18a And they all with one consent began to make excuse.

. . . .

21 So that servant came, and shewed his lord these things. Then the master of the house being angry said to his servant, Go out quickly into the streets and lanes of the city, and bring in hither the poor, and the maimed, and the halt, and the blind.

22 And the servant said, Lord, it is done as thou hast commanded, and yet there is room.

23 And the lord said unto the servant, Go out into the highways and hedges, and compel them to come in, that my house may be filled.

24 For I say unto you, That none of those men which were bidden shall taste of my supper.

KEY VERSE

Whosoever exalteth himself shall be abased; and he that humbleth himself shall be exalted. —**Luke 14:11**

JESUS AND THE JUST REIGN OF GOD

Unit 2: Jesus Ushers in the Reign of God

LESSONS 6–9

LESSON AIMS

After participating in this lesson, each student will be able to:

1. Identify ways a disciple of Jesus demonstrates humility in the extending and receiving of hospitality.

2. Compare and contrast the giving of a banquet in Jesus' day with a contemporary manner of social interaction.

3. Perform one act of Christian charity in the week ahead that involves no expectation of repayment.

LESSON OUTLINE

Introduction

A. Proud to be Humble

In his book *The Life You've Always Wanted*, John Ortberg asks, "We'd like to be humble—but what if no one notices?" If we take pride in our giftedness, why not be proud of our humbleness? And if no one notices how humble we are, shouldn't we point it out?

To anyone with a biblical perspective on humility, the idea of trumpeting humbleness as a prideful accomplishment does not make sense. It is an oxymoron—a self-contradiction. Pride and humility are not good partners. "God resisteth the proud, but giveth grace unto the humble" (James 4:6). This week's lesson takes us to some of Jesus' instructions in this regard.

B. Lesson Background

Today's lesson takes us into a period of time known as the later Perean ministry of Jesus (compare Luke 13:22; John 10:40-42). During this time, in Jesus' third year of ministry, He was invited to a Sabbath-day meal at the home of "one of the chief Pharisees" (Luke 14:1a). As in the lesson from two weeks ago, this proves to be a test as to whether or not Jesus will heal on the Sabbath. Jesus was under close observation (v. 1b), but the subsequent healing seemed to have been done without overt controversy (vv. 2-4). Instead, Luke's focus is on the dynamics of the meal itself. Before diving into today's text, knowing a few things about these village meals-by-invitation will help us understand what was going on there.

The meal at issue in our text happened in a private home, thus sharply limiting the size of the guest list. Luke does not say how many guests were there, but probably no more than about a dozen were at the table, reclining on cushioned benches. Therefore it is a mistake to think of these local dinners as "banquets" in the modern sense of hundreds of guests situated in a hotel ballroom.

The meal would have been served by women of the household or by servants. It is also likely that there were others present who were not at the table, but were standing or sitting around the edges of the room. This arrangement indicated a pecking order: the most-honored guests were at the table, while the less honored were not.

The host presided from a central position at the table, and the closer one was to the host, the more prestigious his status at this dinner. Meals-by-invitation in the village would have been of differing size and scope depending on the occasion. A weekly Sabbath meal (like the one in our text) would have been less elaborate than a wedding feast.

I. Choosing a Place
(LUKE 14:7-11)

A. Bad Action and Consequences (vv. 7-9)

7. And he put forth a parable to those which were bidden, when he marked how they chose out the chief rooms; saying unto them.

The healing of Luke 14:1-6 done, Jesus uses the opportunity of the meal for a teaching parable. This begins not as *a parable* in the usual sense of a little story, but as a contrast between proud, pushy people and those who are lowly and humble.

Jesus has just noticed that the invited guests are vying for *the chief rooms*. This phrase does not refer to guest rooms in the home (it probably doesn't have any), but "room" in the sense of "space." People are jockeying for the best places at the dinner, to be at the table and near the host. This is not a matter of access to food, but of social prestige. It is a little like wanting to sit at the head table at an awards banquet that features visiting dignitaries. Sitting in a highly visible position not only reflects one's social status but also adds to it.

What Do You Think?
> What modern temptations to get "the chief rooms" are most vexing to you? How do you overcome this problem?
>
> Talking Points for Your Discussion
> - Seeking to be noticed with regard to your work at your church
> - Attempting to get a product at a bargain rate before supplies run out
> - Attempting to network with influential people
> - Other

8, 9. When thou art bidden of any man to a wedding, sit not down in the highest room; lest a more honourable man than thou be bidden of him; and he that bade thee and him come and say to thee, Give this man place; and thou begin with shame to take the lowest room.

Rather than identify and embarrass individuals who are in the room at the time, Jesus uses a related and familiar situation for His point: a meal at *a wedding*. The occasional wedding in a rural village is an important social event. It involves pageantry and celebration along with lots of rich food and drink (compare John 2:1-10). The groom's family is expected to host a large dinner the evening before the new couple's first night together. This seems to be the sort of event Jesus has in mind in His illustration.

You may have attended a banquet where the host had assigned the seating as indicated by place cards. More often, though, you may have attended banquets with "open seating," where guests choose their own seats. In Jesus' example, there is a little of both at the hypothetical wedding dinner: the guests have the opportunity to grab the choice places, but the host retains veto power over their choices.

Great social embarrassment may occur if a guest places himself near the host and then a person of higher status arrives. In this case, the former will be asked to vacate his seat for the latter. Since all the other "relatively high" seating positions would be filled at this point, the unfortunate person might be relegated to a much lower place, perhaps to a place that is not even at a table.

B. Good Action and Consequences (vv. 10, 11)

10, 11. But when thou art bidden, go and sit down in the lowest room; that when he that bade thee cometh, he may say unto thee, Friend, go up higher: then shalt thou have worship in the presence of them that sit at meat with thee. For whosoever exalteth himself shall be abased; and he that humbleth himself shall be exalted.

Jesus gives very practical advice: rather than risk the embarrassment of being asked to give up a place of honor, begin instead at a more humble place. If this strategy is followed, there is not only no risk of humiliation, but also there is the possibility of being promoted to a higher place at the table, a public honor. Proverbs 25:6, 7 indicates that what Jesus is teaching is nothing new. The Pharisees, who pride themselves in their meticulous attention to the law, should already know this!

But Jesus is offering far more than social advice here. His parable is intended to compare this situation with a principle in God's kingdom: the self-promoting person will eventually be humbled, whereas the person who acts with humility will eventually be honored (*exalted*). This is an example of what is sometimes called "the great reversal" in the Bible. The world teaches us to push to the front, to seek honor and glory, but God overturns the world's rules and expectations.

Ultimate honor is a gift of God that is not earned through striving for attention. God honors the humble, not the proud (see Luke 1:52; 18:9-14; 1 Peter 5:5). True exaltation is *for* God and *from* God, not a gift we bestow on ourselves (1 Samuel 2:7).

II. Enlarging Your Circle
(LUKE 14:12-14)

A. Inviting for Advantage (v. 12)

12. Then said he also to him that bade him, When thou makest a dinner or a supper, call not thy friends, nor thy brethren, neither thy kinsmen, nor thy rich neighbours; lest they also bid thee again, and a recompence be made thee.

Having used a wedding feast to illustrate the value of humility, Jesus now employs a similar social situation to illustrate another godly principle. We should remember the setting for these teachings: rural, first-century villages. Here there are no fancy restaurants open to the public. There-fore, lavish dinner-events usually are staged in private homes. Such dinners are by invitation only, and there is a lot of reciprocal inviting—if I invite you to my festivities, I expect to be invited to yours.

The guest list usually includes close friends, relatives, and the rich folks in town. Apparently, everyone wants the rich people to come to their festive gatherings, whether they are friends or not. Inviting those who are rich seems to be done with the expectation that the one doing the inviting will, in turn, be invited to the rich man's dinner parties.

The result is something other than genuine hospitality, which has no expectation of *recompence*. As with those who push for the best places at feasts, the whole dinner-party scene is a game involving the village's social ladder. You might climb this ladder by inviting the rich to your event, thus obligating the rich person to include you in one of his high-profile events, where your presence will be respectfully noted. Jesus is about to tell His audience what to do instead.

B. Including from Kindness (vv. 13, 14)

13, 14. But when thou makest a feast, call the poor, the maimed, the lame, the blind: and thou shalt be blessed; for they cannot recompense thee: for thou shalt be recompensed at the resurrection of the just.

Rather than look up the social ladder and devise ways to climb higher on it, Jesus advises looking to those who are on the bottom rung. Instead of inviting rich people whose acquaintance may be to one's benefit, invite *the poor, the maimed, the lame, the blind*. These are the beggars, who have little or no income. They will not be able to stage a lavish dinner-party to invite you to attend in return.

We keep in mind that those in this class of people are despised, even seen as cursed by God for some reason (see John 9:2). From the human viewpoint, they are not objects of pity, but of disgust. But Jesus has God the Father in view here. Those who offer one-way invitations to include the village's most unfortunate residents will be blessed, honored by God. The reward will come *at the resurrection of the just* (compare John 5:29). God loves those whom society rejects, and He cares that we care for them.

HOW TO SAY IT

Isaiah	Eye-*zay*-uh.
Leviticus	Leh-*vit*-ih-kus.
Messiah	Meh-*sigh*-uh.
messianic	mess-ee-*an*-ick.
Perean	Peh-*ree*-un.
Pharisee	*Fair*-ih-see.

❧ THE SMOKING SECTION ❧

God rescued Mary from addictions to alcohol and cocaine. Although her husband is a prominent professional in their community, she does not align herself with the high echelons of society. Instead, she serves homeless and recovering addicts.

When my church family held fellowship dinners, I chose a table and saved seats—excited to spend time with my close friends. Mary, for her part, was never at the "in crowd" table, the one with the Sunday school teachers and worship leaders. Instead, she would always sit with the homeless families that she and her husband had brought with them that week. She helped with their children and made them feel like royalty. At times, I even jokingly referred to the area where she sat as "the smoking section" of the building because of the aroma that accompanied her guests.

Church and community leaders have noticed and honored Mary for her selfless lifestyle. More important is the fact that God sees her. I have seen her too; her example has changed my attitude, and I have been blessed to learn the joy of serving through this humble servant.   —V. E.

III. Snubbing the Supper
(LUKE 14:15-18a, 21-24)

A. Reaction to Jesus (v. 15)

15. And when one of them that sat at meat with him heard these things, he said unto him, Blessed is he that shall eat bread in the kingdom of God.

At least one person in the Pharisee's home understands what Jesus has said thus far. He understands that Jesus is speaking of *the kingdom of God*, which will include a heavenly banquet (see Isaiah 25:6; Luke 13:29; Revelation 19:9). The future banquet is a symbol of God's acceptance and reward of the resurrected, righteous people. This ultimate inclusion by God is also the ultimate blessing.

B. Rebuffed Invitation (vv. 16-18a)

16, 17. Then said he unto him, A certain man made a great supper, and bade many: and sent his servant at supper time to say to them that were bidden, Come; for all things are now ready.

Jesus expands on the guest's reference to the heavenly banquet to tell a story-parable. Although the *certain man* (the host of the *great supper*) is not named, this parable is understood as a portrayal of God—He is the one hosting the feast. As with dinner parties in rural, first-century villages, people are invited (*bade many*). The invitation apparently does not specify anything like "dinner will be served at 6:00 p.m." Instead, the host sends *his servant* to inform invitees when it is time to come.

18a. And they all with one consent began to make excuse.

A most unexpected thing now happens in the parable: the invited guests all *make excuse* for why they can't come! One claims he has a pressing real estate situation (Luke 14:18b). One is involved with new livestock (v. 19). One excuses himself because he is recently married (v. 20). These excuses have two things in common. First, they

Visual for Lesson 8. *Point to this visual as you introduce the discussion question that is associated with verses 13, 14.*

give us the sense that there is a long period of time between the initial invitation and the servant's call; during the interim, the invitees have lost interest. Second, they all show disrespect for the host; other things are more important than honoring the invitation.

It is difficult not to conclude that Jesus intends this parable to be a lesson about the relationship between God, Israel, and the Messiah (Jesus himself). The invitation to be the people of God was issued to Israel hundreds of years earlier (see Leviticus 26:12; Isaiah 42:6; etc.). Now, the Messiah has come, and it is time to join the messianic feast, to follow Him as He ushers in the kingdom of God (Luke 4:43; 17:20, 21). Just as the invited guests in the parable reject the final summons, so Jesus is experiencing the rejection of His message and His person by many religious leaders of Israel.

What Do You Think?
How do we help people see the foolishness of their reasons for resisting Christ's call?
Talking Points for Your Discussion
- Regarding "busyness"
- Regarding personal preferences
- Regarding past negative experiences with church
- Regarding misperceptions of discipleship
- Other

C. Redirected Request (v. 21)

21. So that servant came, and shewed his lord these things. Then the master of the house being angry said to his servant, Go out quickly into the streets and lanes of the city, and bring in hither the poor, and the maimed, and the halt, and the blind.

The servant reports back on the results of his summons: no one is coming. This is not happy news, definitely not what the host expects. His feast is ready. We can imagine that the fatted calf is roasted, the raisin cakes are baked, the wine has been delivered, and the musicians are already playing. The feast cannot be delayed.

Although angry, *the master of the house* orders the servant to invite the village's most unfortunate:

the poor (destitute beggars), *the maimed* (disabled due to injury), *the halt* (unable to walk), and *the blind*. These people are to be found on the main *streets*, perhaps begging, but will also live in the *lanes*, the backstreets of hovels and shacks.

There are no government programs to assist the disabled in Jesus' day. Their lives are hard, miserable, and often short. They are never welcome at fancy meals such as the one where Jesus is giving this teaching. We can imagine their incredulity at this invitation, followed by joyful acceptance.

What Do You Think?
Who are the overlooked people in your community who need to be touched by your church? How will you help correct the situation?
Talking Points for Your Discussion
- Those of a certain economic classification
- Those of a minority racial classification
- Those with physical disabilities
- Those trapped by addiction
- Other

D. Room for More (vv. 22-24)

22. And the servant said, Lord, it is done as thou hast commanded, and yet there is room.

The host's table is large, with room for many guests. Even all of the disabled and poor of the community are not enough to fill it. There is space and food for yet more at this feast. We are reminded of the invitation to join Jesus in the kingdom of God. It is not a matter of running out of admission tickets. There will always be more room. Heaven is not cramped for space (see Revelation 7:9).

23. And the lord said unto the servant, Go out into the highways and hedges, and compel them to come in, that my house may be filled.

The third wave of invitations goes to those in *the highways and hedges.* This is to move beyond the village boundaries and invite anyone who may be found out there. In the larger context, this seems to be a prophecy of the day when the invitation to join God's kingdom is extended beyond the nation of Israel, to the Gentiles (see Matthew 8:11; 28:19). God wants His house to be filled.

What victories has your church experienced by extending invitations beyond its comfort zone? What more can you do in this regard?

Talking Points for Your Discussion

- In ethnic outreach
- In ministry to the destitute
- In ministry to the affluent
- In outreach to the deaf
- Other

24. For I say unto you, That none of those men which were bidden shall taste of my supper.

Jesus' final word is an ominous warning. Those who reject the invitation with various excuses will not be admitted to the feast later. Their decision to decline will be honored and enforced. Jesus is delivering a message to His critics at the Pharisee's house: if you reject me, you will miss the most glorious banquet ever imagined, the table of eternity.

❧ *The Guest List* ❧

If asked to create a list of those you think will be invited to the Great Banquet, what names would you include? Perhaps you would start with those who led you to the Lord. You then might list your faithful brothers and sisters in Christ, those who sit near you in church each week. Then you might cautiously list those of sister congregations, providing their doctrine is good. Perhaps you even would list those who are in streams of Christianity different from your own, providing of course that they know enough truth to be considered "in."

But what about those who have committed unthinkable sins: child molestation, rape, murder, etc.? I once heard a lady talking about her two husbands. She divorced her first husband after discovering that he had molested their children. He served years in prison for this crime, but claimed to be a Christian. Her second spouse was a decent, loving man, but he was an unbeliever. She was deeply troubled at the thought that the first might be in Heaven while the second would not.

Jesus makes this clear: the banquet is open to those who accept His invitation. See Matthew 21:28-32.
—V. E.

Conclusion

A. Avoiding the Spotlight

High-profile athletes are rarely known for their humility. The sports star who acts with humility seems to be the odd exception. One such exception was Roger Maris. In 1961, Maris gained national attention because he was hitting home runs at a pace to break Babe Ruth's record of 60 home runs in a single season. On October 1, 1961, Maris smashed a pitch over the right-field wall of Yankee Stadium, and the record was broken.

If you look this up on the Internet and watch the video of the event, you won't see Maris high-stepping around the bases or calling attention to himself. He looks almost embarrassed as he rounds third base and ducks straight into the dugout. A few seconds later, he reappears to acknowledge the applause of the crowd, but he seems to have been shoved into view by his teammates.

Jesus taught that we should not seek to exalt ourselves. We should take humble positions of service with joy and grace. Paul reminds us that even though Jesus was God, He became like a servant so that we might be saved through His death on the cross (Philippians 2:6-8). May we constantly and consistently examine our lives for ungodly pride and find ways to serve others with humility motivated by Christlike love.

B. Expanding the Circle

Ask yourself a few questions as you consider this lesson. Is my church a welcoming place for people with disabilities? Do I welcome a diversity of races and nationalities in my church? Do I have a desire to share the gospel with those who are not like me? God is the Lord of people of all shapes, sizes, languages, ages, and skin color. Should we be any less welcoming than He?

C. Prayer

Father, may we walk with You in humility and with a heart for serving others. Help us conquer our prideful hearts. We pray in Jesus' name, amen.

D. Thought to Remember

Open the doors of your church a little wider.

INVOLVEMENT LEARNING

Some of the activities below are also found in the helpful student book, Adult Bible Class.
Don't forget to download the free reproducible page from www.standardlesson.com to enhance your lesson!

Into the Lesson

Set up a couple of chairs in the front of your classroom. Post a large sign reading *Reserved for Important People.* Recruit in advance one learner to arrive early and sit first in the back of your space, then, as others arrive, conspicuously move forward to occupy one of the reserved seats. Encourage your recruit to "ham it up" by saying something like, "Sorry, this one's mine" or otherwise act entitled to a reserved chair as he or she motions others to stay away. As class begins, say, "This may seem unusual, because church folks have a tendency to jockey for positions over chairs in the back row, not the front row, right? Be that as it may, today's study is about fighting over perceived entitlements. Let's take a look."

Into the Word

Say, "Jesus was the master of startling truths. Listen to each of the following comments and identify an appropriate verse when I pause." Expected responses are given here in italics, but make sure not to read those since that is what learners are to discover. Learners may select other verses that may be just as appropriate.

1. Those who reject Jesus will miss the most glorious banquet ever imagined, the table of eternity *(v. 24).* 2. The person who acts with humility will eventually be honored *(v. 11).* 3. Inviting the rich person to your event obligates him or her to include you at a high-profile event where your presence would be noted and you might gain respect *(v. 12).* 4. Maybe it's like a queen saying to a little girl, "Here, come sit by me" *(v. 10).* 5. Although the "certain man" is unidentified, this parable (as others) has been understood as a portrayal of God *(v. 16).* 6. Rather than look up the social ladder and devise ways to climb higher, Jesus advises looking down at those on the bottom rung *(vv. 13, 14).* 7. Guests have the opportunity to grab the choice places, but the host retains veto power over their choices. *(vv. 8, 9).* 8. This seems to be a prophecy of the day when the invitation to join God's kingdom will be extended beyond the nation of Israel, to Gentiles *(v. 23).* (*Option:* Put these on a handout to be discussed in small groups.)

Once the above are matched, ask the following questions, pausing after each for discussion: 1. What is there about Jesus' parable regarding a first-century banquet invitation that can be generalized to life in the church? 2. What is Jesus teaching about personal humility? 3. How does Jesus' story of excuse-making relate to those who are rejecting the invitation of the gospel? 4. In what sense does the master's wish to have a full house and his command to compel attendance relate to the preaching and teaching of the gospel?

Alternative: Distribute copies of the "Time to Eat" activity from the reproducible page, which you can download. Have learners complete as indicated. This activity can serve as a bridge to Into Life since it involves application.

Into Life

Ask, "What are some deeds of kindness a person can do this week that lend themselves to the temptation of expecting a similar kindness in return?" Jot responses on the board. After each is offered, immediately ask, "How can we perform this kindness and successfully resist the temptation?" After several responses and rejoinders, ask "Would it be better to stick with doing deeds of kindness where there is no possibility of receiving a service in return (anonymously, etc.)?" Discuss, then challenge the class to select one deed from the list to do in the week ahead.

Alternative: Distribute copies of the "Your Church and Its Circle" activity from the reproducible page. This will help both to (1) identify those who are among the "unlikely" to become a part of your church's fellowship and (2) challenge your learners to leave their comfort zones to reach them.

SHOWING COMPASSION FOR THE POOR

DEVOTIONAL READING: Luke 19:1-10
BACKGROUND SCRIPTURE: Luke 16

LUKE 16:19-31

19 There was a certain rich man, which was clothed in purple and fine linen, and fared sumptuously every day:

20 And there was a certain beggar named Lazarus, which was laid at his gate, full of sores,

21 And desiring to be fed with the crumbs which fell from the rich man's table: moreover the dogs came and licked his sores.

22 And it came to pass, that the beggar died, and was carried by the angels into Abraham's bosom: the rich man also died, and was buried;

23 And in hell he lift up his eyes, being in torments, and seeth Abraham afar off, and Lazarus in his bosom.

24 And he cried and said, Father Abraham, have mercy on me, and send Lazarus, that he may dip the tip of his finger in water, and cool my tongue; for I am tormented in this flame.

25 But Abraham said, Son, remember that thou in thy lifetime receivedst thy good things,

and likewise Lazarus evil things: but now he is comforted, and thou art tormented.

26 And beside all this, between us and you there is a great gulf fixed: so that they which would pass from hence to you cannot; neither can they pass to us, that would come from thence.

27 Then he said, I pray thee therefore, father, that thou wouldest send him to my father's house:

28 For I have five brethren; that he may testify unto them, lest they also come into this place of torment.

29 Abraham saith unto him, They have Moses and the prophets; let them hear them.

30 And he said, Nay, father Abraham: but if one went unto them from the dead, they will repent.

31 And he said unto him, If they hear not Moses and the prophets, neither will they be persuaded, though one rose from the dead.

KEY VERSE

He that is faithful in that which is least is faithful also in much: and he that is unjust in the least is unjust also in much. —**Luke 16:10**

Photo: Comstock / Thinkstock

■ 185

Jesus and the Just Reign of God

Unit 2: Jesus Ushers in the Reign of God

LESSON AIMS

After participating in this lesson, each student will be able to:

1. Retell in his or her own words the account of the rich man and Lazarus.

2. Explain what today's text teaches about caring for the poor and about caring for the lost.

3. Evaluate what his or her church is doing to address the needs of the poor and the lost; plan at least one improvement.

LESSON OUTLINE

Introduction

A. Relief Efforts

As I write this, my Midwestern city has finally reached the end of an epic flood season. The nearby Missouri River had been above flood stage for nearly four months, and several communities were flooded for weeks. The stories of people helping others are both heartbreaking and heartening. Homes and businesses were ruined, and some families lost nearly everything. Helping hands have been extended by those who escaped devastation, offering timely assistance in the form of housing, money, and jobs.

The natural world throws disasters at us all the time: earthquakes, famines, floods, hurricanes, tornadoes, wildfires, and tsunamis. Relief efforts are noteworthy. But what about the ongoing personal disasters in our neighborhoods and communities? What about that family that never seems to rise above grinding poverty? What about the households devastated by alcoholism, unemployment, divorce, or medical expenses? Sometimes we see the megadisasters but not the individual catastrophes.

Today's lesson is set in the time of Jesus, but the contrast between a selfish rich man and a suffering poor man is timeless. It is a story that should cause us to reflect on our own participation in relief efforts, of both physical and spiritual natures, large and small.

B. Lesson Background

This week's lesson comes from a section of Luke that is heavy on parables. Luke 15 offers three parables involving issues of "lost and found," and Luke 16 begins with the parable of the unjust steward. This parable is followed by a brief dialog between Jesus and His opponents (vv. 13-15) and some additional teachings (vv. 16-18). Next comes the parable of the rich man and Lazarus, today's text.

We should pause at this point to acknowledge that some Bible students do not view this story as a parable, but as a real situation describing real people. A primary reason for this conclusion is that Jesus' use of a personal name (Lazarus) breaks the pattern of how He presents parables. Proceeding on the assumption that this is indeed a parable will make us more cautious in the conclusions we draw along the way.

As with all of Jesus' teaching, we should be on the alert for special literary techniques. Two in particular will catch our attention in this parable: *hyperbole* and *foreshadowing*.

Hyperbole is deliberate exaggeration for effect. If I say, "Bob never stops talking," I don't mean that Bob talks every minute of every hour without ceasing, which is obviously impossible. Rather, I would be using hyperbole to create the impression that Bob talks much more than the average person. We want to read the Bible literally, but we must be careful to recognize hyperbole. The parable in today's lesson features two "larger than life" figures that Jesus used to drive home His point.

Foreshadowing, for its part, is an exciting technique where a hint of the future plot is revealed to engage our interest and make us think. The foreshadowing in the parable comes in the last verse, and it is a great one.

Since today's lesson involves a contrast between rich and poor, we should consider what it meant to be classified as *poor* in Bible times. The Bible speaks often of three groups who seem most susceptible to falling into poverty: widows, the fatherless (orphans), and strangers (foreigners; compare Deuteronomy 24:21; Psalm 146:9). We also know from the Gospels that Jesus encountered persons whose disabilities rendered them unable to work and therefore reduced them to begging. This may be the situation with Lazarus, a character in today's lesson.

HOW TO SAY IT

Dives	*Dye*-veez.
Eleazar	El-ih-*a*-zar or E-lih-*a*-zar.
hyperbole	high-**purr**-buh-*lee*.
Lazarus	*Laz*-uh-rus.
Mediterranean	*Med*-uh-tuh-**ray**-nee-un.
Phoenicia	Fuh-*nish*-uh.
Tijuana	*Tee*-uh-**wah**-nuh.
Tyre	Tire.
Tyrian	*Tir*-ee-un.

I. Rich and Poor
(Luke 16:19-21)

A. Life of Indulgence (v. 19)

19. There was a certain rich man, which was clothed in purple and fine linen, and fared sumptuously every day.

The first character in Jesus' parable is *a certain rich man* whose self-indulgent nature is evident in the ways he dresses and eats. His clothes are expensive, since purple dye is costly (compare Acts 16:14). Those in Jesus' audience know about the cities of Phoenicia on the Mediterranean coastline where an ancient process is used for obtaining purple dye from a species of sea snails. The result of this time-consuming process is known as "Tyrian purple" (after the city of Tyre) or "royal purple." The mention of *fine linen* adds to the imagery of luxurious clothing (compare Ezekiel 27:7).

The phrase *fared sumptuously every day* creates a mental image of fine dining with rich food and lavish entertainment seven days per week. Jesus is painting this word picture to create the impression of a self-absorbed individual who devotes his extensive financial resources to nothing but his own enjoyment. We should note in passing that there is a tradition that this rich man's name is *Dives*. This probably comes from a Latin word for "rich," which in the Middle Ages was mistaken to be a personal name.

B. Life of Indigence (vv. 20, 21)

20. And there was a certain beggar named Lazarus, which was laid at his gate, full of sores.

With the introduction of *a certain beggar,* we come to the only character in any of Jesus' parables who is mentioned by name: *Lazarus.* The name Lazarus is a form of the name *Eleazar,* which means "he whom God helps."

The brief nature of this verse makes us wonder how Lazarus ends up at the rich man's gate, etc. Does he have friends who bring him there during the day to beg (compare Acts 3:2), then take him home at night? The picture seems to be that Lazarus has been laid at the entrance to the rich man's residence and abandoned, unable to move to a new location by himself. His loathsome condition reminds us of Job's affliction, being covered with *sores* from head to foot (Job 2:7).

What Do You Think?
What assessments should we make, if any, before extending assistance to those in need? How can you help your church improve in this regard?
Talking Points for Your Discussion
- Regarding the scope of their need
- Regarding their ability to earn a living
- Regarding the reason for their situation
- Regarding assistance already given by others
- Regarding immediate vs. long-term need
- Other

21. And desiring to be fed with the crumbs which fell from the rich man's table: moreover the dogs came and licked his sores.

Apparently, the only food available to poor Lazarus is whatever falls to the floor *from the rich man's table*. These *crumbs* are not the scrapings of leftovers from the pots and dishes, but are scraps of bread, etc., that end up on the floor either accidentally or intentionally. Such "food" (if we can call it that) is normally devoured by dogs (compare Mark 7:28). In effect, Jesus is saying that Lazarus has no choice but to eat the dogs' food. This doglike status of the poor man is heightened by the detail that his sores are licked by dogs.

The positioning of Lazarus at the rich man's gate (v. 20) gives us a picture of this beggar receiving the scraps only after they are swept up and tossed outside after a banquet. Such sweepings would include all the assorted dirt and crud that also is on the floor at the time. What dire straits Lazarus is in!

❧ *THE POOR HAVE NAMES* ❧

Our church family's first mission trip was to the slums of Tijuana, Mexico. There our group of 20 adults and 40 teens mixed concrete and cut wood with handsaws in order to build four simple homes. In the neighborhood where we worked, many families lived on the equivalent of a dollar or two per day. Some families had only strips of cardboard or sheet metal for shelter. Others had stucco homes with leaky roofs. A nonflushing toilet was considered a luxury.

The shock of the poverty quickly passed as we learned the names and personalities of those whom we served. We fell in love with the children and their parents. Although the children played and seemed as happy as many living in more luxurious neighborhoods, the struggles of life were apparent. Medicines were hard to come by, jobs were few, and threats from gangs and other dangers made fear a way of life.

When our assignment was complete, we traveled a few miles north to the glamour and glitz of San Diego. Although we had a recreation day before returning home, many of us could not take pleasure in the excesses of the shopping malls and entertainment opportunities. Our worldview had changed. To us, the poor now had names.

God never says it's wrong to enjoy the blessings He lavishly provides. But it is wrong to use all of our resources on ourselves while ignoring those in need.   —V. E.

II. Paradise and Torment
(LUKE 16:22-26)

A. Same Earthly Outcome (v. 22)

22a. And it came to pass, that the beggar died, and was carried by the angels into Abraham's bosom.

Given the description of exposure to the weather, malnutrition, and infected sores, it is not surprising that the death of Lazarus is part of the story. The fact that he is *carried by the angels into Abraham's bosom* signifies that Lazarus is in a place of favor to Jewish thinking, since the great patriarch Abraham is described as a "friend" of God (see Isaiah 41:8; James 2:23). To be where Abraham is in the afterlife is to be in a place of comfort. For Lazarus, we can assume there will be no more sores, no more cold nights on the street, no more hunger.

22b. The rich man also died, and was buried.

Although not homeless, malnourished, or afflicted with sores, *the rich man also died*, apparently at about the same time. We can imagine a lavish funeral and burial in a family tomb, but these things mean nothing to the bigger picture of the story. Jesus simply affirms the man's death and burial. The man's wealth does not spare him from the fate common to all. Despite their vastly different lifestyles, the earthly outcomes of the rich man and Lazarus are one and the same: they both die.

B. Different Eternal Outcomes (vv. 23-26)

23. And in hell he lift up his eyes, being in torments, and seeth Abraham afar off, and Lazarus in his bosom.

The rich man's death is not said to result in angelic activity as does that of Lazarus. Instead, the rich man's next conscious moment seems to be his awareness that he is *in hell*. Jesus' description obviously has the rich man in the place of punishment in the afterlife, and we can imagine the man's surprise. It isn't supposed to be like this, is it? Rich people are favored by God, aren't they? Shouldn't this favor continue after death?

To make things worse, the rich man is able to see Lazarus off in the distance, in the presence of Abraham. "Isn't that where I should be?" the rich man may ask himself.

24. And he cried and said, Father Abraham, have mercy on me, and send Lazarus, that he may dip the tip of his finger in water, and cool my tongue; for I am tormented in this flame.

As we consider the imagery of these verses, we should be cautious about asking questions that the parable is not designed to answer. There are no answers here to questions such as, "Does this mean that Abraham is in charge of Paradise?" "Will all those who end up in the state of the rich man, the state of torment, be able to converse with those who end up in the state of Lazarus, the state of comfort?" "Will those in torment be able to recognize those who are on the other side?" "Can Lazarus hear what the rich man is saying or see his suffering?" To ask questions that parables are not designed to answer is to distract us from Jesus' teaching point.

We also proceed with caution in the presence of figurative language. Having died and left his body behind to be buried, the rich man no longer has a literal, physical tongue that can be cooled by literal, physical water. Jesus is painting a word picture for the greatest impact on His audience.

A place of torment in the afterlife is very real, as other Scriptures make clear. But Jesus often uses figurative language to make His point—a practice His disciples often cannot grasp (Mark 8:14-21) and find frustrating (John 16:29).

With awareness of this caution, we can at least conclude that there is nothing the rich man can do on his own to relieve his torment. Cannot Lazarus do a small kindness for him?

> *What Do You Think?*
> How should we discuss, if at all, the status of those who have died without Christ?
> *Talking Points for Your Discussion*
> - Regarding discussions with fellow believers
> - Regarding discussions with nonbelievers

25. But Abraham said, Son, remember that thou in thy lifetime receivedst thy good things, and likewise Lazarus evil things: but now he is comforted, and thou art tormented.

As in last week's lesson, we have an example of "the great reversal" of Scripture (see Luke 14:11). This involves an exchange of roles between the rich and the poor, the proud and the humble (compare Luke 1:52, 53; 18:14). Abraham is not presented here as the judge, but as the mouthpiece of God to explain this reversal to the rich man: Lazarus is comforted and the rich man is tormented, the reverse of the circumstances in their lifetimes. There seems to be compassion in Abraham's voice, for he addresses the rich man as *Son,* but there is nothing Abraham can do but explain the situation.

26. And beside all this, between us and you there is a great gulf fixed: so that they which would pass from hence to you cannot; neither can they pass to us, that would come from thence.

Abraham now points out another reason why the rich man's request cannot be honored. We don't know if the *great* part of the *gulf* has to do with its depth, width, or both. The important part is the gulf's impassability. No one can cross it. Things are as they should be: the rich man is in torment and Lazarus is comforted. These states of being cannot be altered in any way.

Therefore, Lazarus can say nothing that has not already been said by these spokesmen for God.

What Do You Think?
 What changes do you need to make in your life
  as you realize that there is no way to cross the
  "great gulf" after death?
Talking Points for Your Discussion
 ▪ Changes in outreach priorities (evangelism and
   benevolence)
 ▪ Changes in upreach priorities (corporate and
   personal worship)
 ▪ Changes in inreach priorities (spiritual growth
   of self and fellow Christians)

III. Return and Rescue
(LUKE 16:27-31)
A. Plan Proposed (vv. 27, 28)

27, 28. Then he said, I pray thee therefore, father, that thou wouldest send him to my father's house: for I have five brethren; that he may testify unto them, lest they also come into this place of torment.

The rich man apparently accepts his fate, but he now has another idea: perhaps Abraham can send Lazarus back to *testify* to the rich man's *five brethren*. We can infer a few things from this request.

First, the man's brothers must be living as the rich man did, neglecting the poor while giving themselves every comfort. Second, since the rich man realizes that his selfish lifestyle is what results in his torment, then his brothers are sure to be punished in the same way. Third, the rich man has a modicum of mercy in his heart (even though he showed no mercy for Lazarus), since he wants family members spared from torment.

Again, however, we are cautious about literal applications from the language of parables. We cannot conclude with certainty, for example, that everyone who dies and ends up in the *place of torment* feels compassion for those still living. The parable is not constructed to address this issue.

B. Plan Rejected (vv. 29-31)

29. Abraham saith unto him, They have Moses and the prophets; let them hear them.

Moses and the prophets often speak of the obligation of the rich to care for the poor (examples:

30. And he said, Nay, father Abraham: but if one went unto them from the dead, they will repent.

The rich man reasons that if Lazarus were sent to his family, then they certainly would listen to him because he had come back *from the dead*. This dramatic return would surely cause the brothers to repent of their evil ways! It is interesting that the rich man does not beg that he himself be the one to return and warn his brothers. In his mind, this is a job for Lazarus, who is obviously favored by God.

31. And he said unto him, If they hear not Moses and the prophets, neither will they be persuaded, though one rose from the dead.

Abraham may or may not have the authority to send Lazarus back. We are not told, and it doesn't matter, for the parable's zinger is now delivered. We now understand that this parable is not just a powerful illustration of the fate of the hard-hearted rich. It is a parable about Jesus himself, a foreshadowing of what is to come. Remember that the Gospel of Luke is "volume one" of a two-volume set. In the second volume, the book of Acts, we find the fulfillment of this parable's prophecy: Even though someone does rise from the dead (Jesus), many family members (the Jews of Jesus' day) still do not believe (see Acts 4:1, 2; 28:23-27).

❧ *JUST ONE MORE CHANCE* . . . ❧

I recently purchased a fast-food beverage that had a "game piece" attached. Although I was not an instant winner, there was a code on the piece that I could use on the company's website in order to get another chance to win something. Those who market products certainly understand the human trait of wanting "just one more chance"!

The rich man wanted an extra chance for his brothers to avoid the punishment that he himself was undergoing. So he suggested something so dramatic that, to his reasoning, it was bound to catch his brothers' attention. But wait—hadn't God already provided numerous second chances? Indeed, God had already gone to great lengths to show the rich man and his brothers how to live.

Today we have even more knowledge in this regard, as the completed New Testament bears witness. But a time comes for each of us when there are no more second chances, when all decisions become final. What can you do today to shine light on the importance of accepting Jesus while the chance to do so remains?   —V. E.

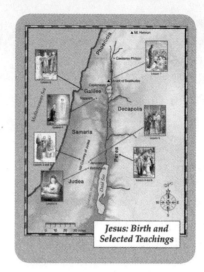

Visual for Lessons 1 & 9

Post this map for the first two units of the quarter to give your learners a geographical perspective.

> **What Do You Think?**
> Having believed that Jesus rose from the dead, how has your life changed? How should it?
> *Talking Points for Your Discussion*
> - Luke 15:11-24
> - Philippians 3:10
> - Colossians 3:1-17
> - Other

Conclusion

A. Saving Dear Ones

Since ancient times, some have wanted to use the details of today's parable as a source of information for details about the afterlife. While it is possible that Jesus is revealing some information in that regard, we should be cautious. To provide such descriptions is not the purpose of this parable, as we have seen. The fact that Jesus predicted His death, died as He had predicted, then rose from the dead should mean that everyone believes in Him. That, in turn, should result in changed behavior toward "the Lazaruses" of the world. But the fact that that is often not the result should not surprise us, since Jesus predicted such an outcome.

But perhaps there is a further application of this parable. The rich man wanted his relatives to be saved, but only after it was too late for him to do anything about it himself. Do you want your brothers and sisters to be saved? Do you want your sons and daughters to be saved? Do you have a passion not to let one precious lamb of your family be lost?

We may be so wrapped up in world evangelism, in national ministries, and in citywide crusades that we neglect those who are dearest to us—our own family members. Ask yourself this question: if you were to die tonight, would you be certain that you had done all you could to convince your closest family members of their need for Jesus? After you die, it is too late for you to witness to them personally.

Let's finish this lesson by writing a prayer that will express our desire to see all of our family members become believers in Christ. Pray for them, name by name; then be resolved to speak to them about Jesus if they are not believers. Don't wait.

B. Prayer

Righteous God, we bring before You our concern for family members who don't know Your Son. Use us as Your instruments to bring the gospel to them so that they might be saved. We pray this in the name of Jesus, the resurrected one who is now seated at Your right hand, amen.

C. Thought to Remember

Remember the poor of both body *and* spirit.

INVOLVEMENT LEARNING

Some of the activities below are also found in the helpful student book, Adult Bible Class.
Don't forget to download the free reproducible page from www.standardlesson.com to enhance your lesson!

Into the Lesson

Option: Place in chairs copies of the "Color Me . . . What?" exercise from the reproducible page, which you can download. Also provide a red- and blue-colored pencil along with a regular pencil with each. Learners can begin working on this as they arrive. This activity will encourage a close reading of the text at the outset.

Display the phrase *Luke: Part II*. Ask, "What is this?" When someone responds "the book of Acts," say, "Yes! And that is where I want us to turn first today." Have Acts 1:1-3 and 13:44-46 read (the former speaks of the resurrection of Jesus, the latter of the rejection of Paul's message). Note, "'Luke: Part II' is a picture of the truth we find at the end of today's text. Let's take a look, by reading our last verse first." Have that verse read aloud, then say, "Let's go back to the beginning."

Into the Word

Ask three of your best readers to take the parts of narrator, Lazarus, and Abraham as they read today's lesson text to the class. Encourage your readers to deliver their parts with dramatic feeling. After the readings, ask everyone to close their Bibles, then divide the class in two and have each side take turns retelling the story. You will interrupt at points with "and then . . ." as a cue for one side to stop the retelling and the other side to start.

Following the retelling, say, "The name of the beggar in today's text is *Lazarus*, a name related to *Eleazar*, meaning 'one whom God helps.' Considering the irony of that choice of names, how would the Jewish leaders of Jesus' day (and perhaps many in today's culture) characterize the 'one whom God helps'?" After discussing, pose the following questions, pausing between each for further discussion: 1. How is that characterization untrue of Lazarus? 2. What is there about the conclusion of Jesus' parable that accurately pictures the "one whom God helps"? 3. How do you sense

that you are "one whom God helps"? How do you expect Him to help you? (Use the commentary to correct misconceptions.)

Alternative: Instead of (or in addition to) using the discussion questions above, create handouts titled "This Story Is Primarily a Lesson About __." Include these choices below the heading:

A. how to deal with the poor.
B. the horrible nature of Hell.
C. how to deal with the lost.
D. condemnation of the idle, callous rich.
E. "For whosoever exalteth himself shall be abased; and he that humbleth himself shall be exalted" (Luke 14:11, last week's study).

Include also these instructions: "Review the five statements, each of which makes a claim regarding the story, then rank-order those statements from '1' (the most supportable) to '5' (the least supportable). Be prepared to defend your rankings."

Expect a lively discussion to result! In the process, be sure to point out the word *primarily* in the heading, recognizing that secondary truths may also be present. Use the commentary to correct misunderstandings.

Into Life

Have a leader from each of your congregation's benevolence and evangelism programs speak very briefly about what your church does in those two areas of ministry outreach. This will allow those leaders a chance to solicit support and receive suggestions from your class regarding opportunities and possibilities. (If they are not available to do so, ask them to provide you a summarizing handout in advance; make copies, distribute, and discuss.)

Option: Distribute copies of the "Choices, Good and Otherwise" activity from the reproducible page to help personalize Jesus' teaching. This should be a take-home activity because it will be somewhat time-consuming to complete.

HEAR AND DO THE WORD

DEVOTIONAL READING: 1 John 3:14-20
BACKGROUND SCRIPTURE: James 1:19-27

JAMES 1:19-27

19 Wherefore, my beloved brethren, let every man be swift to hear, slow to speak, slow to wrath:

20 For the wrath of man worketh not the righteousness of God.

21 Wherefore lay apart all filthiness and superfluity of naughtiness, and receive with meekness the engrafted word, which is able to save your souls.

22 But be ye doers of the word, and not hearers only, deceiving your own selves.

23 For if any be a hearer of the word, and not a doer, he is like unto a man beholding his natural face in a glass:

24 For he beholdeth himself, and goeth his way, and straightway forgetteth what manner of man he was.

25 But whoso looketh into the perfect law of liberty, and continueth therein, he being not a forgetful hearer, but a doer of the work, this man shall be blessed in his deed.

26 If any man among you seem to be religious, and bridleth not his tongue, but deceiveth his own heart, this man's religion is vain.

27 Pure religion and undefiled before God and the Father is this, To visit the fatherless and widows in their affliction, and to keep himself unspotted from the world.

KEY VERSE

Be ye doers of the word, and not hearers only, deceiving your own selves. —**James 1:22**

JESUS AND THE JUST REIGN OF GOD

Unit 3: Live Justly in the Reign of God

LESSONS 10-13

LESSON AIMS

After participating in this lesson, each student will be able to:

1. Recall the behavioral responses to the gospel named in the text.

2. Explain why the gospel requires the responses listed in today's text.

3. Identify the personal behavior most in need of change and make a plan to do so.

LESSON OUTLINE

Introduction
  A. The Camera Does Not Lie
  B. Lesson Background
I. Self-control Needed (JAMES 1:19-21)
  A. Restraining Angry Words (vv. 19, 20)
    Stuff, Vent, or . . .
  B. Receiving God's Word (v. 21)
    How Many Rooms?
II. Hearing and Doing Required (JAMES 1: 22-25)
  A. The Command (v. 22)
  B. The Reasoning (vv. 23-25)
III. Proper Religion Described (JAMES 1:26, 27)
  A. Controlled Speech (v. 26)
  B. Positive Godliness (v. 27)
Conclusion
  A. The Real You
  B. Prayer
  C. Thought to Remember

Introduction

A. The Camera Does Not Lie

The typical person has an idealized self-image in mind, one that he or she tries to refine. Looking at a mirror, one's natural tendency seems to be to adjust hair and posture, pull in the stomach, tilt the head, and smile. The further tendency is to combine the image seen with a memory of his or her appearance at some point in the past.

Then one day I see a photograph of myself. My reactions: "Where did those wrinkles come from? When did I start looking like my father (or mother)? Oh, I look old!" While tricks with photographs are as old as cameras themselves, we also understand why people say, "The camera does not lie." An unretouched photograph acts as a check against my imperfect memory and imagination about how I look.

Getting clear pictures of ourselves involves much more than merely knowing our appearance. Really knowing our true selves means assessing how our thoughts and actions match up with what we claim to believe. There is nothing like our behavior to show what is real and true about us. We can think of conduct as the camera that reveals the real person on the inside.

So—what does the never-lying camera of behavior show us to be in reality? Today's text is about just this issue.

B. Lesson Background

This unit's lessons are taken from the letter of James. Though the author does not draw attention to the fact, he was the James who was a brother of Jesus (compare Matthew 13:55). Jesus' brothers were skeptical of Him during His ministry (John 7:5). But after His resurrection, Jesus appeared to James (1 Corinthians 15:7), and the reality of the resurrection brought him and his brothers to faith.

James became one of the leaders of the church in Jerusalem (Acts 12:17; 15:13; 21:18; Galatians 2:9). Reliable sources outside the Bible tell us that James was highly respected in Jerusalem, even among many who were not Christians. Even so, he was murdered in AD 62 by opponents of Christianity. There are other men by the name of James in the New Testament, and we take care to distinguish between them (Matthew 4:21; 10:3; etc.).

The letter of James is written in a fluent, literate style that reveals a mind that is at home in the Greek culture that dominated the eastern Mediterranean region of the first century AD. Even so, the letter offers us the Jewish outlook of Old Testament wisdom literature, such as the book of Proverbs. The letter's perspective is distinctly Christian as it reflects the emphases of Jesus' teaching, especially that of the Sermon on the Mount.

We see the Jewishness of the letter in its address to "the twelve tribes which are scattered abroad" (James 1:1). These are not simply Jews, but believers in Jesus, the people of God in Christ. They are scattered partly because of persecution (Acts 8:1) and partly because missionaries planted the seed of the gospel outside Palestine, efforts that led still more people to faith in Christ. But after coming to faith, what's next? Today's lesson addresses just this question.

I. Self-control Needed
(JAMES 1:19-21)

A. Restraining Angry Words (vv. 19, 20)

19. Wherefore, my beloved brethren, let every man be swift to hear, slow to speak, slow to wrath.

Those who truly know God express their faith in self-control. James emphasizes that self-control begins with our speech. The instructions here are familiar, reflecting the wisdom of the Old Testament (Proverbs 13:3; 15:1; 29:20).

Self-control in speech begins with being *swift to hear*. Practically, that means listening to others with consideration and empathy. But more specifically, James is telling readers that their first step is to listen to God's Word. Only then can they speak well. The result of quick hearing and slow speaking is that our words can be redirected by the wisdom of God.

A proper self-assessment will restrain our speech and make us better listeners. That in turn leads to a different response with our *wrath* or anger (compare Ecclesiastes 7:9). True faith in God redirects our wrath because we first realize that God,

not we humans, will do the judging and punishing that needs to be done. With the perspective of true faith, we realize that we too are wrongdoers, worthy of judgment and punishment. This is why Jesus famously says, "Judge not, that ye be not judged" (Matthew 7:1).

20. For the wrath of man worketh not the righteousness of God.

At one level it is natural, even right, that humans have wrath or anger. When we witness injustice, and especially when we are wronged ourselves, anger is the consequence. Anger in and of itself is not a sin (see Jesus' anger in Mark 3:5). But fallible humans can neither measure accurately the extent nor formulate the appropriate, just punishment for every wrong. Worse than that, we easily mistake our own motives, justifying our wrath prompted by selfishness as "righteous indignation." Anger tends to make a mess of our own lives and of those around us.

God's anger, however, is different. God does assess right and wrong infallibly. He does measure the punishment for wrong accurately. More than that, God restrains His wrath by His love and mercy, offering forgiveness to the wrongdoer who turns to Him in Christ. God warns of His coming wrath in order to give all the opportunity to repent, be cleansed of guilt, and escape punishment. In all respects God's wrath accomplishes His right way, His righteousness, in the world.

> *What Do You Think?*
> What was an occasion when you saw the very negative impact of a few angry words? What did this experience teach you?
> *Talking Points for Your Discussion*
> - Angry words spoken to you
> - Angry words spoken by you
> - Angry words between other people

❧ STUFF, VENT, OR . . . ❧

I recently participated in a Christian study course designed to help people become free of the hurts they have suffered and lies that they have come to believe as citizens of a fallen world. The class work was carefully designed to get people in

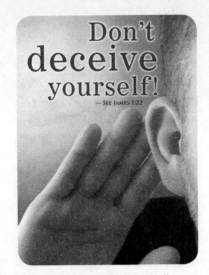

Don't deceive yourself!
— SEE JAMES 1:22

Use this visual as a stimulus for learners to brainstorm common methods of self-deception.

touch with their emotions. As helpful as it was, there was an emphasis (often seen in secular psychology literature) on the need to express anger. The opposite of expressing anger was pejoratively labeled *stuffing.*

Here's where application can get messy. Of course, denying that we have emotions is fruitless and may set us on a path toward a meltdown. But we can acknowledge emotions without venting them on someone else. James clearly tells us God's thoughts here: "the wrath of man worketh not the righteousness of God."

Venting and stuffing are not the only two choices when we are riled, however. A third option is to let God handle our intense emotions. We can present them to God in silent prayer, audible prayer, or by writing them out. This can drain the emotional voltage without harming anyone. If we need to confront someone, we will be better prepared to do so after we've given our emotions to God. Finding our hands around someone else's neck—either figuratively or literally—is a sure sign that we've not submitted the issue to God.—V. E.

B. Receiving God's Word (v. 21)

21. Wherefore lay apart all filthiness and superfluity of naughtiness, and receive with meekness the engrafted word, which is able to save your souls.

The reality of a sinful life is not pretty, and James uses two vivid expressions to describe it. One is *filthiness,* referring not to literal dirt, but to a soiled heart and conscience. Life apart from God is sadly characterized by thoughts and actions that ruin the purpose for which God created humans (compare Revelation 22:11). *Superfluity of naughtiness* simply means an abundance of evil, which characterizes life apart from God. We are reminded of the situation before the great flood: "Every imagination of the thoughts of his heart was only evil continually" (Genesis 6:5).

Of course, most people do not see themselves as soiled or abounding in evil. We imagine ourselves to be relatively pure and good. Not perfect, perhaps, but at least as good as most people, maybe better than most. The change in perspective comes through God's Word. It alone has the power to show us who we really are. But more than that, it has the power to save us from what we are.

So James says that we put aside (*lay apart*) the old life and receive that powerful Word of God. James describes this receiving the Word as being *engrafted,* meaning "planted inside." God has given His Word, and believers have received it. But for its power to be at work, the implanted Word needs to be received again and again.

We acknowledge our need of God's Word *with meekness,* an attitude that says, "I do not have rights or powers that I can assert in this situation." From that perspective, we give up our pretensions of self-sufficiency. We affirm that we need God, that our only hope is to turn to Him. Receiving the implanted word means rightly assessing our deep need for God to do for us what we cannot do for ourselves: cleanse us, instruct us, and empower us.

> *What Do You Think?*
> When you hear God's Word, what helps most for it to become "engrafted" within you?
> *Talking Points for Your Discussion*
> - When listening to a sermon
> - While participating in a group Bible study
> - During personal Bible Study
> - Other

That implanted Word *is able to save your souls.* Certainly it brings salvation from God's righteous anger in final judgment. But it also saves us from the living death of the old life, the here-and-now misery of sin in its filth and abundant wickedness. God wants us to experience salvation that is both now and forever.

❧ *How Many Rooms?* ❧

I recently heard an evangelist to Africa give a colorful explanation for the conflicts a certain Christian was experiencing. The man wanted to know why Jesus didn't fight his battles for him. He wanted to know why the enemy still seemed to have easy access to his life. In reply, the evangelist offered the following illustration.

Consider that your life is like a house with many rooms. When you received Christ, you turned one of them into a very nice guest room for Him. He is a gentleman. When the enemy knocks on your door, Jesus stays in the room you've assigned Him, allowing you to deal with your "company" on your own. Perhaps later you decide to clean out other rooms for the Lord's use. He remains a gentleman, using only the areas of your "house" where you've allowed Him free reign. It is only when you give Him *every* aspect of your life —so that Jesus inhabits the whole house—that He himself will answer the door. As a result, the enemy will not have access to your house again.

Many Christians seem pleased to give God every room "except that one." Such an attitude smacks of a certain arrogance—"I don't need God's help in *that* area; I've got it under control myself." It is only when we realize our powerlessness, however, that we are able to "receive with meekness the engrafted word." The Holy Spirit wants the whole house!   —V. E.

II. Hearing and Doing Required
(JAMES 1:22-25)
A. The Command (v. 22)

22. But be ye doers of the word, and not hearers only, deceiving your own selves.

Merely having God's Word is not enough. It must be put into practice. Reciting the ingredients of a healthy diet is worthless unless we actually follow that healthy diet. When actions do not match words, we doubt whether the person genuinely means what he or she says. So it is especially with God's Word.

Those who *listen* but do not *do* are in a state of self-deception. They pretend to be God's people, but their actions say otherwise. The engrafted Word of God will yield fruit in changed behavior (Matthew 7:15-20). If the behavior has not changed, then the Word has been uprooted or never engrafted in the first place. Our actions are the best indicators of the reality of our hearts.

B. The Reasoning (vv. 23-25)

23. For if any be a hearer of the word, and not a doer, he is like unto a man beholding his natural face in a glass.

James now describes the self-deception of the person who does not act on the Word of God. In the world of the New Testament, people are just as concerned about their appearance as we are today. So mirrors (the meaning of *glass*) are rather common, though being made of polished metal they are not entirely like ours. Even so, these ancient mirrors allow people to check their appearance.

Of course, the purpose of looking in a mirror is to be able to do just that. That is the situation James is describing: one who is examining *his natural face*—that is, the person's physical face—is doing so to get a close, deliberate look. The person takes note of the image in order to make adjustments to improve his or her appearance.

24. For he beholdeth himself, and goeth his way, and straightway forgetteth what manner of man he was.

Looking in the mirror involves being honest about how we look and remembering it as a reference point for the next time we look in that mirror. How foolish to go away from the mirror and remember something false! "Yes, I have a full head of hair!" "No wrinkles—great!" "Why, I look the same as I did when I was a teenager!"

So it is with the person who hears God's Word and does not put it into practice. God's Word

HOW TO SAY IT

equestrian	ih-*kwes*-tree-un.
Mediterranean	*Med*-uh-tuh-**ray**-nee-un.

reveals our true selves, "warts and all" as the old saying goes. It shows us what is wrong and puts us on the path to make it right. Not putting it into practice is akin to the foolish self-deception of looking in a mirror and pretending our real appearance is different. Like the mirror and the camera, God's Word shows our true selves.

What Do You Think?
What differences do you see when you look at yourself in the mirrors of culture and of Scripture? What differences *should* you see?
Talking Points for Your Discussion
- Regarding financial priorities
- Regarding time priorities
- Regarding ethical values
- Other

25. But whoso looketh into the perfect law of liberty, and continueth therein, he being not a forgetful hearer, but a doer of the work, this man shall be blessed in his deed.

James presses his analogy of God's Word as a mirror that reveals one's true self. He speaks of God's *law*, but that word is not limited to the books of law in the Old Testament. God's Word in all its parts is the sure and only guide to right understanding and right living. Although James's readers do not have the full New Testament, they recognize that Jesus came in fulfillment of God's Word. He is the climax of God's all-important instruction of His people.

We tend to think of law as restrictive, but James affirms that God's law gives *liberty*. This is a key theme of Scripture. The God who gave freedom to the Israelite slaves (Exodus 20:2) is the God who gives the commandments that instruct His people in the way of true freedom. Paul reminds us that the true slavery is slavery to sin (Romans 6:15-23).

To enjoy this freedom, we have to do with God's Word what the wise person does with a mirror: pay attention to what it reveals and live accordingly. It is a matter of hearing and doing, not forgetting. What God's Word reveals about us may not be pleasant, but it is true. What is more, God's Word gives the answer to what it reveals about us, the solution to our essential problem.

So James says that the person who acknowledges what God's Word reveals and acts on the Word is the one who *shall be blessed*. This is the way to receive God's favor, to experience life as God designed it to be experienced.

What Do You Think?
Which "listen-and-do" combinations do you struggle most with? How do you plan to improve in these areas?
Talking Points for Your Discussion
- Handling of finances
- Family relationships
- Ministry participation
- Other

III. Proper Religion Described
(JAMES 1:26, 27)
A. Controlled Speech (v. 26)

26. If any man among you seem to be religious, and bridleth not his tongue, but deceiveth his own heart, this man's religion is vain.

The term *religious* is one that people use often but seldom think about. What exactly does it mean *to be religious*? The word that James uses indicates the proper demonstration of respect and devotion to the deity.

But that raises another question: What constitutes proper respect and devotion to the deity? Well, it depends on who the deity is. Pagan gods are seen as selfish, greedy, and unpredictable. Proper devotion to such gods takes the form of a sacrifice that really amounts to a bribe or "protection money." The religious person showing honor to a pagan god does so in hope that the god will be pleased and give a blessing, rather than causing some disaster.

But the one true God as revealed in the Bible is not like the pagan gods. He is just and good in all things. He is generous and forgiving. His wrath burns against evil, but His grace is abundant for those willing to receive it. He takes the side of the weak and helpless—those who recognize their great need for what only He can give.

Proper respect for the one true God consists of behavior that reflects who God is. This involves being obedient to His will, upholding His standards of justice, mercy, grace, and forgiveness. It means acknowledging God's supreme authority in what we say and do.

All that begins with how we use our tongues. Speech that honors God is under control, the way that a horse with a bit and bridle is under the control of an expert equestrian (compare Psalms 34:13; 39:1; 141:3). The speech of a God-honoring person follows the path that God sets. Such speech is filled with love, grace, and forgiveness, but tempered by righteousness and justice.

> *What Do You Think?*
> What are some techniques we can use to control our tongues in difficult situations?
> *Talking Points for Your Discussion*
> ▪ When we are angry
> ▪ When we have been hurt
> ▪ When we are tempted to gossip
> ▪ Other

B. Positive Godliness (v. 27)

27. Pure religion and undefiled before God and the Father is this, To visit the fatherless and widows in their affliction, and to keep himself unspotted from the world.

What begins with words continues with deeds, and James further describes proper devotion to the true God with a short list of representative actions. These are very familiar to Christians of Jewish background, for what James lists is prominent in the Old Testament. Israel's Scriptures name *the fatherless and widows* as special objects of God's favor (example: Psalm 68:5). They are highlighted because they are typical of those in a position of weakness. God is their best and only hope for help in their state of helplessness. So those who know the true God will reflect God's mercy in their own response to the helpless (Isaiah 1:17).

James pairs generosity toward the helpless with being *unspotted* from the world's corruption. Though God is good, just, righteous, and merciful, the world in rebellion against God is anything but those things. We end up bearing the world's filth when we continue in the attitudes and behaviors that the world produces: selfishness, violence, hatred, vindictiveness, etc. God-honoring lives, by contrast, stand out from the world. Such lives reflect God himself rather than the world that runs and hides from Him.

Pure . . . and undefiled is the kind of devotion we seek when we see ourselves and our situation rightly. If we try to split the difference between God and the world, we show that we are holding onto our problem, not embracing our salvation. A grasp of the truth impels us to end the world's kind of life and pursue God's kind.

Conclusion
A. The Real You

Christians in the earliest years of the faith struggled to bring their actions into conformity with the faith that they confessed. In that respect, they were not much different from us today. What do you see about yourself in the true picture of you that emerges from God's Word? Perhaps it reveals the real weakness that lies behind the picture of strength that you try to project. Perhaps it reveals the parts of your life that still reflect the world's outlook instead of the character of the true God. Perhaps it reveals a "motor mouth" with a sensitive accelerator, always speaking before listening. Perhaps it reveals a sense of entitlement that strangles generosity.

In one respect or another, God's Word reveals in all of us our stubborn tendency to run our lives on our terms. If we have confessed that God's way is the only way, our only hope, then it is once again time to assess ourselves in light of God's Word. We do so in order that we may put what we believe into action with the consistency that truly honors the God who has saved us.

B. Prayer

O God, search our hearts and show us who we truly are. You know us better than we know ourselves, and You have shown us the way of life. Strengthen us to live what we confess. In Jesus' name, amen.

C. Thought to Remember

Talk God's talk, and walk God's walk.

INVOLVEMENT LEARNING

Some of the activities below are also found in the helpful student book, Adult Bible Class.
Don't forget to download the free reproducible page from www.standardlesson.com to enhance your lesson!

Into the Lesson

Collect "before they were famous" pictures of celebrities (easy to find on the Internet) and mount the pictures on a poster board with accompanying numbers (or put them in a Power-Point® presentation). As learners arrive, give each a piece of paper. Say, "Identify the celebrities and jot their names with accompanying numbers on this paper." When everyone is finished, reveal the answers. Discuss which pictures were hardest and easiest to identify.

Say, "Unretouched pictures reveal one's true outward appearance at a distinct point in time. Our behavior (actions) creates a 'picture' of who we really are on the inside, which is far more important. In today's lesson we will see how the early Christians were challenged to bring their actions into conformity with the faith they confessed."

Into the Word

Prepare in advance five *causes* index cards with the following entries, one each, but without the verse references you see here: "swift to hear, slow to speak, slow to wrath" *(v. 19)* / "lay apart all filthiness . . . and receive with meekness the engrafted word" *(v. 21)* / "be ye doers of the word, and not hearers only" *(v. 22)* / "bridleth not his tongue" *(v. 26)* / "visit the fatherless and widows . . . to keep himself unspotted from the world" *(v. 27)*.

Also prepare (without verse references) the following five *effects* index cards that will serve, respectively, as counterparts to the five above: "the wrath of man worketh not the righteousness of God" *(v. 20)* / "which is able to save your souls" *(v. 21)* / "deceiving your own selves" *(v. 22)* / "man's religion is vain" *(v. 26)* / "pure religion and undefiled before God" *(v. 27)*.

Distribute the 10 cards among class members as evenly as possible. If your class is smaller than 10 in number, give some learners more than one card, trying not to give cause-and-effect matching cards to the same person. Have learners mingle to find the matches—that is, the causes and effects that go together according to today's text.

When learners have made their matches, affix the matched cards on the board, then read today's text aloud. Discuss the cause-and-effect relationships, adding information from the lesson commentary. (Note that verses 23, 24, not on the cards, are extensions of the effects mentioned in verse 22.) Stress that these actions revealed what was true about the early Christians' hearts.

Into Life

Option 1: Early in the week, secure a photo of each of your learners and enlarge them to 5" x 7". Draw lines on the back of each to resembles a jigsaw puzzle to be cut into four pieces. Give each learner his or her picture, along with scissors and a letter-size envelope. Say, "We discussed at the beginning of class how unretouched photographs are true representations of our outside appearances. Reflecting on our lesson for today, turn your picture over and write in the four segments four behaviors you need to change or implement. When you are finished, cut your puzzle apart."

After learners finish, say, "On the front of your puzzle pieces, write the effects that will occur if you do what is on the back." Encourage learners to take one puzzle piece each day, read the back of it, and then work to accomplish the corresponding goal on the front. When successful, he or she can affix the puzzle piece in a prominent place at home, picture side up. The goal is to have a "new" picture after all four pieces are in place.

Option 2: Distribute copies of the "Here and Now, Hear and Do" activity from the reproducible page to complete individually. Discuss results.

Option 3: Distribute copies of the "The Real Picture" activity from the reproducible page, which you can download. Have learners complete as directed. This is a good option if time is short.

TREAT EVERYONE EQUALLY

DEVOTIONAL READING: Romans 13:8-14
BACKGROUND SCRIPTURE: James 2:1-13

JAMES 2:1-13

1 My brethren, have not the faith of our Lord Jesus Christ, the Lord of glory, with respect of persons.

2 For if there come unto your assembly a man with a gold ring, in goodly apparel, and there come in also a poor man in vile raiment;

3 And ye have respect to him that weareth the gay clothing, and say unto him, Sit thou here in a good place; and say to the poor, Stand thou there, or sit here under my footstool:

4 Are ye not then partial in yourselves, and are become judges of evil thoughts?

5 Hearken, my beloved brethren, Hath not God chosen the poor of this world rich in faith, and heirs of the kingdom which he hath promised to them that love him?

6 But ye have despised the poor. Do not rich men oppress you, and draw you before the judgment seats?

7 Do not they blaspheme that worthy name by the which ye are called?

8 If ye fulfil the royal law according to the scripture, Thou shalt love thy neighbour as thyself, ye do well:

9 But if ye have respect to persons, ye commit sin, and are convinced of the law as transgressors.

10 For whosoever shall keep the whole law, and yet offend in one point, he is guilty of all.

11 For he that said, Do not commit adultery, said also, Do not kill. Now if thou commit no adultery, yet if thou kill, thou art become a transgressor of the law.

12 So speak ye, and so do, as they that shall be judged by the law of liberty.

13 For he shall have judgment without mercy, that hath shewed no mercy; and mercy rejoiceth against judgment.

KEY VERSE

Hearken, my beloved brethren, Hath not God chosen the poor of this world rich in faith, and heirs of the kingdom which he hath promised to them that love him? —**James 2:5**

Jesus and the Just Reign of God

Unit 3: Live Justly in the Reign of God

LESSONS 10–13

LESSON AIMS

After participating in this lesson, each student will be able to:

1. Summarize James's argument that showing favoritism is incompatible with the Christian life.

2. Compare and contrast the biblical concept of "respect of persons" with modern definitions of "discrimination."

3. Propose one way that his or her church can improve in treating people equally, regardless of race, socioeconomic position, membership status, etc.

LESSON OUTLINE

Introduction
  A. Favorite Child?
  B. Lesson Background
I. Problem Identified (JAMES 2:1-4)
  A. Partiality Forbidden (v. 1)
  B. Partiality Illustrated (vv. 2, 3)
  C. Partiality's Implication (v. 4)
    Partiality's End
II. Problem Evaluated (JAMES 2:5-7)
  A. God's Right Action (v. 5)
  B. Readers' Wrong Actions (vv. 6, 7)
III. Problem's Solution (JAMES 2:8-13)
  A. Fulfilling the Law (v. 8)
    Transformational Valuation
  B. Breaking the Law (vv. 9-11)
  C. Liberation by Law (vv. 12, 13)
Conclusion
  A. God's Big Family
  B. Prayer
  C. Thought to Remember

Introduction

A. Favorite Child?

Was there a favorite child in your family? Probably you would rather not answer that question. We realize that when a parent chooses a favorite, children are damaged. Talking about this subject may remind us of some painful experiences.

Some of the world's most famous stories are about the troubles of families with favorites. We think of fairy tales like "Cinderella." We think of biblical accounts like Jacob and Esau, or of Joseph and his brothers. The stories may have happy endings, but only because the problems were overcome.

There are no favorites in God's family. He is "no respecter of persons" (Acts 10:34). But do members of God's family act as if some were God's favorites? Are there some we ignore, exclude, or disrespect by showing favor to others? This may be another question that we would prefer not to answer! James addresses this problem in today's lesson.

B. Lesson Background

Most of us are used to a culture that has a large middle class. Such was not the case in Bible times. Most people earned a meager living by farming or herding, perhaps supplemented with a trade. Earning enough to live day-to-day was the burden for most people. By contrast, a few people had impressive wealth. They were free of worry about food. They had surplus wealth to be spent on fine houses, lavish clothing, and many servants.

Out of their surplus wealth, many people also bought prestige, influence, and power. They distributed favors, and in return they demanded loyalty, honor, and service. A poor family may turn to a rich person for help in a crisis, and the rich person might well rescue the poverty-stricken family by purchasing the family's farmland. Then the poor could only work as laborers on the land of the rich, not as the independent landowners that they had been. Powerful landowners could impose low wages and difficult working conditions.

The Bible speaks of God's regard for the poor while issuing severe warnings for the rich (Luke 6:20-26; lesson 7). This is in part a commentary on the brutal conditions often imposed on the poor by the rich. But as we look closely at the Bible's teaching on this subject, we realize that it is more complex than God's simply taking one side in economic conflict. With no means of self-improvement and no human advocate, the poor person can turn only to God for help (Psalm 35:10; 72:4). By contrast, wealth gives rich people the illusion that they have no need (Luke 12:16-21). Their lives are their own, they think, with no reason to turn to God.

Obviously, either outlook can be taken up by people in any economic circumstance. The poor can seek a human deliverer, ignoring God. The rich can realize their spiritual poverty and turn to God. Even so, the Bible still warns that wealth is deceptive, making it desperately hard to hear God. The Christians whom James addressed lived in this world and faced these problems.

I. Problem Identified
(JAMES 2:1-4)
A. Partiality Forbidden (v. 1)

1. My brethren, have not the faith of our Lord Jesus Christ, the Lord of glory, with respect of persons.

James begins his discussion with a direct command that flows from the very nature of the gospel. The Christian's faith is in the *Lord Jesus Christ.* He alone is *the Lord of glory.* The divine Christ possesses glory far beyond that of any human being. Yet the Lord of glory gave himself in death for all humans, the great and the small.

Therefore, it is impossible to have proper faith in Christ while engaging in *respect of persons.* Though the term *respect* may suggest to our ears a positive regard for others, it translates a word that indicates partiality or favoritism: showing attention and honor to some people and not to others.

HOW TO SAY IT

Deuteronomy	Due-ter-*ahn*-uh-me.
Leviticus	Leh-*vit*-ih-kus.
Moses	*Mo*-zes or *Mo*-zez.
Samaritan	Suh-*mare*-uh-tun.

Such an outlook cannot exist alongside faith in Jesus, the one who died for all.

By the convention of the time, the term *brethren* includes both men and women. This emphasizes that all Christians are part of a family that is drawn together by a tie stronger than earthly blood relationships: the blood of Christ. In this family there can be no favorites.

B. Partiality Illustrated (vv. 2, 3)

2. For if there come unto your assembly a man with a gold ring, in goodly apparel, and there come in also a poor man in vile raiment.

James offers a hypothetical scenario, but one very realistic for people of his time. The *assembly* depicted is the gathering of God's people for prayer and Scripture reading.

A rich person enters. He has more gold than he needs, so he has had some of it fashioned into a decorative ring. His clothing is described with a word that suggests it shines. That can mean that it is exceptionally white, bleached, and laundered to perfection. Or it can indicate that expensive metallic threads have been woven into the fabric. We would say that this man "has money to burn."

Then a second man comes in. He is poor, described simply as being clothed *in vile raiment,* meaning dirty clothing. Ordinary folk have access to water for cleaning their clothes, so this man seems to be especially destitute. Perhaps he has only one set of clothing that he cannot take off for laundering, lest he be naked in the process.

3. And ye have respect to him that weareth the gay clothing, and say unto him, Sit thou here in a good place; and say to the poor, Stand thou there, or sit here under my footstool.

The hypothetical story continues. The church notices the rich man immediately, since his attire displays his wealth (*gay clothing* here is still bright, shining fabric: the same original-language word is used as appears in verse 2). The church ends up welcoming the rich man not because all are welcome, but because he is rich. Chairs are probably few in the homes where the church gathers, so the rich man gets one of the best.

The poor man receives a different kind of welcome. He is told to stand; the chairs are for those better than he. Or worse, he is told to sit on the floor. How can the church do such a thing? The answer could come, "It's just natural. We didn't even think about it." Special honor for the rich is part of the culture. Meanwhile, the poor man is overlooked. There are so many like him, why pay him any attention? From the ordinary, selfish perspective, he is of no benefit or consequence.

What Do You Think?
  What dangers do today's churches face regarding the showing of favoritism? How do we guard ourselves against these?
Talking Points for Your Discussion
  ▪ Programming disproportionately tilted toward a small demographic within the church
  ▪ Policies regarding use of church facilities
  ▪ Inconsistent application of church discipline
  ▪ Other

C. Partiality's Implication (v. 4)

4. Are ye not then partial in yourselves, and are become judges of evil thoughts?

In following customary patterns of responding to rich and poor, the early Christians are unwittingly denying the God whom they claim to serve. Today we would express the idea of being *partial in yourselves* as "discrimination" or "showing prejudice."

The second phrase in the verse makes an equally pointed statement. *Judges of evil thoughts* means "judges who have evil thoughts." If judging is to be objective, based on law and not personal preference, then rich and poor are to be treated equally. Only an evil judge, perhaps one hoping for a bribe or favor from a rich person, shows partiality.

This summary is severe. The person who discriminates in favor of the rich and against the poor is acting in a way opposite to God's story of salvation. God takes the side of the weak against the strong. God responds to the call of the weak who turn to Him in their need. God demands that the strong revise their self-evaluation, realize their weakness, and so submit to Him. Christians who favor those who can do them favors in return are denying what they confess to believe.

What Do You Think?
  What evil thoughts are typically found alongside various types of favoritism? How do we guard ourselves against these?
Talking Points for Your Discussion
  ▪ Economic
  ▪ Racial
  ▪ Cultural
  ▪ Other

❧ PARTIALITY'S END ❧

I have worked with a homeless ministry and have grown in sensitivity to the issues that the poor face, both here and abroad. Therefore, I was not feeling particularly convicted while reading James's teaching about mistreating the poor. Similarly, I grew up in a time and place where racial tension was extreme, and then watched it melt away as a community issue. Therefore, I don't feel that I have a problem with racial prejudice today.

Yes, I found myself reading James and feeling pretty good about the state of my heart . . . until the Holy Spirit reminded me that there are some people whom I still value less than others—those who seem foolish, those who struggle with obesity, and those who don't strike me as attractive. I am stating this as a confession, a twisted mind-set of which I am repenting.

In a culture where there aren't huge class distinctions in most churches, we may feel inclined to skim over this section of God's Word. I would suggest, however, that we ask God to show us which of His children we struggle to value appropriately. To align ourselves with God's heart, we must see every human with the eyes of the heavenly Father, who loves them deeply.   —V. E.

II. Problem Evaluated
(JAMES 2:5-7)
A. God's Right Action (v. 5)

5. Hearken, my beloved brethren, Hath not God chosen the poor of this world rich in faith, and heirs of the kingdom which he hath promised to them that love him?

James now reminds the readers of the way that God's welcoming of the poor is depicted in Scripture. God has *chosen the poor* not by way of preferring one group of people over another, but by the fact that faith grows in a context of need. Only those who realize that they need God will turn to Him, looking to Him to deliver them. The result can be that those who are poor in a material sense are more likely to be the ones who are *rich in faith.* They are the ones likely to respond to God's offer with a desperate, vigorous *yes.*

What Do You Think?
What was a situation where you saw worldly poverty result in richness of faith?
Talking Points for Your Discussion
- In a job-loss and/or home-foreclosure situation
- In a situation involving lack of health insurance
- On the mission field
- Other

The phrase *heirs of the kingdom* reminds us immediately of Jesus' words: "Blessed are the poor in spirit: for theirs is the kingdom of heaven" (Matthew 5:3), and "Blessed be ye poor: for yours is the kingdom of God" (Luke 6:20, see lesson 7). God's kingdom, or the kingdom of Heaven, is the promised, end-time reign or rule of God; it is established with the arrival of the Messiah, God's promised king. Those who receive the kingdom's blessing are those ready to receive what God gives, those who realize that they have deep need.

Note well that James says that this promise is *to them that love him.* The blessing for the poor is for those who respond with faith from the recognition of their need. They love God because they know that He alone is their help.

B. Readers' Wrong Actions (vv. 6, 7)

6. But ye have despised the poor. Do not rich men oppress you, and draw you before the judgment seats?

In a manner inconsistent with their faith, the readers *have despised the poor*, treating them with contempt as described in the hypothetical example of verses 2 and 3. On the other hand, James's readers have reason to be wary of the rich. Their access to power means that they can take advantage of ordinary folk, even using the legal system (*the judgment seats*) to seize their property (Luke 20:47; compare Hebrews 10:34). James's point is not that his readers should be vindictive about such matters. Rather, they should think carefully: in honoring the rich because of their riches, the readers may be aligning themselves with evil.

7. Do not they blaspheme that worthy name by the which ye are called?

From a position of power that refuses to acknowledge God, a person acts with contempt toward everything associated with God. To *blaspheme* is to show contempt with speech. The *name by the which* the readers are called is the name of Jesus, the crucified Lord. In the early generations of Christianity, the Christian gospel is often ridiculed for worshipping a man who had been crucified by Rome, seemingly a criminal without the means to escape the power of the empire. As the rich align themselves with ordinary human power, they show contempt for the kind of power that is characteristic of Christ. They scorn His lowliness.

What Do You Think?
What are some ways to honor Christ when we are discriminated against?
Talking Points for Your Discussion
- At work or school
- As a customer in the economy
- At church
- Other

III. Problem's Solution
(JAMES 2:8-13)
A. Fulfilling the Law (v. 8)

8. If ye fulfil the royal law according to the scripture, Thou shalt love thy neighbour as thyself, ye do well.

James now turns to an argument based on familiar Old Testament passages. Any part of the Word of God can be called *the royal law*, because it expresses the will of the divine king. But here James seems to have in mind Jesus' teaching about the greatest commandments: to love God and to love one's neighbor (Matthew 22:36-40; compare

Leviticus 19:18; Romans 13:9; Galatians 5:14). This commandment is *royal* because it rules many others: all the laws dealing with relationships among humans can be summarized with *love thy neighbour as thyself.*

Loving one's neighbor excludes partiality, of course. Jesus illustrated this truth by telling a story in which a Samaritan—the kind of person despised by much of His audience—generously cared for a victim of a crime (Luke 10:25-37). But the Law of Moses itself is clear in its exclusion of partiality. Unlike other legal codes of the ancient world, the Law of Moses does not provide different levels of protection for different classes of people. Kings and servants, the wealthy and the poor, Israelites and foreigners are subject to the same standards (Numbers 15:15, 16; Deuteronomy 1:17).

What Do You Think?
How have your experiences with favoritism helped you grow spiritually in being able to keep "the royal law"?

Talking Points for Your Discussion
- Discrimination against you
- Discrimination by you
- Discrimination against a friend or family member
- Discrimination stories you have heard

❧ TRANSFORMATIONAL VALUATION ❧

Cinderella becomes a princess because a prince sees something of beauty and worth in her that her own family is blinded to. In *The Velveteen Rabbit,* a stuffed toy becomes real because it is loved. Fictional literature provides many examples of how valuing someone or something transforms them. But what about real life?

The reality is that Jesus has given each of us the highest value possible by shedding His own blood to pay sin's price. For our part, each of us can bring attention to the high value of another human being in various ways. For example, I have noticed that accompanying a senior to the doctor often gets that person better medical attention. I have also noticed that a poor person seeking help receives a more respectful response when accompanied by a "respectable looking" friend.

God's Word lists groups of people who are often disenfranchised (see the Lesson Background to lesson 9), people who need to be served, honored, and protected. Who among the powerless can you speak up for today? The value we give people is often the value we see others assign to them. Let's be like our Father and become assigners of high value.
—V. E.

B. Breaking the Law (vv. 9-11)

9. But if ye have respect to persons, ye commit sin, and are convinced of the law as transgressors.

James expects his readers to grasp this implication. We know that loving our neighbor is a great commandment, summing up much of God's law. God's law allows no partiality. My neighbor is anyone and everyone. Therefore, partiality or discrimination (again, the meaning of *respect to persons*) is a violation of one of the two greatest commandments. The one who shows partiality therefore sins.

10. For whosoever shall keep the whole law, and yet offend in one point, he is guilty of all.

To show the seriousness of this matter of favoritism, James now makes an argument familiar to his readers of Jewish background. The Law of Moses presents itself not as a collection of individual commands, but as a unified whole. It is both many laws and a single unit of law. The standard that God gives His people is not to obey some or much of it, but all of it. So the failure to keep one part is the failure to keep the law in its entirety. Breaking *a* law is breaking *the* law.

11. For he that said, Do not commit adultery, said also, Do not kill. Now if thou commit no adultery, yet if thou kill, thou art become a transgressor of the law.

An illustration establishes James's point. The law forbids both adultery and murder. Keeping the law regarding the former but violating the latter does not leave a person innocent. That person is guilty of breaking the law and so is subject to the punishment due a lawbreaker.

C. Liberation by Law (vv. 12, 13)

12. So speak ye, and so do, as they that shall be judged by the law of liberty.

James summarizes the implication of his argument. Discrimination is serious because it violates a chief commandment: to love one's neighbor. Breaking a single commandment is no small matter; it means breaking the entire law of God. So acting in accord with God's law is of first importance. Thus, James gives a command: in speech and actions, behave as someone who will be judged by God's law, as one who obeys God's law.

Rather than being restrictive, this actually is liberating. James again calls God's law *the law of liberty* (compare James 1:25). As we contemplate God's law, we should experience fear because disobedience invites judgment. But we also experience hope, because obedience brings true freedom (compare Romans 8:2; 1 Peter 2:16).

13. For he shall have judgment without mercy, that hath shewed no mercy; and mercy rejoiceth against judgment.

The law of God is a fearful thing. When we realize that violating one part means violating the whole, we recognize how hopeless our position is, for none of us has kept God's law in every part. Is there a way for our guilt to be removed?

The answer is *yes*. The last part of this verse states the good news of Jesus: in God's mercy, He has provided a means by which we can escape the judgment we deserve. Sinners of all kinds can find forgiveness in Christ. The word translated *rejoiceth against* means something like "overcomes": in Christ, God's mercy overcomes judgment to bring forgiveness.

The way we should live is clear: with forgiveness toward others, like the forgiveness God grants us. The person who shows *no mercy* to others will therefore be denied the mercy that God gives to sinners. Jesus himself taught that the necessary response to God's forgiveness is to be forgiving (Matthew 5:7; 6:14, 15; 18:32-35). If we do not forgive others, have we really received God's forgiveness ourselves?

Conclusion

A. God's Big Family

The divisions between rich and poor were wide in James's time. It was easy to fawn over the rich

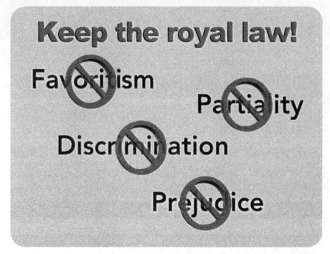

Visual for Lesson 11. *Start a discussion by pointing to this visual as you ask, "What differences in meaning, if any, are there among these four words?"*

and despise the poor. But doing so was contrary to what every part of God's Word teaches.

Today we face similar divisions, still between rich and poor, but also between racial groups, cultures, etc. The easy path for us is to favor those who are like us, with whom we are most familiar and most comfortable. We may mean no harm in doing so, but there is a grim effect of our seemingly innocent behavior: by favoring those like ourselves, we exclude others. Perhaps without realizing it, we keep them from actively belonging to God's family. We make it hard for them to be the church.

It is hard to see and hard to admit, but loving as God loves means deliberately reaching out to those who are unlike us in various ways. God wants to have a big family, so we need to love *all* of our fellow humans. To see others as God sees them—as being worthy of salvation—is our constant challenge.

B. Prayer

God of love and mercy, we depend entirely on Your forgiveness to address You in prayer. We ask by Your mercy that You strengthen us to overcome the patterns of this world by which we ignore members of Your family, our brothers and sisters. Teach us to love one another as You have loved us. In the name of Jesus, amen.

C. Thought to Remember

See others through God's eyes.

INVOLVEMENT LEARNING

Some of the activities below are also found in the helpful student book, Adult Bible Class.
Don't forget to download the free reproducible page from www.standardlesson.com to enhance your lesson!

Into the Lesson

Option: Place in chairs copies of the "How God Looks at People" activity from the reproducible page, which you can download. Learners can begin working on this as they arrive.

Divide the board into three columns. Title the three as follows: *Without Civil Rights / Life Event / After Civil Rights.* Begin by asking learners to brainstorm some ordinary events they participate in on a regular basis; list these in the middle column. Then ask learners to help you fill out the left column as they describe how some people face discriminatory restrictions regarding such life events. (Expect mention of America's civil rights movement of 1955–1968 if your learners are familiar with that era.) Finally, ask learners to help you fill out the right column according to its title.

Say, "Scripture uses some form of the phrase 'respect of persons' numerous times to refer to what we now call *favoritism, discrimination,* or *partiality.* Today we will see how God views those actions and attitudes in light of His revelation to James."

Into the Word

Divide the class into three groups for the following assignments:

Danger Group—Identify what James 2:1-4 says about how churches may be guilty of partiality and the ways to avoid it. Why does favoritism dishonor God?

Contrast Group—Identify the contrast between the rich and the poor in James 2:5-8 and the way God wants us to treat people. How do you see "the great reversal" indicated in these four verses?

Consequences Group—Identify the consequences that arise from the way we treat others as noted in James 2:9-13. Why does committing the one sin of favoritism make a person guilty of breaking the whole law?

When groups are ready, have them read their verses and share findings. The answer to the question for the *Danger Group* should point out that viewing some as more worthy than others puts us in the position of being "judges of evil thoughts" as we minimize the worth of people created in God's image. The answer to the question for the *Contrast Group* should point out the description of "the great reversal" in verse 5; the group may also recall previous discussions of this topic in lessons 8 (Luke 14:11) and 9 (Luke 16:25) and the imperative of the Golden Rule of lesson 7 (Luke 6:31). The answer to the question for the *Consequences Group* should point out the fact that the Law of Moses is a unified whole. Supplement the groups' conclusions with information from the lesson commentary.

Option: Write the following secular definition of discrimination on the board: "Unequal treatment without a rational basis." Compare and contrast this definition with "respect of persons" as discussed in today's text and Deuteronomy 1:17; 16:19; 2 Chronicles 19:7; Proverbs 24:23; Acts 10:34; Romans 2:11; Ephesians 6:9; Colossians 3:25; and 1 Peter 1:17. Ask, "Is the secular definition biblical? Why, or why not?"

Into Life

Review with learners some reasons why people show favoritism, then ask for examples of segments of today's society that are either favored or discriminated against; jot responses on the board under those two headings. Then ask for specific examples of favoritism or discrimination regarding each group. Finally, identify how God's Word directs us to treat each group.

Alternative: Distribute copies of the "Loving My Neighbor" activity from the reproducible page for learners to complete as directed. You may wish to use this alternative if you think the above activity will be too abstract and/or may lead to a heated political discussion. It can also be a take-home exercise.

SHOW YOUR FAITH BY YOUR WORKS

DEVOTIONAL READING: Luke 7:1-10
BACKGROUND SCRIPTURE: James 2:14-26

JAMES 2:14-26

14 What doth it profit, my brethren, though a man say he hath faith, and have not works? can faith save him?

15 If a brother or sister be naked, and destitute of daily food,

16 And one of you say unto them, Depart in peace, be ye warmed and filled; notwithstanding ye give them not those things which are needful to the body; what doth it profit?

17 Even so faith, if it hath not works, is dead, being alone.

18 Yea, a man may say, Thou hast faith, and I have works: shew me thy faith without thy works, and I will shew thee my faith by my works.

19 Thou believest that there is one God; thou doest well: the devils also believe, and tremble.

20 But wilt thou know, O vain man, that faith without works is dead?

21 Was not Abraham our father justified by works, when he had offered Isaac his son upon the altar?

22 Seest thou how faith wrought with his works, and by works was faith made perfect?

23 And the scripture was fulfilled which saith, Abraham believed God, and it was imputed unto him for righteousness: and he was called the Friend of God.

24 Ye see then how that by works a man is justified, and not by faith only.

25 Likewise also was not Rahab the harlot justified by works, when she had received the messengers, and had sent them out another way?

26 For as the body without the spirit is dead, so faith without works is dead also.

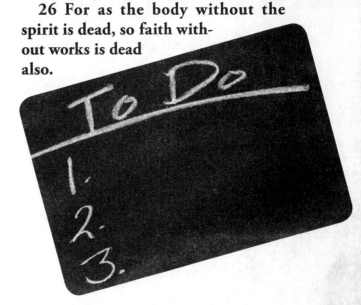

KEY VERSE

As the body without the spirit is dead, so faith without works is dead also. —**James 2:26**

JESUS AND THE JUST REIGN OF GOD

Unit 3: Live Justly in the Reign of God

LESSONS 10–13

LESSON AIMS

After participating in this lesson, each student will be able to:

1. Summarize James's argument that faith and works are inseparable.

2. Compare and contrast James's use of Abraham as an example of works with Paul's use of that patriarch as an example of faith in Romans 4.

3. Identify one way to put faith into action and do so.

LESSON OUTLINE

Introduction

A. Genuine or Counterfeit?

Have you noticed how much paper money (currency) has changed in the last few years? Designs have become more complex, colors have been added, special marks have been included. All these changes have one purpose: to make counterfeiting more difficult.

But even with all these changes, a skilled counterfeiter can still create a fake that can fool many people. It still takes experts to distinguish the genuine from some phonies. One becomes an expert in spotting counterfeit currency by studying the real thing. Skilled experts can see the subtle differences because they know the real article so well.

A parallel problem faced the Christians to whom James wrote. How could they identify true faith? While God alone can know what is in a person's heart, James says that we can identify true faith in ourselves by what it produces.

B. Lesson Background

Evaluating actions in order to distinguish between genuine and counterfeit faith, the theme of today's text, is a well-established one in Scripture. The Old Testament prophets commonly condemned those who confessed faith but acted with disobedience to God (Isaiah 29:13; Ezekiel 33:31). Jesus famously condemned religious leaders of His time for their hypocrisy; they claimed to be faithful to God, but they disobeyed Him habitually (Matthew 6:2, 5, 16; 23:13-33). Paul pointed out at length that all claims to standing with God are empty without deeds directed by godly love (1 Corinthians 13). The Bible is filled with disturbing examples of those who claimed faith in God, but failed to put it into practice.

The context of today's passage gives us a clue about the circumstances that prompted James's discussion of faith and works. James's readers struggled to reflect God's mercy toward the poor (James 2:1-13, last week's lesson). The readers' faith in the God who graciously met their needs was not being expressed in their meeting the needs of others (compare 1 John 3:17, 18). Such a problem cannot go unaddressed!

I. Evaluating Genuine Faith
(James 2:14-19)
A. Questions Posed (vv. 14-16)

14. What doth it profit, my brethren, though a man say he hath faith, and have not works? can faith save him?

James begins by asking two rhetorical questions, expecting negative answers. First he asks about the *profit*, or benefit, of a faith-profession that is not accompanied by actions that reflect that faith. The implication is that such a words-only profession of faith is no faith at all.

Then James moves to a more pointed question. Since the benefit of faith is salvation, what about the kind of faith just described, a faith that yields no actions—can that kind of faith save? Such a faith is an empty statement of agreement with a religious teaching, lacking conviction or commitment. It is merely saying "I believe" without serious thought of what that should entail.

True faith will not yield absolutely perfect obedience. After all, part of our faith is the confession that we are sinners! But true faith must change behavior over time.

15. If a brother or sister be naked, and destitute of daily food.

James moves to a hypothetical but very realistic situation. The readers live in a culture that has a small number of rich people and many, many who are poor. At the subsistence level in which most live, a small crisis can result in abject poverty. Laborers typically are paid a single coin per day in wages, and they commonly buy only enough food for one day's meals. If a day of work must be skipped due to sickness or injury, then a family may have to forego a day's food.

So the image of someone without enough food and/or adequate clothing (*naked* can mean partially or inadequately clothed) is one that the readers doubtless face themselves on occasion or have seen in others. The illustration already hints at what faith must do in this situation.

16. And one of you say unto them, Depart in peace, be ye warmed and filled; notwithstanding ye give them not those things which are needful to the body; what doth it profit?

James points out the emptiness of words of faith that lack the deeds of faith. *Depart in peace* is a standard farewell in Jewish culture. It is a brief prayer that a person will continue to experience the harmony and wholeness that God gives. But where is the sincerity in that statement when the one making it has the means to relieve hunger but offers nothing but words?

We see sarcasm in the phrase *be ye warmed and filled*. Such words express a prayer that God will provide; indeed, Jesus had promised that in God's kingdom the hungry will be filled (Luke 6:21, see lesson 7). Jesus further stated that relief from hunger and inadequate clothing can come through the action of a fellow believer (Matthew 25:35, 36). Why then does the person who has the means not take some practical step to address the need?

In the absence of action, there is no profit or benefit—the same expression as in verse 14. The person claims faith, even prays that God will provide, but this person of "faith" takes no action to do God's will "in earth, as it is in heaven" (Matthew 6:10). Is that real trust in God's promise?

What Do You Think?

What is your church's policy and procedure for addressing the needs of those who request help? How can you help improve or streamline these policies and procedures?

Talking Points for Your Discussion

- Policy issues (what your church will and won't do)
- Procedure issues (what your church does to implement its policy)

B. Proposition Advanced (v. 17)

17. Even so faith, if it hath not works, is dead, being alone.

The words-only "faith" that James has discussed thus far can now be fully characterized. It *is dead*, without life at all. Dead faith is not what we find in one who truly belongs to the living God.

Lying behind James's statement is a key idea in the teaching of the Bible. It is that the world in which we live is God's world, made by Him, and that God is fully committed to this world and to making it His again. A "faith" that has no impact in this world, that takes no action in it, is not a faith directed to the God of the Bible. The God who raised Jesus' dead body to life again is not the God of dead, inactive faith.

As we probe James's discussion of the relationship between faith and works, we may sense a tension with what Paul writes about this. He insists that God makes a person righteous by faith, not by works (see Romans 3:28; Galatians 2:16; Ephesians 2:8, 9), while James says that faith without works is dead. Who is right?

In fact, there is no contradiction between the two biblical writers. Paul's point is to emphasize to Jewish Christians that keeping the rites of the Law of Moses, such as circumcision or dietary regulations, is not what saves them. God saves Gentiles as Gentiles, not requiring that they first become Jews. James on the other hand writes to warn Christians that true faith always expresses itself in actions that reflect God's character and will. James's readers are tempted to neglect needy brothers and sisters while showing favor to the rich (see last week's lesson). Paul, emphasizing salvation by faith apart from works of the Law of Moses, also stresses that people of faith will conform their actions to God's will (Romans 12:1, 2; Galatians 5:16-26).

So both James and Paul view matters in the same way, though from different circumstances. Being Jewish, wealthy, a devout keeper of the law, or anything else does not make us God's people. Faith, not works, makes us His. But that faith always yields a life of obedient conformity to God's will, reflecting God's own nature in our actions.

What Do You Think?

With reference to the "policy and procedure" question of verse 16, what role will you play in your church's benevolence ministry as you put your faith into action in this area?

Talking Points for Your Discussion

- Helping with behind-the-scenes logistics
- Helping in out-front interaction with those receiving help
- Other

C. Objections Anticipated (vv. 18, 19)

18. Yea, a man may say, Thou hast faith, and I have works: shew me thy faith without thy works, and I will shew thee my faith by my works.

Now James draws a contrast with a different point of view to make his point clearer still. He invites us to imagine two people. One has already said something like, "I am not really much of a 'works person.' I am more of a 'faith person.' Works are other people's gift, not mine." Then the second person speaks, the one whom James describes in this verse. That person says, "Really? You have faith, while I have works? Fine. Show me your faith without works. Then I will show you my works, and they will prove that I have faith."

Of course, there is no demonstrating of faith without works. Faith is invisible in and of itself, but the works that James describes are the necessary product of valid faith. Such actions really do speak louder than words. The person who claims faith without works makes an absurd, empty claim.

❧ *VISIBLE INTERCESSION* ❧

Rees Howells was born in Wales in 1879. Greatly influenced by the Welsh Revival of 1904–1905, he came to be known as a powerful prayer warrior and man of faith. His prayers were combined with extreme generosity toward those for whom he interceded. For instance, Howells once paid two full years of rent for a drunkard who had become a Christian so that the man and his family would not be evicted from their home. Such "visible intercession" characterized Howells's life as a missionary to South Africa, founder of a Bible college to train missionaries, etc.

Here's where you should stop reading if you don't want to be convicted: Howells believed that we should ask God to do only what we are willing for Him to do through us.

Think about how you pray for God to intervene in someone's life. When you pray, "Dear God, please help that person," are you willing to be used as the channel through which God's help will come to him or her? What if the reason that God is blessing you today is so that you can be a blessing to someone in need who stands before you tomorrow? God is always seeking those willing to demonstrate their faith through their works on His behalf. Sometimes He finds someone (example: Isaiah 6:8), and sometimes He doesn't (example: Ezekiel 22:30). Will God find you to be a visible intercessor today?   —V. E.

19. Thou believest that there is one God; thou doest well: the devils also believe, and tremble.

James offers a second contrast that lays out still more clearly the absurdity of claiming faith without works. The confession that "God is one" is the essential confession of the Old Testament, differentiating Israel from its pagan neighbors. "Hear, O Israel: The Lord our God is one Lord" (Deuteronomy 6:4) is a defining confession of the Jewish people, including Jewish Christians like James's readers. But what of the person who simply makes this confession and does nothing more?

James affirms that the confession is correct. But then he points out that *the devils* (or demons) believe the same thing! They know who God is; they recognized Jesus' identity (Matthew 8:28, 29; compare Acts 16:16, 17). And even demons react properly regarding their belief about God: they tremble in fear of their coming destruction. The person who claims faith without works is less responsive to God than a demon!

We might paraphrase James's point with the common saying, "Talk is cheap." Saying that we have faith is of no significance at all if we do not act in faith. If demons—who know who God is but refuse to submit to Him—can at least tremble, should not those who claim to belong to God act in ways that please Him?

II. Illustrating Genuine Faith
(JAMES 2:20-26)
A. Abraham (vv. 20-24)

20. But wilt thou know, O vain man, that faith without works is dead?

Does this matter require more proof? Are we not yet convinced *that faith without works is dead*? To lock down his argument further, James now begins a different approach to the problem: examples from the Scriptures.

James addresses a hypothetical conversation partner as a *vain man.* The word *vain* here means "empty" or "without purpose." Any faith that does not act is surely empty and without purpose, and so is the person who claims such faith.

> *What Do You Think?*
> How has someone else's deeds from faith made a lasting difference in your life?
> *Talking Points for Your Discussion*
> ▪ Regarding an act of service for your benefit
> ▪ Regarding an example you followed when faced with the same situation
> ▪ Regarding a need met between third parties

21. Was not Abraham our father justified by works, when he had offered Isaac his son upon the altar?

Abraham, the father of the nation of Israel and the recipient of God's promise to bless all nations (Genesis 12:1-3), is James's first example of true faith. Abraham's faith, of course, was not always at work in his story. Though he willingly left his home for the land God was to show him, he revealed distrust in God when he lied twice to protect himself (12:11-13; 20:1, 2). He revealed further distrust when he took a concubine to conceive a son (16:1-4).

The premier work of faith for Abraham was when he committed himself to sacrifice his son Isaac as God directed (Genesis 22:1-10). God intervened to stop the proceedings (vv. 11, 12), but even before that point Abraham expressed his faith in God's promise when he told his servant that he and Isaac would go to the mountain and return (v. 5). Abraham trusted God's promise that through Isaac a great nation would come to be, so he held to the belief that if God commanded that

HOW TO SAY IT

Abraham	*Ay*-bruh-ham.
Ezekiel	Ee-*zeek*-ee-ul or Ee-*zeek*-yul.
Isaac	*Eye*-zuk.
Isaiah	Eye-*zay*-uh.
Jericho	*Jair*-ih-co.
Rahab	*Ray*-hab.

Isaac be sacrificed, then God would raise him up again (Hebrews 11:19). Only faith could produce a response like this.

So why does James say that Abraham was *justified by works*? When Abraham put faith in God's promise that he would have a son, we are told that it was on the basis of Abraham's faith that God declared that man to be righteous; that is, God *justified* him (Genesis 15:6). But taking us to the end of the story, James shows that Abraham's faith was the kind that produces works. So James can fairly affirm that Abraham was counted righteous because of his works, works that demonstrated the faith that God had seen in him before.

22. Seest thou how faith wrought with his works, and by works was faith made perfect?

James invites us to consider the story of Abraham carefully, to realize that his faith indeed produced actions. The contrast between Abraham's lack of faithful actions in some instances makes James's point all the clearer. Abraham struggled to believe throughout his life. Only when he put his faith in action, climaxing in the amazing story of Isaac's near sacrifice, could it be said that his faith had been *made perfect*, or had achieved its purpose.

What Do You Think?
How does the example of Abraham's near-sacrifice of Isaac help you act on what you believe?
Talking Points for Your Discussion
- Regarding those hard, seemingly "no-win" circumstances
- Regarding how God views obedience
- Recognizing barriers to obedience
- Other

❧ *WHAT YOU SEE IS . . .* ❧

I recently participated in a group coaching session designed to help participants understand themselves. In one exercise, we were asked to review dozens of values and decide which four were our top ones. All of the options were positive characteristics, so it was difficult to decide without the following instruction: "If you don't live it, you don't believe it."

That instruction narrowed down the possible choices in a hurry! In order to claim a value as one of our top four, we had to be able to express how we had lived out that value in the past week.

Generous people don't merely think happy thoughts for others; generous people give to others. Children of the God of compassion and mercy strive to forgive others. The followers of the Lord of love not only do no harm to others, they also do what is in their power to help others. The test of the validity of your faith is simple: Do you live out what you believe?   —V. E.

23. And the scripture was fulfilled which saith, Abraham believed God, and it was imputed unto him for righteousness: and he was called the Friend of God.

James now quotes Genesis 15:6, a passage he alluded to in verse 21, above. Abraham's faith was the basis for God's counting him righteous; that is, that man was considered to be righteous (or justified) by his faith. Abraham's faith was made visible by actions that sprang from that faith. *The scripture was fulfilled* because the faith noted in Genesis 15:16 was made visible by the action of Genesis 22:1-10. The importance of Genesis 15:16 is seen in its being quoted four times in the New Testament (here plus Romans 4:3, 22; and Galatians 3:6).

James uses an expression common among the Jewish people of his time as he refers to Abraham as *the Friend of God* (see 2 Chronicles 20:7; Isaiah 41:8). James's point is that all who live by faith—those putting faith into practice—can be regarded as God's friends as well.

24. Ye see then how that by works a man is justified, and not by faith only.

Had Abraham not done those deeds of faith, would God's promise have been at work in the world through Abraham? Would we conclude that Abraham had faith in God? Indeed, is there such a thing as faith that does not produce actions? James says *no*. Abraham's great deed of faith was a long time in coming, but it demonstrated what God had foreseen: genuine trust in God's promise, trust that Abraham later put on the line. To be counted righteous like Abraham, one needs the kind of faith that leads to action.

B. Rahab (v. 25)

25. Likewise also was not Rahab the harlot justified by works, when she had received the messengers, and had sent them out another way?

James's first biblical example was Abraham, a man and the father of the nation of Israel. Now he turns to Rahab, a woman and a Gentile.

Rahab we know as a *harlot* (prostitute) from ancient Jericho. Having heard of Israel's triumphs in earlier battles, she had come to believe that the true God was with Israel. She was therefore not only afraid of Israel's army, she was ready to assist Israel in its conquest of her city. That meant taking the dangerous step of hiding the Israelite spies who came to Jericho to assess its defenses (Joshua 2:1-13). In the end, she became a part of the Israelite people and an ancestor of King David and Jesus himself (Matthew 1:5).

A pagan prostitute became part of God's people by her faith in Israel's God. But her faith certainly was a faith that resulted in action, action that put Rahab's own life on the line (compare Hebrews 11:31). Without such actions, she would not have become part of Israel and the saga of salvation.

C. Death (v. 26)

26. For as the body without the spirit is dead, so faith without works is dead also.

James offers a final illustration to drive home his point. Every human being is a unity of body (what can be seen) and spirit (what cannot be seen). When the two are separated, there is death. The same is true of *faith without works.* As the visible body is dead without the invisible spirit, so also invisible faith is dead without visible works.

What Do You Think?

What examples can you add to demonstrate how faith is evident in deeds?

Talking Points for Your Discussion

- Beliefs about Scripture
- Beliefs about resurrection
- Beliefs about sin
- Beliefs about grace
- Beliefs about the church

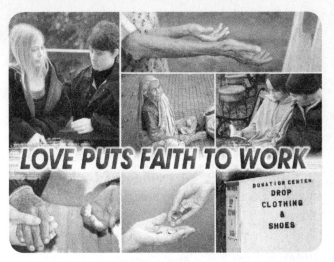

Visual for Lesson 12. *Use this visual to introduce the discussion question that is associated with verse 17.*

Conclusion

A. Living, Working Faith

James takes his readers to school on genuine faith. He teaches them thoroughly what the real article looks like. Real faith, living faith, always works. It is always active. It never leaves a person or the world around the person the same.

If we want to recognize genuine faith, we should first look at ourselves. The assessment of genuine faith is a self-assessment. What actions flow from my faith? Is my life different from what it was before I came to faith in Christ? Do I make excuses about my lack of actions?

Perhaps we should remember that one of the works of genuine faith is prayer. We pray to God only if we know that we need His power to help, only if we believe that He can and will help. We begin by asking God to strengthen our faith and enable us to put it into action. Then we trust Him to sustain us in the adventure that follows.

B. Prayer

O God, we praise You for Your patience with us, Your often workless people. Increase our faith, Lord! Gird us for action in Your world. Make us alive in our faith and works together. We pray in the name of Jesus, the faithful one, amen.

C. Thought to Remember

A workless faith is a worthless faith.

INVOLVEMENT LEARNING

Some of the activities below are also found in the helpful student book, Adult Bible Class.
Don't forget to download the free reproducible page from www.standardlesson.com to enhance your lesson!

Into the Lesson

Summarize how the actions of partiality that were addressed in last week's lesson are contrary to what God desires. Say, "It is important that our behavior reflects what we say we believe about God. Otherwise, we are counterfeit Christians. Today we will see how genuine faith in God produces actions in that regard."

Alternative: Distribute copies of the "Action Test" exercise from the reproducible page, which you can download. When learners are finished, say, "The main thing that should be crystal clear is that *belief about* something naturally leads one to *take action* in relation to that belief. A failure to act on a belief calls into question how genuine that belief really is. Today we will see how genuine faith in God produces actions in that regard."

Into the Word

Divide the board into two columns that are intersected by two rows. Title one column *Having* and the other column *Not Having*, then title the first row *Faith* and the second row *Works*. The result will be that the board is divided into a grid with four sections: having faith / not having faith / having works / not having works. Ask learners to brainstorm what could be put into the four segments. Be prepared to offer important entries that your learners do not mention.

After discussing, say, "When thinking of the terms *faith* and *works* together, what Scripture references come to mind?" If learners mention Romans 4 and James 2, respond that those will be important text references for today; if learners do not mention these two, lead them to those texts now.

Read James 2:14-19. Ask learners to identify what James is saying about faith and works and whether his words speak positively or negatively about each (example: v. 18 speaks positively about works—they demonstrate the validity of faith).

Then read James 2:20-26. Ask learners to identify which truths that the class just identified are illustrated (example: vv. 20, 26 illustrate that faith is dead if not accompanied by works). Use the lesson commentary for further explanations about the role of works in relation to one's faith.

Next, read Romans 4:4-8. Ask learners to find words that appear to be equivalent to either faith or works, then identify whether these words speak positively or negatively (example: in vv. 4, 5, a positive word concerning faith is *righteousness*). Then read Romans 4:13-18, and ask learners to repeat what they did with verses 4-8 (examples: positive words concerning faith are *promise* [v. 13], *grace* [v. 16], *hope* [v. 18]; negative words concerning works are *wrath* and *transgression* [v. 15]).

Use the lesson commentary to lead the class in a discussion of how Romans 4 and James 2 point to the same truths about faith and works. Say, "The emphasis of our text today complements what we studied last week: as Christians our actions should be prompted by our faith in God."

Into Life

Option 1: Say, "Real faith is always active. It never leaves a person or the world around a person the same." Show the brief "History of Traders —a video on sacrifice" (from www.youtube.com, posted by www.RightNow.org). After the video, brainstorm things your group could "trade" in order to serve others. Pick one "trade" your class is willing to make before the end of the month.

Option 2: Distribute copies of the "Faith and Works" acrostic from the reproducible page. Have learners work in pairs to discuss how they will put faith into action in the week ahead.

Option 3: Distribute copies of the "Putting My Faith into Action" commitment statement from the reproducible page. Use this instead of Option 2 if you think your learners prefer to reflect on this alone (that is, "just between me and God").

CONTROL YOUR SPEECH

DEVOTIONAL READING: Proverbs 18:2-13
BACKGROUND SCRIPTURE: James 3:1-12

JAMES 3:1-12

1 My brethren, be not many masters, knowing that we shall receive the greater condemnation.

2 For in many things we offend all. If any man offend not in word, the same is a perfect man, and able also to bridle the whole body.

3 Behold, we put bits in the horses' mouths, that they may obey us; and we turn about their whole body.

4 Behold also the ships, which though they be so great, and are driven of fierce winds, yet are they turned about with a very small helm, whithersoever the governor listeth.

5 Even so the tongue is a little member, and boasteth great things. Behold, how great a matter a little fire kindleth!

6 And the tongue is a fire, a world of iniquity: so is the tongue among our members, that it defileth the whole body,

and setteth on fire the course of nature; and it is set on fire of hell.

7 For every kind of beasts, and of birds, and of serpents, and of things in the sea, is tamed, and hath been tamed of mankind:

8 But the tongue can no man tame; it is an unruly evil, full of deadly poison.

9 Therewith bless we God, even the Father; and therewith curse we men, which are made after the similitude of God.

10 Out of the same mouth proceedeth blessing and cursing. My brethren, these things ought not so to be.

11 Doth a fountain send forth at the same place sweet water and bitter?

12 Can the fig tree, my brethren, bear olive berries? either a vine, figs? so can no fountain both yield salt water and fresh.

KEY VERSE

Out of the same mouth proceedeth blessing and cursing. My brethren, these things ought not so to be.

—James 3:10

JESUS AND THE JUST REIGN OF GOD

Unit 3: Live Justly in the Reign of God

LESSONS 10–13

LESSON AIMS

After participating in this lesson, each student will be able to:

1. List some of the dangers James identifies with improper speech.

2. Compare and contrast today's text with Ephesians 5:4.

3. Identify one speech pattern to bring under control and recruit an accountability partner to help do so.

LESSON OUTLINE

Introduction

A. Free Speech or Costly Speech

In countries that enjoy democratic government, there is no right more cherished than that of free speech. We want to express ourselves, and we want as few restrictions as possible on what we say or how we say it. We believe in the power of freedom of speech, and we want to exercise that power.

But exercising our right to free speech can prove costly. Words freely spoken can hurt feelings, damage reputations, and break relationships. Though we may affirm that "sticks and stones may break my bones, but names will never hurt me," we all know that words *do* hurt.

Free speech may be our right, but costly speech is our experience. All of us can recount instances where someone's words, perhaps our own, did tremendous harm to another. We can spend a lifetime learning to restrain our tongues and still find ourselves saying things that we regret later. Today's text deals with this difficult topic.

B. Lesson Background

The world of the New Testament was filled with speech. Greek and Roman cultures highly prized public speaking, drama, storytelling, and political and philosophical argumentation. Religious teachers—the "self-improvement experts" of the day—traveled from town to town to make speeches to invite people to pay to hear longer, more in-depth instruction. The sons of well-to-do families were trained in rhetoric so that they could offer skilled defense of the family's legal and financial interests. The list goes on.

Jewish culture had a rich tradition of speech as well. The people of Israel had experienced God's speaking to them through His prophets. The words of the law and the prophets were read publicly in the synagogues, committed to memory by the faithful, and recited daily as the need arose. Teachers of the law offered instruction in how God's Word should be lived out, often debating vigorously on points of interpretation. The Jewish tradition of speech had a dark side as well: false prophets who claimed to speak for God, but in fact represented ungodly interests.

Israel's sacred words of Scripture included instruction and warnings about speech. The book of Proverbs, for example, makes numerous statements about wise and unwise speech (Proverbs 10:8, 11, 14, 31; 11:9, 11, 13; 12:18; 15:1, 7; 16:23; 17:28). Of course, knowing the wisdom of speech and practicing it are two very different things.

The situation for James's readers was complex and challenging. They were surrounded by speech, good and bad. They had habits of speech that they had learned through their lifetimes. But as Christians they were entrusted with the greatest message of all: the good news of Jesus. How would these people—people with all the problems that humans have regarding the power of their words —handle the most powerful message of God?

I. Sober Calling
(JAMES 3:1, 2)
A. The Caution (v. 1)

1. My brethren, be not many masters, knowing that we shall receive the greater condemnation.

James begins with a warning about taking the message of God lightly. He speaks kindly, addressing his readers as *brethren* in God's family. But he also speaks sternly: not many should be *masters,* meaning "teachers" (think "schoolmasters") of God's Word. Why would James make such a statement? Is it not true that workers are needed for the harvest of God (Matthew 9:37, 38)?

James is certainly aware of a very troublesome tendency of human nature: to take the things of God and use them for selfish purposes. To be a teacher of God's Word is to be in a prominent position that demands respect. Some aspire to be teachers for the ego gratification that it seems to offer.

To that temptation, James gives a warning: teachers *shall receive the greater condemnation,* meaning that they are subject to greater judgment. Their responsibility before God is magnified, for

HOW TO SAY IT

hyperbole	high-***purr***-buh-*lee*.
Jerusalem	Juh-*roo*-suh-lem.
Publilius Syrus	Puh-*blihl*-ee-uhs *Sigh*-russ.

they proclaim the message of God's salvation. Before anyone decides to use the power of speech to announce God's Word, that person should take a careful inventory of motives. It is a blasphemous contradiction to teach the good news of Christ's unselfish sacrifice out of one's selfish motives (compare Matthew 12:36, 37).

But the Word of God must be proclaimed, and people will answer the call to do so. Note that as James says *we shall receive the greater condemnation,* he is numbering himself among the teachers by the use of the word *we.* The great responsibility of teaching should give us pause, but it should also challenge us to rise to the calling.

> **What Do You Think?**
>   How can James's warning be applied to teaching
>   contexts that do not involve spoken words?
> *Talking Points for Your Discussion*
> - Bible study curriculum (such as the one you're using now)
> - Christian journalism
> - Internet blogs
> - Other

B. The Problem (v. 2)

2. For in many things we offend all. If any man offend not in word, the same is a perfect man, and able also to bridle the whole body.

The challenge of teaching God's Word is twofold: all teachers are sinners, and speech is the most difficult of behaviors to control. Because the Christian carries the Word of God, consistent control of speech for godly ends is vital.

James underlines the issue of universal sinfulness with the statement *in many things we offend all.* Today we might say, "All of us slip up in many ways." We do not intend to sin, but regardless of best intentions, we sin far more than we care to admit. Realizing our sinfulness does not exclude us from teaching God's Word, but it does caution us to consider carefully how we do it. Realizing our sinfulness challenges us to let God change the sinful patterns that persist in us.

So if all people are chronic stumblers, then who are the least stumble-prone? James offers that those who do not stumble with regard to their speech are complete (the sense of the word *perfect* in this context). If one can control one's speech, the most difficult of all behaviors to bring under control, then *the whole body*—the entire person—will be under control.

Who would claim to be such an exceptionally controlled person? No one who takes seriously the warning *in many things we offend all*! But in this realization James makes his point. He invites his readers not to overestimate their ability to control their tongues.

> **What Do You Think?**
> What are some techniques for taming the tongue before words are ever spoken? Which do you find most helpful personally?
>
> *Talking Points for Your Discussion*
> - When angry
> - When hurt
> - When tempted to tell "a little white lie"
> - Other

II. Daunting Challenge
(JAMES 3:3-5)
A. Horses and Bits (v. 3)

3. Behold, we put bits in the horses' mouths, that they may obey us; and we turn about their whole body.

James proceeds to illustrate just how difficult it is to control speech. A horse can be controlled by a skillful rider by use of a relatively tiny bit—a piece of metal attached to the leather bridle and placed in the horse's mouth. The bit-with-bridle causes the mighty horse to obey the rider's every command. This is an impressive level of control, but speech is not so simply brought under restraint as we will see in verse 5.

B. Ships and Rudders (v. 4)

4. Behold also the ships, which though they be so great, and are driven of fierce winds, yet are they turned about with a very small helm, whithersoever the governor listeth.

Bigger than a horse is a sailing ship, and stronger than either a horse or its rider are the winds that drive the ship. But *a very small helm* (rudder) steers a giant ship. Like the horse's bit, the ship's rudder keeps it under control so that it goes wherever *the governor* (helmsman) decides. The tongue, however, is an upside-down version of what James is describing, as our next verse shows.

C. Tongues and Fire (v. 5)

5. Even so the tongue is a little member, and boasteth great things. Behold, how great a matter a little fire kindleth!

Big horses are controlled by small bits; big ships by small rudders. But the tongue, though small, cannot be so easily controlled. In fact, even though it is small, it acts as if it is big in attempting to make itself seem greater than it is as it *boasteth great things*.

Those who aspire to teach should take warning. If their desire is for the prestige that comes from teaching God's Word, then they are on a path in which their speech may control them, not the other way around. Those who know God's grace have no room to brag, for they take seriously their deep, persistent need for God to bless them despite their unworthiness. The "bit" or "rudder" that controls the tongue is a deeply rooted appreciation of God's unmerited favor.

James uses this caution to offer another illustration: the power of fire. A small fire can get out of control quickly, unleashing terrible destructive force. Speech, sadly, can do the same as our next verse shows.

III. Grave Danger
(JAMES 3:6-8)
A. Small and Great (v. 6)

6a. And the tongue is a fire, a world of iniquity: so is the tongue among our members, that it defileth the whole body.

The destructive power of speech rivals that of fire. Compared with the entirety of the human body, the tongue is small. But its potential for unrighteous action is on a global scale, like the entire world in size, James says. Thus the little tongue can cause one's entire body to be corrupt, soiled, and filthy (compare Matthew 15:11).

It does no good to claim that evil speech is "just words," for words can be exceptionally potent.

6b. And setteth on fire the course of nature; and it is set on fire of hell.

James continues the fire comparison. *The course of nature* is a comprehensive expression, like "life as we know it" in our idiom. It signifies the whole of our experience. James insists that evil speech has the power to destroy it all.

Speech has this power because it is ignited by Hell. The Greek term that is translated Hell was originally used to refer to a valley outside Jerusalem where garbage was dumped. Since fires burned constantly there, the image is that of a disgusting, fiery place of imprisonment for evil spirits (compare Matthew 25:41). We are to think of the very depths of wickedness in all its horror. With this image James makes a disturbing point: the power of Satan, which Christ came to defeat, is unleashed in the world through the human tongue.

> *What Do You Think?*
> When have you seen words have the negative impact James describes here? What do these cases teach you?
> *Talking Points for Your Discussion*
> - Political speeches designed to inflame
> - Unguarded speech
> - Advice from (or to) a friend
> - Other

B. Tamed and Untamed (vv. 7, 8)

7. For every kind of beasts, and of birds, and of serpents, and of things in the sea, is tamed, and hath been tamed of mankind.

James introduces yet another comparison. All kinds of creatures, he says, can be trained. His list includes a range of words used in his day to classify these: *beasts* (mostly land mammals), *birds* (including all animals that fly), *serpents* (reptiles and amphibians), and various water animals. He uses an obvious exaggeration (hyperbole) in saying that *every kind . . . hath been tamed*. But the exaggeration serves to emphasize what we have learned to control in contrast with what we have not. Trained animals are a well-known spectacle in the Greco-

Roman world, and skill in taming animals to perform is impressive. But the power to tame has a disturbing limitation, as our next verse shows.

8. But the tongue can no man tame; it is an unruly evil, full of deadly poison.

Animals can be tamed, but can the tongue? No one truly brings speech fully into subjection. Those who aspire to teach God's Word must listen carefully to James's descriptive warnings. Speech is an *unruly evil*. The phrase *full of deadly poison* recalls the words of Psalm 140:3: "They have sharpened their tongues like a serpent; adders' poison is under their lips" (compare Romans 3:13). Words can kill, both as they damage hearts and as they inspire physical violence. That grim reality has been part of human experience from ancient times.

Evil, death, Hell, poison, fire—these are harsh, powerful words. But they are not exaggerations. This is the story of human speech apart from God's grace.

❧ WATCH THOSE WORDS! ❧

When I was in elementary school, the buses carried one load of students home immediately after school and then returned for a second load. It was not a pleasant wait when bullies cut in line, called their fellow students embarrassing names, and teased victims relentlessly. Generally, those being harassed remained silent.

On one occasion, the bullies even went as far as making ridiculous accusations about the parents of the subjects of that day's bullying. Still no reaction, and I remember the sense of powerlessness all of us felt about making them stop. It seemed to cut into the innermost being when one's family was attacked.

Maybe you have experienced something similar. Perhaps you've experienced faultfinding veiled as constructive criticism or conversations comprised of speculations, exaggerations, and gossip. The consequences for those who are the target of damaging comments may be severe indeed.

We answer to a righteous God who expects us to grow in our likeness to Him (Ephesians 4:22-24), so we are expected to guard our words (4:25, 29). When we do, we will have less to retract and more pleasant memories to flood our souls.—C. M. W.

IV. Glaring Contradiction
(JAMES 3:9-12)

A. Problem Noted (vv. 9, 10)

9. Therewith bless we God, even the Father; and therewith curse we men, which are made after the similitude of God.

Someone may read James's discourse and respond, "Well, I admit that my speech is sometimes not as it should be. But I also teach the gospel. Is that not what God wants? I use my 'good' speech to serve Him in that way." To this way of thinking, James gives a rejoinder: speech that does not consistently reflect God's grace contradicts the gospel that the Christian proclaims.

This fact is seen in a devastating statement of contradiction. On the one hand, a believer praises God as a good, loving Father. But on the other hand, that believer also curses another person. And that person, like everyone else, bears the image of God (Genesis 1:27). What does the curse reveal about the heart of the person who utters it? Where is the love and forgiveness of God in such a curse?

Calling for others to be punished by God (cursing them) is completely out of keeping with the identity of Christ's followers. Jesus insisted that those who receive God's forgiveness must extend forgiveness (Matthew 5:7; 6:12; 18:21-35). Doing less suggests that we treat God's mercy with contempt. Such contradictory speech-acts reveal that within the heart of the one who curses others lingers a denial of the gospel message.

What Do You Think?

How do you compare and contrast James's observations about use of the tongue with secular thoughts in this regard?

Talking Points for Your Discussion

- "The best time . . . to hold your tongue is [when] you feel you must say something or bust" (Josh Billings)
- "Man's tongue is soft, and bone doth lack; yet a stroke therewith may break a man's back" (Benjamin Franklin)
- "Give thy thoughts no tongue" (William Shakespeare)

---

10. Out of the same mouth proceedeth blessing and cursing. My brethren, these things ought not so to be.

The contradiction is clear. We might call it "speaking out of both sides of the mouth." What does this person truly believe, who blesses God and curses those who bear God's image? Remembering Jesus' words about taking the beam out of our own eye before attempting to help a brother with a mote in his (Matthew 7:1-5), we realize that we must first ask what our speech reveals about our own hearts.

B. Problem Illustrated (vv. 11, 12)

11. Doth a fountain send forth at the same place sweet water and bitter?

James moves to compare speech with *a fountain* (a spring of water). Since the water's source remains the same, the fountain should yield the same kind of water consistently. How can a fountain produce pleasant-tasting water one moment and then bitter water the next, back and forth? It simply doesn't happen.

A Christian's speech is to be consistent. The image of Jesus as the source of living water perhaps lies in the background of this statement (see John 7:37, 38). The "water" of speech that flows from the believer should consistently reflect the new, everlasting life that Christ has imparted to the believer (compare Proverbs 10:11). The words of our mouths reveal the true content of our hearts.

12. Can the fig tree, my brethren, bear olive berries? either a vine, figs? so can no fountain both yield salt water and fresh.

James underlines the contrasts yet again, to drive the point home. Figs, olives, and grapes (*berries*) are staple foods in the biblical world. Of course, it is the commonest of knowledge that each kind of plant bears only its own kind of fruit. James implies that the Christian's speech must have the same consistency (compare Luke 6:43). If the fruit of plants created by God is consistent, why not the speech of people re-created by God?

James wraps up his argument by clearly stating the answer that is implied in the question of verse 11. Those who say they belong to Christ ought to reflect that belonging in all that they say, not just in their "religious" speech.

❧ WHAT'S WRONG WITH THIS PICTURE? ❧

A mother cradles her infant while she pours out angry words at her because she will not stop crying. A dad talks to his son about the value of sportsmanship, but then blasts the youngster for admitting an error to the umpire and thereby losing the game. What's wrong with these pictures?

Indeed, it is easy to send inconsistent signals in our communications. People who genuinely seek to improve their skills in this area will try to remove such inconsistencies. But the Christian has a higher calling still: we are created in the image of God (Genesis 1:27), and we are to be like Him (Leviticus 11:44 [quoted in 1 Peter 1:15, 16]; Matthew 5:48). How sinful, therefore, to take delight in using our words and our communications inappropriately!

Our speech can be an obvious indication of our authenticity as Christians. We soothe a crying baby. We encourage our children to play fair. And when we do, we model the right picture.

—C. M. W.

Conclusion

A. Words of Grace

The situation of James's audience was not all that much different from ours. We need to confront the reality of our speech so that we can learn to control it. Those who have experienced God's grace should have speech that reflects God's grace.

After studying James's warning that teachers of God's Word "shall receive the greater condemnation," we may want to say, "I certainly do not want to be a teacher! The standard is too high. I can never restrain my speech like this. Just let me be an ordinary Christian who listens to others teach!"

But as James lays bare the realities of our speech and its consequences, we should realize that we are all teachers because of the fact that we bear the name of Christ. Others watch us to see what a Christ-follower does and says. They scrutinize our actions, and they listen to our words. They learn our beliefs more by hearing us speak about ordinary, day-to-day matters than by hearing us speak about Bible doctrine.

When we speak unlovingly with bitterness, vindictiveness, or scorn, we demonstrate a very wrong kind of belief about God—that He too is unloving, vengeful, and unforgiving. If we speak in this way, we invite on ourselves "the greater condemnation" that is due those who teach, because indeed we are teaching something with everything we say.

God's grace is powerful enough to overcome our wayward tongues. As we focus on what God has given us in Christ, the reality of our hearts will flow through our words.

B. Prayer

O holy and gracious God, we praise You with our hearts and our words. By Your grace, please cleanse us of selfishness, anger, and hate. Renew us in Your love. Make our tongues Your instruments. We pray in the name of Jesus, amen.

C. Thought to Remember

"Speech is a mirror of the soul; as a man speaks, so is he."   —Publilius Syrus (first century BC)

Visual for Lesson 13. *Use this visual to start a brainstorming session on various techniques the Christian can use to keep the tongue in check.*

INVOLVEMENT LEARNING

Some of the activities below are also found in the helpful student book, Adult Bible Class.
Don't forget to download the free reproducible page from www.standardlesson.com to enhance your lesson!

Into the Lesson

Have on display the phrase "Sticks and stones may break my bones . . ." as learners arrive. Begin class by asking learners to complete the phrase; expect several to say immediately "but words will never harm me." Then distribute blank index cards and ask learners to brainstorm silently some words that can be harmful to others, writing the words on their cards. Collect the cards without discussing them. Simply say, "We'll come back to these later. First, we have some work to do in wrestling with the dangers of improper speech."

Option: Before learners arrive, place in chairs copies of the "Improper Talk" activity from the reproducible page, which you can download. Those arriving early can begin working on this before class starts.

Into the Word

Divide the class into five small groups of three or four. Give the following assignments: *Not-Many Group*—James 3:1; *Control Group*—James 3:2-5; *Fire Group*—James 3:6; *Untamed Group*—James 3:7, 8; *Hypocritical Group*—James 3:9-12. (If your class is smaller, use fewer groups and combine some passages.) Ask groups to list one danger or challenge of improper speech from their passages.

When groups are finished, have a volunteer from each read the passage at issue and write on the board the danger noted. (Possible responses: *Not-Many Group*, greater condemnation for those who teach; *Control Group*, speech is a most difficult behavior to control; *Fire Group*, the tongue can defile the whole body; *Untamed Group*, an untamed tongue brings evil and even death; *Hypocritical Group*, the tongue is hypocritical because it blesses God and curses people.) Discuss the dangers listed, using information from the lesson commentary to add to the discussion.

Option: Probe deeper by asking every group to be prepared to answer a challenge question that begins "Oh yeah? Well what about . . ." from the next group to follow (with the last of the five groups being challenged by the first group). *Alternative:* You, the teacher, can ask the challenge questions instead, which you have prepared in advance. Possibilities: *Not-Many Group*—"What about the church's need to have many workers for the harvest of God according to Matthew 9:37, 38?" *Control Group*—"Are you saying it's possible to achieve perfection with the tongue in this life?" *Fire Group*—"Aren't you getting the cause and effect reversed?" *Untamed Group*—"If no one can tame the tongue, then why should we wear ourselves out trying?" *Hypocritical Group*—"Was Paul violating the prohibition against cursing others when he wrote 'Cursed is every one that continueth not in all things which are written in the book of the law to do them' in Galatians 3:10?"

Into Life

Read Ephesians 5:4 aloud, then write the following headings on the board: *Filthiness / Foolish Talking / Jesting.* Discuss the implications of each heading, then review the index cards you collected earlier, affixing each under its appropriate heading. Discuss how using such language causes damage before both Christians and non-Christians. Make application where appropriate to the dangers that learners identified earlier.

Brainstorm circumstances where it can be easy to slip up and use the type of language you just identified. Then discuss how a Christian can use uplifting speech in those circumstances. Write those examples under a new heading: *Giving Thanks* (from Ephesians 5:20). *Option:* Distribute copies of the "A Prayer for Perfect Speech" commitment card from the reproducible page. Suggest that each learner recruit an accountability partner for making the intended progress.

Finish with prayers of commitment to watch for opportunities to use speech that blesses others.

JESUS' FULFILLMENT OF SCRIPTURE

Special Features

Lessons

Unit 1: Jesus and the Davidic Covenant

Unit 2: What the Prophets Foretold

Unit 3: Jesus' Use of Scripture

QUARTERLY QUIZ

Use these questions as a pretest or as a review. The answers are on page iv of This Quarter in the Word.

Lesson 1

1. David was called to be king from what previous job? (soldier, priest, shepherd?) *2 Samuel 7:8*

2. God decided that the temple must be built by a descendant of David. T/F. *2 Samuel 7:12, 13*

Lesson 2

1. God promised David that his line would continue for 1,000 years. T/F. *Psalm 89:35, 36*

2. *Emmanuel* means "_____." *Matthew 1:23*

Lesson 3

1. The Messiah would be a priest after whose order? (Levi, Aaron, Melchizedek?) *Psalm 110:4*

2. According to Peter, David was a prophet. T/F. *Acts 2:29, 30*

Lesson 4

1. In Revelation 5, what creatures are used as imagery to describe Jesus in Heaven? (pick two: eagle, lamb, lion, ox, owl?) *Revelation 5:5, 6*

2. Some of the residents of Heaven are pictured as playing harps. T/F. *Revelation 5:8*

Lesson 5

1. Zechariah's prophecy was fulfilled when Jesus entered Jerusalem riding a white horse. T/F. *Zechariah 9:9; Matthew 21:7*

2. The crowd spread branches and _____ on the road before Jesus. *Matthew 21:8*

Lesson 6

1. Isaiah said God's house would be called a house of _____. *Isaiah 56:7*

2. Jesus declared that the temple had become a den of _____. *Mark 11:17*

Lesson 7

1. What is an unusual term Jeremiah uses for the coming Messiah? (Ocean, Door, Branch?) *Jeremiah 23:5*

2. Jesus was tortured with a crown of thorns to mock him as a slave. T/F. *John 19:2, 3*

Lesson 8

1. Hosea prophesied that the Lord would raise up the people on the _____ day. *Hosea 6:2*

2. The first witnesses to the empty tomb of Jesus were a group of women. T/F. *Luke 24:1, 10*

Lesson 9

1. Isaiah prophesied that with the servant's stripes we are _____. *Isaiah 53:5*

2. After His resurrection, Jesus promised His apostles that preaching of the gospel would begin in the city of Rome. T/F. *Luke 24:47*

Lesson 10

1. The Bible teaches that the Lord is never jealous. T/F. *Deuteronomy 6:15*

2. The first temptation of Jesus was based on what? (hunger, thirst, poverty?) *Matthew 4:2, 3*

Lesson 11

1. Isaiah prophesied that the Messiah would be anointed to preach good tidings. T/F. *Isaiah 61:1; Luke 4:18*

2. Returning to His hometown synagogue in _____, Jesus stood and read Scripture. *Luke 4:16*

Lesson 12

1. Jesus was questioned because His disciples did not wash their hands before eating. T/F. *Matthew 15:2*

2. Jesus taught that words coming out of one's mouth come from the _____. *Matthew 15:18*

Lesson 13

1. Jesus was first to give the command "Love thy neighbour as thyself." T/F. *Leviticus 19:18*

2. It is more important to _____ God than to give sacrifices to Him. *Mark 12:33*

QUARTER AT A GLANCE

by Jon Weatherly

D O YOU PREFER to plan or to improvise? Do you lay out steps in advance, or do you make things up on the fly? Most of us probably move back and forth between planning and improvisation, depending on circumstances.

But when someone else is in charge, we like to know that this person has a plan. Starting a construction project, we need detailed drawings and blueprints. Riding in a car, we expect the driver to have a route thoughtfully laid out. Invited to a meal, we hope to be served something other than "whatever falls out of the refrigerator."

Likewise, we hope for a plan in the big picture. Does God have a plan for life, or is it all just random? We hope that there is a plan, especially when life's events seem especially chaotic.

The Bible vigorously affirms that God has a plan for human life. This quarter's lessons remind us that God's plan has the cross of Christ at the center. As we experience life, we find it filled with discouragements, injustice, and suffering. In Christ God takes all of that on himself, enabling us to have meaning, purpose, and hope that reach beyond the worst of the world and welcomes us into God's eternal kingdom.

God's plan is to rule the world through the promised king and son of David, Jesus (**lesson 1**). That king was promised as one who would build the house for the true worship of God, whose own throne God would establish forever. Through generations of hope and disappointment, God's faithful people held fast to that promise.

With Jesus' miraculous birth, marvelous life, torturous death, and triumphant resurrection, God fulfilled His promise. He sent a king who, like His people, was lowly, who ascended the throne as king by freely surrendering His life to those who presumed to rule God's world (**lessons 2, 3**). Riding a lowly donkey, Christ approached Jerusalem as its king (**lesson 5**). He entered Jerusalem's temple as the one who builds the true temple (**lesson 6**). Yet He allowed a pagan ruler to mock His royal status and condemn Him to death (**lesson 7**).

What Christ suffered was the punishment that really belongs to us, His people. He lived and died not just in solidarity with His lowly people but as a substitute for His guilty people. They had failed in the face of temptation, but He was victorious (**lesson 10**). Their rebellion brought them into bondage, but He brought liberation (**lesson 11**). Attempts at self-purification brought them only more blame, but He brought genuine purity (**lesson 12**). Only in Christ can a person find the way to fulfill the very purpose for which God created humanity: to love God with all that one is and to love one's neighbor as oneself (**lesson 13**).

When Christ arose from the dead, He revealed the mystery of God's plan (**lesson 8**). Several despairing women went to His tomb, believing that His death was but another disappointment, another random event in a world where nothing seems to go according to plan. But Christ was triumphant. He had done what He promised, what God had promised. His death and resurrection fulfilled Scripture, for in His death and resurrection every need and hope of humanity, expressed

> **The Bible vigorously affirms that God has a plan for human life.**

throughout the story line of the Bible, was met by the fulfilled promise of God (**lesson 9**).

In the end, all of humanity will bow to the king, the Christ enthroned in the highest place. He alone can open the scroll that represents God's plan for the world. He does so as the lamb once slain, now forever triumphant, one day to stand as judge over all (**lesson 4**).

Indeed, life is not random. God has a plan. The plan is Jesus Christ. Everyone needs to know Him.

GET THE SETTING

by Lloyd M. Pelfrey

THE LESSONS for the next three months are drawn from a wide range of biblical texts—from Leviticus to Revelation! The objective is to present New Testament passages that show how Jesus fulfilled important Old Testament prophecies of the coming Messiah. We may wonder why Jesus was rejected (John 1:11) even though He fulfilled so many prophecies. One answer is that many people expected a Messiah different from who Jesus turned out to be.

A Question of Role

It is frequently said that many in Jesus' day had false ideas about the redemption that the Messiah would bring—that He would be a political hero, one who would restore Israel to be a dominant nation (compare Acts 1:6). These were expectations of peace and prosperity in place of oppression by foreign nations. The results of this view have been stated this way: "They were so enamored with their ideas about the one that God would send that they missed Him when God sent Him."

The fact that there had been several false messiahs before Jesus came caused skepticism about *any* messianic claim. Men with delusions of their own importance were known to persuade others to follow them. Their grand schemes produced death and destruction rather than deliverance (compare Acts 5:36-38; 21:38). Adding to the uncertainty was the number of Messiahs expected.

A Question of Number

Some passages from the Dead Sea Scrolls (most of which date between 150 BC and AD 70) are often interpreted as indicating that there would be two Messiahs: a priestly one from the tribe of Levi and a royal one from the tribe of Judah. Zechariah 6:13 tells of a priest on his throne (lesson 7), and that may be a factor. Rabbinic literature suggests different origins for two Messiahs: one each from the descendants of Joseph and David.

Another source indicates that there could be as many as four Messiahs: Elijah, one from the tribe of Manasseh, one from Ephraim, and a descendant of David. The New Testament stresses, however, that the only Messiah who was to appear is Jesus.

The Answer in Jesus

The apostle John states that he has provided a record of selected signs or miracles so that the reader can "believe that Jesus is the Christ, the Son of God" (John 20:30, 31). It is important to realize that the Hebrew word *Messiah* and the Greek word *Christ* mean the same thing: "anointed" or "anointed one."

John recorded peoples' expectations of this person. Consider the statement of John the Baptist, "I am not the Christ" (John 1:20); such a denial presupposed that the Christ was indeed anticipated. In the same chapter we find a statement of Andrew, who said to brother Simon Peter, "We have found the Messias, . . . the Christ" (1:41).

The declaration of the woman of Samaria strengthens the idea that a singular Messiah was expected: "I know that Messias cometh" (John 4:25). John 7:25-43 goes on to offer a lengthy discussion about the expected Messiah's credentials. Turning to Luke, we encounter Simeon, the aged man in the temple, who was told by the Lord that he would not die until "he had seen the Lord's Christ" (Luke 2:26).

Expectations Today

Some today will believe only in a Messiah who fixes all the bad things that they think He should: eliminating illness, correcting injustice, etc. But it is not our task to put our expectations on Jesus. Rather, it is our task to accept His expectations of us: to live in faithfulness regardless of what happens and to be vigilant for His return. As we do, we echo the words of John as he closed the book of Revelation: "Amen. Even so, come, Lord Jesus."

THIS QUARTER IN THE WORD

Mon, Feb. 24	The Lord Is King	Psalm 93
Tue, Feb. 25	You Are My Son	Psalm 2
Wed, Feb. 26	An Eternal Throne	Psalm 45:1-9
Thu, Feb. 27	God's Heritage	Psalm 94:8-15
Fri, Feb. 28	God's Mercy and Faithfulness	Psalm 98
Sat, Mar. 1	The Messiah Will Reign Forever	Revelation 11:15-19
Sun, Mar. 2	A Throne Established Forever	2 Samuel 7:4-16
Mon, Mar. 3	A Son Named Emmanuel	Matthew 1:22-25
Tue, Mar. 4	The King of the Jews	Matthew 2:1-6
Wed, Mar. 5	Is This the Son of David?	Matthew 12:15-23
Thu, Mar. 6	Hosanna to the Son of David	Matthew 21:12-17
Fri, Mar. 7	Whose Son Is the Messiah?	Matthew 22:41-45
Sat, Mar. 8	Following the Son of David	Mark 10:46-52
Sun, Mar. 9	The Son of David	Psalm 89:35-37; Isaiah 9:6, 7; Matthew 1:18-21
Mon, Mar. 10	Protect Me, O God	Psalm 16:1-6
Tue, Mar. 11	Show Me the Path of Life	Psalm 16:7-11
Wed, Mar. 12	Freed from the Fear of Death	Hebrews 2:14-18
Thu, Mar. 13	The Power of the Resurrection	Philippians 3:7-11
Fri, Mar. 14	The Heavenly Call of God	Philippians 3:12-16
Sat, Mar. 15	Made Both Lord and Messiah	Acts 2:33-36
Sun, Mar. 16	Placed on David's Throne	Psalm 110:1-4; Acts 2:22-27, 29-32

Mon, May 12	Commandments Learned by Rote	Isaiah 29:13-19
Tue, May 13	Testing and Fear	Exodus 20:12-21
Wed, May 14	We Uphold the Law	Romans 3:21-31
Thu, May 15	Fulfilling the Law	Matthew 5:14-20
Fri, May 16	But I Say to You	Matthew 5:27-37
Sat, May 17	Be Perfect	Matthew 5:38-48
Sun, May 18	What Proceeds from the Heart	Matthew 15:1-11, 15-20
Mon, May 19	Love and Commandment-Keeping	Deuteronomy 7:7-16
Tue, May 20	Serving God with Heart and Soul	Deuteronomy 10:12-21
Wed, May 21	Keeping God's Commandments Always	Deuteronomy 11:1-7
Thu, May 22	Relating to Your Neighbor	Leviticus 19:11-17
Fri, May 23	Sin Against a Neighbor or God	1 Kings 8:31-36
Sat, May 24	They Shall Not Be Moved	Psalm 15
Sun, May 25	Loving God and Neighbor	Leviticus 19:18; Deuteronomy 6:4-9; Mark 12:28-34

Answers to the Quarterly Quiz on page 226

Lesson 1—1. shepherd. 2. true. **Lesson 2**—1. false. 2. "God with us." **Lesson 3**—1. Melchizedek. 2. true. **Lesson 4**—1. lion and lamb. 2. true. **Lesson 5**—1. false. 2. garments. **Lesson 6** —1. prayer. 2. thieves. **Lesson 7**—1. Branch. 2. false. **Lesson 8** —1. third. 2. true. **Lesson 9**—1. healed. 2. false. **Lesson 10**— 1. false. 2. hunger. **Lesson 11**—1. true. 2. Nazareth. **Lesson 12** —1. true. 2. heart. **Lesson 13**—1. false. 2. love.

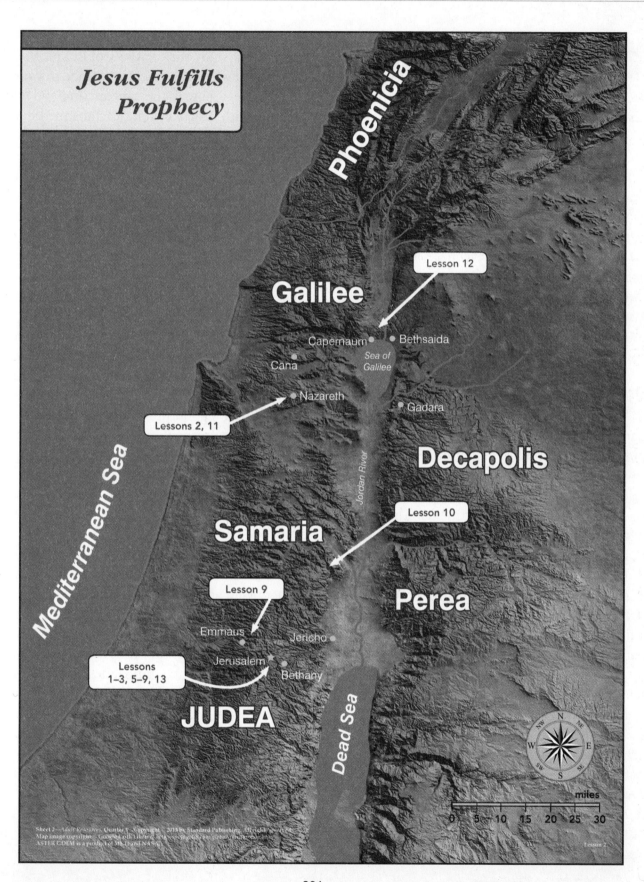

Jesus Fulfills Prophecy

Phoenicia

Galilee

Lesson 12

Capernaum • Bethsaida

Sea of Galilee

Cana

Gadara

Nazareth

Lessons 2, 11

Decapolis

Jordan River

Mediterranean Sea

Samaria

Lesson 10

Lesson 9

Perea

Emmaus

Jericho

Jerusalem

Lessons 1–3, 5–9, 13

Bethany

JUDEA

Dead Sea

miles

0   5   10   15   20   25   30

Lesson 2

LIGHTS, CAMERA, ACTION!

Teacher Tips by Brent Amato

Say you are pondering the best way to teach lesson 8, "The Third Day." As always, you have options. You can lecture, pose discussion questions, do small-group exercises—or you could try something drastically different.

What if your classroom became a theater in which you present a one-act play with the script drawn from Luke 24:1-12, some of your students as the actors, the rest as the audience, and you as the director? Imagine a darkened room called *Disciples' Hideout* where several dejected men are exchanging mournful "if only" remarks when some women burst in excitedly with news that is just too outlandish to believe.

Lights, camera, action! Let's see how such an approach teaches and what it involves.

Drama Engages

How do you know whether or not your students are connecting with your teaching? Acting puts minds and bodies in motion, resulting in an "ownership" of the lesson by your students that other teaching methods can't deliver. "But," you say, "you don't know my students! They would never do this, and even if they went along with it, they don't have a creative bone in their bodies!"

I beg to differ on both counts. Everyone has a little drama in them; it's just that most people don't have a stage. As for audience members, they will be on the edge of their seats, or at least awake and attentive.

Drama Enhances

Four learning styles will be found in your classroom. *Dynamic Learners* are spontaneous and action-oriented; *Innovative Learners* are imaginative and willing to volunteer; *Common-Sense Learners* are experimental and practical; and *Analytic Learners* are systematic and lovers of facts. With variety in your teaching methods, you'll reach all four. Those who are *dynamic* and *inno-*

vative will enjoy the creativity of drama; you'll be amazed at what such students will add to your play! Don't sweat those in the *common sense* and *analytic* camps; with variety in your teaching method, their day will come.

Beyond sensitivity to learning styles is the issue of retention. Educational consultants state that we retain 10 percent of what we hear; 50 percent of what we hear and see; 70 percent of what we hear, see, and say; and 90 percent of what we hear, see, say, and do. Since drama falls in the last category, its usefulness as a teaching method should not be overlooked!

Drama Entertains

I am convinced that effective learning in a Sunday school setting needs a healthy dose of enjoyment. Excitement and emotion fill a theater during a good production. Laughter, which is inevitable during drama, enhances every lesson. Both the audience and the actors come away with a memorable lesson that kept their interest and gave them something to consider.

Preparation

The type of drama we're talking about here is not burdensome in terms of preparation, either for you or your actors. The "Resurrection Pantomime" on the reproducible page for lesson 8 has no lines for the performers to memorize; the participants merely act out what they hear the narrator say. For the *Disciples' Hideout* drama, described above, the written scripts that you will distribute should do no more than excerpt the applicable Scripture for the characters involved. Your creative learners can take it from there!

Give your actors a week or two to think over their parts. The day of the performance, give the actors some time to review their scripts and compare notes. Then "raise the curtain" and enjoy a well-taught class!

An Eternal Kingdom

Devotional Reading: Psalm 98
Background Scripture: 2 Samuel 7

2 Samuel 7:4-16

4 And it came to pass that night, that the word of the LORD came unto Nathan, saying,

5 Go and tell my servant David, Thus saith the LORD, Shalt thou build me an house for me to dwell in?

6 Whereas I have not dwelt in any house since the time that I brought up the children of Israel out of Egypt, even to this day, but have walked in a tent and in a tabernacle.

7 In all the places wherein I have walked with all the children of Israel spake I a word with any of the tribes of Israel, whom I commanded to feed my people Israel, saying, Why build ye not me an house of cedar?

8 Now therefore so shalt thou say unto my servant David, Thus saith the LORD of hosts, I took thee from the sheepcote, from following the sheep, to be ruler over my people, over Israel:

9 And I was with thee whithersoever thou wentest, and have cut off all thine enemies out of thy sight, and have made thee a great name, like unto the name of the great men that are in the earth.

10 Moreover I will appoint a place for my people Israel, and will plant them, that they may dwell in a place of their own, and move no more; neither shall the children of wickedness afflict them any more, as beforetime,

11 And as since the time that I commanded judges to be over my people Israel, and have caused thee to rest from all thine enemies. Also the LORD telleth thee that he will make thee an house.

12 And when thy days be fulfilled, and thou shalt sleep with thy fathers, I will set up thy seed after thee, which shall proceed out of thy bowels, and I will establish his kingdom.

13 He shall build an house for my name, and I will stablish the throne of his kingdom for ever.

14 I will be his father, and he shall be my son. If he commit iniquity, I will chasten him with the rod of men, and with the stripes of the children of men:

15 But my mercy shall not depart away from him, as I took it from Saul, whom I put away before thee.

16 And thine house and thy kingdom shall be established for ever before thee: thy throne shall be established for ever.

KEY VERSE

Thine house and thy kingdom shall be established for ever before thee: thy throne shall be established for ever.

—2 Samuel 7:16

JESUS' FULFILLMENT OF SCRIPTURE

Unit 1: Jesus and the Davidic Covenant

LESSON AIMS

After participating in this lesson, each student will be able to:

1. Summarize God's promise to David.

2. Explain how Jesus brings that promise to its ultimate fulfillment.

3. Write a prayer of self-consecration to help build the temple of the New Testament era (see 1 Corinthians 3:16, 17; 6:19; Ephesians 2:19-22; 1 Peter 2:4, 5).

LESSON OUTLINE

Introduction

A. The Ideal Leader

What constitutes the ideal leader? We might assemble quite a list of traits: expertise, communication skill, honesty, courage, humility, persistence, compassion, levelheadedness. The demands of leadership are many. Success in leadership requires an impressive list of qualities.

Then we can ask, "Who has ever embodied the ideals of leadership?" We might name many famous figures of the past and perhaps some from the present. But many leaders we know of today fall short of the ideal. In fact, it is easier to name a leader's faults than to name an ideal leader.

Our frustration in finding the ideal leader is nothing new. It is reflected throughout history, and especially in the Bible. Much of the Old Testament focuses on the failures of the leaders of God's people. They failed time after time, generation after generation. "When," the faithful ask, "will God send a leader who truly reflects God's own greatness?" Today's text is central to that question.

B. Lesson Background

Today's text marks a high point in Old Testament history. After generations of living in the promised land under the leadership of judges, Israel had begged God to give them a king, so they could be like the mighty nations around them (1 Samuel 8:5-7). God reluctantly pointed Israel to Saul, a man who appeared quite kingly because of his impressive stature and accomplishments on the battlefield (11:14, 15). But Saul willfully disobeyed God. Rejecting Saul as king, God sent the prophet Samuel to the household of Jesse, where Samuel anointed David, the youngest of Jesse's sons, as king (16:1, 11-13).

David rose to prominence soon after he defeated Goliath and won other triumphs on the battlefield. Saul, still on Israel's throne, thought that he had a dangerous rival in David (1 Samuel 18:7-9), so Saul spent the latter years of his life pursuing David off and on to kill him. David hid himself successfully and never attempted to harm Saul directly in retaliation (24:1-7; 26:7-12). Saul was mortally wounded in battle and took his own life (31:4).

With Saul dead, the tribe of Judah acclaimed David as king (2 Samuel 2:4). He led Judah's armies in battle against the Jebusites (5:6, 7), conquered their city Jebus, renamed it Jerusalem, and made it his capital. Soon all Israel affirmed David as king. In the early years of his reign, David enjoyed economic and military success. He built himself a palace in Jerusalem (5:11). To that city he brought the tabernacle, Israel's portable center of worship (6:17).

As 2 Samuel 7 begins, David had surveyed the situation in Jerusalem and announced that it was unfitting for him to live in a palace while God was worshipped in a tent. At first, the prophet Nathan approved David's plan—presumably to build a temple to replace the tabernacle. At this point our text begins; the date is about 1002 BC (1 Chronicles 17:3-14 is parallel).

I. Correction to David
(2 SAMUEL 7:4-7)
A. First Question (vv. 4, 5)

4. And it came to pass that night, that the word of the LORD came unto Nathan, saying.

God is about to speak against David's plans. God does not communicate directly to David, but sends the message through the prophet Nathan. This man also needs a corrective since he has embraced David's wrong thinking (2 Samuel 7:3).

5. Go and tell my servant David, Thus saith the LORD, Shalt thou build me an house for me to dwell in?

The message brings assurance and correction. God's address of David as *my servant* brings to mind the fact that David, unlike Saul, has sought

HOW TO SAY IT

Bethlehem	*Beth*-lih-hem.
bourgeoisie	*burzh*-wah-**zee**.
Davidic	Duh-*vid*-ick.
Goliath	Go-*lye*-uth.
Jebus	*Jee*-bus.
Jebusites	*Jeb*-yuh-sites.
Judah	*Joo*-duh.
Nathan	*Nay*-thun (*th* as in *thin*).

to obey God even when doing so seemed to go against David's own interests. But now David plans to build a house for God, just as David had built a house for himself. Does David, God's servant, presume that he will do God a favor?

What Do You Think?
> When was a time that God corrected one of your plans? How did that corrective come about, and what did you learn from this experience?

Talking Points for Your Discussion
- Regarding a ministry
- Regarding a change in vocation
- Regarding a financial decision
- Other

B. Second Question (vv. 6, 7)

6. Whereas I have not dwelt in any house since the time that I brought up the children of Israel out of Egypt, even to this day, but have walked in a tent and in a tabernacle.

God recounts a bit of history for David. The time frame for bringing *the children of Israel out of Egypt, even to this day* exceeds 400 years. It was God himself who chose the tabernacle as His symbolic dwelling place after that exodus. Although a *house* of sorts came to be in Shiloh (1 Samuel 1), God has never authorized a fixed place such as David wants to construct to replace the tabernacle. The tabernacle, with its design specified in Exodus, was to accommodate Israel's journey to the promised land. The verse ends with the synonyms *tent* and *tabernacle* to emphasize its portable nature.

That portability was deliberate. While the design included many lavish elements, a tent structure by nature is modest compared with a fixed building. The tabernacle's relatively modest, portable design expressed something of God's larger purpose: God's rule even unto David's day is to be manifested not in material grandeur, but in the lives of the lowly who come to Him in their need.

There is no indication in the text that David prayed about his decision to build a temple before announcing it to Nathan (2 Samuel 7:1). Neither is there any indication that that prophet prayed about it before responding to David with his own agreement (7:2). God corrects their presumption.

7. In all the places wherein I have walked with all the children of Israel spake I a word with any of the tribes of Israel, whom I commanded to feed my people Israel, saying, Why build ye not me an house of cedar?

Using repetitive expressions, God emphasizes that He has never even hinted that Israel replace the tabernacle with a grand house, as construction with cedar suggests (compare 2 Samuel 5:11). God's faithfulness to His people has far exceeded their obedience to Him, yet God has not called on anyone to respond by building a temple. The term translated *tribes* probably refers to tribal leaders, those charged by God to ensure the well-being of the people as shepherds do for sheep. David has famously risen to be king above those leaders, but even David is not an exception in this regard.

❧ WHOSE IDEA IS THIS, ANYWAY? ❧

How easy it is to think that an idea we have is so great that it must be from God! (See 1 Kings 22:10-12; Ezekiel 13; etc.) Some go so far as to buttress their "from God" claims by appeals to angelic visitation. Such was the case, for example, of Joseph Smith, who claimed to have received a series of such visitations that began in 1823. The eventual result was *The Book of Mormon,* which remains unsupported by archaeological discoveries and other external evidence.

The history of deceptive voices goes back to the serpent himself in the Garden of Eden (Genesis 3). The serpent's deceivers are still with us today in the form of those who would lead us away from biblical truth. But sometimes the deceptive voice is first heard in the thoughts that originate within our own imaginations.

When David decided that he needed to build a house for the Lord, he must have thought *God surely wants me to do this.* But the voice inside his head telling him to build a temple was his own, not that of the Lord. God's corrective instruction to first Nathan and then to David should give us pause when we think we hear God giving us a mission. It's never a mistake to ask oneself, "Is this the Lord's plan, or is it just mine?"   —C. R. B.

II. Promise to David
(2 SAMUEL 7:8-16)
A. King's Status (vv. 8, 9)

8. Now therefore so shalt thou say unto my servant David, Thus saith the LORD of hosts, I took thee from the sheepcote, from following the sheep, to be ruler over my people, over Israel.

Now God's message takes a positive turn as He reminds David of that man's own history. That history involves God's taking him from lowliness and insignificance to his present power.

The story of David's anointing underlines his insignificance (1 Samuel 16:1-13). God had sent the prophet Samuel to an obscure family in the small village of Bethlehem. There he reviewed each of the sons of Jesse who were present. When none was the one God had chosen, Samuel asked if there was another. Jesse had not bothered to bring his youngest son to Samuel, leaving him to care for the sheep by himself. Apparently, no one thought that David mattered.

But God had chosen David, just as God often chooses the seemingly insignificant throughout biblical history. We think of the aged Abraham, the reluctant Moses, or the timid Gideon—all "heroes of the Bible" who were distinguished by their weaknesses, not their capabilities. The nation Israel itself was just so: a small, insignificant nation among its neighbors, but chosen by God to bring blessing to the nations (Genesis 12:1-3).

Now that David has attained the throne, he still is not in a position to do a favor for God, even as a gesture of thanks. God remains in control of His gifts and His plans. God will show again that His "strength is made perfect in weakness" (2 Corinthians 12:9).

9. And I was with thee whithersoever thou wentest, and have cut off all thine enemies out

of thy sight, and have made thee a great name, like unto the name of the great men that are in the earth.

God was with Israel in the wilderness wandering, represented by the portable tabernacle, and God has been with David in all his endeavors—including his own wilderness wanderings (1 Samuel 23:14–26:25). David has enjoyed victories over enemies that have plagued Israel for centuries. Whatever greatness David has, God has given. It is in this light that God announces that David will not give to God, but God will continue to give to David. David will not have the chance to think of himself as a great builder (compare Daniel 4:28-30).

What Do You Think?

When was a time you were surprised to discover that your service for God turned out to be God's service and blessing for you? What did you learn about God from this experience?

Talking Points for Your Discussion

- Involving a "behind the scenes" ministry
- Involving an "out in front" ministry

B. People's Status (vv. 10, 11a)

10. Moreover I will appoint a place for my people Israel, and will plant them, that they may dwell in a place of their own, and move no more; neither shall the children of wickedness afflict them any more, as beforetime.

What has been true for lowly David is also true for lowly Israel: God promises that His people will have security and permanence in the land that God gives to them. The promise we see here is the same one made generations before through Moses.

David eventually ends up suffering as a result of his failure to remain faithful (2 Samuel 24). A generation later, Solomon will be told that his own idolatry will mean the loss of Israel's unity (1 Kings 11:9-11). Finally, Israel will be taken captive—first the northern tribes in 722 BC, then the southern tribes in 586 BC—because of generations of unfaithfulness (2 Kings 15:29; 25:8-11).

But subsequent reminders of God's promise will show that Israel's unfaithfulness does not

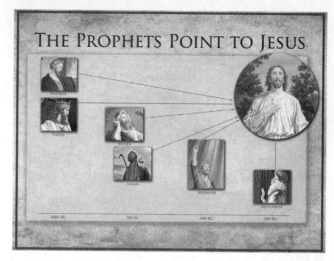

Visual for Lesson 1. *Keep this chart posted throughout the quarter as a reminder of the importance of the Old Testament for learning about Jesus.*

cancel the promise. God promises to restore the captive people, granting them the peace that He has long promised, even though they prove to be unfaithful generation after generation (Deuteronomy 30:1-5). Ultimately this promise is fulfilled not in any political event but through the gospel of Jesus. By this means God gives lasting peace, unshakable security, and genuine prosperity to His people, wherever they are in God's world.

11a. And as since the time that I commanded judges to be over my people Israel, and have caused thee to rest from all thine enemies.

The period of the judges (from about 1380 to 1050 BC) followed Israel's conquest of the promised land, so we might think of that period as the first era of Israel's life as a settled nation. That period was filled with conflict as one nation after another rose against Israel. God delivered Israel through the leadership of judges, but He also allowed threats to arise as Israel sank back into sin.

C. God's Intent (vv. 11b-16)

11b, 12. Also the LORD telleth thee that he will make thee an house. And when thy days be fulfilled, and thou shalt sleep with thy fathers, I will set up thy seed after thee, which shall proceed out of thy bowels, and I will establish his kingdom.

Israel's cry for a king was its response to the upheaval of the era of the judges. After hundreds of years of turmoil, having a king seemed like a good idea (1 Samuel 8:5). But God is the one to deliver the peace that Israel hopes for. David will not build a house (that is, a temple) for God; instead, God will build a house (that is, a kingly dynasty) for David.

We should note well that God's promise is given not because David proves worthy where others do not. Moving beyond 2 Samuel 7, we see David's deep failures: favoritism within his family, sexual immorality, even murder. The promise is to David by God's grace. It is an unmerited gift, given to David despite that man's unworthiness. It is given to Israel despite Israel's unworthiness. Ultimately it is given to all humanity, despite all our unworthiness.

God explains that His promise will come to fruition through a descendant of David, one who will rise to power after David's death. The *King James Version* translates the Hebrew expression literally: David's *seed* is the focus of the promise.

The word *seed*, referring to one's descendant or descendants, has a rich background in earlier texts of the Old Testament. God uses this word repeatedly in Genesis in promises of redemption (Genesis 3:15; 9:9; 12:7; etc.); the patriarchs Abraham, Isaac, and Jacob in particular received promises regarding their "seed." Now David receives a promise that builds on theirs: God will firmly establish the kingdom of one of David's offspring, one physically descended from him.

> ### What Do You Think?
> What are some things your church can do to make sure that its "building" plans are in harmony with God's plan for building His kingdom?
> *Talking Points for Your Discussion*
> - Regarding building spiritual maturity of members
> - Regarding building local outreach programs
> - Regarding building outreach programs abroad
> - Regarding adding church staff
> - Other

13. He shall build an house for my name, and I will stablish the throne of his kingdom for ever.

As we think of the descendants of David, we may naturally think of Solomon as the one who ends up building *an house for my name* since he is the one who built the temple. But Solomon's idolatry ends up meaning that his is not a "forever" kingdom. And Solomon's temple, destroyed generations later, turns out not to be a "forever" house.

The promised king, the builder of the true temple, is none other than Jesus. It is in His death and resurrection that the true temple is built. It is in Jesus that forgiveness becomes available to all who accept Him (Acts 2:38). Jesus is the one who grants that God's Spirit might dwell in us as His body, the temple that will permeate the whole world (John 2:19-21; 4:20-24; 1 Corinthians 3:16, 17; Ephesians 2:19-22).

> ### What Do You Think?
> When was a time your church (past or present) found it necessary to change plans? What made it appear that God was in the change?
> *Talking Points for Your Discussion*
> - Involving a special event
> - Involving a building project
> - Involving an ongoing church program
> - Involving a staff position
> - Other

❧ A TRANSFORMING FORCE ❧

The poor harvests of 1845 and following years affected all of Europe. Within two years, food prices in many places had doubled, farms and businesses went bankrupt, and masses of people were starving. Food riots resulted, then workers' strikes. Such conditions provided fertile soil for the founding of the Communist League in June 1847.

The league's numbers were insignificant at first, Karl Marx's branch in Brussels having only 18 members. But from the leaders of that tiny cell came *The Communist Manifesto*. This document called for the forcible overthrow of the *bourgeoisie* —the supposedly corrupt middle class—and the abolition of private property.

Communism went on to become one of the most powerful ideologies in history. Although it claimed to exalt the lowly, Communism instead ended up creating its own ruling class that was just as corrupt, if not more so, than what it replaced.

How different is the transformational power of God! The "Davidic dynasty" lifts all people of every station in life who place their trust in the ultimate son of David: Jesus. Will you share that power with others today? —C. R. B.

14. I will be his father, and he shall be my son. If he commit iniquity, I will chasten him with the rod of men, and with the stripes of the children of men.

Kings in the pagan nations of the ancient Near East are commonly revered as offspring of the gods. But matters are different in Israel. The king can be spoken of as God's son, but the notion is that God figuratively adopts the king, who serves like a son to do his father's bidding (Psalm 2:7).

The kings that descend from David become God's "sons" in this sense. In particular, God warns that a son will be subject to discipline should he disobey (*commit iniquity*). The ups and downs of Israel's history are explained in just this way in the Old Testament: because of the disobedience of the nation and its kings, God allows rulers and people to suffer at the hands of their enemies, ultimately going into exile. These are *the rod* and *the stripes* that come as discipline to the Davidic kings in later generations.

15. But my mercy shall not depart away from him, as I took it from Saul, whom I put away before thee.

Even if the descendants of David prove unfaithful—as they do—God will not cancel His promise. Even if centuries pass and Israel finds itself without a king—as happens—God will still provide the promised son of David. Saul's disobedience meant the end of his dynasty and the beginning of David's. But David's dynasty, even if it seems to end, will endure by God's promise. This is not a result of David's exceptional goodness; God says that it is a matter of mercy, not merit.

16. And thine house and thy kingdom shall be established for ever before thee: thy throne shall be established for ever.

God's power, not David's attainments, will be the basis for house-building, kingdom-securing, and throne-establishing. What God does will never be undone.

Conclusion

A. Jesus, Son of David

Today's text was a source of hope for Israel for centuries. When rulers were corrupt and enemy nations threatened, God's promise of a great son of David encouraged people to look to a greater future, one secured by God's faithful Word and accomplished by His mighty power.

We recognize that God brings this promise to fulfillment in Jesus. He was and is the promised son of David. He was and is God's Son, having exercised power and authority that God alone possesses. In Jesus, God became present in the world as a human to reclaim what was rightfully His.

Jesus established His rule not through military might but through voluntary lowliness. From that position He defeated the forces of darkness by receiving every evil thing that they could deliver, surrendering himself to die by crucifixion for our sins. In dying, rising, and ascending, He assumed the eternal throne, from which one day He will truly and completely rule all the world (Philippians 2:6-11). From that position He now builds the true temple: His people from every nation.

God's promise to David involved more than David could have imagined. It involves more than we can imagine, except for the amazing good news of Jesus that we now have. Knowing Jesus as king changes everything.

B. Prayer

Our Father, we praise You for Your faithfulness and for Your love that did not spare Your Son. We hail Him as king as we worship as the temple that He is building. In our king's name, amen.

C. Thought to Remember

Honor Jesus as the promised seed of David.

VISUALS FOR THESE LESSONS

The visual pictured in each lesson (example: page 237) is a small reproduction of a large, full-color poster included in the *Adult Resources* packet for the Spring Quarter. That packet also contains the very useful *Presentation Tools* on a CD for teacher use. Order No. 020039214 from your supplier.

INVOLVEMENT LEARNING

Some of the activities below are also found in the helpful student book, Adult Bible Class.
Don't forget to download the free reproducible page from www.standardlesson.com to enhance your lesson!

Into the Lesson

Give each learner an 11" x 2" strip of paper on which you have drawn a simple zigzag line so that one would get the impression of a crown if the ends of the paper were joined. Ask learners to guess what the strip might signify. If no one guesses *crown*, say, "Hold the ends together. Now what do you see?" When someone guesses correctly (or you suggest *crown* if no one else does), point out that the circular nature of a crown is that of something with no end point: an ant could walk around the perimeter of the crown and never reach the end because there is none.

Say, "This circular feature of crowns can remind us of God's eternal kingdom, which goes on and on without end. Such a kingdom is promised in today's text in 2 Samuel 7. Let's take a look."

Into the Word

Give each learner a sheet of paper that has at least 10 empty speech-balloons of varying sizes under the heading "Tell My Servant David." After reading today's text aloud, say, "Go back through the text and write one thing in each balloon that Nathan was directed to relay to King David. Give a verse number for each idea." After several minutes, ask, "From your collection of quotes, what do you think is the most important truth David was to hear and heed?" Jot responses on the board; expect a lively discussion as learners explain and justify their differing choices.

Alternative: Instead of the above, distribute copies of the "Building the House of God" activity from the reproducible page, which you can download. This exercise includes a look at the wider context of today's text.

Into Life

Note to the class that David's intention to build stemmed from contrasting his own fine home with the tabernacle—the portable tent where the ark of the covenant was housed (2 Samuel 7:1, 2). Write this question on the board: "How do the following compare and contrast?" List the following below the question, pausing after writing each to allow time for response before writing the next:

1. David's sense of God's presence; your sense of God's presence (see v. 9).
2. David's plans for a physical temple; your plans for the spiritual temple of the New Testament era.
3. David's sense of security from enemies; your sense of that security.
4. God's assurance of love to David's family (v. 15); God's assurance of love to you.
5. God's promise of a home for ancient Israel; His promise of Heaven for those in Christ (see v. 10).

Assign these texts to four good oral readers: 1 Corinthians 3:16, 17; 1 Corinthians 6:19; Ephesians 2:19-22; 1 Peter 2:4, 5. Introduce the readings of these texts by saying, "God has important things to say about the temple that exists in the Christian era. Hear these."

After the four readings, divide the class as equally as possible into four parts. Ask each fourth of the class to gather around a reader, one each. Say, "Reread your text, then discuss this question: 'How can I reflect in my life this truth about God's temple?'"

Option: After a few minutes, have groups rotate to a different reader to discuss the same question with regard to a different text. Repeat until all groups have considered all four texts. This option obviously requires more time.

Alternative: Distribute copies of the "Being the Temple of God" from the reproducible page, which you can download. Use this exercise instead of the above if you think it more beneficial for your learners to work individually rather than in small groups on these same four texts.

SON OF DAVID

DEVOTIONAL READING: Mark 10:46-52

BACKGROUND SCRIPTURE: Psalm 89; Isaiah 9:1-7;
Matthew 1:18–2:6; Luke 1:26-33

PSALM 89:35-37

35 Once have I sworn by my holiness that I will not lie unto David.

36 His seed shall endure for ever, and his throne as the sun before me.

37 It shall be established for ever as the moon, and as a faithful witness in heaven. Selah.

ISAIAH 9:6, 7

6 For unto us a child is born, unto us a son is given: and the government shall be upon his shoulder: and his name shall be called Wonderful, Counsellor, The mighty God, The everlasting Father, The Prince of Peace.

7 Of the increase of his government and peace there shall be no end, upon  the throne of David, and upon his kingdom, to order it, and to establish it with judgment and with justice from henceforth even for ever. The zeal of the LORD of hosts will perform this.

MATTHEW 1:18-23

18 Now the birth of Jesus Christ was on this wise: When as his mother Mary was espoused to Joseph, before they came together, she was found with child of the Holy Ghost.

19 Then Joseph her husband, being a just man, and not willing to make her a publick example, was minded to put her away privily.

20 But while he thought on these things, behold, the angel of the Lord appeared unto him in a dream, saying, Joseph, thou son of David, fear not to take unto thee Mary thy wife: for that which is conceived in her is of the Holy Ghost.

21 And she shall bring forth a son, and thou shalt call his name JESUS: for he shall save his people from their sins.

22 Now all this was done, that it might be fulfilled which was spoken of the Lord by the prophet, saying,

23 Behold, a virgin shall be with child, and shall bring forth a son, and they shall call his name Emmanuel, which being interpreted is, God with us.

KEY VERSES

She shall bring forth a son, and thou shalt call his name JESUS: for he shall save his people from their sins. Now all this was done, that it might be fulfilled which was spoken of the Lord by the prophet. —**Matthew 1:21, 22**

JESUS' FULFILLMENT OF SCRIPTURE

Unit 1: Jesus and the Davidic Covenant

LESSONS 1–4

LESSON AIMS

After participating in this lesson, each student will be able to:

1. Identify the connections between the texts of the Old and New Testaments in today's lesson.

2. Explain the significance of the genealogical connection between Jesus and David.

3. Sing a song that praises God for His kept promise in Jesus.

LESSON OUTLINE

Introduction
    A. "She Was Never the Same"
    B. Lesson Background
I. Confident Worship (PSALM 89:35-37)
    A. God's Reliability (v. 35)
    B. God's Promise (vv. 36, 37)
II. Confident Hope (ISAIAH 9:6, 7)
    A. Extraordinary Ruler (v. 6)
    B. Eternal Kingdom (v. 7)
        The World Keeps Trying . . . and Failing
III. Confidence Fulfilled (MATTHEW 1:18-23)
    A. Mary's Pregnancy (v. 18)
    B. Joseph's Dilemma (v. 19)
        *It's **Not** "All About Me"*
    C. God's Revelation (vv. 20, 21)
    D. Isaiah's Prophecy (vv. 22, 23)
Conclusion
    A. God Is with Us
    B. Prayer
    C. Thought to Remember

Introduction

A. "She Was Never the Same"

Too many stories end this way. A certain person has a happy life. Then something bad happens: a job loss, a business failure, a broken relationship, the death of a loved one. The conclusion "she was never the same" often is meant to describe a permanent worsening of her state of mind. The person lost hope.

But other hardship stories end differently. After going through similar struggles and making similar adjustments, the change that results in a person is actually a positive one. "She became a stronger person," etc.

Why do hard times drive some to lifelong despair, while others work through despair to a confidence that is stronger because of the hard times? There may be many reasons, but certainly the most important for the believer is the way in which we know God. In hard times, do we perceive God as distant, uninvolved, even uncaring? Or is God present, connected with us?

The Bible is the story of God with His people in hard times. Hard times may not be what we would expect to be the experience of God's people, but the Bible shows otherwise. Through the centuries, they endured disappointment, suffering, and death—outcomes that might have appeared to be no better, if not far worse, than those experienced by their pagan neighbors.

But in the midst of hard times, God promised that He would change the situation. Where His people had been defeated, He would bring victory. Where they had been wronged, He would make things right. Where they suffered, He would comfort.

God fulfills His promise by making His people's hard times His own hard times. In Jesus Christ, God shares our suffering so that we can share in His victory. If we take today's lesson to heart, we can learn how our story can end with "better than before" instead of "never the same."

B. Lesson Background

Last week's lesson focused on the important promise that God made to David in 2 Samuel 7:

that God would send a great descendant of David, whose kingdom God would establish forever, to build the true temple of God. That promise became a centerpiece of hope in ancient Israel. As generation gave way to generation and king succeeded king, the faithful reminded themselves of that promise. They may have seen few signs that indicated God was still in control. It may have appeared that He had abandoned His people to whatever came their way.

But no matter what was happening, God's promise was sure. The writers of the Old Testament often restated the promise of a great king for their own times, and our lesson begins with one such promise.

I. Confident Worship
(PSALM 89:35-37)

Psalm 89 begins with a statement of God's faithfulness (vv. 1-5) and power (vv. 6-18), before turning to a reminder of God's promise to send a great king (vv. 19-37). Forming the climax of the latter section is the first segment of today's lesson text.

Before looking at our text, we should note what follows it: a strongly worded description of the triumph of God's enemies over His people (vv. 38-45), followed by a cry to God to act on His promises and deliver His people (vv. 46-51). The description suggests that this psalm looks back on the destruction of Jerusalem by the Babylonians in 586 BC, from the perspective of those in exile. But the text also speaks to any circumstance in

HOW TO SAY IT

Abraham	*Ay*-bruh-ham.
Ahaz	*Ay*-haz.
Aram	*Air*-um.
Emmanuel	E-*man*-you-el.
Herod	*Hair*-ud.
Immanuel	Ih-*man*-you-el.
Judah	*Joo*-duh.
patriarchs	*pay*-tree-arks.
Selah (*Hebrew*)	*See*-luh.
Syria	*Sear*-ee-uh.

which God's people suffer, showing us that the time of hardship is the time to celebrate God's promises. Psalm 89's many expressions of praise imply that this is a psalm of worship.

A. God's Reliability (v. 35)

35. Once have I sworn by my holiness that I will not lie unto David.

In this part of the psalm, the writer speaks from the perspective of God himself. God affirms the certainty of His faithfulness by reminding the congregation that He is the holy God. Thus God's promise is based on His own character. He is not like fickle humans, who change their minds on a whim or tell lies (compare Numbers 23:19). Because He is the holy God, His promises are like oaths, sworn on His own holiness.

So once God has made a promise to David, will God then turn that promise into a lie? No way! No matter how distant the fulfillment of that promise might seem, God's character makes it sure.

B. God's Promise (vv. 36, 37)

36. His seed shall endure for ever, and his throne as the sun before me.

As the celebration of God's promise continues, the psalm echoes the very words of God's original promise to David. *Seed* is a key word in that promise (2 Samuel 7:12, last week's lesson), reminding us of the many promises in Genesis to the *seed* whom God would send (Genesis 3:15; 12:7; etc.).

Throne is also a key word in the original promise (2 Samuel 7:13, 16) as the symbol of the king's rule, to be established and maintained by God himself. God's promise of a *for ever* king surpasses anything that an ordinary human can accomplish.

37. It shall be established for ever as the moon, and as a faithful witness in heaven. Selah.

For the third time the psalm stresses that God's promise is for a king who rules without end. Like the sun, the moon appears in the sky in an utterly reliable pattern. To human observation, nothing is more permanent than sun and moon. So, God says, His king's throne will be just as permanent.

Of course, we know from the New Testament that the sun and moon are not permanent in an absolute sense (Mark 13:24, 25; 2 Peter 3:10).

What God is doing with this promise is accommodating himself to the human ability to understand: the sun and moon are more enduring than anything else in our daily experience.

The verse ends with *Selah,* a Hebrew word of uncertain meaning. It may be a musical direction to the congregation.

> **What Do You Think?**
> Under what circumstances was a worship experience most helpful in renewing your confidence in a promise of God? Why was that?
>
> *Talking Points for Your Discussion*
> - Involving a national or personal crisis
> - Involving a spiritual "mountaintop experience"
> - Other

II. Confident Hope
(Isaiah 9:6, 7)

Chapters 7–12 of Isaiah are sometimes called The Book of Emmanuel because of their focus on the promised king; His appearance will signify "God with us," the meaning of the word *Emmanuel.* Our section from these chapters opens with a crisis of the eighth century BC: Aram (Syria) and the northern kingdom of Israel have formed a threatening alliance against Judah, Israel's southern kingdom. In reaction, the prophet Isaiah brings a message of hope to Judah's ungodly King Ahaz. He refuses to listen. Even so, God (through Isaiah) makes Ahaz a promise anyway: a child will be born as a sign of God's presence with His people (Isaiah 7:14).

A. Extraordinary Ruler (v. 6)

6. For unto us a child is born, unto us a son is given: and the government shall be upon his shoulder: and his name shall be called Wonderful, Counsellor, The mighty God, The everlasting Father, The Prince of Peace.

The greatest promise of God is not merely that of *a child* whose birth signals the end of a short-term crisis. Rather, God promises to send a king who will surpass what His people have seen in their rulers. As with Psalm 89, the language here about the birth of *a son* reminds us of the prom-

ises to the patriarchs and to David of sons through whom God would bring promised blessings.

This son is clearly marked for rule. He takes the king's responsibility for government, which figuratively rests *upon his shoulder.* Four paired descriptions mark him as extraordinary. First is *Wonderful, Counsellor.* The word *Wonderful* suggests that the child will possess power that belongs to God alone; *Counsellor* indicates that He will be a source of wisdom. Hence, the promised one will have wisdom that can come only from God.

Mighty God depicts the Lord as a great warrior (compare Exodus 15:3). *Everlasting Father* indicates one who cares for His people, protecting and providing without end, as only God can do. *Prince of Peace* indicates that the promised one will establish not just an end to war, but positive harmony and goodwill—the kind of peace that Israel has not known to this point.

> **What Do You Think?**
> Which description of the Messiah offers you the most comfort and hope in a time of crisis? Does it depend on the nature of the crisis? Explain.
>
> *Talking Points for Your Discussion*
> - Wonderful, Counselor
> - Mighty God
> - Everlasting Father
> - Prince of Peace

B. Eternal Kingdom (v. 7)

7. Of the increase of his government and peace there shall be no end, upon the throne of David, and upon his kingdom, to order it, and to establish it with judgment and with justice from henceforth even for ever. The zeal of the Lord of hosts will perform this.

The prophet continues the description to stress that what this promised king will bring, He brings forever. His gifts include the kind of justice that Israel has not seen in its kings.

The throne motif ties to our comments on Psalm 89:36, above. The king who is to sit on this throne could not be more different from the evil, conniving Ahaz. The era of peace that the coming king will usher in could not be more different from the situation that Isaiah and his contemporaries find themselves in. Can anyone but God himself accomplish this? God's ideal for His people is that He is to be their only king and they His true subjects (1 Samuel 8:4-9; 10:17-19). Will the king who is to fulfill the promise of Emmanuel ("God with us") of Isaiah 7:14 be God himself? Our final segment of text has the answer.

❧ THE WORLD KEEPS TRYING . . . AND FAILING ❧

At the end of World War I, the so-called "war to end all wars," many people believed that the way to prevent another war was to form an international parliament. If differences could be talked through, perhaps the human longing for peace would triumph over the temptation to resort to war. The resulting League of Nations held its first meeting on January 16, 1920.

The outbreak of World War II demonstrated that organization's failure, and the league dissolved on April 20, 1946. The peace ideal wasn't really dead, however, because the charter for the United Nations had been signed about 10 months earlier. Yet the ink was barely dry on that document when the UN's failure was being predicted. The second edition of *Encyclopedia of Conflicts Since World War II* lists more than 160 armed conflicts that occurred between 1946 and 2005. The world keeps trying to bring about lasting peace . . . and failing.

There is only one source of lasting peace: the Prince of Peace. Jesus can change the human heart; international organizations cannot. What will have to happen for the world to learn this truth?

—C. R. B.

III. Confidence Fulfilled

(MATTHEW 1:18-23)

We now move several centuries forward from Isaiah's day. Times are still hard for the Jewish people, and Joseph and Mary are not exceptions. Their nation is ruled by King Herod, an evil, conniving proxy ruler for Rome. Israel has endured centuries of domination by cruel, ruthless nations that mock God and persecute the Jews for refusing to conform. But God's promises are still as true as they were when He gave them to Abraham, David, etc.

Those contrasting realities—promises to forefathers on the one hand and centuries of subservience to pagan kingdoms on the other—are what Matthew emphasizes as he opens his story with Jesus' genealogy (Matthew 1:17). Will the child born into this situation somehow fulfill God's promise to end His people's captivity?

A. Mary's Pregnancy (v. 18)

18. Now the birth of Jesus Christ was on this wise: When as his mother Mary was espoused to Joseph, before they came together, she was found with child of the Holy Ghost.

The story of Jesus includes the startling fact that a virgin becomes pregnant by the miraculous work *of the Holy Ghost*. Such a thing is without precedent. God had miraculously granted children to aged, childless couples such as Abraham and Sarah, but never before has a virgin conceived.

Naturally, anyone hearing of Mary's pregnancy will assume that it is the result of sexual activity, not a miracle. In addition to the burden of life under the Romans, Mary will now be burdened with the stigma of immorality. Her hard times are about to become harder still.

B. Joseph's Dilemma (v. 19)

19. Then Joseph her husband, being a just man, and not willing to make her a publick example, was minded to put her away privily.

Joseph, knowing that he is not the father, draws the natural conclusion that Mary has been sexually active with another man. An engagement (betrothal) in their culture is a contractual arrangement between two families; ending it therefore requires a legal process that is recognized by the community.

Under the (apparent) circumstances, Joseph can bring Mary's condition to the community's attention to shame her. But Matthew tells us that Joseph is *just* or righteous; his character is in line with the righteous character of God. So he acts mercifully, seeking to make the dissolution of the engagement as private as possible. He intends to spare Mary undue attention and grief.

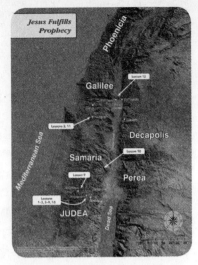

Visual for
Lesson 2

Keep this map posted throughout the quarter to give your learners a geographical perspective.

❧ IT'S NOT *"ALL ABOUT ME"* ❧

Toby Keith's recording of "I Wanna Talk About Me" was at the top of the country music charts in 2001. The song's lyrics tell the tale of a man who listens patiently to his girlfriend's incessant chatter about all the minutiae of her life. He usually does so without complaint, but occasionally he's had enough and responds by saying, in effect, "Every now and then, I'd like for us to talk about the things *I'm* interested in." The song demonstrates the human heart's tendency to self-absorption.

What a difference we see in the heart of Joseph! After learning of Mary's pregnancy, his thoughts were about someone other than himself: how to make a seemingly immoral situation as easy as possible for Mary. Even after being informed of the true state of things, there is no record that Joseph thought or said, "Not me—please find someone else" (contrast Exodus 4:13). When God challenges you to take on a new ministry, are your first thoughts about how the task will affect you?

—C. R. B.

C. God's Revelation (vv. 20, 21)

20. But while he thought on these things, behold, the angel of the Lord appeared unto him in a dream, saying, Joseph, thou son of David, fear not to take unto thee Mary thy wife: for that which is conceived in her is of the Holy Ghost.

We note the sequence: God does not inform Joseph of the source of Mary's pregnancy until *after* that man discovers the fact of the pregnancy on his own. Thus Joseph must go through a certain amount of mental anguish before he learns the truth: *that which is conceived in her is of the Holy Ghost.* Perhaps this sequence is a test of Joseph's character, which we see described in verse 19, above.

What Do You Think?

When was a time that you sensed God calling you to obey Him in a way that seemed contrary to common sense? How did things turn out?

Talking Points for Your Discussion
- A family matter
- A job matter
- A financial matter
- Other

---

21. And she shall bring forth a son, and thou shalt call his name JESUS: for he shall save his people from their sins.

Like Abraham's sons Ishmael and Isaac, this son is to be named according to divine instructions (compare Genesis 16:11; 17:19). The name *Jesus* is derived from the name of Israel's great leader Joshua. Like many Hebrew names, this one makes a declaration about God: "the Lord saves." The angel's message builds on that meaning, declaring that Jesus will *save His people from their sins.*

This announcement is nothing less than that God's promise of the ages is now coming to its fulfillment. Israel and all humanity are in bondage because of rebellion against God. God will now end that bondage by providing deliverance into a kingdom characterized by wisdom and peace, supplied and protected by God's power.

This is the greatest of announcements, but for Joseph it is also a call to serve God in a most unusual way. By telling Joseph that he is the one to name the child, the angel implies that Joseph will serve in the role of the child's father. Joseph is now committed to this child. Acting as father, he will share with Mary the community's scorn for what people will falsely assume to be the couple's mutual immorality.

D. Isaiah's Prophecy (vv. 22, 23)

22. Now all this was done, that it might be fulfilled which was spoken of the Lord by the prophet, saying.

These events are no accident. They fulfill the very plan of God. New Testament writers often cite texts of the Old Testament to show their fulfillment in Jesus. But when they cite those texts, they often refer also to the larger context to which those verses belong, including themes of history and promise. Such is the case with this quotation, as we see next.

23. Behold, a virgin shall be with child, and shall bring forth a son, and they shall call his name Emmanuel, which being interpreted is, God with us.

The text Matthew cites, Isaiah 7:14, is filled with language that connects with Jesus. But it also belongs to its own context—Isaiah's "Book of Emmanuel"—within which we also find Isaiah 9:6, 7, considered above. The connections between the original context and Matthew's application to Jesus are important.

Isaiah's prophecy of a virgin giving birth to a son was delivered in the context of the need for deliverance from the hostile alliance of Aram (Syria) and the northern kingdom of Israel. The people needed a sign of *Emmanuel, which being interpreted is, God with us.* Some students propose that those living in Isaiah's day would have seen this to be a prediction of the birth of Isaiah's own son, with an understanding of that time that *a virgin . . . with child* could refer to a woman who conceives immediately after marrying.

Any expectation along this line is proven wrong by the fuller explanation in Isaiah 9. This child is to be the great king whom God had promised; His greatness will be such that He will have the power of God himself.

With the passage of time, Matthew can say that this promised king has arrived, via the miracle of a virginal conception, to save His people. Jesus is indeed *God* because the subsequent narrative shows that He comes with power and authority that belong to God alone; Jesus is *with us* as He undeservedly takes our sufferings on himself.

At the end of Matthew, Jesus promises to be with His followers to the end of the world (Matthew 28:20). Although Jesus ascends into Heaven after His earthly ministry is over, He remains with us regardless of our circumstances.

Conclusion

A. God Is with Us

The Psalms are songs of praise; yet many of them voice fear, frustration, and complaint. The Prophets are books of hope; yet they often describe the hardships of the faithful. The Bible is brutally honest about the difficulties of the life of faith.

Where is God in all this? He is with us. He was with Israel as they lived under pagan domination. In Jesus, God is with us as one who experienced all the travails of human life. And He is with us as His Holy Spirit lives in us because of Jesus.

B. Prayer

O God, we are amazed that in Jesus You have shared our sufferings and taken the punishment for our sins. May we live as people who know Your constant presence. In Jesus' name, amen.

C. Thought to Remember

God is still with us.

INVOLVEMENT LEARNING

Some of the activities below are also found in the helpful student book, Adult Bible Class.
Don't forget to download the free reproducible page from www.standardlesson.com to enhance your lesson!

Into the Lesson

Write these three definitions on the board before learners arrive, but cover the bottom two so that only the first is visible:

1. "A feeling or consciousness of one's powers or of reliance on one's circumstances."

2. "Faith or belief that one will act in a right, proper, or effective way."

3. "The quality or state of being certain."

After learners gather, point to the first definition (the only one visible) and ask, "What word does this definition apply to?" If no one answers "confidence," uncover the second definition as an additional clue. Uncover the third if needed. If the correct answer is still not forthcoming, say, "C'mon, I have all *confidence* you can get this." Repeat as necessary, stressing the word *confidence* as an obvious hint. When someone answers correctly, uncover all three definitions (if you have not already done so).

Say, "These are obviously general dictionary definitions. As we dig into today's text, we shall see how these definitions apply or do not apply to the words *confidence* and *confident* regarding the state of mind of God's people in hard times."

Into the Word

Distribute handouts that feature the following:

Confidence Fulfilled	*Psalm 89:35-37*
Confident Hope	*Isaiah 9:6, 7*
Confident Worship	*Matthew 1:18-23*

Say, "Look at today's three texts on the right and draw a line to match a topic from the left column to the text that best fits it." Call for conclusions after a few minutes. (The lesson outline on page 242 reveals the answer.)

Next, direct learners' attention to the following three completion statements that are based on the three texts. (You may wish to reproduce these on the backs of the handouts used above.)

1. In Psalm 89 God says His promises are as dependable as the moon. I will use _____ as my constant reminder of God's faithfulness to his promises. 2. In Isaiah 9, God identifies some of the names or descriptors by which His Son the king will be known. My favorite designation for Jesus is _____. 3. In Matthew 1, an angel speaks to Joseph to allay his concerns. If God spoke to me by an angel, the message might be, "_____!"

As you work through the three segments of today's text, pause at appropriate points to allow learners to fill in blanks and explain choices.

Alternative 1: Instead of the above, distribute copies of the "Hello, My Name Is . . ." activity from the reproducible page, which you can download. Have learners fill in the three name tags as you work through each of the three segments of today's text. Discuss.

Alternative 2: For a different way of working through the text, distribute colored pencils and copies of the "God Said It; He Did It" activity on the reproducible page. This can be a small-group exercise. When groups are finished, call for results to be shared with the class as a whole. As each thematic connection is described, immediately ask the other groups if they noticed the same connection. Have groups defend or otherwise explain their choices as appropriate.

Into Life

Distribute copies of R. Kelso Carter's hymn-poem "Standing on the Promises," which is in the public domain. (You can find this in hymnals or on the Internet.) Say, "Circle words and phrases that relate to today's text. Take this with you so you can ponder those grand truths in your times of meditation this week." (Such expressions as "through eternal ages," "promises that cannot fail," and "bound to him eternally" can be readily associated.) Have the class sing this selection to adjourn.

PETER'S REPORT

DEVOTIONAL READING: Psalm 16:7-11
BACKGROUND SCRIPTURE: Psalm 110; Mark 12:35-37; Acts 2:22-36

PSALM 110:1-4

1 The LORD said unto my Lord, Sit thou at my right hand, until I make thine enemies thy footstool.

2 The LORD shall send the rod of thy strength out of Zion: rule thou in the midst of thine enemies.

3 Thy people shall be willing in the day of thy power, in the beauties of holiness from the womb of the morning: thou hast the dew of thy youth.

4 The LORD hath sworn, and will not repent, Thou art a priest for ever after the order of Melchizedek.

ACTS 2:22-27, 29-32

22 Ye men of Israel, hear these words; Jesus of Nazareth, a man approved of God among you by miracles and wonders and signs, which God did by him in the midst of you, as ye yourselves also know:

23 Him, being delivered by the determinate counsel and foreknowledge of God, ye have taken, and by wicked hands have crucified and slain:

24 Whom God hath raised up, having loosed the pains of death: because it was not possible that he should be holden of it.

25 For David speaketh concerning him, I foresaw the Lord always before my face, for he is on my right hand, that I should not be moved:

26 Therefore did my heart rejoice, and my tongue was glad; moreover also my flesh shall rest in hope:

27 Because thou wilt not leave my soul in hell, neither wilt thou suffer thine Holy One to see corruption.

· ·

29 Men and brethren, let me freely speak unto you of the patriarch David, that he is both dead and buried, and his sepulchre is with us unto this day.

30 Therefore being a prophet, and knowing that God had sworn with an oath to him, that of the fruit of his loins, according to the flesh, he would raise up Christ to sit on his throne;

31 He seeing this before spake of the resurrection of Christ, that his soul was not left in hell, neither his flesh did see corruption.

32 This Jesus hath God raised up, whereof we all are witnesses.

KEY VERSE

[David] seeing this before spake of the resurrection of Christ, that his soul was not left in hell, neither his flesh did see corruption. —**Acts 2:31**

JESUS' FULFILLMENT OF SCRIPTURE

Unit 1: Jesus and the Davidic Covenant

LESSONS 1–4

LESSON AIMS

After participating in this lesson, each student will be able to:

1. Identify declarations of God's victory in today's texts.

2. Explain why Jesus' resurrection is the beginning of God's victory and the assurance of God's final victory.

3. Create and carry a reminder to inspire confidence in God's victory whenever difficult circumstances challenge his or her faith.

LESSON OUTLINE

Introduction

A. The Season's Turning Point

For sports fans there is nothing like a championship season for the home team. After such a season, fans may ask themselves, "When was it clear that we had a championship team? What was the turning point in the season?" The faithful may recall different moments when their team came from behind to win against a tough opponent, a key player overcame an injury, or a coach proved the naysayers wrong.

As the people of God look at history, they can ask a similar question: "When was it clearest that God would be victorious?" There are the various "big games" in biblical history: the great flood, the exodus, etc. But the resurrection of Jesus must be considered the ultimate turning point.

The events that led up to that event had moved Jesus' followers from hope to despair. By word and deed, Jesus had appeared to be the great king whom God had promised. But those expectations were dashed when Jesus was arrested and crucified. But His resurrection changed everything, bringing eternal victory to what seemed to be yet another defeat. There could be no greater historical turning point. God's plan had prevailed.

Today we will study two texts that show us Jesus' resurrection to be that definitive turning point. Our texts come from the Psalms (Israel's collection of inspired worship songs) and Acts (the New Testament's history of the first-century church). Though centuries apart, these books reflect similar circumstances: they both address God's people as they lived in what seems to be insignificance, even defeat.

B. Lesson Background

Reading the Psalms and the rest of the Old Testament, we do well to remember that Israel was a small nation with little political or military power in comparison with, at various times, the great powers of Egypt, Assyria, Babylon, and Persia. Yet Israel claimed that its God was the only true God, the ruler over all. How could the true God be worshipped only by the people of a small nation—and not even worshipped consistently by them—while the great powers honored other gods? If Israel's God were the true God, would Israel not be much more powerful than it was?

The answers to such questions can take many forms, but two ideas seem to be at the heart of the matter. First, Israel's God deliberately takes the side of the weak and seemingly insignificant; victory through human weakness means that humans cannot take the credit. Second, Israel's God declared that He was not finished. God promised to retake His world for himself, to make it fully His again, by reversing the effects of human rebellion against Him.

The situation of the first-century church bore similarities to that of Old Testament Israel: Christians were few in number and weak in the eyes of the world. Furthermore, Christians worshipped a man whom the Romans had tortured to death as a criminal. How could such a group have believed itself to be the people of the true God? Today's texts help us answer these questions of both Old Testament Israel, which awaited the fulfillment of God's promise, and of the first-century church, which declared that God had initiated the fulfillment of His greatest promise.

I. Victory Promised
(PSALM 110:1-4)

Psalm 110, written by David, is one of many psalms celebrating the authority that God gave to Israel's king. But as we read this psalm, we remember that the Israel of David's day is a comparatively insignificant nation politically and militarily. Thus we understand that the psalm looks by faith to the future, to the time when God will fulfill the promise to send a great king to rule eternally (2 Samuel 7:4-16, lesson 1).

A. Subdued Enemies (vv. 1, 2)

1. The LORD said unto my Lord, Sit thou at my right hand, until I make thine enemies thy footstool.

The first six words of this verse can be confusing in an English translation—we may wonder if God is talking to himself! We begin to move toward a solution when we realize that the Hebrew text uses different words for the two occurrences of *Lord* that we see here. *The LORD* translates the personal name of God in the Old Testament, often vocalized as Yahweh, while *my Lord* translates a different word.

But what is the identity of this second individual? Some propose that it refers to Israel's king at the time, namely David, as he speaks of himself in the third person. Under this idea, the opening phrase of this psalm means, "This is what the Lord God said to Israel's king."

The complete solution is found in Matthew 22:41-45, where Jesus identifies himself as the second of the two Lords in this psalm. God (through David) is indeed speaking of Israel's king, and that king is ultimately revealed to be the Christ. God's words to Him are an invitation to share the Father's kingly authority. To sit at God's *right hand* is to share His throne, the symbol of that authority. The psalm thus declares that Israel's promised king is to rule by God's appointment and power.

The phrase *until I make thine enemies thy footstool* acknowledges that the world will not be in submission to God's appointed king for a while. But God will defeat the king's enemies. They will end up bowing before the king's feet as if those enemies were a footstool. Israel's God is the true power, and the present situation is temporary. God's enemies seem to prevail only until He acts to bring them into submission to himself and His king. The importance of this verse is seen in the fact that it is quoted eight times in the New Testament (Matthew 22:44; 26:64; Mark 12:36; 14:62; Luke 20:42, 43; 22:69; Acts 2:34, 35; and Hebrews 1:13).

What Do You Think?

Which area of life in the world seems least in submission to God? Why? How should Christians act and react with regard to this rebellion?

Talking Points for Your Discussion

- The entertainment industry
- A country that persecutes Christians
- Governmental policy
- Other

Visual for Lesson 3. *Point to this photo of King David's sepulchre as you discuss the comparison with Jesus in verses 29-32.*

2. The LORD shall send the rod of thy strength out of Zion: rule thou in the midst of thine enemies.

The rod of thy strength is a symbol of the king's authority. From Zion—the mountain on which Jerusalem is built and from which Israel's king rules—God enables His chosen one to rule with authority. It is an authority that stands even though God's people are surrounded by enemies. The Israel of David's day looks forward to that authority being revealed in full as God brings the enemies to submission.

❧ THE POWER OF GOD AND KINGS ❧

The state of monarchy is the supremest thing upon earth; for kings are not only God's lieutenants upon earth, and sit upon God's throne, but even by God himself are called gods. . . . [For someone] to dispute what God may do is blasphemy . . . so is it sedition in subjects to dispute what a king may do in the height of his power.

Those are the words of James I, who was king of England from 1603 to 1625. During his reign, he sought to establish the philosophical and theological foundation for the so-called "divine right of kings."

The act of gaining a leadership position can have a perverse effect. Pride may twist our spirits, encouraging us to believe that we have gained our position by the will of God, regardless of what personal chicanery, deceit, or fraud put us there.

Tragically, leaders in the church and in parachurch organizations have been known to believe that what they do "must" be God's will because they have dedicated their lives to serving God. Even more tragically, their followers may yield in unthinking agreement.

The psalmist reminds us that the ultimate source of all power is God. This means, among other things, that everyone is accountable to Him. We need such reminders!   —C. R. B.

B. Loyal Subjects (v. 3)

3. Thy people shall be willing in the day of thy power, in the beauties of holiness from the womb of the morning: thou hast the dew of thy youth.

God promises to the king the loyalty of his subjects. When the king calls on the people to stand by him for battle, they will answer the call. But the king's authority comes not from military might. Rather, the authority is apparent as he displays *the beauties of holiness*: his belonging to God is what commands his people's allegiance. The king's power will not diminish with time; each new day (*morning*) will mean that the king retains the vitality depicted as *the dew of thy youth*.

C. Eternal Priesthood (v. 4)

4. The LORD hath sworn, and will not repent, Thou art a priest for ever after the order of Melchizedek.

We usually take the word *repent* to mean something like "to be sorry for having sinned," but in this context it means "relent." God's commitment to the king is permanent. The psalmist presents this as an oath, with God declaring the king to be *a priest for ever after the order of Melchizedek*. That man was king of Salem (the settlement that became Jerusalem) and also a priest of God during the time of Abraham (Genesis 14:17-20).

However, Israel's law and history forbid its king to act as priest (compare 2 Chronicles 26:16-18). Although Israelite kings are, in a sense, the nation's leaders in worship, the priestly offices themselves are held by others—those of the tribe of Levi. The verse before us looks forward to something different, to a time when the promised king will also serve as the great high priest. As Hebrews 5:5-10 and 7:1-22 make clear, Jesus is this ultimate priest-king.

II. Victory Achieved
(ACTS 2:22-27, 29-32)

Acts 2 recounts the events of the Day of Pentecost, especially Peter's speech. On that day, the Holy Spirit is poured out on the followers of Jesus in Jerusalem, and the Spirit's presence is miraculously demonstrated as the disciples begin speaking in other languages.

People wonder what they are witnessing. Peter informs them that God's promise to pour out His Spirit on His people is being fulfilled. But why is God doing that now, with these seemingly insignificant people? After quoting the prophet Joel, Peter proceeds to explain the meaning and significance of what is happening.

A. Reviewing Jesus' Story (vv. 22-24)

22. Ye men of Israel, hear these words; Jesus of Nazareth, a man approved of God among you by miracles and wonders and signs, which God did by him in the midst of you, as ye yourselves also know.

Peter summarizes what the crowd already knows about Jesus: that He had been an exceptional worker of miracles (compare John 3:2). Those deeds, Peter elaborates, could have been done only by one having God's approval. But what about Jesus' death? Did that not prove something different about Him, that He had been abandoned by God and defeated by His enemies?

23. Him, being delivered by the determinate counsel and foreknowledge of God, ye have taken, and by wicked hands have crucified and slain.

Jesus' death was no accident, and it was not the result of God's disfavor on Him. Rather, it was the fulfillment of God's deliberate plan (compare Acts 4:28), what God had intended to bring about even before He created the world.

But there is another aspect to the story. The people of Jerusalem, those who are listening to Peter's speech, had called for Jesus' death a few weeks previously. They were among those who rejected the one whom God had sent, handing Him over to be crucified by the pagan Romans. By opposing Jesus, they have aligned themselves with God's enemies. They are guilty of rejecting God's king.

24. Whom God hath raised up, having loosed the pains of death: because it was not possible that he should be holden of it.

God has responded to the rejection and slaying of Jesus with a powerful act: He raised Jesus from the dead. This act vindicated Jesus as God's king, setting right what had been done to Him. It was not possible for Jesus to be held in death's grip; God's promise was simply too great for that to happen.

B. Remembering David's Prophecy (vv. 25-27)

25. For David speaketh concerning him, I foresaw the Lord always before my face, for he is on my right hand, that I should not be moved.

Peter now begins quoting from Psalm 16:8-11. This psalm speaks from King David's perspective, expressing utter confidence in God's protection.

This psalm expresses how all believers should respond in times of adversity: no matter what dangers or threats they confront, they know that God is with them. The quotation begins by saying that God is so close it is as if He is standing right next to David.

Peter is making a significant application of this psalm. His reasoning is that if God has promised to protect King David, then God will all the more protect the great, promised king—Jesus.

> **What Do You Think?**
> What protection by God have you praised Him for most recently? How can you turn this kind of praise into a witness for Him?
> *Talking Points for Your Discussion*
> - Financial protection
> - Physical protection
> - Spiritual protection
> - Other

26. Therefore did my heart rejoice, and my tongue was glad; moreover also my flesh shall rest in hope.

Peter continues to quote Psalm 16. The response of the faithful to God's presence is joy, praise, and confidence for the future. Because God is the protector of the faithful, His people have nothing to fear. Even the worst that can happen to them—death—is no real threat.

27. Because thou wilt not leave my soul in hell, neither wilt thou suffer thine Holy One to see corruption.

The quotation from Psalm 16 continues (see also Acts 13:35). The Old Testament does not provide the reader with a crystal clear notion of life beyond death, but it does affirm the absolute faithfulness of God—faithfulness that extends through all of earthly life and beyond. That is the confidence expressed here by David.

The word translated *hell* refers not to the place of eternal punishment in this context, but simply to the state of death. *Corruption* refers to the physical decay that follows death. David in his day did not believe that death had the final word. The resurrection of Jesus, the *Holy One*, proves the validity of that belief.

> **What Do You Think?**
> How does your belief in Jesus' resurrection make a difference in how you view death in various contexts?
> *Talking Points for Your Discussion*
> - Regarding deaths by accidents
> - Regarding deaths preceded by lengthy suffering
> - Regarding suicide
> - Regarding murder
> - Other

C. Revealing God's Fulfillment (vv. 29-32)

29, 30. Men and brethren, let me freely speak unto you of the patriarch David, that he is both dead and buried, and his sepulchre is with us unto this day. Therefore being a prophet, and knowing that God had sworn with an oath to him, that of the fruit of his loins, according to the flesh, he would raise up Christ to sit on his throne.

Peter expands his comparison of David with Jesus, beginning with the simple, known fact that David died and remains *both dead and buried, and his sepulchre is with us unto this day* (see 1 Kings 2:10). However, the same cannot be said for Jesus! God's promise to protect David was a real promise, but what God planned to do for the promised son of David, *the fruit of his loins, according to the flesh*, was to be even greater. God planned for Jesus to be raised from the dead to sit on David's throne, therefore saying a definitive, final *No!* to the grave and decay. David spoke for all the faithful, but he spoke better than anyone realized concerning the promised king to come (compare Psalm 132:11).

31. He seeing this before spake of the resurrection of Christ, that his soul was not left in hell, neither his flesh did see corruption.

So in Jesus' resurrection, David's hope in God is now fulfilled in an unprecedented way. All the faithful can share David's confidence that God does not abandon them to the grave. Jesus— God's Christ, the promised king—has been delivered from death with an immediacy and finality that surpasses anything that God had done before. God has amazed and surprised His people by raising Jesus from the tomb to appear fully and triumphantly alive to His followers. In a tomb from sundown on Friday to sunrise on Sunday, His life or *soul* was not abandoned to the state of death. *His flesh* did not decay, but was restored to perfect life. Paul will later affirm that David's body indeed decayed after his death, but not so the body of Jesus (Acts 13:34-37).

Peter's argument carries an important implication. In Jesus' resurrection, God demonstrates that He most assuredly acts to protect and preserve. If God has done this for Jesus, then surely He will do the same for all His people. Jesus' resurrection serves as the guarantee that God will also raise us up. Death will have the final word for none of God's people. God's victory, begun in Jesus, will come to completion when God raises all His people at the end of the age (Daniel 12:2; Acts 23:6; Romans 6:5; 1 Corinthians 15; etc.).

❧ THE GREATEST EMANCIPATOR ❧

Abraham Lincoln is regarded by many historians as the greatest U.S. president. Lincoln's role in preserving the Union during America's Civil War is the subject of numerous studies on effective leadership even today, and his actions to end slavery have earned him the designation *the great emancipator*.

Today, the remains of the great emancipator lie in a tomb in Springfield, Illinois. Above the tomb rises a 117-foot obelisk. The tomb itself features polished marble and bronze; statues and plaques honor the president who was felled by an assassin's bullet in 1865. Lincoln's voice lives on in many ways, particularly in his Gettysburg Address—one of the most quoted speeches in American history. Even so, Lincoln is dead.

Jesus also was one who had His life unjustly taken. But when He rose from the dead on the third day, He became history's *greatest* emancipator. His death and resurrection provide freedom from slavery to sin. We serve a Savior who is alive forevermore. The location of Jesus' tomb is uncertain but also irrelevant because it is empty. One day our tombs and graves will be empty and irrelevant as well. Let us live today in recognition of that fact.   —C. R. B.

32. This Jesus hath God raised up, whereof we all are witnesses.

The reason Peter expects his audience to believe the audacious claim of verse 31 is that he and others have seen the resurrected Jesus. They know that Jesus' tomb is empty. He is no longer dead and buried, but alive and active. Jesus' enemies cannot produce the body of a dead Jesus to refute this.

Conclusion
A. Didn't Look Like Much

From a human perspective, Israel was not much of a nation, Jesus was not much of a leader, and the first-century church was not much of a movement. By the numbers—people, money, territory—few of the first Christians amounted to much.

But from God's perspective, the whole of human history is tied up in these seeming "not muches." God worked through tiny Israel to bring lowly Jesus, who built the seemingly insignificant church. While the world went about its business, God was taking back what He had made and deeply loved all along.

B. Prayer

Father, we take heart knowing that Christ has overcome our greatest enemy, death. Give us the confidence that we are secure as Your people no matter what. In Jesus' name, amen.

C. Thought to Remember

Look both backward and forward to Jesus.

HOW TO SAY IT

Assyria	Uh-*sear*-ee-uh.
Babylon	*Bab*-uh-lun.
Egypt	*Ee*-jipt.
Levi	*Lee*-vye.
Melchizedek	Mel-*kiz*-eh-dek.
patriarch	*pay*-tree-ark.
Pentecost	*Pent*-ih-kost.
Persia	*Per*-zhuh.
sepulchre	*sep*-ul-kur.
Yahweh *(Hebrew)*	*Yah*-weh.

INVOLVEMENT LEARNING

Some of the activities below are also found in the helpful student book, Adult Bible Class.
Don't forget to download the free reproducible page from www.standardlesson.com to enhance your lesson!

Into the Lesson

Say, "I'm going to call on some of you to 'give me a letter,' like in an old-time cheer. At the end, I'm going to ask, 'What's that spell?' Then everyone shout out the word." Point to a learner at random as you say "[learner's name], give me a *V*!" Do the same with different learners as you proceed through the letters of the word *victory*. Then with intensity ask the class, "What's that spell?" After the class shouts "victory," say, "Today's texts are simple statements of victory for those who appeared to be losing. Let's see how God planned victory out of the seeming jaws of defeat!"

Option: Before class begins, place in chairs copies of the "The Way of All the Earth" activity from the reproducible page, which you can download. This will help set up the contrast between death and resurrection. At an appropriate point in the Into the Word segment, you can refer to 1 Kings 2:1 to note a key difference between King David and King Jesus, as Peter does in Acts 2:29.

Into the Word

Distribute handouts with the following clauses, one for each of the lesson's 14 verses. Include this instruction: "Identify the verse that best relates to each entry." (Suggested answers are given here in parentheses; do not include these on the handouts.)

From Psalm 110
___ Similar to this guy! *(v. 4)*
___ Some things are ever new! *(v. 3)*
___ Take your seat! *(v. 1)*
___ Rods are for kings! *(v. 2)*

From Acts 2
___ It's no secret! *(v. 22)*
___ Patriarchs are still dead! *(v. 29)*
___ Witnesses are critical to Christian belief! *(v. 32)*
___ What David saw! *(v. 25)*

___ A king who was a prophet too! *(v. 30)*
___ When death didn't mean "decomposition"! *(v. 31)*
___ You stand accused! *(v. 23)*
___ When heart, tongue, and flesh agree! *(v. 26)*
___ Death has just met its match! *(v. 24)*
___ What God will not do! *(v. 27)*.

Have learners work on these in groups of two or three. Call for conclusions when groups are finished. Ask for justifications where disagreements exist. After you finish working through the 14 verses, repeat the cheer from Into the Lesson.

Ask, "In what sense can we say that *Resurrection = Victory*?" After everyone has had a chance to respond, write 1 Corinthians 15:26 on the board: "The last enemy that shall be destroyed is death." Use the fact of Christ's resurrection to discuss implications for our own.

Option: Distribute copies of the "The Way of the Messiah-King" activity from the reproducible page. Form learners into groups of two or three to brainstorm responses. Discuss results; you can give a small prize to members of the group that come up with the most ingenious responses.

Into Life

Give to each learner a copy of the megaphone image below. (You can laminate these onto small cards if you have access to that capability.) Say, "Keep this handy to remind yourself that we are on the winning team. Let this image encourage you when it seems like you are losing. Remember: our ultimate victory is assured!"

Give me a V!

WORTHY IS THE LAMB

DEVOTIONAL READING: Matthew 9:35–10:1
BACKGROUND SCRIPTURE: Revelation 3:7; 5:5-13; 6:12–7:17; 22:16

REVELATION 5:5-13

5 And one of the elders saith unto me, Weep not: behold, the Lion of the tribe of Juda, the Root of David, hath prevailed to open the book, and to loose the seven seals thereof.

6 And I beheld, and, lo, in the midst of the throne and of the four beasts, and in the midst of the elders, stood a Lamb as it had been slain, having seven horns and seven eyes, which are the seven Spirits of God sent forth into all the earth.

7 And he came and took the book out of the right hand of him that sat upon the throne.

8 And when he had taken the book, the four beasts and four and twenty elders fell down before the Lamb, having every one of them harps, and golden vials full of odours, which are the prayers of saints.

9 And they sung a new song, saying, Thou art worthy to take the book, and to open the seals thereof: for thou wast slain, and hast redeemed us to God by thy blood out of every kindred, and tongue, and people, and nation;

10 And hast made us unto our God kings and priests: and we shall reign on the earth.

11 And I beheld, and I heard the voice of many angels round about the throne and the beasts and the elders: and the number of them was ten thousand times ten thousand, and thousands of thousands;

12 Saying with a loud voice, Worthy is the Lamb that was slain to receive power, and riches, and wisdom, and strength, and honour, and glory, and blessing.

13 And every creature which is in heaven, and on the earth, and under the earth, and such as are in the sea, and all that are in them, heard I saying, Blessing, and honour, and glory, and power, be unto him that sitteth upon the throne, and unto the Lamb for ever and ever.

KEY VERSE

Worthy is the Lamb that was slain to receive power, and riches, and wisdom, and strength, and honour, and glory, and blessing. —**Revelation 5:12**

JESUS' FULFILLMENT OF SCRIPTURE

Unit 1: Jesus and the Davidic Covenant

LESSONS 1–4

LESSON AIMS

After participating in this lesson, each student will be able to:

1. Identify elements of the text that stress Christ's rule over the world.

2. Explain God's plan for the world as the saving work of Christ and the sharing of the message of Christ with the entire world.

3. Sign a covenant to be faithful in worship, with a keen appreciation of the Christ he or she worships.

LESSON OUTLINE

Introduction
    A. Beyond Comic-book Images
    B. Lesson Background
 I. The Lamb Appears (REVELATION 5:5-7)
    A. With the Power of a Lion (v. 5)
    B. With the Authority of God (vv. 6, 7)
      Incongruities
II. The Lamb Is Worshipped (REVELATION 5:8-13)
    A. By Beasts and Elders (vv. 8-10)
    B. By a Multitude of Angels (vv. 11, 12)
    C. By Everything in Creation (v. 13)
      A Different Kind of "Universalism"
Conclusion
    A. Our Part in God's Plan
    B. Prayer
    C. Thought to Remember

Introduction

A. Beyond Comic-book Images

Even if you are not a fan, you are probably familiar with the storytelling in superhero comic books. Comic books tell stories of intense conflict. The pictures have vivid colors and exaggerated proportion. The characters, usually having fantastic powers, are part of a story with a clear line between good and evil, between an arch-villain and a superhero, and with the fate of humanity hanging in the balance. Comic books are fantasy, but their appeal to a wide audience of decades past has been renewed in movies that mimic their formula.

Perhaps this formula is popular because humans have a strong desire to see the conflict between good and evil portrayed in a way that reflects their own pain and fears but supplies a decisive ending to the story. Comic-book storytelling gives us what we want to see: heroes who always manage to defeat evil and rescue the helpless.

Critics of the Bible may view the book of Revelation as no more than a comic book, given its vividly colorful word-pictures. These pictures draw clear lines between good and evil, with a superhero victorious in the end. As comic-book superheroes go into battle in issue after issue, so the superhero of Revelation appears in conflict with a supervillain in chapter after chapter.

Such a comparison, however, is quite superficial. The book of Revelation, unlike a comic book, is a God-inspired depiction of the essential conflict of every age: God and His people on the one hand against Satan and the powers of the world on the other. Also unlike comic books, with their stories portraying conflicts seemingly without end, Revelation assures us that the conflict between God and the devil will not go on forever. The book of Revelation is no fantasy. There will be a decisive end in which God is fully victorious. In fact, that end is near.

B. Lesson Background

The book of Revelation is commonly thought to be the most difficult and mysterious in the Bible. But if we consider a few important facts about the book, Revelation's essential message can be very clear to us.

The book itself tells us that its contents were received by John while he was on the remote Mediterranean island of Patmos (Revelation 1:9). For his preaching of the gospel, imperial authorities had sentenced him to exile on that island. Persecution was the lot of many Christians in that day. Faith in Jesus made Christians the object of scorn, ridicule, and even violence. To Christians under persecution, it could seem that all the powers of the world were aligned against them.

Where was God in all of this? Had He abandoned His people? Are the powers of the world really greater than God's power? Revelation answers these persistent questions. Unfolding as a series of visions, the book shows repeatedly that God delivers His people while bringing judgment on those who oppose Him. Of course, persecution of the faithful was nothing new in John's day. So Revelation often borrows images from other biblical books, showing that the experience in the present is very much like the experience of the past.

Our text comes early in Revelation. After introducing the book's themes (chapter 1), the book presents seven short letters to the persecuted churches of Asia Minor, offering encouragement, correction, and warning (chapters 2, 3). Then we are told of John's vision of God's throne (chapter 4). At the throne is presented a scroll or "book," sealed with seven seals (5:1). A search is made for one who can open the book, and none is found (5:2, 3). John begins to weep, fearing that the book will not be opened (5:4). Then our text begins.

I. The Lamb Appears
(REVELATION 5:5-7)

A. With the Power of a Lion (v. 5)

5. And one of the elders saith unto me, Weep not: behold, the Lion of the tribe of Juda, the Root of David, hath prevailed to open the book, and to loose the seven seals thereof.

John's vision thus far has included 24 elders who surround God's throne in worship (Revela-

tion 4:4). These elders seem to provide an image of God's people, gathered in God's presence. One of these figures now explains to John that there is indeed one who can *open the book*. The elder uses terms that remind us of the ancient promise of a great king: *Lion of the tribe of Juda, the Root of David* (Genesis 49:9; Isaiah 11:1). The search that took place in Revelation 5:3, 4 discovered no one able to open the book, but now one is found. He alone has *prevailed* or been victorious.

This description helps us understand the significance of the book: it represents the unfolding of God's plan that brings about His final victory in the world. Thus only God's promised king can open such a book. Looking at the world's awful state today, we might imagine that no one can make it conform to His will. But God's king can and shall.

B. With the Authority of God (vv. 6, 7)

6. And I beheld, and, lo, in the midst of the throne and of the four beasts, and in the midst of the elders, stood a Lamb as it had been slain, having seven horns and seven eyes, which are the seven Spirits of God sent forth into all the earth.

The king who was just described as a victorious lion now appears as a slain lamb. How can both images apply to one being? If we know the good news of Jesus, we have the answer. Jesus is God's king who willingly submitted to death on the cross and rose again. He is the sacrificial lamb who took our sin on himself (Isaiah 53:7-9), becoming utterly victorious as He rose from the dead.

This victorious Lamb has unusual features: *seven horns and seven eyes*. The horns suggest power (Psalm 89:17), while the eyes suggest watchful protection (Zechariah 3:9; 4:10). The fact that the Lamb has seven of each corresponds to the seven churches to whom the book

HOW TO SAY IT

haberdasher	*ha*-burr-*da*-shur.
Mediterranean	*Med*-uh-tuh-*ray*-nee-un.
Patmos	*Pat*-muss.
Zechariah	*Zek*-uh-*rye*-uh.

is addressed (Revelation 1:4). The Lamb manifestly has sufficient power to watch over His people and defeat their enemies.

This powerful Lamb stands in the middle of the throne scene, surrounded by the elders and *the four beasts*, together suggesting the whole of creation. Jesus has authority over God's people and over the entire universe. He has this authority despite the fact that He had been killed, for He has defeated death by His resurrection.

The suffering church is beginning to see the answer to its condition. They are watched over and protected by the Christ who knows what it is like to be persecuted, even to be killed, for the sake of righteousness. His resurrection power is at work in the life of the church, even when everything seems to be going the wrong way.

> **What Do You Think?**
> Which of John's descriptions of Jesus help you most to face daily challenges? Why?
> *Talking Points for Your Discussion*
> - Jesus' absolute power (seven horns)
> - Jesus' absolute awareness (seven eyes)
> - Other

❧ *INCONGRUITIES* ❧

Many things in life seem incongruous. A tiny group of 13 British colonies would become the greatest economic and military power in history. A haberdasher named Harry S. Truman would become the American president who decided to use atomic weapons. A nation founded to offer "life, liberty, and the pursuit of happiness" to its citizens would come to legalize the destruction of infants in the womb. A young man named Bill Gates would become one of the wealthiest men in the world after dropping out of college to start a software company.

The apostle John depicts for us the ultimate incongruity: a Lamb that has been slaughtered —the symbol of weakness and defeat—standing alive and powerful. This Lamb's seven horns and seven eyes enable Him to protect all who place their trust in Him. He exercises His authority over all creation, and no one is able to challenge Him.

God does things that don't make sense to the natural mind. But if we allow Him, He will even do things in our lives that we would never have dreamed to be possible. Are you open to God's incongruities?
—C. R. B.

7. And he came and took the book out of the right hand of him that sat upon the throne.

The Lamb's authority and worthiness to open the book are now demonstrated decisively. The Lamb approaches God's throne and takes the book directly from God's right hand. The Lamb's authority is like God's authority as represented by God's throne: authority over all creation. By that authority the Lamb will fulfill God's purpose, represented by the book that He takes.

II. The Lamb Is Worshipped
(REVELATION 5:8-13)
A. By Beasts and Elders (vv. 8-10)

8a. And when he had taken the book, the four beasts and four and twenty elders fell down before the Lamb,

Previously, those surrounding the throne had fallen in worship before the Lord God (Revelation 4:9, 10). Now they worship the Lamb in the same way. The Lamb's authority is the authority of God himself, and He is worthy of worship in every way that God is.

8b. Having every one of them harps, and golden vials full of odours, which are the prayers of saints.

The beasts and elders hold objects that evoke worship. Their harps suggest worship in song (Psalm 33:2; 43:4; 71:22). They hold *golden vials full of odours* (or incense; compare Revelation 8:3, 4), which the text tells us represent the prayers of God's people. Because smoke from incense rises and creates a pleasing aroma, it was used in Israel's temple as a symbol of prayers rising to God (Psalm 141:2; Luke 1:9, 10).

As the Lamb takes the book or scroll, He will respond to the prayers of God's people—prayers for rescue, for justice, for evil to be defeated, and for God's reign to be realized fully. The Lamb is the one who will bring all this about. So all of

God's people and all of creation join in worshipping Him.

9. And they sung a new song, saying, Thou art worthy to take the book, and to open the seals thereof: for thou wast slain, and hast redeemed us to God by thy blood out of every kindred, and tongue, and people, and nation.

The worshippers' singing is described in terms of *a new song*. God's saving work in Revelation is sometimes described as *new*: the faithful receive a "new name" (Revelation 2:17; 3:12), and God brings about "a new heaven and a new earth" (21:1) and a "new Jerusalem" (3:12; 21:2). Indeed, God declares that in the end He makes "all things new" (21:5).

This newness is the utter change that God brings to the world as He establishes His rule over it. He transforms it from a world of rebellion against Him to submission to Him, from darkness to light, from suffering to joy. So the song that is sung in worship is a new song, reflecting the new reality that God is achieving through Christ, the Lamb.

What Do You Think?
  What kinds of worship songs are especially
    powerful to you in worship? Why is that?
Talking Points for Your Discussion
  ▪ Songs of hope and/or trust
  ▪ Songs of victory
  ▪ Songs of praise
  ▪ Songs of devotion
  ▪ Other

The content of the song reflects the new reality. The Lamb alone is worthy to unseal the book because by His death He has redeemed the people of God. The image of redemption comes from the slave market, implying that humans enslaved in their sin have been freed by Christ's death.

The descriptions *every kindred, and tongue, and people, and nation* pile up to emphasize that God's people ultimately are a global people. As God announced to Abraham, His purpose in calling one nation, Israel, is to bless every nation (Genesis 22:16-18). God's triumph will be global, offering membership in His people to all peoples.

What Do You Think?
  How can you increase your participation in your
    church's efforts to take the gospel to the wide
    diversity of the world's population?
Talking Points for Your Discussion
  ▪ With regard to foreign evangelism
  ▪ With regard to local cross-cultural evangelism
  ▪ With regard to cross-cultural service projects
  ▪ Other

10. And hast made us unto our God kings and priests: and we shall reign on the earth.

The worshippers give thanks that God graciously shares His triumph with His people. Earlier, John saw that the 24 elders were seated and wearing crowns (Revelation 4:4), suggesting that God has appointed them as His regents, carrying out His rule. Entrusted to deliver the saving message of the gospel, Christians are appointed by God to extend His rule to every nation. In that way we have become *kings* who assist the great king (Matthew 16:15-19; Luke 22:30). Of course, our kingship does not invest us with personal authority, for all authority belongs to God and to the Lamb. Our task is to obey the divine king.

Likewise, as those around the throne hold harps and bowls of incense, they take the role of *priests*. Christ's followers, with Christ as high priest, are invested with the priestly roles of worship and intercession, sharing the gospel to bring others to become worshippers of the true God (1 Peter 2:9).

What Do You Think?
  What can you do in the week ahead to fulfill
    your role in Christ's holy and royal priesthood
    (1 Peter 2:5, 9)?
Talking Points for Your Discussion
  ▪ Issues of self (personal holiness, devotional
    time, thought life, etc.)
  ▪ Issues involving others (intercessory prayer,
    service, etc.)
  ▪ Issues involving your church (teaching, etc.)

These exalted roles for God's people stand in sharp contrast with the condition of persecuted Christians like John. As far as the powers of the world are concerned, such people are of no significance. But from the perspective of God's throne, we are His kings and priests. Through them (us) God is making the world His again.

B. By a Multitude of Angels (vv. 11, 12)

11. And I beheld, and I heard the voice of many angels round about the throne and the beasts and the elders: and the number of them was ten thousand times ten thousand, and thousands of thousands.

As the scene continues, the description is like a camera lens zooming out to widen its field of view. Around the throne are *the beasts and the elders,* but beyond them is a numberless crowd of angels. In the Greek language, the highest number-word commonly used is the word for *ten thousand.* So to say *ten thousand times ten thousand* is to offer a number as large as one can describe, and to add thousands to that enhances the description (compare Daniel 7:10; Hebrews 12:22). We might compare our slang word *zillions,* by which we mean a number so large that no one can count it.

Angels are God's messengers and servants. They do not inhabit our earth, but they can visit it at God's command. Sometimes they are pictured as comprising an army that can fight God's enemies (Matthew 26:53). This numberless throng of angels suggests the almighty power of God as all stand by the throne in worship, ready to do His bidding.

12. Saying with a loud voice, Worthy is the Lamb that was slain to receive power, and riches, and wisdom, and strength, and honour, and glory, and blessing.

Our text began with the assertion that only the Lamb is worthy to open the book (v. 5). Now the heavenly assembly joins in proclaiming the full extent of that worthiness. As before, His worthiness is a consequence of giving His life for the sake of the unworthy (v. 9). Because He is *the Lamb that was slain,* He is exalted to the highest position.

The worshippers offer a long list of the things that the Lamb receives, all indicating utter authority to rule (compare 1 Chronicles 29:11). *Power* suggests the ability to accomplish His will. The word *riches* indicates wealth, the possession of all the resources needed to rule. *Wisdom* is the attri-

bute of the noble ruler who brings blessing to those ruled. *Strength* parallels power, suggesting not just abstract power but power at work. *Honour, and glory, and blessing* are what the great ruler receives back from his people, the acclaim that grateful subjects give to a just and powerful king.

Whatever praise the kings of the world receive, it is but a shadow of the praise that the Lamb deserves. John's vision outstrips any scene in which an earthly ruler is acclaimed. The divine Christ, the one who died and rose, is king of kings.

> **What Do You Think?**
> How can churches in your community better work together to honor Christ?
> *Talking Points for Your Discussion*
> - Through community worship services on special occasions (Christmas drama, etc.)
> - Through crisis/disaster response
> - Through ongoing benevolence
> - Other

C. By Everything in Creation (v. 13)

13. And every creature which is in heaven, and on the earth, and under the earth, and such as are in the sea, and all that are in them, heard I saying, Blessing, and honour, and glory, and power, be unto him that sitteth upon the throne, and unto the Lamb for ever and ever.

To this point, the worshipping congregation has been in Heaven—that is, in God's very presence. First we saw those immediately around God's throne, then the throng of angels beyond them. Now the lens of the camera is at the widest possible angle, taking in all that exists.

Again, John uses several expressions to emphasize that praise comes from every part of creation, without exception. *Heaven* here may refer either to the abode of God or to the sky above the earth, and John may intend both. *Under the earth* may refer to the abode of the dead or simply to whatever exists below the physical surface of the earth.

John adds *in the sea* in case we understand *earth* to refer just to dry land. The list ends with *all that are in them,* meaning every created thing in all the places named before. Has any possible place been omitted? We can safely say *no.* All of creation—

literally everything that exists—joins in praise to God. The words of praise echo the words of the heavenly congregation in verse 12. All creation attests that power and praise belong to God and the Lamb *for ever and ever,* a phrase that Revelation uses to emphasize that God's triumph will be eternal, beyond any limit of time.

We now realize more fully the significance of the Lamb's worthiness to open the book. God's plan, as represented by "the book" of verse 5, is to reconcile His world to himself. Christ's death and resurrection puts that plan into action. His people, like kings and priests, carry that plan out in the world. But they are often rejected and persecuted, as Christ himself was. But Christ will faithfully bring God's plan to completion, sharing His triumph with those who belong to Him while bringing righteous judgment on His stubborn enemies.

We can imagine John, the author of Revelation, reading this passage to other Christian prisoners after a long day of forced labor on Patmos. The little band of believers look weak and insignificant. But from God's perspective, they are part of a mighty, universal chorus that proclaims God's glory eternally. Those who imprisoned them may seem to have all the power. But true power belongs to God and to Christ. Christ will bring that victory to completion, and His people will celebrate it with Him forever.

❧ A Different Kind of "Universalism" ❧

The false doctrine of *universalism*—the idea that everyone will eventually be saved, regardless of whether or not they accept Jesus as Savior in this life—occasionally comes back to life to trouble the church. Such was the case in the spring of 2011 with the publication of yet another book that promoted this old idea.

But even as we reject the false doctrine of universalism, we should keep in mind the universal aspect of Revelation's picture: when God brings His plan to consummation, all of creation will acknowledge Christ as the worthy recipient of eternal praise. John is not alone in offering such a picture. Paul says of Christ, "every knee shall bow to me, and every tongue shall confess to God" (Romans 14:11; quoting Isaiah 45:23). Paul's

Visual for Lesson 4. *Start a discussion of verse 12 by pointing to this visual as you ask, "Worthy for what? Why?"*

depiction seems to include both the saved, who bow and confess willingly and joyfully, and the unsaved, whose bowing and confessing is a self-condemning admission of truth they refused to acknowledge while they could still be saved. Make sure you're not in the latter group! —C. R. B.

Conclusion

A. Our Part in God's Plan

Did you notice that you are part of the story that Revelation tells? When our acts of worship are sincere, when our lives are in submission to the one on the throne, we join the chorus that declares the greatness of God and the Lamb. When our lives and our words express the good news of Jesus, we extend God's rule further into the world, to every tribe, language, people, and nation. When we live in submission to the Lamb, we take part in the fulfillment of God's great plan for creation.

B. Prayer

Father, may our lives glorify Your Son, joining the heavenly chorus forever. May Your kingdom come as Your will is done on earth as it is in Heaven. In Jesus' name, amen.

C. Thought to Remember

Don't wait for Heaven.
Celebrate Christ's victory *now!*

INVOLVEMENT LEARNING

Some of the activities below are also found in the helpful student book, Adult Bible Class.
Don't forget to download the free reproducible page from www.standardlesson.com to enhance your lesson!

Into the Lesson

Write this question on the board: "What normal human experiences elicit weeping?" After several responses, say, "In Revelation 5:4, just before today's text begins, we find John weeping for another reason: 'I wept much, because no man was found worthy to open and to read the book, neither to look thereon.' John knew that the book in question was a Word from God, but he was frustrated because it appeared that he had no access to it. We have a Word from God, and it is completely accessible. Let's look."

Into the Word

Give each learner a copy of a blank four-column table that has 14 rows. Say, "We're going to fill in this table by putting the verse number in the first block of each row, followed by a three-word summary. We're following in John's footsteps in being told to 'Write the things which thou hast seen, and the things which are, and the things which shall be hereafter'" (Revelation 1:19).

Continue: "We'll start with an example. First, write *5a* in the first block of the first row to signify *verse 5a*. Then select three words from that partial verse to write in the three blocks, one word per block, that follow in the same row. Here is your clue: The first thing an angel usually says to a human is 'Fear not.' What's the first thing this angel says to John?'" For the three blocks, the correct words are *weep / not / behold*.

Continue with the following stimulus statements; answers are in parentheses. Verse 5b: Who has done what (*Lion* [or *Root*] */ hath / prevailed*)? Verse 5c: What is the Lion able to do (*loose / the / seals* or *loose / seven / seals*)? Verse 6a: What did the creature look like (*a / Lamb / slain*)? Verse 6b: What three things appear in sevens (*horns / eyes / Spirits*)? Verse 7: How does the one on the throne grasp the unopened scroll (*the / right / hand*)? Verse 8: Who were the group of 24 and what did they

do (*elders / fell / down*)? Verse 9a, What were they singing (*a / new / song*)? Verse 9b: How had the Lamb redeemed the many (*by / thy / blood*)? Verse 10: What had the redeemed become (*kings / and / priests*)? Verse 11: How many multiples of 10,000 numbered the angels (*ten / thousand / times*)? Verse 12: What were the angels using to praise the Lamb (*a / loud / voice*)? Verse 13: Other than "in heaven, and on the earth" where were others praising the Lamb? Give two answers on two lines (*under / the / earth* and *in / the / sea*).

You may wish to have learners fill in their tables silently as you voice the clues. When everyone is finished, go over the results as a class. Note that the table is a good summary of today's text.

Into Life

Prepare copies of the following as commitment cards. Add simple clipart of a lamb if possible. Suggest that learners use their cards as Bible bookmarkers, to be seen during daily devotions.

Because He is the slain Lamb sitting on the throne, and because He is worthy by power, riches, wisdom, and strength, I will give Him honor and glory and blessing each week in worship assembly and in life! Signed _____.

Option 1: Before handing out the commitment cards, distribute copies of the "A Time to Weep, A Time Not to Weep" activity from the reproducible page, which you can download. If you choose to have learners complete this individually or in small groups, be sure to allow time for whole-class discussion of results.

Option 2: Distribute copies of the "Joining a Choir of Angels" activity from the reproducible page. Allow a few minutes for class members to suggest titles for other learners who may need their memories jogged. Then encourage personal use of the activity in the week ahead as the instructions suggest.

TRIUMPHANT AND VICTORIOUS

DEVOTIONAL READING: Psalm 47
BACKGROUND SCRIPTURE: Zechariah 9:9, 10; Matthew 21:1-11

ZECHARIAH 9:9, 10

9 Rejoice greatly, O daughter of Zion; shout, O daughter of Jerusalem: behold, thy King cometh unto thee: he is just, and having salvation; lowly, and riding upon an ass, and upon a colt the foal of an ass.

10 And I will cut off the chariot from Ephraim, and the horse from Jerusalem, and the battle bow shall be cut off: and he shall speak peace unto the heathen: and his dominion shall be from sea even to sea, and from river even to the ends of the earth.

MATTHEW 21:1-11

1 And when they drew nigh unto Jerusalem, and were come to Bethphage, unto the mount of Olives, then sent Jesus two disciples,

2 Saying unto them, Go into the village over against you, and straightway ye shall find an ass tied, and a colt with her: loose them, and bring them unto me.

3 And if any man say ought unto you, ye shall say, The Lord hath need of them; and straightway he will send them.

4 All this was done, that it might be fulfilled which was spoken by the prophet, saying,

5 Tell ye the daughter of Sion, Behold, thy King cometh unto thee, meek, and sitting upon an ass, and a colt the foal of an ass.

6 And the disciples went, and did as Jesus commanded them,

7 And brought the ass, and the colt, and put on them their clothes, and they set him thereon.

8 And a very great multitude spread their garments in the way; others cut down branches from the trees, and strawed them in the way.

9 And the multitudes that went before, and that followed, cried, saying, Hosanna to the Son of David: Blessed is he that cometh in the name of the Lord; Hosanna in the highest.

10 And when he was come into Jerusalem, all the city was moved, saying, Who is this?

11 And the multitude said, This is Jesus the prophet of Nazareth of Galilee.

KEY VERSE

The multitudes that went before, and that followed, cried, saying, Hosanna to the Son of David: Blessed is he that cometh in the name of the Lord; Hosanna in the highest. —**Matthew 21:9**

Graphic: Design Pics / Thinkstock

Jesus' Fulfillment of Scripture

Unit 2: What the Prophets Foretold
Lessons 5–9

Lesson Aims

After participating in this lesson, each student will be able to:

1. Tell the key details of Jesus' triumphal entry into Jerusalem in light of Zechariah's prophecy.

2. Explain the combination of humility and royalty that characterizes Jesus.

3. Express how he or she will demonstrate appropriate humility while also recognizing his or her privileged position as a child of King Jesus.

Lesson Outline

Introduction

A. Spotting Royalty

Can those of royal lineage be recognized by their physical appearance? Some in the nineteenth century thought so, as evidenced by the use of the phrase *blue blood* to describe the royal families of Europe. This phrase reflected a folk notion that the royals had a different kind of blood—blood that was blue in color rather than red.

The origin of this strange belief is thought to have come from the appearance of blue veins among members of royalty, the blueness being visible because of the paleness of their untanned skin. The blue veins of common folk, by contrast, were much less visible because their skin was tanned from working outdoors. We see an error in logic here: belief that having conspicuous blue veins (and therefore blue blood) caused one to be of royalty, when it was actually the other way around.

The first king of Israel was Saul, by direct appointment of God (1 Samuel 10:1). But God did not recognize any sense of "royal blood" flowing in that man's veins, as evident by God's choosing someone outside Saul's family to be the successor. Saul's outward appearance had been impressive (10:23), and the prophet Samuel seems to have been evaluating possible successors on that basis when God corrected him (16:5-7). David, the one eventually chosen, also had an impressive appearance (16:12), but that wasn't God's criteria.

God promised that David's house and kingdom would be established forever (2 Samuel 7:16). Thus we sense a royal bloodline here, especially since the lineage leads to and ends with Jesus, king of kings. But we quickly note that all this was due to God's choice and promise. Nationalistic expectations ran high on the day of Jesus' triumphal entry into Jerusalem. Yet it should not have been a time for spotting earthly "blue blood," but of recognizing God's provision for the nation.

B. Lesson Background

This week's lesson examines passages from the prophet Zechariah and the Gospel of Matthew. Zechariah (which means "the Lord remembers") is a very common name in the Bible, with

30 or more men so designated. The Zechariah of the book by that name was called by God to be a prophet, along with Haggai, to urge the Jews to rebuild the temple in Jerusalem (see Ezra 5:1). This Zechariah returned with the freed exiles to Judah to do so in about 536 BC. His recorded prophecies began in 520 BC (Zechariah 1:1) and continued for several years. The temple restoration was completed in 515 BC (Ezra 6:15).

The book of Zechariah is filled with symbolic images, making it difficult to interpret. It is also one of the most messianic of the Old Testament books, with many defining references to the coming Christ. There is an underlying sense in Zechariah's message that the temple had to be finished so that the king could come.

Perhaps some Jews expected the promised king, the promised son of David, to be made known shortly after the rebuilt temple was finished in 515 BC. But God had a plan that required another five and a half centuries before the promised king made His triumphal entry into Jerusalem. Matthew, drawing on Zechariah, interprets that event as nothing less than fulfilled prophecy.

I. The King Is Coming

(ZECHARIAH 9:9, 10)

In addition to rebuilding the altar and the temple in Jerusalem, those who return from exile reinstitute observance of holy days, restart sacrificial offerings, and organize priests to serve in the temple. But surely at least some of the people wonder why they are doing all this. We presume that they want to know what the future holds for Israel.

HOW TO SAY IT

Bethany	*Beth*-uh-nee.
Bethphage	*Beth*-fuh-gee.
Ephraim	*Ee*-fray-im.
Euphrates	You-*fray*-teez.
Jericho	*Jair*-ih-co.
Messiah	Meh-*sigh*-uh.
Messianic	Mess-ee-*an*-ick.
Zechariah	*Zek*-uh-*rye*-uh.
Zion (or Sion)	*Zi*-un.

Zechariah understands that there are bigger issues for his people than temple and land and nation: the people need an ultimate deliverer, a Messiah. To this need for a Savior, Zechariah speaks a word for the future.

A. Mighty and Humble (v. 9)

9. Rejoice greatly, O daughter of Zion; shout, O daughter of Jerusalem: behold, thy King cometh unto thee: he is just, and having salvation; lowly, and riding upon an ass, and upon a colt the foal of an ass.

This verse sets forth three characteristics of the coming king. First, *he is just,* being in complete harmony with the will of God. Second, he comes *having salvation;* the image of this future king is that of one returning from a battle in which his army has been successful and the nation is saved.

Third, he is *lowly,* a gentle and humble king, for he is presented as riding a young donkey. The horse is an animal of war (see the next verse), while the donkey is an animal of peace—an interesting contrast with the second characteristic just described.

What Do You Think?
How can you exhibit the qualities of Jesus noted here?
Talking Points for Your Discussion
- At work or school
- At home
- At church

Before we move on, we can pause to note parallels between the first two phrases. *Rejoice greatly* stands parallel with *shout*—two imperatives intended to mean the same thing. Likewise, *Zion* is a synonym for *Jerusalem.* Parallelism is a feature of Hebrew poetry, and we see similar treatments of *Zion* and *Jerusalem* in Psalms 102:21 and 147:12.

B. Powerful and Peaceful (v. 10)

10. And I will cut off the chariot from Ephraim, and the horse from Jerusalem, and the battle bow shall be cut off: and he shall speak peace unto the heathen: and his dominion shall be from sea even to sea, and from river even to the ends of the earth.

Visual for
Lesson 5

*Start a discussion by turning this statement into a
question: "How will you welcome Jesus today?"*

The designations *Ephraim* and *Jerusalem* represent the entire nation of Israel (compare Isaiah 7:17). Through the use of various images, Zechariah foretells the peace that the coming king will bring to the nation. His arrival signals the day when weapons of war are irrelevant. Through His king, the Lord *shall speak peace*, the end of war.

The territory of this peaceful kingdom is not just for the nation of Israel, but for the entire earth —pictured as being *from sea even to sea* and from *river* (perhaps the Euphrates River) *to the ends of the earth*. His reign will extend throughout the earth; no place will be exempt. There will be no small regional wars, no pockets of resistance. It will be peace, peace, peace, forever and ever!

❧ SPEAKING PEACE ❧

Quakerism got its start in seventeenth-century England. One historic emphasis of the Quakers is their peace testimony from "A Declaration to Charles II," of 1661. This testimony states:

> All bloody principles and practices, we, as to our own particulars, do utterly deny, with all outward wars and strife and fightings with outward weapons, for any end or under any pretence whatsoever. And this is our testimony to the whole world.
>
> . . . .
>
> [T]he spirit of Christ, which leads us into all Truth, will never move us to fight and war against any man with outward weapons, neither for the kingdom of Christ, nor for the kingdoms of this world.

Christians throughout the centuries have held different views on war. Indeed, misguided wars have been fought in the name of Jesus. Examples include the Crusades of the eleventh, twelfth, and thirteenth centuries to retake the holy land from "the infidels" and the wars of Europe in the sixteenth and seventeenth centuries.

When the prophet Zechariah predicted that the Messiah would "speak peace unto the heathen," he was predicting an important part of the Christian message. We may think that Christian pacifists misunderstand how we are to interact with the world in this regard, but "blessed are the peacemakers" (Matthew 5:9) is more than a nice platitude to be memorized along with the rest of the Beatitudes. We each need to ask ourselves, "What is my role in bringing the peace of Christ to those around me?"
—C. R. B.

II. The King Has Come
(MATTHEW 21:1-11)

Our next segment of text opens with Jesus and His disciples on the final leg of their pilgrimage to Jerusalem for Passover. Their arrival in Bethany (see below) is preceded by a walk from Jericho (Matthew 20:29). That is a distance of about 17 miles involving an ascent of some 3,300 feet in elevation. This can be walked in six to eight hours.

A. Direction and Supplication (vv. 1-3)

1a. And when they drew nigh unto Jerusalem, and were come to Bethphage, unto the mount of Olives.

John gives more detail, indicating that Jesus arrives "six days" before the Passover, spending time in the home of Mary, Martha, and Lazarus in Bethany (see John 12:1, 2). The two small villages of Bethany and Bethphage are on the eastern side of Jerusalem. The arrival is late Friday afternoon, for Jesus and His fellow Jews would not travel all the way from Jericho on a Sabbath day, which begins at sundown Friday night.

After the Sabbath, the group arrives at Bethphage (meaning "house of unripe figs"), which is near Bethany (see Mark 11:1). *The mount of Olives* is a north/south ridge that flanks the eastern side of Jerusalem. Bethany and Bethphage are on the far side of this mount, somewhat isolated from the city, yet conveniently close to it.

1b, 2. Then sent Jesus two disciples, saying unto them, Go into the village over against you, and straightway ye shall find an ass tied, and a colt with her: loose them, and bring them unto me.

Jesus now directs two trusted disciples to go into a nearby village (probably Bethphage) and look for a female donkey (a "jenny") that has a young *colt with her*. The expectation that the jenny is tied indicates the donkey is not out grazing or involved in work, but is ready and waiting for Jesus' purposes. She may be fitted with some type of halter that allows her to be tied to a post, readily available for being led back to Jesus. All four of the Gospels mention the younger donkey (compare Mark 11:2; Luke 19:30; John 12:14), but only Matthew includes the detail that there is an older female donkey as well.

3. And if any man say ought unto you, ye shall say, The Lord hath need of them; and straightway he will send them.

Jesus also instructs the disciples what to say if their borrowing of the donkeys is challenged. This gives us the impression that Jesus has prearranged the availability of the two animals. The reason for doing so is explained in the next verse.

> **What Do You Think?**
> When you sense that the Lord "hath need of" something from you, do you have a hard time releasing it to His service? Why, or why not?
> *Talking Points for Your Discussion*
> - Regarding abilities
> - Regarding money or possessions
> - Regarding a family member
> - Other

B. Prophecy and Fulfillment (vv. 4, 5)

4. All this was done, that it might be fulfilled which was spoken by the prophet, saying.

Jesus is aware that He is fulfilling the prophecy of Zechariah concerning the king coming into Jerusalem. In this, Jesus is enacting openly His role as Messiah to complete God's plan. Under-

standing this is important as an answer today to those who claim that Jesus never saw himself as the prophesied Messiah or Christ.

The prophecies of Zechariah and others are not fulfilled by random chance. The events they foresaw are pieces of God's deliberate plan, a plan carried out by Jesus. A key verse in understanding this is Matthew 5:17, which sets the tone for the entire book in the area of prophecy: "Think not that I am come to destroy the law, or the prophets: I am not come to destroy, but to fulfil." There is perfect convergence between the prophets, who were given a glimpse of God's plan, and the Messiah, who enacts the plan centuries later.

5. Tell ye the daughter of Sion, Behold, thy King cometh unto thee, meek, and sitting upon an ass, and a colt the foal of an ass.

So there is no mistake or ambiguity, Matthew gives an abbreviated version of Zechariah's prophecy. We noted earlier that Zion (here spelled *Sion*) is equivalent to Jerusalem. (The *daughter of* part comes from Isaiah 62:11.)

That city is overflowing with Passover pilgrims at this time. This feast temporarily increases Jerusalem's normal population of perhaps 50,000 by several times over. The people of Jerusalem represent the nation of Israel. Here is their king, the one Zechariah foretold. He is not riding a giant stallion with flaring nostrils, but a lowly donkey. We easily imagine Jesus' legs sticking out from the donkey's round belly, with Jesus' feet barely clearing the ground. He is the humble king—a contradiction of terms in the ancient world, but perfect in God's plan.

> **What Do You Think?**
> What do you learn about humility from Jesus that you can apply to your own life?
> *Talking Points for Your Discussion*
> - With regard to what others can see
> - With regard to what only God can see

C. Preparation and Spontaneity (vv. 6-9)

6, 7. And the disciples went, and did as Jesus commanded them, and brought the ass, and the colt, and put on them their clothes, and they set him thereon.

Matthew's account gives an impromptu sense to the preparations. By contrast, a triumphal procession in the city of Rome can take weeks to prepare. The Roman general or emperor receiving "the triumph" rides in a ceremonial chariot specially crafted for the event. The Roman triumphs consist of long parades of dignitaries, captured enemy soldiers and kings, and wagons heavy with the spoils of war. Such carefully planned spectacles sometimes include the erection of a new triumphal arch.

For the case at hand, however, the disciples make do with a borrowed donkey and improvised saddle gear from their own garments. The disciples do not hesitate to follow Jesus' commands by thinking about what they lack!

What Do You Think?

What commands of Jesus are Christians most likely to hesitate in following? Why?

Talking Points for Your Discussion

- Commands about loving one another
- Commands about making disciples
- Commands about helping the poor or others
- Other

---

8. And a very great multitude spread their garments in the way; others cut down branches from the trees, and strawed them in the way.

The nature of this event is contagious, and the crowd responds by paving the triumphal path of Jesus with their own garments and with freshly cut branches. Matthew does not specify the trees used as a source of the branches, but John identifies them as "palm trees" (John 12:13). The phrase *strawed them* brings to mind the spreading of fresh, clean straw in a stable or in a house that has a dirt floor.

The description *a very great multitude* can be understood as "the largest of crowds." Matthew knows of a crowd of 5,000 men (not counting women and children) that came to hear Jesus in Galilee (Matthew 14:21), and this Passover crowd seems to be even larger. This is the biggest thing happening in Jerusalem that day, with perhaps 10,000 or more people lining Jesus' path to the city. It is likely that many are from the Galilee region, come to Jerusalem for Passover.

9. And the multitudes that went before, and that followed, cried, saying, Hosanna to the Son of David: Blessed is he that cometh in the name of the Lord; Hosanna in the highest.

The acclamation of *the multitudes* has three parts, all pointing to Jesus as the promised Messiah. First, the people shout *Hosanna in the highest.* The word *Hosanna* is a Hebrew term that means "save now" (see Psalm 118:25). The people are awaiting God's Savior as promised by Zechariah and the other prophets.

Second, the people acclaim Jesus as *the Son of David,* a clear reference to the line of kings whom God promised to be an eternal dynasty (Psalm 89:3, 4). The crowd seems to know that Jesus is in the line of David (contrast the uncertainty of a previous occasion in John 7:41), and they apparently see Him as the king that Zechariah foresaw.

Third, the crowd gives Jesus a blessing from Psalm 118, a psalm that seems to portray the entry of David and his army into Jerusalem after a successful battle. Thus the crowd shouts *Blessed is he that cometh in the name of the Lord* (Psalm 118:26).

And so we have both sides: Jesus is publicly accepting and enacting His role as God's Messiah, and the Passover pilgrims of Jerusalem are embracing Him as that Messiah—or at least as the Messiah they think He should be. Jesus is the king entering the city as Zechariah foretold over 500 years earlier. Since that prophet's time, Israel has had a city, a temple, and a priesthood. Now the people see their king.

What Do You Think?

If Christ were to come riding into your town, what would people praise Him first for? What would this say about the state of people's hearts?

Talking Points for Your Discussion

- A spiritual issue
- A physical issue
- A relationship issue
- Other

❧ OCCUPY ... WHAT? ❧

The Great Recession of 2007 and the following years snatched away the jobs and savings of millions of Americans. On September 17, 2011, the Occupy Wall Street movement responded as a crowd gathered in New York City's Liberty Square. Originators of the movement said their goal was to fight "the crimes of Wall Street, government controlled by monied interests, and the resulting income inequality, unemployment, environmental destruction, and oppression of people at the front lines of the economic crisis."

The movement spread widely, often with other issues as the focus. Within six months, "Occupy" was demonstrating in hundreds of cities around the world. The phenomenon gave people who thought themselves to have suffered injustice a chance to express their frustration and alienation.

Many first-century Jews, weary of Roman repression, perhaps saw in Jesus the leader who could redress their grievances. Jesus could have staged His triumphal entry as an Occupy Jerusalem movement to play to this expectation, but He didn't. He came to solve a problem much greater than that of Roman dominance. He came to occupy our hearts, not our cities. "The kingdom of God cometh not with observation: . . . for, behold, the kingdom of God is within you" (Luke 17:20, 21).   —C. R. B.

D. Unknown and Identified (vv. 10, 11)

10. And when he was come into Jerusalem, all the city was moved, saying, Who is this?

Many in the joyous crowd are temporary residents of Jerusalem, having come to the city for the Feast of Unleavened Bread and Passover observances. Those who have found lodging outside the city (as Jesus and His disciples have) will walk into Jerusalem each day of the weeklong celebration. On this day, many such pilgrims accompany Jesus into the city, and the commotion is so great that *all the city* notices. The question of the day, though, is not "What's happening?" but *"Who is this?"*

11. And the multitude said, This is Jesus the prophet of Nazareth of Galilee.

Despite the previous acclamation of Jesus as "Son of David," *the multitude* gives a somewhat tame answer to the question of verse 10. The crowd identifies Him by name (*Jesus*), by hometown (*Nazareth of Galilee*), and by special vocation (*prophet*), but there is no language of Jesus as Messiah or king.

Even so, the designation of Jesus as a prophet seems to have a powerful effect on the city; it is the reason the Jewish leaders plot carefully and secretly to have Jesus arrested (see Matthew 21:46). We sometimes forget this aspect of Jesus' identity; we should keep in mind that Jesus spoke as a prophet, proclaiming God's kingdom and calling people to repentance (see Matthew 4:17).

Conclusion

A. Come to Save

The triumphal entry of Jesus was the opening act of what we call Passion Week. That entry was an extraordinary moment of glory for Jesus, but one that He could not savor for long. He was not fooled by the fickle crowd, and He knew the threat posed by the Jewish leadership was real. The cross lay ahead, and His fate was sure. He did not conquer Jerusalem; He did not claim the earthly crown of David; He raised no triumphal arch; He did not lead an army against the Romans. He was dead by the end of the week.

I wonder . . . why do we continue to celebrate Jesus' triumphal entry? Why is it mentioned in all four Gospels and given a day on the church calendar? Maybe the answer is something like this: we celebrate Christ's coming into the city because we so desperately want Him to come again. We want Him to make the words "on earth peace" (Luke 2:14) and "peace in heaven" (19:38) a final reality. We long for Him to come, save us, and take us home. Hosanna to the king! May He be king forever.

B. Prayer

Father, we thank You for sending us our king, mighty in glory, yet humble and meek. We thank You for our Savior, the one who rescues us from our sins. Help us ever to look forward to that great day when He will return to claim us for all eternity. We pray in His name, Jesus, amen.

C. Thought to Remember

Welcome the king into your life.

INVOLVEMENT LEARNING

Some of the activities below are also found in the helpful student book, Adult Bible Class.
Don't forget to download the free reproducible page from www.standardlesson.com to enhance your lesson!

Into the Lesson

Post some pictures of horses around your classroom. (You might find a very inexpensive calendar with horse pictures at this point in the year at a dollar store.) Also display the following matching quiz under the heading "Whose Horse?"

Blackie	a. Alexander the Great
Blueskin	b. George Washington
Bucephalus	c. Napoleon Bonaparte
Marengo	d. Dwight Eisenhower
Traveler	e. Robert E. Lee

After a minute of silent work, discuss answers (*Blackie, d; Blueskin, b; Bucephalus, a; Marengo, c; Traveler, e.*). Say, "Famous generals often rode horses. But we have a different picture today: the greatest king of all time riding a lowly donkey!"

Option: Before class begins, place in chairs copies of the "Zechariah Said What!?" activity from the reproducible page, which you can download. Learners can begin working on this as they arrive.

Into the Word

Set up for a dramatized "person on the street" interview by having your learners seated in facing rows to depict the crowd-lined roadway of today's text. Have learners take turns reading the verses of the two texts aloud; before they do, ask everyone to make a mental effort to "see" the events through the eyes of a first-century person who was familiar with Zechariah's prophecy and was present in Jerusalem as Jesus arrived.

After the texts from Zechariah and Matthew are read, say, "I'm going to play the part of a roving reporter. I have questions for those of you who just witnessed Jesus ride by." (You may wish to tell your learners that one thing that makes dramatized interviews nonthreatening is that participants can avoid being interviewed with responses such as "I didn't really see anything" or "I'm sorry, I don't like to talk politics.")

Add effect by carrying a microphone as you ask the following questions or those of your own devising. 1. "Did the guy who just rode through here match what you expected from Zechariah's prophecy?" (Follow up with "Why?" or "Why not?") 2. "What should a person expect to see when a victorious king rides into a conquered or newly freed city?" 3. "What is there about Zechariah's description of the king that encourages you based on what you just saw?" 4. "Were rejoicing and shouting appropriate for the arrival of the man who just rode through here?" (Follow up with "Why?" or "Why not?") 5. "I understand you were one of those Jesus sent on an errand. What exactly did He tell you to do? Did it make sense?" 6. "What's the point of all these palm branches scattered around here?" 7. "I'm not Jewish, so the word *Hosanna* that the crowd shouted confuses me. What does it mean?" 8. "Some of you seem a little confused about the identity of the man who just rode through. What was the explanation?" (Follow up with "Did it make sense?") 9. "Why are you in Jerusalem today? Did this ruin your plans?" 10. "What did the crowds mean by 'Son of David'?"

Into Life

Give each learner a small image of a donkey. Use this to start a discussion about what has to happen for people to "get off their high horse," as the saying goes, in order to see their need for Jesus. Ask, "How does the concept of *privilege* come into play when one moves from a 'high horse' to a donkey?" Challenge learners to post their images where they will see them often in the week ahead as a reminder of the privileged position of humility we share with our Lord.

Distribute copies of the "Jesus Who?" activity from the reproducible page. Since this calls for very personal reflection, it is best used as a take-home exercise.

JESUS CLEANSES THE TEMPLE

DEVOTIONAL READING: Psalm 27:1-5
BACKGROUND SCRIPTURE: Isaiah 56:6-8; Jeremiah 7:8-15; Mark 11:15-19

ISAIAH 56:6, 7

6 Also the sons of the stranger, that join themselves to the LORD, to serve him, and to love the name of the LORD, to be his servants, every one that keepeth the sabbath from polluting it, and taketh hold of my covenant;

7 Even them will I bring to my holy mountain, and make them joyful in my house of prayer: their burnt offerings and their sacrifices shall be accepted upon mine altar; for mine house shall be called an house of prayer for all people.

JEREMIAH 7:9-11

9 Will ye steal, murder, and commit adultery, and swear falsely, and burn incense unto Baal, and walk after other gods whom ye know not;

10 And come and stand before me in this house, which is called by my name, and say, We are delivered to do all these abominations?

11 Is this house, which is called by my name, become a den of robbers in your eyes? Behold, even I have seen it, saith the LORD.

MARK 11:15-19

15 And they come to Jerusalem: and Jesus went into the temple, and began to cast out them that sold and bought in the temple, and overthrew the tables of the moneychangers, and the seats of them that sold doves;

16 And would not suffer that any man should carry any vessel through the temple.

17 And he taught, saying unto them, Is it not written, My house shall be called of all nations the house of prayer? but ye have made it a den of thieves.

18 And the scribes and chief priests heard it, and sought how they might destroy him: for they feared him, because all the people was astonished at his doctrine.

19 And when even was come, he went out of the city.

KEY VERSE

Is this house, which is called by my name, become a den of robbers in your eyes? —**Jeremiah 7:11**

Photo: iStockphoto / Thinkstock

JESUS' FULFILLMENT OF SCRIPTURE

Unit 2: What the Prophets Foretold
LESSONS 5–9

LESSON AIMS

After participating in this lesson, each student will be able to:

1. Describe the temple cleansing in Mark's Gospel, noting the events that took place and their prophetic significance.

2. Compare and contrast the need for the temple's cleansing with the need for a "cleansing" in one's own life or church.

3. Write a prayer of confession for one needed area of cleansing the temple of 1 Corinthians 6:19.

LESSON OUTLINE

Introduction

A. Getting It Clean

I like having a clean car, and one of my challenges is getting the windows clean inside and out. I use a well-known window cleaner and seem to go through the spray bottles of this product and rolls of paper towels quickly. When I'm finished, the windows of my car always pass the "eye test" for cleanliness. There is no visible grime. Invariably, though, I will be driving in the morning or evening when the sun is at a low angle and will see areas of the windshield that are not clear. Despite all my careful efforts, I still end up with some smears.

Then I wonder if I'm being too picky. How clean is clean enough? Should I care that certain sunlight conditions reveal a few smudges? We all have different standards of cleanliness. Some people keep themselves fastidiously clean to the point of obsession. Others are more satisfied with a general appearance of being clean. Still others seem not to care much if their clothes, etc., are clean at all.

In today's lesson, Jesus and the prophets will help us understand cleanliness from God's perspective. This is not a lesson about washing cars or personal hygiene. It is about spiritual purpose. It is about scrubbing clean the house of God.

B. Lesson Background

The thoughts of the prophets Isaiah and Jeremiah that are included in this week's lesson come from books that are right next to each other in our Bibles. Because of this proximity, we may think that their authors were colleagues, but they were not. Their ministries were separated by many years and addressed different historical situations.

Isaiah began his lengthy prophetic ministry in about 740 BC (see Isaiah 6:1). Today's text from Isaiah comes from the part commonly known as the Book of Consolation, namely Isaiah 40–66. Some prophecies in this section address the time when God's chosen servant (Jesus) will come to restore justice and bear the sins of the people (see Isaiah 42:1; 53:11).

Jeremiah's lengthy prophetic ministry began about 626 BC, or some 55 years after the end of Isaiah's ministry. The Assyrian menace of Isaiah's day was gone, only to be replaced by threats from Babylon. Jeremiah's relentless warnings always seemed to fall on deaf ears. Persecuted by his own people, Jeremiah lived to see the fall of Jerusalem in 586 BC (Jeremiah 52). The text from Jeremiah in today's lesson comes from his message at the gate of the temple, where he warned that the mere presence of that grand, 400-year-old edifice was no guarantee of blessing or protection by the Lord.

Jesus' action of cleansing the temple occurred some 600 years after the time of Jeremiah. The temple of Jesus' day was the second such structure of the Israelites, completed by Zerubbabel in 515 BC (Ezra 6:15) and expanded by King Herod and his successors just before and during the time of Jesus (John 2:20). Herod's version of the temple was an architectural wonder, having huge courtyards and beautiful stonework. Yet beneath the temple's splendid exterior was a crass commercialism that profited at the expense of those on pilgrimage to Jerusalem for the Passover observance. This problem needed to be addressed.

I. Worldwide Focus
(ISAIAH 56:6, 7)

A. For Everyone (v. 6)

6. Also the sons of the stranger, that join themselves to the LORD, to serve him, and to love the name of the LORD, to be his servants, every one that keepeth the sabbath from polluting it, and taketh hold of my covenant.

A consistent vision in the prophecies of Isaiah is that of Jerusalem as a center of justice, "The city of righteousness, the faithful city" (Isaiah 1:26). Even so, the prophet is well aware that the Jerusalem of his day falls far short of this ideal.

Isaiah also sees the temple of Jerusalem as a center of worship for all people, not just the nation of Israel (Isaiah 2:3). *The sons of the stranger* are Gentiles, those who are not part of the nation of Israel. Isaiah prophesies a future when these outsiders will be welcomed as part of the people of God.

Three characteristics are given to describe that future reality. The first is that the included Gentiles will *join themselves to the Lord*—not as conquered people, but as those who make a deliberate

choice for commitment to the God of Israel. This commitment is defined immediately in terms of the Gentiles' dedication *to serve* the Lord, devotion to *the name of the Lord,* and willingness to be the Lord's *servants.* These might seem repetitive, but there are distinct concepts here.

First, to be dedicated to the Lord's service has the sense of exclusive worship; this echoes the First Commandment: "Thou shalt have no other gods before me" (Exodus 20:3). *To love the name of the Lord* reminds us of the Third Commandment: "Thou shalt not take the name of the Lord thy God in vain" (Exodus 20:7). *To be his servants* is literally to be the Lord's slaves, fully sold out to doing His will. That reminds us of Jesus' choice for the greatest commandment: "thou shalt love the Lord thy God with all thy heart, and with all thy soul, and with all thy mind, and with all thy strength" (Mark 12:29, 30; compare Deuteronomy 6:5; see lesson 13).

A second characteristic of the included Gentiles is their respect for *the sabbath.* This respect involves much more than a commitment to attend a worship service. It is a commitment to honor God's instructions for a day where everything slows down to allow for rest and reflection, away from the pressures and frenzy of labor.

The third characteristic is all-encompassing: to take *hold of [God's] covenant.* This is the bottom line. To be included among the people of the Lord, one must commit to a covenant relationship with Him. In the most basic sense, this is expressed in the Old Testament as "I will walk among you, and will be your God, and ye shall be my people" (Leviticus 26:12; see also Jeremiah 11:4; Ezekiel 36:28).

HOW TO SAY IT

Bethany	*Beth*-uh-nee.
denarii	dih-*nair*-ee or dih-*nair*-eye.
Herod	*Hair*-ud.
Josephus	Jo-*see*-fus.
shekels	*she*-kulz.
Tyre	Tire.
Tyrian	*Tir*-ee-un.
Zerubbabel	Zeh-*rub*-uh-bul.

Churches often have difficulty adjusting to change. Some have split over styles of worship. Increasing informality in clothing styles has created tension in others. Changing demographics in the neighborhood can create problems or opportunities, depending on one's viewpoint. For example, take the case of a certain big-city congregation that had a large campus featuring a 1,000-seat sanctuary. As the years passed, this once-thriving congregation dwindled to a few dozen worshippers as the surrounding community changed from being mostly white to being predominantly people of Asian descent.

The church tried to adapt by inviting Christians of Asian descent to worship in the small chapel on the campus. Soon the chapel was bursting at the seams as those believers outgrew their meeting area. Even so, the original congregation (or what was left of it) kept meeting in the cavernous auditorium, which only gave increasing testimony to that group's declining numbers.

Isaiah challenged the people of his day to see that God wanted the doors of His house open even to Gentiles. The Bible sets forth our responsibility to recognize that the gospel is for everyone. Are we limiting our fellowship only to Christians who are "like us"? —C. R. B.

What Do You Think?
What roadblocks do churches erect that restrict inclusion of "the stranger"? How do we tear down these roadblocks?
Talking Points for Your Discussion
- Regarding routines and traditions
- Regarding stances on political issues
- Regarding worship styles
- Other

B. For Prayer (v. 7)

7. Even them will I bring to my holy mountain, and make them joyful in my house of prayer: their burnt offerings and their sacrifices shall be accepted upon mine altar; for mine house shall be called an house of prayer for all people.

The *holy mountain* is the temple location in Jerusalem. Isaiah's prophecy understands this to be a future place of joy, a place for proper sacrifices, and a place for prayer. Our impression of the functions of the temple might naturally include the first two of these three (see Psalm 100 and 1 Kings 8:62-64, respectively). What we may forget is that the temple is to be seen as a place of prayer; this function of the temple was offered to Gentiles from the beginning of its existence (see 1 Kings 8:41-43).

The marvelous thing about Isaiah's prophecy is that the temple will be understood to be a *house of prayer for all people.* Isaiah's ideal is more than that of a restored Israel—he sees a future when all nations will be united in worship of the Lord. As we shall see later in this lesson, the God-intended function of the Jerusalem temple as a worldwide house of prayer is a factor in Jesus' furious cleansing of the temple of His day.

II. Corrupt Den
(Jeremiah 7:9-11)

A. Lawbreakers' Lack of Shame (vv. 9, 10)

9, 10. Will ye steal, murder, and commit adultery, and swear falsely, and burn incense unto Baal, and walk after other gods whom ye know not; and come and stand before me in this house, which is called by my name, and say, We are delivered to do all these abominations?

Isaiah's grand vision of the temple as a place dedicated to prayer for all people clashes with the harsh reality of the temple in Jeremiah's day. Rather than functioning as a place where people get right with God through prayer and sacrifice, the temple seems to have become a sanctuary for those who break commandments with impunity. The abominations that the people feel free to commit are all specifics from the Ten Commandments: theft (Eighth Commandment), murder (Sixth), adultery (Seventh), swear falsely (Ninth), and worship of other gods (First).

The blatant hypocrisy of this situation is shocking! Jeremiah describes people whose sins are public knowledge, but who still present themselves as temple worshippers in good standing.

B. The Lord's Full Awareness (v. 11)

11. Is this house, which is called by my name, become a den of robbers in your eyes? Behold, even I have seen it, saith the LORD.

Things are so bad that the temple can be characterized as *a den of robbers*. People seem to be under the illusion that the temple in and of itself has the power to protect them no matter what they do (see Jeremiah 7:4). But God knows what is plotted behind the closed doors of the human heart. The fact that the temple does not provide "magical" protection for unrepentant sinners will be apparent when God allows the temple to be destroyed.

Let us keep two thoughts in mind as we come to our primary lesson text: (1) Isaiah's ideal vision of the temple as *a house of prayer*, and (2) Jeremiah's evaluation of the temple of his day as *a den of robbers*.

III. Cleansed Temple
(MARK 11:15-19)

A. Commerce Halted (vv. 15, 16)

15, 16. And they come to Jerusalem: and Jesus went into the temple, and began to cast out them that sold and bought in the temple, and overthrew the tables of the moneychangers, and the seats of them that sold doves; and would not suffer that any man should carry any vessel through the temple.

Jesus entered Jerusalem triumphantly (last week's lesson) the day before the action we see here. Having done a reconnaissance of the temple after that triumphal entry, He has returned after spending the night in Bethany. The word *they* refers to Jesus and the Twelve (Mark 11:11).

Herod's grandly remodeled temple has acres of space in its courtyards. These courtyards seem to be given over to commercial activities in Jesus' day. Thousands of pilgrims are in Jerusalem for Passover; most are Jews, but there are Gentiles in town as well. The local merchants seize upon this annual opportunity with gusto. They set up shop inside the temple's courtyards to conduct two businesses that are specifically mentioned by Mark.

First, there are *the moneychangers*. These people exchange the coins of foreigners for the only kind acceptable for paying the temple tax: the silver shekels of the city of Tyre. This is not a service of the temple, but a for-profit business. Even with competition, it is likely that these moneychangers make a substantial profit on each transaction. Those visitors to Jerusalem who do not otherwise have access to Tyrian shekels have little choice but to fork over their silver denarii or other coins at unfavorable exchange rates in order to get the coins that are acceptable in the temple.

Second, there are merchants who sell birds and animals that can be used in the temple to fulfill the pilgrims' sacrificial needs. These animals are raised for this purpose in the pastures of the surrounding villages. Josephus, a first-century Jewish historian, claims that over 250,000 lambs were sacrificed during Passover in AD 66, a staggering number! Even when we acknowledge that historian's penchant for exaggeration, this is big business at Passover time, undoubtedly including pens for sheep, etc. (compare John 2:14).

For the visitor to the temple, this is a little like buying a meal in an airport for us. Because those at the airport are a "captive audience," the food vendors are able to charge high prices. While everyone resents such an arrangement, it has been the accepted arrangement for temple worshippers. But Jesus does not accept this situation. He does not tolerate a temple turned into a shop for sharp currency exchangers and a market for overpriced livestock. So He drives out both *them that sold and bought in the temple*, bringing the bustling commerce there to a halt, at least temporarily.

B. Leaders Shaken (vv. 17-19)

17. And he taught, saying unto them, Is it not written, My house shall be called of all nations the house of prayer? but ye have made it a den of thieves.

Jesus uses His bold action for teaching, recalling the words of Isaiah and Jeremiah. Isaiah's hopeful vision of the temple as an international *house of prayer* is unfulfilled. Instead, the temple of Jesus' day has become again the temple of Jeremiah's day, *a den of thieves*. The word *den* brings to mind the image of a cave in which dangerous predators might live. The thieves can be thought of as financial predators.

Jesus' pronouncement also has two dire implications. First, it indicts the leaders of the temple as criminal coconspirators. The fact that these leaders tolerate the commercialism suggests that they profit from the sharp practices, perhaps "getting a cut" of the proceeds. Second, Jesus' pronouncement foreshadows a future for the temple of His day similar to that of the temple of Jeremiah's day. As the first temple was destroyed back then, so also Herod's temple will be destroyed—which

ends up happening at the hands of the Romans in AD 70. God is not to be mocked. His holy mountain, His designated house of prayer, is a travesty, and (as Jeremiah said) God has been watching.

❧ WAS IT REALLY "JUST BUSINESS"? ❧

In July 1897, two ships carrying miners with bags of gold from the Yukon sailed into port in Seattle and San Francisco. When word got out, the great Klondike Gold Rush was on!

Those who intended to profit from the discovery of gold quickly divided themselves into two groups: *the stampeders* (that is, the miners or prospectors) and *the outfitters*. In less than six months, 100,000 stampeders had headed off for the Alaskan Yukon, but only about a third completed the difficult trip. Of those who did, only about 4,000 found any gold at all.

As things turned out, most of those to "get rich quick" were the outfitters—those who sold supplies to the miners. Each miner was required to have about a ton of supplies before the Northwest Mounted Police allowed him to cross the border into Canada. As you can imagine, profiteering at the expense of the eager stampeders was rampant.

One way to view that situation is that it was "just business"—after all, none of the stampeders was being *forced* to buy supplies at inflated prices, right? The same could be said of the merchants (outfitters) in the temple precincts. Were they not merely providing a valuable service to those who could voluntarily choose not to trade with them? Jesus looked at the situation in the temple a bit deeper than that, and so should we.   —C. R. B.

18, 19. And the scribes and chief priests heard it, and sought how they might destroy him: for they feared him, because all the people was astonished at his doctrine. And when even was come, he went out of the city.

We wonder what happens at the temple just after Jesus cleanses it. We can imagine that the moneychangers and merchants straighten things up and return to "business as usual" as soon as He leaves. Jesus has no legal authority to change anything, and greed has been trumping holiness in this place for a long time.

What Do You Think?

What can we do to ensure that various kinds of "greed" do not trump holiness in the church?

Talking Points for Your Discussion

- Regarding "approval greed" (watered-down messages, etc.)
- Regarding "safety greed" (hoarding funds instead of using them for ministry, etc.)
- Other

There is a consequence, however, when *the scribes and chief priests* hear about Jesus' action. They are not pleased, so they continue to seek *how they might destroy him.* We say "continue" because Jewish leaders were plotting to kill Jesus even before this episode (see John 11:45-53). The temple operation is their livelihood. Jesus' challenge is a threat, made more dangerous because of His popularity. We can imagine onlookers cheering the one who is not afraid to confront extortionist practices.

Conclusion

A. The Church Off Target

Having served on the ministry staffs of several congregations, I know how easy it is for a church to get off target. Sometimes the diversions that present themselves seem like the right thing to do. Establish a day care center? Let's do it! Maintain a cemetery for the membership? Yes! Sponsor a softball team? It's what the people want!

Well-intentioned projects and programs may be worthy of consideration, but not at the expense of the core ministries of the church. These core ministries have been expressed in various ways, but a simplified (some would say oversimplified) categorization is that the core ministries can be grouped in terms of *outreach* (Matthew 28:19, 20), *upreach* (John 4:23, 24), and *inreach* (Ephesians 4:11-13).

Sometimes a church needs to clear the clutter and clarify its priorities. As hard as it may be to do, sometimes we need to purge our programs in order to get back on target. But be forewarned: as Jesus' cleansing of the temple met with opposition, a reevaluation of church programs and activities may cause turmoil and congregational strife. Even

so, a failure to clear the clutter may indicate that a church has lost its "first love," with the resulting danger of losing its light (Revelation 2:4, 5).

B. The Christian Off Target

The personal life of a Christian believer may be a smaller version of the cluttered church. Many of us struggle to get (or stay) on target with God's will. We are easily distracted by seemingly worthy things, so we forget to pray. We may even get to the point of neglecting to meet with other believers for worship (Hebrews 10:25). A lack of focus is sometimes clarified by a traumatic event that puts things in perspective—we end up realizing that busyness does not equal godliness, that overcommitment leads to commitment breakdown, etc. Is there a cluttered area of your life that hinders you from serving your Lord fully? Paul's question in 1 Corinthians 6:19 can help us evaluate our lives: "What? know ye not that your body is the temple of the Holy Ghost which is in you?"

C. Prayer

Holy God, may our churches be dedicated to Your service only. May our lives be focused on doing Your will. Cleanse us of distractions through the power of Your Holy Spirit. We pray this in the name of the fearless Jesus, amen.

D. Thought to Remember

Keep God's temple clean.

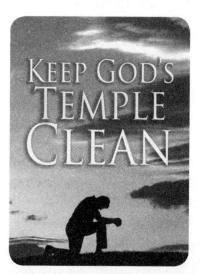

Visual for Lesson 6

Point to this visual as you pose the discussion question associated with verses 18, 19.

INVOLVEMENT LEARNING

Some of the activities below are also found in the helpful student book, Adult Bible Class.
Don't forget to download the free reproducible page from www.standardlesson.com to enhance your lesson!

Into the Lesson

Have a variety of cleaning products (soaps, sprays, etc.) and implements (mop, broom, etc.) on display. As each learner arrives and moves toward a chair, approach with a whisk broom and say, "Here, let me clean that seat for you." Quickly make an exaggerated show of brushing the chair. As you begin class, say, "April is a traditional time for spring cleaning. Today's text reveals implications of spiritual cleanliness. Let's take a look."

Into the Word

Have one learner read aloud Isaiah 56:6, 7 and another read Jeremiah 7:9-11. Summarize the opposite ways that the Old Testament temple is characterized in these two passages: ideally as a "house of prayer," but in reality as "a den of robbers." Then read Mark 11:15-19 aloud as you point out the reality of the situation in Jesus' day, hundreds of years after Isaiah and Jeremiah.

Next, give each learner a handout titled *"House of Prayer* or *Den of Robbers?"* On the left, have reproduced the floor plan of the temple of Jesus' day (easy to find on the Internet or a Bible atlas). On the right, have a generic outline of a human figure with "1 Corinthians 6:19" printed underneath it.

Draw learners' attention to the courtyard areas of the temple complex where Jesus most likely undertook the "cleansing." Then pose this discussion question, printed on the bottom of the handout: "What could the temple leaders of Jesus' day have done (1) to ensure that the peoples' offerings and sacrifices were acceptable to God while (2) not enriching themselves in the process and (3) not introducing noisy distractions for people who were praying in the temple area?" Follow up by asking, "Why did the temple officials of Jesus' day not see the problem of Jeremiah 7:9-11 in their practices?" Be prepared to give some modern examples of how people tend to rationalize behavior.

Into Life

Point to the human figure on the handout and comment further that the two outcomes "house of prayer" or "den of robbers" are definite possibilities for the temple of the New Testament era—us.

Form learners into small groups, then pose this question: "What are some things that do not belong in the temple of the New Testament era?" Have learners jot their ideas outside the outline of the human figure on the handout.

After a few minutes, discuss conclusions. Some obvious entries will be behaviors such as adultery, lying, and thievery. Entries involving attitude can be greed, thinking evil thoughts of others (as the scribes and chief priests did), etc.

Shift the discussion to the positive by saying, "Now think of some things that *do* belong in the temple of the New Testament era." Have learners jot their ideas inside the outline of the human figure. Some obvious entries are servant attitude, reverence for God's Word, joy, prayer, sacrificial offerings, righteous indignation over sin, and concern for pure doctrine.

Alternative: Instead of the above, have learners complete the "From Then to Now" activity on the reproducible page, which you can download.

Option: Expand this discussion by having learners complete the "Wash Me!" exercise on the reproducible page. Learners should work individually since the exercise calls for personal evaluation. Conduct a whole-class discussion as you ask, "Which passage do you find most convicting? Why?" Do not put anyone on the spot, but be prepared to answer the question yourself.

To conclude, give each learner a photo of your class beneath which you have reproduced Psalm 51, David's expression of "feeling dirty" because of his sin. Comment: "Each of us has had the occasion when the petitions of David reflected our own. Post this where you can use it in your prayer occasions for a time. Memorize verse 10."

A MESSIANIC PRIEST-KING

DEVOTIONAL READING: Hebrews 7:11-19
BACKGROUND SCRIPTURE: Jeremiah 23:5, 6; Zechariah 6:9-15;
John 19:1-5; Hebrews 7:13

JEREMIAH 23:5, 6

5 Behold, the days come, saith the LORD, that I will raise unto David a righteous Branch, and a King shall reign and prosper, and shall execute judgment and justice in the earth.

6 In his days Judah shall be saved, and Israel shall dwell safely: and this is his name whereby he shall be called, THE LORD OUR RIGHTEOUSNESS.

ZECHARIAH 6:9-15

9 And the word of the LORD came unto me, saying,

10 Take of them of the captivity, even of Heldai, of Tobijah, and of Jedaiah, which are come from Babylon, and come thou the same day, and go into the house of Josiah the son of Zephaniah;

11 Then take silver and gold, and make crowns, and set them upon the head of Joshua the son of Josedech, the high priest;

12 And speak unto him, saying, Thus speaketh the LORD of hosts, saying, Behold the man whose name is The BRANCH; and he shall grow up out of his place, and he shall build the temple of the LORD:

13 Even he shall build the temple of the LORD; and he shall bear the glory, and shall sit and rule upon his throne; and he shall be a priest upon his throne: and the counsel of peace shall be between them both.

14 And the crowns shall be to Helem, and to Tobijah, and to Jedaiah, and to Hen the son of Zephaniah, for a memorial in the temple of the LORD.

15 And they that are far off shall come and build in the temple of the LORD, and ye shall know that the LORD of hosts hath sent me unto you. And this shall come to pass, if ye will diligently obey the voice of the LORD your God.

JOHN 19:1-5

1 Then Pilate therefore took Jesus, and scourged him.

2 And the soldiers platted a crown of thorns, and put it on his head, and they put on him a purple robe,

3 And said, Hail, King of the Jews! and they smote him with their hands.

4 Pilate therefore went forth again, and saith unto them, Behold, I bring him forth to you, that ye may know that I find no fault in him.

5 Then came Jesus forth, wearing the crown of thorns, and the purple robe. And Pilate saith unto them, Behold the man!

KEY VERSE

[The soldiers] said, Hail, King of the Jews! and they smote him with their hands. —**John 19:3**

JESUS' FULFILLMENT OF SCRIPTURE

Unit 2: What the Prophets Foretold

LESSONS 5–9

LESSON AIMS

After participating in this lesson, each student will be able to:

1. List what Pilate and the soldiers did to Jesus.

2. Explain the significance of "branch" imagery as applied to Jesus.

3. Attend a Good Friday service in the week ahead.

LESSON OUTLINE

Introduction

A. Branches

When my family lived in the Seattle area, we occasionally hiked a favorite trail that wound through a forest of red cedar trees. Such trees are cousins of the giant redwoods of California and can easily reach 200 feet in height. That little forest, now protected, had been logged in the nineteenth century. Today, one can still see the colossal, dead stumps—some over 6 feet wide—of giant trees cut down long ago.

But not all of the stumps died. Some have sprouted, and some of the resulting trees are now over a century old. The newer trees are not yet 200 feet tall, but eventually they will be if left alone. The seeds of the stumps yielded both the possibility and the fact of new life. That is the vital imagery of this week's lesson.

B. Lesson Background

The Old Testament portions of our lesson come from Jeremiah and Zechariah. The ministry contexts of those two prophets were discussed in lessons 6 and 5, respectively, so that information need not be repeated here. Instead, we will take a brief look at the Old Testament's puzzling way of referring to the promised Messiah as *the branch*.

For some, the word *branch* creates a mental image of a tree limb that has fallen in the yard during a windstorm, a fallen branch. Others may envision a suburban bank, a branch office. Still others may think of a subfield of a major field of study, such as microbiology as a branch of biology.

None of these ideas really captures the biblical concept of the Messiah as *the branch*. The concept is more along the lines of new growth—a fresh, green manifestation of life. It is an idea of "the new coming out of the old."

A vivid example is found in Isaiah 6. Many of us are familiar with verses 1-8 of that chapter, which describe the prophet's dramatic call. But the verses that follow may not be as familiar: Isaiah's ministry was to be met with hard hearts, and devastation would result. But then comes a glimmer of hope. Though fallen Israel would be like the mere stump of a once-great tree, within this seemingly dead stump was "the holy seed" (v. 13) This was the latent branch, the sprout, the hope for Israel's renewal and restoration: the Messiah.

The apostle John was an eyewitness to the ministry of Jesus, and John was very familiar with Old Testament prophecies about Jesus (example: John 19:37). John probably wrote his Gospel after the destruction of Jerusalem and its temple in AD 70 by the Romans, creating some interesting parallels between John's perspectives and those of the prophets who worked centuries before him.

I. The Righteous Branch-King
(JEREMIAH 23:5, 6)

The overall tone of the book of Jeremiah is that of doom and warning. Expressions of "woe" are frequent (examples: Jeremiah 4:13; 10:19) as befitting Jeremiah's life situation. Yet there are passages in his book that reveal a sparkling, vibrant hope for the future, and 23:5, 6 is one of them.

A. Heir of David (v. 5)

5. Behold, the days come, saith the LORD, that I will raise unto David a righteous Branch, and a King shall reign and prosper, and shall execute judgment and justice in the earth.

There are several places in the Old Testament where the coming Messiah is referred to as a (or the) *Branch* (examples: Isaiah 4:2; Zechariah 3:8), but the passage before us gives us the fullest picture of the one to come. We are told first that the Branch will be raised up by the Lord, provided by God himself. Second, this person will be *unto David,* meaning an heir in the line of that king.

Third, this heir will be righteous, one who follows God in heart and conduct. Fourth, the Branch will be *a King* whose reign will be prosperous. Fifth, the Branch will also be a judge, called to enact justice. Surely there has never been one yet to rule as the Branch will!

B. Savior of Israel (v. 6)

6. In his days Judah shall be saved, and Israel shall dwell safely: and this is his name whereby he shall be called, THE LORD OUR RIGHTEOUSNESS.

Both the person of the Branch and the time of His arrival are important. Here we are told that He will appear at the appropriate time (*in his days*), at a time of crisis when Judah/Israel needs to be rescued from danger. This timing is determined by the Lord, for He is the one who sends the Branch on the rescue mission.

The way the Branch is identified is significant for Jeremiah's people. The king of Judah at the time is Zedekiah, whose name means "righteousness," and he is the last king of Judah (see Jeremiah 21:1; 24:8). The designation of the branch-king as *our Righteousness* comes across rather literally from the Hebrew as *Zedkenuah.* The similarity between that designation and the name Zedekiah is therefore a rebuke to Zedekiah, who follows the evil ways of previous kings (2 Kings 24:19). His eventual rebellion against the king of Babylon leads directly to the destruction of Jerusalem in 586 BC.

Zedekiah's selfish and stubborn ways reveal his lack of trust in the Lord. The coming king, by contrast, will speak for all the people in His right words and right actions; He truly will be *The Lord our Righteousness.*

> **What Do You Think?**
> How will you allow the Lord to become "your righteousness" more and more on a daily basis? Why is it important for this to happen?
> *Talking Points for Your Discussion*
> - Psalm 45:7
> - Matthew 5:20
> - 1 Timothy 4:7
> - Titus 2:12

II. The Building Branch-King
(ZECHARIAH 6:9-15)

We now move to Zechariah, a prophet in Jerusalem after the return from exile of 538 BC. His book divides into two main parts. The first part (1:7 –6:8) describes a series of night visions on February 15, 519 BC, in Jerusalem. Their overall theme is that God has arranged everything needed for the temple rebuilding to be finished, a task the people accomplish in 515 BC. Today's text marks the beginning of the second main part of the book.

A. Crowns of Gold and Silver (vv. 9-11)

9. And the word of the LORD came unto me, saying.

This short verse tells us that what is about to follow is an *oracle*, a communication received directly from the Lord himself (see also Zechariah 4:8; 7:4; 8:1, 18). In this case, the oracle is a directed action, as we shall see.

10, 11. Take of them of the captivity, even of Heldai, of Tobijah, and of Jedaiah, which are come from Babylon, and come thou the same day, and go into the house of Josiah the son of Zephaniah; then take silver and gold, and make crowns, and set them upon the head of Joshua the son of Josedech, the high priest.

Zechariah is instructed to receive three Jewish leaders who also have returned to Jerusalem from captivity. The men Heldai, Tobijah, and Jedaiah are difficult to identify. The listing here is not quite the same as in verse 14, and some students think that these are titles rather than proper names. The wording of these verses is rather complicated, but the sense seems to be that these three men are to supply the *silver and gold* that Zechariah is to use to *make crowns*.

This action is to take place in *the house of Josiah the son of Zephaniah*. Zephaniah is the name of a prophet who lived over 100 years before this episode (Zephaniah 1:1), but we don't know if there is any connection between that man and the son mentioned here. This son, Josiah, may be a metalsmith who is capable of working gold and silver into suitable crowns. This Josiah also seems to be a returnee from exile, and he has been in Jerusalem long enough to establish a house and home.

More than one crown is fashioned, and at least one of these is to be placed on *the head of Joshua the son of Josedech*. We say "at least one" because the plural word *them* does not appear in the Hebrew. Many printings of the *King James Version* indicate such absent words in italics—words for which the translators have to make a "best guess" for smooth reading—and that is the case here.

Ezra 3:8 and Haggai 1:14 tell us that the Joshua in view is the high priest who returned with Zerubbabel to rebuild the temple in Jerusalem. This Joshua is a direct descendant of Hilkiah, a high priest in the seventh century BC (see 1 Chronicles 6:13-15, where Josedech's name is given as Jehozadak). In his day, Hilkiah was a leader of the reforms resulting from his finding "the book of the law" in the temple, which was probably a copy of Deuteronomy (see 2 Kings 22:8; 23:24).

In Ezra's account of the return from exile, Zerubbabel and Joshua are seen as partners in the project to restore the temple (see Ezra 5:2). To place a crown on Joshua's head does not make him a king—the action is symbolic. It may signify Joshua's equal partnership with Zerubbabel, who is the governor (Haggai 1:1) and is in the royal lineage of David (Matthew 1:12, 13). Christians understand the placing of this crown on a priest as a prophetic act that points to Jesus the Messiah, who will be both priest and king.

❧ *WHAT OUR CROWN COST* ❧

In 1907, King Edward VII of England called on the Royal Asscher Diamond Company in Amsterdam to cut and polish the famed Cullinan diamond. That procedure was necessary to make the resulting, smaller stones suitable for inclusion in Great Britain's crown jewels. At 3,106 carats (almost 1 pound, 6 ounces), the Cullinan was the largest diamond discovered up to that time.

Before an audience, Joseph Asscher struck the stone. But his blade broke, leaving the diamond unchanged. After making stronger tools, he tried again. Asscher later said his adrenaline was so strong that he had to check the result several times before he could believe that he had done it right.

HOW TO SAY IT

Heldai	*Hell*-day-eye.
Helem	*Hee*-lim.
Hilkiah	Hill-*kye*-uh.
Jedaiah	Jeh-*day*-yah.
Jehozadak	Jeh-*hawz*-uh-dek.
Josedech	*Jahss*-uh-dek.
Tobijah	Toe-*buy*-juh.
Zechariah	Zek-uh-**rye**-uh.
Zedekiah	Zed-uh-*kye*-uh.
Zedkenuah	Zed-keh-*new*-uh.
Zerubbabel	Zeh-*rub*-uh-bul.

Today's text tells us nothing about Josiah's adrenalin level or state of mind as he set about his task of working with gold and silver to make suitable crowns. But we do have very accurate information about what Jesus went through mentally and physically as He endured the agony of the cross in order that we might have "the crown of life" (James 1:12) and "a crown of glory" (1 Peter 5:4). May we never forget what our crowns cost the Lord of glory, the one who wears "many crowns" (Revelation 19:12).   —C. R. B.

B. Temple of Glory and Peace (vv. 12-15)

12. And speak unto him, saying, Thus speaketh the LORD of hosts, saying, Behold the man whose name is The BRANCH; and he shall grow up out of his place, and he shall build the temple of the LORD.

A fuller purpose of the crown-making is now given: the crowns are in preparation for *The Branch.* This designation recalls the prophecies of Isaiah and Jeremiah concerning the coming Messiah. We wonder if Zechariah anticipated that the branch-king would be revealed in his day. Historical hindsight tells us that his prophecy was of one greater than either Zerubbabel the governor or Joshua the high priest.

Zechariah's description of the branch-king is very striking. For one thing, Zechariah uses the word for the noun *branch* as a verb when he says *he shall grow up.* Very literally, we could translate this as "the branch will branch out." The branch-king is not passive, but active and dynamic.

A second striking feature of this verse is Zechariah's prophecy that the branch-king will be a temple builder. The temple of Zechariah's day is only partially rebuilt at this point in time, but it will be finished in four years or less. When that happens, everyone who is aware of this prophecy at the time should realize that that temple is temporary. The coming branch-king will build the true, eternal temple of the Lord (see Mark 14:58; compare Acts 7:48).

Perhaps the most startling thing in this verse, though, is the command *Behold the man,* which is an eerie foreshadowing of Pilate's words about Jesus (see John 19:5, below). The clarity of Zecha-

Visual for Lesson 7

Point to this visual as you introduce the discussion question associated with verses 4, 5.

riah's vision speaks to the prophet's knowledge of the future as revealed to him by God.

13. Even he shall build the temple of the LORD; and he shall bear the glory, and shall sit and rule upon his throne; and he shall be a priest upon his throne: and the counsel of peace shall be between them both.

The temple of the coming branch-king will be something far greater than the sanctuary in Jerusalem. This new arrangement will have three distinctives. First, the branch-king, who occupies the temple, *shall bear the glory.* While this language might be applied to an ordinary king, it speaks more to the honor and glory given to God as king (see Psalm 104:1, 2; compare John 1:14).

Second, the new temple will contain a throne room (see Psalm 9:7), a suitable place from which the branch-king can reign; this was not a feature of the temple of Solomon or the temple as rebuilt by Zerubbabel. Third, the king in the new temple will also *be a priest.* This combination of priest and king is unthinkable for the Jews of Zechariah's day. To them, the king needs to be from the tribe of Judah and a descendant of David, while a priest must be from the tribe of Levi. The authors of the New Testament see these two offices combined in the person of Jesus (see Hebrews 7:14-17).

The Jerusalem temple is not a royal palace for a Jewish king, but serves as a kind of dwelling for God, something of Heaven on earth (Exodus 25:8; Psalm 132:7, 8). In the day of the branch-king, temple and palace come together (*the counsel of peace shall be between them both*). Zechariah foresees a king who dwells in the temple as His palace, for He will be the Lord God.

> **What Do You Think?**
> As part of the "holy priesthood" serving in "a spiritual house," what "spiritual sacrifices" can you offer to God this week that will be most pleasing to Him (1 Peter 2:5)? Be specific.
> *Talking Points for Your Discussion*
> - Time investment in prayer
> - Time investment in Bible study
> - Time investment in the lives of others
> - Romans 12:1

14. And the crowns shall be to Helem, and to Tobijah, and to Jedaiah, and to Hen the son of Zephaniah, for a memorial in the temple of the LORD.

After the crowns are placed on the head of Joshua the high priest, they are to be taken to the temple by the three men mentioned here and displayed *for a memorial*. Perhaps this is a way of helping the people remember that it is the Lord who has allowed them to return to Jerusalem and rebuild His house, the temple. *Helem* seems to be another name for Heldai, and *Hen* seems to be a nickname for Josiah (v. 10).

15. And they that are far off shall come and build in the temple of the LORD, and ye shall know that the LORD of hosts hath sent me unto you. And this shall come to pass, if ye will diligently obey the voice of the LORD your God.

Zechariah now shifts back to his vision of the future temple of the branch-king. A new detail is included: this temple will be constructed with the assistance of *they that are far off*. While it is possible that this refers to the Jewish exiles still in Babylon, it is more likely that it refers to those who are "far off" in a spiritual sense, meaning non-Jewish (Gentile) peoples. This future temple will be comprised of all people (compare 1 Corinthians 3:16, 17; Ephesians 2:19-22). The Messiah will be the king of all nations, not just Israel, and His house will be for all people, not just the Jews (Revelation 11:15).

> **What Do You Think?**
> Who are the "far off" groups that your church is or should be trying to reach? What differences in approach are needed to reach these?
> *Talking Points for Your Discussion*
> - Those "far off" in distance but not in culture
> - Those "far off" in culture but not in distance
> - Those "far off" in both culture and distance

III. The Broken Branch-King
(JOHN 19:1-5)

We now move about 550 years forward in time to the trials of Jesus. These trials witness a power struggle between the Jewish authorities, who demand Jesus' death, and Pilate, the Roman governor who uses the occasion to humiliate both them and Jesus. A focus of their debate is the claim that Jesus is a king (John 18:33, 37; compare 19:15, 19).

A. Brutalized (vv. 1-3)

1. Then Pilate therefore took Jesus, and scourged him.

We are at the point in the drama where Pilate has Jesus brutally whipped by soldiers. The Romans use whips embedded with pieces of bone or metal to increase the pain and bodily harm.

2, 3. And the soldiers platted a crown of thorns, and put it on his head, and they put on him a purple robe, and said, Hail, King of the Jews! and they smote him with their hands.

Roman legionnaires are battle-hardened and desensitized to violence. They are known for their cruelty and thus are feared by occupied peoples such as the Jews. These men follow the governor's orders in flogging Jesus (probably ripping the flesh of His back raw), but then take their brutality further: they weave a wreath of thorny branches and jam it onto Jesus' head. This "crown" probably does not feature small thorns such as we find on rosebushes; rather, it more likely consists of the two-inch thorns of the acacia bush. Even if Jesus has a full head of hair, that will not protect Him from the thorns penetrating His scalp.

The soldiers add to this mocking coronation by dressing Jesus in *a purple robe*. This is a costly garment and indicates that their cruel fun is also quite serious (compare Luke 23:11). They then disrespect Jesus further by pretending to honor Him as the *King of the Jews* as they strike Him. It is obvious that there is no real honor in their actions, and they are not inclined to show honor to a Jewish king under any circumstances. They are mocking both Jesus and the Jews at the same time.

> ### What Do You Think?
> What is it about human nature that tempts people to "join the crowd" in wrongdoing? How do you resist that temptation?
>
> *Talking Points for Your Discussion*
> - Exodus 23:2; 32:1-6
> - Numbers 25:1-3
> - Matthew 20:31
> - Luke 23:18, 19
> - Acts 14:19; 19:29; 21:27-32

B. Ridiculed (vv. 4, 5)

4, 5. Pilate therefore went forth again, and saith unto them, Behold, I bring him forth to you, that ye may know that I find no fault in him. Then came Jesus forth, wearing the crown of thorns, and the purple robe. And Pilate saith unto them, Behold the man!

It is difficult to know Pilate's intentions here. Is he trying to placate the Jews by punishing Jesus but not executing Him? Or is he ramping up the intensity of the situation to show them his absolute power over both Jesus and them? If an innocent man can be brutalized this way, what protection does any Jew have from these Romans?

In any case, John presents Jesus in a way that should drive us to tears. Here is a man who has done nothing wrong, by Pilate's own admission. Yet Pilate not only orders Jesus to be horribly abused, but also presents Him as an object of ridicule. Unwittingly, Pilate ties this all to Zechariah's prophecy with the striking statement, *Behold the man!* Here He is indeed, the sacrificial Lamb who takes away the sin of the world (John 1:29). The mighty branch of Jeremiah and Zechariah is here, and Pilate ironically speaks of Him as a king (19:15). But there is no majesty and glory for Jesus—not yet.

> ### What Do You Think?
> How will you help people "behold the man" Jesus this week as He lives in you? Be specific.
>
> *Talking Points for Your Discussion*
> - In acts of sacrificial love
> - In use of the tongue
> - Other

❧ PRICE VS. VALUE ❧

Oscar Wilde (1854–1900) is credited with defining a cynic as "a man who knows the price of everything and the value of nothing." We can see in this definition a focus on the short term (price) at the expense of the long term (value).

Pilate demonstrated this trade-off. He coldly weighed the price to himself of allowing an innocent man to go free when his Jewish subjects wanted the prisoner crucified. In so doing, Pilate set aside the bigger pictures of the value of the accused man, the value of right judgments, etc.

The question for us is whether we do the same thing. Does our behavior testify that we value our relationship with Christ more than the earthly price of following Him (Acts 5:27-29, 40-42)?

—C. R. B.

Conclusion

A. Behold the Man!

Pilate and Jesus were real men. The real soldiers were sadistic brutes. The blood on the pavement was really that of Jesus. The crown of thorns caused real pain. This all really happened.

Behold the man! He suffered and died for you and for me. As the prophecies confirm, this was God's plan for our salvation: a king who would die, rise again, and be exalted to reign forever. He did, and He does.

B. Prayer

O God, may we see past the cost of the momentary sufferings of this life as we value Jesus as our king forever. We pray in His honored name, amen.

C. Thought to Remember

We serve a king who suffered for us.

INVOLVEMENT LEARNING

Some of the activities below are also found in the helpful student book, Adult Bible Class.
Don't forget to download the free reproducible page from www.standardlesson.com to enhance your lesson!

Into the Lesson

Start with a guessing game to introduce today's main topic. Divide the class into two teams, and use the toss of a coin to see which goes first. Tell them you will give a series of definitions that all apply to the same word. Each team gets one guess during its turn as to what the word is. The clues you will give are (1) "an area of knowledge that may be considered apart from related areas"; (2) "a part of a computer program executed as a result of a program decision"; (3) "a stream that flows into another usually larger stream"; (4) "a division of a family descending from a particular ancestor"; (5) "a separate but dependent part of a central organization"; (6) "a side road or way."

If no one has guessed *branch* after the six clues above, give the final clue for both groups to see who can answer first: "a secondary shoot or stem arising from the main trunk of a tree." Then say, "Various Old Testament prophecies about the Messiah refer to Him as a *Branch*. Let's take a closer look to see how Jesus fulfilled two of those prophecies."

Into the Word

Distribute on handouts the following assignments to three teams of three or four. If your class is larger than 12 in size, form more groups and give duplicate assignments. (See the lesson commentary for expected responses.)

Righteous-Branch Group. Read Jeremiah 23:5, 6, and answer the following questions: 1. From which king is the Messiah to be descended? 2. Who will raise the Messiah up? 3. What kind of king is He to be? 4. Why can the designation *Savior* be applied to Him? 5. How do Acts 13:22, 23 and Revelation 19:11 make a case for Jesus' being the one who fulfills Jeremiah's prophecy?

Building-Branch Group. Read Zechariah 6:9-15, and answer the following questions: 1. What is made with the gold and silver taken from the exiles returned from captivity? 2. Who is Joshua,

and what is done to him? 3. In what way is the Messiah to be like a priest? like a king? 4. What is so unusual about the picture of "a priest upon his throne"? 5. How do John 2:18, 19 and Hebrews 5:5, 6; 8:1 make a case for Jesus' being the one who fulfills Zechariah's prophecy?

Broken-Branch Group. Read John 19:1-5 and answer the following questions: 1. How does Pilate treat the one he calls "the king of the Jews" (compare John 19:15, 19)? 2. What are the four ways the Roman soldiers mock Jesus in terms of kingship? 3. What is Pilate's opinion concerning Jesus' guilt? 4. How do Pilate's words echo the prophecy about the Messiah in Zechariah 6:12? 5. How do Isaiah 50:6 and 53:2-5 make a case for Jesus' being the one who fulfills prophecy?

Ask groups to present their conclusions for a whole-class discussion. Pay particular attention to each group's proposed answers to its question 5.

Alternative: Instead of the above, distribute copies of the "The Messiah, Predicted and Present" from the reproducible page, which you can download. Learners can work in pairs to complete it.

Option: After either alternative above, distribute copies of the "The Messiah Described" activity from the reproducible page. Use this easy "look up" exercise to introduce a deeper discussion about the nature and role of Jesus.

Into Life

Before class, find out if your church or another one nearby is having a Good Friday service. Supply details to your learners and encourage them to attend. Ask for volunteers who have attended such a service in the past to share how it helped them prepare for Easter Sunday.

Option: Distribute copies of the "Honoring the Messiah" activity from the reproducible page. Use this as a thought stimulus for learners to name one way they will honor Jesus this week for His sacrifice.

THE THIRD DAY

DEVOTIONAL READING: 1 Corinthians 15:12-20

BACKGROUND SCRIPTURE: Hosea 6:1-3; Luke 24:1-12

HOSEA 6:1-3

1 Come, and let us return unto the LORD: for he hath torn, and he will heal us; he hath smitten, and he will bind us up.

2 After two days will he revive us: in the third day he will raise us up, and we shall live in his sight.

3 Then shall we know, if we follow on to know the LORD: his going forth is prepared as the morning; and he shall come unto us as the rain, as the latter and former rain unto the earth.

LUKE 24:1-12

1 Now upon the first day of the week, very early in the morning, they came unto the sepulchre, bringing the spices which they had prepared, and certain others with them.

2 And they found the stone rolled away from the sepulchre.

3 And they entered in, and found not the body of the Lord Jesus.

4 And it came to pass, as they were much perplexed thereabout, behold, two men stood by them in shining garments:

5 And as they were afraid, and bowed down their faces to the earth, they said unto them, Why seek ye the living among the dead?

6 He is not here, but is risen: remember how he spake unto you when he was yet in Galilee,

7 Saying, The Son of man must be delivered into the hands of sinful men, and be crucified, and the third day rise again.

8 And they remembered his words,

9 And returned from the sepulchre, and told all these things unto the eleven, and to all the rest.

10 It was Mary Magdalene, and Joanna, and Mary the mother of James, and other women that were with them, which told these things unto the apostles.

11 And their words seemed to them as idle tales, and they believed them not.

12 Then arose Peter, and ran unto the sepulchre; and stooping down, he beheld the linen clothes laid by themselves, and departed, wondering in himself at that which was come to pass.

KEY VERSES

Remember how he spake unto you when he was yet in Galilee, saying, The Son of man must be delivered into the hands of sinful men, and be crucified, and the third day rise again. —Luke 24:6, 7

JESUS' FULFILLMENT OF SCRIPTURE

Unit 2: What the Prophets Foretold

LESSONS 5–9

LESSON AIMS

After participating in this lesson, each student will be able to:

1. Identify actions and attitudes of belief and disbelief on the third day after Jesus' crucifixion.

2. Explain the relationship between Hosea 6:1-3 and Luke 24:1-12.

3. Write an answer for someone who might ask him or her about reasons for believing in Christ's resurrection and the significance of such belief.

LESSON OUTLINE

Introduction

A. Nothing, Reincarnation, or Resurrection

What happens after we die? There are three primary answers proposed for this question, and all three were taught by various groups in Jesus' day.

First, some thought that death was the absolute end—when all aspects of our being ceased to exist. This was the view of the Sadducees, the party of the high priest (see Acts 22:30–23:9). This view, sometimes called *nihilism* ("nothingness"), is shared by atheists and secularists today.

Second, some thought that the dead person's soul was recycled into a new body to begin a new life after death. This view was taught by famous Greek philosophers such as Pythagoras and Plato; the view may have had some adherents among the first-century Jews. This view is widely known today as *reincarnation*; it is a feature of Eastern religions such as Hinduism.

The third option is *resurrection*. This was the view of the Pharisees (Acts 23:8) and most of the Jewish people in Jesus' day. This view sees an existence beyond death in which one's soul will be brought back to life with a new, immortal body (see 1 Corinthians 15:52). In Christian thought, resurrection is followed by a judgment (Hebrews 9:27).

There are other viewpoints, of course, but those seem to be "the big three." As we reflect on these, we should keep in mind that (1) the resurrection of Jesus was a victory over death, for He will never die again (Romans 6:9), and (2) Jesus' resurrection opens the door to eternal life for all (Philippians 3:21). These are not abstract ideas of philosophy, but truths that are based on historical events in the life of Jesus and foreseen by Old Testament prophets like Hosea.

B. Lesson Background

The prophet Hosea had a ministry of several decades in the latter half of the eighth century BC. His career overlapped about the first third of the prophet Isaiah's. Hosea's ministry, however, was to the kings and people of the northern kingdom of Israel, whereas Isaiah spoke to the people of the southern kingdom of Judah. The name *Hosea* means "salvation" and is the same as the original name of Joshua, which was Oshea (Numbers 13:16; the name *Joshua* is also spelled *Jehoshua*).

Hosea's book begins with the account of his marriage to a prostitute and the birth of children (chapters 1–3). The marriage itself illustrates the Lord's relationship with Israel (the faithful husband with the unfaithful wife). The rest of the book (chapters 4–14) sets forth various oracles that point out the sins of the people and call them to repentance. Today's lesson, from chapter 6, is part of one of those calls to repentance.

The New Testament portion of our lesson takes us to part of Luke's account of Jesus' resurrection. The common thread between our Old and New Testament texts is that they both deal with *the third day.*

I. Revived on the Third Day
(Hosea 6:1-3)
A. The Lord's Intent (vv. 1, 2)

1. Come, and let us return unto the LORD: for he hath torn, and he will heal us; he hath smitten, and he will bind us up.

The exhortation *Come, and let us return unto the Lord* marks a shift in tone from the strident condemnation of Hosea 5. This is not a call for physical relocation, but for a spiritual reorientation—a turn of hearts toward God (compare Joel 2:12). Such a call is a frequent refrain in Hosea.

HOW TO SAY IT

Arimathaea	*Air*-uh-muh-***thee***-uh (*th* as in *thin*).
Bethany	*Beth*-uh-nee.
Galilee	*Gal*-uh-lee.
Herod	*Hair*-ud.
Hosea	Ho-*zay*-uh.
Jehoshua	Je-*hosh*-you-uh.
Judas	*Joo*-dus.
Magdalene	*Mag*-duh-leen or Mag-duh-*lee*-nee.
nihilism	***nee***-huh-*lih*-zum.
Oshea	O-*shay*-uh.
Pythagoras	Pi-*thag*-o-rus.
Sadducees	*Sad*-you-seez.
sepulchre	*sep*-ul-kur.

What Do You Think?
In what ways have you seen people "return unto the Lord"? How have these affected you?
Talking Points for Your Discussion
- In personal holiness (1 Peter 1:15, 16)
- In regular worship (Hebrews 10:25)
- In proper attitudes (1 John 2:9-11)
- In financial stewardship (2 Corinthians 9:6, 7)
- Other

Despite the peril of the rising Assyrian empire, the people of Israel ignore Hosea's pleadings (see Hosea 11:5). The people's wickedness is described in terms of their unfaithfulness ("spirit of whoredoms," 5:4), their pride (7:10), and their sinful deeds ("iniquity," 14:1). There is quite a bit of overlap between these three problem areas, and taken together they describe a very serious situation.

Hosea does not scold Israel as an outsider, but includes himself—note the three occurrences of the word *us*—in this address. His plea is that God is the one who is allowing (even causing) the current national calamities, for He is the one who has *torn* and *smitten*. The people cannot save themselves or avoid God's punishing actions, for only the Lord can *heal* and *bind*, not pagan nations such as Egypt and Assyria (Hosea 7:11).

Hosea's message is disheartening and encouraging at the same time. The future of Israel hinges solely on its willingness to repent. The turmoil within the northern kingdom of Israel in Hosea's day can be seen in 2 Kings 15:17-31; 17:1-23.

2. After two days will he revive us: in the third day he will raise us up, and we shall live in his sight.

Hosea now restates this tearing/healing, striking-down/binding-up prophecy in terms of death and burial. His view of the future is that the destruction of Israel will come at the hands of the Assyrians (see Hosea 9:3, where this is likened to a return to the bondage of Egypt). This could be thought of as a national death.

Over time, however, there will be a national revival. First day: dead. Second day: beginning to revive. Third day: returned to life. This restoration is pictured as living in the Lord's *sight*, meaning the people will have the favor of God on their nation. While Hosea's promises apply directly to Israel's future, the language of *the third day* is prophetic of Jesus' death, burial, and resurrection.

B. The Lord's Reliability (v. 3)

3. Then shall we know, if we follow on to know the LORD: his going forth is prepared as the morning; and he shall come unto us as the rain, as the latter and former rain unto the earth.

The result of the national reorientation is that Israel will *know the Lord*, meaning the people will experience the blessings of God. Hosea describes this in terms of the regular cycles of nature. *The morning* features the unfailing, daily appearance of the sun. The rains of which Hosea speaks are the appropriate seasonal showers necessary for successful crops (*latter* and *former* refer to the winter and spring rains, respectively). The picture is of a future when God's blessings are regular and plentiful.

What Do You Think?

What "showers of blessings" does the risen Lord provide regularly? Why is it important to reflect on these?

Talking Points for Your Discussion

- Showers on you personally
- Showers on family members
- Showers on your church
- Showers on unbelievers
- Other

II. Surprised on the Third Day
(LUKE 24:1-8)

A. Faithful Women (vv. 1-3)

1. Now upon the first day of the week, very early in the morning, they came unto the sepulchre, bringing the spices which they had prepared, and certain others with them.

The *they* of this verse is the group of women disciples of Jesus who have followed Him from Galilee (Luke 23:55). This group seems to be led by Mary Magdalene (Luke 24:10; compare Matthew 28:1; Mark 16:1; John 20:1).

The Jewish custom of Jesus' day is not to use names for the days of the week, but to designate them by numbers. This is reckoned in relation to the Sabbath day (which does have a name), the seventh and last day of the week. After the Sabbath, the cycle begins anew with *the first day of the week,* which we call Sunday.

Jesus died and was buried late Friday afternoon. The burial was rushed because the Sabbath was about to begin, at sundown (Luke 23:53, 54). These women are not satisfied with the hasty burial, so they are determined to honor Jesus by giving His body a fitting preparation (23:56). As these women had ministered to Jesus during His life (see Luke 8:1-3), so they seek to care for His body in death.

2. And they found the stone rolled away from the sepulchre.

Jesus was buried in a tomb "that was hewn in stone" (Luke 23:53), not a hole dug in the ground. This *sepulchre* is therefore a man-made cave, carved into the soft limestone in a hillside outside of Jerusalem. It has been provided by Joseph of Arimathaea, a member of the Jewish high council and also a secret follower of Jesus (Luke 23:50, 51; compare John 19:38). Joseph may have intended this cave to serve a tomb for himself and family members, although it was unused before Jesus' interment (Luke 23:53).

Mark 16:3 records that the women are worried about the practical aspect of opening the tomb, for they know that a large stone had been rolled across its entrance. This turns out to be no problem, though, because the stone has already been *rolled away* when they arrive.

3. And they entered in, and found not the body of the Lord Jesus.

Much is left unsaid here, but we can imagine the dismay of the women. They probably are not relieved to find the tomb open, for this can be an indication that grave robbers have been at work, with the desecration of their Lord's body resulting. The fears of the women seem to be realized when they enter the tomb and discover that the body is missing. The conclusion they draw is that the body of Jesus has been moved, if not stolen (John 20:13-15).

B. Shining Men (vv. 4-8)

4. And it came to pass, as they were much perplexed thereabout, behold, two men stood by them in shining garments.

We easily imagine the women's mixture of reactions: outrage over the missing body, sadness at the disrespect, and fear that something devious is afoot. All the emotions are summarized as their being *much perplexed*.

As the women ponder the situation, *two men* are present with them. These are not ordinary men, though, for their garments are shining in an unusual way (compare Acts 1:10). These beings may look like men, but they are angels (see Matthew 28:2, 3; compare Luke 24:23).

5, 6a. And as they were afraid, and bowed down their faces to the earth, they said unto them, Why seek ye the living among the dead? He is not here, but is risen.

The women are understandably fearful at this situation, so they break eye contact as they bow down. It is left to the angels to speak first, and they ask a question that is also a revelation: *"Why seek ye the living among the dead?"* This is not intended to mock the women, but to explain. There has been no grave robbing. There is no need to anoint the body and wrap it with spices. There is no corpse in the tomb because Jesus is not dead, He is risen. Their master is alive!

What Do You Think?
In what ways can churches be guilty of seeking "the living among the dead" today? How do we guard against this?
Talking Points for Your Discussion
- Clinging to outmoded traditions
- Dwelling on past achievements
- Failing to discern cultural trends
- Other

6b, 7. Remember how he spake unto you when he was yet in Galilee, saying, The Son of man must be delivered into the hands of sinful men, and be crucified, and the third day rise again.

The women will understand what has happened if they remember what Jesus prophesied about himself while they were still *in Galilee* (see Luke 9:22, 44; compare 24:46). The fact that the angels challenge the women to *remember* indicates that the women had heard the prediction previously.

There are three parts to this prophecy, now fulfilled. First, Jesus was to *be delivered into the hands of sinful men;* that happened when He was betrayed and bound over to the Romans for trial. Second, Jesus was predicted to be put to death via crucifixion; that too came to pass. Third, Jesus would not remain dead, but would be raised to life on *the third day* following the crucifixion (compare Acts 10:39, 40).

While Hosea's prophecy of a third-day resurrection is not quoted here, it is part of the pattern of the prophets who foresaw the resurrection of the Messiah (see Luke 24:46). Jesus also tied this to the experience of Jonah (see Matthew 12:40).

8. And they remembered his words.

The earliest preaching of the gospel includes the facts of Jesus' burial and many hours in the tomb. A first-century formulation of this preaching is that Christ "was buried, and that he rose again the third day according to the scriptures" (1 Corinthians 15:4). The combination of "burial" and "third day" is important because it proves that Jesus had been dead—His physical body truly died. This is remembered by these initial witnesses and others of the first-century church; they have passed the facts on for us to remember as well.

What Do You Think?
What was a time that remembering a promise of Scripture helped you overcome a rough patch in life? Which Scripture was it?
Talking Points for Your Discussion
- After the death of a loved one
- During a divorce
- After a job loss
- During a health crisis
- Other

❧ WHEN MEMORY FAILS ❧

Memory often seems to play tricks on us. This seems all the more so as we get older (and I'm speaking from experience here). Once I came out of a grocery store, walked to my car, and reached into my pocket for the keys. They weren't there. *Where are my keys?* Then I remembered I had put them in my coat pocket because they would be easier to reach instead of diving into my front pants pocket. We all have stories like that.

We may wonder how the women at the tomb could have possibly forgotten something as important as Jesus' prediction of His resurrection. Research tells us that memory failure, at any age, can be due to distractions that catch our attention, causing what we want to remember to be displaced. For the women in our text, Jesus' recent crucifixion was certainly a traumatic distraction of the highest order!

More foundationally, however, the women's failure to remember Jesus' predictions of resurrection can be tied to a general failure on the part of the disciples to comprehend the predictions (compare Mark 9:9, 10; John 12:16). Recall happened only by means of an angelic appearance.

Remembering Jesus' death and resurrection should stand behind all our actions. We dare not let anything push that precious memory aside.

—J. B. N.

III. Amazed on the Third Day
(LUKE 24:9-12)

A. Disbelieving Apostles (vv. 9-11)

9. And returned from the sepulchre, and told all these things unto the eleven, and to all the rest.

The women return to the place where the remaining apostles (11 because of no Judas) are staying. We do not know for sure where this is, but a likely place is the house of Mary, the mother of John Mark (see Acts 12:12), or less likely, the home of Mary, Martha, and Lazarus in nearby Bethany (see John 12:1-3).

Wherever the location, the phrase *all the rest* indicates others besides the apostles are present—perhaps as many as the 120 who gather before the Day of Pentecost (see Acts 1:15). The women relate everything they have witnessed: the rolled-away stone, the empty tomb, the dazzling angels, and the message to remember the prophecy of Jesus.

What Do You Think?
 What holds Christians back from sharing the
   message of Jesus' resurrection more freely?
   How can we overcome this problem?
Talking Points for Your Discussion
 ▪ Regarding how we think others will perceive us
 ▪ Regarding fear of inadequate Bible knowledge
 ▪ Regarding concern for "chasing people off"
 ▪ Other

10, 11. It was Mary Magdalene, and Joanna, and Mary the mother of James, and other women that were with them, which told these things unto the apostles. And their words seemed to them as idle tales, and they believed them not.

The language of Luke indicates there are at least five women. Three are named. *Mary Magdalene* is recorded by the Gospels as being present at the crucifixion of Jesus, at His burial, and at the empty tomb early Sunday morning. She was delivered from demon possession by Jesus, which helps us understand her devotion to Him (Luke 8:2). *Joanna* is the wife of an official in the household of Herod, the king of Galilee (8:3).

Mary the mother of James is further defined as being "the mother of James and Joses" in Matthew 27:56. This may be the writers' way of referring to Mary, the mother of Jesus, for she had sons named James and Joses (Mark 6:3). It would be odd, however, that Jesus' mother would not be identified as such at this point rather than by the names of two of Jesus' half-brothers (compare Acts 1:14). So it is more likely that the Mary in view here is a different woman from Galilee.

In any case, these women are followers of Jesus. But that is not enough to make their account of the empty tomb credible to the rest. Instead, those gathered (including the apostles) dismiss their story *as idle tales*. We can imagine the disappointment and hurt these faithful women must feel at not being believed.

❧ *WHEN A VIEWPOINT MUST CHANGE* ❧

I recently read a book about the assassination of President James A. Garfield and the medical treatment he received after being shot. The year was

1881, and most physicians still discounted Joseph Lister's theories on germs. Without washing their hands, doctors stuck fingers into Garfield's wound to find the bullet. When Garfield died some 11 weeks later, it wasn't the bullet that killed him, but the infection introduced by the filthy fingers.

When Lister tried to remonstrate with Garfield's physicians, they scornfully replied that they would become the laughingstock of future generations if they changed their procedures because of the alleged presence of things that no one had ever seen (germs). Those doctors "knew what they knew," and if new ideas didn't fit into their theoretical structure, then the new ideas had to be nonsense. We see the same mind-set in our text.

We have a choice to make: either we can allow the evidence of Jesus' resurrection to shape and change our view of reality, or we can allow a pre-existing view that "the dead stay dead" to dismiss Jesus' resurrection as fiction. Which choice do you make?   —J. B. N.

B. Wary Peter (v. 12)

12. Then arose Peter, and ran unto the sepulchre; and stooping down, he beheld the linen clothes laid by themselves, and departed, wondering in himself at that which was come to pass.

Although verse 11 counts Peter among the disbelievers, he is curious enough to run *unto the sepulchre* to see for himself (compare John 20:1-3). He too finds an empty tomb. The additional mention of abandoned grave clothes is an important detail, for body stealers would not have taken the time to unwrap Jesus' body and leave *the linen clothes* behind. Peter's reaction to all this is similar to that of the women when they encountered the angels: he wonders *at that which was come to pass*, meaning that these things do not yet make sense to him. But soon they will, for he will see the Lord Jesus face to face (Luke 24:34).

Conclusion

A. Waiting for Jesus

Waiting. Mary Magdalene and the other women could only wait as they watched Jesus die (Matthew 27:55, 56; Mark 15:40, 41; Luke 23:49;

John 19:25-27). At least two of the women could only watch as Jesus was buried hastily (Matthew 27:59-61). Constrained by the laws of the Jewish Sabbath, the women disciples of Jesus could only wait to give His body the burial preparation they thought it deserved.

And so they did wait. They waited until Sunday morning. Then the unimaginable happened: they learned that Jesus was no longer dead.

We wait for Jesus in many ways. Hosea had a glimpse of Him, but that prophet was hundreds of years early. Many of the disciples of Jesus were awaiting a Messiah when they met Him. Today we wait to be united with Him in the place He has prepared for us, our heavenly home.

We can wait because we know He lives, that death was not the end for Jesus. The tomb was empty because He is risen, never again to die. And we, His disciples today, will also be raised from our own graves to be with Him forever.

B. Prayer

Father, we believe the testimony of the women, that Your Son's tomb was empty because He had been brought back to life. We believe He is risen and exalted to Your right hand. May He come quickly to take us home. In His name, amen.

C. Thought to Remember

We await our own resurrections
because we know He lives.

Visual for Lesson 8. *Point to the five-word acrostic on this visual as you ask, "Which of these five speaks most to your heart today? Why?"*

INVOLVEMENT LEARNING

Some of the activities below are also found in the helpful student book, Adult Bible Class.
Don't forget to download the free reproducible page from www.standardlesson.com to enhance your lesson!

Into the Lesson

Have on display as learners arrive the question *What happens after we die?* Use this question to summarize the three primary answers of *nothingness, reincarnation,* and *resurrection* from the lesson's Introduction. As you talk about *nothingness,* illustrate by drawing on the board a line with a dot at the beginning and at the end. While discussing *reincarnation,* draw a circle. For *resurrection,* have a dot at the start of a line that continues off the board. Make a transition by saying, "The story of Jesus' resurrection gives us reasons to believe in our own resurrection. Let's take a closer look at the resurrection account."

Into the Word

Introduce the text from Hosea by summarizing that man's prophetic ministry (see the Lesson Background). Also say, "As Hosea called people to repentance, he also offered a word of prophetic hope about a coming resurrection. See if you can identify that as we listen to Hosea 6:1-3." Select a learner to read those three verses, then ask which verse relates to the resurrection. When someone says "verse 2," read it again. Then state, "The passage from Luke 24 will show us how this prophecy was fulfilled."

Distribute a handout titled "Do You Believe?" Have printed on the handout three columns with these headings, one each: Luke 24 / Actions / Emotions. List the following references down the first column: verse 1 / verses 2-4a / verses 4b-5a / verses 5b-7 / verse 8 / verses 9, 10 / verse 11 / verse 12. Include these instructions: "To the right of the indicated verses, briefly describe the actions taken and the probable emotions felt."

As you distribute the handouts, form learners into groups of three or four to work together. Appropriate entries for the "Actions" column are listed in the text. Possible entries for the "Emotions" column are grief (v. 1); perplexity (vv. 2-4a); fear (vv. 4b-5a); hope (vv. 5b-7); joy (v. 8); excitement (vv. 9, 10); skepticism (v. 11); and wonder (v. 12).

When groups finish, say, "Sometimes when a question is answered, the answer serves to raise other questions. What does your 'sanctified imagination' suggest regarding questions that *could* have occurred but are not attested in the text?" *(Possibilities: "Where is Jesus now?" "Should we tell anyone else about all this?" "Is Jesus angry with us?" "Should we pray?" "Why didn't we understand this when Jesus predicted it?" etc.)* Discuss.

Option: Before class, ask six or more learners (preferably with some acting ability) to rehearse the "Resurrection Pantomime" script from the reproducible page, which you can download. Introduce the scene by saying, "We are fortunate to have a talented pantomime team with us today to act out an episode involving Jesus' resurrection. Pay close attention as they show us what that first Resurrection Sunday might have looked like."

Lead in applause for the performance when finished. Then review the days on which Jesus died (Friday), was in the tomb (Saturday), and was resurrected (Sunday) to make the point that Jesus arose on "the third day" as Hosea prophesied.

Into Life

Pose this scenario: "Suppose you had a friend who told you that he just can't believe that Jesus really came back from the dead. Your friend's main objection is that he thinks it was a hoax perpetrated by the disciples. How would you use the texts we studied today to dispel that idea?" If your learners don't mention such things as the fulfillment of prophecy, the women's grief, the disciples' reluctance to believe in it, and the grave clothes left behind, be sure to suggest these yourself.

Close with prayer praising God for His wonderful power in raising Jesus from the dead and for the hope it gives you.

FROM SUFFERING TO GLORY

DEVOTIONAL READING: John 1:10-18

BACKGROUND SCRIPTURE: Isaiah 52:13–53:12; Luke 24:25-27, 44-50

ISAIAH 53:3-8

3 He is despised and rejected of men; a man of sorrows, and acquainted with grief: and we hid as it were our faces from him; he was despised, and we esteemed him not.

4 Surely he hath borne our griefs, and carried our sorrows: yet we did esteem him stricken, smitten of God, and afflicted.

5 But he was wounded for our transgressions, he was bruised for our iniquities: the chastisement of our peace was upon him; and with his stripes we are healed.

6 All we like sheep have gone astray; we have turned every one to his own way; and the LORD hath laid on him the iniquity of us all.

7 He was oppressed, and he was afflicted, yet he opened not his mouth: he is brought as a lamb to the slaughter, and as a sheep before her shearers is dumb, so he openeth not his mouth.

8 He was taken from prison and from judgment: and who shall declare his generation? for he was cut off out of the land of the living: for the transgression of my people was he stricken.

LUKE 24:25-27, 44-47

25 Then he said unto them, O fools, and slow of heart to believe all that the prophets have spoken:

26 Ought not Christ to have suffered these things, and to enter into his glory?

27 And beginning at Moses and all the prophets, he expounded unto them in all the scriptures the things concerning himself.

· ·

44 And he said unto them, These are the words which I spake unto you, while I was yet with you, that all things must be fulfilled, which were written in the law of Moses, and in the prophets, and in the psalms, concerning me.

45 Then opened he their understanding, that they might understand the scriptures,

46 And said unto them, Thus it is written, and thus it behoved Christ to suffer, and to rise from the dead the third day:

47 And that repentance and remission of sins should be preached in his name among all nations, beginning at Jerusalem.

KEY VERSE

Beginning at Moses and all the prophets, he expounded unto them in all the scriptures the things concerning himself. —**Luke 24:27**

JESUS' FULFILLMENT OF SCRIPTURE

Unit 2: What the Prophets Foretold

LESSONS 5–9

LESSON AIMS

After participating in this lesson, each student will be able to:

1. List the elements of Isaiah's prediction of Jesus' humiliation.

2. Suggest reasons why Jesus' disciples were "slow of heart to believe" the prophecies about Jesus.

3. Identify a personal "slow of heart" shortcoming and write a prayer for change.

LESSON OUTLINE

Introduction

A. The Scapegoat

In the business world, there is a phenomenon called *scapegoating*. This happens when an employee leaves a company; problems are then blamed on the departed one for a few months. (This can happen with churches too.)

The scapegoat concept comes from the Bible: on the annual Day of Atonement, the high priest was to lay his hands on the head of a goat, confess the sins of the people, then release the goat into the wilderness to be the scapegoat ("escape goat") that took away the sins of the people. This ritual therefore was understood to be a transfer of the people's sins to the goat (Leviticus 16:7-10, 20-22).

This idea of transfer of guilt for sins is at the heart of the sacrificial system used by the Israelites. There were many kinds of sacrifices, but the most potent were those that involved killing an animal by shedding its blood. For example, a goat was to be killed on the Day of Atonement (before the other goat, the scapegoat, was released into the wilderness), and its blood used in an atonement ritual (Leviticus 16:15-19). The concepts of transfer of guilt and sacrificial shedding of blood are keys to understanding the atoning effect of Jesus' death. Today's lesson demonstrates that the idea of the sacrificial death for God's chosen one was prophesied over 700 years before it happened.

B. Lesson Background

While the early chapters of Isaiah celebrate *Immanuel*, the special child to be given as a sign of God's presence (Isaiah 7:14; 8:8; 9:6), the latter half of the book presents the Messiah as the servant, the one designated for a special ministry for the Lord (see Isaiah 42:1-4; 50:10; etc.). The most detailed prophecies about the role of the servant of the Lord are found in Isaiah 53, parts of which are in today's text. Here we learn something of how the Messiah is to bear the sins of the people, as the scapegoat did at the tabernacle.

Our lesson today also addresses two sections from the Gospel of Luke. The two passages have a similar theme (Jesus' resurrection), but from different settings.

I. Suffering for Others

(ISAIAH 53:3-8)

The first passage of our lesson is part of a section beginning in Isaiah 52:13 that discusses the "servant" of the Lord. Isaiah 42–53 is characterized by its Servant Songs, and the one beginning in 52:13 is quoted multiple times in the New Testament as a description of Jesus' ministry, death, and burial (see Matthew 8:17; Luke 22:37; Acts 8:26-35; 1 Peter 2:22).

The last half of Isaiah 53:2 emphasizes the "comeliness" this servant is to lack. At first glance, this seems to be a very odd picture of the Messiah: people will not be attracted to Him! Isaiah 53:3 begins to tell us why.

A. Man of Sorrows (vv. 3-5)

3. He is despised and rejected of men; a man of sorrows, and acquainted with grief: and we hid as it were our faces from him; he was despised, and we esteemed him not.

In some of the most poignant words in all of Scripture, the Messiah is described as one whose situation is so dire that people cannot bear to look at Him. Isaiah paints a horrific picture in this regard: the Messiah *is despised,* meaning He has lost all respect; He is *rejected,* meaning He has been expelled from the community; He is not *esteemed,* meaning opinions of Him are very low.

Isaiah also describes the inner turmoil of the Messiah. He is *a man of sorrows,* meaning He is not immune to great pain and humiliation. He internalizes these things at a deep level. He is *acquainted with grief,* meaning emotional pain floods His soul.

4. Surely he hath borne our griefs, and carried our sorrows: yet we did esteem him stricken, smitten of God, and afflicted.

The description of the Messiah's great personal pain continues. Also included is an explanation for the reason: the *griefs* and *sorrows* of the Messiah are not of His own making—they are neither self-caused nor deserved. He bears the griefs and sorrows for us, as our surrogate, our scapegoat.

People do not easily accept this relationship. Horror at His condition is self-excused because people believe that since God is punishing Him, then He is rightly *stricken, smitten,* and *afflicted.* People know that God never acts unjustly, so they naturally reason that this man must have done something to deserve the punishment. However, Isaiah's use of the word *our* (twice) does not allow us to escape our culpability.

What Do You Think?

What griefs and sorrows do you need to turn over to Christ today? Why?

Talking Points for Your Discussion
- A sorrow of the spirit
- A sorrow of the body
- A sorrow of your family
- A sorrow of your church

---

5. But he was wounded for our transgressions, he was bruised for our iniquities: the chastisement of our peace was upon him; and with his stripes we are healed.

The prophet moves from the emotional pain of the Messiah to His physical torture. He has done nothing to deserve being *wounded* and *bruised;* rather, He suffers because of *our transgressions* and *our iniquities.* He gains nothing personally from His *chastisement;* rather, it happens for *our peace.* This peace is the Hebrew word *shalom,* indicating a complete, restful relationship. The Messiah is our peace, the one who allows our relationship with God to be restored by removing the barrier of sin (see Romans 5:1; Ephesians 2:14).

HOW TO SAY IT

Apollinarius	Uh-*pawl*-uh-**nair**-ee-us.
Arius	*Air*-ee-us.
Emmaus	Em-*may*-us.
Eutyches	*You*-tuh-kess.
Immanuel	Ih-*man*-you-el.
Ketuvim (*Hebrew*)	*Ket*-you-vim.
Nevi'im (*Hebrew*)	*Neh*-vih-im.
Nestorius	Neh-*stawr*-ee-us.
Niebuhr	*Nee*-bore.
Pilate	*Pie*-lut.
shalom (*Hebrew*)	shah-*lome*.
Torah (*Hebrew*)	*Tor*-uh.

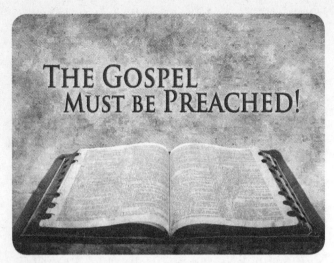

THE GOSPEL MUST BE PREACHED!

Visual for Lessons 9 & 11. *Point to this visual as you introduce the discussion question that is associated with verse 47.*

One of the most powerful concepts in the Bible is found in the phrase *with his stripes we are healed.* This happened in the brutal, bloody flogging and subsequent crucifixion that Jesus endured at the hands of His Roman torturers (see John 19:1). On the surface, this seems like nonsense. How can all this suffering result in our healing?

Peter, an eyewitness, helps us understand when he quotes this verse and comments that Jesus "bare our sins in his own body on the tree, that we, being dead to sins, should live unto righteousness" (1 Peter 2:24). This is the concept of *atonement*, which is at the heart of everything Christian. We cannot save ourselves from the consequences of our sins; we cannot make things right with God on our own. So God provides the perfect, once-for-all sacrifice in the person of His Son (Hebrews 9:26; 10:12; see 1 John 2:2). Jesus voluntarily takes the punishment we deserve. May we never lose this core, irreplaceable truth!

❧ THE NATURE OF CHRIST ❧

Students of the Bible have been debating the nature of Christ for almost 2,000 years. This was particularly true in the early centuries of the church. Some, such as Arius and Nestorius, saw Jesus as fully human but less than fully divine. Others, such as Apollinarius and Eutyches, saw Jesus as fully divine but not fully human.

Critics opposed all four of these teachers, labeling them heretics. Some of the most strident opposition came against the latter two. If Jesus were not fully human, then how could He have been "in all points tempted like as we are, yet without sin" (Hebrews 4:15)? If He did not have a full human nature to be nailed to the cross, then how can He be the perfect sacrifice for my sin? As some of the early church fathers phrased it, "What the Son of God did not assume, He could not redeem."

Isaiah is just as emphatic when he tells us that the coming one would bear our grief, take our sorrows, and be wounded and bruised on our behalf. Only the fully God and fully human Jesus could do that.   —J. B. N.

B. Innocent Lamb (vv. 6-8)

6. All we like sheep have gone astray; we have turned every one to his own way; and the LORD hath laid on him the iniquity of us all.

Isaiah continues this prophecy of the Messiah by shifting to an analogy well known to his people: the realm of sheep and shepherds. First, he characterizes us as being like sheep that ignore their shepherd and wander off. This is a way of describing our sinfulness, a willful rejection of God's rules and guidance. God chooses to lay the guilt for our iniquity upon the Messiah. The one who is not guilty becomes the target of punishment for those who are guilty.

What Do You Think?
In what ways did people willfully fail to follow the shepherd, Jesus, in the first century? How do these compare and contrast with similar failures that we see today?
Talking Points for Your Discussion
- John 6:60-66
- 2 Timothy 4:10a
- 2 John 9
- 3 John 9-11
- Other

7. He was oppressed, and he was afflicted, yet he opened not his mouth: he is brought as a lamb to the slaughter, and as a sheep before her shearers is dumb, so he openeth not his mouth.

The sheep analogy continues, but shifts from us (the guilty, straying sheep) to the Messiah as a lamb to be slaughtered (see Revelation 5:6) and a shaggy sheep ready to be sheared of its wool. In both cases, the emphasis is on the docile, cooperative nature of sheep. Jesus, aware of the horror He would suffer on the cross, went to His death with a docile dignity (see Luke 18:31-33). A remarkable fulfillment of this prophecy comes at the trials of Jesus, where He offers no defense. This causes Pilate to marvel (see Matthew 27:12-14). Isaiah foresees both the trials and execution of the Messiah (see Acts 8:30-35, which quotes our text).

8a. He was taken from prison and from judgment: and who shall declare his generation?

This verse is harder to understand, but the impression is that of "justice perverted" regarding Jesus' trials. The reference to *his generation* seems to be a prophetic indictment against Jesus' fellow Jews, who not only failed to protest His condemnation to death but demanded it (Luke 23:21).

8b. for he was cut off out of the land of the living: for the transgression of my people was he stricken.

Isaiah ends this section with a summation of this incredible vision: the servant of the Lord will be killed *for the transgression of* God's own people. The great tragedy is that the majority of Jewish people do not accept this role for their Messiah and therefore reject Jesus. In so doing, they reject God's provision for their salvation.

II. Prophesied to Suffer
(LUKE 24:25-27)

Only Luke gives us the wonderful story of the two disciples walking to Emmaus (Luke 24:13-35). They are joined in their walk by a stranger, and the two tell this man about the recent events in Jerusalem involving Jesus' death. This is a very sad thing for the two disciples (v. 17), for they had hoped that Jesus would be the one to redeem their nation (v. 21). The stranger is none other than the risen Jesus, but the two are prevented from recognizing Him (v. 16).

A. From Suffering to Glory (vv. 25, 26)

25, 26. Then he said unto them, O fools, and slow of heart to believe all that the prophets
have spoken: ought not Christ to have suffered these things, and to enter into his glory?

The still-incognito Jesus seizes the opportunity to explain to the two that they have misunderstood the Christ's God-ordained role. Jesus' summary of God's plan is very simple: the prophets foresaw that the Christ would suffer and enter His glory.

Some readers think that Jesus is being quite harsh as He calls the two *fools, and slow of heart to believe.* But the fact that these two will invite this (for now) stranger to stay with them (v. 29) indicates that they are more intrigued than offended. There is a certain "shock value" to Jesus' technique, and we see its success when the two later say to each other, "Did not our heart burn within us, while he talked with us by the way?" (v. 32).

> *What Do You Think?*
> What can happen if we fail to discern the presence of Christ in our lives? How do we correct or avoid this problem?
> *Talking Points for Your Discussion*
> - At work or school
> - At home
> - When traveling
> - Other

B. From Prophecy to History (v. 27)

27. And beginning at Moses and all the prophets, he expounded unto them in all the scriptures the things concerning himself.

Although the disciples still do not know who the stranger is, He gives them a lesson about himself based on Scripture. He begins with *Moses* (meaning the five books of Moses, which are Genesis through Deuteronomy) and walks through *the prophets*, the writings of God's Old Testament spokesmen like Isaiah. Oh, how we wish we had a transcript of this conversation! It is not hard to imagine, though, that our earlier text from Isaiah 53 is a key part of Jesus' lesson.

Reflecting on this encounter later, the two disciples admit that this was an emotional time for them (Luke 24:32). Even before they were allowed to recognize their Master, they had sensed something supernatural and wonderful.

III. Promises to Preach

(LUKE 24:44-47)

In the intervening text, Jesus agrees to stay with the two disciples (Luke 24:28, 29), and He reveals His identity while breaking bread. After Jesus disappears, the two disciples return hastily to Jerusalem to tell others about their meeting with the risen Jesus. As they relate their story, it receives an unexpected confirmation: Jesus appears to all who are gathered (Luke 24:36).

A. Understanding the Scripture (vv. 44, 45)

44. And he said unto them, These are the words which I spake unto you, while I was yet with you, that all things must be fulfilled, which were written in the law of Moses, and in the prophets, and in the psalms, concerning me.

After dealing with His followers' doubts, Jesus helps them understand the purpose of His ministry, His death, and His resurrection. From this we learn a key principle in the Christian understanding of the Old Testament. As Jesus once said to His critics, these earlier Scriptures "testify of me" (John 5:39). Jesus is the prophesied Messiah, and His disciples already believe this (see Matthew 16:16; Mark 8:29). The problem is their misconception about what God's Messiah is intended to be and do. They and, it seems, all of the Jewish people of their day have missed passages like Isaiah 53 that speak of a Messiah's being sent to save souls rather than liberate a nation.

The fact that Jesus refers to what is *written in the law of Moses, and in the prophets, and in the psalms* indicates that He is drawing on the entirety of the Old Testament, since that's how the people of His day categorized the sections of Scripture. Modern Jews refer to these three sections of the Hebrew Bible as *Torah* (law), *Nevi'im* (prophets), and *Kethuvim* (writings), respectively. These three together have all the same books that we have in our Old Testament, although our English Bibles arrange the 39 books differently.

The entirety of the Old Testament bears witness to the Messiah. Without this Old Testament background, our understanding of Jesus and His purpose would be limited and inadequate. There is important continuity between the Old and the New Testaments, and the connecting link is the Messiah. He is the one promised by the Old Testament and revealed to us in the four Gospels.

45. Then opened he their understanding, that they might understand the scriptures.

We do not have Jesus physically sitting with us and answering our questions about Scriptures today. Yet there is a sense that He is still opening our understanding so that we may appreciate the message of the Bible as He did on that day in Jerusalem. This is one of the purposes of the book of Luke (and its companion volume, Acts), written to show us how Jesus understood himself and how His story was preached by the first-century church. We believe today that the Holy Spirit works through Scriptures to help us understand meanings and applications (see Ephesians 1:17, 18).

What Do You Think?

What are some ways to correct misunderstandings people hold about Jesus today?

Talking Points for Your Discussion

- Misunderstandings held by fellow Christians
- Misunderstandings held by unbelieving seekers
- Misunderstandings held by nonseekers

B. Evangelizing the Nations (vv. 46, 47)

46. And said unto them, Thus it is written, and thus it behoved Christ to suffer, and to rise from the dead the third day.

This verse gives us a clear way to understand how Jesus sees His role in the prophecies and in history. First, the intentions of God were written, and then they are fulfilled in the person of Jesus. It has been necessary for Him *to suffer* (die on the cross) *and to rise from the dead the third day.* (For the prophecies about the third day, see last week's lesson.) While His death was cruel and unjust, it was not random. As Isaiah foresaw, His suffering is our salvation, for "with his stripes we are healed" (Isaiah 53:5).

❧ THE CENTRALITY OF THE CROSS ❧

H. Richard Niebuhr (1894–1962) was one of the most significant American theologians of the first half of the twentieth century. Reacting against classical theological liberalism, he and brother Reinhold were leading figures in the development of neoorthodoxy (a viewpoint that many evangelicals today would still consider too liberal).

The Niebuhrs wanted to resist the pious optimism of liberalism, the viewpoint that "every day in every way mankind is getting better and better." Richard and his brother criticized the liberal "social gospel" as portraying an idealistic picture of human perfection and inaccurate presumptions about human progress. In his 1937 book *The Kingdom of God in America,* Richard Niebuhr pilloried the social gospel as teaching that "A God without wrath brought men without sin into a kingdom without judgment through the ministrations of a Christ without a cross."

Christianity is centered on the cross. Jesus himself stated He had to suffer and be killed. He fulfilled the prophets because He knew the nature of humanity. Let no one tell you otherwise: we are not without sin, and we cannot be saved without the cross.   —J. B. N.

47. And that repentance and remission of sins should be preached in his name among all nations, beginning at Jerusalem.

Jesus takes things one step further as He gives His gathered disciples their marching orders. The colossal events of the previous week are the basis for the continuing mission of His church: to preach a message of *repentance and remission of sins* everywhere (compare Acts 1:8).

This message is possible because the death of Christ serves as a sacrifice for our sins. The resurrection of Christ verifies God's acceptance of His sacrifice in that regard.

What Do You Think?
How will you fill a role in proclaiming the message of Christ "among all nations"?
Talking Points for Your Discussion
- Direct roles (personal witness, etc.)
- Indirect roles (financial support of missionaries, etc.)

Conclusion
A. The Wonder of Prophecy

The "Scopes Trial" of 1925 received widespread attention, becoming a referendum on the merits of the theory of evolution. Some saw it as a contest between Christian belief and atheism. The attorney for the evolution side was Clarence Darrow (1857–1938), perhaps the most celebrated lawyer of his day. Less remembered are two later debates that involved Darrow in the 1930s. His opponent in these was P. H. Welshimer (1873–1957), minister of the First Christian Church in Canton, Ohio.

Darrow had debated many people on the merits of the Christian faith, and his great intellect served him well. His opponents were usually not prepared to meet his challenges. Welshimer, however, employed a tactic Darrow had not encountered before: Welshimer focused on the unity of the Bible as a book of prophecy as he laid out some of the wondrous prophecies of the Old Testament that found fulfillment in Jesus Christ. Darrow had no answer for this approach and admitted as much to Welshimer in private. (Unfortunately, Darrow died a few weeks after the second debate and never had a chance to read the books on prophecy suggested by Welshimer.)

Prophecy and fulfillment are inconceivable unless there is a God who is orchestrating them. The intentions of God must be communicated, and then the intended events must take place. We have only a vague idea of how God accomplishes this, but we can marvel nonetheless. God lost us when we sinned, but He was unwilling to allow us to remain lost. We are restored to Him through His grace and mercy in the atoning death of His Son—all planned and revealed ahead of time through God's messengers, the prophets.

B. Prayer

Holy God, we are amazed at Your plan for our salvation through Jesus, a plan prophesied hundreds of years in advance. We humble ourselves in the presence of Jesus, the prophesied one, amen.

C. Thought to Remember
Our salvation in Jesus was prophesied.

INVOLVEMENT LEARNING

*Some of the activities below are also found in the helpful student book, Adult Bible Class.
Don't forget to download the free reproducible page from www.standardlesson.com to enhance your lesson!*

Into the Lesson

Option: Place in chairs copies of the "What Happened to Jesus" puzzle from the reproducible page, which you can download. Learners can begin working on this as they arrive.

Distribute copies of an optical illusion that features different pictures that can be seen, depending on where one focuses. (Find this on an optical illusions website or from a library book.) Ask learners to tell what they see. As you get more than one answer, ask learners if they can refocus to see the other picture. Then say, "Once you focus on one picture, it's often hard to see the other one. That's what happened to Jesus' disciples. They were so focused on seeing a Messiah who would be a conquering king that they failed to notice the prophecies that revealed He would also be a suffering servant. Let's take a look at one such prophecy."

Into the Word

Bring the six objects listed below; have attached to each an index card with these instructions: *a mask or veil*—Read Isaiah 53:3 and explain why anyone would want to hide his or her face from the Messiah; *a pillowcase stuffed with a few heavy objects and labeled "our griefs and sorrows"*—Read Isaiah 53:4 and describe the what the Messiah did with our griefs and sorrows; *a bandage*—Read Isaiah 53:5 and tell what happened to the Messiah so that we could be healed; *a toy sheep*—Read Isaiah 53:6 and demonstrate what happened to the Messiah because of what we sheep did; *a sock puppet*—Read Isaiah 53:7 and act out how the Messiah responded when He was falsely accused; *scissors plus a sheet of paper with a line drawn across the word **Alive***—Read Isaiah 53:8 and demonstrate what happened to the Messiah because of our transgressions.

Distribute the six objects to individuals or small groups; allow a few minutes for reading the assigned verses and deciding how to use the objects

to explain them. After an individual or group makes its presentation, have everyone read the verse aloud. Discuss why this would be a difficult passage for the disciples to associate with the Messiah. (Feel free to change the objects and instructions based on the size and nature of your class.)

Give two of your "sharper" students each a handout with these identical instructions: "Read your assigned passage and prepare a summary of the setting, main characters, and what happened." Assign one to work on Luke 24:13-24 and the other on Luke 24:33-43. Provide each a copy of relevant sections from the lesson commentary as aids.

As those two work on their assignments, divide the remainder of the class in half. Assign Luke 24:25-27 to one half and Luke 24:44-47 to the other. Then give everyone in both groups handouts with these questions (or display them on the board or by PowerPoint®): 1. What was the first thing Jesus said and why did He say it? 2. What portions of Old Testament Scripture did He use to explain things? 3. What did He help His hearers understand that they had not understood before? 4. Why were they unable to understand this on their own?

After the individuals and groups finish, ask the learner working on Luke 24:13-24 to sketch the setting, main characters, and what happened to set the stage for discussion of verses 25-27. Do likewise for verses 33-43 regarding verses 44-47.

Into Life

Hand each learner a bandage. Distribute markers and ask them to draw stripes on their bandages. Encourage learners to place their bandages in a prominent place this week to help them remember that "with his stripes we are healed."

Option: Distribute as take-home work copies of the "What Needs to Happen to Me" activity from the reproducible page. Challenge learners to complete this exercise in a time of solitary prayer in the week ahead.

JESUS RESISTS TEMPTATION

DEVOTIONAL READING: Psalm 91:1-12
BACKGROUND SCRIPTURE: Deuteronomy 6:13-16; 8:3;
Psalm 91:11, 12; Matthew 4:1-11

DEUTERONOMY 6:13-16

13 Thou shalt fear the LORD thy God, and serve him, and shalt swear by his name.

14 Ye shall not go after other gods, of the gods of the people which are round about you;

15 (For the LORD thy God is a jealous God among you) lest the anger of the LORD thy God be kindled against thee, and destroy thee from off the face of the earth.

16 Ye shall not tempt the LORD your God, as ye tempted him in Massah.

MATTHEW 4:1-11

1 Then was Jesus led up of the Spirit into the wilderness to be tempted of the devil.

2 And when he had fasted forty days and forty nights, he was afterward an hungred.

3 And when the tempter came to him, he said, If thou be the Son of God, command that these stones be made bread.

4 But he answered and said, It is written, Man shall not live by bread alone, but by every word that proceedeth out of the mouth of God.

5 Then the devil taketh him up into the holy city, and setteth him on a pinnacle of the temple,

6 And saith unto him, If thou be the Son of God, cast thyself down: for it is written, He shall give his angels charge concerning thee: and in their hands they shall bear thee up, lest at any time thou dash thy foot against a stone.

7 Jesus said unto him, It is written again, Thou shalt not tempt the Lord thy God.

8 Again, the devil taketh him up into an exceeding high mountain, and sheweth him all the kingdoms of the world, and the glory of them;

9 And saith unto him, All these things will I give thee, if thou wilt fall down and worship me.

10 Then saith Jesus unto him, Get thee hence, Satan: for it is written, Thou shalt worship the Lord thy God, and him only shalt thou serve.

11 Then the devil leaveth him, and, behold, angels came and ministered unto him.

KEY VERSE

[Jesus] answered and said, It is written, Man shall not live by bread alone, but by every word that proceedeth out of the mouth of God. —**Matthew 4:4**

Jesus' Fulfillment of Scripture

Unit 3: Jesus' Use of Scripture

Lessons 10–13

Lesson Aims

After participating in this lesson, each student will be able to:

1. Recount the key events of Jesus' temptation.
2. Explain the significance of Jesus' successful resistance of the devil's tempting.
3. Identify a temptation that he or she is susceptible to and locate at least one Scripture passage to commit to memory to combat the temptation.

Lesson Outline

Introduction

A. Sunday School on Trial

Churches are abandoning Sunday school at an alarming rate. Those who approve this trend are heard to say, "Young people and many adults sit behind desks all week. How can we expect them to sit for an hour on Sunday morning right before sitting through an hour of worship?" It is better, they propose, to simplify Sundays by eliminating Sunday school altogether. Children will receive instruction at youth group meetings, and adults have small-group programs during the week.

An unfortunate consequence of canceling Sunday school is that many believers never receive comprehensive biblical instruction. Though youth and small-group curriculum may be Bible-based, it is often topical in nature. So unless preachers work through the books of the Bible comprehensively in sermons, the average believer might never receive instruction on certain sections of the Bible.

Today's passages provide compelling reasons to take Bible instruction seriously. When facing important decisions about the shape of His life and ministry, it was Jesus' familiarity with God's Word that triumphed over the devil's temptations.

B. Lesson Background

Two layers of context furnish the background of today's passages. Our first passage is from Deuteronomy. The reason we have this book is that God's people, Israel, did not remain faithful to Him. After God delivered the Israelites from Egypt, He gave them His law and then led them toward the promised land.

Unfortunately, that generation got cold feet. After a preliminary inspection of the promised land, the people feared the land's inhabitants more than they trusted God's power (Numbers 13:26–14:4). So God refused that generation of Israelites entrance into the land and chose the next generation for that task instead. Deuteronomy is Moses' "sermon" to those of the second generation.

In this sermon, Moses reminded the people of the failures of the first generation and instructed them on how to follow God's law faithfully. Deuteronomy 6:13-16 is a key part of that instruction.

Our second passage comes at the very beginning of Jesus' ministry. At about age 30 (Luke 3:23), He was baptized by John the Baptist (Matthew 3:13-17; Mark 1:9-11; Luke 3:21, 22), who received a sign of Jesus' identity when the Holy Spirit descended "from heaven like a dove" on Jesus (John 1:29-34). This set the stage for Jesus' extremely challenging ministry. But that ministry was preceded by a test of His faithfulness to be the kind of Messiah that God had called Him to be.

I. Israel's Task
(DEUTERONOMY 6:13-16)

Moses' sermon to the second generation of Israelites after the exodus includes a restatement of the Ten Commandments (compare Exodus 20:1-17 with Deuteronomy 5:1-21). The focus of Deuteronomy 6, which immediately follows, further stresses those ten in various ways.

A. Fear God Alone (vv. 13, 14)

13. Thou shalt fear the LORD thy God, and serve him, and shalt swear by his name.

If the second generation of Israelites is to succeed where the first generation failed, its success will have to be grounded in fear of the one true God. In this context, *fear* does not first and foremost mean "terror." When speaking about deity, the word *fear* often conveys the idea of "worship." When Jonah is asked to give an account, he says he is one who fears "the God of heaven" (Jonah 1:9), and this is a statement of religious devotion more than one of being afraid of God. Indeed, Jonah appears to be the only person on the boat who is *not* afraid of what God is doing at the time (1:5).

HOW TO SAY IT

Ashtaroth	*Ash*-tuh-rawth.
Baal	*Bay*-ul.
Chemosh	*Kee*-mosh.
Habakkuk	Huh-*back*-kuk.
Massah	*Mass*-uh.
Meribah	*Mehr*-ih-buh.
Milcom	*Mill*-com.
Molech	*Mo*-lek.

There certainly are times when God's people are truly afraid before God's power (example: Exodus 20:18, 19). But the usage of the word *fear* likely parallels the meaning of the other verbs in the verse before us: the Israelites must *serve* God and *swear by his name* alone. They need to find their motivation, purpose, and surety in the God who has led them from Egypt.

What Do You Think?
  What are some ways to demonstrate appropriate "fear" of God in daily life?
Talking Points for Your Discussion
  ▪ In lifestyle choices
  ▪ In prioritizing use of time and resources
  ▪ In service opportunities
  ▪ Other

❧ RELATING TO GOD ❧

When I was just a wee lad, my parents bought me an illustrated Bible storybook. I went through it several times, but the story of Abraham confused me. The book stated that "Abraham feared God," but I couldn't understand why. As a young boy, I didn't fear God. God was my friend. Why was Abraham afraid of God? I didn't get it.

Perhaps my confusion can be traced to a revival of religion in America at the time (the 1950s). Popular gospel songs seemed to encourage a cheap, superficial relationship with God. One Hollywood star remarked, "I love God; and when you get to know Him, you'll find He's a livin' doll." God was seen as a great Santa Claus in the sky, a doting grandfather who overlooked our childish ways.

God is neither a wrathful monster to be feared nor just a good ol' fishing buddy. A proper relationship with God requires respect, honor, and worship. Cowering fear is not required, but genuine repentance in the face of pure holiness is. Fear in the sense of "terror" or "dread" comes into the picture when we fail to repent (see Hebrews 10:31). God is not a terror to those who repent in the name of His Son, Jesus. —J. B. N.

14. Ye shall not go after other gods, of the gods of the people which are round about you.

One alternative to trusting God is to trust one's own strength and resources. However, the second generation of Israelites consists of the children of runaway slaves, so it probably has not had any military training. Therefore, the most attractive alternative will be to worship *the gods of the people which are round about*. These include Baal, Ashtaroth, Molech (or Milcom), and Chemosh (examples: Leviticus 20:1-5; Judges 2:13; 1 Kings 11:33). Such fictitious gods will vie for Israelite allegiance.

What Do You Think?

What are some of "the gods of the people" that challenge our loyalty to the one true God? How can we better resist these challenges?

Talking Points for Your Discussion
- Career aspirations
- Material possessions
- Personal accomplishments
- Entertainment choices
- Other

B. Remember God's Jealousy (v. 15)

15. (For the LORD thy God is a jealous God among you) lest the anger of the LORD thy God be kindled against thee, and destroy thee from off the face of the earth.

The exodus generation and the one that follows are told multiple times that their *God is a jealous God* (see Exodus 20:5; 34:14; Deuteronomy 4:24; 5:9; 6:15; and Joshua 24:19). In each case, this means that God does not tolerate His people's courting of other gods.

The consequence for religious promiscuity is being destroyed *from off the face of the earth*. This seems quite severe, and it is. But God has good reasons. He is forming Israel to be a people that He can use to bless all nations. Israel is central to His strategy for dealing with the global havoc of sin. For God so loves the world that He raises up the Israelites, defeats the Egyptians, and rids the promised land of its pagan inhabitants. He is not doing all this just so the Israelites will fall into the same traps of the other nations! He is doing it so that Israel will become a nation like none other.

If the Israelites abandon their unique identity, they will be useless to God and the world. The only

fitting thing to do in such a case is what God is about to do to the promised land's current inhabitants as the Israelites prepare to enter the area.

C. Don't Tempt God (v. 16)

16. Ye shall not tempt the LORD your God, as ye tempted him in Massah.

In Exodus 17:1-7, the first generation tested God's patience by complaining about not having water to drink at a place Moses called *Massah* and *Meribah* (which mean "testing" and "quarreling," respectively). The people had threatened to stone Moses, and they questioned whether God was even with them. Though God did provide water on that occasion, the fact that they pushed the limits of His patience is evident in the psalmist's reflection on this event. Psalm 95:8-11 tells us that this testing of God was one of the main reasons He did not allow that generation to enter the promised land (compare Hebrews 3:15-19).

II. Jesus' Temptation
(MATTHEW 4:1-11)

The first generation of Israelites failed the test of faith of Numbers 13, even though the people had gone through the baptismal waters of the Red Sea (1 Corinthians 10:1, 2). The result was 40 years of wilderness wandering and more testing (Deuteronomy 8:2). After emerging from His own baptismal waters (Matthew 3:13-17), it is now time for Jesus to be tested in a wilderness.

A. Setting (vv. 1, 2)

1. Then was Jesus led up of the Spirit into the wilderness to be tempted of the devil.

The forthcoming test has a parallel in the book of Job: the devil does the tempting, while God allows it. God sometimes accomplishes His purposes through actions of evil agents (Job 1:6-12; 2:1-7; Isaiah 10:5, 6; Habakkuk 1:6-11), although God himself never tempts (James 1:13). We keep in mind that God is in control, not Satan.

2. And when he had fasted forty days and forty nights, he was afterward an hungred.

Some students see Jesus' hunger and thirst in His 40-day wilderness setting to echo Israel's 40-year wilderness experience (Exodus 16:3; 17:1-7). We remember, however, that Israel's testing came at the beginning of that nation's wilderness experience, with many years of wandering as the result of failure to be faithful. Jesus' testing, by contrast, comes at the end of His wilderness experience.

What Do You Think?

What kinds of situations tend to become occasions for temptation for you? What steps can you take to avoid such situations?

Talking Points for Your Discussion

- When hungry
- When alone
- At work or school
- During periods of transition
- Other

B. First (vv. 3, 4)

3. And when the tempter came to him, he said, If thou be the Son of God, command that these stones be made bread.

The temptations we are studying have been interpreted quite narrowly to apply only to how Jesus will use His power as God's Son, that is, as God in the flesh. Will He use this power for His own selfish purposes, or will He use it only to do God's will? From this perspective, the temptation in this verse is whether Jesus will use His divine abilities to feed himself.

As true as it is that Jesus is fully human and fully divine during His earthly ministry, the designation *Son of God* also has a wider meaning. Psalm 2 refers to an Israelite king as God's son. Jews and (later) Christians see this psalm applying also to the Messiah (example: Hebrews 1:5), so the devil may also be testing Jesus by tempting Him to become a Messiah different from what God is calling Him to be.

The Jews expect the Messiah to restore Israel's fortunes so that, among other things, they will hunger no more (compare Ezekiel 34:29). We see a connection here with the people's attempt to install Jesus as king after He feeds the 5,000 (John 6:5-15). Alone with His disciples after that miracle, Jesus asks them who they think Him to be. When Peter proclaims Jesus as "the Christ" (which is the Greek word for Messiah), Jesus informs the disciples of His forthcoming sufferings. This implies that Jesus is not the kind of Messiah that the people are waiting for (Luke 9:18-22).

4. But he answered and said, It is written, Man shall not live by bread alone, but by every word that proceedeth out of the mouth of God.

Though Jesus is willing to feed the crowds on certain occasions, He does not make that the main focus of His ministry. There will come a time when He returns to bring His kingdom in full when every mouth is fed, but the cross must come first.

Jesus therefore responds to the devil by quoting Deuteronomy 8:3. It is doubly appropriate for Jesus to quote from this verse because here Moses tells the Israelites that God tested them with hunger in the desert for 40 years precisely to teach them that they must *not live by bread alone* but by God's Word.

Jesus does not complain about lack of food or being the kind of Messiah whom God calls Him to be. In rejecting this temptation, Jesus shows the tempter and all others that people are to live *by every word that proceedeth out of the mouth of God*. Jesus models this sense of priorities throughout His earthly ministry (compare John 4:31-34). God sends Jesus to be the bread of life (John 6:25-59).

C. Second (vv. 5-7)

5, 6. Then the devil taketh him up into the holy city, and setteth him on a pinnacle of the temple, and saith unto him, If thou be the Son of God, cast thyself down: for it is written, He shall give his angels charge concerning thee: and in their hands they shall bear thee up, lest at any time thou dash thy foot against a stone.

Jesus has just resisted the tempter by quoting Scripture, so the devil adapts his strategy along that line. Since Jesus wants His messiahship to be shaped by God's Word, the devil tempts Him by quoting from God's Word—specifically Psalm 91:11, 12. This psalm, as a whole, discusses God's protection for those who seek refuge in Him alone.

This temptation may also be a challenge to what kind of Messiah Jesus is to be. Many Jews expect a nationalistic Messiah who will storm Jerusalem in dramatic fashion. In that regard, what better place

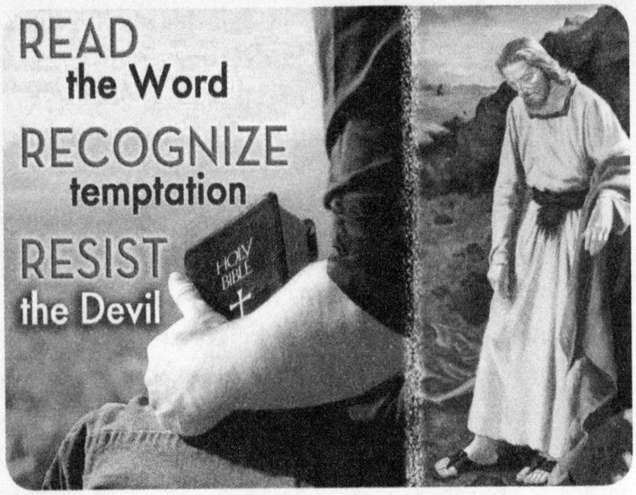

Visual for Lesson 10. *Start a discussion by pointing to this visual as you ask, "Are these the three most important* Rs *of Christianity? Why, or why not?"*

to make such a grand entrance than at the sacred temple? Since the Messiah's refuge must be in God, then God's own Word indicates that a dramatic event at Jerusalem like the one the devil is proposing will certainly be endorsed by the Lord's angelic entourage, right?

7. Jesus said unto him, It is written again, Thou shalt not tempt the Lord thy God.

Of course, God's Word nowhere says that His people should expect Him to show up each and every time they try to make a point by placing their lives on the line. Trust in God means being willing to leave one's life in His hands whenever being faithful to His Word requires doing so (compare Daniel 3:16-18).

Faith that God *can* do something does not guarantee that God *will* do something. To try to force God's hand by expecting Him to bail us out is to tempt (test) God. But we are not in a position to do that. So Jesus responds to the devil's improperly quoted Scripture with a properly quoted one of His own: Deuteronomy 6:16, discussed above.

If Jesus is not going to multiply bread in order to become a bread-king Messiah (the first temptation), then He also is not going to make a dramatic entrance into Jerusalem to become a military-king Messiah. Though Jesus is able to secure God's protection, He knows that the messiahship to which He is called means relinquishing such protection in order to endure great abuse at the hands of men at the cross (Matthew 26:53, 54).

Testing God

The bestselling book *Games People Play* was published in 1964. When I first heard about it, I thought it was about various parlor games for adults to enjoy, and I looked forward to getting a copy. But I was mistaken. Instead, it was a book about the psychological games people indulge in to manipulate others.

Unfortunately, Christians have been known to try that with God. An acquaintance of mine once used an apple tree in his yard to test God's approval of a certain plan. The man prayed, "God, if You don't want me to do what I am planning to do, then tomorrow I want to see oranges on this apple tree." There were no oranges on the tree the next day, so the man took that as God's approval of what the man wanted to do.

Christians sometimes justify their testing of God by calling it "putting out a fleece" (see Judges 6:36-40). But make no mistake: God will not allow himself to be manipulated. Requiring Him to perform a miracle to stop you from doing what you plan to do is spiritually dangerous.—J. B. N.

D. Third (vv. 8-11)

8, 9. Again, the devil taketh him up into an exceeding high mountain, and sheweth him all the kingdoms of the world, and the glory of them; and saith unto him, All these things will I give thee, if thou wilt fall down and worship me.

These two verses raise several questions, not all of which can be answered with certainty. We don't know which *exceeding high mountain* the devil takes Jesus to. Since no mountain on earth allows one to see *all the kingdoms of the world*, perhaps we should not take this in an overly literal way. *All the kingdoms* may refer to a representative sampling that points to the global scope of the devil's influence.

Whatever temporary power the devil has over the nations, he has with God's permission. Therefore Jesus can refer to the devil as "the prince of this world" (John 12:31; 14:30; 16:11), and Paul can call him "the god of this world" (2 Corinthians 4:4). The New Testament makes it clear, however, that God places all powers under Jesus' feet as a result of His death, resurrection, and ascension (1 Corinthians 15:24-28).

Yet even at this early stage in Jesus' ministry, the devil is beginning to lose whatever control he has. So the devil is not here offering something that Jesus does not already have coming as an entitlement. The devil is offering, rather, a shortcut that will get Jesus there more quickly. But this offer is really no offer at all. For Jesus to submit to the devil implies that Jesus will gain a quick position of authority over the earth, but still under the spiritual powers and principalities (compare Colossians 2:15). Yet Christ's rightful place is at the right hand of the Father in Heaven, with all powers (including the devil) beneath Him. Some shortcuts can only get us to a destination that falls short of God's will.

What Do You Think?
Under what circumstances do desires for power become sinful temptations? How can we handle such temptations?

Talking Points for Your Discussion
- Desire for power in politics or at work (2 Samuel 15; 1 Kings 1:5-10)
- Desire for power in the church (1 Timothy 3:1; 3 John 9)
- Other

10. Then saith Jesus unto him, Get thee hence, Satan: for it is written, Thou shalt worship the Lord thy God, and him only shalt thou serve.

Jesus sees right through the devil's scheme and dismisses him with a final quotation from Scripture. Drawing on Deuteronomy 6:13, discussed above, Jesus reminds him of what he already knows. The true Messiah, like any true servant of the one true God, will worship and serve only that God.

What Do You Think?
When was a time that recalling a Bible verse helped you overcome temptation?

Talking Points for Your Discussion
- Regarding a temptation at work or school
- Regarding a temptation when alone
- Regarding a temptation involving a recreational activity
- Other

11. Then the devil leaveth him, and, behold, angels came and ministered unto him.

Satan has no choice but to leave. The truth of God's Word triumphs over all the lies and shortcuts that the false gods of this world have to offer.

The devil had suggested that Jesus could test God's willingness to send angels to assist Him. The Father does now indeed send angels, but not because Jesus took the devil's bait. Quite the opposite!

Conclusion
A. Sword of the Spirit
Ephesians 6:12 reminds us that our struggle is "not against flesh and blood, but against . . . the rulers of the darkness of this world." The equipment that Paul urges us to wear in this struggle is largely defensive in nature (vv. 13-16). The only offensive weapon we possess is "the sword of the Spirit, which is the word of God" (v. 17).

Jesus used that weapon effectively to counterattack in the face of temptation. We must do the same. But to be able to use it, we have to know it. The Spirit will guide us to use God's Word at the appropriate time, but we must take the time to learn it first. Sunday school is a good place to accomplish this, but it is not the only place or even the best place. Personal study is crucial in order that one might be "approved unto God, a workman that needeth not to be ashamed, rightly dividing the word of truth" (2 Timothy 2:15).

To know God's Word, we must read it, meditate on it, and internalize it. Then when we need it most, it will be there for us.

B. Prayer
Lord God, we confess that You alone offer the words of life and that You alone know what is in our best interest. Protect us from the devil's lies. Keep us alert to shortcuts that lead only to our destruction. Help us seek Your kingdom, Your way, in the manner of Your Son, Jesus. In His name we pray, amen.

C. Thought to Remember
God's Word triumphs over the lies of this world.

INVOLVEMENT LEARNING

Some of the activities below are also found in the helpful student book, Adult Bible Class.
Don't forget to download the free reproducible page from www.standardlesson.com to enhance your lesson!

Into the Lesson

Display some tempting treats where everyone can see them. Post a "Do Not Touch" sign next to them. When everyone is settled in, ask, "Was anyone tempted to ignore the sign and help yourself?" Allow time for response. Then say, "Since you are adults, you aren't too likely to help yourself to treats such as these without permission—especially when everyone is watching! Yet there are other things that do tempt us every day, and the temptation can be stronger when we're alone. Today we're going to see how Satan tempted Jesus and how Jesus responded." Remove the sign and invite learners to help themselves to the treats.

Alternative: Instead of the above, distribute copies of the "Satan Says" activity from the reproducible page, which you can download. Have learners work on this exercise in pairs. Ask study partners to share with each other what temptation they struggle with most. If you think that your learners will resist sharing at such a personal level, request instead that they identify what temptation to sin they see most in the culture at large on a daily basis. Make a transition by saying, "Jesus also had to deal with serious temptation. In today's lesson, we'll see how He handled it."

Into the Word

Use the Lesson Background to explain the context for both passages in today's text. Emphasize that Deuteronomy was Moses' sermon to the generation preparing to enter the promised land. He did not want them to refuse to trust God as did the previous generation. Then state, "It will be interesting to see how Jesus uses verses from Deuteronomy to fight off Satan's temptation during His own time in the wilderness."

Form learners into three small groups of three of four. Distribute the following assignments to the groups. (Larger classes can form additional groups and give duplicate assignments.)

Temptation Group A. Read Deuteronomy 6:13-16 and answer these questions: 1. What did Moses tell the people to do? 2. How is "fear the Lord" similar to "worship Him"? 3. What did Moses tell the people *not* to do? Why? 4. What sin of the previous generation tested God's patience (compare Exodus 17:1-7)?

Temptation Group B. Read Matthew 4:1-4 and answer these questions: 1. Why did Jesus go into the wilderness? 2. What was Satan ultimately trying to get Jesus to do in the temptation to turn stones into bread? 3. What does Jesus' use of Deuteronomy 8:3 tell us about what kind of Messiah He came to be?

Temptation Group C. Read Matthew 4:5-11 and answer these questions: 1. How did the devil use Scripture to try to get Jesus to make a dramatic statement about who He was? 2. In what way would it have been a tempting or testing of God for Jesus to fall for the devil's temptation of verse 6? 3. How did Jesus' use of Deuteronomy 6:13 serve to resist temptation to take a shortcut as Messiah?

Review each group's conclusions during a whole-class discussion. Use the commentary to add insight and correct misconceptions.

Into Life

Ask, "When Jesus faced Satan's three temptations, how did He fight them off?" As learners mention His use of Scripture, share a Scripture that you find personally helpful when tempted. Then ask volunteers to share verses that give them strength and comfort.

Option: Have Hebrews 4:12 read aloud. Comment: "No matter how sharp the Word of God is, its sharpness is of little use if we're not ready to use this sword. One way to keep this sharp sword 'at the ready' is to memorize Scripture." Distribute copies of the "Ready to Resist" activity from the reproducible page. Allow learners time to complete it as indicated.

JESUS' MISSION ON EARTH

DEVOTIONAL READING: John 10:1-10
BACKGROUND SCRIPTURE: Leviticus 25:8-55; Isaiah 61; Luke 4:14-21

ISAIAH 61:1-3

1 The Spirit of the Lord GOD is upon me; because the LORD hath anointed me to preach good tidings unto the meek; he hath sent me to bind up the brokenhearted, to proclaim liberty to the captives, and the opening of the prison to them that are bound;

2 To proclaim the acceptable year of the LORD, and the day of vengeance of our God; to comfort all that mourn;

3 To appoint unto them that mourn in Zion, to give unto them beauty for ashes, the oil of joy for mourning, the garment of praise for the spirit of heaviness; that they might be called trees of righteousness, the planting of the LORD, that he might be glorified.

LUKE 4:14-21

14 And Jesus returned in the power of the Spirit into Galilee: and there went out a fame of him through all the region round about.

15 And he taught in their synagogues, being glorified of all.

16 And he came to Nazareth, where he had been brought up: and, as his custom was, he went into the synagogue on the sabbath day, and stood up for to read.

17 And there was delivered unto him the book of the prophet Esaias. And when he had opened the book, he found the place where it was written,

18 The Spirit of the Lord is upon me, because he hath anointed me to preach the gospel to the poor; he hath sent me to heal the brokenhearted, to preach deliverance to the captives, and recovering of sight to the blind, to set at liberty them that are bruised,

19 To preach the acceptable year of the Lord.

20 And he closed the book, and he gave it again to the minister, and sat down. And the eyes of all them that were in the synagogue were fastened on him.

21 And he began to say unto them, This day is this scripture fulfilled in your ears.

KEY VERSE

He began to say unto them, This day is this scripture fulfilled in your ears. —Luke 4:21

JESUS' FULFILLMENT OF SCRIPTURE

Unit 3: Jesus' Use of Scripture

LESSONS 10–13

LESSON AIMS

After participating in this lesson, each student will be able to:

1. Summarize the purpose of Jesus' earthly ministry as He expressed it in Nazareth.

2. Explain how Isaiah's prophecy informs our understanding of salvation.

3. Prepare a presentation of the good news of Jesus that can be used to proclaim this news to someone in the coming week.

LESSON OUTLINE

Introduction

A. Which Comes First?

The twentieth century saw Christians from various traditions engaged in debate regarding what the church's primary focus should be. Should we concentrate first on people's souls and then address their material needs after they convert? Or should we act to meet their physical needs first in hopes that they will appreciate our generosity and will be drawn to our salvation message about Jesus as a result? And what should we do if people only pretend to listen to our spiritual teaching because they want to keep receiving material blessings from us?

Such debates continue into the twenty-first century. A central issue in the debate is whether Jesus focused on one or the other during His earthly ministry. Today's Scriptures help us wrestle with this issue by exploring the biblical story line in this regard, a story line that spans the Old and New Testaments. It begins with God's teaching of Israel through Moses, it continues with the prophecy of Isaiah, and it finds its ultimate expression in Jesus.

B. Lesson Background

Behind today's passages from Isaiah and Luke stands Leviticus 25:8-55, which discusses the year of jubilee concept. Since Isaiah and Luke's discussion of the year of the Lord is best understood in this light, this invites us to review the passage from Leviticus in its own context.

A primary reason that people of the ancient world did not flourish was that most of the world's power and resources were concentrated in the hands of a few wealthy persons, who often used their power oppressively. This was the Israelites' experience as slaves in Egypt. So when God freed them from Egypt, He taught them His ways and formed them into a people who would exhibit His justice. Even before God brought the Israelites into the promised land, He knew that some people would fall into hardship in that "land of milk and honey." To keep that from happening, He established a procedure that, if followed, would prevent the land and people from falling under the permanent control of a few.

That procedure was the concept of a year of jubilee. Every fiftieth year—the jubilee year—the poor who had had to serve as hired hands as indentured servants were to be released to return home (Leviticus 25:13, 39-43, 54), and land was to revert to ancestral ownership (25:28, 31). That year, when the Israelites' physical and economic freedoms were reset, is the backdrop of "the acceptable year of the Lord"—the year prophesied by Isaiah and then announced by Jesus. This understanding allows us to appreciate fully the good news that was proclaimed by the prophet and fulfilled by the Messiah.

I. Prophecy
(ISAIAH 61:1-3)

Isaiah prophesied during the reigns of four kings (Isaiah 1:1), meaning that his prophetic ministry lasted from perhaps 740 to 681 BC. Much of the book that bears his name is occupied with God's condemnation of the unrighteous and His wrath on them. Crossing into chapter 40, however, takes the reader into what is commonly called the Book of Comfort or the Book of Consolation within Isaiah. Our Old Testament text today is from this section.

A. Good News for the Meek (v. 1)

1. The Spirit of the Lord GOD is upon me; because the LORD hath anointed me to preach good tidings unto the meek; he hath sent me to bind up the brokenhearted, to proclaim liberty to the captives, and the opening of the prison to them that are bound.

As Isaiah announces relief for *the meek, the brokenhearted, the captives,* and *them that are bound,* we wonder who these persons are. As Isaiah prophesies in the eighth century BC, a lot has changed since the time of Moses' teaching about jubilee in Leviticus 25. God's ideal for how the Israelites are to order their lives as 12 tribes under His rule has been replaced with a monarchy similar to that of other nations (see 1 Samuel 8). The Israelites have rejected God's plan for them, replacing it with a worldly system in which a king has great power over the people (since the tribes fall under

his jurisdiction) and land can be redistributed according to royal whim. As a result, the jubilee law seems to have been fully eclipsed.

In addition, worship of the Lord as the one true God of Israel has been compromised by worship of the fictitious gods of other peoples. As a result, God has determined to punish His people by placing the northern tribes under the jurisdiction of the Assyrians (in the eighth century BC) and the southern tribes under the Babylonians (in the sixth century BC). The Israelites end up as vassals of ruthless emperors who claim the promised land for themselves as they take the people captive. Even when the Israelites are allowed to work their own land, a good deal of their produce is absorbed into the ruling empires' storehouses.

The Babylonians, in particular, make a point of removing prominent Israelites from their land in Palestine and relocating them to Babylon, where they are forced to serve the Babylonian empire (compare 2 Kings 24:14). The Israelites end up downtrodden, having lost land, liberty, and hope. (This lies in the future from Isaiah's perspective.)

But the story does not end there! God raises up the prophet Isaiah in advance to proclaim good news to the enslaved Israelites wherever they are or will be. God hears their cry, and He plans to act on their behalf (compare Isaiah 11:11).

B. The Year of the Lord (v. 2)

2. To proclaim the acceptable year of the LORD, and the day of vengeance of our God; to comfort all that mourn.

The freedom announced by Isaiah is not restricted only to the opening of prison cells. *The acceptable year of the Lord* involves much more! In jubilee fashion, it means restoration of inheritance.

Israelites have mourned since the beginning of the subjugation of the northern tribes to the Assyrians (Isaiah 7:17-20). Many lose hope in 722 BC when taken captive to Assyria. More still will lose hope in 586 BC, long after Isaiah's day, when Jerusalem falls to the Babylonians. The people cry out to God to remember them and His promise to them. When the prophet announces *comfort* to *all that mourn*, he is indicating that God plans to grant them the core desires of their hearts.

God's deliverance also means *vengeance* on enemies. The fact that God punishes Israel by means of the Assyrians does not mean that God approves the Assyrians' unjust actions. He promises their demise (Isaiah 10:5, 12); He plans to raise up Babylon to punish them (10:24-27; etc.). Later, Persia will punish Babylon (13:19; 14:22; etc.).

C. Reversal of Fortune (v. 3)

3. To appoint unto them that mourn in Zion, to give unto them beauty for ashes, the oil of joy for mourning, the garment of praise for the spirit of heaviness; that they might be called trees of righteousness, the planting of the LORD, that he might be glorified.

God's liberation of the Israelites will mean both *freedom from* and *freedom for*. As God frees the people from *ashes, mourning,* and *heaviness*, He is also freeing them for *beauty, joy,* and *praise*. He will free them to be His own planting in this world so that He himself *might be glorified*.

It is not as if God needs His ego affirmed by reestablishing Israel. Rather, God is replanting Israel as His chosen people so that He can use

HOW TO SAY IT

Assyrians	Uh-*sear*-e-unz.
Babylonians	Bab-ih-*low*-nee-unz.
Esaias	E-*zay*-us.
Galilean	Gal-uh-*lee*-un.
Galilee	*Gal*-uh-lee.
Isaiah	Eye-*zay*-uh.
Nazareth	*Naz*-uh-reth.
Shema	*She*-muh.
synagogue	*sin*-uh-gog.
Torah (Hebrew)	*Tor*-uh.

them to be His witness to all nations, that all nations might come to know Him. God is preparing Old Testament Israel to usher in the Messiah —Jesus Christ.

II. Fulfillment
(LUKE 4:14-21)

Our New Testament text takes us hundreds of years forward from Isaiah's time. Jesus is just beginning His Galilean ministry, having recently endured His temptations in the wilderness (Luke 4:1-13; covered in last week's lesson from Matthew's perspective). Therefore the passage to follow comes very early in Jesus' public ministry.

A. Jesus Teaches (vv. 14, 15)

14. And Jesus returned in the power of the Spirit into Galilee: and there went out a fame of him through all the region round about.

When we read that *Jesus returned*, we naturally wonder "from where?" Luke 3:1-3, 21; 4:1 indicate that He has been to the Jordan River and a wilderness area. But John 1:19–4:42 indicates His actions elsewhere before He comes *in the power of the Spirit into Galilee*. The reason Jesus' fame is spreading *through all the region round about* is noted in John 4:45.

❧ HIS POWER, OUR POWER ❧

More than 7 billion people live on the planet as I write this. As of 5:00 p.m. today, more than 267 million e-mails have been sent and nearly 3 million blogs have been posted. Tweets exceed 206 million, and there have been more than 2.6 billion Google searches—and the day isn't over!

Jesus didn't have Internet access or global satellite communications as tools to spread His message, yet His fame spread quickly. Yes, He came with a powerful message. But more importantly, He came with the power of the Holy Spirit.

The Holy Spirit, who undergirded Jesus in His day, now lives within us as Christians (Romans 8:1-17). The Spirit brings us power to resist the enemy of our souls, power to communicate truth with clarity, and power to demonstrate God's love. Do you draw on that power, or do you rely on your own strength?   —V. E.

15. And he taught in their synagogues, being glorified of all.

Jesus is now "about thirty years of age" according to Luke 3:23. He had interacted with Jewish scholars when He was only 12 years old, impressing them with uncommon insight into the things of God (2:42, 46, 47). Now, some 18 years later, the student has become the teacher.

We should be careful not to misinterpret the phrase *being glorified of all*. Though we commonly attribute glory as belonging to God alone, we should not assume that Jesus' hearers are praising Him as deity so early in His ministry. *Being glorified* at this point more likely means that people speak well of His reputation as established thus far.

B. Jesus Reads (vv. 16-19)

16. And he came to Nazareth, where he had been brought up: and, as his custom was, he went into the synagogue on the sabbath day, and stood up for to read.

The focus now shifts from the region of Galilee in general to the town of Nazareth in particular. This is Jesus' hometown, *where he had been brought up* (compare Matthew 2:23). He is now at the local synagogue, where He likely received the most instruction while growing up.

One might expect this to be a happy occasion, but homecomings may be less than happy when children surpass their parents and teachers. That Jesus returns to this sort of resentment is clear in Luke 4:22-28. The confrontation about to take place is all the more public due to the fact that it happens on a Sabbath. Though synagogue activity occurs throughout the week, *the sabbath day* (which is Saturday) draws the most people. It is

in this context that Jesus takes the initiative by assuming the role of one of the readers.

17. And there was delivered unto him the book of the prophet Esaias. And when he had opened the book, he found the place where it was written.

If this synagogue service matches our historical records of Jewish worship of the day, the proceedings likely include the following five activities: reciting *the Shema* (Deuteronomy 6:4-9); reading from the Torah (that is, Genesis through Deuteronomy); reading from the Prophets; commenting on the readings; and a closing benediction.

Jesus takes a leading role in part three of this gathering, since Esaias (another spelling of Isaiah) is a reading from the Prophets. We are not told whether Jesus chooses the particular passage or if it is assigned to Him.

> *What Do You Think?*
> What percentage of Bible-instruction time should churches devote to teaching the Old Testament? Why do you say that?
> *Talking Points for Your Discussion*
> - In sermons
> - In classrooms
> - Other

18, 19. The Spirit of the Lord is upon me, because He hath anointed me to preach the gospel to the poor; he hath sent me to heal the brokenhearted, to preach deliverance to the captives, and recovering of sight to the blind, to set at liberty them that are bruised, to preach the acceptable year of the Lord.

Jesus proceeds to read Isaiah 61:1, 2. Whether He is assigned this passage or chooses it himself, the selection could not be more appropriate! When we read of *the Spirit of the Lord* being on Jesus, we may think of the Spirit's visible manifestation in the form of a dove at Jesus' recent baptism (Luke 3:21, 22). But in truth, Jesus, as God's Son, has had God's Spirit all along.

The Hebrew word *Messiah* and the Greek word *Christ* both mean "anointed." The anointing is, among other things, *to preach the gospel*, meaning "good news."

We discussed earlier what this passage meant to the Israelites in Isaiah's day as a commentary on Israel's jubilee law. Given the background of this topic as Jesus reads, we wonder whether the Torah reading for the day is from Leviticus 25, which teaches about the jubilee year.

What Do You Think?
    What does Isaiah 61:1, 2 say about the priorities
        the church is to have today?
Talking Points for Your Discussion
   ▪ Concerning the content of preaching
   ▪ Concerning the content of teaching
   ▪ Concerning the nature of benevolent ministries
   ▪ Concerning the audience(s) to be addressed
   ▪ Other

C. Jesus Fulfills (vv. 20, 21)

20. And he closed the book, and he gave it again to the minister, and sat down. And the eyes of all them that were in the synagogue were fastened on him.

There is no dozing off during the service this day! How can the people be anything but alert and expectant given Jesus' spreading fame and His reading of a passage as rich as Isaiah 61:1, 2? Surely this hometown teacher has something powerful to say about this passage! Rather than look to the regular teachers to offer commentary on the day's reading, all eyes are on Jesus.

We note in passing that standing may be the normal posture for reading Scripture (Nehemiah 8:1-5), with sitting the normal posture for teaching (see Luke 5:3; Acts 16:13; etc.).

21. And he began to say unto them, This day is this scripture fulfilled in your ears.

In one sentence, Jesus offers an answer to the questions the people likely have swirling inside their heads: Does Jesus think He is special? Does He see himself as a teacher or prophet of Israel?

In the verses that follow (not in today's text), we learn that Jesus knows the thoughts of the audience and that the people are not kindly disposed toward His sublime claims. When He exposes their negative thoughts, they are enraged and seek to drive Him out of town and throw Him off a cliff (Luke 4:29).

What Do You Think?
    Are crowds of opinionated people as fickle today
        as they seemed to be in Jesus' time? What
        does this tell us, if anything, about how and
        where the church should focus its efforts?
Talking Points for Your Discussion
   ▪ Issues of social media (Twitter, etc.)
   ▪ Issues of crossing cultural lines
   ▪ Issues involving the pace of modern life
   ▪ Other

Yet our lesson today is not about how Jesus is received back home, but what He is in fact claiming that His ministry is all about. When the Jews in Jesus' hometown read Isaiah 61, what do they think that passage is saying? Certainly God had already punished the Assyrians and Babylonians for oppressing His people. Certainly the Jews were sent back to their homeland to rebuild the temple. All of that is ancient history at this point. So what is Isaiah saying to their day, and what do they hear Jesus to be claiming for himself?

A bit more history is necessary. By the late seventh century BC, God had brought about the promised downfall of the Assyrian Empire. All of its territory (including Judah) was absorbed into the Babylonian Empire. That situation did not last long because the Persians took control of the Babylonian realm by the late sixth century BC. Eventually this empire was overtaken by the Greeks in the fourth century BC; the Greeks in turn were subdued by the Romans in the first century BC.

By the time of Jesus, then, deliverance is no longer sought from the enemies of Isaiah's day. The first-century Jews instead expect to be freed from Roman control. They expect the coming Messiah to break the stranglehold that Roman tribute has on their economy and to vanquish the ominous presence of Roman soldiers in their sacred cities, not least of which is Jerusalem (compare Acts 1:6). Of course, the Romans themselves are not the only oppressors: some Jews have become collaborators, profiting at the expense of their own people (example: Luke 5:27).

As in Isaiah's day, *freedom from* implies *freedom for.* The people expect the Messiah to free them from political oppression so that they can live prosperous lives in God's kingdom. Many devout Jews undoubtedly expect each family to have its own land, plenty of food on the table, and clothes on their backs. The ideal culture would be characterized by justice in the courts, purity of worship, and a positive witness to the nations. It is nothing less than all of this that Jesus is claiming to fulfill, but not in the way people expect.

❧ *Where's [Insert Your Name]?* ❧

For years children (and often their parents) have delighted in the Where's Waldo? series of books. Somewhere present on every elaborately decorated page-spread is a tiny, camouflaged cartoon character. One may have to spend time searching for him, but then, that's the point of the book. Waldo is there—somewhere.

Jesus found himself in the pages of Isaiah. Jesus knew His identity and His destiny. He lived it out, fulfilling everything prophesied of Him. Because of His alignment with the Father's heart, Jesus was unwavering in His mission.

We too can find ourselves in the pages of God's Word. We can identify ourselves by our spiritual giftedness (Ephesians 4:11). Perhaps you are one who will lead many to righteousness (Daniel 12:3), one who has a heart for those in need (Acts 6:1-6), one who will be an extender of hospitality (Acts 16:14, 15), or—the possibilities are almost endless. What could be more satisfying than living a life that uses all one's talents and spiritual gifts for God's glory? You are a precious child of God, and He will help you find your place in the pages of the work for His kingdom.   —V. E.

Conclusion

A. From and For

This lesson began by rehearsing the debate about whether salvation is concerned first with spiritual matters or with bodily matters. Sometimes the debate is framed in terms of how Jesus was concerned with religion or with politics and social justice. It is true that Jesus did not pursue politics and/or social justice the way certain Jews wanted Him to in the first century. He did not overthrow the Roman Empire and establish a new earthly kingdom with himself on the throne instead of Caesar.

Yet Jesus was indeed concerned with social justice and political practices as He came to liberate people spiritually from the worldly powers that had bound them for centuries. True liberation is won not by beating the system at its own game but by pioneering a new system that is not subject to the limitations of the old one. To this end, Jesus began incorporating people into a kingdom that is not limited by geography or ethnicity. Jesus was freeing people *from* primary allegiance to worldly nationhood and economic systems *for* incorporation into the church, of which He is head.

The church should be the place that models where true justice is rendered and where no spiritual or physical need goes unaddressed. To the world, this system is not the wave of the future. But we know that the jubilee we have begun to experience will come in full when Jesus returns in glory. That's when Jesus' enemies are fully subdued, when God and His kingdom stand alone.

B. Prayer

Father, we rejoice that Jesus has made possible our eternal freedoms *from* and *for*. Make us bold to proclaim those freedoms in His name, amen.

C. Thought to Remember

Eternal freedom is available to everyone!

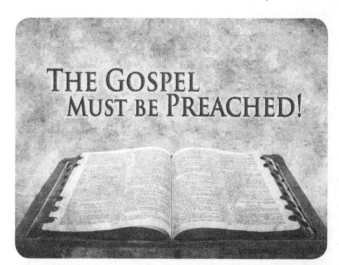

Visual for Lessons 9 & 11. *Point to this visual as you introduce the discussion question associated with verses 18 and 19.*

INVOLVEMENT LEARNING

Some of the activities below are also found in the helpful student book, Adult Bible Class.
Don't forget to download the free reproducible page from www.standardlesson.com to enhance your lesson!

Into the Lesson

Distribute index cards as learners arrive, one each. Say, "Please write on your card the name of the place you consider to be your hometown." Collect the cards and read a few out loud to see if the class can guess whose hometown it is.

For those whose hometowns are different from where they currently live, ask them to tell about the last time they visited it and their impressions of it now. Ask, "Would you like to live there again? Why, or why not?"

Make a transition to the study of the lesson text by saying, "Early in His ministry, Jesus returned to His hometown of Nazareth and declared what His mission would be. Today, we'll take a look at what He said and what that signified."

Into the Word

Secure a guest speaker (either a class member or someone else in your congregation) to prepare a five-minute talk on the year of jubilee concept (see the Lesson Background). Introduce the guest speaker by stating, "Our guest speaker [person's name] is going to give us valuable background information that will help us understand the two texts in today's lesson."

Form learners into groups of four or five. Give each group this same instruction: "Read Luke 4:14-21 and try to imagine that everyone in your group grew up in Nazareth at the time Jesus lived there. Collectively, you are being interviewed as a 'focus group' by a reporter. How would you answer the following questions about what took place in the synagogue?" (Note: not all responses can be found in the text; some will require use of one's imagination.) 1. Jesus taught in other synagogues before He came back to Nazareth. What had you heard about Him regarding those occasions? 2. When you knew Jesus growing up in Nazareth, what kind of a boy was He? 3. When Jesus came back to town, where did He go and

what did He do? 4. When Jesus took the book of Isaiah at the synagogue, did it seem like He was looking for the specific passage in Isaiah that He ended up reading? Why, or why not? 5. What was the specific content of the passage Jesus read? 6. What was the audience's reaction when Jesus finished reading and sat down? 7. What was the first thing Jesus said after He sat down? 8. How did the audience appear to react to what He said? 9. What claim did Jesus appear to be making?

Have each group appoint a spokesperson. The spokespersons will take turns offering their respective group's responses to the questions. The spokespersons can offer both majority and minority reactions, as in "Most of us believed . . . , but some of us believed . . ."

Option: Before doing the above, ask learners to close their Bibles and listen carefully as someone reads Isaiah 61:1-3 aloud. Then distribute copies of the "The Messiah's Mission" activity from the reproducible page, which you can download. Ask learners to work quickly to complete the puzzle and discover the Messiah's mission. Encourage them not to use their Bibles unless absolutely stumped. As you review the answers, ask learners to name specific ways Jesus fulfilled this prophecy in order to bring salvation to the world.

Into Life

Have learners work in pairs to discuss specific ways that Jesus has ministered to them according to the promises of Isaiah 61:1-3. These ministries may include being set free from certain addictive sins, healing of broken hearts, etc. Encourage learners to practice with each other how they can share their testimonies with non-Christian friends.

Option: Distribute copies of the "Our Mission" activity from the reproducible page. Encourage learners to use this as a stimulus to minister for Jesus to others in the week ahead. Close with a prayer that asks for God's strength to that end.

JESUS' TEACHING ON THE LAW

DEVOTIONAL READING: Matthew 5:14-20
BACKGROUND SCRIPTURE: Exodus 20; Isaiah 29:13, 14;
Matthew 5:17-48; 15:1-20; Romans 3:31

MATTHEW 15:1-11, 15-20

1 Then came to Jesus scribes and Pharisees, which were of Jerusalem, saying,

2 Why do thy disciples transgress the tradition of the elders? for they wash not their hands when they eat bread.

3 But he answered and said unto them, Why do ye also transgress the commandment of God by your tradition?

4 For God commanded, saying, Honour thy father and mother: and, He that curseth father or mother, let him die the death.

5 But ye say, Whosoever shall say to his father or his mother, It is a gift, by whatsoever thou mightest be profited by me;

6 And honour not his father or his mother, he shall be free. Thus have ye made the commandment of God of none effect by your tradition.

7 Ye hypocrites, well did Esaias prophesy of you, saying,

8 This people draweth nigh unto me with their mouth, and honoureth me with their lips; but their heart is far from me.

9 But in vain they do worship me, teaching for doctrines the commandments of men.

10 And he called the multitude, and said unto them, Hear, and understand:

11 Not that which goeth into the mouth defileth a man; but that which cometh out of the mouth, this defileth a man.

· ·

15 Then answered Peter and said unto him, Declare unto us this parable.

16 And Jesus said, Are ye also yet without understanding?

17 Do not ye yet understand, that whatsoever entereth in at the mouth goeth into the belly, and is cast out into the draught?

18 But those things which proceed out of the mouth come forth from the heart; and they defile the man.

19 For out of the heart proceed evil thoughts, murders, adulteries, fornications, thefts, false witness, blasphemies:

20 These are the things which defile a man: but to eat with unwashen hands defileth not a man.

KEY VERSES

This people draweth nigh unto me with their mouth, and honoureth me with their lips; but their heart is far from me. But in vain they do worship me, teaching for doctrines the commandments of men.

—Matthew 15:8, 9

JESUS' FULFILLMENT OF SCRIPTURE

Unit 3: Jesus' Use of Scripture
LESSONS 10–13

LESSON AIMS

After participating in this lesson, each student will be able to:

1. Summarize the conflict between Jesus and His opponents regarding the nature of "tradition."

2. Explain how the Pharisees' attempts to enforce law-keeping actually resulted in nullifying God's Word.

3. Analyze some personal, family, or church traditions to see whether they need to be discarded or revised in order to keep God's Word more perfectly.

LESSON OUTLINE

Introduction

A. Telephone Game 2.0

My children came home from a youth group activity excited to teach my wife and me a new game that they had learned. Everyone sits in a circle, and each person writes a phrase on a piece of paper. Each then passes his or her paper to the person on the left, who draws a picture that represents the phrase. After everyone has drawn a picture, the papers are to be folded so that the original phrases are hidden, then papers are passed one person to the left. Each person then writes out a phrase that represents the picture he or she has received. Papers are refolded so that only this phrase is visible, then papers are passed again to the left to repeat the cycle.

This process continues until each person receives back his or her original piece of paper. Papers are then unfolded to behold the often comical transformation of the original phrases into something quite different. My wife and I recognized this game as a creative adaptation of the old "telephone game" that we learned growing up.

The principle conveyed by these games is that a message often changes over time as it is passed along. This is especially true when the message has been passed across changing cultures over a long period. By the time of Jesus, something like this had happened to the laws that God gave His people on Mount Sinai many centuries earlier.

B. Lesson Background

Today's lesson focuses on a confrontation Jesus had with scribes and Pharisees over the meaning of the cleanness laws of the old covenant. Debates regarding these laws were common in the first century. Since the religious authorities tried to pull Jesus into these sharp debates, it is helpful to understand why they occurred in the first place.

The best way to understand debates of the first century AD regarding God's law is to sketch the contours of the law's complex history. God first revealed His laws, through Moses, on Mount Sinai; the recipients were the Israelites after their deliverance from bondage in Egypt. These laws were tailored to a people that God was bringing into the promised land to live as free people. Each tribe and family had its own God-given land, and God's law showed them how to use their freedom to reflect His holiness and justice. But the passing of the centuries saw the Israelites refusing to live according to God's laws, so He punished them by handing them over to other nations (see the Lesson Background of last week's study).

Since many of the laws delivered through Moses were directly connected with life in the promised land free from foreign domination, the first-century Jews struggled to know how to apply such laws under Roman occupation. For example, the Sabbath laws stressed the need for everyone to rest—whether slave or free, foreigner or native. Under the Romans, however, the full application of Sabbath laws was not always possible. Therefore, the common people relied on the scribes and Pharisees for interpretation and application of God's law.

Problems arose, however, when the religious authorities ended up placing their interpretations on the same level as the laws themselves. Today's text is an example of this. (Mark 7:1-23 is parallel.)

What Do You Think?

How do modern expectations and lifestyles make it difficult for us to live by biblical teachings?

Talking Points for Your Discussion

- Regarding attitudes toward wealth
- Regarding entertainment choices
- Regarding cultural ways of determining "right" from "wrong"
- Regarding laws or workplace policies that reflect an unchristian worldview
- Other

I. Accusation
(MATTHEW 15:1, 2)

A. Authorities Arrive (v. 1)

1. Then came to Jesus scribes and Pharisees, which were of Jerusalem, saying.

Jesus' conversation partners in our passage are Jewish leaders from Jerusalem. The designation *Pharisees* means "the separated ones," and they are very strict in their interpretation and appli-

cation of God's law (compare Acts 26:5). *Scribes,* who are often associated with Pharisees in the New Testament, study and make copies of the law as their occupation. It matters that they are coming from Jerusalem, for that city is the religious power center. Scribes and Pharisees from there see themselves as the guardians of proper religious instruction. So when they hear about strange teaching coming out of the small villages scattered about Palestine, they send envoys to gather information and, if need be, set matters straight.

Jesus already has had head-on collisions with the religious authorities, and they are already plotting to kill Him (Matthew 12:14). Their presence in this passage is thus an ominous sign.

B. Authorities Confront (v. 2)

2. Why do thy disciples transgress the tradition of the elders? for they wash not their hands when they eat bread.

The Jewish leaders who wish to silence Jesus launch this particular attack at the level of *the tradition of the elders.* The elders being referred to are probably the religious authorities back in Jerusalem; they are very careful to wash their hands ritually before eating (see explanation in Mark 7:3, 4). It is likely that these elders and/or their predecessors have developed this tradition out of genuine concern to uphold the cleanness laws of the Old Testament.

What Do You Think?

In what ways can a church tradition that was developed to address a genuine need become counterproductive or even antiscriptural over time?

Talking Points for Your Discussion

- Regarding resources needed to continue the tradition
- Regarding witness to the community
- Regarding changes in demographics of the church itself
- Other

The book of Leviticus places great emphasis on ritual purity or cleanness, so the scribes and

Pharisees are not without biblical support. Their problem is that the Scriptures do not require ritual hand-washing before eating (compare Exodus 30:17-21; Leviticus 15:11). Rather, this is a tradition above and beyond that of the Law of Moses. The religious authorities also miss the point of the original meaning of passages about ritual cleanness, as we shall see.

II. Rebuke
(MATTHEW 15:3-9)
A. Hypocrisy (vv. 3-6)

3. But he answered and said unto them, Why do ye also transgress the commandment of God by your tradition?

Before setting the record straight on the issue of ritual cleanness itself, Jesus confronts the larger problem of *tradition*: although these leaders present themselves as guardians of the Law of Moses, their traditions sometimes end up undermining that very law. Jesus is now putting this practice on trial.

What Do You Think?

How can we ensure that our traditions do not break God's commands?

Talking Points for Your Discussion

- Matters of the faith vs. matters of expediency
- Misunderstandings of biblical principles
- Levels of spiritual maturity (1 Corinthians 8:9-13)
- Personal preferences vs. personal convictions (Romans 14:1-9)
- Other

---

4. For God commanded, saying, Honour thy father and mother: and, He that curseth father or mother, let him die the death.

Jesus picks as His case study two interrelated laws that are relatively clear-cut. The command to honor one's parents is stated in Exodus 20:12 and Deuteronomy 5:16. The punishment of death for cursing one's parents is recorded in Leviticus 20:9; the fact that the death penalty is invoked for such behavior emphasizes that this law is extremely important to God.

5, 6. But ye say, Whosoever shall say to his father or his mother, It is a gift, by whatsoever thou mightest be profited by me; and honour not his father or his mother, he shall be free. Thus have ye made the commandment of God of none effect by your tradition.

Though the religious authorities pay lip service to God's command to honor parents, they also endorse a tradition that accomplishes exactly the opposite. Many Christians learn as young children the command to honor their parents. As children, we are taught to obey our parents, so we (ideally) do our chores, mind our manners, and do not talk back. But we must remember that the command to honor father and mother originally also included the idea of seeing to the needs of aging parents.

But the teachers of the law provide a loophole that enables opting out of this responsibility. In Mark 7:11, this loophole is called *Corban*, which means "offering to God." This legal sleight of hand involves (1) dedicating some or all of one's income to God, thereby making it ineligible for nonreligious use while (2) retaining possession of the money to provide for one's own needs. Since caring for parents can be classified as "nonreligious," Corban allows personal funds to be exempted from use in providing for parents' needs.

The religious authorities apparently do not believe that caring for parents is a deeply religious obligation, but Jesus disagrees. His rebuke is quite sharp. Paul follows Jesus in this by rebuking those who do not provide care for their own families. He even calls such care a way to show "piety," the neglect of which is worse than the offenses of infidels (1 Timothy 5:4-8).

What Do You Think?

What challenges do Christians today have in meeting responsibilities both to God and family? How can the church assist in this regard?

Talking Points for Your Discussion

- Financial responsibilities in relation to governmental assistance programs
- End of life issues
- Time-management responsibilities
- 1 Timothy 5:8

B. Fulfillment (vv. 7-9)

7. Ye hypocrites, well did Esaias prophesy of you, saying.

Hypocrites are those who say one thing but do another. Their words do not match their actions, and Jesus is about to explain why the scribes and Pharisees are in this camp. The prophet Esaias (Isaiah) encountered their same mind-set in his day, and the words he spoke in identifying this problem are timeless.

8, 9. This people draweth nigh unto me with their mouth, and honoureth me with their lips; but their heart is far from me. But in vain they do worship me, teaching for doctrines the commandments of men.

Jesus quotes from Isaiah 29:13, and the situation Isaiah faced in the eighth century BC has parallels to that of the first century AD. To begin with, this quotation is part of a prophecy beginning in Isaiah 29:1, which addresses the people of Jerusalem specifically. In Isaiah's day, they worshipped God with great pomp and enthusiasm, but then they treated needy people unfairly in the courts and otherwise failed to address their economic situation as the law required (Isaiah 1:12-17). This is like the hypocrisy of the scribes and Pharisees who teach high principles yet neglect needy parents. When words do not match actions, we can be sure that one's behavior is the real indicator of where one's heart truly is.

These deviant activities had their own deviant leaders in Isaiah's day. Someone was convincing the Israelites that their sinful way of life was acceptable. Someone was deceiving the people with persuasive teachings that were deeply hypocritical. Isaiah 28:7, 14 names these perpetrators as the rulers, priests, and false prophets. Isaiah's insights were relevant not only to His time and place, but also to first-century Jerusalem and to us today.

❧ *GODLY DISCERNMENT* ❧

Renowned science-fiction author Isaac Asimov (1920–1992) created The Three Laws of Robotics, which are employed throughout many of his stories. Those laws are (1) a robot may not injure a human being or, through inaction, allow a human being to come to harm, (2) a robot must obey the

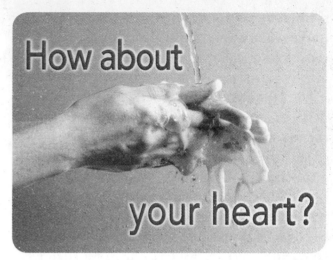

Visual for Lesson 12. *Start a discussion by pointing to this visual as you ask, "How can we make sure that cleanliness of heart is the greater priority?"*

orders given to it by human beings, except where such orders would conflict with the First Law, and (3) a robot must protect its own existence as long as such protection does not conflict with the First or Second Laws. The characters in his fictional books wrestle with the application of these laws—and eventually an additional Zeroth Law—in situations of ever-increasing complexity.

Part of the appeal of such fictional works is that they have a certain tie-in to reality. Our reality is that families, companies, and governments create rules to establish and maintain order within their boundaries. Although we don't always appreciate rules, a world without them would be chaotic.

As we wrestle with the application of laws and rules in situations of moral and ethical complexity, we *must* keep in mind that God's laws supersede human laws. This calls for discernment, especially in being able to recognize where interpretations of God's laws end up merely negating those laws. See also Acts 4:19 and 5:29.   —V. E.

III. Clarification
(MATTHEW 15:10, 11, 15-20)
A. Public Explanation (vv. 10, 11)

10. And he called the multitude, and said unto them, Hear, and understand.

Jesus addresses three groups in Matthew 15. First, He engages His accusers: the scribes and Pharisees; His word to them is one of judgment on their faulty teaching and example. Now He turns to the wider crowd to set the record straight. In verse 15, He will finish His teaching by addressing His most immediate followers.

11. Not that which goeth into the mouth defileth a man; but that which cometh out of the mouth, this defileth a man.

Jesus' main point is simple. People are not clean or unclean in God's eyes based on what enters their bodies—by way of their hands or otherwise. If that were the case, then only the wealthy could be consistently clean in a legal way because many people do not have water to spare for such purposes. To have enough water to be able to wash at every meal is a luxury unavailable to many people in ancient times.

We take care to realize that the issue is not that of removal of dirt as such. In reality, Old Testament purity laws seldom have to do with dirt. Some purity laws have to do with blood primarily because life is in the blood, making it sacred to God (Genesis 9:4). Some purity laws have to do with vessels that are set apart for sacred purposes; because these are sacred, they cannot be allowed to make contact with anything else (Leviticus 6:24-30). Such laws are designed to create Israel to be a set-apart people who take God's holiness seriously and do not defile themselves with the sins of their neighbors.

The concept of religious cleanness has to do with holiness, not dirt (compare 1 Peter 3:21). God wants people to live holy lives so He can dwell among them; when that happens, they will be shining examples to the world. By focusing on legal cleanliness before eating, the Pharisees unfortunately miss the heart of purity: *that which cometh out of the mouth, this defileth a man.* Since the teaching coming from the mouths of the Pharisees is wrong, they themselves are judged by Jesus to be

HOW TO SAY IT

Berea	Buh-*ree*-uh.
Corban	*Kor*-bun.
Esaias	E-*zay*-us.
Isaiah	Eye-*zay*-uh.
Pharisees	*Fair*-ih-seez.

a "generation of vipers" and "evil" because "out of the abundance of the heart the mouth speaketh" (Matthew 12:34, 35).

B. Private Explanation (vv. 15-20)

15. Then answered Peter and said unto him, Declare unto us this parable.

As is their custom, Jesus' followers press Him to explain His teaching (compare Matthew 13:36; Luke 8:9). We are fortunate to be able to read these follow-up discussions because some of Jesus' richest teachings are found in them.

16. And Jesus said, Are ye also yet without understanding?

Jesus' followers are slow learners. But we should not look down our noses at them when a teaching seems obvious to us today. They have been under the influence of confused teaching about purity for a while. Even simple truths can seem quite complex after one's mind has been clouded by rival teachings that seemed persuasive earlier.

17. Do not ye yet understand, that whatsoever entereth in at the mouth goeth into the belly, and is cast out into the draught?

So Jesus begins with basic biology. To put it in modern terms, whatever enters the body works its way through the digestive system, and whatever the body finds useless leaves the body. Jesus' point is that everything that enters the human body leaves the body without making a significant difference in the life of the one who is eating.

Of course, we know today that harmful bacteria exists, and so we take care to wash our hands whenever appropriate to avoid germs that can lead to sickness. Jesus is not talking about this. Rather, He is responding to the faulty reasoning of the scribes and Pharisees regarding purity before God.

18. But those things which proceed out of the mouth come forth from the heart; and they defile the man.

The right place to focus is *the heart.* Ancient Jews do not view the heart as the primary place of their feelings; rather, they locate feelings in the intestines, similar to how we use the word *gut,* as in "I had a gut feeling." For the ancient Jew, the heart is the intellectual seat. They refer to the heart in the way we often refer to the mind or brain, although they probably do not disconnect feelings from the intellect the way moderns often do.

These observations are important for not missing what Jesus is saying here. By *heart* He likely refers to one's inner disposition—what people think, especially when they believe that no one else knows those thoughts. Someone who truly honors God seeks God's heart. When a person's heart is in tune with God, the rest of his or her life will reflect that fact (1 Timothy 1:5).

19, 20. For out of the heart proceed evil thoughts, murders, adulteries, fornications, thefts, false witness, blasphemies: these are the things which defile a man: but to eat with unwashen hands defileth not a man.

The state of a person's heart prompts all his or her behaviors, and Jesus lists several sinful actions that should be obvious in that regard. Most importantly, these things have nothing to do with whether or not people wash their hands ceremonially before eating.

❧ WHAT GOES INTO YOUR HEART? ❧

More than 900,000 copies of Fred Stoeker's book *Every Man's Battle* have been sold around the world. While I am happy that his book is helping so many, I am grieved that its message is so badly needed. The book was written to help people fight the pervasive temptation of pornography. Here are some statistics of a few years ago:

* The adult film industry generates annual revenues exceeding $13 billion in the U.S.
* There are more than 420 million pornographic web pages.
* There are 68 million search-engine requests for pornography daily.
* Those addicted to pornography include 50 percent of Christian men and 20 percent of Christian women.

Pornography degrades attitudes about sex to being that of a self-centered thrill. It leads to adultery and ruined marriages. At its most vile, pornography is used to "season" trafficked women and children into the sex business.

As Jesus discusses the evil behaviors that spring "out of the heart," we do well to stop and ask ourselves how the seed for those evil behaviors was ever planted in the heart in the first place. "Thy word have I hid in mine heart, that I might not sin against thee" (Psalm 119:11).   —V. E.

> *What Do You Think?*
> As Christians, how do we make sure that our witness is primarily in light of what we *do* rather than in light of what we *don't do*?
> *Talking Points for Your Discussion*
> - Examining attitudes about God's expectations
> - Examining attitudes toward other people
> - Examining traditional expectations about "correct" Christian behavior
> - Other

Conclusion

A. Beyond Telephone Games

The old telephone game and its contemporary successors are comical because of how bad humans are at passing along information accurately. Too much is "lost in translation" from one person to another. Human traditions are like this and religious traditions are no different.

Believers have been entrusted by God with the good news of God's kingdom. We must be careful to pass this message along faithfully. We must humbly admit that we are prone to confuse important information. We must return to the Scriptures constantly to evaluate what we hear, even from respected teachers. The Christians in Berea did this for the apostle Paul (Acts 17:10, 11), and we should continue to do so today. Failure to do this may mean missing out on the profound teachings of Jesus.

B. Prayer

Lord God, please make us clean from the inside out. Purify us by the truth of Your Word and the power of Your Spirit. Give us ears to hear the simple truths of Your Scriptures and discernment to know when human traditions have taken their place. In Jesus' name, amen.

C. Thought to Remember

Let God's Word purify you
from the inside out.

INVOLVEMENT LEARNING

Some of the activities below are also found in the helpful student book, Adult Bible Class.
Don't forget to download the free reproducible page from www.standardlesson.com to enhance your lesson!

Into the Lesson

Have the following questions displayed as learners arrive: *Prayer before meals? Ate together as a family? Good manners enforced? Clean-your-plate Club?* To begin, have learners pair off and discuss what dinnertime traditions were followed in the family in which they grew up. After a few minutes, ask, "Would three of you like to share with the whole class some dinnertime traditions you followed as a child but no longer do as an adult?" (Stress *three* as a limit to keep this segment from dragging out.)

After discussion, make a transition by saying, "Traditions can be useful as a means to achieve a good end. But when a tradition becomes an end in and of itself, trouble looms. Let's see what today's lesson has to say about a certain tradition."

Into the Word

Distribute copies of a handout titled "Who Implied What?" Under the title, have three columns designated Topic / What the Pharisees Implied / What Jesus Implied. Also include the following four entries as four rows under the Topic column: 1. Washing hands (Matthew 15:1, 2, 10, 11, 19, 20). 2. Supporting parents (Matthew 15:3-6). 3. Worshipping God (Matthew 15:7-9). 4. Being defiled (Matthew 15:11, 15-20).

Form learners into small groups of three or four to complete the rows according to the column designations. If time is short, have half the groups work on rows 1 and 4 only while other groups complete rows 2 and 3. Stress that the challenge is to move beyond what both the Pharisees and Jesus *actually said* to what they *implied* by what they said. Call for conclusions in a whole-class discussion.

Possible entries for the Pharisees column: *1. Everyone who doesn't practice ritualistic hand washing is in the wrong because we're right on the basis of the positions of authority we hold. 2. Money dedicated to God is just that, and you needn't feel guilty if you have no money left over to support your elderly parents. 3. As long as people are doing all the things we teach, everything is fine. 4. God values purity! If a person eats with the impurity of unwashed hands, how can anything else about that person possibly be pure?*

Possible entries for the Jesus column: *1. Unclean hands won't make an unclean heart, but an unclean heart can certainly result in hands that are unclean with the stain of innocent blood. 2. You Pharisees have made a mistake in separating "money dedicated to God" from "supporting parents"; when you support your needy parents, you **are** dedicating money to God. 3. The fact that I have to quote Isaiah 29:13 means that you Pharisees—of all people!—are ignoring a lesson of history. 4. Make sure you distinguish the means from the ends—don't get them reversed!*

Alternative: If you use a teaching method other than the above, distribute copies of the "Missing the Mark" activity from the reproducible page, which you can download, for learners to use as a personal note-taker throughout the lesson.

Into Life

Returning to the subject of family dinnertime traditions at the beginning of class, have learners pair off and discuss current family traditions (in any area) that should be changed or modified to align more closely with God's Word. Discuss how to deal with resistance to change. Distribute blank index cards and ask learners to jot their ideas for later reference. (Stress that you will not collect the cards.)

Option: Distribute copies of the "What Was Your Tradition?" activity from the reproducible page. Give students a few minutes to work on this individually before you discuss it as a class. Try to keep the discussion from becoming a gripe session by encouraging (even insisting) students to find Scriptures to support their positions.

THE GREATEST COMMANDMENT

DEVOTIONAL READING: Psalm 15
BACKGROUND SCRIPTURE: Leviticus 19:18;
Deuteronomy 4:35; 6:1-9; Mark 12:28-34

LEVITICUS 19:18

18 Thou shalt not avenge, nor bear any grudge against the children of thy people, but thou shalt love thy neighbour as thyself: I am the LORD.

DEUTERONOMY 6:4-9

4 Hear, O Israel: The LORD our God is one LORD:

5 And thou shalt love the LORD thy God with all thine heart, and with all thy soul, and with all thy might.

6 And these words, which I command thee this day, shall be in thine heart:

7 And thou shalt teach them diligently unto thy children, and shalt talk of them when thou sittest in thine house, and when thou walkest by the way, and when thou liest down, and when thou risest up.

8 And thou shalt bind them for a sign upon thine hand, and they shall be as frontlets between thine eyes.

9 And thou shalt write them upon the posts of thy house, and on thy gates.

MARK 12:28-34

28 And one of the scribes came, and having heard them reasoning together, and perceiving that he had answered them well, asked him, Which is the first commandment of all?

29 And Jesus answered him, The first of all the commandments is, Hear, O Israel; The Lord our God is one Lord:

30 And thou shalt love the Lord thy God with all thy heart, and with all thy soul, and with all thy mind, and with all thy strength: this is the first commandment.

31 And the second is like, namely this, Thou shalt love thy neighbour as thyself. There is none other commandment greater than these.

32 And the scribe said unto him, Well, Master, thou hast said the truth: for there is one God; and there is none other but he:

33 And to love him with all the heart, and with all the understanding, and with all the soul, and with all the strength, and to love his neighbour as himself, is more than all whole burnt offerings and sacrifices.

34 And when Jesus saw that he answered discreetly, he said unto him, Thou art not far from the kingdom of God. And no man after that durst ask him any question.

KEY VERSES

Thou shalt love the Lord thy God with all thy heart, and with all thy soul, and with all thy mind, and with all thy strength: this is the first commandment. And the second is like, namely this, Thou shalt love thy neighbour as thyself. There is none other commandment greater than these. —**Mark 12:30, 31**

JESUS' FULFILLMENT OF SCRIPTURE

Unit 3: Jesus' Use of Scripture

LESSONS 10–13

LESSON AIMS

After participating in this lesson, each student will be able to:

1. Recite from memory the two greatest commandments.

2. Explain why the two greatest commandments are so important.

3. Suggest a way to keep the greatest commandments always in mind at home, place of work, and church.

LESSON OUTLINE

Introduction
  A. Some Things Remain the Same
  B. Lesson Background
I. Love in the Old Testament (LEVITICUS 19:18; DEUTERONOMY 6:4-9)
  A. Toward Neighbor (v. 18)
    Close to Home
  B. Toward God (vv. 4, 5)
  C. In Heart and Teaching (vv. 6-9)
II. Love in the New Testament (MARK 12: 28-34)
  A. Scribe's Question (v. 28)
  B. Jesus' Answer (vv. 29-31)
    My Sad Failure
  C. Scribe's Agreement (vv. 32, 33)
  D. Jesus' Approval (v. 34)
Conclusion
  A. Not as Different as It Appears
  B. Prayer
  C. Thought to Remember

Introduction

A. Some Things Remain the Same

When one compares what it meant to be God's people during Old Testament times with New Testament times, we notice that many things change. God's people are no longer focused on trying to live in Palestine. The practice of circumcision is no longer associated with incorporation into God's people. Animal sacrifice is no longer required or even adequate to atone for sin.

Instead we see that God's people are scattered throughout the world in mission (Matthew 28:19, 20); baptism is now associated with the circumcision of the heart as people are incorporated into the church (Colossians 2:11, 12); and the death of Jesus brought an end to the old sacrificial system (Hebrews 10:11-14).

We ought to be careful, however, not to emphasize the differences at the expense of the similarities. For example, God cares about the heart —one's "internal life"—in both eras. Both old and new covenants reveal God to be a loving God; this truth was used to expose the false distinction offered by Marcion, a bishop of the second century AD, who sharply contrasted what he saw as the loving God of the New Testament with the wrathful God of the Old Testament.

The church of Marcion's day wisely identified his teaching as false and dangerous. The truth is, God always has been a loving God. Central to God's desire for His people is that they model His love toward others.

B. Lesson Background

Our first Old Testament text comes from Leviticus. This book includes many laws that Moses received from God on Mount Sinai; Moses was responsible for passing these on to the Israelites who left Egypt. Leviticus 19:18 is located in the heart of the Holiness Code of that book. This section, spanning chapters 17 to 26, instructed the ancient Israelites how to live holy lives before their holy God.

Our second Old Testament passage is from Deuteronomy. Though Leviticus and Deuteronomy both belong to Torah, the five books of

Moses, they were addressed to different audiences. After the first generation of Israelites was not allowed to enter the promised land, Moses had to present God's laws anew to the second generation, which would enter instead. That's where Deuteronomy comes in.

After recounting the failure of the first generation in Deuteronomy 1–3, Moses prepared the second generation to renew the covenant in chapters 4–11. Our passage in chapter 6 was a key part of that preparation, and Jesus later acknowledged its ongoing relevance for His followers.

Though only one generation separates our two Old Testament passages, a millennium separates those two from our text of Mark 12:28-34. These verses feature Jesus having one of His most congenial conversations with a Jewish leader. Since Mark 11:27, Jesus had been challenged by priests, scribes, elders, Pharisees, Herodians, and Sadducees. They had been coming at Him from every angle, trying to find fault. But the scribe in today's text asked Jesus a frank question and received a frank answer. That answer drew upon the two Old Testament passages to which we now turn.

I. Love in the Old Testament
(LEVITICUS 19:18; DEUTERONOMY 6:4-9)

A. Toward Neighbor (v. 18)

18. Thou shalt not avenge, nor bear any grudge against the children of thy people, but thou shalt love thy neighbour as thyself: I am the LORD.

To *love thy neighbour as thyself* is closely connected with the golden rule: do unto others as you would have them do unto you (Matthew 7:12; Luke 6:31). But this connection can confuse the purpose behind neighbor love, as if we should love others only because we want favorable treatment in return.

Another way to miss the thrust of this passage is to focus on the *thyself* part. In a culture of self-obsession, it is easy for us to hear this passage saying that we must first focus on loving ourselves because, if we cannot do that, then we will be unable to love our neighbors. But that is not what this passage is saying either.

This passage presumes that humans are accustomed to putting their own needs first. God is telling the people, through Moses, to think that way about other people. This especially applies to fellow Israelites, to whom the term *neighbour* refers (same as *the children of thy people*). In the Law of Moses, non-Israelites who live in the land are referred to as "strangers." An example is Leviticus 19:34, and there God commands the Israelites to love them as well.

There is one more way to miss the thrust of this passage, and that is by ignoring how it begins and ends. It begins by commanding the original readers not to avenge themselves or to hold grudges (compare Deuteronomy 32:35; quoted in Romans 12:19 and Hebrews 10:30); this implies that the neighbors to be loved aren't just friends or neutral parties, but also include enemies.

The passage ends with the reminder that *the Lord* is the one who gives this command; it is not optional. The love that God's people are to express is grounded not in self-interest but in the identity and nature of God.

What Do You Think?
Does "thou shalt not avenge" mean that God's people cannot take a neighbor to court to redress a wrong? Why, or why not?
Talking Points for Your Discussion
- Exodus 22:9
- 1 Corinthians 6:1-11
- Civil vs. criminal cases

❧ CLOSE TO HOME ❧

Think about how we feel about criminals—even international terrorists—as the news reports them. Sure their crimes are egregious, *but what have they ever done to me?* We watch, shake our heads, and finish our suppers. Now compare that with the intense emotion we feel when a neighbor's dog digs up our yard or a friend at church betrays a confidence. The truth is, we are more easily hurt when the offense is closer to home.

I have witnessed people in the same family or the same church merely putting up with each other for years rather than forgiving. They can't carry each other's burdens because their arms are full of grudges. I've heard people speak as if forgiveness were an add-on to the Christian walk —an extra credit assignment, if you will.

In truth, love and forgiveness are linked. Those two stand at the core of God's heart. We cannot say we love the God who forgives us in Christ while failing to forgive others, who are created in His image as we are. See Matthew 18:21-35.   —V. E.

B. Toward God (vv. 4, 5)

4. Hear, O Israel: The LORD our God is one LORD.

As important as Leviticus 19 is to the ancient Israelite, the passage before us is arguably more so. Even today, Deuteronomy 6:4 is the centerpiece of a prayer that orthodox Jews pray every morning and evening. It is called *the Shema*, taking its name from the first Hebrew word of this verse, which we see translated as *hear*.

In the original language, there is no verb in the statement *The Lord our God is one Lord*. Many editions of the *King James Version* designate this absence by putting the word *is* in italics. The question is exactly where this implied verb should be placed. Is it implied for the first half of this statement, for the second half, or for both? These alternatives can yield translations such as "The Lord is our God, the Lord alone" or "The Lord our God, the Lord is one" or "The Lord is our God, the Lord is one," respectively. The first possibility focuses on the fact that Israel has one and only one God, the second focuses on God's unity, while the third incorporates both ideas.

We will see where Jesus puts the verb *is* when we get to Mark 12:29. But at this point we can affirm that all three alternatives are true and foundational for the instruction to follow.

5. And thou shalt love the LORD thy God with all thine heart, and with all thy soul, and with all thy might.

This passage can be read in two ways as saying the ancient Israelite is to love God with one's entire being. One is the familiar way of saying that *heart* stands for the inner self, *soul* stands for the spiritual self, and *might* stands for the physical self. Another way is to say that *heart* stands for the inner being, *soul* stands for that which makes one a living being, and *might* stands for the excess of one's being; it is as if to say that one must love God with one's inner self, one's whole life, and everything that flows forth from one's being.

Though the second is arguably closer to the original language and the worldview of the ancient Israelite, both yield the same result. There is no aspect of who one is that should not be directed to loving God. God cares for everything His people say, think, feel, do, and produce. The threefold phrase is His reminder not to place any aspect of life outside one's devotion to Him.

What Do You Think?
How can the church help people devote themselves ever more fully to loving God?
Talking Points for Your Discussion
- In use of time and material resources
- In interactions with other people
- In lifestyle choices
- Other

C. In Heart and Teaching (vv. 6-9)

6. And these words, which I command thee this day, shall be in thine heart.

Because Jeremiah later prophesies that the new covenant will be written on our hearts (Jeremiah 31:31-33; quoted in Hebrews 8:8-12; 10:16, 17), some have concluded that the old covenant was concerned only with external rituals, not with the heart. Yet here we see clearly that God wants His old covenant laws to be on His people's hearts. God requires His people to love Him with every fiber of their being. It is better to interpret Jeremiah as saying that even though God intended His old covenant to be written on every Israelite heart, it did not happen due to the people's unfaithfulness. Many followed the rituals but were not devoted to God from the inside out (Isaiah 29:13; etc.). According to Jeremiah, that will not be the case under the new covenant.

7. And thou shalt teach them diligently unto thy children, and shalt talk of them when thou sittest in thine house, and when thou walkest by the way, and when thou liest down, and when thou risest up.

If God's commands are to permeate the lives of His people, each generation must pass those decrees to the next; there must be no breach in transmitting them. For this reason, God instructs the Israelites to talk about His laws everywhere and all the time. Any time is a good time to discuss God's commands!

We should realize that Sunday school and youth group are not enough. The world fills our heads with lies so often that unless we constantly remind one another of what it means to follow Jesus, we will gradually forget and thereby fail to pass along the message that God has given us.

8, 9. And thou shalt bind them for a sign upon thine hand, and they shall be as frontlets between thine eyes. And thou shalt write them upon the posts of thy house, and on thy gates.

God also knows that word of mouth is not enough. Therefore He gives His people several imperatives in terms of visual aids for remembering His commands. The people are to inscribe those decrees on planks of wood or chunks of stone that they walk by daily, whether inside their homes or outside on the gateways of their towns. They are to write them on paper and bind them onto hands or foreheads. Still today, orthodox Jews bind on their hands and heads little scrolls called *phylacteries*. These can be seen in pictures of people praying at the Wailing Wall in Jerusalem.

These forms of reminder correspond with the times when God's people should convey His commands. When at home, people can convey the decrees as they meditate on Scriptures fastened to hands and heads. When entering or leaving a house or village, people will remember to talk about the commands while on the move.

II. Love in the New Testament
(MARK 12:28-34)
A. Scribe's Question (v. 28)

28. And one of the scribes came, and having heard them reasoning together, and perceiving that he had answered them well, asked him, Which is the first commandment of all?

Jesus has just finished answering difficult questions designed to trap Him (see Mark 12:13-27).

This man's question seems no different at first since Matthew 22:35 (which is parallel) says that he is "tempting" Jesus. Jewish tradition counts more than 600 commands in the Law of Moses, and this man wants to know which commandment Jesus considers to be most important.

B. Jesus' Answer (vv. 29-31)

29, 30. And Jesus answered him, The first of all the commandments is, Hear, O Israel; The Lord our God is one Lord: and thou shalt love the Lord thy God with all thy heart, and with all thy soul, and with all thy mind, and with all thy strength: this is the first commandment.

Jesus begins His answer by citing *the Shema* (see Deuteronomy 6:4, above). In so doing, He adds the term *mind* to the aspects of the human life that ought to love God. This may be an effort to counteract some Greek ideas that had become more prominent in Palestine as a result of the Greek occupation of 333 to 63 BC. In the Jewish worldview, the heart is the intellectual seat, the place from which one's deepest thoughts originate. The Greeks are more likely to speak of the mind as the thinking organ. So Jesus may be expanding the formula so that no part of oneself can be exempted from loving God.

What Do You Think?
How does our love for God serve as a foundation for all other aspects of our faith?
Talking Points for Your Discussion
- Regarding self-image
- Regarding ethical responsibility
- Regarding stewardship
- Regarding sense of purpose in life
- Other

---

31. And the second is like, namely this, Thou shalt love thy neighbour as thyself. There is none other commandment greater than these.

Jesus is not content to answer the scribe's question at the level of love for God only. People may profess love for God yet have little regard for their neighbor. Yet Jesus knows that these two cannot be separated. It is improper to say that people should love God as the first move, then love their neighbor whenever they get around to it. There is no way to love God truly without truly loving one's neighbor as well. We encounter God in our neighbor and show love for God by loving our neighbors (Matthew 25:31-46). We cannot love God without loving one another (1 John 4:7-12).

What Do You Think?

How can the church do better at helping people see the connection between expressing love for neighbor and love for God?

Talking Points for Your Discussion
- With regard to one's heart
- With regard to one's soul
- With regard to one's mind
- With regard to one's strength

❧ MY SAD FAILURE ❧

There he was, stiff-legged but resolved against the bitter blasts of icy wind. The tall, unshaven man in his worn jacket, jeans, and flip-flops trudged toward the supermarket entrance. Nothing says "homeless" like flip-flops in an ice storm!

I tried to follow him, rehearsing how to begin. I caught sight of him again as he left the bakery section, eating a donut as he trudged forward with painful, plodding steps. I knew there was a high-end boot shop just a few stores down. I decided what I would say: "Excuse me sir, it's so very cold out today. May I get you a pair of boots?"

Before I could do that, however, another thought intruded: *What if I offend him? make him angry? Who do I think I am?* And so I dawdled, caught in the old "paralysis of analysis," and I lost sight of him. I walked quickly through the store. Nothing. I waited outside in my car. He was gone.

When my children were young, I made sure they had proper shoes and clothing for the weather. Why did I not make a similar attempt with this man? What possible momentary awkwardness could outweigh the pain and damage of frostbite? Father, forgive me for not loving this man, whom Your Son died for. Align my heart with Yours and save me from fear or anything else that would hinder me from fulfilling Your desire to love in deed as well as in word.   —V. E.

C. Scribe's Agreement (vv. 32, 33)

32, 33. And the scribe said unto him, Well, Master, thou hast said the truth: for there is one God; and there is none other but he: and to love him with all the heart, and with all the understanding, and with all the soul, and with all the strength, and to love his neighbour as himself, is more than all whole burnt offerings and sacrifices.

As much as Jesus and the scribes have butted heads, He is united with this one regarding the centrality of love. This particular scribe also adds commentary on the Shema. We noted above that the second clause of the Shema could mean that God is a unity or that there is only one God. This scribe clearly sides with the second in claiming that there is none other than He.

This scribe also connects the centrality of love with the words of the prophets. Several of them emphasize that God cares more for how His people treat one another than what sacrifices they offer to Him (Isaiah 1:11-17; Hosea 6:6; Micah 6:7, 8). Jesus says the same in Matthew 9:13 and 12:7.

What Do You Think?

Why do we sometimes fail to show genuine love to neighbors? How can we do better?

Talking Points for Your Discussion
- Barriers of past experiences
- Allowing the urgent to displace the important
- Barriers of suspicion
- Fears of becoming too involved
- Other

D. Jesus' Approval (v. 34)

34. And when Jesus saw that he answered discreetly, he said unto him, Thou art not far from the kingdom of God. And no man after that durst ask him any question.

Jesus is impressed with the scribe's response! Although the scribe started by "tempting" Jesus (Matthew 22:35), the man ends up acknowledging that Jesus teaches the truth. In fact, this man's acknowledgement means that he is on the path to understanding God's heart; this puts the scribe close to Jesus' preaching about *the kingdom of God*.

Given the context described in Mark 12:28, this encounter seems to take place within earshot of others of the Jewish religious hierarchy. If so, this scribe is demonstrating a certain amount of courage in staking out an area of agreement with Jesus! The Jewish authorities often appear in packs and are emboldened by one another's obstinacy to the truths of Jesus. This scribe seems to be an exception (compare John 3:1-12; 7:50-52; 19:39).

Now that Jesus has shown himself to be adept at escaping traps and is orthodox by Old Testament standards, the questioning comes to an end. If Jesus' enemies are going to take Him down, they will have to find some other way.

Conclusion

A. Not as Different as It Appears

God wants His people to be set apart by their love for Him and for one another. Is it not true, however, that differences between the Old and New Testaments mean that God wanted something quite different in this regard from Old Testament Israel? How else can we explain the Old Testament focus on Palestine, circumcision, and sacrifices?

An analogy to parenting is instructive. When parents ask different things of their children at different stages in their development, it does not mean that the parents' ultimate desires for their children are constantly changing. When my children were toddlers, I blocked their access to electrical outlets and warned that they must never touch them. As they grew older, I removed the plastic protectors and taught the children that it is OK to stick appliance plugs into the outlets, but

Visual for Lesson 13. *Point to this visual and ask, "What acts of piety, etc., do people try to substitute for what Jesus says is most important?"*

they must never remove the faceplate. Now that they are becoming adults, I am teaching them that it is appropriate to switch off the circuit breaker, remove the faceplate, detach wires, and install a new outlet when the old one needs to be replaced. Though I have taught my children three different ways of relating to electrical outlets, what I have wanted of them from the beginning has never changed.

The same can be said about the way God has related to His people during different times. He has always wanted to form a people after the teachings of Jesus, empower them by His Spirit, and send them to make disciples of all nations. But many preliminary preparations had to be made through Abraham, Moses, etc.

Those preparations included shaping the ancient Israelites into a set-apart people in relative isolation in Palestine. When the time was right, God sent Jesus to finish their formation so they could in turn be sent to the nations in mission. God's loving plan for this world does not change. May our loving part in it match His.

B. Prayer

Lord God, we thank You for Your constancy! Empower us to love as You draw us deeper into Your own love. In Jesus' name, amen.

C. Thought to Remember

Love God and neighbor.

HOW TO SAY IT

Herodians	Heh-*roe*-dee-unz.
Marcion	*Mahr*-shuhn.
Pharisees	*Fair*-ih-seez.
phylacteries	fih-*lak*-ter-eez.
Sadducees	*Sad*-you-seez.
Shema	*She*-muh.
Sinai	*Sigh*-nye or *Sigh*-nay-eye.
Torah (*Hebrew*)	*Tor*-uh.

INVOLVEMENT LEARNING

Some of the activities below are also found in the helpful student book, Adult Bible Class.
Don't forget to download the free reproducible page from www.standardlesson.com to enhance your lesson!

Into the Lesson

Ask learners to raise their hands if they wish they knew more Scriptures by heart. Then say, "Let's take the opportunity to do that right now as we work on 'the first commandment' as Jesus stated it in Mark 12:30." Ask learners to repeat the following after you: "Thou shalt love the Lord thy God with all thy heart, and with all thy soul, and with all thy mind, and with all thy strength." Pause after each comma as a signal for learners to repeat the phrase you just vocalized.

Option: Find on the Internet the hand gestures of American Sign Language for the words *love, God, heart, soul, mind,* and *strength*; have learners imitate those gestures as you model them when you come to the words they represent.

Repeat this a few times, picking up speed with each repetition. Make a transition by saying, "Now let's find out why this particular verse is so important to memorize."

Into the Word

Recruit two learners in advance to conduct a "Point, Counterpoint" exchange. Provide a realistic setting by providing two lecterns for the antagonists. The first presenter will offer the following points: 1. "The Old Testament was all about external behavior; the New Testament is about a person's inner being." *[Quotes Jeremiah 7:3; Romans 2:29; and/or similar.]* 2. "The only way for children to grow into decent adults is through strict discipline." *[Quotes Proverbs 22:15; 23:13; 29:15.]* 3. "It is impossible to identify one or two commandments that are greater than the others since they are all important." *[Quotes James 2:11.]* 4. "Jesus thought it was not possible for a scribe or Pharisee to be part of the kingdom of God." *[Quotes Matthew 15:12-14 and/or 23:13.]*

After offering a point above, the first debater will fall silent while the second debater offers the corresponding counterpoint: 1. "Are you not guilty of quoting Scripture selectively? Consider Leviticus 19:18 and Deuteronomy 6:4-6." *[Quotes them.]* "Even the external behavior of Deuteronomy 6:8, 9 is intended to shape one's inner being." *[Quotes the two verses.]* 2. "Have you overlooked Deuteronomy 6:7?" *[Quotes it.]* 3. "Your concern to uphold the importance of all God's commands is noteworthy, but we should also consider Mark 12:28-31." *[Quotes it.]* 4. "Again, I fear that you are quoting Scripture selectively. We should also consider Mark 12:32-34." *[Quotes it.]*

The wording of the points and counterpoints can be modified as you or the debaters see fit. After each point and corresponding counterpoint is presented, pause the exchange as you ask the class, "Are there any additional reactions regarding the passage(s) that the 'point' debater quoted?"

Option: After the above, say, "Love for God and neighbor stand at the center of the Old Testament law. Let's examine other passages that pick up on these imperatives." Distribute copies of the "The Imperative of Love" activity from the reproducible page, which you can download. Have learners complete it as indicated. When everyone is finished, ask, "Which of these texts hit you the hardest? Why?" Allow time for personal sharing.

Into Life

Say, "Now let's see how well your memory is holding up" as you repeat the memorization exercise of the Into the Lesson segment. After a few repetitions, add Mark 12:31; repeat both verses together a few times, picking up speed as you go. After a brief time of whole-class repetition, pair learners off to practice their memorization with one another.

Option: As learners finish practicing in pairs, distribute copies of the "Remembering to Love" activity from the reproducible page. Encourage learners to post it in a prominent place as a daily memory challenge for the week ahead.

THE PEOPLE OF GOD
SET PRIORITIES

Special Features

*Note: Special Features are minimized this quarter because there are 14 lessons instead
of the usual 13. Some lessons are shorter than normal for the same reason.*

Lessons

Unit 1: Hope and Confidence Come from God

Unit 2: Living as a Community of Believers

Unit 3: Bearing One Another's Burdens

QUARTERLY QUIZ

Use these questions as a pretest or as a review. The answers are on page iv of This Quarter in the Word.

Lesson 1
1. Haggai's work was to encourage the people of Jerusalem to finish the _____. *Haggai 1:2*
2. Haggai declared that the Lord had called for a flood on the land. T/F. *Haggai 1:11*

Lesson 2
1. Haggai prophesied during the reign of which Persian king? (Cyrus, Darius, Xerxes?) *Haggai 1:15*
2. The name of the Jewish governor of Judea in the time of Haggai was _____. *Haggai 2:2*

Lesson 3
1. The people of Judea had their crops reduced by blasting, mildew, and _____. *Haggai 2:17*
2. What trees did Haggai mention? (pick three: apple, fig, pomegranate, cherry, olive?) *Haggai 2:19*

Lesson 4
1. Who prophesied at the same time as Zechariah? (Ezekiel, Haggai, Jonah?) *Ezra 5:1*
2. Zechariah's visit with an angel began by seeing a silver candlestick. T/F. *Zechariah 4:2*

Lesson 5
1. Paul refers to Peter as "Cephas." T/F. *1 Corinthians 1:12*
2. Paul had baptized only one person in the Corinthian church. T/F. *1 Corinthians 1:14-16*

Lesson 6
1. What sin did Paul say is "against" the body? (idolatry, fornication, stealing?) *1 Corinthians 6:18*
2. Paul says that "your body is the _____ of the Holy Ghost." *1 Corinthians 6:19*

Lesson 7
1. Eating meat sacrificed to _____ was a problem in Corinth. *1 Corinthians 8:4*
2. Paul warned that misused liberty could become a stumblingblock. T/F. *1 Corinthians 8:9*

Lesson 8
1. When there is a temptation, _____ will provide a way to escape. *1 Corinthians 10:13*
2. Paul said that sacrificing to idols is equivalent to sacrificing to devils. T/F. *1 Corinthians 10:20*

Lesson 9
1. Paul claimed that he never spoke in tongues. T/F. *1 Corinthians 14:18*
2. Paul desired that "all things be done unto" what? (law, edifying, time?) *1 Corinthians 14:26*

Lesson 10
1. Paul understood that when he suffered, he shared the sufferings of _____. *2 Corinthians 1:5*
2. Under great pressure, Paul even had despaired for his life. T/F. *2 Corinthians 1:8*

Lesson 11
1. Paul was determined to make another visit to Corinth "in heaviness." T/F. *2 Corinthians 2:1*
2. Paul admitted that he was unaware of Satan's devices (tactics). T/F. *2 Corinthians 2:11*

Lesson 12
1. Paul described possession of the gospel as being a ____ in earthen vessels. *2 Corinthians 4:7*
2. Paul rejoiced that his ministry had been without serious troubles. T/F. *2 Corinthians 4:8*

Lesson 13
1. Paul had a spiritual armor of what? (light, patience, righteousness?) *2 Corinthians 6:7*
2. Paul was exceeding joyful in tribulation. T/F. *2 Corinthians 7:4*

Lesson 14
1. Who delivered Paul's request to the Corinthians? (Titus, Luke, Demas?) *2 Corinthians 8:6*
2. Paul did not desire equality of resources between churches. T/F. *2 Corinthians 8:14*

THIS QUARTER IN THE WORD

Answers to the Quarterly Quiz on page 338

Lesson 1—1. temple (or Lord's house). 2. false. **Lesson 2**—1. Darius. 2. Zerubbabel. **Lesson 3**—1. hail. 2. fig, pomegranate, olive. **Lesson 4**—1. Haggai. 2. false. **Lesson 5**—1. true. 2. false. **Lesson 6**—1. fornication. 2. temple. **Lesson 7**—1. idols. 2. true. **Lesson 8**—1. God. 2. true. **Lesson 9**—1. false. 2. edifying. **Lesson 10**—1. Christ. 2. true. **Lesson 11**—1. false. 2. false. **Lesson 12**—1. treasure. 2. false. **Lesson 13**—1. righteousness. 2. true. **Lesson 14**—1. Titus. 2. false.

i

Mon, June 23	**Being of the Same Mind**	Philippians 4:1-7
Tue, June 24	**Empowered by the Same Spirit**	1 Corinthians 12:4-11
Wed, June 25	**Maintaining the Unity of the Spirit**	Ephesians 4:1-6
Thu, June 26	**Many Members in One Body**	1 Corinthians 12:12-20
Fri, June 27	**No Dissension Within the Body**	1 Corinthians 12:21-26
Sat, June 28	**Members of the Body of Christ**	1 Corinthians 12:27-31
Sun, June 29	**Agreement Without Divisions**	1 Corinthians 1:10-17; 3:4-9
Mon, June 30	**Building Up the Body of Christ**	Ephesians 4:7-16
Tue, July 1	**Building Up the Beloved**	2 Corinthians 12:14-21
Wed, July 2	**Sincerity and Truth in the Body**	1 Corinthians 5:1-8
Thu, July 3	**Dissociating from Immorality in the Body**	1 Corinthians 5:9-13
Fri, July 4	**Washed, Sanctified, and Justified**	1 Corinthians 6:1-11
Sat, July 5	**A Particular Gift from God**	1 Corinthians 7:1-9
Sun, July 6	**Glorify God in Your Body**	1 Corinthians 6:12-20
Mon, July 7	**Regulations for the Interim**	Hebrews 9:1-10
Tue, July 8	**Human Commands and Teachings**	Colossians 2:16-23
Wed, July 9	**Faith and Knowledge**	2 Peter 1:2-11
Thu, July 10	**Grow in Grace and Knowledge**	2 Peter 3:14-18
Fri, July 11	**Honoring and Giving Thanks to God**	Romans 14:1-6
Sat, July 12	**Accountable to God**	Romans 14:7-12
Sun, July 13	**Liberty or Stumbling Block?**	1 Corinthians 8
Mon, July 14	**Turning Aside from God's Commands**	Exodus 32:1-10
Tue, July 15	**Warning About Turning from God**	Deuteronomy 7:1-6
Wed, July 16	**Putting the Lord to the Test**	Acts 5:1-11
Thu, July 17	**Search with Heart and Soul**	Deuteronomy 4:25-31
Fri, July 18	**Holding Firm to the End**	Hebrews 3:7-14
Sat, July 19	**Examples that Deter from Evil**	1 Corinthians 10:1-5
Sun, July 20	**God's Faithfulness in Our Testing**	1 Corinthians 10:6-22

Mon, July 21	**Imitate What Is Good**	3 John 2-12
Tue, July 22	**Doing the Right Thing**	James 4:13-17
Wed, July 23	**Complete in Everything Good**	Hebrews 13:16-21
Thu, July 24	**Devoted to Good Works**	Titus 3:8-14
Fri, July 25	**So All Learn and Are Encouraged**	1 Corinthians 14:27-33
Sat, July 26	**All Done Decently and in Order**	1 Corinthians 14:37-40
Sun, July 27	**Praying with Spirit and Mind**	1 Corinthians 14:13-26
Mon, July 28	**Our Refuge and Strength**	Psalm 46
Tue, July 29	**The Shield of Your Help**	Deuteronomy 33:24-29
Wed, July 30	**O Lord, We Rely on You**	2 Chronicles 14:1-12
Thu, July 31	**Support the Weak**	Acts 20:28-35
Fri, Aug. 1	**Admonish, Encourage, Help, and Do Good**	1 Thessalonians 5:12-22
Sat, Aug. 2	**A Cause for Giving Thanks**	Philemon 3-7
Sun, Aug. 3	**The God Who Consoles Us**	2 Corinthians 1:3-11
Mon, Aug. 4	**Sin and Forgiveness**	Acts 13:36-41
Tue, Aug. 5	**Confession and Forgiveness**	1 John 1:5-10
Wed, Aug. 6	**Repentance and Forgiveness**	Luke 17:1-6
Thu, Aug. 7	**Redemption and Forgiveness**	Ephesians 1:3-10
Fri, Aug. 8	**Grace and Justification**	Romans 5:15-21
Sat, Aug. 9	**Speaking as Persons of Sincerity**	2 Corinthians 2:12-17
Sun, Aug. 10	**Forgiving and Consoling**	2 Corinthians 1:23–2:11
Mon, Aug. 11	**Enduring Troubles and Calamities**	Psalm 71:17-24
Tue, Aug. 12	**Finding Grace in the Wilderness**	Jeremiah 31:1-6
Wed, Aug. 13	**Sharing Christ's Sufferings and Glory**	1 Peter 4:12-19
Thu, Aug. 14	**Standing Fast in God's True Grace**	1 Peter 5:8-14
Fri, Aug. 15	**Walking in Truth and Love**	2 John 1-9
Sat, Aug. 16	**Waiting for the Lord's Mercy**	Jude 17-25
Sun, Aug. 17	**Proclaiming Jesus Christ as Lord**	2 Corinthians 4:1-15

OBEY THE LORD

DEVOTIONAL READING: Luke 19:41-48
BACKGROUND SCRIPTURE: Haggai 1:1-11

HAGGAI 1:1-11

1 In the second year of Darius the king, in the sixth month, in the first day of the month, came the word of the LORD by Haggai the prophet unto Zerubbabel the son of Shealtiel, governor of Judah, and to Joshua the son of Josedech, the high priest, saying,

2 Thus speaketh the LORD of hosts, saying, This people say, The time is not come, the time that the LORD's house should be built.

3 Then came the word of the LORD by Haggai the prophet, saying,

4 Is it time for you, O ye, to dwell in your cieled houses, and this house lie waste?

5 Now therefore thus saith the LORD of hosts; Consider your ways.

6 Ye have sown much, and bring in little; ye eat, but ye have not enough; ye drink, but ye are not filled with drink; ye clothe you, but there is none warm; and he that earneth wages earneth wages to put it into a bag with holes.

7 Thus saith the LORD of hosts; Consider your ways.

8 Go up to the mountain, and bring wood, and build the house; and I will take pleasure in it, and I will be glorified, saith the LORD.

9 Ye looked for much, and, lo, it came to little; and when ye brought it home, I did blow upon it. Why? saith the LORD of hosts. Because of mine house that is waste, and ye run every man unto his own house.

10 Therefore the heaven over you is stayed from dew, and the earth is stayed from her fruit.

11 And I called for a drought upon the land, and upon the mountains, and upon the corn, and upon the new wine, and upon the oil, and upon that which the ground bringeth forth, and upon men, and upon cattle, and upon all the labour of the hands.

KEY VERSES

Then came the word of the LORD by Haggai the prophet, saying, Is it time for you, O ye, to dwell in your cieled houses, and this house lie waste? —**Haggai 1:3, 4**

THE PEOPLE OF GOD SET PRIORITIES

Unit 1: Hope and Confidence Come from God

LESSONS 1–4

LESSON AIMS

After participating in this lesson, each student will be able to:

1. Summarize the Lord's message to the people through Haggai.

2. Explain why the people had not made the rebuilding of the temple a priority after its reconstruction was halted following the return from exile.

3. Identify one ministry that needs to have a higher priority in his or her life and make a plan to change.

LESSON OUTLINE

Introduction

A. Sleeping Through Life

"Rip Van Winkle" is American author Washington Irving's humorous short story about a man who hikes to the mountains one day to get away from his nagging wife. He lies down to take a nap—and doesn't wake up until 20 years have passed! When Rip returns home, he finds that his wife has died, his children have grown, and many other changes have taken place. Eventually, he realizes what has happened and that he has indeed slept through 20 years of his life.

The focus of the ministries of Haggai and Zechariah was to challenge God's people to wake up from 16 years of spiritual slumber, years that had left God's house unfinished and the people themselves unfulfilled. Thus their problem (unlike that of Rip Van Winkle) was not that of confronting changes that had occurred during that time; rather, their problem was that nothing had changed because they had neglected to make the completion of God's house a priority.

B. Lesson Background

Haggai and Zechariah lived in the post-exilic period of Old Testament history. The "exilic" part of this phrase refers to the tragedy of the Babylonian exile. That deportation occurred in stages, culminating in 586 BC when the Babylonians under King Nebuchadnezzar destroyed the city of Jerusalem. Palestine had been under Babylonian domination for some two decades preceding that tragedy (example: Daniel 1).

In 539 BC, Cyrus of Persia conquered the Babylonians, and Persia became the dominant power in the ancient Near East. Soon afterward, Cyrus issued a decree that allowed Jews who so desired to return home and rebuild their house of worship (2 Chronicles 36:22, 23, same as Ezra 1:1-3). It is worth noting that the prophet Isaiah had predicted the rise of Cyrus (by name) and described what that king would do on behalf of God's people (Isaiah 44:24–45:6). That was about 150 years before Cyrus ever appeared on the stage of world history!

So in 538 BC some 50,000 Jews traveled to Judah to begin the task of rebuilding the temple

(Ezra 2:64, 65). Within two years of their arrival, they had completed the important step of setting the foundation in place.

But then opposition to the rebuilding effort surfaced, and the people's enthusiasm began to wane. This opposition originated with those who already resided in the territory when the Jews arrived back—people who had moved in and taken up residence in the land after God's people were exiled. They did not welcome the return of God's people, so these opponents "weakened the hands of the people of Judah, and troubled them in building, and hired counsellors against them, to frustrate their purpose. . . . Then ceased the work of the house of God which is at Jerusalem. So it ceased unto the second year of the reign of Darius king of Persia" (Ezra 4:4, 5, 24).

The temple remained unfinished for 16 years. As time passed, it became easier and easier to let the task remain undone. It seemed more practical for the people to focus on rebuilding their own homes and pursue their own interests.

The prophets Haggai and Zechariah appeared on the scene in the midst of the people's complacency (Ezra 5:1). These men were raised up by the Lord to shake the people out of their lethargy, to stir them to act in order to finish rebuilding the temple. Although the book of Haggai is placed within the Minor Prophets because of its length (only Obadiah is shorter), Haggai played a major role in conveying God's message to a people who had become indifferent to His work.

HOW TO SAY IT

Babylonian	Bab-ih-*low*-nee-un.
Cyrus	*Sigh*-russ.
Darius Hystaspes	Duh-*rye*-us Hiss-*tas*-pus.
Habakkuk	Huh-*back*-kuk.
Haggai	*Hag*-eye or *Hag*-ay-eye.
Josedech	*Jahss*-uh-dek.
Nebuchadnezzar	*Neb*-yuh-kud-**nez**-er.
Obadiah	O-buh-*dye*-uh.
Persia	*Per*-zhuh.
Shealtiel	She-*al*-tee-el.
Zechariah	*Zek*-uh-**rye**-uh.
Zerubbabel	Zeh-*rub*-uh-bul.

I. Setting
(HAGGAI 1:1, 2)
A. Date (v. 1)

1. In the second year of Darius the king, in the sixth month, in the first day of the month, came the word of the LORD by Haggai the prophet unto Zerubbabel the son of Shealtiel, governor of Judah, and to Joshua the son of Josedech, the high priest, saying.

Not all prophetic books begin with such precise dating information! The Darius mentioned in this regard is Darius I (also called Darius Hystaspes or Darius the Great). Reigning from 522 to 486 BC, he is the third ruler during the Persian period. Combining *the second year of Darius the king* (compare Ezra 4:24) with *the first day* of *the sixth month* yields a date of August 29, 520 BC.

The timing of *the word of the Lord* as it comes to Haggai is important in various ways. The sixth month is important because this is the time of year when certain crops are harvested; the problems the people have been having in this regard is a topic Haggai will address shortly. The first day of a month is the day of the new moon, a day for special sacrifices (Numbers 28:11-15). First Samuel 20:18-24 records a feast marking the occasion, and some students find it noteworthy that Haggai, whose name means "festival," receives his prophetic revelation on a festival day. Furthermore, 2 Kings 4:22, 23 indicates that the first of the month (new moon) is considered an appropriate time to consult a prophet. Thus the time is right for a prophet to come forward and speak the Word of God.

The recipients of the Lord's word, the governor and the high priest, are also mentioned. These men are the two primary leaders of God's people during the first return of captives from Babylon (Ezra 5:2). Each man has a specific role to fill: Zerubbabel as governor is the political leader, and Joshua as high priest is the spiritual leader.

B. Dilemma (v. 2)

2. Thus speaketh the LORD of hosts, saying, This people say, The time is not come, the time that the LORD's house should be built.

Haggai gets to the heart of the Lord's message right away. The Lord's words begin by quoting the people's words: *The time is not come, the time that the Lord's house should be built.* As noted in the Lesson Background, 16 years have now elapsed since the foundation of the temple was laid by those who first returned from exile in Babylon. The enthusiasm that characterized the beginning of this noble task has long ago been replaced by an apathetic "It's just not the right time to build" attitude.

What Do You Think?

How do we recognize when *strategic delay* has become *procrastination* in the church today? How do we overcome this problem or prevent it from happening in the first place?

Talking Points for Your Discussion

- In changing/updating a program or format
- In adding a staff member
- In starting a new Bible study class
- Other

❧ *GETTING USED TO IT?* ❧

When I was a youngster, our house had a porch that wasn't really a porch. It was merely a rectangle of cinder blocks of about 3' x 5', with the rectangle being filled with sand. For some reason, no concrete slab had been poured on top of it. One had to walk across the sand to get into the house. In the process, of course, sand was tracked in.

We had a long rug just inside the doorway, and naturally that rug bore the brunt of what was tracked in. It was often my job to hang that rug over a clothesline and beat it to get the sand out. But no matter how much I beat it, there was always more sand in it. I would finally give up, take the rug back inside, and repeat the process some other time.

When I was in high school, my dad had a contractor pour the needed slab. By that time we had lived there almost 15 years! It's amazing what one gets used to over time. A job delayed, an unsightly nuisance—but that's just "how it is." Yet when we get around to correcting the problem, we ask ourselves, "Why didn't I do this sooner?" Regarding issues of the Lord, that's a question we best ask ourselves before God does! —J. B. N.

II. Failing
(HAGGAI 1:3-6)
A. Ungodly Priorities (vv. 3, 4)

3, 4. Then came the word of the LORD by Haggai the prophet, saying, Is it time for you, O ye, to dwell in your cieled houses, and this house lie waste?

Haggai confronts the people by drawing attention to their actions. They seem to have plenty of time to build their *cieled houses*. They have invested much time and expense to make sure their homes look their best. The word *cieled* brings to mind the word *ceiling*; the Hebrew word means "cover" and may refer either to covering a house with a roof or paneling its sides. Whatever the specific reference, it is clear that the people's houses are finished while the Lord's house—the temple—is not.

Of course, the issue here is not really a matter of having the time to complete the temple; it is, rather, a matter of being willing to *make* the time to do so. If the people had really wanted to complete the Lord's house, they would have done so long before now. The problem is simply one of misplaced priorities. The people's own houses are completed because that is where the people's priorities have been focused.

What Do You Think?

How do you determine which tasks are most important? What role do others have in helping you set priorities?

Talking Points for Your Discussion

- Regarding personal needs (Matthew 6:33)
- Regarding the needs of immediate family members (1 Timothy 5:8)
- Regarding the needs of fellow Christians (Luke 6:42; Acts 6:1-4)
- Regarding the needs of the congregation as a whole (Revelation 3:1-3)

B. Unhappy People (vv. 5, 6)

5. Now therefore thus saith the LORD of hosts; Consider your ways.

Haggai proceeds to offer the Lord's message to the people about an issue that goes much deeper than the houses to which the prophet has referred. The challenge is brief but compelling: *Consider your ways*. The Hebrew for this phrase is most insightful: literally, it may be rendered as "Set your heart upon your ways." It is repeated in verse 7, and the command to simply "set your heart" (literal Hebrew) is given in Haggai 2:15, 18. The problem is the condition of the people's hearts. Their hearts are not passionate about the Lord's work. Their hearts are consumed by the pursuit of their own agendas rather than the Lord's.

What Do You Think?

How do we instill passion for the Lord's work?
What will be your part in doing so?

Talking Points for Your Discussion

- The role of prayer
- The role of Scripture
- The role of the Holy Spirit
- The role of teaching and preaching
- Other

---

6. Ye have sown much, and bring in little; ye eat, but ye have not enough; ye drink, but ye are not filled with drink; ye clothe you, but there is none warm; and he that earneth wages, earneth wages to put it into a bag with holes.

Since the people are so concerned with the material side of life, Haggai challenges them to consider whether that aspect of life is really worth the priority time and attention that the people have been giving it. The prophet observes that the peoples' investment in the necessities of life (food, drink, and clothing) has yielded inadequate returns—they have *sown much* but *bring in little*. Haggai's words describe the condition of all too many today who are doing the same. Isaiah addresses this issue as well: "Wherefore do ye spend . . . your labour for that which satisfieth not?" (Isaiah 55:2).

In addition, whatever *wages* the people receive from their labors is used up so quickly that it seems as if each person's *bag* has *holes* in it. We can identify with owning purses or wallets that seem to have such holes! There is a specific reason for these circumstances in Haggai's time, which the prophet addresses in the next section.

The late 1990s saw rapid growth of the Internet, and market values for technology stocks soared in tandem. Then the bubble burst early in the year 2000, and market values of technology stocks plummeted. Investors' losses were heavy.

A similar thing happened in the U.S. housing market. Fueled by easy credit, low downpayments, and subprime loans, housing prices seemed to be on an ever-upward trajectory. Many bought houses they could not really afford. People turned their houses into virtual ATM machines as they borrowed against their homes' increasing market value.

But then the bubble began to burst in 2007. Home values fell, people lost jobs, and many found themselves stuck with payments they could not afford on houses that were worth less than what was owed. Massive foreclosures followed, and the downward spiral continued. Some areas of the U.S. saw housing values drop by 50 percent.

Both cases above started out as "feeding frenzies" as people jumped on board with little regard for the time-tested fundamentals of those markets. Forgetting or ignoring such fundamentals is always fraught with peril. Over the course of many years, Haggai's audience also had disregarded the most vital of all fundamentals: the need to focus first on God. How does God figure into your financial planning?   —J. B. N.

III. Finishing
(HAGGAI 1:7-11)
A. Rethinking Priorities (vv. 7, 8)

7, 8. Thus saith the LORD of hosts; Consider your ways. Go up to the mountain, and bring wood, and build the house; and I will take pleasure in it, and I will be glorified, saith the LORD.

Once more the prophet offers the challenge given in verse 5: *Consider your ways*. Here the challenge is followed by an action step that God's people need to take in order to reverse the frustrating circumstances highlighted in verse 6. The task of rebuilding the Lord's house, which the people originally set out to do with such zeal, must be resumed and completed.

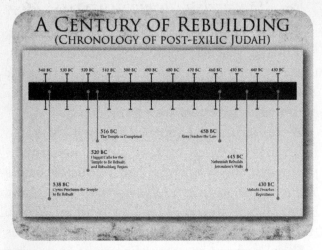

A CENTURY OF REBUILDING
(CHRONOLOGY OF POST-EXILIC JUDAH)

540 BC 530 BC 520 BC 510 BC 500 BC 490 BC 480 BC 470 BC 460 BC 450 BC 440 BC 430 BC

516 BC
The Temple is Completed

458 BC
Ezra Teaches the Law

520 BC
Haggai Calls for the
Temple to Be Rebuilt,
and Rebuilding Begins

445 BC
Nehemiah Rebuilds
Jerusalem's Walls

538 BC
Cyrus Proclaims the Temple
to Be Rebuilt

430 BC
Malachi Preaches
Repentance

Visual for Lesson 1. *Keep this chart posted throughout the first unit of the quarter to give your learners a chronological perspective.*

No mention is made of bringing any stone for the project, probably because stone is available locally. Solomon had to import wood from Lebanon for constructing the first temple (1 Kings 5), but locally available wood may suffice now since the second temple will not be as grandiose. Nehemiah 8:15 refers to various trees that are available locally during the post-exilic period to provide wood for constructing booths in observance of the Feast of Tabernacles. Clearly, the resources for finishing the temple are accessible; the people simply need to take the time and go get them.

The Lord then declares through Haggai a result of the rebuilding efforts: when the house of the Lord is completed, He *will take pleasure in it* and *will be glorified*. Completing the temple will ultimately be an act honoring the Lord. In reaching that milestone, the people will discover the fulfillment that has eluded them for so long.

It is important to note that God's desire for being honored and glorified is not a selfish desire on His part. He knows that honoring Him allows us to experience to the fullest degree the purpose for which the people exist as beings created in His image. When we ignore that aspect of who we are, then not only do our purses and wallets have holes in them but our souls do as well.

B. Remembering the Lord (vv. 9-11)

9. Ye looked for much, and, lo, it came to little; and when ye brought it home, I did blow

upon it. Why? saith the LORD of hosts. Because of mine house that is waste, and ye run every man unto his own house.

Haggai elaborates on the frustrations described previously in verse 6. *Why* have these situations occurred? This is not a matter of "bad luck" or a random "bad year" for crops. It is, rather, because God's people have not made His house a priority; instead, each of them has been preoccupied with *his own house*.

It is noteworthy that Haggai pictures the people as "running" (literal Hebrew) to their own homes. This captures the sense of urgency with which the people have been treating their own affairs. "Let's get the work on our houses done; let's not waste a minute's time" is their attitude. But concerning the Lord's house, their pace is zero.

What Do You Think?
  How do Haggai's indicators of wrong priorities apply to our situation? How do we address this problem?
Talking Points for Your Discussion
  ▪ Reasons vs. excuses
  ▪ Thinking vs. feeling
  ▪ Blind spots
  ▪ Other

---

10. Therefore the heaven over you is stayed from dew, and the earth is stayed from her fruit.

Words such as *because* in verse 9 and *therefore* in this verse highlight the cause-and-effect relationship between the people's failure to make God's work a priority and the failure of their crops. Such a relationship is tied to the special covenant that exists between God and these people. They are His "holy nation" (Exodus 19:5, 6). God has promised material blessings to His people if they obey Him faithfully (Deuteronomy 28:1-6). But He also has promised to discipline them by withholding those same blessings if they turn from Him in rebellion and disobedience (28:15-19).

Haggai's description of how *the heaven* and *the earth* are being affected seems to be a fulfillment of Deuteronomy 28:23: "And thy heaven that is over thy head shall be brass, and the earth that is under thee shall be iron." The fact that heaven and earth are hindered from providing what the people need also seems to be tied to Moses' words in Deuteronomy 30:19, where he declares to the Israelites, "I call heaven and earth to record this day against you, that I have set before you life and death, blessing and cursing: therefore choose life, that both thou and thy seed may live" (compare 4:26). Now, declares Haggai, heaven and earth are speaking by their silence in not providing *dew* and *fruit*. This testifies to the failure of God's people to honor and obey Him.

11. And I called for a drought upon the land, and upon the mountains, and upon the corn, and upon the new wine, and upon the oil, and upon that which the ground bringeth forth, and upon men, and upon cattle, and upon all the labour of the hands.

Here Haggai notes specific crops that have been affected by *a drought* that the Lord has brought about. *Corn* refers to various grains that grow in the valleys, while grapes used to produce *the new wine* and olives used to produce *the oil* grow on the mountains. In Deuteronomy 7:13, corn, wine, and oil are all mentioned in a promise of blessing, while in Joel 1:10 these three are pictured as being in scarce supply within a description of the Lord's judgment.

Ultimately, the people suffer in every aspect of their lives as a consequence of neglecting the Lord's work. A curse on the ground followed sin in the Garden of Eden (Genesis 3:17-19), and the series of events noted by Haggai is tied to the people's disobedience to the covenant between God and Israel. The good news in the midst of all of this distress is that the God of the covenant can and will reverse the conditions of His people. But first, the people must reverse their priorities. The covenant promises of blessing have not been revoked! There is hope—but the people will have to make serious changes.

Conclusion

A. Room for Caution

Today's study notes the link between obedience to God and material prosperity that was a vital part of the covenant relationship that existed between God and Old Testament Israel. We should be cautious about carrying over such a link and applying it to God's people today (Christians). Nowhere does the New Testament establish the kind of strong connection between obedience and material prosperity that we see evidenced, for example, in today's text from Haggai.

As with many such topics, balance seems to be a worthy goal. Yes, God will take care of His people (example: Matthew 6:33). But we are also told that "all that will live godly in Christ Jesus shall suffer persecution" (2 Timothy 3:12). The lack of material prosperity rather than its abundance may, in some cases, be an indication that one is serving God faithfully. Even so, the issue of priorities still confronts us today (Luke 17:7, 8).

What Do You Think?
  Are there *any* negative circumstances today that Christians can safely say are a result of God's withholding of blessings? How does Hebrews 12:3-13 relate to this issue, if at all?
Talking Points for Your Discussion
  ▪ Matthew 5:3-12, 45
  ▪ Luke 13:1-5
  ▪ John 9:1-3
  ▪ James 2:5; 4:2
  ▪ Revelation 2:9
  ▪ Other

B. Prayer

Father, the unbelieving world beckons us with so many urgencies that at times it becomes difficult to make spiritual matters a priority. May each of us consider our ways and seek to align our priorities with Yours. In Jesus' name, amen.

C. Thought to Remember

Now is the right time to do what God desires.

VISUALS FOR THESE LESSONS

The visual pictured in each lesson (example: page 346) is a small reproduction of a large, full-color poster included in the *Adult Resources* packet for the Summer Quarter. That packet also contains the very useful *Presentation Tools* on a CD for teacher use. Order No. 020049214 from your supplier.

INVOLVEMENT LEARNING

Some of the activities below are also found in the helpful student book, Adult Bible Class.
Don't forget to download the free reproducible page from www.standardlesson.com to enhance your lesson!

Into the Lesson

Before learners arrive, write on the board some either/or preference choices of approximately equal cost. Examples: *hot beverages or cold? light-colored clothing or dark? ketchup or mustard?* Pair off learners as they arrive to discuss their preferences.

After allowing some to share their choices, ask learners to consider one more choice: *read your Bible or watch TV?* Don't ask for a response; instead ask, "How is this choice different from the others on the board?" Discuss the difference between *preferences* and *priorities.* Then say, "The people in today's lesson were making wrong choices in their life priorities. Let's see what Haggai had to say to them."

Into the Word

Deliver a short lecture on the Lesson Background to introduce the historical information relevant to the lessons in the first unit. *Option:* Before the lecture, say, "There will be a quiz afterward, so please listen closely." After the lecture, distribute copies of the "This or That?" activity from the reproducible page, which you can download. Have learners work on it quickly, individually or in pairs. Then form three groups and distribute the following assignments, one each.

The Rebuke Group: Read Haggai 1:1-4. 1. Whom did the Lord rebuke through Haggai? 2. What did the Lord quote the people as saying? 3. What had they been doing instead of building the temple? 4. Why might they have made that choice?

The Results Group: Read Haggai 1:5, 6, 9-11. 1. What problems had the people experienced related to the weather? their harvest? their physical comfort? 2. What illustration did the Lord use to explain their disappearing wages? 3. Why had all this happened? 4. How should this information have encouraged them to change their ways?

The Requirement Group: Read Haggai 1:5, 7, 8. 1. What was the advice the Lord gave twice? 2. If the people followed the Lord's advice, how would they change their priorities? 3. What were the practical instructions the Lord gave? 4. In what two ways would those actions benefit the Lord?

Follow this activity by leading the class in discussing the following questions: 1. In what important way did the people have their priorities in the wrong place? 2. What may have caused them to make that wrong choice? 3. How were they suffering as a result of their mixed-up priorities? 4. What did they need to do to make things right with the Lord?

Into Life

Introduce the following two scenarios either verbally to the class as a whole or on handouts to groups. Ask learners to suggest how the individuals can better prioritize their lives and the possible consequences if they don't.

A. Between running a home business, chauffeuring her three teens to various activities, and overseeing the church's benevolence program, Gina rarely has a minute to herself. Her husband is concerned that she's not taking good care of herself and is overcommitted. Since Gina enjoys all of her activities, it's hard for her to see how she can change her life.

B. Derek is a gifted athlete who devotes much of his spare time to playing various sports, refereeing soccer games, and coaching a Little League team. However, his wife is unhappy that he isn't spending more time with her. Derek really enjoys everything he is doing and is glad for the opportunity to mentor young boys, but he also doesn't want his wife to be unhappy.

Option: Distribute copies of the "Good, Better, Best" activity from the reproducible page. Have learners pair off to use this as a discussion starter regarding their own struggles with setting priorities. If you think this exercise is too personal for your class, distribute it as a take-home activity.

TRUST GOD'S PROMISES

DEVOTIONAL READING: Psalm 27:7-14
BACKGROUND SCRIPTURE: Haggai 1:12–2:9

HAGGAI 1:12-15

12 Then Zerubbabel the son of Shealtiel, and Joshua the son of Josedech, the high priest, with all the remnant of the people, obeyed the voice of the LORD their God, and the words of Haggai the prophet, as the LORD their God had sent him, and the people did fear before the LORD.

13 Then spake Haggai the LORD's messenger in the LORD's message unto the people, saying, I am with you, saith the LORD.

14 And the LORD stirred up the spirit of Zerubbabel the son of Shealtiel, governor of Judah, and the spirit of Joshua the son of Josedech, the high priest, and the spirit of all the remnant of the people; and they came and did work in the house of the LORD of hosts, their God,

15 In the four and twentieth day of the sixth month, in the second year of Darius the king.

HAGGAI 2:1-9

1 In the seventh month, in the one and twentieth day of the month, came the word of the LORD by the prophet Haggai, saying,

2 Speak now to Zerubbabel the son of Shealtiel, governor of Judah, and to Joshua the son of Josedech, the high priest, and to the residue of the people, saying,

3 Who is left among you that saw this house in her first glory? and how do ye see it now? is it not in your eyes in comparison of it as nothing?

4 Yet now be strong, O Zerubbabel, saith the LORD; and be strong, O Joshua, son of Josedech, the high priest; and be strong, all ye people of the land, saith the LORD, and work: for I am with you, saith the LORD of hosts:

5 According to the word that I covenanted with you when ye came out of Egypt, so my spirit remaineth among you: fear ye not.

6 For thus saith the LORD of hosts; Yet once, it is a little while, and I will shake the heavens, and the earth, and the sea, and the dry land;

7 And I will shake all nations, and the desire of all nations shall come: and I will fill this house with glory, saith the LORD of hosts.

8 The silver is mine, and the gold is mine, saith the LORD of hosts.

9 The glory of this latter house shall be greater than of the former, saith the LORD of hosts: and in this place will I give peace, saith the LORD of hosts.

KEY VERSE

The glory of this latter house shall be greater than of the former, saith the LORD of hosts: and in this place will I give peace, saith the LORD of hosts. —**Haggai 2:9**

THE PEOPLE OF GOD SET PRIORITIES

Unit 1: Hope and Confidence Come from God

LESSON AIMS

After participating in this lesson, each student will be able to:

1. Summarize the promises God gave to His people and their leaders as they began to rebuild the temple.

2. Explain why the new temple seemed "as nothing" when compared with Solomon's and how, in spite of that, it would come to have "greater glory" than Solomon's temple.

3. Identify one area in which he or she can take the lead in rebuilding a neglected ministry of his or her congregation and make a plan to do so.

LESSON OUTLINE

Introduction

A. Extreme Makeover: Temple Edition

The television program *Extreme Makeover: Home Edition* has had many devoted fans since it first aired in December 2003. The people selected for the makeovers have been living in much less than ideal conditions. Often they have seen their own homes deteriorate while they sacrificed in service to others. So the makeover team enters a deficient house and rebuilds, leaving the occupants stunned at the beauty of their new residence.

Last week's study introduced us to the Old Testament prophet Haggai, who challenged the people to finish rebuilding the temple. Today's text features Haggai continuing his encouragement to the people, but with a different focus—a focus to think in terms of an extreme makeover.

B. Lesson Background

Today's lesson begins where last week's ended, at Haggai 1:12, and the year is still 520 BC. Since the background is the same, that information need not be repeated here. Even so, a bit more can be said about the larger historical context.

The book of Haggai is set in the period of Persian dominance, which began with the rise of Cyrus in 539 BC. Persian expansion to the west was eventually halted by defeats at the battles of Marathon (490 BC) and Salamis (480 BC). These battles occurred within the time gap between the last verse of Ezra 6 and the first verse of Ezra 7. The book of Esther is set within this time frame as well.

Persia was overthrown by Alexander the Great of Greece in the 330s BC. Thus the existence of Persia as a superpower in the ancient Near East lasted a bare 200 years. Her rise and collapse was foreseen some 30 years prior to the ministry of Haggai (Daniel 7:1, 5; 8:1-7, 20; 11:2). God was using these historical currents to protect His people.

I. Building a Temple
(HAGGAI 1:12-15)
A. Obedience Offered (v. 12)

12. Then Zerubbabel the son of Shealtiel, and Joshua the son of Josedech, the high priest, with

all the remnant of the people, obeyed the voice of the LORD their God, and the words of Haggai the prophet, as the LORD their God had sent him, and the people did fear before the LORD.

We met the two leaders Zerubbabel and Joshua in last week's lesson (compare Ezra 3:2, 8; 4:3; 5:2; Nehemiah 12:1). That study indicted the people for their failure to give God's house the attention it deserved, but the prophecy was addressed to the people through these two leaders.

At the center of Haggai's message is his command to "consider [literally, 'set the heart upon'] your ways" (Haggai 1:5, 7). These words are indeed taken to heart as the verse before us records the reactions of the leaders along with *all the remnant of the people* as they obey *the voice of the Lord their God*.

The term *remnant* is an important one in Old Testament prophecy. In particular, Isaiah speaks of the significance of the remnant, which describes those who are left after an act of God's judgment, such as the Babylonian captivity (Isaiah 10:20-23; 11:11, 16; 46:3). What characterizes the true remnant, however, is not just that they survive to return to the land but that they have returned to the Lord. That Haggai's audience has done just that is clear from the language used in the verse before us: they have chosen to obey the Lord's word. By so doing, they acknowledge that Haggai is indeed the Lord's messenger.

❧ THE VALUE OF A REMNANT ❧

Some time ago, my wife's stepmother worked in a fabric-remnant store. The store had many varieties of remnants of bolts of cloth—various kinds of cloth, patterns, and sizes. Such remnants were the leftovers after customers had purchased most of the fabric from the bolts.

These remnants were of little value to the typical fabric store. Fabric customers usually want multiple yards of cloth to make clothing, so the leftover at the end of a bolt was deemed not worth keeping in stock. There was little chance that someone would come in wanting such a small amount of a particular kind and pattern of cloth.

But rather than throw the cloth out, fabric stores would sell them to remnant stores for a very small price. Since the remnant stores did not have a huge investment in their stock, they too could sell these pieces for a very low price.

When our daughters were still small, my wife could pick up a piece of remnant cloth for 50 cents and make a dress or shirt for one of them. Our daughters wound up with a number of items of clothing that were made with little expense. So—what's a remnant worth? As raw material, next to nothing. But in the hands of a skilled craftsman, a remnant can become very useful. There is no greater craftsman than God! He can and will do great things with the remnants of His people in any era. Expect it!   —J. B. N.

Furthermore, the verse notes that the people have an attitude of *fear before the Lord*. Such an attitude seems not to have characterized the people over the past 16 years, the time during which the temple remained unfinished. Now, however, the people's spiritual slumber is over; they are awakened by the challenge of Haggai. Their change of heart may well be captured in the phrase *the Lord their God*. At the beginning of Haggai's proclamation, the Lord refers to "this people" (Haggai 1:2), not "my people" to acknowledge them as His. But now the people choose to take God's messenger—and therefore God himself—seriously.

What Do You Think?
How should fear of the Lord manifest itself in the various ministries of the church? What problems can arise if such fear is absent?
Talking Points for Your Discussion
▪ Evangelism
▪ Worship
▪ Teaching
▪ Benevolence
▪ Other

B. Assurance Affirmed (v. 13)

13. Then spake Haggai the LORD's messenger in the LORD's message unto the people, saying, I am with you, saith the LORD.

The words of the prophet are no longer words of rebuke and chastisement from the Lord; now they have the tone of encouragement and support. No greater assurance can be offered to any individual or group than when the Lord says *I am with you* (also Haggai 2:4, below).

C. Spirits Stirred (vv. 14, 15)

14, 15. And the LORD stirred up the spirit of Zerubbabel the son of Shealtiel, governor of Judah, and the spirit of Joshua the son of Josedech, the high priest, and the spirit of all the remnant of the people; and they came and did work in the house of the LORD of hosts, their God, in the four and twentieth day of the sixth month, in the second year of Darius the king.

Evidence of the Lord's presence is shown by His action in stirring up the spirit of the same people who are highlighted as obedient in verse 12. When God's people respond in obedience to His Word, then He is ready to bless them and accomplish great things through them.

> *What Do You Think?*
> How do we distinguish between times when God expects us to move forward vs. times when He wants us to wait for Him to do something?
> *Talking Points for Your Discussion*
> - The role of prayer
> - Open and closed doors of opportunity
> - The relevance of biblical examples (Exodus 14:15; Acts 1:4; etc.)
> - Other

The date of *the four and twentieth day of the sixth month, in the second year of Darius the king* computes to be September 21, 520 BC. Thus we see

HOW TO SAY IT

Cassiodorus	*Ka*-see-uh-***dawr***-us.
Cyrus	*Sigh*-russ.
Darius	Duh-*rye*-us.
Haggai	*Hag*-eye or *Hag*-ay-eye.
Josedech	*Jahss*-uh-dek.
Salamis	*Sal*-uh-mis.
Shealtiel	She-*al*-tee-el.
Solomon	*Sol*-o-mun.
Zechariah	*Zek*-uh-***rye***-uh.
Zerubbabel	Zeh-*rub*-uh-bul.

an elapse of less than a month between the times when Haggai begins speaking the word of the Lord and the people's move to action. Even so, the prophet Zechariah will speak his own prophecy in just a few weeks regarding the people's need to repent and return to the Lord (Zechariah 1:1-7).

> *What Do You Think?*
> How do we recognize when a church is slipping into indifference? What has to happen to change course?
> *Talking Points for Your Discussion*
> - Regarding attendance and giving patterns
> - Regarding inward vs. outward focus
> - Regarding engagement with culture
> - Regarding programming
> - Other

II. Blessing a Temple
(HAGGAI 2:1-9)

A. Former House (vv. 1-3)

1. In the seventh month, in the one and twentieth day of the month, came the word of the LORD by the prophet Haggai, saying.

This date computes to October 17, 520 BC. Therefore Haggai receives a new *word of the Lord* less than a month after the restart of the building project noted in Haggai 1:14, 15.

2, 3. Speak now to Zerubbabel the son of Shealtiel, governor of Judah, and to Joshua the son of Josedech, the high priest, and to the residue of the people, saying, Who is left among you that saw this house in her first glory? and how do ye see it now? is it not in your eyes in comparison of it as nothing?

Those addressed are the same as before: the primary leaders (*Zerubbabel* and *Joshua*) and *the residue* (or remnant) *of the people.* The phrase *this house in her first glory* refers to Solomon's temple, which the Babylonians had destroyed some 66 years earlier, in 586 BC. Thus, there are some in Haggai's audience who are old enough to recall the majesty of that structure; they also can recall the indescribable heartache of seeing it ravaged by pagans. The Lord (through Haggai) asks these older folks to compare that temple with the one rising up before them now. Despite the fact that the Persians provide the necessary resources for rebuilding—first with the support of Cyrus (Ezra 1:1-8) and later with that of Darius (6:1-12)—it is clear that this second temple will not measure up to Solomon's.

This truth seems to have become evident after the foundation of the first temple was laid. Ezra 3:10-13 records the mixture of emotions at the dedication of the foundation, with many people shouting for joy while the older ones in the group wept. Apparently, there are some older folks still around who are able to recall with fondness the "good old days" of the splendor of Solomon's temple. Perhaps these individuals are now tempted to give up the rebuilding effort yet again since realistic expectations must admit that the grandeur of the new structure will not match that of the old. The leaders, Zerubbabel and Joshua, may be feeling this pressure as well, since they are addressed in the next verse.

What Do You Think?

What role, if any, should "realistic expectations" play in how the church is led?

Talking Points for Your Discussion

- In building programs
- In attendance
- In giving
- In spiritual growth
- Other

❧ DOES IT SEEM AS NOTHING? ❧

Gregor Mendel was an Austrian monk who studied and taught physics in his monastery. From 1859 to 1863, he experimented with hybridizing peas and discovered principles of heredity that are still regarded as the foundation of the modern field of genetics. The monumental impact of his studies came from little peas.

Cassiodorus, a Roman statesman and writer who became a monk in retirement, lived in Italy in the sixth century AD. That was a time when much of the literature of the ancient world was being destroyed by German barbarians as well as by neglect. He saved many manuscripts and had

monks in his monastery copy them, thus preserving much of the literature of the ancient world for us today. Because of his seemingly small effort, many later monasteries became some of the best libraries in medieval Europe.

What projects for the Lord are you involved with? Do they "seem as nothing"? When we yield to God's will, our projects and acts of service may yield a significance in the longer view of things that we can scarcely imagine. Pray for it!

—J. B. N.

B. Present Task (vv. 4, 5)

4. Yet now be strong, O Zerubbabel, saith the LORD; and be strong, O Joshua, son of Josedech, the high priest; and be strong, all ye people of the land, saith the LORD, and work: for I am with you, saith the LORD of hosts.

The Lord's exhortation to both leaders and people is exactly the same: *be strong* for the *work*. Then the assurance of Haggai 1:13 is repeated: *I am with you.*

The exhortation *be strong* may seem to be overly simple advice in a situation like this, but in truth it is precisely what the people need to hear. The lack of strength (both spiritual and physical) in the face of opposition had caused the initial attempt to rebuild the temple to slow down and eventually stop all together (Ezra 4; compare Nehemiah 4). The people must recognize that the strength they need is not that of their own; the Lord is indeed with them. He will continue to empower their efforts as they move forward together in faith and obedience.

5. According to the word that I covenanted with you when ye came out of Egypt, so my Spirit remaineth among you: fear ye not.

The Lord adds to the exhortation of the previous verse a reminder of a promise He made to their ancestors who had emerged from bondage in Egypt. He had promised to be with them, and the power of His Spirit has been manifested at different times (examples: Exodus 31:1-5; Judges 6:34, 35; 15:14, 15).

We should note that the people whom God now addresses are not the ones who *came out of Egypt,* but their descendants. God's promises to the

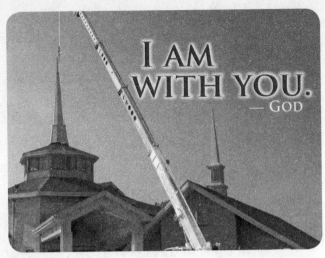

Visual for Lesson 2. *Point to this visual as you ask, "How do we know if God is 'with us' in our spiritual and physical building projects?"*

ancestors have not been nullified, in spite of all the obstacles and setbacks that those in Haggai's audience have experienced. And in a sense, Haggai's audience has emerged from its own "Egypt": the bondage of being held captive in Babylon.

C. Future Plan (vv. 6-9)

6. For thus saith the LORD of hosts; Yet once, it is a little while, and I will shake the heavens, and the earth, and the sea, and the dry land.

If the people are becoming discouraged because of the apparent inferiority of the second temple, then the Lord now offers a glimpse of what He has in store for this structure. His announcement of His intention to *shake the heavens, and the earth, and the sea, and the dry land* may bring to mind Exodus 19:18, where Mount Sinai "quaked greatly" when the Lord descended upon it. Now, however, Haggai pictures a coming shaking that will be worldwide in its impact.

The prediction of future shaking to occur in *a little while* makes us wonder to what event the Lord refers. We note that this verse is quoted in Hebrews, where the writer urges his readers not to "refuse" Jesus, the mediator of a new covenant (Hebrews 12:24-26). In verse 27, the writer focuses on the word *once* in analyzing the promise found in the book of Haggai: "And this word, Yet once more, signifieth the removing of those things that are shaken, as of things that are made, that those things which cannot be shaken may

remain." Thus the writer of Hebrews seems to be describing the events surrounding the return of Jesus. How, then, does this fit with Haggai's phrase *a little while*, which he uttered in 520 BC (now over 2,500 years ago)?

The writer of Hebrews, as do other New Testament writers, treats the entire church age as taking place within the "last days." Note, for example, Hebrews 1:2, which states that God has spoken to us through Jesus His Son "in these last days." A series of shakings is associated with the first coming of Jesus: there are physical shakings at the times of His death (Matthew 27:50, 51) and resurrection (28:1, 2). There also is the spiritual upheaval brought about by the gospel's impact when it is preached; opponents of the gospel note that Paul and Silas have "turned the world upside down" (Acts 17:6).

Of course, a shaking of the entire universe will take place when Jesus returns, as noted in 2 Peter 3:10-13. Only those who are in the kingdom that "cannot be shaken" (Hebrews 12:27, 28) will be prepared for that day.

7. And I will shake all nations, and the desire of all nations shall come: and I will fill this house with glory, saith the LORD of hosts.

Some students understand *the desire of all nations* to be a description of Jesus as the one whom the nations hunger and long for (even though they may not be willing to acknowledge that as such). But since the verb *shall come* is plural in Hebrew, others suggest that what is desired are the "forces of the Gentiles" of Isaiah 60:5 being brought in honor of and in service to Jesus— with the word *forces* perhaps figurative in terms of "strength" or "wealth." (In Haggai's own time, the wealth of the nation of Persia is being used to contribute to the rebuilding of the temple; see comments on the next verse.)

With either interpretation, a reference to the messianic age is in view. The promise *I will fill this house with glory* is then to be seen as fulfilled when Jesus enters the second temple (as elaborately refurbished by Herod the Great) and conducts some of His teaching ministry there (Luke 19:47; John 2:13-17; 7:14; 8:2). The presence of Emmanuel, meaning "God with us" (Matthew

1:22, 23), is what will make this second temple superior to Solomon's.

8. The silver is mine, and the gold is mine, saith the LORD of hosts.

Solomon's temple had been built using extensive amounts of gold (1 Kings 6:19-35). Gold was in great abundance throughout Solomon's reign (note its frequent mention in 10:14-21), and he had "made silver to be in Jerusalem as stones, . . . for abundance" (10:27). Yet who really owned these precious metals? If Haggai's listeners are concerned about whether they will have sufficient resources to finish their task, they are to remember that the Lord owns all resources; He will make certain the people have what they need.

> *What Do You Think?*
> How do we avoid crossing the line from *functional relevance* to *undue extravagance* in deciding how to equip our church buildings?
> *Talking Points for Your Discussion*
> ▪ Audio-visual capabilities
> ▪ Internet access in classrooms
> ▪ Wireless parent notification system
> ▪ Other

9. The glory of this latter house shall be greater than of the former, saith the LORD of hosts: and in this place will I give peace, saith the LORD of hosts.

As in verse 7 above, the promise of glory is given. But here the Lord affirms that *the glory of this latter house shall be greater than of the former.* As previously noted, this greater glory will occur because the Messiah, Jesus, will enter and teach there. As John tells us, "And the Word was made flesh, and dwelt among us, (and we beheld his glory, the glory as of the only begotten of the Father,) full of grace and truth" (John 1:14). The presence of the one "greater than Solomon" (Matthew 12:42) is what will make the glory of the second temple greater than that of the first.

God's message concludes with the promise of peace. The name Jerusalem, where the temple is located, means "city of peace." Peace with God is often highlighted as a purpose for Jesus' coming into the world (Luke 2:13, 14; John 16:33;

Romans 5:1; Ephesians 2:14-18). The Prince of Peace (Isaiah 9:6), who brings about peace between us and God, achieves this by means of His death and resurrection. In so doing, He can grant His followers entrance into the eternal city of peace, the new Jerusalem (Revelation 21:2).

Conclusion
A. Surviving the Shaking

The houses that the makeover team constructs on the television show *Extreme Makeover: Home Edition* are exceptionally beautiful. They also show a high quality workmanship. A viewer can see the work being done by people who know what they're doing and that they are building something that will last.

Of course, those houses won't last. No matter how structurally sound a house or any other building may be at completion, it cannot last forever. No earthquake has to occur—any structure will deteriorate as time passes, and various parts will need to be repaired or replaced. This is bound to occur with whatever belongs to the category of "things that are shaken" (Hebrews 12:27).

By contrast, Christians are "receiving a kingdom which cannot be moved" (Hebrews 12:28). Those who belong to that kingdom know the peace promised at the conclusion of today's text. Although the world around us may shake and the world's treasures and valuables age and decay, we remain firm and unmoved.

We trust in the promises of the God who does not change. As David expressed it so well, "Truly my soul waiteth upon God: from him cometh my salvation. He only is my rock and my salvation; he is my defence; I shall not be greatly moved" (Psalm 62:1, 2).

B. Prayer

Father, may our attitude today echo that of H. F. Lyte: "Change and decay in all around I see; O Thou who changest not, abide with me!" In Jesus' name, amen.

C. Thought to Remember

God's promises are unshakable.

INVOLVEMENT LEARNING

Some of the activities below are also found in the helpful student book, Adult Bible Class.
Don't forget to download the free reproducible page from www.standardlesson.com to enhance your lesson!

Into the Lesson

Have a bowl of peanuts on display. Point to it as you ask learners to suggest uses of peanuts other than for eating. Then say, "While we usually think of using peanuts in food, George Washington Carver came up with dozens of other products that could be made from peanuts. Even something so small and unimpressive looking as a peanut contains a multitude of ways to bless people. In today's lesson, God reminds the people of Judah that even though the temple they were building would not be as impressive as Solomon's temple, it was to exceed Solomon's in a certain way. Let's find out how and why."

Alternative: Introduce one of God's promises from today's lesson by distributing copies of the "Crossout Quiz" activity from the reproducible page, which you can download. When learners have completed it, say, "Let's find out why the second temple, which was much less impressive in appearance than the first, was to have much more glory than Solomon's temple."

Into the Word

Distribute handouts of today's text along with blue and red pens. Say, "We are going to mark the verses so you can see the promises God gave and the people's obedience to Him. Use red pens for God's promises, blue pens for actions of obedience." Read the text aloud, pausing after each verse to allow learners to mark them accordingly. The verses with God's promises are 1:13; 2:4, 5, 6, 7, 8 (implied promise that God would provide the resources they needed), and 9. Those with the people's obedience are 1:12, 14, 15. Review all the promises God made in this passage. Then ask, "Which promises were helpful for Haggai's day, and which ones gave hope for the future?" Discuss.

Divide the class in two, an *Agree Group* and a *Disagree Group*. Give the *Agree Group* the following instructions on a handout: "Develop an argu-

ment to support the propositions that (1) Solomon was the greatest king of Israel and (2) Solomon's temple brought the most glory to Israel. To support your arguments, research these Scriptures: (1) 1 Kings 3:1-15; 10:14-29; and (2) 1 Kings 6:14-38; Haggai 2:1-3.

Give the *Disagree Group* the following instructions on a handout: "Develop an argument to disprove the propositions that (1) Solomon was the greatest king of Israel and (2) Solomon's temple brought the most glory to Israel. To support your arguments, research these Scriptures: (1) 1 Kings 11:1-6; Matthew 12:42; and (2) Haggai 2:3, 6-9; John 2:13-22; 7:14.

After several minutes, have one spokesperson from each group come to the front. Read *Proposition 1* and allow the groups to respond; do the same with *Proposition 2*. Then ask, "Which side of this debate would God be on?" Discuss. (If you have a large class, form four groups and assign each to agree or disagree with just one of the propositions.)

Into Life

Have someone who has been part of your fellowship for many years participate in an interview about what your congregation was like in the past. Let this person know in advance that you'll be asking these questions: "What do you remember about the earlier days of the church? How has the building in which we meet changed over the years? Is there a ministry that we used to do that we no longer do?" Allow time for questions.

Lead a discussion by asking, "Is there anything we used to do that we should do again?" (Be careful not to stir up controversy!) If there is interest in doing so, encourage learners to become involved in reviving that ministry with approval of the church's leadership. Distribute copies of the "Temple Then, Temple Now" activity from the reproducible page as a take-home exercise.

LIVE PURE LIVES

DEVOTIONAL READING: 1 Peter 1:13-21
BACKGROUND SCRIPTURE: Haggai 2:10-19

HAGGAI 2:10-19

10 In the four and twentieth day of the ninth month, in the second year of Darius, came the word of the LORD by Haggai the prophet, saying,

11 Thus saith the LORD of hosts; Ask now the priests concerning the law, saying,

12 If one bear holy flesh in the skirt of his garment, and with his skirt do touch bread, or pottage, or wine, or oil, or any meat, shall it be holy? And the priests answered and said, No.

13 Then said Haggai, If one that is unclean by a dead body touch any of these, shall it be unclean? And the priests answered and said, It shall be unclean.

14 Then answered Haggai, and said, So is this people, and so is this nation before me, saith the LORD; and so is every work of their hands; and that which they offer there is unclean.

15 And now, I pray you, consider from this day and upward, from before a stone was laid upon a stone in the temple of the LORD:

16 Since those days were, when one came to an heap of twenty measures, there were but ten: when one came to the pressfat for to draw out fifty vessels out of the press, there were but twenty.

17 I smote you with blasting and with mildew and with hail in all the labours of your hands; yet ye turned not to me, saith the LORD.

18 Consider now from this day and upward, from the four and twentieth day of the ninth month, even from the day that the foundation of the LORD's temple was laid, consider it.

19 Is the seed yet in the barn? yea, as yet the vine, and the fig tree, and the pomegranate, and the olive tree, hath not brought forth: from this day will I bless you.

KEY VERSE

Is the seed yet in the barn? yea, as yet the vine, and the fig tree, and the pomegranate, and the olive tree, hath not brought forth: from this day will I bless you. —**Haggai 2:19**

THE PEOPLE OF GOD SET PRIORITIES

Unit 1: Hope and Confidence Come from God

LESSONS 1–4

LESSON AIMS

After participating in this lesson, each student will be able to:

1. Explain God's instructions through Haggai about purity and its impact on the rebuilding of the temple.

2. Compare and contrast the effects of the people's impurity on their "success" with the impact purity and impurity have on people's successes and failures today.

3. Identify one area in his or her life where purity is compromised and make a plan for change.

LESSON OUTLINE

Introduction

A. Some Assembly Required

I'm not much of a handyman, and the three words *some assembly required* strike fear into me more than they do most people. Not being very mechanically minded, I find even the simplest instructions on how to put something together to be quite a challenge. My wife is much more proficient at such tasks; so whenever one of our grandsons comes to me with a request to help assemble something, I have just three words: *Go see Grandma.* Thankfully, God's instructions to us on how to live lives pleasing to Him are "user friendly." We can see clearly in Scripture what He requires of us.

Today's lesson continues our studies of Haggai's challenge to God's people to complete the rebuilding of the temple. Of course, following a plan is essential in rebuilding a temple (or any structure for that matter). But God's people also needed to embrace His plan for rebuilding their lives and shaping them according to His master design. Leaving captivity in Babylon to return to the promised land was an important step; leaving spiritual captivity to return to God was another.

B. Lesson Background

As was the case with last week's lesson, today's Scripture text begins where the previous week's ended. Therefore the lesson background of those two lessons is the same for this one, so that information need not be repeated here. Instead, we will take a brief look at the wider context of the Persian Empire of Darius I (reigned 522–486 BC), within which the Judeans of today's study lived.

According to the Greek historian Herodotus (484–425 BC), Darius gained the Persian throne by intrigue and assassination following the death of Cambyses. As a result, the leaders of various provinces in the Persian Empire viewed the kingship of Darius to be illegitimate, so the years 522–518 BC, during which time the prophet Haggai ministered, saw Darius occupied with putting down rebellions.

With so much going on at the time, it's easy to imagine that Darius was not in the mood to have "just one more thing" on his plate when he received the letter described in Ezra 5. His strongly worded response in Ezra 6 left no doubt regarding his viewpoint on the rebuilding of the temple: it had to proceed! The royal treasury was to support the project; anyone found opposing the effort was subject to the death penalty. (We take care to note that Darius I is not the same Darius of Daniel 5:31–6:28.)

I. Asking Questions
(HAGGAI 2:10-13)
A. About Purity (vv. 10-12)

10. In the four and twentieth day of the ninth month, in the second year of Darius, came the word of the LORD by Haggai the prophet, saying.

Each of our texts from Haggai thus far in this unit has included a dating of the time when the events recorded occur (Haggai 1:1, 15; 2:1). The date in the verse before us computes to December 18, 520 BC. This is just over two months after Haggai's second message to God's people (2:1) and about three months after work on the temple resumed (1:14, 15).

11. Thus saith the LORD of hosts; Ask now the priests concerning the law, saying.

To this point, Haggai's messages from the Lord have been directed to the leaders (the governor Zerubbabel and the high priest Joshua) and to the remnant who have traveled to Judah to rebuild the temple (Haggai 1:1; 2:2). Nothing has been said until now about any priests besides Joshua. It is clear from Ezra 2:36-39, 70, however, that many priests were among those who came back from Babylon. Their role as spiritual leaders of God's people is still a very necessary one in Haggai's day.

While priests are often associated with officiating at the animal sacrifices that are carried out in accordance with the Law of Moses, they are also appointed as teachers of that law (Leviticus 10:8-11). The Lord (through Haggai) now addresses the priests as He probes their understanding regarding a question about holiness or purity.

12. If one bear holy flesh in the skirt of his garment, and with his skirt do touch bread, or

pottage, or wine, or oil, or any meat, shall it be holy? And the priests answered and said, No.

A hypothetical situation is presented regarding the transfer of holiness when certain things come in contact with one another. *Holy flesh* is sacred or consecrated meat; *the skirt of his garment* refers to the edge of clothing that can be folded back to form a kind of pouch for carrying that meat; *pottage* is stew. The issue presented to the priests by means of these images is essentially this: can holiness or purity be passed along to other items (such as *bread, or pottage, or wine, or oil, or any meat*) by secondary contact?

The law declares that various holy objects make other items that they touch to be holy as well. For example, anything that comes in contact with a consecrated altar becomes holy (Exodus 29:37; compare Matthew 23:19). All of the objects within the tabernacle were set apart to be holy, and anything they touched became holy (Exodus 30:29; compare Ezekiel 44:19).

According to the Law of Moses, consecrated meat makes a garment holy by contact with it (Leviticus 6:24-27). But secondary contact—such as between that garment and anything else—will not make another object holy in turn. Holiness cannot be passed along by further contact, therefore the priests correctly answer *no* to the Lord's question. We could say "holiness is not infectious."

> **What Do You Think?**
> How have you seen associations between people affect the purity or holiness of those involved? What have you learned from these observations?
> *Talking Points for Your Discussion*
> - Family members
> - Friends
> - Colleagues or classmates
> - Other

B. About Defilement (v. 13)

13. Then said Haggai, If one that is unclean by a dead body touch any of these, shall it be unclean? And the priests answered and said, It shall be unclean.

While purity or holiness is not easily passed through contact, such is not the case with defilement or uncleanness. The Law of Moses states that a person becomes unclean when touching *a dead body* (Leviticus 11:8, 24, 25; Numbers 19:11). Will an item mentioned in Haggai 2:12 above then become unclean if that unclean person touches it? The priests correctly reply *it shall be unclean*. Any object touched by an unclean person is made unclean (Numbers 19:22). Thus according to the law, ceremonial impurity or uncleanness is transmitted much more easily than purity.

> **What Do You Think?**
> What warnings did you receive as a child about "the company you keep"? How is that counsel still relevant to you as an adult? Why?
>
> *Talking Points for Your Discussion*
> - Associating with certain individuals
> - Going to certain places
> - Participating in certain activities
> - Other

Purity, as defined by the Law of Moses, requires that proper precautions are to be taken to make certain that all areas of life are acceptable to God. This is a vital part of the covenant relationship between God and Israel. He has called Israel to be His holy people (Leviticus 19:2), and His continual presence with His people is to be acknowledged by avoidance of anything that violates His standards of holiness. The key to maintaining purity is separation from anything impure.

> **What Do You Think?**
> When have you seen the purity or impurity of one person have an impact on a larger group? How has that experience influenced you personally?
>
> *Talking Points for Your Discussion*
> - In the church
> - In politics or government
> - In business
> - Other

❧ *THAT WHICH CONTAMINATES* ❧

There is an old preacher's story about a group of young people that was planning an expedition to see a working coal mine. Members of the group had been told that conditions down in the mine were rather dirty and that they should wear clothing suitable for such a venture.

Everyone except one wore work clothes, or at least clothes that would not suffer unduly from contact with coal dust. The one exception was a girl who always liked to appear prettily attired—she came to the mine wearing a white dress. The veteran miner who would guide them on their tour told the girl that that was not appropriate clothing for a trip into a mine.

"But I like this dress," the girl replied. "What's to prevent me from wearing a white dress into the mine?"

"Nothing can prevent you from wearing a white dress *into* the mine," responded the miner. "But there is a lot that will prevent you from wearing a white dress *out of* the mine."

Physical and spiritual impurities seem to have this in common: both transfer much more easily than their respective purities. —J. B. N.

II. Applying the Answers
(HAGGAI 2:14-19)
A. The People's Problem (v. 14)

14. Then answered Haggai, and said, So is this people, and so is this nation before me, saith the LORD; and so is every work of their hands; and that which they offer there is unclean.

The Lord's evaluation of the people is quite negative! How do we harmonize such an assessment with the encouraging, more positive tone that we saw in the text of last week's lesson? There we noted God's challenge to the people to "be strong" (Haggai 2:4) and His assurance that His Spirit remains among them (v. 5). Thus they are not to fear (v. 5). Those words were spoken approximately two months before the situation described in today's text (comparing Haggai 2:1 with 2:10). Has something changed since that time?

Perhaps over those two months God's people have drifted back into some of the apathy that Haggai addressed in his first message (Haggai 1:2-11). As we will see in the upcoming verses in our text today, there apparently has been little change in the people's material prosperity since restarting the building effort. This may contribute to the return of a disinterested spirit.

At any rate, God's people need to understand that their obedience to Him is not to be governed by the level of their material well-being. They are not to obey God simply on the basis that they expect life to get better if they do. Such an "unclean attitude" translates into unclean or unacceptable worship, affecting any offerings the people may bring. Perhaps Haggai is pointing to the altar on which sacrifices are being offered when he relates the Lord's message that *that which they offer there is unclean.*

> **What Do You Think?**
> How have attitudes about what is "unclean" changed over time? How do you ensure that your outlook matches God's?
> *Talking Points for Your Discussion*
> - In language
> - In clothing styles
> - Other

B. The Lord's Punishment (vv. 15-17)

15, 16. And now, I pray you, consider from this day and upward, from before a stone was laid upon a stone in the temple of the LORD: since those days were, when one came to an heap of twenty measures, there were but ten: when one came to the pressfat for to draw out fifty vessels out of the press, there were but twenty.

Once again Haggai uses the word *consider*, though it is not part of the phrase "consider your ways" used earlier (Haggai 1:5, 7; lesson 1). This time it is *consider from this day and upward.* To look at time *upward* seems a bit unusual to us, and the Hebrew wording seems to have the sense of "from this day backward." This appears to be the proper understanding given that the prophet proceeds to speak of how the people's circumstances were *from before a stone was laid upon a stone in the temple of the Lord* (compare Ezra 3).

As noted in the Lesson Background for lesson 1, the foundation of the second temple was laid 16 years before Haggai's current prophesying. Here, however, the prophet seems to allude to

his audience's more recent (*since those days*) frustrations with agricultural failures. The language is reminiscent of Haggai's words in Haggai 1:5-11, where he describes the Lord as having withheld certain material blessings (particularly agricultural bounty) from the people because of their failure to give attention to completing His house.

Haggai uses numerical amounts to depict the people's disappointment. A *heap* of grain results from the process of winnowing as threshed grain is tossed into the air. The worthless, lighter chaff (the outer husks of the grain) drifts away while the grain itself, which is heavier, falls to the ground in a heap. Imagine the disappointment of those who go to all that work expecting *twenty measures* of grain, but ending up with only half that much!

The *pressfat* is the winepress where grapes are processed to produce wine. Here too the results of one's labors are far from satisfactory; the individual expects *fifty vessels out of the press*, but ends up with only *twenty* instead.

17. I smote you with blasting and with mildew and with hail in all the labours of your hands; yet ye turned not to me, saith the LORD.

The crop failures and other setbacks the people have experienced are not simply the result of "bad luck." God himself has been behind these outcomes. The *blasting* likely refers to a disease that has, along with *mildew* and *hail*, devastated the people's crops. The blasting and mildew are mentioned among the covenant curses in Deuteronomy 28:22.

God's motivation for bringing these conditions about is to stir His covenant people to repentance. But He observes, no doubt with deep sadness, that *ye turned not to me.* Such language is reminiscent of the prophet Amos's indictment of the Lord's people in Amos 4:1-11. Five times within those verses Amos cites various circumstances that God has brought upon His people to discipline them. At the end of each of these descriptions comes the tragic refrain, "Yet have ye not returned unto me" (vv. 6, 8, 9, 10, 11).

❧ THE LORD STILL CONTROLS ❧

A former student of mine was married to a wheat farmer, and from year to year she told me of the lack of rain, the destructive hail, and other problems. Finally I asked her, "With all these problems, how can you afford to continue to do this?" She replied that a good harvest could compensate for more than one bad harvest.

Over the decades, farmers have been able to give themselves an edge in this regard. I remember back in my college days that 100 bushels of corn from an acre was considered a bumper crop. But with improved fertilizers and new methods of planting, now it is not unusual for a farmer to get 200 bushels an acre. I recall talking with one man who said farmers would be lucky to get 125 bushels per acre during a certain year when there was virtually no rain all summer. Not as much as they had hoped, but certainly far more than was typical 40 years earlier!

Despite all the advances in farming, farmers can still go bankrupt if the weather doesn't cooperate for an extended period of time. God controls the weather. He does so now just as He did in Palestine 2,500 years ago. Whenever He desires, He can frustrate the plans of anyone in order to bring that person back to a realization of who is in control. May He not have to do so with us!

—J. B. N.

C. The Lord's Provision (vv. 18, 19)

18. Consider now from this day and upward, from the four and twentieth day of the ninth month, even from the day that the foundation of the LORD's temple was laid, consider it.

It is still December 18, 520 BC (compare v. 10, above) as the prophet again challenges God's people to look to the past for an important history lesson.

HOW TO SAY IT

Amos	*Ay*-mus.
Cambyses	Kam-*bye*-seez.
Darius	Duh-*rye*-us.
Ezra	*Ez*-ruh.
Haggai	*Hag*-eye or *Hag*-ay-eye.
Herodotus	Heh-*rod*-uh-tus.
Leviticus	Leh-*vit*-ih-kus.
Persian	*Per*-zhuhn.
Zerubbabel	Zeh-*rub*-uh-bul.

son. They are to look back as far as *the day that the foundation of the Lord's temple was laid*.

Since there have been two layings of the foundation of the temple (1 Kings 6:37 and Ezra 3:10), we may wonder which one Haggai has in view. Most likely he is describing what has transpired in the people's recent experiences. The people have become increasingly discouraged over the lack of productivity in their land. In the verse before us, they are being encouraged to trust God to reverse that condition and provide abundance for His people once more. This leads to the promise of the next verse.

19. Is the seed yet in the barn? yea, as yet the vine, and the fig tree, and the pomegranate, and the olive tree, hath not brought forth: from this day will I bless you.

The timing of Haggai's message is important for understanding this verse. The date of December 18 (Haggai 2:10, 18) marks roughly a two-month interval since the prophet's previous words from the Lord (2:1). The early rains begin in mid-October, followed by plowing and sowing. Therefore the reasons for answering *no* to the Lord's question *Is the seed yet in the barn?* is that (1) all seed that has been set aside for sowing has been sown and (2) harvesting of wheat and barley crops will not even begin for at least another three months.

Harvesting that involves *the vine, and the fig tree, and the pomegranate, and the olive tree* does not begin for another six months. So the fact that these *hath not brought forth* is not surprising. Yet God's promise is clear: *from this day will I bless you.* An abundant harvest will come in due time as blessing from the Lord in response to His people's commitment to making His work their priority.

Conclusion

A. Purity Then

Impurity seems to flourish in so many areas of life today. One of the great ironies of modern society is that people can become so passionate about keeping water, air, and food free from contamination, yet exhibit an alarming apathy regarding moral and spiritual purity. God has always been concerned that His people—whether in Old or New Testament times—live pure lives. But when we come to a text such as today's and read about the purity laws reflected there (especially in Haggai 2:11-13), we may wonder about the reasoning behind such laws. How can purity or impurity depend on what someone touches? Aren't those qualities matters of the heart (Mark 7:1-23)? Why did God enforce such strict requirements?

To address this question, we must go back to the covenant that God made with the Israelites at Mount Sinai. There He declared Israel to be His "peculiar treasure . . . above all people" and His "holy nation" (Exodus 19:5, 6). The principle of holiness was taught to the people through every detail of life (examples: Leviticus 11:1–12:8).

Even so, some of the laws may seem to make no sense to us today. Possible examples in this regard are Exodus 23:19 (prohibition against cooking a kid [a baby goat] in its mother's milk); Leviticus 11:6, 7 (prohibition from eating hare [rabbits] and swine); Leviticus 19:27b (prohibition against trimming one's beard in a certain way); and Deuteronomy 27:5 (use of iron tools forbidden when constructing an altar). Why such commandments? In many cases, God was concerned that His people not imitate the practices and traditions of the surrounding peoples—imitation that could have opened the door to involvement with pagan religious practices.

The laws concerning the transmission of purity and impurity, which are part of Haggai's message in today's text, were for the benefit of God's people. Essentially, these laws were meant to emphasize that impurity or defilement is much easier to transmit than purity or holiness. The principle is that *one maintains purity by separation; defilement results from exposure to that which is defiled.*

Visual for Lessons 3 & 6. *Start a discussion by pointing to this visual as you ask, "What can we do to make purity more intentional?"*

B. Purity Now

That principle is emphasized in the New Testament as well, even though Christians are not subject to the laws of the Old Testament as the people of that era were (Colossians 2:14). James tells us that one aspect of "pure religion" is keeping oneself "unspotted from the world" (James 1:27). Paul sets forth separation principles to the Corinthians, who had their own issues with matters of purity (1 Corinthians 5:9-13; 2 Corinthians 6:14–7:1).

God wants His people in the new covenant age to be as passionate about purity as He wanted the Israelites to be under the old covenant. Jesus offered a vivid challenge in this regard when He said to pluck out one's right eye should it become offensive (Matthew 5:29). We are not to trifle with sin or compromise with it! Like a gangrenous infection in one's body, sin must be dealt with in one way—complete, total elimination.

Purity is that important.

C. Prayer

Father, the psalmist teaches us, "Wherewithal shall a young man cleanse his way? by taking heed thereto according to thy word" (Psalm 119:9). In a world increasingly impure, help us maintain purity in every part of life. In Jesus' name, amen.

D. Thought to Remember

Purity must be intentional.

INVOLVEMENT LEARNING

Some of the activities below are also found in the helpful student book, Adult Bible Class.
Don't forget to download the free reproducible page from www.standardlesson.com to enhance your lesson!

Into the Lesson

Distribute handouts of the following quote and discussion questions: "In forfeiting the sanctity of sex by casual, nondiscriminatory 'making out' and 'sleeping around,' we forfeit something we cannot well do without. There is dullness, monotony, sheer boredom in all of life when virginity and purity are no longer protected and prized" (Elisabeth Elliot). 1. How does the culture's message differ from this statement about sexual purity? 2. What are some results for those who listen to culture's message rather than God's?

Have learners pair off to discuss the two questions. After a few minutes, ask volunteers to share conclusions. Then say, "Issues of holiness and purity confront God's people in all centuries. This was no less true for the ancient Judeans, who needed a refresher course in holiness in order to receive God's blessing, as we will see in today's lesson."

Into the Word

If your class numbers eight or fewer, divide it in half and give each group one of the following two assignments. For a larger class, create more groups and give duplicate assignments.

Assignment—Clean or Unclean? Read Haggai 2:10-14. 1. What could make a person or thing unclean? 2. Under what circumstances, if any, could something unholy be made clean by coming in contact with something holy? 3. How does disobedience lead to impurity? (Further Scripture resources are Exodus 29:37; 30:29; Leviticus 6:24-27; Ezekiel 44:19; and Matthew 23:19.)

Assignment—Successful or Unsuccessful? Read Haggai 2:15-19. 1. What kept the Judeans from flourishing? 2. How was lack of diligence in building the temple connected with a lack of success in producing crops? 3. What was the Lord's purpose for smiting the crops? 4. How did Haggai's message give the people hope for success in the future? (Also see Deuteronomy 28:22; Haggai 1:4-8.)

Alternative: Enlist in advance a creative person to help prepare the signs and props needed for the "Purity Pantomime" on the reproducible page, which you can download. The pantomime needs five participants, although you may wish to reserve the role of Narrator for yourself.

Give to each cast member a copy of the script. Allow only a minute or two for each actor to look it over. (Being pantomimes, there are no lines to memorize; participants will merely act out what they hear the Narrator say). Ask participants to leave their scripts at their chairs before commencing the skit. (The reproducible page notes the option for an additional pantomime.)

After the performance(s), pose some of the questions listed above for discussion. Also note elements of "dramatic license" that are not in the text.

Into Life

Prepare in advance three poster boards with these titles, one each: *Marriage/Relationships, Work, Health.* Have two columns headed *Success* and *Failure* below each title. Form learners into three groups, giving each a poster plus markers.

Say, "Write in the columns various actions we can take that will result in either success or failure, depending on whether or not we live pure and godly lives. For example, committing adultery could result in the failure of a marriage. You will have only two minutes to come up with as many ideas as possible before passing your poster to the next group clockwise." After you call "time's up" three times, discuss results. Make sure to probe how the listed successes and failures relate to purity and impurity.

Give each learner an index card. Encourage everyone to write down one way to pursue greater purity and godliness in the area of marriage and/or relationships, work, or healthy living. Suggest that learners keep their cards handy in the week ahead as a reminder and prayer stimulus.

HOPE FOR A NEW DAY

DEVOTIONAL READING: Psalm 43
BACKGROUND SCRIPTURE: Nehemiah 7:1-7; Haggai 2:20-23; Zechariah 4

HAGGAI 2:23

23 In that day, saith the LORD of hosts, will I take thee, O Zerubbabel, my servant, the son of Shealtiel, saith the LORD, and will make thee as a signet: for I have chosen thee, saith the LORD of hosts.

ZECHARIAH 4:1-3, 6-14

1 And the angel that talked with me came again, and waked me, as a man that is wakened out of his sleep,

2 And said unto me, What seest thou? And I said, I have looked, and behold a candlestick all of gold, with a bowl upon the top of it, and his seven lamps thereon, and seven pipes to the seven lamps, which are upon the top thereof:

3 And two olive trees by it, one upon the right side of the bowl, and the other upon the left side thereof.

· ·

6 Then he answered and spake unto me, saying, This is the word of the LORD unto Zerubbabel, saying, Not by might, nor by power, but by my spirit, saith the LORD of hosts.

7 Who art thou, O great mountain? before Zerubbabel thou shalt become a plain: and he

shall bring forth the headstone thereof with shoutings, crying, Grace, grace unto it.

8 Moreover the word of the LORD came unto me, saying,

9 The hands of Zerubbabel have laid the foundation of this house; his hands shall also finish it; and thou shalt know that the LORD of hosts hath sent me unto you.

10 For who hath despised the day of small things? for they shall rejoice, and shall see the plummet in the hand of Zerubbabel with those seven; they are the eyes of the LORD, which run to and fro through the whole earth.

11 Then answered I, and said unto him, What are these two olive trees upon the right side of the candlestick and upon the left side thereof?

12 And I answered again, and said unto him, What be these two olive branches which through the two golden pipes empty the golden oil out of themselves?

13 And he answered me and said, Knowest thou not what these be? And I said, No, my lord.

14 Then said he, These are the two anointed ones, that stand by the Lord of the whole earth.

KEY VERSE

This is the word of the LORD unto Zerubbabel, saying, Not by might, nor by power, but by my spirit, saith the LORD of hosts. —**Zechariah 4:6**

THE PEOPLE OF GOD SET PRIORITIES

Unit 1: Hope and Confidence Come from God

LESSONS 1–4

LESSON AIMS

After participating in this lesson, each student will be able to:

1. Describe God's plan for and revelation to Zerubbabel.

2. Tell how Zerubbabel's life illustrates that God sometimes works through "small things" and unimpressive agents to do His will.

3. Make a list of some "small things" that are dedicated to the Lord and commit to praying daily that God would use them in powerful ways for His glory.

LESSON OUTLINE

Introduction

A. One Day at a Time

In the January 2012 edition of his newsletter *The Encouraging Leader,* basketball coach Jamy Bechler comments on the importance of small, daily victories in achieving major goals. If your long-term goal is to pay off a credit card debt, don't stop at the mall today. If you want to lose 20 pounds, then bypass your usual after-dinner piece of pie. Big goals need to be tackled in small increments. Win the little battles, says Bechler, and eventually you'll win the war.

Today's lesson is the last in this unit of studies that focuses on the rebuilding of the temple in the post-exilic period of Old Testament history. Most of today's text comes from the book of Zechariah, who was a contemporary of Haggai (lessons 1-3). Like Haggai, Zechariah encouraged God's people to faithfulness in completing the rebuilding project that had been on hold for some 16 years. The day of victory and achievement would come only by means of a day-by-day devotion to carrying out God's plan. The same principle holds true for Christian service today.

B. Lesson Background

The fact that Zechariah was a contemporary of Haggai is clear from the dates mentioned in their books (compare Zechariah 1:1 with Haggai 1:1). These two prophets are also mentioned together in Ezra 5:1, 2, where they are described as "helping" those who worked on rebuilding the temple.

The first major section of the book of Zechariah (that is, 1:1–6:8) consists of eight visions given at night to the prophet. All were messages to challenge and encourage those involved in rebuilding the temple. As Haggai did, Zechariah conveyed special messages to the leaders of the people, namely Zerubbabel and Joshua. The fourth of the eighth visions, recorded in Zechariah 3, concerned Joshua. Today's lesson from chapter 4 describes the fifth of these visions and offers a message especially intended to encourage Zerubbabel.

Before we turn to our text from Zechariah, we will consider a single verse from Haggai. The final message in this book is addressed to Zerubbabel, governor of those who returned from Babylonian captivity. The message begins with another promise from God to "shake the heavens and the earth" (Haggai 2:21), repeating an earlier promise found in 2:6 (covered in lesson 2). The effect of the shaking is more specifically defined in 2:21, 22: kingdoms and chariots, along with their horses and riders, will one day "come down, every one by the sword of his brother." Amidst all of this predicted turmoil, a promise was given to Zerubbabel.

I. Special Man
(HAGGAI 2:23)

A. Zerubbabel's Designation (v. 23a)

23a. In that day, saith the LORD of hosts, will I take thee, O Zerubbabel, my servant, the son of Shealtiel, saith the LORD.

Zerubbabel has been noted previously as governor of Judah (Haggai 1:1, 14; 2:2, 21). Now he is designated by the Lord as *my servant*. The designation "servant of the Lord" is used of such noteworthy individuals as Moses (Deuteronomy 34:5; Joshua 1:1), Joshua (Joshua 24:29), and David (1 Kings 11:13; superscription to Psalm 18). It also carries important implications regarding Jesus, especially in Isaiah 40–55. Regarding *Shealtiel*, see Matthew 1:12 (where the spelling is *Salathiel*).

B. Zerubbabel's Selection (v. 23b)

23b. And will make thee as a signet: for I have chosen thee, saith the LORD of hosts.

In the remainder of the verse, God reveals His plan involving His servant Zerubbabel. The word *signet* refers to a signet ring. An important symbol of a ruler's authority in ancient times, it is used by the ruler to authorize official documents. Note the similarities between the words *signet* and *signature*.

The prophet Jeremiah had used signet-ring language to depict how God would treat King Jehoiachin of Judah, who was Zerubbabel's grandfather: "Though Coniah [another name for Jehoiachin] the son of Jehoiakim king of Judah were the signet upon my right hand, yet would I pluck thee thence; and I will give thee into the hand of them that seek thy life, and into the hand of them whose face thou fearest" (Jeremiah 22:24,

25). God's removal of Jehoiachin represented His judgment on that evil king (2 Kings 24:8, 9). By contrast, God's intention to make Zerubbabel *as a signet* represents the reversal of judgment imposed on that man's grandfather.

What Do You Think?

When was a time you realized that you would not have accomplished something without God's help? How does that affect your prayer life now?

Talking Points for Your Discussion

- A reconciled relationship
- A change in a sin habit
- An area of ministry or service
- Other

The fact that this is to happen "in that day" (Haggai 2:23a), the day God will "shake the heavens and the earth" (v. 21), makes us wonder exactly what day is in view. The messianic implications of this promise were considered in lesson 2, where the predicted shaking of the heavens and the earth is also addressed. Certainly worth highlighting is the fact that Jehoiachin and Zerubbabel are included in the ancestry of Jesus in Matthew 1:12, 13 (with different spellings). As also noted in lesson 2, the ancient Near East is subject to much turmoil between the time of Zerubbabel and the birth of Jesus. But God's promise holds true and is fulfilled in Zerubbabel's descendant Jesus Christ, God's chosen one and ultimate servant.

II. A Special Message
(ZECHARIAH 4:1-3, 6-14)

A. Zechariah Sees (vv. 1-3)

1. And the angel that talked with me came again, and waked me, as a man that is wakened out of his sleep.

An angel is present to serve as a kind of "tour guide" when Zechariah sees the prophetic visions granted to him (1:7-9; etc.). As the fifth of the eight night visions begins here, the angel comes to wake Zechariah *as a man that is wakened out of his sleep.* Zechariah may be sleeping because of the fact that the visions all come at night; another possibility is that Zechariah sleeps between visions because the intensity of the experience to this point may have worn him out (compare Daniel 8:15-18, 27).

2. And said unto me, What seest thou? And I said, I have looked, and behold a candlestick all of gold, with a bowl upon the top of it, and his seven lamps thereon, and seven pipes to the seven lamps, which are upon the top thereof.

Zechariah describes *a candlestick all of gold* in answer to the angel's question. The Hebrew word translated *candlestick* is *menorah,* familiar because of its association with the Jewish holiday of Hanukkah. An ordinary lamp is a small bowl of olive oil with a wick for the flame, but what Zechariah sees is no ordinary lamp!

The menorah Zechariah beholds has *a bowl upon the top of it* with *seven lamps thereon,* but we are not told exactly how these are arranged. Perhaps the menorah of the Jerusalem temple in the first century AD offers a possibility. The Arch of Titus in Rome pictures this menorah as part of the spoils that the Roman general Titus brought back after he conquered Jerusalem in AD 70.

Zechariah also sees *seven pipes.* Apparently these carry oil from the bowl to the lamps.

3. And two olive trees by it, one upon the right side of the bowl, and the other upon the left side thereof.

The significance of the *two olive trees* will be addressed in commentary on verse 14, below.

B. Zechariah Hears (vv. 6, 7)

6. Then he answered and spake unto me, saying, This is the word of the LORD unto Zerubbabel, saying, Not by might, nor by power, but by my spirit, saith the LORD of hosts.

Verses 4 and 5, not in today's text, record Zechariah's admission that he does not know the significance of what he sees. So the angel proceeds to convey the primary lesson of this vision.

We should keep in mind that the issue Zechariah is facing is also that of his colleague Haggai: completing the Jerusalem temple. The essence of the message here is the same as when Haggai challenges Zerubbabel to "be strong" (Haggai 2:4). Haggai reminds Zerubbabel and the builders that the Lord's Spirit remains among them (v. 5), and this assurance is what Zechariah conveys in the verse before us. The oil for the lamps apparently symbolizes the power of God's Spirit. This symbolism is seen also where the idea of "anointing" (usually done with oil) is linked with God's Spirit (compare Isaiah 61:1; Acts 10:38).

As noted in lesson 2, it is clear that this second temple will not possess the grandeur of Solomon's renowned temple. But those engaged in the important task of rebuilding do possess the most important "building material" of all: the power of the Spirit of God. This will more than compensate for whatever material resources or manpower the people seem to lack as they rebuild.

7. Who art thou, O great mountain? before Zerubbabel thou shalt become a plain: and he shall bring forth the headstone thereof with shoutings, crying, Grace, grace unto it.

In lesson 1, we saw Haggai's challenge to the people to go to the mountains to obtain timber for the rebuilding effort (Haggai 1:8). Here, however, the term *mountain* may picture the various obstacles being faced during the work. We are reminded of Jesus' teaching about the power of faith to move mountains (Mark 11:23).

Once the obstacles represented by the mountain are leveled, Zerubbabel is then pictured as bringing *forth the headstone.* This is the topmost stone, the last stone to be set in place. When this is done, the building is finished! No wonder this step will be accompanied by a shout of triumph: *Grace, grace unto it.* The reference to grace highlights the special favor of the Lord, blessing His completed house.

> *What Do You Think?*
> What have you learned from overcoming obstacles?
> How does that help you face other challenges?
> *Talking Points for Your Discussion*
> - Educational pursuits
> - Vocational pursuits
> - Spiritual pursuits
> - Family plans
> - Other

C. Zechariah Speaks (vv. 8-10)

8, 9. Moreover the word of the LORD came unto me, saying, The hands of Zerubbabel have laid the foundation of this house; his hands

shall also finish it; and thou shalt know that the LORD of hosts hath sent me unto you.

The promise of verse 7 is now restated in language that is much more direct. Zerubbabel, who was involved in laying the temple's foundation some 16 years earlier (Ezra 3:8-11), will finish the project he started. He will do so in spite of the setbacks (4:4, 5). The completion of *this house* will validate Zerubbabel's leadership and ministry, but it will also provide evidence that Zechariah has served as the Lord's faithful messenger.

> *What Do You Think?*
>
> What have you seen leaders do to lead a congregation through a building project successfully?
>
> *Talking Points for Your Discussion*
> - In casting the vision of the project
> - During the planning stage
> - When encountering unexpected problems
> - In wrestling with the financial element
> - Other

10. For who hath despised the day of small things? for they shall rejoice, and shall see the plummet in the hand of Zerubbabel with those seven; they are the eyes of the LORD, which run to and fro through the whole earth.

Zechariah then receives a rhetorical question to pass along: *Who hath despised the day of small things?* It can be restated, "Who has the nerve to despise the day of small things?" The question is aimed at those doubters who question the worth of a rebuilt temple, since it obviously will be inferior to Solomon's temple. Size, however, should not be the standard by which success is measured in God's work (compare Matthew 13:31-33).

> *What Do You Think?*
>
> When was a time you were surprised that what appeared to be a "small thing" ended up having a far-reaching impact? How do you pass this lesson along to others?
>
> *Talking Points for Your Discussion*
> - Something done or not done
> - Something said or not said
> - Other

A *plummet,* or plumb line, is a weight suspended on a string so that the string will hang straight. It is used to ensure that a wall is perfectly vertical. To see this item *in the hand of Zerubbabel* is similar to seeing him bring the headstone of verse 7. In both instances, he is carrying out his role as primary leader of the rebuilding project, here as an inspector of the work.

> *What Do You Think?*
>
> In what ways can and should the Bible serve as "an inspector of the work" for building projects?
>
> *Talking Points for Your Discussion*
> - For incurring (or not incurring) debt
> - For encouraging financial giving
> - For encouraging participation in the labor
> - For encouraging participation in the planning
> - For engaging in prayer
> - Other

The conclusion of this verse is difficult. It appears to read as if *those seven* (which refers to *the eyes of the Lord*) are *in the hand of Zerubbabel.* The Hebrew text, however, indicates that the phrase *those seven* is actually the subject of this portion of the verse. Rearranged in this manner, the verse says, "They—those seven, the eyes of the Lord, which run to and fro through the whole earth—shall rejoice and shall see the plummet in the hand of Zerubbabel."

According to Revelation 5:6, the Lamb in the center of the heavenly throne has "seven eyes, which are the seven Spirits of God sent forth into all the earth." This suggests watchful protection. Thus the Spirit, who has already been described as the one empowering Zerubbabel's efforts (Zechariah 4:6), is now pictured as taking great joy in seeing Zerubbabel's work completed (compare 3:9).

❧ NOT A SMALL THING ❧

I have had the pleasure of touring the Cathedral Basilica of St. Louis. It is stunning in its architectural beauty and artistry—definitely not a "small thing"! Its extensive collection of mosaics is made up of more than 40,000,000 pieces of glass. Some artisans spent their entire adult lives creating the massive stained-glass masterpieces.

Our tour guide was sensitive to the controversies that surround such a work. He acknowledged that some say that the funds required to build such a structure would have better been used to help the poor. But he went on to observe that the artwork had served an educational purpose that might not be obvious to visitors today: the mosaics depicting stories from Scripture were designed to instruct the mostly illiterate parishioners who worshipped there in the cathedral's early years.

I was struck by the sacrifice required to create such a structure. I was touched by our tour guide's reverence. God is worthy of our adoration, sacrifice, and reverence, which at times can be expressed through art and craftsmanship.

Although I have never worshipped in a church building with lavish décor, I have worshipped in many churches where the praise and passion for God was lavish and even expensive—expensive in the sense that some had become believers at great personal cost. God was eager to have the second, more modest temple completed. But He is even more eager to see the completion of the third temple, the one in 2 Corinthians 6:16. Do we share His eagerness, or do we treat it as a "small thing"?
—V. E.

D. Zechariah Asks (vv. 11, 12)

11. Then answered I, and said unto him, What are these two olive trees upon the right side of the candlestick and upon the left side thereof?

This is the second time Zechariah asks the angel about the *two olive trees*, one on either side of the candlestick in his vision. The first time is in verse 4, not in today's text.

12. And I answered again, and said unto him, What be these two olive branches, which through the two golden pipes empty the golden oil out of themselves?

In addition, Zechariah queries the angel about some details not noted in the earlier description of the candlestick: there are *two olive branches* that are the source of the oil in the bowl (v. 2, above). Zechariah also observes that the oil itself is *golden,* meaning that it is obviously of the finest quality.

E. The Angel Answers (vv. 13, 14)

13. And he answered me and said, Knowest thou not what these be? And I said, No, my lord.

The angel responds as he did in verse 5 (not in today's text), by answering Zechariah's question with the question *Knowest thou not what these be?* Again, as in verse 5, Zechariah admits his ignorance.

14. Then said he, These are the two anointed ones, that stand by the Lord of the whole earth.

The two branches represent Zerubbabel and Joshua, the primary leaders of God's people at this time (Ezra 3:2, 8; 4:3; 5:2; Haggai 1:1, 12, 14; 2:2, 4). Both men are specifically challenged and encouraged by both Haggai and Zechariah. The latter has already seen a vision concerning a special promise given to Joshua, the high priest, in Zechariah 3; the focus is on Zerubbabel and God's promises to him in Zechariah 4.

The important roles carried out by Zerubbabel and Joshua are captured in the description of them as *anointed ones.* The Hebrew word translated *anointed* is not the one from which comes the term *Messiah.* In this case, it is literally "sons of oil." This seems to highlight how both Zerubbabel and Joshua are instruments of the Lord through whom His "oil" (the Holy Spirit) flows in order to accomplish His holy purposes. The Lord empowers each man for his special task, and because of that neither man will fail.

❧ *MAGIC FORMULAS?* ❧

At times it seems there are nearly as many how-to books on success as there are success stories

HOW TO SAY IT

Babylonian	Bab-ih-*low*-nee-un.
Coniah	Ko-*nye*-uh.
Haggai	*Hag*-eye or *Hag*-ay-eye.
Hanukkah	*Hahn*-uh-kuh.
Jehoiachin	Jeh-*hoy*-uh-kin.
Jehoiakim	Jeh-*hoy*-uh-kim.
menorah	meh-*nor*-uh.
Shealtiel	She-*al*-tee-el.
Zechariah	*Zek*-uh-*rye*-uh.
Zerubbabel	Zeh-*rub*-uh-bul.

themselves. A quick search produced the following eye-catching titles: *If You Know & Do These You Must Prosper: A Winners Manual on 21ˢᵗ Century Prosperity; The 100 Absolutely Unbreakable Laws of Business Success;* and *Nuts! Southwest Airlines' Crazy Recipe for Business and Personal Success.* Whenever a group or an individual achieves something, others clamor to know the "magic formula" of the processes, protocols, and programs used to achieve the success. Hence the books.

Obstacles seemed insurmountable during the rebuilding of the temple, and for some 16 years the project went nowhere. But by means of angelic counsel, Zechariah discovered the key to success in that endeavor: empowerment by God's Holy Spirit.

Secular how-to books do not include the Holy Spirit as part of their formulas. But success in endeavors for God *always* involves our obedience to the Spirit's leading and our trust in His power—and there's nothing "magic" about it.

What is God asking of you today? Be assured that what He asks of you, His Spirit fully equips you to do. Focusing on the obstacles brings discouragement (see Nehemiah 4:10); focusing instead on the Holy Spirit, who gives wisdom and strength, wins the day.   —V. E.

Conclusion

A. Big Blessings in Small Places

"For who hath despised the day of small things?" The question from Zechariah 4:10 has great relevance to Christian service today. Often we see much attention paid to the megachurches and the impact of their ministries. Certainly other churches and their leaders can learn much from what these congregations have achieved (as long as these churches and leaders are careful to measure everything by the standard of Scripture).

However, we dare not "despise" or overlook the efforts of smaller churches or ministries. We dare not consider their endeavors as being in some way inferior to what larger churches are doing. As both Haggai and Zechariah emphasized to their audiences, size is not a measuring stick as to whether a given work is pleasing to God or is being empowered by His Spirit.

DO NOT DESPISE THE DAY OF SMALL THINGS

Visual for Lesson 4

Start a discussion by pointing to this visual as you ask the first question that is associated with verse 10.

"Small things," especially small churches, have played a big part in this writer's life and in his Christian walk. The church where I grew up in south central Indiana has never been and likely will not become a megachurch. It is a country church, blessed over the years with faithful people who have served the Lord diligently. Their influence helped mold and shape me and encouraged me to consider full-time Christian service.

In the middle of my junior year of Bible college, I began preaching at another small country church that is about an hour east of Lexington, Kentucky. This congregation also will most likely never appear on a list of megachurches, but it certainly helped this young preacher in a "mega" way! I can never forget or "despise" the influence of these two small churches. Theirs was not the "might" or "power" that is impressive to some, but they were (and still are) places where God's Spirit is at work.

B. Prayer

Father, in the midst of our attempts to do big things for You, help us not to forget the importance of small things! Use us, we pray, as instruments through which the oil of Your Spirit flows. In Jesus' name, amen.

C. Thought to Remember

As Zerubbabel's hands accomplished God's purpose, so may ours.

INVOLVEMENT LEARNING

Some of the activities below are also found in the helpful student book, Adult Bible Class.
Don't forget to download the free reproducible page from www.standardlesson.com to enhance your lesson!

Into the Lesson

Distribute handouts of the following "Who said it?" matching activity.

__ A. Don't confuse fame with success. Madonna is one; Helen Keller is the other.

__ B. Formula for success: rise early, work hard, strike oil.

__ C. I don't know the key to success, but the key to failure is trying to please everybody.

__ D. The person who makes a success of living is the one who sees his goal steadily and aims for it unswervingly. That is dedication.

__ E. Action is the foundational key to all success.

__ F. Luck is a matter of preparation meeting opportunity.

1. Cecil B. DeMille; 2. Oprah Winfrey; 3. J. Paul Getty; 4. Erma Bombeck; 5. Bill Cosby; 6. Pablo Picasso. *(Answers: A-4, B-3, C-5, D-1, E-6, F-2.)*

Give a small prize to those who get all answers correct; express congratulations for being "successful." Then say, "In today's lesson, Zerubbabel doesn't need to memorize any quotes from famous people to know that he will be successful in rebuilding the temple. Let's find out why."

Into the Word

Option: Before the exercise below, distribute copies of the "The Z's Have It!" activity from the reproducible page, which you can download. Tell learners that this is a closed-Bible self-test. After two minutes, ask learners to set their handouts aside; correct answers will be discussed later.

Bring to class the following items: a large class ring, a menorah or candlestick, two jars of olives, image of a dove, picture of a mountain, a container with one or more small things (aspirin, button, safety pin, etc.). Form six groups and distribute handouts of the following assignments along with the props indicated. (Smaller classes can form fewer groups and give more than one assignment per group.)

Ring Group: Read Haggai 2:23 and explain the significance of the fact that God would make Zerubbabel His signet. *Menorah Group:* Read Zechariah 4:1, 2 and explain what the candlestick and seven lamps symbolize. *Jars of Olives Group:* Read Zechariah 4:3, 11-14 and explain who the two olive branches represent. *Dove Group:* Read Zechariah 4:6 and explain how the presence of the Holy Spirit was a message of encouragement. *Mountain Group:* Read Zechariah 4:7 and explain how a mountain turning into a plain represents victory in the context of the passage. *Small Things Group:* Read Zechariah 4:8-10 and describe the attitude one is to have regarding that which seems "small."

Allow time for each group to prepare and present conclusions. Expected responses may not be apparent in all cases from the assigned passages themselves. In that light, you may wish to include as hints the additional passages from Scripture that are noted in the lesson commentary, depending on the nature of your class.

If you used the "The Z's Have It!" option above, discuss answers at this point.

Into Life

Tell your class that you have one more "success quote" that agrees with one idea in today's lesson. Write on the board, "Success is the sum of small efforts, repeated day in and day out" (Robert Collier). Ask, "What are some 'small' daily habits that will help us in our Christian lives?" After discussion ask, "How can the neglect of these 'small' things lead to 'big' problems?" Discuss.

Option: Distribute copies of the "Small Things Make a Big Difference" activity from the reproducible page, to be completed as indicated. This can be a take-home exercise if you think one or more subject areas will be too controversial or too personal. Encourage learners to select a ministry to pray for daily so that God will use the "small" thing in a "big" way.

PURSUE UNITY IN CHRIST

DEVOTIONAL READING: 1 Corinthians 12:12-20
BACKGROUND SCRIPTURE: 1 Corinthians 1:10-17; 3:1-17

1 CORINTHIANS 1:10-17

10 Now I beseech you, brethren, by the name of our Lord Jesus Christ, that ye all speak the same thing, and that there be no divisions among you; but that ye be perfectly joined together in the same mind and in the same judgment.

11 For it hath been declared unto me of you, my brethren, by them which are of the house of Chloe, that there are contentions among you.

12 Now this I say, that every one of you saith, I am of Paul; and I of Apollos; and I of Cephas; and I of Christ.

13 Is Christ divided? was Paul crucified for you? or were ye baptized in the name of Paul?

14 I thank God that I baptized none of you, but Crispus and Gaius;

15 Lest any should say that I had baptized in mine own name.

16 And I baptized also the household of Stephanas: besides, I know not whether I baptized any other.

17 For Christ sent me not to baptize, but to preach the gospel: not with wisdom of words, lest the cross of Christ should be made of none effect.

1 CORINTHIANS 3:4-9

4 For while one saith, I am of Paul; and another, I am of Apollos; are ye not carnal?

5 Who then is Paul, and who is Apollos, but ministers by whom ye believed, even as the Lord gave to every man?

6 I have planted, Apollos watered; but God gave the increase.

7 So then neither is he that planteth any thing, neither he that watereth; but God that giveth the increase.

8 Now he that planteth and he that watereth are one: and every man shall receive his own reward according to his own labour.

9 For we are labourers together with God: ye are God's husbandry, ye are God's building.

KEY VERSE

Now I beseech you, brethren, by the name of our Lord Jesus Christ, that ye all speak the same thing, and that there be no divisions among you; but that ye be perfectly joined together in the same mind and in the same judgment. —**1 Corinthians 1:10**

THE PEOPLE OF GOD SET PRIORITIES

Unit 2: Living as a Community of Believers

LESSONS 5–9

LESSON AIMS

After participating in this lesson, each student will be able to:

1. Tell what problems resulted in Corinth when believers put too much importance on the role of human leaders.

2. Explain how one ought to look at the role of leaders in the local church.

3. Write a prayer for the ministry staff of his or her church that God would bless their work and that the congregation would rally behind them to bring glory to God.

LESSON OUTLINE

Introduction

A. Surprised by Unity

At the end of a worship service in some British churches, those gathered say "The Grace" together. This traditional benediction is based on the final verse of 2 Corinthians: "The grace of the Lord Jesus Christ, and the love of God, and the communion of the Holy Ghost, be with you all." I have taught this to the churches I have ministered with in the United States.

My father and stepmother learned this as members of a church I was preaching for in Seattle. They did not think much about it until they took an Alaskan cruise. On Sunday aboard the ship, they attended a Protestant worship service led by an Anglican priest. Much of this service was strange to them, but the priest closed the service by having those gathered say "The Grace." And my parents knew it! Suddenly, they felt an unexpected kinship with the other Christians gathered that morning. They were surprised at being able to share in an element of unity familiar to them.

Unfortunately, church disunity exists. We sometimes idealize the churches of the first century as authoritative exemplars of unity for churches today. It is true that first-century churches have much to teach us about unity, but we should not sugarcoat the reality that those churches had problems too. *Exhibit A* in this regard was the church in Corinth.

B. Lesson Background

Paul's second missionary journey began as a trip to visit the congregations he had planted on his first journey (Acts 15:36). After doing so (15:41), the restless Paul desired to move on to new territory with the message of the gospel.

God influenced Paul's itinerary through a vision that directed him to cross the Aegean Sea to the region known as Macedonia (Acts 16:9, 10). He eventually arrived in Corinth in about AD 52, where he remained for some 18 months (see 18:11, 18). Corinth was a busy and wealthy center of trade in Paul's day, a cosmopolitan city with residents from many regions. It was a place of lax morals and influential pagan religions.

Acts 18:4 tells us that Corinth had a synagogue (as was the case in most of the large trading cities of the Roman Empire). Paul began his preaching in that synagogue, which was composed of both Jews and Greeks (vv. 4, 5). But opposition caused him to leave and focus on the Gentiles of the city (vv. 6, 7). Nevertheless, there was a strong contingent of Jewish believers in the Corinthian church (v. 8), and it was to this mixed congregation that Paul wrote the two Corinthian letters while on his third missionary journey. The four or so years that elapsed between Paul's time in Corinth and his first letter back saw ungodly trends develop—trends that needed to be corrected.

I. Divided Church
(1 CORINTHIANS 1:10-12)
A. God's Ideal (v. 10)

10. Now I beseech you, brethren, by the name of our Lord Jesus Christ, that ye all speak the same thing, and that there be no divisions among you; but that ye be perfectly joined together in the same mind and in the same judgment.

Paul is thankful for his Corinthian brethren in Christ (1 Corinthians 1:4). We should remember this as we work through today's lesson, because Paul has some difficult things to say to them. He does not wish to come across as one who merely criticizes, but as one who cares deeply and seeks to correct problems for the Corinthians' benefit (compare 2 Corinthians 13:10).

The verse before us begins this corrective agenda, and Paul uses a strong phrase to open: *I beseech you.* He is speaking of serious matters—matters so important that he makes his exhortation in *the name of our Lord Jesus Christ.* This invokes Paul's authority as an apostle, one commissioned by the risen Lord himself (compare 1 Corinthians 1:1; 9:1; 2 Corinthians 1:1; 12:12; 10:8; 13:10).

Paul desires unity in the Corinthian church in what the people say and do. Unity in the church is desirable both for the peace of the congregation and the effectiveness of its message to unbelievers. This is God's ideal.

B. Sad Reality (vv. 11, 12)

11. For it hath been declared unto me of you, my brethren, by them which are of the house of Chloe, that there are contentions among you.

Paul acknowledges learning of *contentions* within the church at Corinth. This is not mere rumor. It has been reported to Paul directly *by them which are of the house of Chloe*—family members or workers involved with her business dealings. We have no information about Chloe except her name, but she is obviously known to the Corinthians, probably a member of the congregation. It is not common to speak of "the house of [a woman]" in the first century, so perhaps she has no husband.

Paul is not yet speaking to the actual divisions within the church, but of the contentious spirit that is resulting in and from the divisions. The issues in church fights are sometimes trivial (even ridiculous) in and of themselves. Often more deadly is the desire to dominate that lurks underneath the surface issues. The tone of this verse indicates that Paul is deeply disappointed that the Corinthians allow such a spirit to exist in their congregation.

12. Now this I say, that every one of you saith, I am of Paul; and I of Apollos; and I of Cephas; and I of Christ.

A spirit of partisanship has infected the congregation, and Paul knows of at least four factions that have arisen. One group claims to be followers *of Paul.* This faction may consist of those who came into the church during the apostle's "year and six months" stay in Corinth (Acts 18:11). It's not hard to imagine that those who had received the gospel from Paul himself are now claiming some sort of elite status. Others claim allegiance to *Apollos,* a capable teacher who ministered in Corinth after Paul (see Acts 18:24–19:1).

A third group declares for *Cephas*; this is Simon Peter (see John 1:42). We have no evidence that this great apostle ever visited Corinth, so perhaps the members of this faction have learned "how to do church" where Peter ministered in Jerusalem (Acts 1:15; 2:14; Galatians 2:1, 7-9) before they came to Corinth.

The fourth group is the most puzzling: its adherents claim to be the party *of Christ*. Isn't this what Paul should want for all of the Corinthians? The answer is *yes* in the sense of allegiance to Christ as Lord, but *no* in terms of separating into a party that divides the church—a party that perhaps claims to have a relationship with Christ that others lack.

What Do You Think?

What reasons for church disunity in the Bible still present themselves today? How can proper handling of such challenges result in a church that is even stronger than before?

Talking Points for Your Discussion

- Acts 6:1-7
- Acts 15:36-40
- Philippians 4:2, 3
- 3 John 9, 10

❧ *Unity Through Uniformity?* ❧

We humans tend to gravitate toward those who see things the way we do. When that happens, the result can be an "us versus them" mind-set. Doctrinal and procedural disagreements in the church are important to work out, but we all know of people who are better at shedding "heat" than "light" during dialogue. Temperament research may help us avoid this problem. I remember when I first learned about differences in decision-making styles. At that time it hit me—"Oh, my husband doesn't do things the way he does just to annoy me! He's actually wired differently than I am."

Did the "I am of . . . " divisions in Corinth get their start in a clash of temperaments? It's hard to say. But becoming aware of the tendencies of differing temperaments can help us grow in sensitivity and respect for those who process information differently from the way we do.

As we strive to "be perfectly joined together in the same mind and in the same judgment" (v. 10), we can't miss seeing God's love of diversity. We work counter to His plan if we try to achieve unity through uniformity.

—V. E.

II. Frustrated Apostle
(1 CORINTHIANS 1:13-17)
A. Rhetorical Questions (v. 13)

13. Is Christ divided? was Paul crucified for you? or were ye baptized in the name of Paul?

Paul drives his point home with three rhetorical questions. A good principle for proper reading of the Bible is to recognize questions like this and answer them as we go. *Is Christ divided?* Answer: no. *Was Paul crucified for you?* Answer: no. *Were ye baptized in the name of Paul?* Answer: no.

The questions and the expected answers emphasize two things. First, activities that cause the church to be divided should be questioned (compare Romans 16:17), since Christ intended that His followers "be one" (see John 17:20-23). Paul's language is vivid, for the word translated *divided* has the sense of being cut into pieces.

Second, Paul refuses to allow human leaders to usurp the place of Jesus Christ. Our ultimate master is the one who died for our sins and rose from the grave. He is the head of the church (Ephesians 5:23). It is Christ who loved the church and gave His life for her (5:25). Paul's great reminder here is the name of the one the Corinthians were baptized into, and that is the name *Jesus Christ* (compare Acts 19:5). This is the common experience, regardless of who did the baptizing.

B. Reality Check (vv. 14-17)

14, 15. I thank God that I baptized none of you, but Crispus and Gaius; lest any should say that I had baptized in mine own name.

Those tempted to see themselves as an "of Paul" elite must grapple with the fact that Paul did not personally baptize everyone who responded positively to his gospel preaching. Since that is the case, then any "of Paul" faction logically should be subdivided into (1) those converted by Paul's preaching **and** baptized by him (the more elite) and (2) those converted by Paul's preaching **but not** baptized by him (the less elite).

The absurdity of any such subdivision becomes sharper still as Paul reminds his readers that any baptisms he had administered were not in his *own name*; he is no more than God's instrument in their salvation experience, not its author. Paul uses a bit of hyperbole (exaggeration for effect) as he says he *baptized none of you*. He quickly tempers this statement with the two exceptions of *Crispus* (see Acts 18:8) and *Gaius* (see Romans 16:23).

16. And I baptized also the household of Stephanas: besides, I know not whether I baptized any other.

Recalling baptizing *the household of Stephanas* as well (1 Corinthians 16:15), Paul's point is that it doesn't matter who was baptized by his hands rather than someone else's. If he cannot remember all whom he baptized, then why should "converted by Paul himself" be a rallying point for a faction within the church?

17. For Christ sent me not to baptize, but to preach the gospel: not with wisdom of words, lest the cross of Christ should be made of none effect.

Paul is not minimizing the importance of baptism but is reminding the Corinthians of his chief contribution to their church: he had been there *to preach the gospel*. He brought them the good news of Christ's atoning death for their sins (1 Corinthians 1:23; 15:3) and of their chance for reconciliation with God (2 Corinthians 5:18-21).

The fact that Paul's preaching had not been with *wisdom of words* means that his preaching had not been based on Greek philosophical wisdom (1 Corinthians 1:20). Paul knows that truth is not determined by the best philosophical argument (2:1-5). Rather, truth is found in the simple gospel message that originates with God (1:24, 25).

III. Corrected Thinking
(1 CORINTHIANS 3:4-9)
A. Roles of Servants (vv. 4, 5)

4, 5. For while one saith, I am of Paul; and another, I am of Apollos; are ye not carnal? Who then is Paul, and who is Apollos, but min- isters by whom ye believed, even as the Lord gave to every man?

Our lesson now moves to chapter 3, where Paul continues his discussion of the Corinthian church's divisions. In chapter 2 (not in today's text), Paul reminds the readers that his message is not a masterpiece of human wisdom, but a spiritual message given and confirmed by God's Spirit (1 Corinthians 2:4, 5). Paul exhorts the Corinthians to live as spiritually driven people, to have the "mind of Christ" (2:16).

Yet this is not the case in Corinth. The Corinthians are not acting as spiritual people, but as *carnal* people. This means they are being controlled by human lusts and weaknesses rather than depending on God's Spirit for strength and guidance. To be distracted by political maneuvers within the congregation makes them no better than nonbelievers who seek power and control.

We also see here that the two primary parties within the Corinthian church seem to be "the Paulites" and "the Apollosites." We don't know who the primary minister of the church is at this point, but many preachers can identify with the situation of "the ghosts of preachers past." We can imagine the bickering! "Paul taught us these hymns, and we don't need any new ones." "Apollos used this translation of Isaiah, so any other version is wrong." Where does it stop? When does it end?

> *What Do You Think?*
> Is it a sign of disunity for people to seek out their church's previous minister to conduct marriage ceremonies or funerals? Why, or why not?
> *Talking Points for Your Discussion*
> * Reasons for such requests
> * Frequency of such requests
> * Reactions by the previous minister to such requests
> * Other

Paul says it must cease, and it can stop if the Corinthians remember that he and Apollos serve the same Lord. They are God's gifts to the church, and the Lord never intends them to be the focus of partisan loyalties or the cause of division.

B. Role of God (vv. 6, 7)

6, 7. I have planted, Apollos watered; but God gave the increase. So then neither is he that planteth any thing, neither he that watereth; but God that giveth the increase.

These two verses deserve close attention, for they go against the grain of much popular wisdom in the church these days. Paul gives a little history lesson by using a farming metaphor: he is the one who *planted*—he put the seed in the ground. By this, he means that he was the one who initially brought the word of God, the message of the gospel (compare Luke 8:11), to Corinth (Acts 18:1-8). Paul's message had been received by some in Corinth, and they banded together to form a church. It is in this sense that the Corinthian church was planted by Paul himself.

But Paul's time in Corinth ended after 18 months (Acts 18:11). He was followed by Apollos (19:1), an able teacher whose ministry *watered* the new believers. By this, Paul means that Apollos helped the faith and knowledge of the Corin-

HOW TO SAY IT

Aegean	A-*jee*-un.
Alexandria	Al-iks-*an*-dree-uh.
Apollos	Uh-*pahl*-us.
Cephas	*See*-fus.
Chloe	*Klo*-ee.
Corinthians	Ko-*rin*-thee-unz (*th* as in *thin*).
Crispus	*Kris*-pus.
Gaius	*Gay*-us.
hyperbole	high-**purr**-buh-*lee*.
Macedonia	Mass-eh-*doe*-nee-uh.
Tarsus	*Tar*-sus.

thians to grow by teaching them in greater depth. There was no conflict in these two roles.

Paul and Apollos were both willing and effective servants of the Word, but the Corinthian church is growing not because of their winsome personalities or even because of their powerful preaching and teaching. In the end, God is the one who gives *the increase*.

A farmer can till the soil, plant the seed, and water the ground. But the farmer cannot make the plants grow; that is a work of God. When planting churches, we can do demographic studies of neighborhoods, hire talented ministry staff, and build marvelous buildings in superb locations. We can have ministers who write books and appear on television. But a church will not grow unless God causes growth. We can be willing and useful servants in this task, but God is still in control.

❧ GOING TO WORK WITH OUR FATHER ❧

Many corporations participate in "Take our daughters and sons to work day." The goal is to get young people thinking about their future. This is not an employer or employee productivity program. In fact, it's apparent that the employer is exempting the employee from normal work expectations in order to serve a larger societal goal.

There may be something of a paradigm here regarding our contributions to the kingdom of God. When God invites us to join Him at work, it doesn't mean that He needs our help. In fact, our "help" may serve at times to delay what He wants to accomplish. Although God commissions His children to be His fellow laborers, we dare not take ourselves too seriously.

Instead of creating spiritual résumés that take credit for successes in the church, we should assess our situations by thinking of ourselves as children going to work with our Father. Any fruit from the day comes from Him.   —V. E.

C. Outcome for the Corinthians (vv. 8, 9)

8, 9. Now he that planteth and he that watereth are one: and every man shall receive his own reward according to his own labour. For we are labourers together with God: ye are God's husbandry, ye are God's building.

The farming analogy continues. Paul makes the point that the planter of a field and the one who waters that field are engaged in the same overall task: bringing plants to a harvestable state.

What Do You Think?

What do you see as your primary area of Christian service in Paul's farming analogy? Why?

Talking Points for Your Discussion

- Planting
- Watering
- Other area not mentioned by Paul

We are careful not to misunderstand what Paul means by *every man shall receive his own reward according to his own labour.* He is not teaching salvation by works (compare Ephesians 2:8, 9). The *reward* here is the fruit of the labor: new believers who hear the gospel and maturing believers who are growing in the Word. For those engaged in ministry, there is nothing more rewarding or satisfying than a church growing both numerically and spiritually. But we in the church, all of us, *are God's husbandry,* the place of action.

In a final word picture, Paul switches from agriculture to architecture. We, the church, are also *God's building,* an intentional, unified structure with Jesus as the cornerstone (see Ephesians 2:19-22; 1 Peter 2:4-6).

Conclusion

A. Corinthian Divisions Today

While the exact causes of the divisions among the Corinthians are unknown to us, our lesson gives us the names of four individuals who were used as rallying cries: Paul, Apollos, Cephas, and Christ. Using a little "sanctified imagination," let's consider what these factions within the Corinthian church might have looked like and see if they match with any groups in our own experience.

Those who claimed to be "of Paul" might have been the original converts of the apostle, the charter members. Perhaps they wanted a church frozen in time, unchanged from the day Paul left. Because of their tenure, this group had great influence, so their resistance to change dominated.

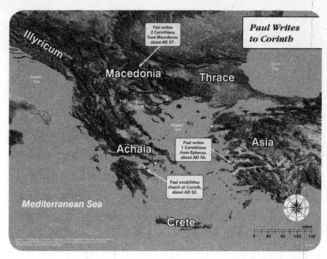

Visual for Lesson 5. *For a geographical perspective, keep this map posted throughout your studies of the lessons of units 2 and 3.*

Those "of Apollos" perhaps were converts who came into the church after Paul left and Apollos arrived. The background of Apollos was Alexandria (Acts 18:24), so he did things differently from Paul, who was from Tarsus (21:39). Apollos had a different preaching style. His admirers might have thought that Paul's methods needed an upgrade so that the church could keep moving forward.

Corinth had a transient population, and those who claimed to be "of Cephas" could have been Christians who had learned from that great apostle before they came to Corinth. Perhaps they believed that the church in Corinth did not measure up to their former church.

The group "of Christ" perhaps claimed some sort of spiritual superiority. Yet Paul's general conclusion was that all of the Corinthians were spiritual babies (1 Corinthians 3:1-3). Their quarreling was evidence of this.

As we shall see in future lessons, the Corinthians had plenty of doctrinal problems. Correct doctrine is important, but so is unity.

B. Prayer

Holy God, may our hearts be undivided in our devotion to You. May we never be satisfied with divisions in our church, which is the body of Your Son, Jesus. In His name we pray, amen.

C. Thought to Remember

Submitting to Christ brings unity.

INVOLVEMENT LEARNING

Some of the activities below are also found in the helpful student book, Adult Bible Class.
Don't forget to download the free reproducible page from www.standardlesson.com to enhance your lesson!

Into the Lesson

Prepare four large (at least 15") squares with the following affirmations, one each: *I am of Paul / I am of Apollos / I am of Cephas / I am of Christ.* On the other sides of the four squares, have these words respectively, one each: *WE / ARE / HIS / CHURCH* with the **HIS** in bold lettering.

Hand the four squares to four learners, asking them to keep the affirmation sides up. Ask those four to go to four sides of your meeting space and hold the affirmations in view. Comment: "This is what a divided church looks like: no close fellowship, each person joining his or her own little clique." Then ask your learners to bring the squares front and center and hold them against a wall with the other sides showing so that *WE ARE* **HIS** *CHURCH* is revealed.

As the learners hold their squares, tape them together. Comment, "As Paul will show us in today's text, we are to be unified in a certain way. Let's look at 1 Corinthians 1 and 3 for a picture of what might divide us and how we can avoid this problem."

Into the Word

Prepare in advance a copy of each of the 14 verses of today's lesson text; cut the verses into logical parts, depending on phrasing. For example, verse 10 can be divided obviously after the words *brethren, Christ, same thing,* and *among you,* yielding five parts for this verse. Put all segments of this verse into an envelope. Do the same with all other verses, so you end up with 14 envelopes.

Give 14 learners one envelope each, with these directions: "Take the strips out of your envelope and put them together to make one of the verses of today's text. Have your verse ready to read when I call for it." Provide tape to hold the segments together. You may or may not allow learners to use their Bibles for this, depending on the nature of your class. If your class is smaller than 14 in size, use fewer than 14 envelopes, with some or all envelopes containing more than one verse.

After a few minutes, call a learner at random to come to the front and read his or her verse. Repeat until all verses are read. Then ask learners who are not up front (because they did not receive an envelope) to suggest, without using Bibles, how to arrange the verses to be in biblical order; have those standing up front switch places to do so. Repeat the request until the result is correct.

After asking readers to be seated, ask, "In what ways did our activity reflect the divisions and the unity Paul writes of in the text?" Possible responses may include the observations that (1) verses of Scripture lose their impact when mixed and confused, just as the church does when its members are "mixed and confused" and (2) it took the group working together to accomplish the task at hand. If a learner suggests an idea you do not understand, simply ask, "I am unclear; how do you see that as related to Paul's ideas?"

Into Life

Display the back (blank) side of a child's jigsaw puzzle that you have put together. Ask learners to write on each puzzle piece the name of someone who holds a leadership position in your congregation. Then ask someone to read 1 Corinthians 3:10, introducing it as "Paul's prayer for church leaders." Ask class members to volunteer to take pieces of the puzzle home for a daily prayer for unity-in-purpose for those named.

Alternative: Distribute copies of the "Only God Can Make It Grow" activity from the reproducible page, which you can download. Assign learners to work in pairs to complete this, taking care not to allow family members to be paired up. If time is short, have learners work on only one of the three entries of their choice.

Distribute copies of the "Dramatis Personae" activity as a take-home exercise.

GLORIFY GOD WITH YOUR BODY

DEVOTIONAL READING: Ephesians 4:7-16
BACKGROUND SCRIPTURE: 1 Corinthians 6:12–7:40

1 CORINTHIANS 6:12-20

12 All things are lawful unto me, but all things are not expedient: all things are lawful for me, but I will not be brought under the power of any.

13 Meats for the belly, and the belly for meats: but God shall destroy both it and them. Now the body is not for fornication, but for the Lord; and the Lord for the body.

14 And God hath both raised up the Lord, and will also raise up us by his own power.

15 Know ye not that your bodies are the members of Christ? shall I then take the members of Christ, and make them the members of an harlot? God forbid.

16 What? know ye not that he which is joined to an harlot is one body? for two, saith he, shall be one flesh.

17 But he that is joined unto the Lord is one spirit.

18 Flee fornication. Every sin that a man doeth is without the body; but he that committeth fornication sinneth against his own body.

19 What? know ye not that your body is the temple of the Holy Ghost which is in you, which ye have of God, and ye are not your own?

20 For ye are bought with a price: therefore glorify God in your body, and in your spirit, which are God's.

KEY VERSE

Know ye not that your body is the temple of the Holy Ghost which is in you, which ye have of God, and ye are not your own? —**1 Corinthians 6:19**

THE PEOPLE OF GOD SET PRIORITIES

Unit 2: Living as a Community of Believers

LESSONS 5–9

LESSON AIMS

After participating in this lesson, each student will be able to:

1. Summarize Paul's argument about not allowing Christian liberty to become a license for immorality.

2. Compare and contrast the problem of sexual immorality in Corinth with sexual immorality in one's own community.

3. Suggest ways to encourage young adult believers to remain sexually pure.

LESSON OUTLINE

Introduction

A. Slogans as Half-Truths

Since I don't have a refrigerator in my office, I plaster my magnets on file cabinets instead. (Yes, I confess that I am a "magnet person.") My favorites are from states or foreign countries I have visited. One magnet I particularly like is from New Hampshire, shaped like a license plate and emblazoned with the state's official motto: *Live Free or Die.* What a bold slogan!

I wonder how far New Hampshirites are willing to push this ideal. Do they believe they should be free not to pay any taxes whatsoever? Do they believe they are free to drive without a driver's license? Do they feel free to litter with impunity?

The answer to these questions for the vast majority is, of course, *no.* The residents of this proud state (as other states) have both defined and accepted limits to their personal freedoms. That fact does not detract from the spirit of the slogan, however. It is a spirit that expresses a desire to live where freedom flourishes, where there are no unnecessary restrictions.

One of the things Paul seems to have been battling in the Corinthian church was the ill-advised use of slogans. Such mottoes appear to have been used by various factions within the church to champion their causes and batter their opponents. We should be careful of doing doctrine by slogan. Without context, slogans can be half-truths, as today's lesson makes clear.

B. Lesson Background

Today's lesson deals with the touchy subject of sexual immorality and a misunderstanding in the Corinthian church regarding the damage it can cause. We need to consider as a backdrop the standards of morality in the Greco-Roman culture of the first century, which were different from what is accepted today.

Consider the issue of prostitution (harlotry) as an example. In the vast majority of American and Canadian cities today, to pay for sex is seen as both illegal and immoral—and an adulterous violation of marriage vows for a married person. The ancient Greeks did not see it this way. For them, adultery was a narrower concept. Adultery was committed when a married woman engaged in sexual activity with anyone other than her husband; if a married man had relations with another man's wife, that too was wrong. But if a married man visited a prostitute, well, that was to be expected.

Thus Greek marital expectations regarding fidelity were more for the wife than for the husband—a double standard. Public parties might include prostitutes to entertain the men after the wives were excused from the banquet. This was not considered improper or sexually immoral.

In contrast, Christian preachers like Paul taught a much broader definition of what constituted sexual immorality: *any* sexual activity outside of marriage was sinful and forbidden. Shockingly, some members of the church at Corinth were engaging in illicit sexual activity that even the pagan Gentiles disapproved of (1 Corinthians 5:1)! Paul would not stand for this, for he saw sexual sin as a threat to the unity and purity of the entire body of Christ.

I. Consecrated Bodies
(1 CORINTHIANS 6:12-16)
A. Controlling (vv. 12-14)

12. All things are lawful unto me, but all things are not expedient: all things are lawful for me, but I will not be brought under the power of any.

A recognized difficulty in understanding the book of 1 Corinthians is Paul's handling of (what appear to be) slogans. These are not his slogans, but are short statements that the various factions in the Corinthian church seem to be using to define themselves and their agendas. Therefore when we see Paul cite a slogan, we must be careful not to take it out of context as an absolute rule that he himself is promoting, for his intent may be quite the opposite.

HOW TO SAY IT

Corinth	*Kor*-inth.
Corinthians	Ko-*rin*-thee-unz (*th* as in *thin*).
Myanmar	*Myawn*-mawr.

But how do we know if and where Paul quotes a Corinthian slogan if he doesn't preface it with something like "you say that . . ."? Jay Smith proposes several telltale indicators, and we can summarize four of them here. Slogans (1) are brief, pithy statements usually in the present tense, (2) are often repeated, (3) feature wording that is inconsistent with the way Paul usually writes, and/or (4) are followed by a counterpoint.

We see all four indicators here in the phrase *all things are lawful unto me.* This phrase (1) is brief and pithy, (2) is repeated both here (with identical Greek wording) and in 1 Corinthians 10:23 (with very similar Greek wording), (3) does not have an expected conjunction between it and the preceding verse, and (4) is followed by counterstatements both here and in 10:23.

Passages such as Galatians 2:15, 16 indicate that this slogan probably has its roots in the teachings of Paul himself as he has proclaimed freedom in Christ. But some are distorting Paul's teaching to be something arrogant like, "I can do anything I want to do, and no one has a right to criticize me!"

What Do You Think?
How can we help Christians see the fallacies in the secular thinking that "people have the right to do whatever they want with their bodies"?
Talking Points for Your Discussion
- Regarding sexual practices
- Regarding the exercise of free speech
- Regarding substance abuse
- Regarding modesty (personal appearance)
- Other

The Christian way is based on grace, not on keeping laws. But it is also a way of life that strives for holiness and righteousness. Paul expresses this here in two ways. First, disregard for life-guiding rules is not always *expedient.* God's rules (laws) for living are designed for our benefit, not as oppressive restrictions that spoil our fun. Why not commit adultery? Because it will destroy the trust on which marriage is built and wreck one's family life. To commit sin is never to our benefit.

Paul's second reason to reject the *all things are lawful* slogan is that he refuses to be dominated and controlled by sinful behavior. Christ frees the Christian believer from this bondage, so why allow sin back on the throne of our lives? The attitude that says, "I can do no wrong" is opening the door for the power of sin to reassert itself. Paul addresses the addictive, enslaving power of sin more fully in Romans 6:16–7:6.

13a. Meats for the belly, and the belly for meats: but God shall destroy both it and them.

We come to another simplistic slogan: *meats for the belly, and the belly for meats.* (The word *meats* refers to food in general, not just the flesh of animals.) As with the previous slogan, this one is probably based on Paul's teaching, but expressed in a distorted way. Paul does not require Gentile Christians to follow the Jewish food laws (compare Mark 7:19), but freedom from restrictive food laws is being flaunted in the Corinthian church.

Everyone should realize that an "anything and everything goes" attitude regarding dietary decisions can cause problems that affect the unity of the church. In the final analysis, neither food nor our digestive systems are eternal; both exist under that power of God to create and destroy.

Paul will address this issue in more depth later in the letter; we'll see that in next week's lesson. But before we move on, we should also note that the issue is probably not just that of the kinds of food being eaten, but also the amount (the issue of gluttony; see Proverbs 23:20, 21).

What Do You Think?

What cherished slogans should you reevaluate?

Talking Points for Your Discussion

- Slogans regarding the use of money
- Slogans regarding attitudes toward food
- Slogans regarding how one should view self
- Church slogans
- Other

❧ *CHERRY PICKING* ❧

It was a beautiful summer day in northern California. The two cherry trees we had planted were producing their first crop, so we climbed into the playhouse we had built between the trees and picked a large bowl of the luscious red fruit.

Our son was the most enthusiastic. As I left picking to return to other chores, I saw him settle onto a lawn chair, bowl in lap. "Don't eat too many," I warned, "or you will get a stomachache."

He was unconcerned. But later, after hours of feeling sick, he had a thorough understanding of my purpose in warning him. Memory of this lingers decades later; he will not eat cherries today.

God created this world and filled it with things for us to enjoy. His commands are not to keep us from fun, but to protect us from harm. Like the good Father He is, He steers us from the dangers. Often we want to cherry-pick our way through the Bible, accepting the things that seem pleasant to us while rejecting the rest. Perhaps we think we have found a better formula for abundant life than God has offered. Perhaps we see Him as stern and withholding, instead of as the giver of every good gift. Whatever our reasons, we can choose to trust and obey His ways, or we can learn from our physical and spiritual stomachaches. —V. E.

13b, 14. Now the body is not for fornication, but for the Lord; and the Lord for the body. And God hath both raised up the Lord, and will also raise up us by his own power.

If we continue the logic some Corinthians are using in verse 13a, we would have "the body is for fornication and fornication for the body." In other words, the human body has natural desires for food and sex, so why put any restrictions on them? But Paul will not have this. *The body is not for fornication.* Our bodies were created so we can worship and serve *the Lord.*

In effect, Paul is replacing the Corinthian's defective slogan with one that puts everything together properly: The body is for the Lord, and the Lord is for the body. We surrender our bodies along with all their appetites to the Lord's service, and He commits himself to us. The fulfillment of the latter is seen in resurrection: Christ's human body was raised from death by God, and our bodies will likewise be raised, the great hope of eternal life for believers. Resurrection is being denied by some in Corinth, but Paul saves his fuller discussion of this false teaching for later (1 Corinthians 15).

We also recognize a deeper sense of *body* at issue here: the body of Christ as the church. This is the direction of Paul's discussion in the verses to follow.

B. Restricting (vv. 15, 16)

15. Know ye not that your bodies are the members of Christ? shall I then take the members of Christ, and make them the members of an harlot? God forbid.

It is important to grasp what *members* means here. For Paul and his readers, this word refers to a body part such as an arm, leg, hand, ear, or toe. Paul is fond of picturing the church as a human body with Christ as its head (see Romans 12:4, 5; 1 Corinthians 12:27; Ephesians 5:30). So when he refers to *the members of Christ*, he means "the parts of the church body, which belong to Christ."

This power of association within the church body can be warped and damaged by improper associations. Chief among such associations is involvement with harlots (prostitutes). Paul is not advising that his readers cease all contact with the non-Christians of their community. Rather, he is saying that inappropriate *sexual* contact must cease (see 1 Corinthians 5:9, 10).

16. What? know ye not that he which is joined to an harlot is one body? for two, saith he, shall be one flesh.

Paul continues his argument using forthright terms. Sexual contact involves a physical joining of bodies, and Paul approaches this fact by drawing on the Genesis account of the creation of man and woman, who are joined as *one flesh* (Genesis 2:24; compare Matthew 19:5). God's plan for creation includes intimacy between husband and wife within the marriage relationship.

However, if the husband has sexual relations with a harlot (prostitute), the result is to bring an improper "wife" into the marriage. This is both sexually immoral and destructive to the family unit. By logical extension, sexual contact with a harlot introduces the same into the church body, and this cannot be. Paul's underlying point is that things we do with our personal bodies will affect the church as a body, to which we belong as members.

II. Consecrated Spirits
(1 CORINTHIANS 6:17-20)

A. Connection with the Lord (vv. 17, 18)

17. But he that is joined unto the Lord is one spirit.

Paul uses the image of improper intimacy above to contrast with an image of a proper relationship: spiritual intimacy *unto the Lord* (compare John 17:21-23). The implication here is that sexual immorality not only soils a marriage, it introduces moral filth into one's relationship with God. The moment of physical pleasure that an immoral act may bring must be considered in the context of the lasting damage it causes. It is not possible to separate a Christian's sexual behavior from his or her relationship with the Lord, and this spiritual dimension must be the controlling factor.

18. Flee fornication. Every sin that a man doeth is without the body; but he that committeth fornication sinneth against his own body.

Paul's language here is telling. He does not say "resist," but *flee* (contrast James 4:7); it is not "be strong and stand your ground" but "run away!" This is powerful (see also 1 Corinthians 10:14; 1 Timothy 6:11; 2 Timothy 2:22).

Here, Paul again uses candid language to justify this strong warning as he puts sexual sin in a unique category of wrongdoing. Other sins are *without the body*, meaning they are external. For example, stealing may use the hands to accomplish the sin, but it is still "outside." Sexual sin, by contrast, is *against* the body because of the intimate union between those engaged in it.

What Do You Think?
If we are to "flee fornication," then how do we bring the message of the gospel to those mired in the sex trade?
Talking Points for Your Discussion
- Context in which we bring the gospel
- Safeguards to enact when bringing the gospel
- Lessons learned by those who are experienced in this area of gospel outreach
- Other

Visual for Lessons 3 & 6. *Start a discussion by pointing to this visual as you ask the question associated with verse 20.*

❧ TAKING FLIGHT ❧

Nineteen million. That is the number of new infections of sexually transmitted diseases (STDs) reported each year in the U.S. according to the Centers for Disease Control and Prevention. This statistic represents only three types of STDs, which means it's only a fraction of the true numbers. This figure also does not take into account those who do not seek medical attention.

STDs can cause problems ranging from pain to infertility to death. Yet a sexualized culture does not say, "Stop the immoral behavior that results in STDs," but rather, "Go ahead and have fun, but make sure you do it safely." A culture with sexual norms that are far below God's standard does not seem to realize that *every* sexual act outside of a marriage between one man and one woman results in a spiritual disease known as *sin*. Spiritually speaking, there is no "safe sex" outside of marriage.

Commercials, entertainment dialogue, and supermarket conversations that would have embarrassed us a few decades ago now tempt us to reevaluate what is "normal." We must assume that we will face sexual temptation, and we must be prepared to take flight immediately when it presents itself. Given the attention to this issue we find in the Word of God, we know that sexual immorality has always been a weapon of destruction the enemy wants to use against us. But with God's help, we can overcome. See 1 Corinthians 10:13. —V. E.

B. Temple of the Spirit (vv. 19, 20)

19. What? know ye not that your body is the temple of the Holy Ghost which is in you, which ye have of God, and ye are not your own?

This verse is quoted often by those who strive to take care of their bodies through exercise and diet. We are certainly called to be stewards of the marvelous bodies God has given to us (see 3 John 2), but that is not the point here. We should note that the word *your* is plural while the word *body* is singular in the original language. Paul is talking about the body of Christ, the church, of which we are members.

This body is none other than *the temple of the Holy Ghost* (compare 1 Corinthians 3:16; 2 Corinthians 6:16). The church is the dwelling place of God's Holy Spirit. The Spirit inhabits the church corporately and each believer individually (Romans 8:9). Once this is understood, then one can grasp why engaging with a prostitute is starkly inconsistent with the Christian life. How can a vessel of the Holy Spirit take part in such an unholy act? Such activity is not merely one of illicit physical pleasure, it is also an act of spiritual desecration and violation.

> **What Do You Think?**
> In what ways have you seen an individual's sin harm the larger body of Christ? What kinds of "damage control" can church leaders undertake in such cases?
> *Talking Points for Your Discussion*
> - Sins involving sexual misconduct
> - Sins involving financial misconduct
> - Sins involving substance abuse
> - Seemingly "little" sins (gossip, etc.)

20. For ye are bought with a price: therefore glorify God in your body, and in your spirit, which are God's.

Paul concludes this section by reminding the Corinthians of the great price that has been paid for their spiritual freedom: the agonizing, sacrificial death of God's own Son on a Roman cross (see Romans 8:3). There are many implications to the cross-work of Jesus. It is a demonstration of God's love for us (5:8). It serves as an atonement for our sins, a sacrifice we could never make our-selves (3:25). It has a once-for-all quality that does not need to be repeated (6:10).

The word picture Paul is using is from the slave markets of cities like ancient Corinth. Everyone in the Corinthian church knows of the place in their city where people are bought and sold like livestock. Some in this church may have suffered this dehumanizing experience personally. Some may be slave owners, perhaps struggling in their hearts to reconcile that fact with their new Christian faith. Paul says that God has bought them all, having purchased their spiritual freedom through Christ's death.

The Corinthians have not been purchased by Christ's death just to be enslaved all over again. They have been bought in order that they might be free from the bondage of sin, free forever. They have been made free so that they might *glorify God* with both their spirits and bodies in every way. As this is true for the larger body of Christ, so it is true for each individual member who makes up this body.

What Do You Think?
  What challenges in our culture work against our glorifying God with our bodies? How do we overcome these challenges?
Talking Points for Your Discussion
  ▪ Activities that culture says are good, but are not
  ▪ Activities that culture says are not good, but are

Conclusion

A. Independence and the Body of Christ

I recently returned from a trip to Myanmar (Burma) where I was privileged to teach in a grad-uate program at one of the Christian colleges. While in the airport in Yangon waiting for my flight to Mandalay, I had a conversation with the only other Westerner in the terminal, a woman from Paris.

She had come to Myanmar, alone, on a spiritual quest: to visit Buddhist shrines (of which there are thousands), to pray and meditate at these places, and perhaps to gain enlightenment from one of the Buddhist teachers. It was quickly clear in our conversation that her only understanding of the church was the formalistic and spiritually lifeless Roman Catholicism she had encountered in her native France. (Interestingly, she seemed not to be able to understand that I was a Christian but not a Catholic.) It seemed to me that she was searching for spiritual fulfillment and connection with God that she had never encountered in her homeland. I wonder what she found on her solitary quest.

Spirituality can be both very personal and very selfish; some folks want a private relationship with God that excludes others. But this is not how the church is intended to be. The church is the body of Christ, the temple of the Holy Spirit, the fellow-ship of the saved. Our joys and hopes are part of this body's life. Our times of worship are strength-ened by joining with the body in corporate praise. Our understanding of God's Word is matured by sitting under the wise teachers of the church.

Working against this, the spirit of today ele-vates and celebrates personal freedom and inde-pendence. We are encouraged to question any and every limit to our autonomy in our quest for personal fulfillment. We are to despise any barri-ers to the exploration of our individuality. Laws that were once seen as expressions of shared moral standards are now attacked as unwanted limits to personal freedom and privacy.

But the sins we commit, even in private, are part of the life of the body. The sinful act does not have to be committed on Sunday morning or inside the church building in order to bring its taint upon the body of Christ. When we sin, we violate not only our own bodies, we also infect the body of Christ—the church that was bought at the cost of the death of God's Son.

B. Prayer

Father, You have given us so much! The church is Your gift, redeemed by the blood of Your Son. You have given us Your Holy Spirit to inhabit the church and our lives. Lord, enable us to keep our-selves and our church pure. In Jesus' name, amen.

C. Thought to Remember

What we do with our bodies
affects our spiritual well-being.

INVOLVEMENT LEARNING

Some of the activities below are also found in the helpful student book, Adult Bible Class.
Don't forget to download the free reproducible page from www.standardlesson.com to enhance your lesson!

Into the Lesson

Prepare three poster strips, to be used as flash cards, that feature the following slogans, one each: *If it feels good, do it / Better dead than red / What happens in Vegas stays in Vegas.* As you hold up each flash card in turn, ask, "What flaw do you see in this statement?" Discuss.

Make a transition by saying, "Some in the Corinthian church were sloganeering their faith. Some of the slogans appeared to summarize doctrinal truth. But flaws revealed themselves when Paul put them under the microscope of Scripture. Let's take a look at their slogans . . . and ours."

Option: Before class begins, place in chairs copies of the "When Good Things Are Bad Things" activity from the reproducible page, which you can download. This will help prime your learners' thinking for today's study; it will be used further below.

Into the Word

Have today's text read aloud, switching readers every two verses. Then give each learner a strip of poster board that measures at least 3" by 20" along with a marker. Say, "Look at today's text and come up with a slogan for the individual Christian. Write it on your strip along with the verse number. If you finish quickly, put a second one on the back." If learners need an example, point to verse 20 and say, "In this verse I see *Act valuable; you are!*"

Collect the strips after a few minutes, shuffle them, then use them as flash cards, calling for critique of each statement. For any slogan drawing only positive comments, ask, "Is there any problems with this slogan?" For any slogan drawing only negative comments, do the opposite.

Alternative: Prepare all the slogans yourself, entering them on the poster strips described above. Some possibilities: *Good choices are not always good choices* (v. 12); *Be the master, not mastered* (v. 12); *Sometimes an exercise of rights is an exercise of wrongs* (v. 12); *Rise up with Jesus* (v. 14); *It's a membership card worth having* (v. 15); *One + One = One* (v. 16); *When in doubt, run way out* (v. 18); *Make room for the Spirit and He will make room for you* (v. 19); *To honor God in deed is to honor God indeed* (see v. 20). Have learners analyze the slogans per above.

After either alternative, draw on the board two large, simple human outlines. Write *I live in Corinth* on one, *I live in [name of your community]* on the other. Ask, "What might each of these individuals be thinking regarding sexual behavior in relation to so-called 'community standards'?" Jot responses on the board. Responses will undoubtedly fall into subcategories of Christian and non-Christian thought. Expect comments such as "sexual immorality is rampant" and "whatever consenting adults do with one another is their own business, as long as it does not hurt anyone else." Compare and contrast the idea of "community standards" with today's text.

Option: If you used the option under Into the Lesson, draw learners' attention back to that handout. As a result of the study thus far, discuss adjustments learners think they should make to the thoughts they previously jotted down.

Into Life

Give each learner a simple poster-board "coin" that has the word *Choice* on one side and the word *Consequence* on the other. Ask, "What is the inevitable relationship between the two sides of this coin?" After comments, say, "Carry this coin with you for a time as a reminder that every choice has a consequence and that many consequences can be traced back to voluntary choices, either good or bad. Whenever a choice is to be made, touch this coin and remember Paul's warnings."

Alternative: Distribute copies of the "Price Tags" activity from the reproducible page. Have learners work in pairs to complete this. If time is short, distribute as a take-home activity.

EXERCISE FREEDOM WITH CAUTION

DEVOTIONAL READING: Romans 14:7-12
BACKGROUND SCRIPTURE: 1 Corinthians 8, 9

1 CORINTHIANS 8

1 Now as touching things offered unto idols, we know that we all have knowledge. Knowledge puffeth up, but charity edifieth.

2 And if any man think that he knoweth any thing, he knoweth nothing yet as he ought to know.

3 But if any man love God, the same is known of him.

4 As concerning therefore the eating of those things that are offered in sacrifice unto idols, we know that an idol is nothing in the world, and that there is none other God but one.

5 For though there be that are called gods, whether in heaven or in earth, (as there be gods many, and lords many,)

6 But to us there is but one God, the Father, of whom are all things, and we in him; and one Lord Jesus Christ, by whom are all things, and we by him.

7 Howbeit there is not in every man that knowledge: for some with conscience of the idol unto this hour eat it as a thing offered unto an idol; and their conscience being weak is defiled.

8 But meat commendeth us not to God: for neither, if we eat, are we the better; neither, if we eat not, are we the worse.

9 But take heed lest by any means this liberty of yours become a stumblingblock to them that are weak.

10 For if any man see thee which hast knowledge sit at meat in the idol's temple, shall not the conscience of him which is weak be emboldened to eat those things which are offered to idols;

11 And through thy knowledge shall the weak brother perish, for whom Christ died?

12 But when ye sin so against the brethren, and wound their weak conscience, ye sin against Christ.

13 Wherefore, if meat make my brother to offend, I will eat no flesh while the world standeth, lest I make my brother to offend.

KEY VERSE

But take heed lest by any means this liberty of yours become a stumblingblock to them that are weak.

—1 Corinthians 8:9

THE PEOPLE OF GOD SET PRIORITIES

Unit 2: Living as a Community of Believers

LESSONS 5–9

LESSON AIMS

After participating in this lesson, each student will be able to:

1. Explain why the issue of eating meat sacrificed to idols was a problem for the Corinthian Christians.

2. Explain how the issue of meat sacrificed to idols translates into issues in the church today.

3. Identify a behavior in his or her life that may cause others to stumble and make a plan to eliminate it.

LESSON OUTLINE

Introduction

A. Idols as Chic Decorations

People decorate their homes to project a certain image, and this is often carefully planned and executed. With this in mind, I have been surprised over the years to find many Christian homes using pagan idols as decorative elements. A recent trend is to decorate with an Asian theme and include a figurine of a chubby, smiling Buddha.

Some Buddhists reject the idea that they are idol worshippers, claiming to use the statues only as an aid for their prayers and acts of devotion to the Buddha. But this understanding is similar to the idol worship in the Greek cities of Paul's world. When a citizen of Corinth went to the temple of Apollo to worship, he did not believe that the statue in the temple was the actual god Apollo; rather, he believed that it represented a spiritual reality behind the statue. The idol served as a point of contact and focus with the god.

Christians don't include statuettes of the Buddha in their decorating scheme with the intent of doing Buddhist worship. They believe these idols are harmless, inert objects. Yet more than once I have been in a home where a statuette of the Buddha had a little pan in front of it, and incense had been burned in the pan. This bothered me. It is too much like the Buddhist shrines I have seen in Myanmar, where incense is burned as a real act of worship by real Buddhists who believe the idol represents a real god.

Buddha statuettes, native American worship art, zodiac symbols, tiki carvings—should we view decorating with idol artifacts as being no more than innocent acts of chic ornamentation? Can we play with idols without causing problems for ourselves or others?

B. Lesson Background

The Corinth of Paul's day featured many temples devoted to the worship of fictitious deities. These temples hosted religious festivals at various times when wealthy patrons would bring animals to be sacrificed. In the process, the carcasses of these animals would be divided three ways. A small portion would be burned as an offering in the temple. Another portion would be reserved for the priests or priestesses of the temple. The biggest portion, though, would be made available to the public at large, who could dine on the meat free of charge at the festival meal. Leftover meat might be available for purchase in a butcher shop associated with a temple.

For the poor of the city, the chance to eat meat was an opportunity to be seized. Meat was expensive and not normally available to the lower classes. The pleasure of such a rare treat could override any pangs of conscience about hanging out at a pagan temple in order to get a meal that included meat that had been sacrificed to a pagan god or goddess. This seems to be the main issue in 1 Corinthians 8, the focus of this week's lesson. (The issue of private, at-home eating of meat that had been purchased at the pagan temple's butcher shop seems to be more the context of Paul's instructions in 1 Corinthians 10, next week's lesson.)

No one in the Corinthian church claimed it was permissible to participate in the rituals of the pagan temples by taking an animal there for sacrifice. The question concerned the surplus of meat generated through these rituals: was its consumption an accommodation with paganism?

Before we dive into this issue, we should revisit the deliberations of the famous Jerusalem Council of Acts 15. There, Paul had met with other Christian leaders some five years before he wrote 1 Corinthians. The chief issue discussed was circumcision for Gentiles, which the council decided was unnecessary. Often overlooked, however, is that the council also instructed Gentile Christians to "abstain from meats offered to idols" (Acts 15:29). Therefore this was not a new issue.

HOW TO SAY IT

Buddha	*Bew*-duh.
Buddhists	*Bew*-dists.
Deuteronomy	Due-ter-*ahn*-uh-me.
Isaiah	Eye-*zay*-uh.
Leviticus	Leh-*vit*-ih-kus.
monotheism	***maw***-nuh-the-*ih*-zum (*th* as in *thin*).
Myanmar	*Myawn*-mawhr.

I. Primacy of Love
(1 CORINTHIANS 8:1-3)
A. Two Paths (vv. 1, 2)

1. Now as touching things offered unto idols, we know that we all have knowledge. Knowledge puffeth up, but charity edifieth.

As discussed in the previous lesson, Paul sometimes quotes brief slogans that seem to be circulating among the Corinthians. One such slogan is in the verse before us: *we all have knowledge.* This is an obvious truth, for everyone has a certain amount of knowledge. At the most basic level, knowledge is "information." A higher level of knowledge can be called "comprehension," a deeper understanding of a subject. Paul does not dispute the slogan *we all have knowledge.* But he wants the reader to consider the nature of knowledge and how it can be misused.

What Do You Think?
  What well-intentioned slogans have you seen churches use that caused confusion or harm? How do we avoid this problem?
Talking Points for Your Discussion
  ▪ Slogans that summarize doctrinal beliefs
  ▪ Slogans that summarize church practices
  ▪ Other

The warning *knowledge puffeth up* means that its possession can lead to self-importance and pride. It is possible for a person to acquire and hoard information to gain advantage over others, even in a church situation. An outward focus on *charity*, meaning love for others, is the needed corrective to an undue inward focus on knowledge.

How is this working in Corinth? Paul's issue with knowledge has to do with the matter of food *offered unto idols.* Most if not all of the Corinthian Christians have been instructed about the true nature of idols: they are lifeless objects of stone, metal, or wood (see v. 4, below). That's good knowledge! The problem is that at least some of the Corinthians are using this knowledge to rationalize questionable behavior: participation in the food events at the pagan temples (see the Lesson Background). Since pagan worship of idols is a sham, what harm is there in getting some free food, especially meat?

2. And if any man think that he knoweth any thing, he knoweth nothing yet as he ought to know.

In effect, Paul now says, "You aren't as smart as you think you are." The Corinthians' correct understanding regarding the bogus nature of idols is leading to problems. The problem isn't the presence of the knowledge as such, but lack of wisdom in its application. Wisdom is the judicious use of knowledge. If true knowledge regarding the phony nature of idols is somehow leading to spiritual problems among members of the congregation, then such knowledge is being used unwisely.

> *What Do You Think?*
> What safeguards can we adopt to ensure that we exercise our knowledge of God's truth in ways that demonstrate love and humility?
> *Talking Points for Your Discussion*
> - In situations of doctrinal disagreement
> - In guiding a Christian who is new to the faith
> - In sharing with an unbeliever
> - Other

❧ *COTTON-CANDY CHRISTIANITY* ❧

Do you remember going to the fair when you were a child? Part of this experience was to beg our parents for some cotton candy. The inflated price of the treat didn't reflect the cost of the ingredients, which was next to nothing. It was not only the price that was inflated: cotton candy is merely a small amount of sugar that is heated and spun into an airy bundle of fluffy fibers. (The machine that produces this cavity-inducing convection was coinvented by a dentist!) There is very little food value in cotton candy, but it has caught the fancy of fairgoers for decades.

For Paul, knowledge can be like cotton candy. It's easy to get caught up in the sweet feeling that our knowledge brings us. Knowledge can cause us to be puffed up. We get self-inflated, sure of ourselves because of what we "know." We may see this especially in recent college graduates who believe they know more than other, less-educated people.

The more degrees we have, the more puffed-up we may become. On the other hand, folks without such degrees can be puffed up with their common-sense knowledge, disdaining "that high-falutin' stuff" that eggheads learn in college.

Surely none of this would happen in our church, would it? What knowledge of a spiritual nature might lead us into cotton-candy Christianity?

—C. R. B.

B. Desired Result (v. 3)

3. But if any man love God, the same is known of him.

Turning from human knowledge to divine knowledge, Paul points out that God knows those who love Him. The implication of Paul's statement is that God is not fooled by empty claims of devotion. He is not impressed by our knowledge, but by what is in our hearts. The smartest person in the church is not necessarily the most blessed by or devoted to God.

II. Primacy of God
(1 CORINTHIANS 8:4-8)
A. Looking Up (vv. 4-6)

4. As concerning therefore the eating of those things that are offered in sacrifice unto idols, we know that an idol is nothing in the world, and that there is none other God but one.

Paul seems to quote two Corinthian slogans in this verse. Both have the ring of truth but are dangerous if used in the wrong context. The first slogan, *an idol is nothing in the world,* recognizes that idols are physical objects having no power. The second slogan, *there is none other God but one,* recognizes just that. This second slogan can even be considered a loose quotation of Scripture (see Deuteronomy 6:4; Isaiah 44:6; 45:14).

Putting these two together in the context of eating *those things that are offered in sacrifice unto idols* would seem to lead to the conclusion that there is nothing wrong with eating food at pagan temple festivals (therefore being a passive participant). On a logical level, this makes sense. But our actions can have unintended consequences, and this is Paul's next point.

5, 6. For though there be that are called gods, whether in heaven or in earth, (as there be gods many, and lords many,) but to us there is but one God, the Father, of whom are all things, and we in him; and one Lord Jesus Christ, by whom are all things, and we by him.

Paul takes the opportunity to do a little teaching on the central doctrine of monotheism, which is the idea that there is only one God. Paul does not deny the reality of powerful spiritual beings *in heaven or in earth* (compare Ephesians 3:10; 6:12). He concedes there are *gods many, and lords many* that are recognized and even worshipped by the pagan world. Paul is not interested in discussing all of these, though. He wants our attention on the main point: the oneness of God.

Christians believe in one God. We may not fully understand the relationship within the Trinity of Father, Son, and the Holy Spirit as being three and at the same time one. But at the end of the day we still affirm that there is only one God.

We can see this unity of God in the descriptive phrases (which are nearly identical) that Paul applies to the Father and the Son. Paul says of the Father that all things are *of* Him; concerning the Son, all things are *by* Him. Of the Father, Paul says we are *in* Him; of the Son, that we are *by* Him.

If we look at these phrasings closely, we see that the difference is our perspective rather than the nature of Father and Son within the Trinity. Rather than divide God into two, Paul acknowledges the singularity of God. Because there is only one God, the idols worshipped in the many pagan temples cannot be true gods.

B. Looking Around (vv. 7, 8)

7. Howbeit there is not in every man that knowledge: for some with conscience of the idol unto this hour eat it as a thing offered unto an idol; and their conscience being weak is defiled.

Paul now uses the fact of the uniqueness and oneness of God to address the problem in Corinth. Some of the Christians there have not yet reached this level of understanding about God. While they believe in Jesus as Savior and worship the Father, their former beliefs about other gods, beliefs held for many years, may still be fresh.

Such folks need to stay away from the pagan temples because those are places of spiritual danger for them. Hanging around those temples may result in being drawn back into former lifestyles. For "enlightened" Christians—those who know that "an idol is nothing" (v. 4)—to participate in a meal at the pagan temple therefore carries potential negative consequences when witnessed by those whose conscience is *weak* in this regard. Paul needs to instruct those who are more mature doctrinally on how to handle the issue.

8. But meat commendeth us not to God: for neither, if we eat, are we the better; neither, if we eat not, are we the worse.

Meat (food) in and of itself is not the issue, for it cannot bring us closer to God. Whether our pizza is vegetarian or loaded with pepperoni does not affect how God views us and forms no barrier in our relationship with Him. We may make food choices based on health or other factors, but the food itself is physical, not spiritual. However, that does not mean there are no spiritual implications to our food choices, and that is what Paul discusses next.

III. Primacy of Witness

(1 CORINTHIANS 8:9-13)

A. What Can Happen (vv. 9-12)

9. But take heed lest by any means this liberty of yours become a stumblingblock to them that are weak.

Can freedom be abused? Paul's answer: of course! We may be firm advocates for human rights, but there are times when an exercise of our own rights can cause problems for others. This can be a touchy matter within the church. Things that I do without the slightest twinge of conscience may *become a stumblingblock* to others.

We remind ourselves that we do not live in isolation. The church is a community, a fellowship of believers. We must be aware that activities that one person sees as harmless may be damaging to others. This is particularly true of a person who has been delivered from the deep abyss of a certain type of sin. One person might be indifferent to violent content in movies, but this same content might tempt another to return to a life of violence. Paul's reminder is that the spiritual safety of our Christian brothers and sisters is always more important that the exercise of our rights in Christian liberty. Romans 14:1-21 expands on this.

10, 11. For if any man see thee which hast knowledge sit at meat in the idol's temple, shall not the conscience of him which is weak be emboldened to eat those things which are offered to idols; and through thy knowledge shall the weak brother perish, for whom Christ died?

Paul now gets very specific about the issue at hand. Suppose a church member who has a mature knowledge about the spurious nature of idols socializes at the pagan temple and takes a meal there. What if this is seen by another Christian who was recently delivered from the full-blown worship of idols? The action on the part of the first Christian may result in the second Christian's falling back into the sin of idol worship!

Paul is leading up to this stern warning for those who are more mature: are you not endangering the faith of one *for whom Christ died?* Christ loves this less enlightened one—*the conscience of him which is weak*—so much that He gave His life so that this person can have eternal salvation. Are you willing to risk this individual's faith so that you might exercise your liberty? This should not be. This cannot be (compare Romans 14:15).

12. But when ye sin so against the brethren, and wound their weak conscience, ye sin against Christ.

Paul's passionate tone rises. Not only will the thoughtless participation in the pagan temple's food event be a sin against the one with a *weak conscience,* it will also be a *sin against Christ* himself. If you damage another believer's relationship with the Lord, the Lord notices!

Sometimes Paul's arguments here are misused in situations of disagreement within a church. Dale tells Lindsay that she must not engage in a certain activity for the sake of his own weak conscience. In such a case, the self-identified "weak brother" is using Paul's warning as leverage to control another person's behavior, to limit her liberty. This is the road to legalism and is an inappropriate use of what Paul is saying. (We also note that Paul may use the word *weak* in different senses in other contexts; compare 1 Corinthians 1:27; 2 Corinthians 13:9.)

What Do You Think?

What are some ways to show consideration for the conscience of a fellow Christian?

Talking Points for Your Discussion
- Regarding recreational choices
- Regarding sensitivity to former temptations
- Regarding misunderstanding of biblical teachings on Christian living
- Other

B. What Should Happen (v. 13)

13. Wherefore, if meat make my brother to offend, I will eat no flesh while the world standeth, lest I make my brother to offend.

Paul takes his stand: he pledges that he will give up eating meat altogether rather than have his food choices lead to sin in another believer (compare Romans 14:21). We note that the word *offend* in this context means "to cause someone to sin."

Although he does not quote it, this is Paul's application of Jesus' second great commandment,

"Thou shalt love thy neighbour as thyself" (Matthew 22:39). We would not appreciate another church member leading us into sin, so why would we do it to anyone else?

❧ *WITHIN THE CALL OF DUTY* ❧

U.S. Marine Corporal Dakota L. Meyer was maintaining security on a patrol point in an Afghan village on September 8, 2009, when members of his team were ambushed. Dozens of the enemy opened fire from concealed positions in buildings and the hills above them. With members of his team trapped, Corporal Meyer took the initiative to disrupt the attack.

With a fellow Marine driving a gun-truck, Meyer manned an exposed machine gun as they headed into the village under heavy fire. Meyer risked his life time and time again on five trips during a six-hour battle, rescuing numerous U.S. and Afghan military personnel in the process. For his actions that day, Meyer was awarded the Congressional Medal of Honor "for conspicuous gallantry . . . above and beyond the call of duty."

While we may admire the courage of Corporal Meyer and others like him, we remind ourselves that Jesus said that everything we do for Him is *within* our call of duty (Luke 17:10). He performed the duty set before Him by the Father in going to the cross. Surely we can do our own duty in setting aside personal preferences for the sake of another Christian's conscience!   —C. R. B.

Conclusion

A. Three Examples

A rite of passage for many children is learning there is no Santa Claus. This revelation sometimes comes rudely from older children who enjoy belittling the beliefs of younger siblings. In this case, superior knowledge does not translate into superior maturity, for this "enlightenment" can be done in a very hurtful manner.

While ministering in California, I often stopped at a coffee shop next to the church on my way to the office. When the weather was nice, I would sit in the outdoor courtyard and do some early morning reading. This ritual ended when another man

Visual for Lesson 7. *Point to this visual as you introduce the discussion question that is associated with verse 12.*

began to use the courtyard to smoke a powerful cigar while enjoying his latte. He was breaking no laws, but the odor was nauseating. But before I could speak with him about this, another patron did so and was treated very poorly by cigar man. He was using a freedom in a very selfish manner.

I remember a Jewish friend telling me of her daughter's actions at dinner one day. The young woman had become a Christian and believed she was liberated from her Jewish roots. Her parents were somewhat indifferent to all this. But a crisis occurred when the daughter had her parents over for dinner and served ham. From the daughter's perspective, this was an expression of her right to eat formerly forbidden food (Leviticus 11:7; Deuteronomy 14:8). Her parents found this deeply offensive.

A right application of what Paul was teaching would have made each of these three situations better. Sometimes the assertion of our rights as Christians is really just selfishness. Oh, to be part of a congregation where members love each other so much that this never becomes an issue!

B. Prayer

Father, may we never be the cause of the fall by one of the precious souls for whom Your Son gave His life. Help us to love our brothers and sisters as much as You do. In Jesus' name, amen.

C. Thought to Remember

Be a building block, not a stumbling block.

INVOLVEMENT LEARNING

Some of the activities below are also found in the helpful student book, Adult Bible Class.
Don't forget to download the free reproducible page from www.standardlesson.com to enhance your lesson!

Into the Lesson

Post a large sign that reads *FREE MEAT!* In smaller letters underneath, have *Ask No Questions* in parentheses. (*Option:* Also display three or four cans of meat.) As learners react, say, "Today we take the availability of meat for granted. But that was not true in the first century." Use the Lesson Background to explain why meat was a rare commodity in the first century—especially for the poor—reserved for special occasions.

Into the Word

Give each learner a handout of the Christian principles (truisms) listed below. Say, "First, go through the statements and identify the verse or verses of today's text that each is drawn from. Then rank these statements from 1 (highest) to 10 (lowest) based on how important you think they are to daily life in our culture." (*Option:* Have learners complete this in study pairs or small groups.)

A. Knowledge tends to make one feel self-important. B. The essence of love is that it builds others up rather than tearing them down. C. Even a well-informed person has gaps in his or her knowledge. D. The person who truly loves God can be assured of the reverse. E. Food does not relate to spiritual life. F. The exercise of one's rights must be controlled by concern for others. G. To sin against others is to sin against Christ. H. Certain personal rights must be set aside if exercising them creates a stumbling block for another. I. Believing that there is one God who makes life possible is the starting point for wrestling with day-to-day dilemmas. J. Beliefs can have powerful effects in one's life even when what is believed is not true.

Possible answers to verse sources, although learners may make a good case for others: A, verse 1; B, verse 1; C, verse 2; D, verse 3; E, verse 8; F, verse 9; G, verse 12; H, verse 9; I, verses 4b-6; J, verse 7. Wrestling with the learners' rank-orderings will result in a discussion of the truths Paul teaches.

Into Life

Discuss one or more of the following scenarios. (*Option:* Form learners into small groups for the discussion; if using this option, reproduce the scenarios on handouts.)

At the movies. You are standing in line at a theater for a movie—one that is known to be filled with crude and violent situations, yet also featuring an uplifting moral lesson. A new Christian from your congregation, headed for a different film, walks by and sees you. He says, "Why, I can't believe you're going to see that!" What do you do now? What should you have done differently, if anything, before getting in that line?

Casino. While standing in a checkout line, you are chatting with someone about your plan to accompany your dad to a casino. Then you notice behind you an acquaintance whose spouse is a member of Gamblers Anonymous. He has obviously overheard your plans but says nothing. What do you do now? What should you have done differently, if anything, before making your plans?

New neighbors. Some neighbors are planning a "welcome to the neighborhood" dinner for a new family moving in. That new family happens to be Muslim by faith. At the planning meeting, you say, "We need to be careful not to include food that would be offensive to our new neighbors." Another planner, a relatively new Christian, says, "Well, I hope they don't think they're too good to eat what we eat!" How do you proceed?

Alternative: Instead of discussing the scenarios above, distribute copies of the "Knowing and Acting" activity from the reproducible page, which you can download. Have learners complete this in small groups or study pairs. The challenges are stated in the third person ("Christians should") rather than the first person ("I should") to foster nonthreatening discussion.

Distribute copies of the "Dig In?" activity from the reproducible page as a take-home exercise.

OVERCOME TEMPTATION

DEVOTIONAL READING: Hebrews 3:7-14
BACKGROUND SCRIPTURE: 1 Corinthians 10:1-22

1 CORINTHIANS 10:6-22

6 Now these things were our examples, to the intent we should not lust after evil things, as they also lusted.

7 Neither be ye idolaters, as were some of them; as it is written, The people sat down to eat and drink, and rose up to play.

8 Neither let us commit fornication, as some of them committed, and fell in one day three and twenty thousand.

9 Neither let us tempt Christ, as some of them also tempted, and were destroyed of serpents.

10 Neither murmur ye, as some of them also murmured, and were destroyed of the destroyer.

11 Now all these things happened unto them for ensamples: and they are written for our admonition, upon whom the ends of the world are come.

12 Wherefore let him that thinketh he standeth take heed lest he fall.

13 There hath no temptation taken you but such as is common to man: but God is faithful, who will not suffer you to be tempted above that ye are able; but will with the temptation

also make a way to escape, that ye may be able to bear it.

14 Wherefore, my dearly beloved, flee from idolatry.

15 I speak as to wise men; judge ye what I say.

16 The cup of blessing which we bless, is it not the communion of the blood of Christ? The bread which we break, is it not the communion of the body of Christ?

17 For we being many are one bread, and one body: for we are all partakers of that one bread.

18 Behold Israel after the flesh: are not they which eat of the sacrifices partakers of the altar?

19 What say I then? that the idol is any thing, or that which is offered in sacrifice to idols is any thing?

20 But I say, that the things which the Gentiles sacrifice, they sacrifice to devils, and not to God: and I would not that ye should have fellowship with devils.

21 Ye cannot drink the cup of the Lord, and the cup of devils: ye cannot be partakers of the Lord's table, and of the table of devils.

22 Do we provoke the Lord to jealousy? are we stronger than he?

KEY VERSE

There hath no temptation taken you but such as is common to man: but God is faithful, who will not suffer you to be tempted above that ye are able; but will with the temptation also make a way to escape, that ye may be able to bear it. —**1 Corinthians 10:13**

THE PEOPLE OF GOD SET PRIORITIES

Unit 2: Living as a Community of Believers

LESSONS 5–9

LESSON AIMS

After participating in this lesson, each student will be able to:

1. Tell how Paul used Hebrew history and the church's experience with the Lord's Supper to teach about resisting temptation.

2. Describe the nature and causes of temptation.

3. Recruit an accountability partner for mutual support in resisting temptation.

LESSON OUTLINE

Introduction

A. The Medicine of Immortality?

Ignatius of Antioch, a leader in the early church, called the Lord's Supper the "medicine of immortality, the antidote against dying." He was writing about AD 110, a little over 50 years after Paul wrote 1 Corinthians. Ignatius believed and taught that partaking of the Lord's Supper gave Christians almost magical protection against life's ultimate troubles. This idea later developed into what is called *sacramentalism*, a belief that eating the bread and drinking the cup of the Lord's Supper is essential to maintaining one's salvation. To be barred from partaking (excommunication) was effectively to lose one's salvation.

But defective views of the Lord's Supper did not begin with Ignatius of Antioch. At least some of the Corinthian Christians of Paul's day held one or more false understandings in this area. Part of Paul's response was to warn them by drawing on incidents from the history of Israel. This week's lesson will explore those examples.

B. Lesson Background

Two areas of background information will better help us understand today's lesson. First, it is useful to review the wilderness experience of the nation of Israel since it forms the backdrop for Paul's teaching in 1 Corinthians 10. Perhaps some may idealize that experience as being somewhat like a weekend camping trip that was extended for 40 years. Everything was the same, week by week, as people lived in tents. Their clothes and shoes never wore out, so they never got new ones (Deuteronomy 29:5). They gathered manna and ate it daily (Numbers 11:6; Deuteronomy 8:3).

But it wasn't that simple; things weren't always the same. During this period, the people of Israel had many points of contact with other small nations and tribes (Numbers 14:45; 25:16-18; Deuteronomy 23:3). Encounters with peoples outside the covenant are the basis for some of the lessons Paul teaches in 1 Corinthians 10.

A second background item that can help us understand this lesson is to note Paul's use of an interpretation method known as *typology*. The essence of typology is that certain persons, places, things, or events in the Old Testament serve as patterns (or "types") that can help us understand various persons, places, things, or events in the New Testament.

A good example is King David as a "type" of the Messiah or Christ. Certainly, David did not measure up to Jesus in essential nature, character, or importance, but David's kingship provides many patterns that help us understand Jesus as the true Messiah, sent by the Father. For example, when Psalm 2:7 says "Thou art my Son," we understand this as having been written about David, but it is applied more fully to Jesus in Hebrews 1:5. Typology figures heavily into Paul's method of teaching in 1 Corinthians 10.

I. Lessons from History
(1 CORINTHIANS 10:6-13)
A. Examples of Sin (vv. 6-11)

6. Now these things were our examples, to the intent we should not lust after evil things, as they also lusted.

In the five verses just before this one, Paul compares Israel's Red Sea deliverance with Christian baptism and compares Israel's miraculous provision of food (manna) and drink (water from the rock) with the Lord's Supper. His point is that even though the people of Israel had these marvelous things (which were "types" of baptism and the Lord's Supper; see the Lesson Background), God was not pleased with the people. As a result, the Israelites "were overthrown in the wilderness" (1 Corinthians 10:5).

These incidents serve as *our examples.* The Greek word translated *examples* here is *typoi,* which comes into English rather directly as *types.* Paul thus uses

HOW TO SAY IT

Antioch	*An*-tee-ock.
Baalpeor	Bay-al-*pe*-or.
Ignatius	Ig-*nay*-shus.
Ouija	*Wee*-juh.
typology	tie-*paw*-luh-gee.
Wicca	*Wih*-kuh.

events from the Old Testament as lessons of warning: we are not to *lust after evil things* as the Israelites in the wilderness did, lest we be subject to God's wrath as Israel was. Paul then proceeds to offer four examples from the history of Israel in the wilderness.

7. Neither be ye idolaters, as were some of them; as it is written, The people sat down to eat and drink, and rose up to play.

Paul's first example is from the notorious golden calf incident, where the Israelites demanded that Aaron make an idol for them to worship (see Exodus 32; compare Deuteronomy 9:7-21). This took place during the most important event in the history of Israel: the receiving of the law by Moses on Mount Sinai. Paul even quotes Exodus 32:6, *The people sat down to eat and drink, and rose up to play.* The polite word *play* carries the sense that the people of Israel were having a giant party that included drunkenness and sexual immorality.

Paul is not being subtle here; even a blockhead can see the parallel with the Corinthian situation. The incident of the golden calf involved both idol worship and sexual immorality, the great dangers of the pagan temples of the city of Corinth (see the Lesson Background of last week's lesson).

❧ AMERICAN IDOL(ATRY)? ❧

American Idol first aired on June 11, 2002, quickly becoming one of the most popular TV shows ever. The show is a singing competition for amateurs. Celebrity judges eliminate contestants in the early stages, but the winners are determined by viewers who vote by telephone, Internet, and text messaging. By the tenth season, the total of votes was around 750 million! Winners typically receive lucrative recording contracts. Jeff Zucker, an executive for a rival network, declared *American Idol* to be "the most impactful show in the history of television."

Has adoration of top contestants by *American Idol* fans reached the stage of being literal idolatry? Such a question can be answered only on a fan by fan basis. In any case, the dedicated following the program has gained does say something about Americans' unhealthy tendency to venerate celebrities. What would have to happen for us to get as excited about our faith as the world does about the contestants on *American Idol*? —C. R. B.

8. Neither let us commit fornication, as some of them committed, and fell in one day three and twenty thousand.

Paul's second example is the Baalpeor incident of Numbers 25:1-9. This is another notorious episode of idolatry in the history of Israel. It began with illicit sex with non-Israelite women, which led to idolatrous worship with them. The result was death on a massive scale. This should be a stark lesson for the Corinthians who are being tempted in the same two areas.

> **What Do You Think?**
> Which happens more often: *idolatry leads to other sins* or *other sins lead to idolatry*? Or is such a distinction unimportant? Explain.
> *Talking Points for Your Discussion*
> - In your personal, day-to-day observations
> - In the country as a whole
> - In the differing cultural contexts of other countries

9. Neither let us tempt Christ, as some of them also tempted, and were destroyed of serpents.

Paul's third example is from Numbers 21:4-9, the incident of the serpents in the wilderness. In this case, the people of Israel complained against both Moses and the Lord, implying that the former life in Egyptian slavery was to be preferred. In particular, the people complained about the manna God was providing, calling it "light bread" (v. 5). The Lord's response was to send a plague of poisonous snakes, causing many deaths. This disaster was mitigated when the people repented and looked upon a brass serpent that the Lord had directed Moses to make (compare John 3:14).

Paul's lesson here is that the Corinthians' abuse of the Lord's Supper is a testing of the patience of the Lord, here expressed as to *tempt Christ*. The Corinthians should understand that God's willingness to endure the abuse of His patience may result in disaster.

10. Neither murmur ye, as some of them also murmured, and were destroyed of the destroyer.

The fourth example from the history of Israel is an incident of grumbling against Moses. Grumbling and murmuring was an ongoing problem for the Israelites during the trip to the promised land. Paul's reference is Numbers 14:37, where 10 of the 12 men sent to spy out the land of Canaan were struck down by a plague from the Lord. Mention of *the destroyer* reflects Exodus 12:23.

The Israelites' grumbling against Moses is like the Corinthians' grumbling against Paul. Both cases are, in effect, grumbling against God. Those Corinthians who are inclined to ignore Paul as an unwelcome, outside meddler are being forewarned that they should heed what he has to say!

11. Now all these things happened unto them for ensamples: and they are written for our admonition, upon whom the ends of the world are come.

These incidents have not been recorded because they are part of a glorious history of Israel—quite the opposite! They are recorded as cautionary *ensamples* (an older word for "examples") to future generations, and they now serve that function in the Corinthian situation. The mix of idolatry, sexual immorality, and rebellion against God-ordained authority resulted in a 40-year delay for the ancient people of Israel, and that mix is present in an eerily similar way in the church at Corinth. Paul wants the Corinthians to heed these lessons from history.

Paul uses grand terminology at the end of this verse: the Corinthians are part of the larger body of Christ, the church as a whole, the new covenant people *upon whom the ends of the world are come*. Paul's readers should appreciate that the historical accounts of faith failures serve as enduring warnings for the church age.

B. Cautions for Corinthians (vv. 12, 13)

12. Wherefore let him that thinketh he standeth take heed lest he fall.

Paul offers sound advice: don't overestimate your spiritual strength. This is akin to the old saying, "Don't play with fire or you will get burned." Paul is not speaking to folks who are constantly in the presence of temptations due to life circumstances. In that regard, we can imagine the situation of a woman in the church at Corinth whose unbelieving husband demands she attend events at pagan temples. Such a believer is not playing with fire voluntarily; she is being forced toward the furnace. Paul has in mind, rather, the believer who acts arrogantly, trusting in his or her spiritual maturity and strength to enter the lions' den of paganism voluntarily and not be consumed.

13. There hath no temptation taken you but such as is common to man: but God is faithful, who will not suffer you to be tempted above that ye are able; but will with the temptation also make a way to escape, that ye may be able to bear it.

This is a well-known verse, but we should take a careful look at what it means. Sometimes it has been used to teach that there is no excuse for ever yielding to temptation, because to commit a sin implies that one has not drawn on God's help to resist that sin. While this idea has some merit, it is not really what Paul is teaching here. The promise is not about an infusion of spiritual strength to resist, but about having *a way to escape.*

Let's apply this to the Corinthian situation. What would be a way to escape the temptation of participating in idolatrous activities at a pagan temple? How about this: *Don't go!* We should never underestimate the power of temptation (that is what the four examples from Israel's history are intended to demonstrate). Often the best way to defeat temptation is to avoid it altogether.

However, we should not lose sight of another fundamental truth here: God does not desert us in our times of temptation and trial. He stands with us. He will not abandon us. He will walk with us until we can extricate ourselves from the tempting situation. God wants us to have victory over sin, and this means to resist and escape temptation.

What Do You Think?

Is it useful to try to identify in advance possible escape routes for various kinds of temptations? Or is this more of a "wait and see what God will provide" issue? Explain.

Talking Points for Your Discussion
- Regarding temptations of the body
- Regarding temptations of the spirit

II. Application of the Lessons
(1 CORINTHIANS 10:14-22)
A. Fleeing from Idolatry (vv. 14, 15)

14, 15. Wherefore, my dearly beloved, flee from idolatry. I speak as to wise men; judge ye what I say.

By speaking *as to wise men,* Paul is calling on the Corinthians to exercise wisdom. To *flee from idolatry* is the wise path. The opposite is to invite temptation by participating in activities of the pagan temples, the places of idol worship. To join in activities there—even activities that do not involve worship as such—is unwise, foolish. Paul wants his readers to take this matter seriously, to examine carefully what he says. This is not a light matter! The salvation of some believers may be at stake.

B. Connecting in Communion (vv. 16, 17)

16, 17. The cup of blessing which we bless, is it not the communion of the blood of Christ? The bread which we break, is it not the communion of the body of Christ? For we being many are one bread, and one body: for we are all partakers of that one bread.

Paul now returns to the Lord's Supper as a way to understand the danger of flirting with idolatry. He reminds the Corinthians that the Lord's Supper is a communal meal, a symbolic sharing in *the blood of Christ* and *the body of Christ.* The Lord's Supper has a built-in symbol of unity: the single loaf of bread that is shared by *all partakers.* This connectedness is not incidental, but purposeful and meaningful (compare Romans 12:5). Paul's implication is that the communal meals at a pagan temple, using food dedicated to an idol, also speak to a unity of worship—idolatrous worship.

C. Wrestling with Reality (vv. 18-22)

18. Behold Israel after the flesh: are not they which eat of the sacrifices partakers of the altar?

Paul briefly returns to consider *Israel after the flesh,* the historic people of that nation, to point out that they ate some of the meat from certain sacrifices offered at the altar of the tabernacle (see Leviticus 7:15, 16). This was a shared meal with great spiritual significance, performing a duty to the Lord that also gave them communion with the God of Israel. This was a central purpose of the tabernacle and its successor, the temple: a place where sacrifices could be offered.

19, 20. What say I then? that the idol is any thing, or that which is offered in sacrifice to idols is any thing? But I say, that the things which the Gentiles sacrifice, they sacrifice to devils, and not to God: and I would not that ye should have fellowship with devils.

Using irony, Paul points out that some of the spiritual realities of the Jewish temple in Jerusalem are also present in the pagan temples of Corinth. The worshippers of Apollo, etc., also offer sacrifices involving a spiritual presence, but in those cases the sacrifices are made *to devils, and not to God.* While it is surely true that the idols of the pagan temples are inanimate creations of stone and wood, Paul warns that there is a demonic presence behind them. Just because the pagan gods are fictitious does not mean they do not represent powerful, evil spiritual forces (compare Revelation 9:20).

> *What Do You Think?*
> What experiences have you had, or personally know of people having had, with demonic spiritual forces? How have these affected you?
> *Talking Points for Your Discussion*
> - Ouija board
> - Witchcraft/Wicca
> - Fortune-telling
> - Other

21. Ye cannot drink the cup of the Lord, and the cup of devils: ye cannot be partakers of the Lord's table, and of the table of devils.

This verse has one of the most profound statements in the book of 1 Corinthians. In modern idiom, we might put it this way: "You cannot share yourself with both the Lord and the demons." Our relationship with God must be exclusive. There can be no such thing as a part-time, Sunday-only Christian.

Paul is drawing a direct contrast between the pagan celebrations—spiritually enlivened by the demonic realm—and the celebrations of the Lord's Supper practiced by the Corinthians. Both

are intended to have a powerful spiritual impact on participants. The temples of the gods do not sponsor meals merely as free entertainment. They do so to honor their gods, and Paul warns that demonic powers lurk behind these events.

Paul's statement here is similar to Jesus' teaching that we cannot serve God and mammon (Matthew 6:24). There can be no divided loyalties in the Christian walk. There is one God (Ephesians 4:6) and all other gods, whether mammon or Apollo, are false. This does not mean they are "fake" with no spiritual power (compare Acts 16:16-18 19:13-16). If we allow ourselves to think otherwise, we are truly setting ourselves up for a fall (1 Corinthians 10:12). We must guard our hearts, not inviting temptations and compromise.

> *What Do You Think?*
> Has Paul's argument shifted from one of *right use of liberty* to a matter of *right versus wrong*? Why, or why not?
> *Talking Points for Your Discussion*
> - Reasons the argument has shifted
> - Reasons the argument has not shifted

❧ *BELONGING* ❧

What determines or indicates where we belong or don't belong? In the not too distant past, one could find places in America where skin color was the criteria in this regard. Even today, gender may be the determining factor. Humans have a long history of creating rules, expressed or implied, that say, "We'll invite you, you, and you because you are like us. Everyone else—stay away."

The Lord's Supper is inclusive because all who confess Jesus as Lord are invited to partake. As we do, we are saying we are one in Christ regardless of differences in culture, language, nationality, race, gender, socioeconomic level, education, or any of the other distinctions by which the world divides people into categories of *us* and *them*. The unity of the body of Christ transcends all such categories.

Yet the Lord's Supper by nature also witnesses to exclusion and distinction. As we partake, we say, "By being united *with* Christ, we are united *against* the world that rejects Him." Think of how odd and self-contradictory it is to partake of the loaf and cup only to join in an unholy activity of the world an hour later! Our partaking of the Lord's Supper should make a profound statement about where our allegiance lies. —C. R. B.

> **What Do You Think?**
> What guardrails can we erect to keep us from dividing our loyalties in various areas of life?
> *Talking Points for Your Discussion*
> - Family
> - Vocation
> - Hobbies
> - Other

22. Do we provoke the Lord to jealousy? are we stronger than he?

Paul ends this section with two rhetorical questions, the answers to which should be obvious. As God desired the allegiance of Old Testament Israel, so He desires ours. To shift our allegiance to idols or other things will *provoke the Lord to jealousy* (compare Exodus 20:5; 34:14; Deuteronomy 4:24; 5:9; 6:15). This is the lesson of the four examples from Israel's history.

These two questions boil down to the folly of pitting our strength against the mighty power of the Creator of the universe. In the final analysis, God commands that we "flee from idolatry" (1 Corinthians 10:14). This is a constant refrain in the Old Testament, and the Christian way does not require any less. The new covenant through Jesus' blood has not changed this. We must guard our hearts and give them only to the Lord.

Conclusion

A. Seduction to Sin

On the blog "Waiter Rant," this observation was made: "Seduction . . . isn't making someone do what they don't want to do. Seduction is enticing someone into doing what they secretly want to do already." This statement occurs in the context of a waiter enticing a foursome of women to have dessert after an expensive dinner. He presumed that the four truly wanted calorie-laden desserts but were denying themselves this pleasure. The

Visual for Lesson 8. *Challenge your learners to answer this question both in terms of them as individuals and the congregation as a whole.*

waiter, using patience and the power of suggestion, eventually convinced all four to order dessert, adding $33 to their bill. When paying their tab, one of the women moaned, "I can't believe I ate that. . . . You are the devil."

We are surrounded by temptations. These come from advertisements, from the Internet, from friends, from those closest to us. None of these wears the face of a devil or demon. But just as Paul warned the Corinthians, we are to be careful lest we fall into old patterns of sin.

Temptation to sin may also come through us. Remember that some of our fellow believers have been delivered from horrendous, destructive patterns of sin. They may fall back into them easily through a bad witness on our part. We must never be the cause of the fall of a brother or sister (Romans 14:20; 1 Corinthians 8:13). Let us work daily to keep our lives pure and unspotted from the world (James 1:27) and to keep everyone in our fellowship in the same condition (Jude 23).

B. Prayer

Holy God, may we flee from sin. May we be strong to resist temptation. May we never think we can mix our allegiance to You with service to the gods of this world. In Jesus' name, amen.

C. Thought to Remember

Falling to temptation is not inevitable.
God always provides a way out.

INVOLVEMENT LEARNING

Some of the activities below are also found in the helpful student book, Adult Bible Class.
Don't forget to download the free reproducible page from www.standardlesson.com to enhance your lesson!

Into the Lesson

First Corinthians 10:1-5, which precedes today's text, sets the context for the bad examples Paul cites in the verses that follow. Have a good oral reader read those verses aloud. Then ask, "Thinking about the bigger picture, what was it that displeased God?" The expected summation is that although all the Israelites of the exodus received the same evidences of God's presence and power, many chose to disbelieve and disobey. Say, "Today's lesson warns us of the consequences of ignoring God. Let's take a look."

Into the Word

Create in advance five index cards, each of which has the phrase *Friends, I don't want you to be ignorant regarding* followed by one of these five topics: *sexual immorality / grumbling / tempting (testing) God / the Lord's Supper / idolatry*. If your class is larger than five, create additional (duplicate) sets of cards so that when you distribute the cards each learner will have at least one.

Distribute the cards as evenly as possible among learners; for those who receive more than one card, make sure the cards are not duplicates. Say, "Fill out your card or cards based on today's text. As you do, ask yourself what problem Paul sees or implies and what solution is in order."

Collect the completed cards. Arrange them in the order the topics are addressed in the text. Use the cards to work down through the topics, pointing out good observations on the cards and using the commentary to fill in missing information.

Before working down through the topics, explain the concept of *typology* (see the Lesson Background) as Paul uses that method to discuss persons, places, things, and/or events in the New Testament in light of persons, places, things, and/or events in the Old Testament. As you work through the topics, ask at appropriate points, "What is the Old Testament element that Paul is using here to stand behind a New Testament parallel, if any?" If learners seem to be having a hard time grasping the concept of *typology,* use the case of John the Baptist in relation to Elijah to illustrate further (Malachi 4:5, 6; Matthew 17:10-13; Luke 1:17).

Option: Do all the above, but instead of having a whole-class evaluation of the cards, distribute the completed cards as evenly as possible to small groups of two to four. If you created more than five cards, spread duplicate topics as evenly as possible. Ask groups to evaluate the entries on the cards in order to supply missing information and correct misconceptions. After groups finish, call for conclusions. If two or more groups have the same topic (if you created more than five cards), compare and contrast their responses.

Alternative: Instead of the above, distribute copies of the "As Some of Them" activity from the reproducible page, which you can download. You can use this in one of two ways: either (1) have learners work down the four entries of the bad example column first (individually or in small groups) to set the stage for class discussion regarding how Paul uses these examples, or (2) have learners use the chart as a note taker, completing in tandem the bad example and higher standard entries for each example as they encounter them in the progression of the lesson.

Into Life

Explain the accountability-partner concept, which involves being available to be called for encouragement by another who is having trouble resisting destructive, sinful behavior. Ask if anyone has had experience with this practice; discuss procedures and outcomes. Encourage learners to form such partnerships.

Distribute copies of the "How Not to Fall" activity from the reproducible page as a take-home exercise.

SEEK THE GOOD OF OTHERS

DEVOTIONAL READING: Titus 3:8-14
BACKGROUND SCRIPTURE: 1 Corinthians 14:13-26

1 CORINTHIANS 14:13-26

13 Wherefore let him that speaketh in an unknown tongue pray that he may interpret.

14 For if I pray in an unknown tongue, my spirit prayeth, but my understanding is unfruitful.

15 What is it then? I will pray with the spirit, and I will pray with the understanding also: I will sing with the spirit, and I will sing with the understanding also.

16 Else when thou shalt bless with the spirit, how shall he that occupieth the room of the unlearned say Amen at thy giving of thanks, seeing he understandeth not what thou sayest?

17 For thou verily givest thanks well, but the other is not edified.

18 I thank my God, I speak with tongues more than ye all:

19 Yet in the church I had rather speak five words with my understanding, that by my voice I might teach others also, than ten thousand words in an unknown tongue.

20 Brethren, be not children in understanding: howbeit in malice be ye children, but in understanding be men.

21 In the law it is written, With men of other tongues and other lips will I speak unto this people; and yet for all that will they not hear me, saith the Lord.

22 Wherefore tongues are for a sign, not to them that believe, but to them that believe not: but prophesying serveth not for them that believe not, but for them which believe.

23 If therefore the whole church be come together into one place, and all speak with tongues, and there come in those that are unlearned, or unbelievers, will they not say that ye are mad?

24 But if all prophesy, and there come in one that believeth not, or one unlearned, he is convinced of all, he is judged of all:

25 And thus are the secrets of his heart made manifest; and so falling down on his face he will worship God, and report that God is in you of a truth.

26 How is it then, brethren? when ye come together, every one of you hath a psalm, hath a doctrine, hath a tongue, hath a revelation, hath an interpretation. Let all things be done unto edifying.

KEY VERSE

How is it then, brethren? when ye come together, every one of you hath a psalm, hath a doctrine, hath a tongue, hath a revelation, hath an interpretation. Let all things be done unto edifying.

—1 Corinthians 14:26

THE PEOPLE OF GOD SET PRIORITIES

Unit 2: Living as a Community of Believers

Lessons 5–9

LESSON AIMS

After participating in this lesson, each student will be able to:

1. Explain the role of speaking in tongues in the Corinthians' (or other first-century) worship experience.

2. Compare and contrast speaking in tongues with contemporary activities that may be personally rewarding to the one practicing it, but is of little help to others without being explained first.

3. Identify one practice in his or her church's conduct of worship services that is a barrier to unbelievers and discuss with church leaders a plan for change.

LESSON OUTLINE

Introduction

A. Birth of a Movement

In 1906, William J. Seymour opened the Apostolic Faith Mission church in a modest, two-story building south of the Los Angeles city hall. Seymour was preaching a new type of message, and the church was quickly flooded with people. Seymour proposed that becoming a Christian was a three-step process: (1) salvation by faith, (2) cleansing sanctification of the believer by the Holy Spirit, and (3) filling of the believer by the Holy Spirit in a miraculous way.

The most prominent of the miraculous works of the Holy Spirit was said to be the ability to speak in tongues—ecstatic languages of prayer and worship. Seymour and others declared that this was a restoration of the gifts of the first-century church as depicted in the book of Acts. What Seymour launched came to be known as *the Azusa Street Revival*, which lasted until about 1915.

Many churches came into being as a result, and these came to be known as Pentecostal churches. Later, a similar movement of people known as *charismatics* began to develop within many denominations. Charismatics often encountered hostility in churches that did not accept the practice of speaking in tongues. Despite opposition, the charismatic movement has grown. It is estimated that 500 million Christians today are charismatic or Pentecostal —25 percent of all Christians worldwide.

The practice of speaking in tongues was controversial in Paul's day. It is still controversial today because many believe that the miraculous spiritual gifts, including the ability to speak in tongues, ceased with the completion of the New Testament; this is known as *cessationism*, and is the position of this commentary. But even though we no longer have such gifts, there are principles in Paul's instructions about them that still apply.

B. Lesson Background

Paul wrote letters to the churches in Rome, Corinth, the region of Galatia, Ephesus, Philippi, Colosse, and Thessalonica. Yet in all of his letters, Paul addressed the issue of speaking in tongues only with the church in Corinth, and only in

1 Corinthians. (The other New Testament texts that address this subject are Acts 2:4; 10:46; 19:6.) Paul's lengthy discussion of tongues in 1 Corinthians indicates that this was a point of controversy within the Corinthian church.

Scholars within Pentecostal churches generally divide the phenomenon into two categories. One category is *glossolalia*, defined as a worship language that does not communicate by itself, but needs interpretation. Sometimes this is called a prayer language (based on 1 Corinthians 14:14), a worship language (based on 14:15), or the language of angels (based on 13:1). The other general category is *xenoglossia*, the miraculous ability to speak in an existing foreign language that the speaker has not studied. The purpose is usually for evangelism, as in Acts 2.

One thing to keep in mind as we study this lesson is that not everyone in the Corinthian church spoke in tongues. We can see this fact in a series of seven rhetorical questions that Paul asks in 1 Corinthians 12:29, 30. The sixth of these is "Do all speak in tongues?" The expected answer to this and to the other six questions is *no.*

Paul has already said several things about speaking in tongues in 1 Corinthians 14 by the time we get to the opening *wherefore* of today's text: it is speaking to God (v. 2a), is a spiritual mystery (v. 2b), and is primarily for self-edification (v. 4). Paul also expressed a personal desire that all the Corinthians speak in tongues (v. 5), but he further taught that prophesying was to be preferred over speaking in tongues "except he interpret" (v. 5).

I. Problem
(1 CORINTHIANS 14:13-17)
A. Unfruitfulness (vv. 13, 14)

13, 14. Wherefore let him that speaketh in an unknown tongue pray that he may interpret. For if I pray in an unknown tongue, my spirit prayeth, but my understanding is unfruitful.

The translators have added the word *unknown* for the sake of clarity here. Such additions are clearly indicated by use of italics in most editions of the *King James Version*. Taken literally, the word translated *tongue* refers to the muscle-

organ located in the bottom of the mouth. But in the Bible, *tongue* is more often used in a non-literal sense to refer to an organized pattern of human speech, or what we call *language*. What Paul is referring to in the two verses before us, and what the KJV translators recognized, is a practice of people seeming to speak in a language (organized speech) that was unknown to themselves or to their hearers.

Paul sees this uninterpreted activity within a church service to be *unfruitful*, unhelpful, unedifying. Therefore, he asks that any speaking in tongues be interpreted. He has more to say about this below, as we shall see.

B. Understanding (vv. 15-17)

15. What is it then? I will pray with the spirit, and I will pray with the understanding also: I will sing with the spirit, and I will sing with the understanding also.

In the view of the KJV translators, *the spirit* Paul speaks of here is the human spirit, as indicated by its lack of being capitalized: *spirit*, not *Spirit*. This is the correct translation, and it allows us to understand this verse better. Paul is not in favor of mindless activity—speaking that is understood by neither the speaker nor the hearers. He wants praying and singing that is spiritual and *with the understanding also*. He wants the mind to be aware of what the mouth is saying.

What Do You Think?
What can the church do to help people pray and sing with greater understanding?
Talking Points for Your Discussion
- The role of faith in prayer and singing
- The role of humility in prayer and singing
- The role of persistence in prayer and singing
- The content of prayer and song
- Other

16, 17. Else when thou shalt bless with the spirit, how shall he that occupieth the room of the unlearned say Amen at thy giving of thanks, seeing he understandeth not what thou sayest? For thou verily givest thanks well, but the other is not edified.

Paul gives a very practical reason for his instruction for praying in a way that others can understand, a reason that might seem almost comical: if someone is praying publicly in unintelligible speech, how will anyone know when it is time (or if it is appropriate) to say *Amen*? (*Amen* means "may it be true" or "let it be so"). In particular, Paul has in mind *the unlearned,* someone without the gift of tongues and/or their interpretation.

Central to Paul's point is the issue of edification. This word is borrowed from the sphere of house construction, where it literally means "build up." Paul's question is this: how is an unlearned person spiritually built up in any way by hearing someone pray in a tongue that the unlearned person cannot understand? This is a clarifying question of purpose.

What Do You Think?

What steps can the church take to make the gospel more intelligible to an uncomprehending world?

Talking Points for Your Discussion

- Spiritual jargon
- Biblical terms that culture misdefines
- Cultural awareness
- Other

❧ *IDENTIFYING THE PROBLEM* ❧

Have you heard about Joe, who was afraid his wife was losing her hearing? Joe told the family doctor that his wife refused to have her hearing checked. The doctor suggested that Joe perform a hearing test at home. He was to call to his wife from another room. If she did not answer, he would move a few feet closer and call again. He was to repeat this test until she responded.

So one evening while his wife was preparing their meal, Joe stood down the hall and called, "Rose, what's for dinner?" No answer. Joe moved a few feet closer and tried again. Still no answer. After several attempts, Joe was at the doorway to the kitchen when he again asked, "Rose, what's for dinner?" With exasperation in her voice, she responded, "For the sixth time, it's steak, potatoes, and green beans!"

Rose was not the one with the hearing problem! This silly story illustrates the fact that communication problems aren't always what we think they are. Those Corinthians speaking in tongues might have been edifying themselves, but others in the church couldn't understand. So Paul told them, in effect, "If you're not communicating, you're missing the point!" What applications of the principle to contemporary church life can you think of?

—C. R. B.

II. Solution
(1 CORINTHIANS 14:18-26)
A. What Paul Wants (vv. 18-20)

18, 19. I thank my God, I speak with tongues more than ye all: yet in the church I had rather speak five words with my understanding, that by my voice I might teach others also, than ten thousand words in an unknown tongue.

Paul continues by stating a fact that some may find surprising: *I speak with tongues more than ye all.* There is no one more invested in speaking in tongues than the apostle himself, the very one who had planted the church in Corinth.

Despite his own proficiency in the tongues area, Paul points the readers in a different direction. He notes that to speak *an unknown tongue* is not to speak with understanding. *Five words* that are understood are to be preferred over *ten thousand words* that are without meaning to the hearers. Paul's goal in the speaking of intelligible words is the teaching of others. The unintelligible words of tongues may be impressive and exciting, but they do not benefit others since such words convey no useful content.

20. Brethren, be not children in understanding: howbeit in malice be ye children, but in understanding be men.

Paul adds to his point by introducing a difference between children and adults. It is OK to have a childlike innocence when it comes to *malice* (evil), but it is not OK to be childish regarding the matter at hand. The Corinthians need to grow up when it comes to the issue of communicating with *understanding* (compare 1 Corinthians 13:11; Ephesians 4:14). The implication is that there is a certain childishness regarding the issue of speaking in tongues the way the Corinthians are approaching it. Speaking in tongues may provide a personal faith experience, but there are deeper issues one must grasp.

> ### What Do You Think?
> What has helped you grow most from spiritual childishness to maturity? What can you do to help others in this regard?
> *Talking Points for Your Discussion*
> - Selflessness
> - Personal holiness
> - Scripture knowledge
> - Prayer habits
> - Other

B. What the Law Says (vv. 21, 22)

21, 22a. In the law it is written, With men of other tongues and other lips will I speak unto this people; and yet for all that will they not hear me, saith the Lord. Wherefore tongues are for a sign, not to them that believe, but to them that believe not.

Paul offers a loose quotation of Isaiah 28:11, 12. Ministering 700 years before, Isaiah warned that a time was coming when the Israelites would hear the foreign languages (*other tongues and other lips*) of oppressors such as the Assyrians (compare Deuteronomy 28:49). This was to happen when the people proved themselves faithless by refusing to listen to the Lord's prophets time after time.

The fulfilled prediction that God's people were indeed given over to the control of those having

HOW TO SAY IT

Assyrians	Uh-*sear*-e-unz.
Colosse	Ko-*lahss*-ee.
Corinth	*Kor*-inth.
Corinthians	Ko-*rin*-thee-unz (*th* as in *thin*).
Ephesus	*Ef*-uh-sus.
Galatia	Guh-*lay*-shuh.
glossolalia	glaw-suh-**lay**-lee-uh.
Philippi	Fih-*lip*-pie or *Fil*-ih-pie.
Thessalonica	*Thess*-uh-lo-**nye**-kuh (*th* as in *thin*).
xenoglossia	zen-uh-**glaw**-see-uh.

other tongues and other lips therefore served as a sign of God's judgment on the faithlessness of His people in that day. Similarly, speaking in tongues may end up serving *for a sign* in the church at Corinth to lead *them that believe not* to conclude that God is absent from the gathering (see 1 Corinthians 14:23, below).

22b. But prophesying serveth not for them that believe not, but for them which believe.

The appropriate context for the use of tongues just established in verse 22a is now contrasted with that of *prophesying*. Opinions vary regarding what exactly this activity is, but it is clearly something different from speaking in tongues or interpretation of tongues.

In the context of the first-century church, to prophesy can involve predicting the future (Acts 11:28; 21:10-12), but that does not seem to be its primary function. More broadly, those who prophesy "speaketh unto men to edification, and exhortation . . . that all may learn, and all may be comforted" (1 Corinthians 14:3, 31). Prophesying therefore seems to involve a teaching function, perhaps something akin to the act of preaching the Word today.

To be able to prophesy, as being able to speak in tongues, is a spiritual gift (Romans 12:6; 1 Corinthians 12:10; 13:2; compare 1 Timothy 4:14). The first-century church does not view prophets as belonging solely to Old Testament times, but acknowledges prophets of their own day (see Acts 13:1; 15:32; 21:9). Since the gift of prophetic speech serves as a witness within the body of believers rather than *for them that believe not*, its primary function seems to be to bring believers to maturity. As it is exercised primarily in that regard, it can have an additional good benefit, as verse 24 below shows.

C. What the Impact Is (vv. 23-26)

23. If therefore the whole church be come together into one place, and all speak with tongues, and there come in those that are unlearned, or unbelievers, will they not say that ye are mad?

Having explained a potential effect of speaking in tongues as a sign for unbelievers, Paul proceeds to warn of an additional danger as he sets up a hypothetical situation. Imagine that *the whole church* is gathered for worship in *one place*. Then while everyone is speaking in tongues, *there come in those that are unlearned, or unbelievers*. As these folks witness everyone else there speaking in tongues, what will they think? They will conclude that everyone is *mad* (insane)!

To present the church as a group of people all speaking in tongues at once will be interpreted as mayhem—surely a negative witness. Paul poses this hypothetical scenario because it is more than hypothetical. This is what is actually going on in the Corinthian church. The chaotic nature of their gatherings has become a deterrent for visitors. (Paul describes the orderly use of tongues in verses 26-28, not in today's text.)

> ### What Do You Think?
> What safeguards can the church adopt to ensure orderly participation when a worship service includes an open time of "sharing"?
> ### Talking Points for Your Discussion
> - Before-the-fact policy to prevent problems
> - After-the-fact intervention to correct ongoing problems

24, 25. But if all prophesy, and there come in one that believeth not, or one unlearned, he is convinced of all, he is judged of all: and thus are the secrets of his heart made manifest; and so falling down on his face he will worship God, and report that God is in you of a truth.

Paul presents an alternative scenario. Imagine that *one that believeth not, or one unlearned* comes to a gathering where the church members *all prophesy*, speaking the Word of God in intelligible ways. Paul proposes that the unbeliever in such a case will be *convinced*. Such a person will see the positive impact that the prophesying of the gospel message is having on the gathered believers (*that God is in you*).

As a result, this person will feel *judged* that the sin in his or her life is unacceptable. Such an unbeliever will then fall down to *worship God*. (Paul describes the orderly use of prophesying in verses 29-33, not in today's text.)

> ### What Do You Think?
> What are some things the church of today can do to demonstrate a genuine openness for unbelievers who walk in?
> ### Talking Points for Your Discussion
> - In teaching methods
> - In music styles
> - In fellowship
> - In building layouts
> - Other

By contrast, the chaos of many believers speaking in tongues at the same time is like a trumpet giving "an uncertain sound" (1 Corinthians 14:8). This is military imagery. Roman armies use trumpeters to relay signals to troops prepared for battle. The success of an army in battle depends on clear signals, and this is the message for the Corinthians. As much as one might enjoy speaking in tongues on a personal level, clear communication via intelligible words should be the priority.

26. How is it then, brethren? when ye come together, every one of you hath a psalm, hath a doctrine, hath a tongue, hath a revelation, hath an interpretation. Let all things be done unto edifying.

A few verses later, Paul will end this chapter with the imperatives "forbid not to speak with tongues. Let all things be done decently and in order" (1 Corinthians 14:39b, 40). Some planning is necessary to make that happen, and Paul proceeds to outline the thinking that should go into that planning in the verse before us.

Before we examine Paul's thoughts in detail, a couple of cautions are in order. First, the phrasing *every one of you hath . . . , hath . . . ,* etc., should not be taken to mean that each and every one of the Corinthians is to come to a worship service with all of the things listed. Rather, the idea is more like "some have this, some have that" (compare 1 Corinthians 12:8-10). Second, we should not interpret the verse before us as "the" God-ordained pattern for worship services, but as a hypothetical way of how good planning can work.

The *psalm* someone might cite or sing may be from the Old Testament, or it may be a Christian hymn that is known to the congregation. For someone to present *a doctrine* indicates a teaching time. This may involve using Scripture, repeating a teaching received from Paul, etc. Then someone can speak in *a tongue,* which must be followed by *an interpretation* (see v. 27); if there is no one available to interpret, then tongues speaking should not occur (v. 28).

Paul also desires that speaking time be allowed for someone having *a revelation.* Opinions differ as to whether being enabled to speak revelations is the same as being enabled to prophesy. The fact that 1 Corinthians 14:6 mentions speaking both "by revelation, . . . or by prophesying" leads some to conclude that those are distinct concepts. Others think, however, that the concepts are synonymous or nearly so. The important principle that applies either way is that we are to *let all things be done unto edifying.*

Recalling from comments on verse 17 that *edify* is related to *build,* we see the connection with 1 Corinthians 3:9, where Paul refers to his readers as "God's building." That building, the church, is constructed by God himself (see Ephesians 2:19-22), but it is also built up by leaders of the church.

⚜ *EVERYTHING IN ORDER* ⚜

The Burj Khalifa is the tallest building in the world, rising more than 2,700 feet over the city of Dubai. More than 30 on-site contracting companies were involved in the construction. At one time, more than 12,000 workers were on site daily.

Imagine the confusion if the first contractors to arrive on the scene were plumbers. What if the interior decorators showed up before excavation had even started? Obviously, such an approach would have been downright laughable. Millions of man-hours went into the building's construction, much of it devoted to ensuring that workers and materials for each phase arrived on site at the right time.

Paul's instructions to those who made up "God's building" in Corinth were intended to bring order from confusion. Orderly worship doesn't just happen; it takes planning to ensure that everyone is on the same page. We should not be any less concerned about this today than Paul was in the first century. —C. R. B.

Visual for Lesson 9. *Start a discussion by pointing to this visual as you ask, "What else does worship do? Why?*

Conclusion
A. Building Up the Church

Paul's sage advice "Let all things be done unto edifying" (v. 26) can be used in many situations. It challenges us to evaluate our church activities by a simple question: *Does it build up the church or tear it down?*

Consider how this test applies to your own church and how you relate to it on a personal level. What issues are important to you? music styles? preaching methods? Sunday school options? Do you want changes to suit your own preferences? When does voicing your preferences cross the line from building up the church to tearing it down?

These are hard questions! We move toward the right answers when we realize that the abiding value of 1 Corinthians 14 is not so much doctrinal instruction about the gift of speaking in tongues but about how we understand the priority of edification in the church.

B. Prayer

Father, may we love the church as much as You do. May we resist selfishness as we seek to build up others within our congregation. May You bless our church as You give it unity and a clarity of purpose. In the name of Jesus, amen.

C. Thought to Remember

Always ask, "Does it edify?"

INVOLVEMENT LEARNING

Some of the activities below are also found in the helpful student book, Adult Bible Class.
Don't forget to download the free reproducible page from www.standardlesson.com to enhance your lesson!

Into the Lesson

Option: Place in chairs copies of the "Interpret This!" activity from the reproducible page, which you can download. Learners can begin working on this as they arrive, but most will find it too difficult to solve without help from you. This fact will help set the tone of today's study.

Recruit someone who is fluent in a language other than English to read today's lesson text in that other language. *Alternative:* Download from the Internet an audio segment of Scripture being read in another language (perhaps John 3:16) to play to the class. After either, ask if anyone understood what was read. You may have one or two who say *yes*, but to the vast majority you can ask, "Did that reading do anything to build up your knowledge of Christ?" The obvious answer of *no* will serve as a transition as you observe, "Paul had something important to say about unintelligible speech, and his thoughts still apply today."

Into the Word

Assign these three texts to good oral readers, one each: Acts 2:1-12; Acts 10:43-48; and Acts 19:1-7. After the readings, say, "Besides 1 Corinthians 12–14, these are the only other New Testament texts that address speaking in tongues. What do you see God doing on those occasions?" Allow free response, assuming someone will note that God was empowering the gospel to be presented in a miraculous way. Then have today's lesson text read aloud.

Divide your class in half, designating one of the halves to be the *Problem Group* and the other half as the *Solution Group*. Assign portions of today's text to each group based on the problem/solution outline in the commentary. Say, "Your tasks are to identify either the problem that existed in Corinth or the solution to the problem, depending on your group's designation. In a few minutes, I will call for you to present your conclusions. But be warned:

right after you present your conclusion regarding the problem or solution, a 'contrarian Christian' is going to say, 'No—you've got it all wrong.' Then the contrarian will present an alternative viewpoint. You will have a chance at rebuttal."

Arrange in advance for one of your learners to be the "contrarian Christian" above, who will come prepared to offer alternatives. These should be provably wrong when the text is read closely, which is the intent. Examples: "the problem," according to your contrarian, was that not enough people were speaking in tongues, there were too many interpreters present, etc.; "the solution" could be the opposites of these. Your contrarian can enhance the believability of the alternative viewpoints by quoting "proof texts" out of context. This will challenge learners to demonstrate why the "proof texts" are misapplied.

Close this segment by stressing Paul's concerns to "Let all things be done unto edifying" (1 Corinthians 14:26) and "Let all things be done decently and in order" (v. 40, not in today's lesson text).

Into Life

Ask, "What elements of our worship assemblies may be off-putting to 'those that are unlearned, or unbelievers' per 1 Corinthians 14:23?" Encourage brainstorming, but be cautious about raising controversial issues. After a short discussion say, "Based on these ideas, what recommendations can we make to those who plan our assemblies?" Record suggestions to deliver to these planners.

Suggest that learners carry the following question with them to ponder in the week ahead: "What am I doing or saying that may dissuade the 'unlearned' or 'unbelievers' from coming to our worship assemblies?" *Option:* Distribute copies of the "If I Speak . . ." activity from the reproducible page as learners depart. This exercise will challenge learners to ponder their use of the tongue in ways other than speaking in tongues.

COMFORT IN TIMES OF TROUBLE

DEVOTIONAL READING: Psalm 46
BACKGROUND SCRIPTURE: 2 Corinthians 1:3-11

2 CORINTHIANS 1:3-11

3 Blessed be God, even the Father of our Lord Jesus Christ, the Father of mercies, and the God of all comfort;

4 Who comforteth us in all our tribulation, that we may be able to comfort them which are in any trouble, by the comfort wherewith we ourselves are comforted of God.

5 For as the sufferings of Christ abound in us, so our consolation also aboundeth by Christ.

6 And whether we be afflicted, it is for your consolation and salvation, which is effectual in the enduring of the same sufferings which we also suffer: or whether we be comforted, it is for your consolation and salvation.

7 And our hope of you is stedfast, knowing, that as ye are partakers of the sufferings, so shall ye be also of the consolation.

8 For we would not, brethren, have you ignorant of our trouble which came to us in Asia, that we were pressed out of measure, above strength, insomuch that we despaired even of life:

9 But we had the sentence of death in ourselves, that we should not trust in ourselves, but in God which raiseth the dead:

10 Who delivered us from so great a death, and doth deliver: in whom we trust that he will yet deliver us;

11 Ye also helping together by prayer for us, that for the gift bestowed upon us by the means of many persons thanks may be given by many on our behalf.

KEY VERSE

Our hope of you is stedfast, knowing, that as ye are partakers of the sufferings, so shall ye be also of the consolation. —2 Corinthians 1:7

Photo: Ingram Publishing / Thinkstock

THE PEOPLE OF GOD SET PRIORITIES

Unit 3: Bearing One Another's Burdens

LESSONS 10–14

LESSON AIMS

After participating in this lesson, each student will be able to:

1. Describe the nature of the suffering and the consolation that Paul discusses.

2. Explain the relationships between suffering, comfort, and prayer in the life of the Christian.

3. Write a letter of encouragement to a missionary supported by his or her church, including a prayer of consolation similar to what Paul describes.

LESSON OUTLINE

Introduction

A. Xtreme Christianity?

Have you noticed how many things are described as "extreme" these days? The trend seems to have started with so-called *extreme sports*: snowboarding, mountain-bike racing, etc. Then advertisers latched onto the word *extreme* to promote features of various products, products said to have *extreme flavor, extreme comfort, extreme value,* etc. And at its own extreme, the first letter of the word *extreme* is dropped, with an *xtreme* result!

What about the exercise of our Christian faith? Is there such a thing as *xtreme Christianity*? If so, what does it look like? Today's text has answers.

B. Lesson Background

Paul wrote letters to the church at Corinth in response to several problems. Our previous five lessons considered the first such letter, 1 Corinthians, written from Ephesus in about AD 56. That letter contains many strong statements about the church's failure to live out the gospel message.

Paul then seems to have made a brief trip from Ephesus to Corinth to see how the church was responding to his instructions. Apparently, that visit was not a great success (see 2 Corinthians 2:1; compare 7:8; 13:2).

At about the same time, Paul also faced great difficulties while in Ephesus. Acts 19:23–20:1 tells us of a massive protest—nearly a riot—against him and the gospel. This happened after Paul had sent two of his key assistants ahead of him to Macedonia (Acts 19:22), so he was left without the support of two of his most trusted associates during this trying time.

All this meant that Paul was saddled with enormous mental and emotional burdens as he left Ephesus and traveled toward Macedonia (Acts 20:1). Along the way, Paul undoubtedly wondered about the fate of the great church in Corinth. What would he find there as a result of his diverting time and energy to Ephesus? Arriving at Troas, Paul expected to find his friend Titus, but he was not there—another setback (2 Corinthians 2:13). Paul was at best discouraged, at worst deeply depressed. "For, when we were come into Macedonia, our flesh had no rest, but we were troubled on every side; without were fightings, within were fears" (7:5).

But Paul eventually received good news. Arriving in Macedonia (AD 57), he at last met up with Titus, who informed him of the Corinthian church's positive regard for Paul and repentance (2 Corinthians 7:6-8). There was still more for that church to do, but the commitment of their faith was reaffirmed.

Events and circumstances caused Paul to reflect deeply on what it means to face hardship in following Jesus. The results of Paul's reflections are found in several passages of 2 Corinthians. One such passage is our text for today.

I. Reality of God's Comfort
(2 Corinthians 1:3-7)
A. Thanking the Father (vv. 3, 4)

3. Blessed be God, even the Father of our Lord Jesus Christ, the Father of mercies, and the God of all comfort.

In Paul's time, letters typically begin with a greeting that is followed by a prayer of thanksgiving for the welfare of the addressees. Paul usually begins his letters the same way. Paul's prayers are no mere formality; they express profound gratitude for the things that he writes about in the sections that follow. That is certainly the case here.

Paul begins his prayer with an extended, focused description of God. That God should be *blessed* means that God is to be spoken well of by all. The God worthy of such praise is none other than *the Father of our Lord Jesus Christ,* the one sent into the world to live and die as a human.

That death was not just a "normal" experience of human suffering, however. It was the means by which God made forgiveness available to stub-

HOW TO SAY IT

Corinth	*Kor*-inth.
Corinthians	Ko-*rin*-thee-unz (*th* as in *thin*).
Ephesus	*Ef*-uh-sus.
Macedonia	Mass-eh-*doe*-nee-uh.
Titus	*Ty*-tus.
Troas	*Tro*-az.

born, rebellious humans. God is therefore also *the Father of mercies,* the source of that compassionate forgiveness. In Christ, God demonstrates the profound level of concern and commitment that He has for those created in His image.

God's concern and commitment goes beyond His extending of forgiving mercy. He is also *the God of all comfort.* He knows that His people experience discouragement, suffering, and setbacks of all kinds. In His committed love, God addresses His people's suffering not always by taking it away but by granting encouragement and sustaining strength that they (we) need in order to endure. Whatever the problem God's people face, in the long run God's comfort is greater.

4. Who comforteth us in all our tribulation, that we may be able to comfort them which are in any trouble, by the comfort wherewith we ourselves are comforted of God.

Note how Paul uses various forms of the word *comfort* five times in this verse and the one preceding. God's comfort surely is central to Paul's thanksgiving!

As the God of comfort, He ministers to His people in every situation of *tribulation,* a word simply meaning "trouble." Large or small, instances of trouble in the lives of God's people are met with His encouragement and sustenance. He proves himself faithful to His people by acting in this way. The God who gave His Son in death for His people will surely not abandon His people in times of trouble (Romans 8:32).

We who have received God's comfort become the agents of His comfort to others. Paul notes later how the presence of other Christians has encouraged him at critical times (2 Corinthians 7:6, 7, 13). He stresses that the church, the body of Christ, carries out Christ's work in the world. If comfort comes from the God of comfort, then it surely comes through those who belong to God through Christ.

Certainly we can see how this works in everyday life. When times are hardest is when we often receive the greatest encouragement, the keenest wisdom, the deepest understanding from people who have been through similar situations. When we connect with someone who is experiencing in the present what we have experienced in the past, we sense an immediate closeness with that person.

This connection is surely based on and combined with a strong, Spirit-empowered impulse to provide empathy, encouragement, and reassurance. God's love and comfort are made real and tangible as His people become vessels that carry to others what God has already given to them.

> **What Do You Think?**
> In what circumstances do you experience God's comfort the most? How have these experiences helped you to extend His comfort to others?
>
> *Talking Points for Your Discussion*
> - Family situations
> - Church situations
> - Job situations
> - Other

❧ BLESSED, AND BLESSING OTHERS ❧

Chuck and Pat, a young Christian couple, lost their baby Mary to a congenital heart defect when she was only a month old. When Mary's grandparents came to console the couple a few hours later, they were accompanied by a man and woman whom Chuck and Pat had never met. They explained their reason for requesting to come: they too had lost a baby at an early age, and they wanted Chuck and Pat to know that others had a sense of the pain they were feeling. This selfless act stirred up painful memories, but the consolation they offered helped Chuck and Pat begin to heal.

Chuck and Pat found their life paths crossing those of other hurting parents numerous times in the years that followed. In the process, Chuck and Pat shared the blessing they had received years earlier from those previously unknown friends, who were doing what Paul speaks of in today's text.

We should not say that such tragedies come upon us so that grief-stricken parents can be prodded into comforting others. However, we will find ourselves being prepared to help others see how God's grace works even in the most difficult circumstances as we experience God's comfort through others in the midst of our own suffering.

—C. R. B.

B. Standing with Christ (vv. 5-7)

5. For as the sufferings of Christ abound in us, so our consolation also aboundeth by Christ.

Belonging to Christ means experiencing what Christ experienced as well as receiving all that Christ gives. This is the great insight that Paul shares from his reflection on the gospel and his recent experiences.

At the core of the gospel is the truth that those who belong to Christ have been united with Christ (Romans 6:4-6; Colossians 2:12). That means that we enjoy all the blessings of Christ's supreme rule (Ephesians 2:6; Colossians 3:1). But being united with Christ means also sharing in His sufferings (2 Corinthians 4:10; Philippians 3:10, 11). Such sufferings are not signs that God has abandoned us. Rather, they are signs that we truly belong to Christ, the Christ who died on the cross.

God is faithful to those who suffer for being united with Christ. God's comfort and encouragement are always greater than suffering. Again and again, we can point to instances where the most powerful testimony to the truth of the gospel comes from those who have suffered deeply, but who also have experienced God's comfort in even greater abundance. This is the extreme, abundant life to which the Christian is called, a life that deeply reflects Christ's own life.

> **What Do You Think?**
> What are some ways to keep from sinking into a "pity party" when we suffer for Christ? Which have you found most helpful in this regard?
>
> *Talking Points for Your Discussion*
> - Methods that involve your fellow Christians
> - Methods that don't involve your fellow Christians

6. And whether we be afflicted, it is for your consolation and salvation, which is effectual in the enduring of the same sufferings which we also suffer: or whether we be comforted, it is for your consolation and salvation.

The cross teaches us about our suffering and God's comfort. Christ did not suffer merely for the sake of suffering, as if pain and hardship were good things in and of themselves. No, Christ suffered on behalf of others. He took on himself the punishment that we deserve. He suffered so that we can have God's blessing.

So it is, in a sense, for Paul. God does not put Paul through hard times merely to "toughen him up." His sufferings are for the sake of others. He suffers as he travels, experiencing dangers and hardships to preach the gospel. He suffers emotionally as he experiences the ups and downs of working with new believers. Experiencing all these things, Paul becomes all the more able to minister the gospel to hurting people, to be the vessel of God's encouragement to the suffering. Through his own sufferings Paul is developing the tenacious endurance that enables him not just to overcome hardship personally but to provide a seasoned example to others who are suffering.

United with Christ, who died for others, Paul's suffering is for the sake of others too. So is ours. In hardships big and small, God is shaping us to be the vessels of His merciful comfort to people who will have experiences like ours. He is using us as Christ's body in the world to make the work of the cross real in others' lives.

7. And our hope of you is stedfast, knowing, that as ye are partakers of the sufferings, so shall ye be also of the consolation.

What does all this mean for the Corinthian Christians? They have been through significant hardships—many of their own making—as they have struggled with sinful habits and attitudes. Paul's forceful, even harsh, admonitions to the Corinthians have provoked deep feelings of resentment among some (2 Corinthians 10:10). But God's Word has proven to be more powerful than the old sinful lifestyle.

What Do You Think?
When was a time you resented an admonishment from a fellow Christian at first, only to realize later that his or her counsel was exactly what you needed to hear?

Talking Points for Your Discussion
▪ Regarding something you did
▪ Regarding something you failed to do
▪ Regarding an attitude
▪ Other

So, Paul says, he has a firm, unshakable hope for the Corinthians. He sees not a group of wavering, shallow, inconsistent converts. He sees, rather, people who have been joined with Christ and who are now learning what it means to belong to Him. Their sufferings are a sign of their union with Christ. So it is all the more sure that God will provide everything that they need to endure and grow, becoming the people whom God calls them to be in Christ.

II. Reliance on God's Strength
(2 CORINTHIANS 1:8-11)
A. Burdened Heavily (v. 8)

8. For we would not, brethren, have you ignorant of our trouble which came to us in Asia, that we were pressed out of measure, above strength, insomuch that we despaired even of life.

Paul now moves from providing a thankful overview of God's comfort to describing his own experience. He does not try to hide the harsh realities of his life. He does not want the Corinthians to be ignorant of his troubles, imagining that his life is somehow protected from suffering. Rather, he wants them to know all about it.

Even so, Paul does not narrate all the specific circumstances here. Some of those we learn elsewhere in 2 Corinthians, and some we learn from Acts. Undoubtedly, many other specific events are unknown to us. Rather than sharing the details now, Paul shares the effect that the hardships have had on him. His suffering, he says, has exceeded what he could have endured on his own. The suffering has been beyond the limits of natural strength. Had Paul known beforehand what he was to face, he would have said that it was more than he could possibly bear (compare Acts 9:16).

The full extent of Paul's suffering is captured at the end of the verse: *we despaired even of life.* It is hard for us to imagine that Paul, a towering figure of spiritual strength, would reach such a point. But this is what he expresses. At some point, hope had left him. The pressures, disappointments, and threats had seemed too great at certain times (compare 2 Corinthians 11:23-29).

B. Delivered Providentially (vv. 9, 10)

9. But we had the sentence of death in ourselves, that we should not trust in ourselves, but in God which raiseth the dead.

Paul doesn't mince words: his situations of suffering and despair have felt like *the sentence of death*. He has found himself living moment by moment with an overwhelming sense of having been defeated by his hardships.

But God's power can shine brightest in dark situations. When there is no way out in human terms, the almighty God can provide a way. Think of Jesus. No one's situation looked more hopeless than His: abandoned by His followers; arrested and condemned; and publicly mocked, tortured, and killed by the imperial Roman authorities. Among Jesus' own words was a cry of anguish that God had abandoned Him (Matthew 27:46).

Yet God raised Jesus from the dead, victorious over death and all His enemies. In the death and resurrection of Christ, God shows His people that He is faithful to them not by preventing every instance of suffering but by giving them His resurrection life in the very midst of suffering.

The power of Christ's resurrection is what God gives to His suffering people. It is a power greater than death itself. As God empowers His people in suffering, the story of Jesus is reenacted in our lives. In the contrast between our weakness and God's power, the true, divine magnitude of God's power is made clear to us and to those around us. When we face hardship, our weakness is the setting in which God demonstrates His supreme power (2 Corinthians 4:7, lesson 12).

So for the suffering believer, the question is whom to trust. Do we rely on ourselves or on God? The question is deceptively easy. We are weak; He is strong. Surely we will trust God! But to do so in suffering, when all that we see and feel indicates that we are alone, is an act of great faith. Paul's experiences have taught him the overwhelming need for such faith and the overwhelming faithfulness of God toward His people. Now Paul's experiences become the means by which others' faith can be strengthened for similar situations.

10. Who delivered us from so great a death, and doth deliver: in whom we trust that he will yet deliver us.

Paul's experience of suffering has been a foretaste of death itself. But God's encouraging, strengthening comfort is a foretaste of the resurrection of the dead. Such experiences strengthen Paul's confident faith in God. If God can deliver him as He has done thus far, and if God can raise Christ from the dead, then surely God will be faithful and powerful to deliver Paul and all God's people from every situation that they face.

Paul's circumstances in Asia—primarily in the city of Ephesus—have refined his faith. He can now relate his experiences to those of others who suffer, providing them with strong encouragement from God. Paul can look forward to the future with great confidence not because his suffering is over but because God will be just as faithful in the future as He has been so far. Paul's confidence that "all things work together for good" (Romans 8:28) is based on these insights. God's faithfulness is greater than our circumstances and our weaknesses. He is the foundation of the believer's confidence in every situation.

Early in World War II, thousands of American troops surrendered to the Japanese in the Philippines. Those who survived the infamous Bataan Death March faced death by malnutrition and disease that awaited them as prisoners of war. To make matters worse, the guards would kill nine prisoners for each prisoner who escaped.

For such prisoners to despair of life is easy to understand; many undoubtedly gave up on God under those circumstances. But Paul's reaction was just the opposite. In the depths of his despair, he realized that there was no one to trust but the God who raises the dead. God does not always choose to deliver His people from physical death in trying circumstances. But God is the source of strength in such times nonetheless. May Paul be our model when such times come.   —C. R. B.

C. Celebrating Thankfully (v. 11)

11. Ye also helping together by prayer for us, that for the gift bestowed upon us by the means of many persons thanks may be given by many on our behalf.

God's faithfulness is constant and sure. But the Scriptures teach us that God often responds to His people only when they pray to Him and ask. So Paul urges the Corinthian church to join with him in praying for God's future deliverance for Paul and those who work alongside him. The result of such prayers will be that God will be praised and thanked for what He does. The thanksgiving that Paul offers in today's text will be repeated by many as they join him in praying for God's deliverance and then witnessing what God does.

This helps us understand the seeming paradox between God's constant faithfulness and the biblical command to pray that God act on His people's behalf. God wants to give us His blessings: power through the Holy Spirit, comfort in suffering, abundant life now and forever. But we may recognize that these are indeed God's gifts only when we ask Him for them. God responds to our prayers in part because our prayers move us to recognize His gifts. When we pray and see God's answer, we are able to acknowledge God's action as we thank Him for His abundant faithfulness.

Visual for Lesson 10. *Point to this visual as you introduce the discussion question that is associated with verse 10.*

Conclusion

A. Power to Overcome Suffering

Some may caricature the Christian life as dull and bland. Christians are known for what "thou shalt not" do. Christians are often characterized as withdrawn, timid, and fearful. Others may search for what they think should be the ideal Christian life: a life without difficulty. Are not God's promises of protection and blessing sure? Do not the hardships in a Christian's life indicate a lack of faith?

Paul shows us that neither characterization is true. The gospel begins with Jesus, with His death and resurrection. The power at work in Him is also at work in us. Like Christ, we live under a sentence of death. But like Him, we have God's resurrection power on our side. That power does not insulate us from suffering. Rather, that power enables us to overcome it. As it does, we can see that God himself is the one at work in us.

B. Prayer

Almighty God, as You have forgiven us in Christ, also please comfort us in Him to face hardships we experience in His name. May You be praised because the world sees Your power at work in us. We pray in Jesus' name, amen!

C. Thought to Remember

When in trouble, look up.

INVOLVEMENT LEARNING

Some of the activities below are also found in the helpful student book, Adult Bible Class.
Don't forget to download the free reproducible page from www.standardlesson.com to enhance your lesson!

Into the Lesson

Ask learners what sufferings they have experienced over the past six months. Jot responses on the board; keep this list on the board for the end of the lesson. (*Alternative:* Have learners identify sufferings of Bible characters instead.)

After you have a fairly sizable list, ask learners to comment on their emotional and spiritual state in the midst of the sufferings noted (or to imagine the emotional and spiritual state of the Bible characters). Say, "As we consider the sufferings of Paul and the Corinthians in today's lesson, we will see how God can respond to and use our sufferings."

Into the Word

Divide the class into four groups and give each a piece of poster board that has one of these four headings: *Paul's Sufferings (Acts 19:22-31; 20:1; 2 Corinthians 2:13; 7:5) / Corinthians' Sufferings (2 Corinthians 2:1-11; 7:8) / God's Response to Suffering (2 Corinthians 1:3-11) / How God Uses Suffering (2 Corinthians 1:3-11).* Say, "List items and issues from the Scripture references that correlate with the title of your chart." (For smaller classes, combine the first two and/or the last two charts.)

After groups finish, begin discussion by reading aloud verses 8 and 9 of today's text. Say, "In order to understand Paul's references in these verses, we must consider texts outside of today's lesson to supply details." Ask the group dealing with Paul's sufferings to share discoveries. Repeat the procedure for the group that explored the Corinthians' sufferings. Be prepared to add important details that the groups do not mention.

Say, "Now that we have a pretty good idea of what Paul and the Corinthians were going through, let's look at God's response to their suffering and how He used it for His greater purpose." Ask a volunteer to read the entirety of today's text aloud. Then ask the remaining two groups to share their conclusions.

The *God's Response* group should note that He responds with comfort (vv. 3, 4a, 5b) as well as hope and deliverance (vv. 7a, 10). The *God Uses* group should address His greater purposes in allowing and responding to suffering: His comfort allows those receiving it to pass it along (v. 4); suffering connects us with the sufferings of Christ, which is comforting in that Christians receive all that Christ gives through His suffering (v. 5); passed-along comfort allows the sufferer to endure (v. 6); suffering on the part of some can give hope to others who realize that they are not alone in suffering (v. 7); suffering that is "pressed out of measure, above strength" forces reliance on God's ability and willingness to deliver (vv. 8-10); the mutual prayer support of those who suffer results in God's being glorified (v. 11).

Option: Before discussing groups' conclusions, distribute copies of the "Suffering Has Purpose" activity from the reproducible page, which you can download. Suggest that learners fill out the acrostic as you work through the text, resulting in the activity's being a note-taker on today's lesson. At the conclusion of the discussion of the four groups' findings, work through the nine lines of the acrostic to explore learners' insights.

Into Life

Direct learners' attention back to the list of sufferings from the beginning of the lesson. Ask, "How can God's purposes be accomplished through this one?" as you point to each entry in turn. Conclude by reading Romans 8:28.

Alternative: Distribute copies of the "Prayer of Encouragement" activity from the reproducible page. Say, "Let's put 2 Corinthians 1:11 into action as we compose prayer letters of encouragement to missionaries we support." Collect completed prayer letters for conversion (by scanning) into an electronic format for e-mailing to those missionaries.

FORGIVENESS AND RESTORATION

DEVOTIONAL READING: Luke 17:1-6
BACKGROUND SCRIPTURE: 2 Corinthians 1:23–2:17

2 CORINTHIANS 1:23, 24

23 Moreover I call God for a record upon my soul, that to spare you I came not as yet unto Corinth.

24 Not for that we have dominion over your faith, but are helpers of your joy: for by faith ye stand.

2 CORINTHIANS 2:1-11

1 But I determined this with myself, that I would not come again to you in heaviness.

2 For if I make you sorry, who is he then that maketh me glad, but the same which is made sorry by me?

3 And I wrote this same unto you, lest, when I came, I should have sorrow from them of whom I ought to rejoice; having confidence in you all, that my joy is the joy of you all.

4 For out of much affliction and anguish of heart I wrote unto you with many tears; not that ye should be grieved, but that ye might know the love which I have more abundantly unto you.

5 But if any have caused grief, he hath not grieved me, but in part: that I may not overcharge you all.

6 Sufficient to such a man is this punishment, which was inflicted of many.

7 So that contrariwise ye ought rather to forgive him, and comfort him, lest perhaps such a one should be swallowed up with overmuch sorrow.

8 Wherefore I beseech you that ye would confirm your love toward him.

9 For to this end also did I write, that I might know the proof of you, whether ye be obedient in all things.

10 To whom ye forgive any thing, I forgive also: for if I forgave any thing, to whom I forgave it, for your sakes forgave I it in the person of Christ;

11 Lest Satan should get an advantage of us: for we are not ignorant of his devices.

KEY VERSE

To whom ye forgive any thing, I forgive also: for if I forgave any thing, to whom I forgave it, for your sakes forgave I it in the person of Christ. —**2 Corinthians 2:10**

Photo: iStockphoto / Thinkstock

THE PEOPLE OF GOD SET PRIORITIES

Unit 3: Bearing One Another's Burdens

LESSONS 10–14

LESSON AIMS

After participating in this lesson, each student will be able to:

1. Tell what the issue in Corinth was that caused Paul to write a letter instead of conducting a personal visit.

2. Explain how the gospel demands redemptive responses toward people in either sin or repentance.

3. Develop a plan of reconciliation that can be followed to restore a wayward believer to fellowship with the church. Discuss the plan with church leadership.

LESSON OUTLINE

Introduction

A. "Don't Judge Me!"

Today in places where Christianity once dominated the culture, few people know the Bible well. But it seems that everyone in those cultures still knows one biblical commandment: "Judge not" (Matthew 7:1). Judging others is bad form in our world because it is "intolerant."

But the Bible's stance on judgment is not as simple as a flippant "judge not" sound bite would suggest, especially when one reads the rest of Matthew 7. The point of departure for proper understanding here is the fact that God is the ultimate judge. He sets the final standard of judgment. All humans are subject to His judgment and His standard. There is a judgment to face, and for many it will be a terrible one. Yet God's desire is not to judge but to forgive. For this reason, He sent His Son to die to pay sin's penalty so we can be forgiven. God sends His people around the world with this message of forgiveness.

If we do not accept that we are subject to God's judgment, then we will never be able to accept His forgiveness or even sense a need for it. That reality keeps God's judgment in the forefront of the Christian message. For that reason, Christianity will always strike many people as judgmental and negative. But in truth, forgiveness has no meaning unless it is cast against the alternative of judgment. That is why the emphasis of the Christian message is on forgiveness.

Sadly, though, some forget the reality of judgment after they receive forgiveness. Instead of living as grateful people who want to serve the one who forgave them, they fall back into the old habits of rebellion and evil, what the Bible calls *sin*. They treat their forgiveness not as precious and life-changing but as cheap and inconsequential.

God's response to such contempt for His great gift is persistence in drawing the contemptuous back to repentance. That process can be painful, for it means bringing the backslider to a renewed awareness of the consequences of God's righteous judgment. When God shows us the reality of judgment, it's because He wants us to turn to Him while there is still time.

B. Lesson Background

Paul's letters to the church at Corinth addressed several specific problems. One of the most important had to do with a man who was carrying on a sexual relationship with his father's wife (1 Corinthians 5:1). Paul gave the church very specific instructions regarding that situation: the man had to be separated from fellowship with the church (5:2, 11-13). The purpose of that punishment, which Paul compared with turning the man over to Satan, was to provoke the man to repent and end his sinful behavior (5:5).

That message was difficult for the Corinthian church to receive. It appears that many in the church resented Paul's instruction, so Paul had to pay them a visit "in heaviness" to address the situation (2 Corinthians 2:1, part of today's text). The church decided to follow Paul's instruction after that visit. As a result, the immoral individual was separated from church fellowship (today's lesson).

While awaiting the outcome of all this, Paul planned yet another visit to Corinth, apparently announcing it in advance. But as explained in today's text, he cancelled his plans for specific reasons.

I. Changed Plans
(2 CORINTHIANS 1:23–2:4)

A. To Spare Them Pain (v. 23)

23. Moreover I call God for a record upon my soul, that to spare you I came not as yet unto Corinth.

Paul responds to the suspicious critics regarding his change in plans (see the Lesson Background) by calling on God as his witness (compare Romans 1:9; 2 Corinthians 11:31; Philippians 1:8; 1 Thessalonians 2:5, 10). Because God alone knows a person's motives, He alone can provide

HOW TO SAY IT

Corinth	*Kor*-inth.
Corinthians	Ko-*rin*-thee-unz (*th* as in *thin*).
Ezekiel	Ee-*zeek*-ee-ul or Ee-*zeek*-yul.
Philippians	Fih-*lip*-ee-unz.
Thessalonians	*Thess*-uh-*lo*-nee-unz (*th* as in *thin*).

testimony for why Paul's plans have changed. With the phrase *upon my soul*, Paul says that he is willing for God to take his very life if he is being untruthful.

The reason for changing his plans, Paul says, is *to spare you*. As the apostle assesses the situation in Corinth, he realizes that another visit would cause shame and sorrow rather than provoking the needed repentance. Repentance and reconciliation are Paul's priorities.

B. To Give Them Joy (v. 24)

24. Not for that we have dominion over your faith, but are helpers of your joy: for by faith ye stand.

If some in Corinth interpret Paul's actions as a power play, Paul insists that this is not the case. Having *dominion over* others has no place in the life of a Christ-follower. Jesus said that those who want to act this way are like Gentiles or pagans, those who do not know God (Mark 10:42). Jesus has set the standard for His people: He came to serve others (v. 45).

Instead, Paul refers to himself as one of the *helpers of your joy*. He ministers alongside God for one aim: to bring the true joy of salvation into the lives of others. Such joy comes only by standing firm in one's faith in Jesus.

C. To Avoid a Repeat (2:1-3)

2:1. But I determined this with myself, that I would not come again to you in heaviness.

Paul's priorities guide his decision. He has already made one visit to Corinth that has provoked sorrow or *heaviness*. His overarching aim is joy through reconciliation that comes from repentance. If another visit will not bring that about, then he will not make another visit (1 Corinthians 4:21; 2 Corinthians 12:21).

2. For if I make you sorry, who is he then that maketh me glad, but the same which is made sorry by me?

As the one who had first brought the gospel to Corinth, Paul has a special relationship with the Corinthian church and a special responsibility. No one can be the leader of that church in the same sense as he has been. Even so, his relationship with them is a relationship of equals, of brothers and sisters in Christ.

When that relationship functions as it should, the result is joy to all. Following the "helper" idea of 2 Corinthians 1:24 above, Paul says that the Corinthians should bring joy to him as he does to them. He cannot bear to bring them unnecessary, unproductive sorrow, so he decides not to repeat the "in heaviness" visit.

3. And I wrote this same unto you, lest, when I came, I should have sorrow from them of whom I ought to rejoice; having confidence in you all, that my joy is the joy of you all.

Paul's decision to write to the Corinthians is controlled by the same aim as a visit would be: to bring joy by provoking repentance and reconciliation. Paul may be reflecting on his writing of 1 Corinthians here, as in that letter he directly addressed the problem of the immoral man (1 Corinthians 5; compare 2 Corinthians 12:21). Or he may be referring to another letter that he wrote after 1 Corinthians, one that we do not have.

In either case, Paul stresses that the intent of the earlier correspondence was to rectify a situation before he arrived there personally. Paul wants his readers to understand the truth of their problem, to address it directly, to lead the sinful man to repentance, and so to restore the joy that they should share with Paul.

> *What Do You Think?*
> When did a Christian outside your congregation help lift your spirits in trying circumstances involving your church as a whole? What could be your role in doing likewise?
> *Talking Points for Your Discussion*
> ▪ During a financial crisis
> ▪ During a time of leadership turmoil
> ▪ During the stress of a building campaign
> ▪ Other

D. To Show Abundant Love (v. 4)

4. For out of much affliction and anguish of heart I wrote unto you with many tears; not that ye should be grieved, but that ye might know the love which I have more abundantly unto you.

Paul's choices have been difficult at every step. Even so, his previous correspondence, stern though it was, was no power trip on his part. Rather, it was an expression of love—tough love that tells the truth. As such, it had caused Paul *much affliction and anguish of heart* to write. While its message was difficult to hear, its aim was not to inflict pain but to convey the truth in love—truth that would lead to the repentance that brings joy.

Paul's actions, past and present, reflect what the gospel demands. God's people warn of His judgment so that others can receive His forgiveness. If our motives are to attain power by provoking pain, then we have stepped outside the gospel's boundaries. If we are aiming at the joy-filled goal of reconciliation between God and sinners, then our hearts will be burdened but our consciences clear in warning of God's judgment (compare Ezekiel 3:16-27).

> *What Do You Think?*
> In what area are you most likely to tell someone a hard thing that he or she needs to hear—to speak the truth in love? What adjustments do you need to make in this regard?
> *Talking Points for Your Discussion*
> ▪ Doctrinal issues
> ▪ Moral issues
> ▪ Health issues
> ▪ Family issues
> ▪ Other

❧ TOUGH LOVE ❧

The phrase *tough love* has been around since 1968, when a book of that title was published. Tough love is strong discipline to correct the behavior of someone whose life is spiraling down to destruction. Tough love is used today in many family situations—out-of-control teenagers, substance-addicted adults, etc. It is generally a response of last resort, when nothing else seems to work.

Tough love demands that family members cease being enablers of the destructive behavior to be corrected. Family members are respectful toward the erring loved one but also demand respect in return. Those implementing tough love remain strong even when (or especially when) the hurt in their heart tempts them to give in or "make an exception." Tough love sometimes involves sending a child to a facility that can do what the parents seem unable to do.

From a Christian perspective, a mere change of behavior that makes life "less crazy" for all involved is not the goal of tough love. The heart of the erring one must change. The course of action the apostle Paul recommended to the church in Corinth was designed to bring their sinning church member to repentance. From the penitent heart would come the changed, life-giving behavior they desired. An eternal destiny was at stake. It always is!   —C. R. B.

II. Changed Hearts
(2 CORINTHIANS 2:5-11)
A. Punishment Succeeds (vv. 5, 6)

5. But if any have caused grief, he hath not grieved me, but in part: that I may not overcharge you all.

As we will see below, Paul's counsel has in fact brought about what he has been seeking: the repentance of the immoral individual. But as a prelude to discussing that, Paul explains who the aggrieved parties really are. The apostle himself has suffered anguish by the man's immorality (1 Corinthians 5), but the Corinthian church has suffered even more. Paul has been grieved *in part,* and he takes care not to overstate this (*that I may not overcharge*). He can rightly say that it is the Corinthians (*you all*) who have suffered the greater sorrow. When one member of the church defies the will of God, the entire church suffers.

6. Sufficient to such a man is this punishment, which was inflicted of many.

In his first letter (and probably during his visit "in heaviness" mentioned above), Paul had called for the man to be punished by exclusion from the fellowship (1 Corinthians 5:2, 13). Eventually, the church acted properly: the *many* who carried the burden of grief for the man's sin took the necessary, painful action. Their action was *sufficient,* and the next verse reveals what should happen next.

B. Love Comforts (vv. 7, 8)

7. So that contrariwise ye ought rather to forgive him, and comfort him, lest perhaps such a one should be swallowed up with overmuch sorrow.

Because the man has repented and ended his immorality, the time for forgiveness has come. He is to be welcomed back into the fellowship of the Corinthian church, receiving the encouraging comfort that believers give to each other as God's people (2 Corinthians 1:4). To continue his punishment would be to add sorrow where it is no longer needed.

The lesson for the church is clear. Sin leads to condemnation, but forgiveness means freedom from condemnation. God's judgment needs to be made clear to the unrepentant, but those who recognize their sin should not remain in sorrow over sin. Repentance means an end to sorrow and the beginning of rejoicing and celebrating with God, just as Jesus taught (Luke 15:7, 10, 32).

8. Wherefore I beseech you that ye would confirm your love toward him.

So Paul urges that the church welcome the repentant man back in a way that shows the meaning of the entire story. Love, not vindictiveness, has motivated the action to separate the guilty party from the fellowship. The goal was his repentance and restoration, to be reconciled to God and God's people. A welcoming return will conclude this "love story" appropriately.

Visual for Lessons 11 & 13. *Point to this visual as you ask, "Where has the church slipped up in this regard? How can we do better?"*

C. Testing Ends (vv. 9, 10)

9. For to this end also did I write, that I might know the proof of you, whether ye be obedient in all things.

The instructions Paul had given in 1 Corinthians 5:2, 13 were a test for the man who needed to repent. But they were also a test for the church. Are the church's members genuinely committed to the gospel and so to each other's welfare before God? Are they ready to listen to Paul and obey what the good news of Jesus compels? Clearly, obedience has not been easy for the Corinthians. But they prove faithful in the end.

> **What Do You Think?**
> In what area does the church seem to have the most difficulty in implementing the process of church discipline? Why is that?
> *Talking Points for Your Discussion*
> - Area of doctrinal defection (1 Timothy 6:3, 4)
> - Area of moral defection (1 Corinthians 5)
> - Area of divisiveness (Romans 16:17)

10. To whom ye forgive any thing, I forgive also: for if I forgave any thing, to whom I forgave it, for your sakes forgave I it in the person of Christ.

Paul now removes any doubt that he holds any lingering grudge against the repentant man. What the church has forgiven, he also forgives. Those who think Paul to be power-hungry and vindictive are mistaken. Paul has taken great care to avoid even the appearance of impropriety in that regard (see 1 Corinthians 9:12; 2 Corinthians 6:3; 8:21; etc.). He stands with the church in its faithfulness: first to encourage the man's repentance, then to welcome him home as a member of God's family.

In the end, Paul and the Corinthian Christians all forgive for the same reason: Christ. Christ forgives us despite the trouble and pain that we cause Him. Christ forgives freely and fully. He does not hold a grudge against those repenting, but insists that they be welcomed by God's people with celebration. Those who follow Christ are compelled to forgive as they have been forgiven (Matthew 6:12). To do less is to deny the Christ whom we claim to follow (18:21-35).

> **What Do You Think?**
> What should forgiveness extended to a repentant backslider "say" to various people?
> *Talking Points for Your Discussion*
> - To the one being forgiven
> - To the ones doing the forgiving
> - To outside observers who are Christians
> - To outside observers who are not Christians

D. Danger Remains (v. 11)

11. Lest Satan should get an advantage of us: for we are not ignorant of his devices.

Paul referred to disfellowshipping the immoral man as delivering "such an one unto Satan" (1 Corinthians 5:5). That meant that the church was to treat him as if he were not part of God's people, but Satan's. The goal was for the man to understand the consequences of his sin and repent. Now a failure to forgive and welcome the man back would be a concession to the wiles of Satan. When the church lets habitual sin go unaddressed, the devil's work moves forward. But the same is true when the church does not recognize repentance. If we condemn those whom Christ has saved, we do not do Christ's work, but the opposite.

Conclusion

A. Judgment Replaced with Joy

For Christians to announce God's pending judgment is a warning that comes from love. To stress the reality of judgment is a difficult, tear-inducing necessity when people remain ensnared in sin. The aim is not condemnation but salvation. God is the judge, but His people must lovingly and clearly announce what God does as judge—and how that judgment can be replaced with joy.

B. Prayer

O God, we stand as Your people only by Your mercy. Make us agents of that mercy, conscious of Your holy judgment. In Jesus' name, amen.

C. Thought to Remember

Repentance compels forgiveness.

INVOLVEMENT LEARNING

Some of the activities below are also found in the helpful student book, Adult Bible Class.
Don't forget to download the free reproducible page from www.standardlesson.com to enhance your lesson!

Into the Lesson

Discuss as a class the following scenarios, which you have reproduced on handouts. (*Option*: If you have a larger class, form small groups to discuss one scenario each.)

Scenario 1. You ask a coworker to trade shifts with you, but she refuses. What would be a judgmental response? What would be a response of grace?

Scenario 2. A coworker asks you to trade shifts with her a couple of weeks after you asked the same of her but she refused. What would be a judgmental response? What would be a response of grace?

Scenario 3. You're in slow traffic when a man in an SUV drives on the shoulder and cuts you off. A few minutes later you see his car at the side of the road with the hood up. What would be a judgmental reaction? What would be a reaction of grace?

Scenario 4. Christmas is approaching, so you are in a shopping mall parking lot waiting for a parking space to come open. When one does, a car from the other direction zips in to take it although you've been waiting several minutes. What would be a judgmental reaction? What would be a reaction of grace?

Say, "In today's lesson we will see that while it is important for us to understand God's judgment, His desire *for* us and *from* us is grace and forgiveness."

Alternative: Before learners arrive, place in chairs copies of the "Judge Ye This!" matching exercise from the reproducible page, which you can download. Discuss results.

Into the Word

Say, "As we read today's text, be alert for two reasons Paul wrote his previous letter to the Corinthians." Have learners take turns reading the verses of the text. The two reasons are found in verses 3 and 9. Say, "We will reconsider these verses a bit later."

Form learners into pairs. Give each pair a piece of poster board with one of the following passages written on it. Ask learners to summarize their verses in as few words as possible—no more than two sentences. If your class is small, give more than one assignment to pairs. (Do not include the comments in italics, which indicate the focus of each reference.)

A. 1 Corinthians 5:1, 2, 11-13 (*instructions for handling immorality in the church*); **B**. 1 Corinthians 5:5 (*purpose of the instructions*); **C**. 2 Corinthians 1:23, 24 (*reason for not visiting again*); **D**. 2 Corinthians 2:1 (*chose not to make another visit in heaviness*); **E**. 2 Corinthians 2:2-4 (*wanted visit to be mutually edifying*); **F**. 2 Corinthians 2:5 (*sin caused grief for all, not just for the sinner*); **G**. 2 Corinthians 2:6-9 (*punishment sufficient; welcome the repentant person back*); **H**. 2 Corinthians 2:10, 11 (*forgiveness granted is grounded in forgiveness in view of Christ*).

When pairs are finished, have them affix their summaries in correct order on a wall. Discuss each summary's significance in light of *judgment* and *forgiveness*. (Example: "Was withholding fellowship from the immoral man an act of *judgment* or *forgiveness*? Why?") Remind learners of the heart of the gospel: to reconcile people to God.

Into Life

Say, "Assume that Jesus himself is pointing verses 3 and 9 right at our church like this: 'When I, Jesus, return in glory, I do not want to have sorrow from them of whom I ought to rejoice' (v. 3 reworded), and 'I, Jesus, want to know the proof of you, whether ye be obedient in all things' (v. 9 reworded). What can we do to make sure Jesus is pleased with us both right now and when He returns?" Jot ideas on the board.

Alternative: Distribute copies of the "The Ministry of Reconciliation" activity from the reproducible page. This can be a small-group exercise. Caution learners not to use real names.

TREASURE IN EARTHEN VESSELS

DEVOTIONAL READING: Jude 17-25

BACKGROUND SCRIPTURE: 2 Corinthians 4:1-15

2 CORINTHIANS 4:1-15

1 Therefore seeing we have this ministry, as we have received mercy, we faint not;

2 But have renounced the hidden things of dishonesty, not walking in craftiness, nor handling the word of God deceitfully; but by manifestation of the truth commending ourselves to every man's conscience in the sight of God.

3 But if our gospel be hid, it is hid to them that are lost:

4 In whom the god of this world hath blinded the minds of them which believe not, lest the light of the glorious gospel of Christ, who is the image of God, should shine unto them.

5 For we preach not ourselves, but Christ Jesus the Lord; and ourselves your servants for Jesus' sake.

6 For God, who commanded the light to shine out of darkness, hath shined in our hearts, to give the light of the knowledge of the glory of God in the face of Jesus Christ.

7 But we have this treasure in earthen vessels, that the excellency of the power may be of God, and not of us.

8 We are troubled on every side, yet not distressed; we are perplexed, but not in despair;

9 Persecuted, but not forsaken; cast down, but not destroyed;

10 Always bearing about in the body the dying of the Lord Jesus, that the life also of Jesus might be made manifest in our body.

11 For we which live are always delivered unto death for Jesus' sake, that the life also of Jesus might be made manifest in our mortal flesh.

12 So then death worketh in us, but life in you.

13 We having the same spirit of faith, according as it is written, I believed, and therefore have I spoken; we also believe, and therefore speak;

14 Knowing that he which raised up the Lord Jesus shall raise up us also by Jesus, and shall present us with you.

15 For all things are for your sakes, that the abundant grace might through the thanksgiving of many redound to the glory of God.

KEY VERSES

We are troubled on every side, yet not distressed; we are perplexed, but not in despair; persecuted, but not forsaken; cast down, but not destroyed. —**2 Corinthians 4:8, 9**

THE PEOPLE OF GOD SET PRIORITIES

Unit 3: Bearing One Another's Burdens

LESSONS 10–14

LESSON AIMS

After participating in this lesson, each student will be able to:

1. Identify the character traits that accompany the genuine proclamation of the gospel.

2. Explain how those character traits arise from faith in the gospel.

3. Identify one character trait to improve to reflect the gospel and make a plan for doing so.

LESSON OUTLINE

Introduction
    A. Knockoff Religion
    B. Lesson Background
I. Glory of the Gospel (2 CORINTHIANS 4:1-6)
    A. In Honest Service (vv. 1, 2)
    B. In the World's Rejection (vv. 3, 4)
    Preaching the Pure Gospel
    C. In the Light of God (vv. 5, 6)
II. Humility of the Messenger (2 CORINTHIANS 4:7-12)
    A. God's Treasure (v. 7)
    B. Paul's Hardships (vv. 8, 9)
    C. Jesus' Death and Life (vv. 10-12)
III. Persistence of Faith (2 CORINTHIANS 4:13-15)
    A. Confident in Resurrection (vv. 13, 14)
    B. Benefit for Many (v. 15)
Conclusion
    A. Hardship with Hope
    B. Prayer
    C. Thought to Remember

Introduction

A. Knockoff Religion

Can you tell the difference between an authentic product and an imitation? Although many imitations are sold with full disclosure to that effect, some very expensive "designer" brands of clothes, handbags, and watches are often imitated by dishonest manufacturers that use cheaper materials and processes. Then disreputable merchants sell these imitations as if they were authentic, but for much less money. In popular terms, the counterfeits are called *knockoffs*.

Most things that people value can be imitated with cheap, unsatisfying knockoffs. The message of God is one of those. Knockoff versions of Christianity pop up like weeds in the human landscape. Many people engage in bogus proclamations of cheap gospels that weakly imitate the real thing.

Of course, the true gospel is just that because it comes from God, and it depicts what actually happened. The gospel must be proclaimed by people whose lives reflect its truth, messengers whose lives have been changed by the gospel first. Only then can the real message have a real proclamation.

B. Lesson Background

Paul's two letters to the Corinthian church were, in part, responses to criticisms of his own ministry. Some (many?) in Corinth saw Paul as bold and powerful in his letters, but base and weak in person (2 Corinthians 10:1, 10). They preferred powerful, eloquent teachers (compare 11:6).

Paul responded to these criticisms, but he did more than just defend himself. He also explained the real nature of the gospel and what it means to follow Jesus. The power of the true gospel is not in the skill of the messenger, but in the message itself and in the messenger's deep, personal commitment to the message.

That commitment will give the messenger a transformed character, one that reflects the message. That character reflects Christ's lowliness in becoming human and giving His life. It reflects Christ's loving persistence in enduring suffering for the sake of others. It reflects the honesty of those who know they stand before the all-knowing God.

I. Glory of the Gospel

(2 CORINTHIANS 4:1-6)

A. In Honest Service (vv. 1, 2)

1. Therefore seeing we have this ministry, as we have received mercy, we faint not.

Paul proceeds to explain the kind of life that the gospel demands of those who proclaim it. He describes himself as entrusted by God with a *ministry*. This word literally means "service," the duties that a servant performs for a master. So Paul begins with the understanding that he, like all believers, has been called to serve almighty God.

The Christian's obligation to serve God has its basis not just in the fact of His role as Creator, but in His mercy as Redeemer. God has given His people not the punishment that we deserve but the forgiveness that we need. We serve from an obligation transformed by gratitude.

Such an outlook makes authentic service persistent. In light of God's great mercy, discouragement cannot defeat the believer. If God has already given His people something much better than they deserve, He will not abandon us in our struggles.

2. But have renounced the hidden things of dishonesty, not walking in craftiness, nor handling the word of God deceitfully; but by manifestation of the truth commending ourselves to every man's conscience in the sight of God.

Many religious teachers of Paul's day are notorious for their dishonest, self-serving schemes. Paul, by contrast, insists that God's truth cannot be joined to any falsehood or deception. Those who know that they stand before God can never be less than honest in all their dealings. So nothing about Paul's ministry is cleverly deceptive or tricky. (Note the playful irony in 2 Corinthians 12:16: "being crafty, I caught you with guile!") Rather, Paul's ministry is focused on making the truth of the gospel clear, teaching it through a life that is consistently submissive to that truth.

HOW TO SAY IT

Corinth	*Kor*-inth.
Corinthians	Ko-*rin*-thee-unz (*th* as in *thin*).
Ephesians	Ee-*fee*-zhunz.

The Corinthians have more than Paul's words as proof of his integrity. Paul had lived among them for many months (Acts 18:11). They had seen his life up close, for an extended period. They should be able to give their own testimony as to his honesty before God and people.

B. In the World's Rejection (vv. 3, 4)

3. But if our gospel be hid, it is hid to them that are lost.

"Well," Paul's opponents might say, "if honest teaching is all that the gospel needs, why are there so many who do not believe? Perhaps Paul with his simple honesty is not as effective as he says."

Indeed, many people do not believe. But that, Paul notes, is not because the message is wrongly proclaimed. It is not that the gospel needs a boost from eloquent, learned presentation. No, those who disbelieve do so because they persist in their lost condition. Neither the message nor the messenger is at fault, but the one hearing the message and refusing to heed it (compare 1 Corinthians 1:18).

4. In whom the god of this world hath blinded the minds of them which believe not, lest the light of the glorious gospel of Christ, who is the image of God, should shine unto them.

The condition of those who reject God's message can rightly be called blindness. It is a blindness that they choose as they continue to follow a knockoff god, *the god of this world,* Satan, the great opponent (compare Ephesians 2:2). Resisting change, the unbeliever lets the devil have his way, and so the unbeliever becomes (or remains) blind to the truth. Meanwhile, *the light of the glorious gospel of Christ* continues to shine as a bright beacon to reveal the God of light.

This description of the gospel is very personal for Paul. He had once been just such a spiritually blind unbeliever. But when Christ appeared to him in bright light and spoke to him, Paul (as Saul) listened and believed (Acts 9:3-6). Paul's spiritual blindness was lifted, even as he became physically blinded for a time (9:9). Paul can speak with authority about both sides of the divide!

When people reject the gospel, does that mean that the gospel is weak or that it has been wrongly presented? Not at all! It simply demonstrates the persistent power of the devil to tempt people to keep the blindness they choose to embrace. But the devil need not prevail in anyone's life. The light of the gospel is clear, and Paul is proof that one can leave darkness and blindness for the light.

What Do You Think?

What approaches or techniques can we use to break through a person's defenses so the gospel is not "hid" from him or her?

Talking Points for Your Discussion

- When the resistance is emotional in nature
- When the resistance is due to faulty thinking
- Other

Preaching the Pure Gospel

An American missionary traveled to the African country to which God had called him. On arrival, he began getting acquainted with other Americans who were doing missionary work there. Since he was new at mission work and had only "book learning" to guide his efforts, he thought perhaps he could learn from others more experienced in presenting the gospel to that culture.

One missionary he spoke with had been in the country for 25 years and was ministering to a small group of Christians who were the results of his work. That missionary explained the small number of converts by saying, "We're preaching the pure gospel, and Satan is hindering it."

The work of another long-term missionary, however, had yielded a large numbers of converts and a significant cadre of indigenous ministers and teachers who were leading their congregations. That missionary said his work was prospering because, "We're preaching the pure gospel, and God is blessing it."

Which missionary was right? Perhaps both!

Paul was preaching the pure gospel, and he saw Satan hindering his work. However, his work for Christ was being blessed, as we know from the letters he wrote to many of the churches that got their start because of his witness. Perhaps the lesson we can learn is the one the apostle himself had learned: we do the work God has called us to do and act in the spirit of Christ as we do it. The results are up to Him. —C. R. B.

C. In the Light of God (vv. 5, 6)

5. For we preach not ourselves, but Christ Jesus the Lord; and ourselves your servants for Jesus' sake.

The focus of the message, Paul says, is not the messenger. It is Christ. When the messenger is less, Christ can be more (compare John 3:30). Insofar as Paul or any preacher of the gospel matters, it is only as a servant for the benefit of the people to whom the message is delivered.

It is most fitting that the messenger of Christ's gospel should be a servant. Jesus declared himself to be the servant of all, the one who gave His life for others (Mark 10:45). When the messenger is a servant for others, then Jesus, the servant-king, is proclaimed by the messenger's word and by the messenger's character.

6. For God, who commanded the light to shine out of darkness, hath shined in our hearts, to give the light of the knowledge of the glory of God in the face of Jesus Christ.

The God who is able to say "Let there be light" in a physical sense (Genesis 1:3) can also bring *light to shine out of darkness* in a spiritual sense (Matthew 4:16, quoting Isaiah 9:2). The light of the gospel shines outward as the gospel is preached. But it also shines inward on the hearts of those who receive it. We can see that the gospel

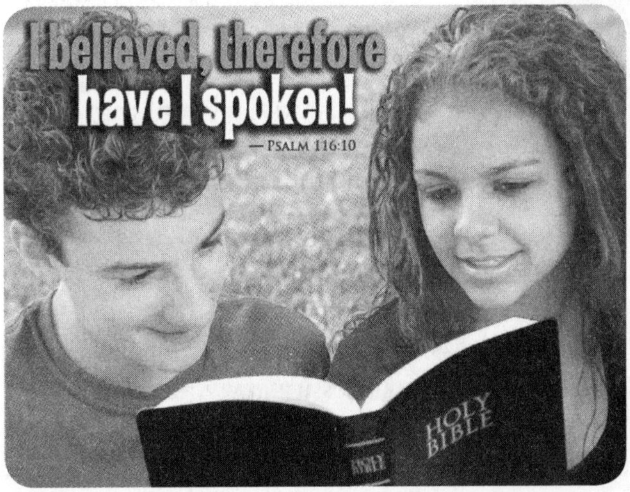

Visual for Lesson 12. *Point to this visual as you introduce the discussion question that is associated with verse 13.*

is God's light in both ways: the truth proclaimed publicly and the change effected inwardly.

Witnessing the transformation of others is a key part of recognizing that the good news of Jesus is truly God's message of salvation. Every aspect of the gospel demands that the person who believes and proclaims it must be sincerely committed, oriented to service for others, and ready to endure hardships faithfully.

> **What Do You Think?**
> When was a time you saw the light of the gospel drive back spiritual darkness in a most powerful way? What did you learn from this experience?
> *Talking Points for Your Discussion*
> - Episode of cross-cultural evangelism
> - Episode of evangelism on your part
> - As the result of a sermon
> - As the result of extending benevolence
> - Other

II. Humility of the Messenger
(2 Corinthians 4:7-12)
A. God's Treasure (v. 7)

7. But we have this treasure in earthen vessels, that the excellency of the power may be of God, and not of us.

The lowliness of God's messengers is the very thing that displays the glory of God's message. Paul compares himself and everyone who carries the gospel with the articles of pottery (*earthen vessels*) that are so common in his day. Such containers are relatively inexpensive and completely ordinary. Within such ordinary-looking vessels resides an exceptionally valuable treasure: the gospel. Its value is all the more obvious because it stands in contrast with its container.

This vivid image captures the essence of Paul's point. The gospel is priceless, for it is God's good news, God's saving light. Those who believe it and proclaim it are by necessity lowly, for they follow the Lord who surrendered His privileges to give His life for His people. Therefore, all the power is in the treasure, the gospel message, not in the earthen vessel, the messenger. That makes clear where the real glory lies.

B. Paul's Hardships (vv. 8, 9)

8. We are troubled on every side, yet not distressed; we are perplexed, but not in despair.

Life for the earthen vessel that contains the gospel treasure is a life of paradox, filled with contrasts as sharp as the one between the treasure and the pottery. Christ's earthen vessels experience trouble of all kinds, the perplexity of deeply confusing situations. But we are not crushed by the trouble, not confused to the point of giving up. The maker of the earthen vessel ensures that the pot does not crack.

9. Persecuted, but not forsaken; cast down, but not destroyed.

The paradoxes continue. Christ's earthen vessels are *persecuted*—deliberately harassed because of the faith. But we always have God himself on our side. We may feel as if we have been *cast down* violently to the ground. But unlike a typical clay pot, we do not shatter when we fall. The power of God assures that we remain whole.

> **What Do You Think?**
> What one thing most keeps you going for Christ in your darkest hours? Does your answer change as the years pass? Why?
> *Talking Points for Your Discussion*
> - A promise of God
> - An example of a Bible character
> - An example of someone in church history
> - Strength from fellow Christians
> - Other

C. Jesus' Death and Life (vv. 10-12)

10. Always bearing about in the body the dying of the Lord Jesus, that the life also of Jesus might be made manifest in our body.

Paul expresses the foundational paradox directly. Jesus is Lord, the author of life. Yet Jesus surrendered to death. But thereby He rose from the dead and granted resurrection life to us. Now we are to live the same way, experiencing all the world's troubles while showing Christ-given life as we endure and overcome.

11. For we which live are always delivered unto death for Jesus' sake, that the life also of Jesus might be made manifest in our mortal flesh.

The lives of people who belong to Jesus will inevitably conform to the pattern of Jesus' life. We will give our lives for the sake of others—not as He did in dying for others' sins, but in giving time, talent, and treasure to serve others in Jesus' name. In so doing, we allow Jesus' life to become clear to the world as it shines through our lowly service.

12. So then death worketh in us, but life in you.

Paul's words here make sense when we remember that he speaks as a messenger of the gospel to those who have received the message. The lowly, self-sacrificial life of the messenger resembles the death of Christ; through that self-sacrificial life, those who receive the message receive the life of Christ. Those who carry the gospel serve in the image of Jesus, bringing life through death.

III. Persistence of Faith
(2 CORINTHIANS 4:13-15)

A. Confident in Resurrection (vv. 13, 14)

13. We having the same spirit of faith, according as it is written, I believed, and therefore have I spoken; we also believe, and therefore speak.

The hardships that Paul describes in 2 Corinthians are considerable, but so is the faith that sustains him. Paul quotes Psalm 116:10 to show that the faith of the self-sacrificial Christ-follower is like the faith expressed in that psalm, which witnesses to and celebrates an occasion when God rescued His people from deadly peril. The psalmist trusted God and so called out to Him for help. God's utter faithfulness is what sustains His people in hardship.

What Do You Think?
What words of testimony do you speak because of what you believe?
Talking Points for Your Discussion
- Regarding God's protection
- Regarding God's comfort
- Regarding hope sustained
- Regarding victories observed

14. Knowing that he which raised up the Lord Jesus shall raise up us also by Jesus, and shall present us with you.

We have reason to believe in God's faithfulness even more than the psalmist! By raising Jesus from the dead, God demonstrated that there are no limits on what He can do to deliver His people from peril. Having raised Christ, He will certainly raise us as well (Romans 8:11; 1 Corinthians 6:14; 15:15, 20).

Paul's stress on God's final raising of believers from the dead means being gathered together in God's presence. He will see His people safely through to their destination, which is eternity in His presence.

B. Benefit for Many (v. 15)

15. For all things are for your sakes, that the abundant grace might through the thanksgiving of many redound to the glory of God.

As gospel messengers pour out their lives in service, those who receive the gospel become part of the multitude that will praise God forever. In that way, the messengers' lives serve others and in the end serve and glorify God. In that way, the messengers' lives reflect the message of the risen Jesus.

Conclusion
A. Hardship with Hope

The authentic life of a Christ-follower is a lowly life of honest, persistent service. By living for and sharing the gospel, Christians experience hardship but ultimately share the eternal life of God as well. Is there a better, more meaningful life that one can live?

B. Prayer

Gracious God, You have bought us at great cost: the life of Your Son. We give You our lives to be conformed to His image. Focus our goals and dreams on Your purposes. Make us Your earthen vessels and fill us with Your treasure. In the name of Jesus, amen.

C. Thought to Remember

Hardship for Christ is worth it!

INVOLVEMENT LEARNING

Some of the activities below are also found in the helpful student book, Adult Bible Class.
Don't forget to download the free reproducible page from www.standardlesson.com to enhance your lesson!

Into the Lesson

Option: Place in chairs copies of the "The True Gospel" activity from the reproducible page, which you can download. Learners can begin working on this as they arrive.

Prepare in advance a PowerPoint® presentation of genuine and knockoff handbags and shoes. Begin by saying, "I'm going to show you two handbags or two pairs of shoes on each slide. See if you can determine which is genuine and which is the imitation or knockoff." Pause after each slide to give learners the opportunity to do so, then reveal the correct answer. *Alternative 1:* If you do not have PowerPoint® capability, do the above with handouts. Adjust the presentation accordingly. (Images are easy to find on the Internet.)

Alternative 2: Have these two phrases on the board as learners arrive: *name-it-and-claim-it gospel / salvation-by-knowledge gospel (Gnosticism).* Ask learners what they know about these two "gospels." If learners do not do so, identify areas where they depart from Scripture, which you have researched in advance.

After any of the above, say, "Today's lesson is about the true message of God: the gospel of Jesus Christ. The gospel must be proclaimed by those whose lives reflect its truth."

Into the Word

Draw a vertical line down the middle of the board to form two columns. Above one write *True Gospel*; above the other write *Knockoff Gospel*. Assign the lesson's 15 verses to learners as evenly as possible. Ask learners to read their verses aloud. During the pause between verses, ask what characteristics of either the true gospel or a knockoff gospel they detect; jot responses in the appropriate columns. Expected responses for *True Gospel*: mercy (v. 1), honesty (v. 2), preaches Christ as Lord (v. 5), servants for Christ (v. 5), light of knowledge of the glory of God shines in the heart (v. 6), focuses on God (v. 7), messengers not abandoned by God (vv. 8, 9), messengers willing to suffer to make Christ known (vv. 10-12), and confidence in resurrection (vv. 13, 14). Expected responses for *Knockoff Gospel*: uses deception (v. 2), distorts the Word of God (v. 2); messengers are blind to truth (v. 4); messengers preach self (v. 5).

Spend a few minutes elaborating on the concept of *knockoff gospel*, focusing on the fact that its characteristics can be centered on the messenger. If you used the second alternative activity to begin class, relate these characteristics to those particular knockoff gospels. Discuss how the characteristics of both the *true gospel* and *knockoff gospels* are transforming, considering how the characteristics listed in the first column on the board reveal a life changed for the better, while those on the right reveal the opposite.

Say, "Today's lesson has taught us that every aspect of the gospel demands that the person who believes and proclaims it must be sincerely committed, oriented to service for others, and ready to endure hardships faithfully."

Into Life

Say, "We've identified several characteristics of the true gospel today. Now let's identify some specific disciplines that will help us develop those characteristics in our own lives." Divide learners into groups of three and assign a characteristic from the *True Gospel* side of the board to each group. Ask groups to identify at least one specific way Christians can develop that particular characteristic. (Example: Instead of expecting thanks for acts of service, Christians can offer thanks to God, since it is His love that compels the service.)

Option: Distribute copies of the "Improving My Witness" activity from the reproducible page. This will foster personal reflection on the characteristics learners may need to develop. If time is short, this can be a take-home activity.

AN APPEAL FOR RECONCILIATION

DEVOTIONAL READING: 2 Corinthians 5:16-21
BACKGROUND SCRIPTURE: 2 Corinthians 6:1–7:4

2 CORINTHIANS 6:1-13

1 We then, as workers together with him, beseech you also that ye receive not the grace of God in vain.

2 (For he saith, I have heard thee in a time accepted, and in the day of salvation have I succoured thee: behold, now is the accepted time; behold, now is the day of salvation.)

3 Giving no offence in any thing, that the ministry be not blamed:

4 But in all things approving ourselves as the ministers of God, in much patience, in afflictions, in necessities, in distresses,

5 In stripes, in imprisonments, in tumults, in labours, in watchings, in fastings;

6 By pureness, by knowledge, by longsuffering, by kindness, by the Holy Ghost, by love unfeigned,

7 By the word of truth, by the power of God, by the armour of righteousness on the right hand and on the left,

8 By honour and dishonour, by evil report and good report: as deceivers, and yet true;

9 As unknown, and yet well known; as dying, and, behold, we live; as chastened, and not killed;

10 As sorrowful, yet alway rejoicing; as poor, yet making many rich; as having nothing, and yet possessing all things.

11 O ye Corinthians, our mouth is open unto you, our heart is enlarged.

12 Ye are not straitened in us, but ye are straitened in your own bowels.

13 Now for a recompence in the same, (I speak as unto my children,) be ye also enlarged.

2 CORINTHIANS 7:1-4

1 Having therefore these promises, dearly beloved, let us cleanse ourselves from all filthiness of the flesh and spirit, perfecting holiness in the fear of God.

2 Receive us; we have wronged no man, we have corrupted no man, we have defrauded no man.

3 I speak not this to condemn you: for I have said before, that ye are in our hearts to die and live with you.

4 Great is my boldness of speech toward you, great is my glorying of you: I am filled with comfort, I am exceeding joyful in all our tribulation.

KEY VERSE

Receive us; we have wronged no man, we have corrupted no man, we have defrauded no man.
—2 Corinthians 7:2

THE PEOPLE OF GOD SET PRIORITIES

Unit 3: Bearing One Another's Burdens

LESSONS 10–14

LESSON AIMS

After participating in this lesson, each student will be able to:

1. Describe some of the hardships Paul endured for ministry.

2. Tell how enduring hardship for the gospel enhances one's credibility in proclaiming the gospel.

3. Evaluate his or her own willingness to endure hardship for Christ's sake and make needed adjustments.

LESSON OUTLINE

Introduction

A. Various Fights

In television's early days, broadcasters quickly discovered that boxing was inexpensive to air and was popular with audiences. So began the "Saturday Night Fights" that were common television fare in the 1950s. Unfortunately, churches have been known for their "Sunday Morning Fights," with rivalry and rancor tarnishing the good news of Jesus. Such fights go all the way back to the first century. Given the availability of the apostles themselves, we may find it surprising that church fights would have happened back then. But they did. Today's text addresses one such.

B. Lesson Background

Paul faced opposition from one or more factions within the Corinthian church. We can sketch some of their characteristics by reading his letters to that church. His opponents claimed superior spiritual status and knowledge (1 Corinthians 8:1, 2). Some taught that immoral behavior was of no consequence (5:1, 2; 6:9-13). Some denied that God raises the dead (15:12).

Furthermore, some opponents minimized or denied Paul's authority as an apostle (2 Corinthians 6:8; 11:5; 12:11, 12). Some characterized him as powerful in his letters, but unimpressive in person (10:9, 10)—perhaps downright crazy (5:13). Some insisted that Jewish identity was vital to a true relationship with God (11:22).

The combination of doctrinal deviations and power struggles created big problems at Corinth! Paul worked hard to straighten things out. When he wrote 2 Corinthians, it appears that he had largely succeeded. Not all had given up the false teaching, but to those who had, Paul had the message of today's text.

I. Corinthians' Need
(2 CORINTHIANS 6:1, 2)

A. What Not to Do (v. 1)

1. We then, as workers together with him, beseech you also that ye receive not the grace of God in vain.

Today's text comes just after a long segment on the subject of reconciliation (2 Corinthians 5:11-21). In this light, Paul reminded his readers of the Christians' standing with God: we belong to Him through His grace, not our goodness. To receive God's grace and then to be unforgiving is to make His grace *vain* or empty. His forgiveness compels us to forgive others (Matthew 6:12).

Paul offers this reminder as a fellow laborer with God. Paul applies the exalted designation *workers together with him* to anyone who serves the Lord in truth (compare 1 Corinthians 3:9; 1 Thessalonians 3:2). But to be God's fellow laborer with consistency, one has to follow God's lead in extending forgiveness.

What Do You Think?
Under what circumstances do Christians find it hardest to extend forgiveness? Why is that?
Talking Points for Your Discussion
- Wrongs done to oneself personally
- Wrongs done against a family member
- Wrongs done against the church
- Other

B. What to Realize (v. 2)

2. (For he saith, I have heard thee in a time accepted, and in the day of salvation have I succoured thee: behold, now is the accepted time; behold, now is the day of salvation.)

Paul quotes Isaiah 49:8. That text speaks of God's response to His people's cry for help, giving them the salvation that they needed but did not deserve. The apostle then affirms that the time of salvation of which Isaiah spoke centuries ago has truly come! The word *now* makes an emphatic point: because God is now gathering all kinds of people to be His, those so gathered must be united with others whom God is gathering. There can be no divisions within the one people of God.

II. Paul's Hardships
(2 CORINTHIANS 6:3-10)
A. Without Offense (v. 3)

3. Giving no offence in any thing, that the ministry be not blamed.

Paul begins to describe his own efforts in bringing reconciliation. In doing so, he is also describing a characteristic of the life of any Christian who is devoted to the gospel.

While not compromising on the truth of the gospel, Paul works diligently to avoid doing anything that would offend others and thus hinder their receptivity to the gospel message. For example, he has not accepted payment from those to whom he preached the gospel in Corinth—although it was his right to do so—in order that more would listen to his message (1 Corinthians 9:7-18). Paul's all-the-time goal is to create an opening for the gospel in others' lives (10:32, 33).

B. In Suffering (vv. 4, 5)

4. But in all things approving ourselves as the ministers of God, in much patience, in afflictions, in necessities, in distresses.

Instead of giving offense, Paul says, he shows that he is what he claims to be—one of the genuine *ministers of God.* The apostle proceeds to demonstrate this fact with a long list of reasons and characteristics. Persisting in these, Paul says, demonstrates that he is genuinely God's servant (the meaning of *minister*).

The list begins with *patience,* implying not just a willingness to wait, but the positive ability to endure hardship. As Christ endured the cross, so His people endure hardships out of love for others. Next come three words suggesting hardship: *afflictions,* troubles of all kinds; *necessities,* experiences of need and deprivation; and *distresses,* situations of great pressure. These come to believers because they belong to the suffering Christ. Like Christ, a true believer is willing to undergo such hardships for the sake of restoring fellowship with others.

5. In stripes, in imprisonments, in tumults, in labours, in watchings, in fastings.

The list of hardships continues. *Stripes* are wounds from beatings; Paul has been beaten numerous times during his ministry (2 Corinthians 11:24, 25). *Imprisonments* are another punishment Paul has suffered (Acts 16:23). *Tumults* are civil disturbances or riots; Paul experienced these as well, especially just before he wrote 2 Corinthians (see Acts 19:23-41). All these reflect the rejection that Christ himself experienced. Enduring such things is the price the believer may have to pay in the service of seeing God's people united.

The list continues with *labours,* referring to tiring work of all kinds. *Watchings* refers to sleep deprivation. *Fastings* are not simply voluntary times without food, but going hungry for any reason. Again, such hardships are Paul's experience for the gospel. All reflect Christ's own life. All define what the faithful may undergo in being servants of Christ's reconciling work.

What Do You Think?

What hardships have you seen Christians suffer recently in the cause of Christ? How should this affect your prayer life?

Talking Points for Your Discussion

- Job discrimination
- Social ostracism
- Outright violence
- Other

C. With Godly Character (vv. 6, 7)

6. By pureness, by knowledge, by longsuffering, by kindness, by the Holy Ghost, by love unfeigned.

The focus now shifts to the character traits and resources needed to endure the hardships. *Pureness* refers to moral cleanliness—being wholly devoted to right living. *Knowledge* here is comprehension of the true God, knowing Him through Jesus Christ. *Longsuffering* is the ability to remain calm and endure under pressure or suffering. In the New Testament, this is a quality based on confident trust in God. *Kindness* means being devoted to actions that benefit other people.

These qualities are the result of the Holy Spirit's work in reshaping the believer to be conformed to Christ's image, empowering us to do God's work. None of the qualities listed here can exist in earnest without divine empowerment.

Love unfeigned is unhypocritical love. There is nothing fake about it. Paul can appeal to his history with the Corinthian Christians as an example. His consistent love for them reflects God's constancy and sets an example for their own response to God's love in loving others.

7. By the word of truth, by the power of God, by the armour of righteousness on the right hand and on the left.

Both the truthful message and God's power are at work to motivate and enable His people. Paul uses the image of armor to illustrate God's powerful protection (compare Romans 13:12; Ephesians 6:11-17; 1 Thessalonians 5:8). With *the armour of righteousness,* God's people are protected to do His righteous work in the world. It is sufficient for every situation: both sides, right and left, are protected.

❧ POWER TO OVERCOME ❧

Parents who intervene in disputes between their children hear excuses ready to be offered. "But Dad, he started it!" "But Mom, I was just minding my own business when she . . ." Most such excuses have one thing in common: the situation is the fault of someone else.

Adults often have the same mind-set. Perhaps using words that are more elegant than those of children, we excuse ourselves for our part in a disagreement or for a failure by pointing the finger elsewhere. The other person offended me, I was having a bad day, her personality is abrasive, the circumstances conspired against me—on and on it goes. Problems are never really *our* fault, are they?

Paul described an array of difficulties that faced the Corinthians and their relationship with him. But he did not point out the problems merely so he could distance himself in a "not my fault" kind of way. Rather, he engaged the problems and problem people as he listed several factors working in his favor.

Within Paul's list is "the power of God." This is what outweighed all the problems and personalities arrayed against him. When tough times come, will we use excuses to point fingers elsewhere, or will we look to the power of God to enable us to resolve the problem?   —C. R. B.

HOW TO SAY IT

Corinth	*Kor*-inth.
Corinthians	Ko-*rin*-thee-unz (*th* as in *thin*).
Isaiah	Eye-*zay*-uh.

D. Under Vexing Circumstances (vv. 8-10)

8. By honour and dishonour, by evil report and good report: as deceivers, and yet true.

The right and left sides of a soldier (v. 7) suggest contrasting kinds of situations that believers working for reconciliation face. Some people, speaking with bitter hostility, attempt to dishonor the reconcilers. Others, however, honor reconcilers as God's workers. Some people speak slanderously, while others commend. Some characterize reconcilers as deceivers even as those reconcilers are speaking the truth.

All who pursue reconciliation will experience these extremes. But they also experience the joy of seeing former enemies become friends.

What Do You Think?

How have you seen God empower people to fulfill the call for reconciliation? What did you learn from this?

Talking Points for Your Discussion

- Within families
- Within the church
- Between friends
- In society in general
- Other

---

9. As unknown, and yet well known; as dying, and, behold, we live; as chastened, and not killed.

As far as the world is concerned, Christians are completely insignificant. But from God's perspective, they are the famous ones, heralded for doing God's work. Their lives of hardship seem like an unending struggle of death, yet in them Christ's resurrection life is truly at work. They may appear to be under harsh discipline, but they cannot be stopped (Psalm 118:18).

10. As sorrowful, yet alway rejoicing; as poor, yet making many rich; as having nothing, and yet possessing all things.

The contrasts continue, expressing the paradoxes of the life of faith. Paul has much sorrow in his ministry, largely due to the struggles that his churches face. Why endure such heartache? For the joy that accompanies it! Seeing people come to faith and mature in faith, seeing people who have

Visual for Lessons 11 & 13. *Point to this visual as you ask, "How does neglect of attempting to reconcile give Satan an advantage?"*

been enemies become brothers and sisters—these are sources of incomparable joy.

Paul can honestly say that he has lived as a poor man. His practice is to support himself with his trade while preaching the gospel at no cost (1 Corinthians 9:1-18). Choosing to follow Christ always means choosing not to pursue wealth, for as Jesus put it, "No man can serve two masters. . . . Ye cannot serve God and mammon" (Matthew 6:24). But those who live for the gospel know that God's treasury is at their disposal, now and forever (6:33). We Christians seem to have nothing, but in Christ the whole world is ours forever.

III. Paul's Proposal
(2 CORINTHIANS 6:11-13; 7:1-4)

A. What Has Happened (vv. 11, 12)

11. O ye Corinthians, our mouth is open unto you, our heart is enlarged.

Paul has spoken to the Corinthians with complete honesty and frankness. Confident in Christ, he can take the risk of complete disclosure. He has no secrets.

Paul's open mouth mirrors his open heart. Christ's love makes the human heart big enough to welcome anyone, even an enemy. As God loved us when we were in rebellion against Him, so His Spirit teaches us to love our enemies. When enemies become part of God's family, the real power of the gospel is displayed.

12. Ye are not straitened in us, but ye are straitened in your own bowels.

The intestines (*bowels*) are seen as the center of compassion and mercy in Greek culture. So Paul is saying to his opponents in Corinth, "You have lacked compassion for us, but we have not lacked it for you." He is completely ready for reconciliation, his heart made open by God's love.

B. What Needs to Happen (6:13; 7:1, 2a)

13. Now for a recompence in the same, (I speak as unto my children,) be ye also enlarged.

If Paul has been honest and forgiving, should not those in the Corinthian church be so as well? Such would be a fair trade for what he has done in bringing them the saving message of Jesus. They are his children in the faith (1 Corinthians 4:14). They should respond to his open heart with their own open hearts. Actually, it is more than a fair trade, since Paul has brought much more to the Corinthians than they can ever give back in exchange. Being reconciled to him is the least that they can do in response to what they have received!

7:1, 2a. Having therefore these promises, dearly beloved, let us cleanse ourselves from all filthiness of the flesh and spirit, perfecting holiness in the fear of God. Receive us.

The phrase *these promises* refers to God's intent to "be their God," "receive you," and "be a Father unto you" (2 Corinthians 6:16-18). Christians receive the fulfillment of all these promises. That fact should motivate the lifelong responses of (1) eliminating the selfish, hostile attitudes of the old life, and (2) replacing those with devotion to God as His distinct people who respect Him utterly.

With a renewed outlook, the Corinthians will find reconciliation not just possible but inevitable. On this basis Paul can challenge them to *receive us*.

What Do You Think?
Having been "washed . . . in the blood of the lamb" (Revelation 7:14), what can Christians do to cleanse themselves from all unholiness?
Talking Points for Your Discussion
- Regarding the flesh
- Regarding the spirit

C. What to Realize (vv. 2b-4)

2b. We have wronged no man, we have corrupted no man, we have defrauded no man.

Paul again reminds his readers of his own commitment to Christ. Despite any accusations, Paul has been honest and loving toward all (compare 1 Samuel 12:3). His life reflects Christ's own life. There is no reason to be hostile toward someone with such commitment.

3. I speak not this to condemn you: for I have said before, that ye are in our hearts to die and live with you.

Paul's words have been harsh. Yet they come not from anger but from deep commitment to Christ and to the Corinthians. Paul speaks with power because of the powerful love that he has for them, a love like Christ's that is willing to die for others.

4. Great is my boldness of speech toward you, great is my glorying of you: I am filled with comfort, I am exceeding joyful in all our tribulation.

Where does all this bold speech come from? Paul's determination to be reconciled has only one source: commitment to Christ. So he can endure any hardship and undertake any task to see God's work through to its fulfillment.

Conclusion

A. When Enemies Become Family

Some churches may be known for their fights (compare 2 Corinthians 12:20), but the true story of the church is forgiveness. In Christ, enemies become family. If Christ's love lives in us, then we can do no less than love all those for whom Christ died. To refuse to be reconciled is to blaspheme the cross of Christ. To pursue reconciliation is to glorify it.

B. Prayer

Father, Your Son died for us, unworthy sinners. Strengthen us to demonstrate Your mercy as we work to reconcile. In Jesus' name, amen.

C. Thought to Remember

Work for reconciliation—God did!

INVOLVEMENT LEARNING

Some of the activities below are also found in the helpful student book, Adult Bible Class.
Don't forget to download the free reproducible page from www.standardlesson.com to enhance your lesson!

Into the Lesson

Have the sentence *I have rights!* displayed on the board as learners arrive. Ask learners to name various "rights" they believe they have or are entitled to. Record responses on the board. Discuss what determines a person's "rights." Then say, "In today's lesson we will identify the 'rights' Paul had as a messenger of the gospel of Christ and see how they apply to our own lives."

Into the Word

Affix to the walls four poster boards that feature the following headings, one each: 1. What was wrong with the relationship between Paul and the Corinthians? How did Paul describe the result? 2. What was Paul's manner of conduct? Why did he conduct himself that way? 3. How should the Corinthians have responded to Paul's initiative? 4. Why was reconciliation so important to Paul?

Divide the class into four groups and number them according to the questions above, which you will assign for research. Give each group one of the following handouts of Scripture references for the research: *Group 1*—2 Corinthians 6:8, 12b (see also 10:10, not in today's text); *Group 2*—2 Corinthians 6:3-12a; 7:2b-4; *Group 3*—2 Corinthians 6:1-3, 13; 7:1, 2a; *Group 4*—2 Corinthians 6:1-3; 7:1. Say, "Examine your assigned texts to answer the questions. As you find the answers, record them on the corresponding chart."

When groups finish, review the charts. *Group 1's* should reflect the fact that the Corinthians denied or minimized Paul's authority as an apostle; they were assassinating Paul's character and contradicting his teachings. The result was closed hearts.

Group 2's findings should emphasize that Paul's manner of conduct was driven by his desire for reconciliation, he with the Corinthians and the Corinthians with one another. Paul's response was, in essence, "Look at my track record and you'll see I have conducted myself properly."

Group 3's findings should highlight the necessities of holiness and open hearts. Also point out that Paul's attitudes and actions of pureness, knowledge, etc. (6:6) are examples to follow. These are possible by the word of truth, the power of God, and the armor of righteousness (6:7).

Group 4's findings should highlight the fact that reconciliation was important because salvation was at stake. Paul was the spiritual mentor of the Corinthians. If they could not be reconciled to him, then they probably would no longer accept his gospel teaching. Failure to reconcile might mean that the Corinthians saw no need to devote their lives to "perfecting holiness in the fear of God" (7:1).

Into Life

Say, "We have one question left to answer: What do we need to learn from this lesson?" (*Option 1* below will supply some starting points for the discussion.) Lead the discussion to 2 Corinthians 7:1, reading it aloud. Write "perfecting holiness in the fear of God" on the board.

Call learners' attention to the original list of "rights" recorded on the board. Say, "In light of today's lesson, it seems that we should talk more about our *responsibilities* as Christians rather than our 'rights.' What are some responsibilities?" (Possible responses: turning the other cheek, serving others, accepting suffering for the gospel). Say, "Paul's message was validated by his willingness to give up 'worldly rights' for 'kingdom responsibilities.' Are you willing to do the same?" Discuss.

Option 1: Introduce the application of the lesson above by distributing the "Fellow Laborers in the Kingdom" activity from the reproducible page, which you can download. Learners should be able to complete this quickly.

Option 2: As a further challenge, distribute as a take-home activity copies of the "Am I Willing?" confessional on the reproducible page.

GENEROSITY IN THE MIDST OF POVERTY

DEVOTIONAL READING: 1 Corinthians 13:1-7
BACKGROUND SCRIPTURE: 2 Corinthians 8, 9

2 CORINTHIANS 8:1-14

1 Moreover, brethren, we do you to wit of the grace of God bestowed on the churches of Macedonia;

2 How that in a great trial of affliction the abundance of their joy and their deep poverty abounded unto the riches of their liberality.

3 For to their power, I bear record, yea, and beyond their power they were willing of themselves;

4 Praying us with much intreaty that we would receive the gift, and take upon us the fellowship of the ministering to the saints.

5 And this they did, not as we hoped, but first gave their own selves to the Lord, and unto us by the will of God.

6 Insomuch that we desired Titus, that as he had begun, so he would also finish in you the same grace also.

7 Therefore, as ye abound in every thing, in faith, and utterance, and knowledge, and in all diligence, and in your love to us, see that ye abound in this grace also.

8 I speak not by commandment, but by occasion of the forwardness of others, and to prove the sincerity of your love.

9 For ye know the grace of our Lord Jesus Christ, that, though he was rich, yet for your sakes he became poor, that ye through his poverty might be rich.

10 And herein I give my advice: for this is expedient for you, who have begun before, not only to do, but also to be forward a year ago.

11 Now therefore perform the doing of it; that as there was a readiness to will, so there may be a performance also out of that which ye have.

12 For if there be first a willing mind, it is accepted according to that a man hath, and not according to that he hath not.

13 For I mean not that other men be eased, and ye burdened:

14 But by an equality, that now at this time your abundance may be a supply for their want, that their abundance also may be a supply for your want: that there may be equality.

KEY VERSE

As ye abound in every thing, in faith, and utterance, and knowledge, and in all diligence, and in your love to us, see that ye abound in this grace also. —**2 Corinthians 8:7**

THE PEOPLE OF GOD SET PRIORITIES

Unit 3: Bearing One Another's Burdens

LESSONS 10–14

LESSON AIMS

After participating in this lesson, each student will be able to:

1. Summarize the circumstances of Paul's appeal to the Corinthians for generosity.

2. Explain self-sacrificial generosity as a necessary outcome of faith in Jesus.

3. Make a plan for exercising generosity as an expression of faith in Jesus.

LESSON OUTLINE

Introduction

A. Epic Generosity

One of the world's favorite stories is Victor Hugo's *Les Misérables*. First as a novel and later as a musical stage play, it has fascinated audiences for generations.

Les Misérables is the story of Jean Valjean, a poor man who is imprisoned for stealing a loaf of bread. Finally released from prison, he is given refuge by a saintly bishop of the church. Valjean repays the man's generosity by stealing his silverware! But when the police capture Valjean, the bishop says that the silverware was a gift to the man. Stunned by the bishop's gracious generosity, Valjean becomes a changed man. In the rest of the story, he becomes a person of humble, heroic generosity.

Perhaps what makes *Les Misérables* so beloved is that it exemplifies the grace of God. Though we have rejected God's generosity, He still freely offers us forgiveness by His grace. Having received that forgiveness, a person can never be the same. God's gracious generosity begets the same generosity in His people.

B. Lesson Background

While on his third missionary journey, the apostle Paul planned to receive a collection for the poor of Jerusalem—the offering to be received from churches he had planted (Romans 15:25-32; 1 Corinthians 16:1-4). It seems that the Jerusalem church had little left to help its own people after years of sponsoring missionaries, enduring famines, and suffering persecution. So Paul planned an offering as a practical response to the need.

Beyond meeting needs of the recipients, such an offering would be a powerful demonstration of the church's unity. Paul's congregations had many Gentiles, while the Jerusalem church had a very high percentage of Jews. The offering would express a unity in Christ that transcended differences in ethnicity or geography.

As Paul wrote about his plan in his second letter to the church at Corinth, he was probably in the province of Macedonia, more than 100 miles to the north of that city (2 Corinthians 7:5; 8:1;

9:2-4). Paul had established churches in Macedonia on his second missionary journey (Acts 16:9–17:15). He had planted the church in Corinth in Achaia to the south on this same journey (Acts 18:1-18; 2 Corinthians 9:2).

I. Macedonian Example
(2 CORINTHIANS 8:1-5)

A. Gracious Giving (vv. 1, 2)

1. Moreover, brethren, we do you to wit of the grace of God bestowed on the churches of Macedonia.

Paul begins by describing how *the churches of Macedonia* have responded to his appeal for a collection (*do you to wit* means "to make known to you"). In so doing, he begins not by speaking of the Macedonians' generosity as such but by noting that they have received *the grace of God*. Generosity is itself a gift of God, the means by which His people can participate as givers in God's own plan of gracious giving.

2. How that in a great trial of affliction the abundance of their joy and their deep poverty abounded unto the riches of their liberality.

Because Christian generosity is based on God's unchanging grace, one's generosity remains (or should remain) strong regardless of circumstances. Macedonia is an excellent example. The churches in this area have been under great pressure, both from persecution and from their own lack of material wealth. But their generous spirit is rich, flowing from *their joy* in knowing Jesus. If believers under such pressure can give so generously, certainly the Corinthians can do so as well.

B. Impressive Initiative (vv. 3-5)

3. For to their power, I bear record, yea, and beyond their power they were willing of themselves.

HOW TO SAY IT

Achaia	Uh-*kay*-uh.
Les Misérables	Lay Mee-zay-*rah*-bl.
Macedonia	Mass-eh-*doe*-nee-uh.
Titus	*Ty*-tus.

Logically, one expects that people will be generous only up *to their power* to give. This should be especially so of those who are themselves in need. But Paul serves as a witness to the fact that the poverty-stricken Macedonians have given above and beyond that point!

What Do You Think?
What does it look like for people to give "beyond their power"? How are you doing in this regard?
Talking Points for Your Discussion
- Regarding tangible gifts (money, etc.)
- Regarding intangible gifts (time, etc.)

The exceptional generosity of the Macedonians has not been forced. They have responded freely, by their own choice. Paul understands that a forced response would not be genuine. Real generosity shows itself when people reckon with and freely respond to God's grace.

4. Praying us with much intreaty that we would receive the gift, and take upon us the fellowship of the ministering to the saints.

The Macedonians are far from reluctant to give! Paul combines several words to emphasize that they enthusiastically insist on being exceptionally generous. The word *praying* as used here refers to requests not to God but to other people—in this case, to Paul and his assistants (*us*). Those requests have come with much urging, or *intreaty*.

Those who are to be the recipients of the collection really need it (Romans 15:26). But Paul restates a larger purpose for the collection: it will be a tangible expression of the common bond between believers. It is a concrete action of service to others. The recipients, just as the givers, are *the saints*—the people of God set apart by His grace (compare 2 Corinthians 9:1). Here is an opportunity for a powerful expression of what it means to follow Jesus (compare Matthew 25:34-40).

5. And this they did, not as we hoped, but first gave their own selves to the Lord, and unto us by the will of God.

In fulfilling their deep desire to participate in the collection, the Macedonian Christians far surpass (*not as we hoped*) Paul's expectations! They give not just an offering of money but *their own selves*. Someone has said that money is "coined life" because it takes the time and energy of life to obtain it. The Macedonian Christians' give with an attitude that they are sharing themselves with their brothers and sisters in Jerusalem, as if they are neighbors sharing the ups and downs of life together.

The Macedonian Christians have this attitude because they are giving themselves first and foremost *to the Lord*. If Christ's Spirit lives in every believer, if believers together constitute Christ's body, then generosity toward other Christians expresses generosity toward the Lord Jesus.

The Macedonians' generosity also expresses a grateful response to Paul for bringing the gospel to them. Paul has given himself freely and generously in preaching to the Macedonians; now they are giving themselves *unto us* (Paul and his traveling companions). Such self-giving is submission to the will of the God who gave himself for us on the cross of Christ.

❧ *THOSE WHO GIVE MOST* ❧

We tend to marvel at the million-dollar gifts of wealthy benefactors to charitable organizations. While we may commend such donors, the poorest people in America actually give a bigger percentage of their income. According to the U.S. Bureau of Labor Statistics, the richest 20 percent of Americans give only 2.1 percent of their income while the poorest 20 percent of Americans give 4.3 percent. Perhaps equally surprising is the fact that in difficult times the generosity of the poor declines less than that of those richer.

What compels the poor to be so generous? The attitude of a 40-year-old unemployed single mother is revealing: "I believe that the more I give, the more I receive, and that God loves a cheerful giver." Arthur Brooks, author of a book that analyzes American generosity, sees a strong connection between religious faith and generosity.

What Paul wrote about the generosity of the Macedonian Christians tells us this is not a new phenomenon—see also Mark 12:41-44. The key is likely to be found in the fact that they "first gave their own selves to the Lord." How are we doing in that regard?　　　　　　　—C. R. B.

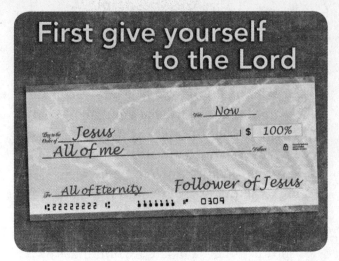

Visual for Lesson 14. *Point to this visual as you ask, "How do we keep from 'writing checks' that Jesus 'can't cash'?"*

II. Corinthian Challenge
(2 CORINTHIANS 8:6-9)

A. Complete the Commitment (v. 6)

6. Insomuch that we desired Titus, that as he had begun, so he would also finish in you the same grace also.

The Macedonian Christians' generosity encourages Paul to move forward with the planned collection. If the churches in Macedonia can respond so exceptionally, then Corinth must be challenged to do so as well. So Paul is sending Titus to deliver the letter we are now reading to the believers in Corinth to prepare them to make their own contributions. The Corinthians have already made plans to do so, but Titus will help them finish what they have started.

By referring to the Corinthians' forthcoming gift as *the same grace also*, Paul is stressing that this offering is not forced. It will be an act of generosity, an act on the Corinthians' part that imitates the grace of God.

B. Pass the Test (vv. 7-9)

7. Therefore, as ye abound in every thing, in faith, and utterance, and knowledge, and in all diligence, and in your love to us, see that ye abound in this grace also.

For all its shortcomings, the church at Corinth is one of the great churches of Christianity's first generation. Paul can speak honestly of the believers there as having responded to the gospel in abundance: in their deep *faith*, in their *utterance*, in *knowledge* of God (1 Corinthians 1:5), in *diligence* in putting faith in action, and especially in their *love* for Paul and all the fellowship of faith. It is from this perspective that Paul urges them to participate in the collection as part of their avid embrace of the Christian faith.

But there is another aspect to Paul's instructions. Yes, the Corinthians are exemplary in many ways, but some (many?) think too highly of themselves. In his first letter, Paul warned about overestimating one's spiritual state (compare 1 Corinthians 8:1, 2; 13:4). To those in danger in this regard, the verse before us is a pointed challenge: now is the time to practice what you have bragged about.

The readers will respond properly when they recognize that mature Christian virtue is no sign of personal superiority. Such virtue is, rather, the sign of God's superiority, for Christian virtue is the simple, honest, still unworthy response to God's redeeming grace (see 2 Corinthians 9:12).

8. I speak not by commandment, but by occasion of the forwardness of others, and to prove the sincerity of your love.

Paul stresses that he is not ordering the Corinthians to contribute. Their offering should be voluntary. But he affirms that he is challenging them by discussing the Macedonians (*others*). Their example will be the test of the Corinthians' response. A generous response will prove that their love for Christ is genuine not just in words but also deeds.

What Do You Think?

What's the difference between "encouragement" to give and "undue pressure" to give? How do we keep from crossing that line?

Talking Points for Your Discussion
- Giving vs. tithing
- Test of fellowship
- Test of leadership
- Guilt trips
- Other

---

9. For ye know the grace of our Lord Jesus Christ, that, though he was rich, yet for your sakes he became poor, that ye through his poverty might be rich.

Paul now retells the gospel story briefly but pointedly. Christ *was rich* in the fact that He enjoyed equality with God the Father—supreme, unsurpassable power and glory. But for the sake of sinners, He set aside those privileges to become human, even suffering an undeserved death for our sake. By that means, we humans, who are genuinely *poor* in comparison with Christ, become rich, receiving the treasure of God's kingdom now and forever.

Summarizing the gospel in a sentence, Paul thus provides the unassailable foundation for Christian generosity. When the Corinthians realize what Christ has done for them, they will be utterly compelled to be generous. We glorify Christ by imitating His generosity. We can never equal it, but we can reflect it.

III. Important Work
(2 CORINTHIANS 8:10-12)
A. That Was Then (v. 10)

10. And herein I give my advice: for this is expedient for you, who have begun before, not only to do, but also to be forward a year ago.

Paul expresses confidence in the Corinthians' commitment to the offering. What he is saying is not a command but is counsel on how to proceed. This is fitting for the Corinthians because they had committed to the collection *a year ago*. The phrase *to be forward* indicates their strong willingness to participate. The condition of the heart must be right for the gift to matter beyond that of meeting a need of the recipient.

B. This Is Now (vv. 11, 12)

11. Now therefore perform the doing of it; that as there was a readiness to will, so there may be a performance also out of that which ye have.

The Corinthians' contribution has been planned for some time now (1 Corinthians 16:1-4). Now, Paul says, the time has come to put the plan back into action, finishing what they have begun. Generosity starts in the heart, but it must be acted upon to be real generosity, just as God's love was expressed in the real action of Christ's incarnation, death, and resurrection.

12. For if there be first a willing mind, it is accepted according to that a man hath, and not according to that he hath not.

Perhaps the Corinthians' initial enthusiasm for the collection has given way to discouragement as they face the limitations of their resources. There is evidence, for example, that a famine affects Corinth not long before the writing of 2 Corinthians. Paul acknowledges that the Corinthians have limited means: they can give only from what they have. Their important response, however, is not the amount that they give but their willingness to share from what they have. Among God's people, the response of love is always outward, but the size of love is found within the mind and heart.

What Do You Think?
Considering all the giving requests you receive weekly, how do you decide which to support and in what amounts?
Talking Points for Your Discussion
- Evaluating your ability to give
- Evaluating the need
- Evaluating the credibility of the recipient
- Evaluating the "kingdom impact" of the gift
- Evaluating Christian vs. secular causes
- Other

IV. Desired Outcome
(2 CORINTHIANS 8:13, 14)
A. Not Burden . . . (v. 13)

13. For I mean not that other men be eased, and ye burdened.

Used to high taxes, sharp business practices, and dishonest religious teachers, some may wonder whether the collection's purpose is to make certain people rich at the expense of others. But Paul assures the Corinthians otherwise.

B. . . . But Equality (v. 14)

14. But by an equality, that now at this time your abundance may be a supply for their want, that their abundance also may be a supply for your want: that there may be equality.

Whatever the limits of their resources, the Corinthian Christians have more at their disposal than do the Jerusalem Christians. From the Corinthians' *abundance* can come an amount that will meet the need in Jerusalem. Paul assures his readers that were the tables turned, the Jerusalem church would respond similarly. In fact, it was from the Jerusalem church's generous sharing of their spiritual resources that the Corinthians have become part of God's family (Romans 15:27).

The *equality* that Paul desires is not absolute economic parity, where every Christian has exactly the same amount of material goods. Rather, he desires an equality of sufficiency, where all have at least what they need because all are ready to share with those who have not. God provides His people with sufficient resources so this can happen.

What Do You Think?
What would have to happen for our church to implement Paul's idea of equality?
Talking Points for Your Discussion
- Educational (Bible study) steps
- Issues of privacy and embarrassment
- Evaluating levels of need
- Other

Conclusion
A. The Best Reason to Give

What makes people generous? Some give for the good feeling they experience. Some give to make a name for themselves. Some give to honor someone who gave to them in the past.

Christian generosity is founded on the last of those reasons (see 2 Corinthians 9:12). Followers of Jesus are generous because Jesus was supremely generous with them. When that truth gets inside us, it turns our world upside down.

B. Prayer

Father, You have been generous to us beyond measure! May our hearts and our gifts reflect the grace of Christ, in whose name we pray, amen.

C. Thought to Remember

You cannot outgive God, but try to do so anyway!

NVOLVEMENT LEARNING

Some of the activities below are also found in the helpful student book, Adult Bible Class.
Don't forget to download the free reproducible page from www.standardlesson.com to enhance your lesson!

Into the Lesson

Ask learners to share a time when someone showed great generosity toward them. Discuss how it felt to have someone express such generosity. After a time of sharing, say, "Today we will look at a challenge to generosity and develop a plan to extend generosity to others."

Into the Word

Before learners arrive, have on display four banners with these four phrases (one each): *Macedonian Example / Corinthian Challenge / Important Work / Desired Outcome.* Hang banners over separate sections of the board. The banners can be made quickly and easily using blank newsprint (or similar) and felt-tip markers.

Read 2 Corinthians 8:1-5 aloud. Ask learners to identify various aspects of the Macedonians' example of generosity; jot responses on the board under the *Macedonian Example* banner. (Possible responses: endured great hardship; had a generous spirit; gave beyond their means; gave sacrificially; had given themselves to God first; responded out of gratitude for the gospel message; etc.)

Discuss how these facts made the Macedonians an example to other churches. Say, "Even though no one would have faulted the Macedonians for a lesser participation in the collection, they understood the grace they were extending in their offering. But sometimes it's easier to plan a gift than it is to follow through with the action. Were the Corinthians wavering in this regard? Let's see."

Read 2 Corinthians 8:6-9 aloud. Ask learners to identify aspects of the challenge Paul issued to the Corinthians; jot responses on the board under that banner. (Possible responses: Paul sent Titus to encourage them to give; Paul did not mandate that they contribute; generosity is founded in Christ's work; etc.) Discuss how Paul's challenge may have affected the Corinthians. Say, "Paul wants the Corinthians to understand that generosity is a way of reflecting God's grace in Christ. This leads to the apostle's advice to the Corinthians."

Read 2 Corinthians 8:10-12 aloud. Ask learners how the past connects with the present in Paul's line of thought; jot responses on the board under the *Important Work* banner. (Possible responses: desire expressed should match follow-through; changing financial status is not as important as willingness; etc.). Say, "Paul's 'that was then, this is now' line of thought is air tight! But one last thing needed to be addressed: the issue of outcome."

Read 2 Corinthians 8:13, 14 aloud, then write the word *reciprocity* on the board. Ask, "How does this word relate to the two verses just read?" Jot responses under the last banner. (Expected response: just as the Corinthians were about to extend help, they could expect other churches to respond likewise to future needs of the Corinthians.) *Caution:* When discussing Paul's desire "that there may be equality" (v. 14), do not allow the discussion to become political; keep the discussion focused on Christian obligation.

Option: Ask learners to close their Bibles as you announce that you will now test them on what was just studied. Distribute copies of the "A Generous Spirit" activity from the reproducible page, which you can download; have learners complete as indicated. Stress that this is a self-test only; you will not collect the completed tests. Go over results as a class, allowing learners to score their own work.

Into Life

Discuss the financial need of a church, a parachurch organization, or an individual. Create and implement a plan to help meet that need.

Option: Prior to the above, distribute copies of the "Giving as the Corinthians" activity from the reproducible page. This exercise will help learners grapple with how to apply the apostle Paul's desires for a twenty-first-century context.